The Practice of Satire in England, 1658–1770

The Practice of Satire in England, 1658–1770

ASHLEY MARSHALL

The Johns Hopkins University Press

Baltimore

© 2013 The Johns Hopkins University Press
All rights reserved. Published 2013
Printed in the United States of America on acid-free paper
2 4 6 8 9 7 5 3 1

The Johns Hopkins University Press
2715 North Charles Street
Baltimore, Maryland 21218-4363
www.press.jhu.edu

Library of Congress Cataloging-in-Publication Data

Marshall, Ashley.
The practice of satire in England, 1658–1770 / Ashley Marshall.
p. cm.
Includes bibliographical references and index.
ISBN 978-1-4214-0816-3 (hdbk. : alk. paper)—ISBN 978-1-4214-0817-0 (electronic)—
ISBN 1-4214-0816-3 (hdbk. : alk. paper)—ISBN 1-4214-0817-1 (electronic)
1. Satire, English—History and criticism. 2. English literature—18th century—History and criticism.
3. English literature—17th century—History and criticism. I. Title.
PR935.M37 2013
827 409—dc23   2012025275

A catalog record for this book is available from the British Library.

*Special discounts are available for bulk purchases of this book. For more information,
please contact Special Sales at 410-516-6936 or specialsales@press.jhu.edu.*

The Johns Hopkins University Press uses environmentally friendly book materials,
including recycled text paper that is composed of at least 30 percent
post-consumer waste, whenever possible.

For Rob Hume

There can be no adequate criticism that is not solidly based on the history of the art with which it is concerned.

—R. S. Crane, "History versus Criticism in the Study of Literature"

This study is devoted to answering a simple question: how was satire conceived by writers and readers ca. 1658–1770? The long eighteenth century is generally hailed as the great age of satire, and as such it has received much critical attention. That attention, however, has been devoted almost exclusively to those works that have stood the test of time. In 1940, David Worcester cheerfully proclaimed that theories of satire should derive from those texts that have "risen to the top" and that the works below, "graduated from acidulous gruel to a thick sludge of hell-broth," are useful only insofar as they contribute to our appreciation of their betters. Scholars in the past half-century have not exactly echoed Worcester's sentiments, but from Ian Jack to Fredric Bogel, "eighteenth-century satire" has implied *Mac Flecknoe, Absalom and Achitophel, A Tale of a Tub, Gulliver's Travels, The Dunciad,* Pope's Moral Essays, and a small number of other much-celebrated works. Interpretations of particular canonical texts have been of high quality, but those works have been almost entirely removed from their contexts. The argument of this book is that if we are not reading the "hell-broth" alongside the canonical masterworks, then we are misrepresenting the culture of satire in the eighteenth century. The scope and diversity of that culture is enormous, dauntingly complex, and until now largely unknown: scholars rightly proclaim that this is the great age of satire and then overlook much of what makes it so spectacular.

"Satire" in the long eighteenth century is a multifarious phenomenon, or rather a set of multifarious phenomena, and it exists in vast quantities. Before going any further, I should explain what I mean by a "satire," a point taken up in some detail in chapter 1. I have included in this study those works that have long been treated as satirical or partly satirical, as well as those that were originally identified as satires by their authors. The resultant list includes more than three thousand works, satires written in numerous forms for a variety of reasons. Much of this material circulated anonymously; a lot of it is crudely executed, coarse, and not very literary. Taken item by item, these works often have little to recommend them, but taken as a whole, they represent a heterogeneity unparalleled by any other period in literary history. They also reveal an exciting set of trends and patterns that force us to rethink our conclusions about satire as a mode and about the works and writers we most cherish.

As for how the canonical works will figure in a study based on extensive reading in the realm of "hell-broth," three points are worth stressing. The first is that this is not a book of interpretations; critics have for the most part soundly explicated the satires they cover, and except in a few instances I am not directly challenging established readings of the principal canonical works. Second, this study is not just devoted to treating the headliners alongside the dreck; it also demonstrates the need to attend to more of the major writers' work. Dryden is a radically different satirist in the 1690s than he had been in the late 1670s and early 1680s. To read only *Mac Flecknoe* and *Absalom and Achitophel*, glancing briefly at the *Discourse concerning the Original and Progress of Satire*, is to miss a huge shift in his practice and what that alteration has to tell us about satire more broadly. The third point is simply that the major authors and their most important satires do loom large in this study. They are not being ousted to make room for the likes of John Ayloffe, Arthur Maynwaring, Ned Ward, and Robert Lloyd. This is not a "recuperation" of the minor works; the welter of satiric material is meant to provide the context within which to understand Dryden, Swift, Pope, and company. Though the major writers did become famous, and though pieces like *Gulliver's Travels* and *The Dunciad* were definitely sensations, our favored "Augustans" did not exist in a vacuum, and extracting them from the world in which they wrote and were read has caused a variety of problems.

What do we gain from restoring the much-admired works to the satiric milieu (or, more accurately, milieus) whence they came? One of the more important lessons of this study is that the presumed interrelatedness of the major works is neither helpful nor true. Reading Dryden, Swift, Pope, and other canonical satirists in isolation from their contexts has led scholars to understand their works as connected enterprises, examples of what is still too often termed "Augustan satire." To date, no one has sufficiently grappled with the heterogeneity of satiric practice in the long eighteenth century, even among the luminaries most extensively studied. Dryden, Swift, Pope, Gay, and Fielding are the premier "Augustans," and they are frequently grouped together, but they have fundamentally different satiric practices and purposes. *The Rape of the Lock* is not doing what *Absalom and Achitophel* or *Mac Flecknoe* had done; Fielding's oft-cited tolerance resembles Swift's rage not a whit; the Dean's propagandistic works are a world away from Pope's Moral Essays; and both *Gulliver's Travels* and *The Beggar's Opera* are one-offs that have little satiric commonality with anything else produced in this century. These differences matter. For one thing, we ought to be trying to do justice to these authors—to get them right. For another, we need to appreciate that, say, Swift, for the most part, very much "fits" in his satiric milieu, whereas Pope and Gay are relative outliers. Stressing correspondences between

Fielding and the "Scriblerians" is also unwise. Fielding has great range as a satirist, and as of the 1740s he is among the more prominent practitioners of a sympathetic mode of satire—a mode that is beginning to flourish during the heyday of the "Scriblerians," a period frequently associated with *punitive* satires. Recognizing the importance of sympathetic satire is much more difficult if we insist on overemphasizing Fielding's affinities with Pope's circle. The major works do not often seem to "go" together, and neither do they typify the practice of the time. Literary critics are fond of seeking categories and continuities, but the practice of satire in the long eighteenth century actually makes a good deal more sense if we refrain from trying to see it as a single mode.

Modern scholars usually seem to assume that this "mode" of eighteenth-century satire is marked either by underlying unity or by organic development. Discussions of satire, in other words, leave one with the impression either that little changes from 1660 to 1690 to 1730 and so on or that the changes can be described in evolutionary terms (Dryden and Rochester begetting Pope and Swift, the Scriblerians begetting Fielding and Sterne). Neither model accords well with the evidence. I carried out my investigation chronologically, and what I discovered is the presence of much diversity not reducible to a simple trajectory. Perhaps more than any other type of writing, satire is crucially dependent upon its immediate extrinsic circumstances. One of the points to which I return throughout is the vital significance of chronology. Satiric practice changes several times over the course of this period, and these shifts are non-evolutionary, unpredictable, and (depending on the instance) somewhere between partially and totally inexplicable. These changes can, however, be traced with some precision. Transformations in satiric practice are messy but undeniable, and to ignore or oversimplify them is to miss much of what makes eighteenth-century satire so remarkable. The bottom line is that we cannot legitimately talk about satiric practice in this period in terms of a single mode with lasting markers. To characterize "eighteenth-century satire" as a unitary concept is, in point of fact, well-nigh impossible.

What we can define with some confidence are the subperiods that constitute the broader span covered in this book. I argue that we should avoid generalizations made on the basis of limited evidence and that this material is much more confusing than anyone looking at the canonical works could realize—but also that there are drastic changes from subperiod to subperiod and that those changes make sense. I survey satiric practice in chapters 3 through 7, and each of those chapters focuses on a particular span of years that has a coherence and a character all its own. What we find in the reign of Charles II is quite unlike what we find in the 1690s; the kinds of satire that dominate in the reign of Queen Anne have precious little to do with those prominent in the later 1710s and early 1720s. The late 1720s and the 1730s are best not lumped together with what comes before or after; the 1760s are again another world entirely. Within each subperiod we find diversity and inconsistency, as will become apparent to readers struggling to process the many and varied details in each of the survey chapters. But out of that confusion some order does spring.

With all respect to my numerous and distinguished predecessors in this field, I suggest that singling out a few texts has drastically shrunk and simplified a big world. Resituating canonical masterpieces in the full complexity of their original setting will, I believe, transform the way we conceive of satire in this period. I realize that looking at vast quantities of noncanonical satire is not in itself an exciting prospect. For my part, reading the hundreds of examples of Worcester's "hell-broth" turned out to be less tedious and a great deal more fun than anticipated. Some of these satires are admittedly pretty awful, but many are not, and the picture that emerges from looking at the whole lot of them is quite unlike what critics of "Augustan satire" describe.

Carrying out this survey surprised me. I did not read the primary material with any expectations about the particular conclusions it would generate, but if I had tried to guess I could only have guessed very wrong. The culture of satire was far messier and more exciting than our representations of it would lead one to believe, and contemporary writers and readers would have had a much different sense of what satire is than what one finds in modern accounts of "satire." For writers and readers of the long eighteenth century, satire was energetic, often outrageous, confusing, and richly varied. My aim is to re-create the sense of chaotic but vibrant diversity that the original audiences enjoyed. This is not a study of the best eighteenth-century satires. It is rather an account of the culture of satire as writers and readers would have understood, produced, and experienced it between 1658 and 1770.

The plans for what became this book were laid in the spring of 2005, and since then it has been through more iterations than I have been able to count. I owe special gratitude to the people who have given me help beyond what anyone can be reasonably expected to give. My principal debt is to Rob Hume, who not only kept me in graduate school but also "saved" me from modernism and taught me to love the eighteenth century. He uncomplainingly read version after version of this book, bloodying up every page every time until I got it right, and improved my prose and my spirit at every step of the way. I am also deeply beholden to Howard Weinbrot and Tom Lockwood, who read a 567-page version of the manuscript with characteristic rigor, and characteristic generosity. Howard returned the manuscript in short order, having marked all but five of the pages (which had no doubt stuck to their predecessors). Tom wrote more than twenty pages of single-spaced comments, all insightful and spot on. He also deserves more general thanks for encouraging me to do less finger-wagging and to be less gloomy. John Harwood and I had many conversations about what I could and could not do in this enterprise. His hard questions made this a better book; his unwavering confidence in the project helped get it off the ground. I am also extremely grateful to Ron Paulson, who read the whole of the manuscript in its later stages, pushing me to sharpen my conceptual terminology and to make a long list of other useful changes.

The first version of this book was written at The Pennsylvania State University, and I benefited enormously from its splendid library and electronic resources. I am particularly grateful to Bill Brockman for his unfailing support in the acquisition of books, microfilm collections, and databases without which this study would have been impossible. In completing the first draft of this book, I was greatly helped by a Mellon/ACLS dissertation fellowship, and substantial revisions were carried out while I held an ACLS New Faculty Fellowship at Johns Hopkins University.

I want to express my appreciation to the department and university of which I became a member during the latter stages of completing this manuscript for publication. The University of Nevada, Reno, has been a wonderful place to start my career: friendly, helpful, welcoming, and energizing. I am deeply grateful for important financial support generously given to me by the College of Liberal Arts through its Scholarly and Creative Activities Grant Program and for the moral support and advice of my departmental colleagues and chair, Eric Rasmussen.

Along the way, I have received sustenance and counsel from a number of people. For rigorous readings in the early stages, I am grateful to Laura Knoppers and Philip Jenkins. Tom Minsker devoted considerable time and energy to solving formatting problems that would in his absence have defeated me. For Tom's tireless and cheerful assistance, for his much-tested but never exhausted patience, and for every time he said, "Let's try it this way," I am grateful. To David Spielman I owe a special thanks, for serving as a sounding board and for never really believing that I would head for the bus station.

Countless friends, strangers, teachers, and colleagues have answered questions, offered advice, and given the kind of collegial assistance that makes this such a rewarding profession. I cannot specify every kindness I have received, and I fear I will be forgetting some benefactors unintentionally, but all of the following should know that I am grateful for help and for friendship: Eve Bannet, Lance Bertelsen, Marshall Brown, Bob Burkholder, Vin Carretta, Robert Clark, Scott Dawson, Alan Downie, Bob and Carey Eckhardt, Chris Fox, Julian Fung, Patricia Gael, Dustin Griffin, Kathryn Grossman, Brean Hammond, Earle Havens, Kit Hume, Paul Hunter, Nick Joukovsky, Matt Kinservik, Jack Lynch, Nancy Mace, Bob Mahony, Doug Mao, Jim May, Don Mell, Judy Milhous, Andreas Mueller, Hugh Ormsby-Lennon and Margaret Boerner, Leah Orr, Joe Pappa, Alex Pettit, Adam Potkay, Hermann Real, Ric Reverand, John Richetti, Pat Rogers, Peter Sabor, Robin Schulze, Geoff Sill, Cal Winton, and James Woolley. To that list must be added the late Bert Goldgar, whose erudition was matched only by his generosity, and also the late Ray Nelson, for taking me as I was.

Finally, I should like to thank my family—my parents, Judy and Pat Brogan and Cliff and Christine Crain; my grandparents, Rufus and Evelyn Hall; and the whole lot—for trying to understand why I do what I do, and for believing in it. Everything in my life is done partly in memory of my brother, Stephen (1972–2001): *ave atque vale.*

My primary material comes from a variety of sources. A high proportion is first editions obtained electronically through Early English Books Online (EEBO) or Eighteenth-Century Collections Online (ECCO). The place of publication of seventeenth- and eighteenth-century texts is London unless otherwise specified. Where good modern scholarly editions exist, I have used them (e.g., the "California" Dryden; the Oxford editions of Butler, Buckingham, Churchill, and others; the Twickenham Pope; the Harold Williams edition of Swift's poetry; the Wesleyan edition of Fielding). Many poems from the period 1660–1714 are quoted from John Harold Wilson's *Court Satires of the Restoration* or the seven-volume "Yale" *Poems on Affairs of State*. Titles are given in whatever form my source renders them, which produces occasional oddities (e.g., *The Beaux Stratagem* without an apostrophe, *The Wives' Excuse* with an editorially added apostrophe). Unless otherwise stated, dates are for the first printed edition of nondramatic satires. When there is a significant gap between composition and publication, I give both dates if known. For plays, I give the date of first performance. If the publication date is not the same year as initial performance, I give both.

Because I have systematically paid attention to the cost of buying satires, many prices are cited. For those unfamiliar with Britain's pre-1971 nondecimal currency, there were 12 pennies (*d*) to the shilling (*s*) and 20 shillings to the pound (£). A 1*d* broadside therefore cost less than a tenth of the price of a 1*s* play. There is no valid way of providing a single multiplier that gives a present-day buying power equivalent for an eighteenth-century price. Readers should be aware, however, that a 5*s* novel sounds cheap but was actually far from affordable for any but elite buyers. As I explain in chapter 1, applying a multiplier anywhere from two hundred to three hundred times the late seventeenth- or early eighteenth-century price yields a reasonable approximation of present-day value. On this basis, a 5*s* novel may be calculated as costing £50–75 in our terms.

Price Symbol Key

The following symbols indicate the source from which I have derived the prices of satires where known.

* = *The Luttrell File*
† = advertisement
‡ = *The Term Catalogues*
no symbol = price from title page

The Practice of Satire in England, 1658–1770

CHAPTER ONE

Canonical and Noncanonical Satire, 1658–1770

Some Questions of Definition, Aims, and Method

◇◇◇◇◇◇◇◇◇◇◇◇◇◇◇◇◇◇◇◇◇◇◇◇◇◇◇

In Poetry the Height we know;
'Tis only infinite below.

—Swift, *On Poetry: A Rapsody*, ll. 391–392

The period between the return of Charles II to the throne and the deaths of Pope and Swift has long been acclaimed the golden epoch of satire, and this *aetas mirabilis* has enjoyed much critical attention in the past seventy years. Book after book, article after article, has sought to characterize "Augustan satire" and its most famous practitioners, especially Dryden, Swift, Pope, Fielding, and Johnson. A small number of major works have formed the center of modern satire studies. From them—and, for the most part, only from them—our conclusions about satire have derived. This book began out of a conviction that we need to resituate the canonical masterpieces amid the hundreds upon hundreds of other works that constitute the contexts in which they were originally written and read, and that doing so would compel a drastic revision of the standard literary history of eighteenth-century satire.

Focusing on a few largely atypical works and assuming their interconnectedness means missing much of what makes the culture of satire in the long eighteenth century so exciting. Proofs are in puddings, and the utility of a broader investigation will have to be demonstrated by the survey chapters. My objectives in the first four sections of this chapter are: to confront the vexed issue of definition (I); to explain my decision to adopt an approach of broad, multigenre coverage (II); to identify the canon used by modern scholars, the evidentiary basis on which our conclusions have rested (III); and to give some indication of the magnitude and diversity of the primary material on which this book is based (IV). Section IV also includes an investigation of the format and price of satire as it circulated in this period, carried out in order to call attention to the implications of material contexts for dissemination and imagined audience. The point, most broadly, is to make clear how little we have seen and understood of what turns out to be a massive and variegated body of writing and to appreciate the economic contexts of that corpus. Section V offers an explanation of the method and organization of the book, and in the final section I argue for the utility of a taxonomic approach to this material and provide some sense of what sort of conclusions such a survey can generate.

I. The "Definition" Quagmire and the Problem of Descriptive Terminology

Because this is a project based on inclusiveness rather than exclusiveness, the first question to address is what counts as "satire." On what works is this study based and why? Definitions are numerous, exhibit a considerable amount of agreement, and prove surprisingly unhelpful for reasons we need briefly to explore.

Satire critics often begin their discussions by observing that satire is hard to pin down conceptually. Not without reason has it been called "that most protean literary something."[1] Difficulties notwithstanding, most scholars believe that they have some notion of what "satire" is and what its central characteristics are. In *Anatomy of Criticism*, Northrop Frye argued that "essential to satire . . . is an object of attack" plus "wit or humor"—pretty standard criteria.[2] What Frye viewed as requisite remains central for a great number of critics: "literary satire," says Linda A. Morris, "is understood to be work that relies upon humor to expose both human and institutional failures."[3] Eighteenth-century writers and readers had a fairly varied sense of what "satire" meant and what it could include, but most modern definitions (implicit or explicit) tend to be narrower and more restrictive, describing satire in ways that do not allow for the messy reality of historical practice.

Most modern definitions reflect at least five basic assumptions about satire. (1) It is a *literary* art. (2) It *attacks* its targets, with varying degrees of seriousness or intensity. Brian A. Connery and Kirk Combe insist that "satirists specialize in demolition projects," and George A. Test concludes, "That satire is an attack is probably the least debatable claim that one can make about it."[4] (3) Its targets are *real*—they represent, in Edward W. Rosenheim's words, "discernible historical particulars."[5] (4) It is to some extent *humorous*. (5) It is essentially a *negative* enterprise, generally seen as reflecting a sour view of human nature. Some critics suggest that little good can come of satire: the satirist, says Leonard Feinberg, believes that there "are many things wrong in the world" and that "nothing much is likely to be done about it."[6] In the mid-twentieth century, satire was regarded by many critics as a moral art, and some in the tradition of Maynard Mack still stress satire's moral basis and its reformative potential, though Dustin Griffin and others have usefully warned against overemphasizing its "moral intensity."[7]

The still-current definitional principles work passably well when applied to some of the satires most commonly studied by literary critics. Pope's *Dunciad* (1728, 1729,

1743) is a punitive and sometimes lively put-down of mostly obscure hack poets and political writers, written out of contempt for a development (the burgeoning of "low" culture) that is unlikely to be stopped, and it is a literary masterpiece penned by a brilliant technician. The problem is that our definitional assumptions tend to derive from a small number of works, and if one reads more than a few carefully selected satires, those assumptions quickly come to seem inadequate. Many satirists seem less concerned with literary form and aesthetics than with content and immediate impact. Much of this satire is not terribly funny, some of it is written not to punish or reform a target but to instruct like-minded readers (and hence is positive, not negative, in thrust), and "attack" is a crude oversimplification or simply not true in a substantial number of cases.

Critics have opinions about what is "essential" to this kind of writing, about what it must and must not do, but (naturally) counterexamples abound if we want to find them. Introducing a 2007 volume on satire, Ruben Quintero states flatly that satirists "write not merely out of personal indignation, but with a sense of moral vocation and with a concern for the public interest," and he then quotes Pope.[8] Pope's Moral Essays nicely bear out Quintero's assertion, but what of Rochester's *On Poet Ninny* or the satire in Sterne's *Tristram Shandy*? The first is hardly motivated by "concern for the public interest," and the latter has nothing in it of indignation. This raises an obvious question. If satire cannot be easily identified on the basis of the standard set of components, then what counts as satire? Using a definition to generate a list of primary sources is a bad idea, but having completed a pass through some three thousand satiric works, I will with due caution offer a descriptive characterization (not a definition) of my own.

Satire involves some kind of critique and needs a target—that is point one. The critique can be of particular people, of types, of institutions, of modes of behavior, or of any number of other things; it can be explicit or not. I am deliberately using a milder term than "attack," which has misleading implications concerning motive, negativity, and the degree of hostility behind the satire. Satire is not only critique, of course, and not all critique is satire. Satire involves an element of critique, but beyond that, it needs something else. Critics have tended to use a formula in which satire equals attack or ridicule plus humor or wit. I would suggest a more open set of formulae, including but not limited to critique plus distortion, critique plus humorous ridicule, or critique plus gratuitousness in motive.

This nondefinition is valid, but I have doubts about the practical utility of any such discussion. Attempts to encapsulate satire tend to be overly exclusionary or highly inclusionary. Neither helps. In the first case, we find ourselves in the position of Elder Olson, who arrived at a definition of comedy on the basis of which he disallows *Much Ado*, *As You Like It*, and seven other of Shakespeare's fourteen so-called comedies.[9]

Many of the best satire critics have invoked a narrow definition only to dispense with it in practice, as in the simultaneous assumptions that satire is motivated by righteous indignation and that *The Rape of the Lock* is satiric. Abandoning a restrictive definition is better than adhering to it, but what is the point of generating a definition only to leave it behind?

Neither is too broad a concept useful. A set of concepts capacious enough to apply to everything in practice help us with nothing. Definitional principles that are equally appropriate for Rochester's *Satyre against Reason and Mankind*, Dryden's *The Kind Keeper*, Defoe's *Jure Divino*, Johnson's *London*, and Garrick's *Lethe*—all identified as satires by their authors—are unlikely to illumine any of the texts. Common ground there is some, but what do we gain by overemphasizing it? Howard D. Weinbrot opens his important study of "Menippean satire" with an abbreviated but lengthy list of works to which critics have applied that label—he gives thirty-five titles, among which are *Praise of Folly*, Johnson's *Dictionary*, *Alice in Wonderland*, and *The Waste Land*. A genre that includes such a range of exemplars, he rightly observes, "is less baggy than bulbous."[10] Our concept of satire needs to be able to accommodate works labeled "satire" and contemporaneous enterprises manifestly similar in design, but at some point a generalized definition becomes useless. The struggle to "explain" satire is unlikely to be resolved by the development of a new and improved, more expansive definition to replace the bad old definitions of yesteryear. We need conceptual flexibility, not one definition fits all.

Lacking a rigorous definition, then, how does one generate a list of titles to be surveyed? For this study, I adopted a practical approach. My primary source list includes any work (1) labeled a "satire" by its author or (2) that we have cause to believe was understood by contemporaries as a satire or (3) that has been treated as satirical by modern critics. The inclusion of works belonging to the first category is hard to dispute, poorly though many of them fit standard definitions. The second and third categories are less clear cut. Evidence of contemporary recognition of satire tends to come in diaries, letters, and responses; when a satire is included on this basis I have given the source of the characterization. The third category is messy but relatively unproblematic. Most of these works are widely accepted as belonging to the satiric pantheon; in cases where I have reservations (such as *The Rape of the Lock*) I say so. Taking works from all three categories makes for a long list, and while another scholar might quibble over the inclusion or exclusion of particular satires, what cannot be contested is the enormousness of the body of material with which we are dealing. Reflected in these works is a wide range of aims and motives: satire is written from many different standpoints, with varying degrees of intensity and hostility, and for very different reasons. What I try to provide in this book is a kind of taxonomical classification, one that permits us to identify the aims and to discuss the operational modes of a multifarious phenomenon over a period of more than a century.

This brings me to a vexing terminological problem. My study is avowedly taxonomic, but the works involved do not classify tidily into descriptive genera. I employ a lot of useful "terms of the time" (e.g., Horatian, Juvenalian, mock heroic, lampoon, libel, invective) but they do not provide sufficiently helpful characterizations of hundreds of particular satires, many of which will be unfamiliar to a lot of readers. Travesties, for example, vary from the teasing to the viciously hostile, so the "travesty" label, while useful in signaling a work's reductive intent, tells us only so much about what the work really is. Not wishing to create a lot of pigeonholes into which to cram every exemplar, I have freely employed descriptors designed to convey tone and apparent intention, such as "lightweight," "savage," "farcical," "dark," and "glum." Obviously these are subjective terms. They reflect my own sense of what the author is trying to do and the dominant tone of the enterprise, and many enterprises are not consistent. "Harsh satire" and "sympathetic satire" are the ends of a long continuum, but some works (e.g., "distributive justice satires") do not map onto a single point of that continuum. A reader may disagree with my characterization of a particular work, and of course there are borderline cases; a satire that is amusing to one reader can seem upsetting to another. I have tried to be consistent in my application of adjectival descriptors—without claiming that these terms have precise literary definitions. Again, my aim is practical: elucidatory labels such as "affectionate," "dark" (i.e., negative and pessimistic), "cynical," "cheerful," and "hard-hitting" are helpful in establishing the character of a satire, especially an unfamiliar one.

II. Genre versus Mode

This book is a study not of "satires" but of the practice of satire—the uses and manifestations of the satiric. I agree with Alastair Fowler that what we are dealing with is a mode (or rather a set of modes) that inhabit multiple genres. "Satire," Fowler observes, "is the most problematic mode to the taxonomist," having never corresponded to a single genre or kind.[11] Modal terms are usually adjectival—a satiric pamphlet, a satiric play, and so on. Formal verse satire is a genre within a mode, and its exemplars share consistent markers—something we do not find in any other genre satire tends to inhabit. Offering a helpful theory of formal verse satire is possible in a way that usefully "explaining" narrative or dramatic satire is not. But this does not mean that everything except poetry should be ignored.

My inclusion of fiction and drama may disconcert readers who feel that those genres are beyond the satiric pale. I disagree. Most studies of satire privilege verse, which would not be a problem if conclusions were presented as generically specific. Instead, what we are usually told is that "Restoration satire does X," with reference to a few poems by Dryden, Rochester, Butler, and Oldham. In the realm of "Augustan" satire, some nonpoetry gets attention—such as *A Tale of a Tub* and *Gulliver's Travels*—but not much. Writing more than forty years ago, Ronald Paulson made a powerful case in *Satire and the Novel in Eighteenth-Century England* for recognizing the presence of satire in novels, even though the novels themselves are not "satires." Plays have at least equal claim to satiric status. Playwrights of the time quite regularly apply the label "satire" to their works, as for example Congreve's *Double-Dealer*, Fielding's *Modern Husband*, and Dodsley's *Toy-Shop*. Dryden's testimony seems particularly significant on the issue of inclusivity. The author of a theoretical essay on satire largely concerning Roman formal verse, he nevertheless does not regard "satire" and "drama" as mutually exclusive concepts. In the *Discourse*, he comments on "*Roman Theatrical Satire*"; in the seventies he had defended the *Kind Keeper* as "an honest Satyre" and praised Wycherley's *Plain-Dealer* as "one of the most bold, most general, and most useful Satyres which has ever been presented on the *English* Theater."[12] Dryden was the author of two of the most celebrated satiric poems of the long eighteenth century, he was one of the principal theorists of satire, and he definitely allows for the possibility that a play can be a satire.

Even if one grants this possibility, there remains the difficulty that many satiric or partially satiric plays and novels do not seem to be centrally defined by their satiric content or to be "satire" as we generally conceive it. What percentage of the whole needs to be satiric for a work to be legitimately discussable? No one would deny that *Mac Flecknoe* is a satire, and most would agree that *Tristram Shandy* is satirical without being "a satire," but a lot of works fall somewhere in between. There is no tidy boundary. The presence of characters and plot usually dilutes whatever satire coexists with them. Such is the case in Fielding's novels and in the "softer" satiric drama of the 1760s, though not all satiric plays and novels work that way—see Southerne's *The Wives' Excuse*, Smollett's *Ferdinand Count Fathom*, and Macklin's *The Man of the World*. I admit the problem posed by works that are "satirical" rather than "satires," though the diversity of works labeled "satire" in this period suggests that eighteenth-century writers were not working in what they regarded as a clear-cut genre with established rules. They evidently classified "satire" much more loosely than a modern, definition-bound critic is inclined to do: Defoe calls *Jure Divino* "a satire," though most modern scholars would be inclined to label it merely a poem with some satiric elements.

Scholars of eighteenth-century satire have tended to privilege verse satires over satiric plays or novels, but the exclusion of fiction and drama often seems arbitrary. Most critics would count *The Rehearsal* and *The Way of the World* as satire, and some of Fielding's plays are regularly treated that way. Claiming that Thomas Duffett's burlesques are satiric or treating Macklin and Foote as dramatic satirists is unlikely to raise hackles. Readers who object to the inclusion of *Tom Jones* but accept a section on Smollett without hesitation are obviously not troubled by the admixture of satire, plot, and characters. The problem seems to be less generic categorization than the type of satire presented in a particular play or novel. Matthew J. Kinservik's conclusion seems about right: "A play characterized by cynicism, attack, and negative examples is normally called 'satiric,' whereas one that features exemplary characters, sympathy, and benevolence is generally considered 'sentimental.' This strikes me as a false distinction. The difference lies in the dramatic emphasis, not in the ostensible didactic effect on spectators."[13] Take Shadwell's *Squire of Alsatia*, which represents a kind of satiric venture remote from, say, *The Dunciad* or even something like Foote's *Minor*, but also unquestionably displays a didactic, satiric agenda of a sort that became common in late seventeenth- and early eighteenth-century comedy. On what basis do we have the right to ignore it? Excluding all works not self-labeled as satire is no saner for drama and fiction than it is for verse.

Satire's relationship to genre has always been a complicated one. Genre theory tends to assume that genre determines outcome, and this brings us to the crux of the issue. Satire is a purposive mode, and its purposes can dominate the genre it inhabits—or not. Where the satiric mode dominates, then formal genre no longer controls the results or response. In that case a genre is simply a vehicle for satire—witness *The Fall of Mortimer* and Smollett's *Adventures of an Atom*, "pure" satires that happen to take the form of a play and a prose narrative. The unperformed ballad operas written against Walpole are satires, not satiric ballad operas. Satire can dominate the genre it inhabits, but it can also be an incidental presence in that genre, built into generic structures that have a distinct form, a set of expectations, and strongly defined characteristics of their own. Most modern scholars respond principally to *Joseph Andrews* and *Tom Jones* as novels, only secondarily as satiric works, and rightly so. Fiction that does much with semiplausible characterization and "real life" tends to embed satire in a not purely satiric context. The same is true of most drama. Whereas a poem or prose squib can be *only* satire, the addition of plot and character significantly changes the satiric effect. The result is not necessarily softer satire—Sarah Fielding's *Volume the Last* is not "soft"—but it is diluted.

Beyond these broad points about characterization and dilution, can we theorize what happens to satire when it enters multiple genres? I admit to having doubts about the utility of any single theory for satire in all genres (never mind all times). The nature and characteristics and tendencies of formal verse satire have been well explicated, but when satire appears in plays and novels, it does so in different ways and to different degrees, a point to which I return in chapter 7. As satiric fiction, *Roderick*

Random is not *Humphry Clinker* is not *Tristram Shandy*. A crucial question seems to be the extent to which genre or mode dominates: does genre control response, or is the presence of satire more important than genre? The issue is one of proportion: a novel that is 90 percent satire we can safely label a satire, and a novel that is 20 percent satire is only incidentally satiric. But where is the dividing line? Probably we need to think in terms of a spectrum and to answer the question of generic versus modal dominance on a case-by-case basis.

In practice what this means is that I move freely among genres in this study but without pretending that the satiric effect is dominant where that is manifestly not the case. I regard Fielding's fiction as satiric, and I discuss his uses of satire in *Joseph Andrews* and *Tom Jones* without calling those works "satires." Granting generic differences and their importance to audience response, an attempt to reconstruct eighteenth-century attitudes toward satire cannot reasonably ignore all but verse and selected prose. If we are looking for where and how satire appeared, then we need to take it in all its manifestations.

III. The Modern Critical Canon and Its Implications

Selectivity is the critical norm, and in some ways eighteenth-century satire has had broader representation than other territories (see the big five Romantic poets), but discussions have nevertheless been both conceptually and quantitatively narrow. This section is devoted to an analysis of the canon treated by satire scholars. These critics make no claim to exhaustiveness, and the rich readings of particular texts and writers that they supply would not be possible without a high degree of selectivity. All I wish to suggest is that such studies implicitly or explicitly project a theory of "eighteenth-century satire," and that theory is necessarily limited insofar as it comes off a small number of works.

Inclusivity of the sort I am attempting here would of course have been all but impossible only a few years ago. The smallness of the canon stems in part from real difficulties in finding and reading the many noncanonical works. Someone writing a generation or even a decade ago could have spent years trying to turn up printed texts in libraries without ever finding all of the sources that a scholar today can readily obtain from Early English Books Online and Eighteenth-Century Collections Online. EEBO and ECCO, as well as the English Short Title Catalogue (ESTC) and other resources, have revolutionized potentialities for research in this period. We now have the means to find and read virtually all satires printed in the long eighteenth century, and that access has opened up a new world.

What is the extent and nature of the modern critical canon? Magnitude first: on what foundation have conclusions about satire been based? This is not a subjective question; we can quantify citations in illustrative if imperfect ways. Although I refer to a range of critics and books throughout this study, my statistics in this section are derived from eleven accounts written by ten satire scholars. David Worcester's *The Art of Satire* (1940) was the first general satire book to be taken at all seriously, so I begin with him. I also include James Sutherland's *English Satire* and Alvin B. Kernan's *The Plot of Satire*, whose focuses—like that of *The Art of Satire*—are not exclusively eighteenth century, but which draw heavily on examples from this period and have been influential on successive generations of eighteenth-century satire scholars. The list includes particularly important books, especially those by Ronald Paulson, Claude Rawson, and Dustin Griffin, and representatives from each decade following Worcester. Other studies could be used, but adding or substituting different books would not meaningfully alter the statistical patterns I wish to highlight here. Not part of this list are some excellent accounts of specific types of satire or subperiods within the century—for example, Thomas Lockwood's *Post-Augustan Satire* (1979), Vincent Carretta's *The Snarling Muse* (1983) and *George III and the Satirists from Hogarth to Byron* (1990), Harold Love's *English Clandestine Satire 1660–1702* (2004), and Howard D. Weinbrot's *Menippean Satire Reconsidered* (2005). Neither do I include single-author studies like Maynard Mack on Pope or Irvin Ehrenpreis on Swift, which of course include a wider array of works but do not attempt to describe "eighteenth-century satire."

A word about the citation statistics in table 1.1 and how they were generated. I distinguish among (1) works mentioned only once and strictly in passing, (2) works referred to in passing on more than one occasion, (3) works given short analysis (anywhere from half a page to a few pages), and (4) works given more substantial time and attention (a lengthy section or chapter). This is not a perfect system—where is the line between "short" and "substantial"?—but I have tried to be fair and consistent. I do not include texts referred to as contrastive examples to satire or otherwise as nonsatiric. I count the original *Poems on Affairs of State* as a single work when it is cited that way; the same is true of Marvell's "Painter" poems, Young's *Love of Fame* series, the various *Dunciads*, the Moral Essays, and the Horatian imitations. *The Epistle to Arbuthnot* and the *Epilogue to the Satires* are counted separately because they are commonly referred to individually. To reiterate an important point: few of these critics profess to be dealing with a lot of satires and authors, and I am not so unsporting as to conclude in triumph that my predecessors did not achieve what they did not attempt. Each of these books was written with its own agenda, and the best studies (by Paulson, Rawson, and Griffin, in particular) will deservedly remain touchstones for eighteenth-century scholars for decades to come. My aim is to generate quantitative statistics that allow us to see more precisely what has been privileged, in terms of particular works, kinds of satire, and genre.

TABLE I.I
Citation counts for eleven general satire studies

Study	Works mentioned once	Works mentioned more than once	Works briefly discussed[a]	Works analyzed at length[b]	Total
Worcester, *Art of Satire* (1940)	25	9	5	0	39
Jack, *Augustan Satire* (1952)	14	7	0	8	29
Sutherland, *English Satire* (1958)	36	8	20	1	65
Kernan, *The Plot of Satire* (1965)	7	3	5	4	19
Paulson, *The Fictions of Satire* (1967)	24	10	9	6	49
Paulson, *Satire and the Novel in Eighteenth-Century England* (1967)	19	13	24	10	66
Bloom and Bloom, *Satire's Persuasive Voice* (1979)	35	11	31	4	81
Seidel, *The Satiric Inheritance* (1979)	3	3	4	8	18
Rawson, *Satire and Sentiment* (1994)	25	10	12	4	51
Griffin, *Satire* (1994)	20	12	16	1	49
Bogel, *The Difference Satire Makes* (2001)	8	10	6	7	31

Note: This does not include works that are cited in footnotes and endnotes but not also in the main text. Those numbers are usually fairly small: Worcester (4); Sutherland (4); Kernan (2); Paulson (5 each in *Fictions* and *Satire and the Novel*); Seidel (2); Rawson (11); and Bogel (3). The figures for Jack (13) and Griffin (20) are slightly higher, and the Blooms refer to an additional 60 works in their notes.

[a]Discussion ranges from half a page to a short section.

[b]Discussion ranges from a long section to a chapter.

The table gives us figures on a study-by-study basis. The average number of eighteenth-century works *referred* to as satires, whether once or multiple times (columns 1 and 2), is roughly 28; the average number of works *discussed*, whether briefly or at considerable length (columns 3 and 4), is just 17. Omitting Paulson's *Satire and the Novel* and the Blooms' book would reduce the average to just 13 satires actually discussed. More telling are the results if we calculate citation statistics for the total canon, drawing on all eleven of these books.

Only 94 works have been mentioned in more than one of these accounts. The pool is not only small but also highly selective. The most conspicuous form of selectivity is in the realm of author coverage. The average number of writers mentioned in these studies is 25. Worcester refers to 23 satirists, as does Jack; Sutherland, to 30; Kernan, to 10; Paulson, to 18 (*Fictions*) and 24 (*Satire and the Novel*); the Blooms, to 75 (39 of those in notes); Seidel, to only 7; Rawson, to 18; Griffin, to 36; and Bogel, to just 6. Of the 94 works alluded to by more than one critic, 21 are Swift's, 10 are Pope's (including *Peri Bathous* and *Memoirs of Scriblerus*), and 6 are Dryden's. Ten are Fielding's, 3 are Johnson's, and Gay and Smollett each contribute 3 to the count. (Only 2 of the 94 works are by female writers—Sarah Fielding's *David Simple* and Lennox's *The Female Quixote*.) The math is striking: of the 94 works discussed in multiple satire studies, 34 (36%) are by the major "Scriblerian" trio, Pope, Swift, and Gay; 37 (39%) are by the "Augustan" heavyweights, Dryden, Swift, and Pope. Dryden, Swift, Pope, and Fielding account for 47 of the works (50%). If we add Gay, Johnson, and Smollett, the group is responsible for 56 of the works (60%). Roughly 60 percent of the primary material studied in accounts of eighteenth-century satire, in other words, was produced by seven satirists, and half of the satires mentioned in more than one of these studies are by just four writers.

Not all genres fare equally well. That verse satire dominates the list is not surprising; 49 of the 94 works cited by more than one critic are poems (that is, more than half). Prose satire is a broad category, including anything from *The Rehearsal Transpros'd* to *Peri Bathous* to *Tristram Shandy*, and it also receives relatively substantial coverage: 29 of the works fall under this heading, including 10 by Swift, 4 by Fielding, and 3 by Smollett. Five satirical or sometimes satirical journals are cited. The generic loser on the list is drama: only 11 dramatic satires are referred to by more than one scholar, and 4 of those are Fielding's. Other noteworthy playwrights are entirely unrepresented. None of Dryden's plays makes this list, and neither does anything by Shadwell, Southerne, Macklin, or Foote. I grant that adding *The Kind Keeper* and *Amphitryon* might not significantly alter our theories, but the problem is bigger than a particular work or set of works.

Vast amounts of satiric material have been expunged from our literary history. Let us take, for example, the 1690s, a decade little admired by satire scholars. I have read some 160 datable satires first published or apparently composed in this decade. This total includes such obvious items as Dryden's translation of Juvenal and Persius (1693)[14] and Garth's *Dispensary* (1699). It also includes a flock of plays: the anonymous *The Female Wits* (satirizing Delarivier Manley and others); Southerne's *The Wives' Excuse* and *The Maid's Last Prayer*; Shadwell's *The Scowrers*; Behn's *The Widdow Ranter*; Dryden's *Amphitryon*; Congreve's *The Old Batchelour*, *The Double-Dealer*, and *Love for Love*; and Vanbrugh's *The Relapse* and *The Provok'd Wife*. Miscellaneous items include Tutchin's *The Tribe of Levi*, Ward's *The Poet's Ramble after Riches* and the beginning of his *London Spy*, and Defoe's *A New Discovery of an Old Intreague* and *An Encomium upon a Parliament*. A large number of satires were being written and circulated. The first collection of *Poems on Affairs of State* appeared in 1689 and the last in 1716, printing hundreds of poems from the mid-seventeenth century to the time of publication. Massive though these volumes are, they contain nothing like all the poems now known to survive in manuscript. More than five hundred topical verse satires on state affairs have survived from the period 1688 to 1697 alone.[15] The seven-volume twentieth-century collection of the same title represents only a small selection of what is to be found in the original volumes of *Poems on Affairs of State*. A lot happened in satire in this decade, but the modern canon reflects almost none of this activity—the nineties being part of the black hole that separates *Absalom and Achitophel* from *A Tale of a Tub*.

That the canonical works of Dryden, Pope, Swift and a few others count, while the low-culture or nonliterary dreck does not, is inherited wisdom. In 1940, Worcester genially pronounced the irrelevance of inferior samples: "In thinking of satire," he ruled, "we should consider the hundreds of works that have risen to the top. The millions below . . . are interesting only insofar as they help to explain the principles of great satire."[16] Nothing else in later satire studies quite matches Worcester's ringing endorsement of a purely evaluative system of selection, but other scholars have, at least implicitly, followed his lead. Jack observes that any study of a long period must be either "extremely general or extremely selective," and he admits to his being the latter: "Since I wished to avoid byways and concentrate on the central poems of the period, several of the poems selected themselves."[17] When Bogel states that his study "focuses mostly on canonical texts by male authors,"[18] we can guess to which writers he is referring. The writers generally thought of as "Tories" have dominated our accounts of the period as a whole, and broadly speaking this is true in treatments of satire as well.

Most literary critics would readily acknowledge that they discuss what is good and ignore what is less good, disagreeing with me only on the question of whether this selectivity represents a problem. Are the scores of noncanonical satires simply inferior examples of a mode perfected by Dryden, Swift, and Pope? If so, then adding them to our field of vision only makes for thankless drudgery, an exercise in wading through muck to find what we already knew existed. Another way of asking the question: can the major writers tell us how to read the period? Some critics seem to assume so. In the satire chapter of *The Cambridge Companion to English Literature, 1650–1740*, Michael Seidel "proves" a series of claims about satire by stating each of his points and asserting its application to Dryden, Pope, and Swift.[19] Obviously we need to ask how well these conclusions hold up if we extend our test sample beyond those three writers.

The truth is that the canonical masterpieces are not representative of satiric practice in this period. J. Paul Hunter is one of a few critics who have recognized the rich messiness of writing. In his discussion of poetry in the long eighteenth century, he reminds us that others beyond Dryden and Pope were writing, others to whom posterity has been unkind. Ultimately, however, he concludes that "Pope from his youth set the tone for virtually everything that happened in poetry" and that—in the case of Dryden, then Pope, and yet later Johnson—"a single figure tended to dominate, indeed virtually rule, the world of writing" in their respective periods.[20] Pope was extremely important; many of his contemporaries feared or resented him, and others were prepared to be obsequious. He certainly had a reputation, as well as indisputable influence on later eighteenth-century poets. But at least in the realm of satire, there are decided dangers to assuming that his work "set the tone," which means that in excluding the majority of satires we are losing more than bulk. The works of Mayn-waring, Dodsley, Garrick, and many other satirists are not second-rate exemplars of what is now thought of as "Augustan" satire. They represent fundamentally different enterprises from each other and from the kind of satire described by modern critics.

Satire scholars have singled out the great works and then forgotten that much has been erased, and if anything, that represents a problem greater than selectivity. We operate as though what we are discussing is all there is, and that leads us to treat the works in our canon as somehow connected, as vital links in an evolutionary chain. Literary critics are often of a mind to sort everything into a few categories, to dem-onstrate shared concept, to describe a "mode." In the literary history of satire, Swift and Pope follow Dryden; Fielding and Johnson and Sterne follow Pope and Swift. Lumping *Absalom and Achitophel* with *A Tale of a Tub* under the heading of "Augus-tan" satire takes both works out of their original contexts and, considerably different though they are, invites us to find commonalities that we may be all too inclined to exaggerate. The connection from Dryden to Swift is cloudy, dubious, and insubstan-tial; the spate of Carolean clandestine satires have little to do with what happens after 1700; the assumption that Pope and Swift are twin satirists is a falsification; the rela-tionship of satire in the 1710s to that of the 1730s is tenuous. *Absalom and Achitophel, A Tale, The Dunciad,* and the other much-studied works need to be understood as chronologically remote examples of a widely practiced and multifarious form. One of the principal conclusions of this book is that the assumed interconnectedness of the great satires is an ex post facto critical construct—and not a useful one.

Radical contextual oversimplification has produced a set of generalizations that we now have the resources to test with relative ease. Reading more satires changes things. I am not suggesting that we replace Swift and Pope on our undergraduate syllabi with Ned Ward and Robert Gould, and I certainly do not wish to demean the canonical works. In my opinion *Absalom and Achitophel* is one of the most brilliant satiric poems in the language, and Swift and Sterne are inspired singularities the likes of which we may never see again. I can well understand the impulse to highlight the masterpieces and filter out the rest, but in this case exercising quality control does nothing but viti-ate the culture we mean to describe. What makes this the Age of Satire is not (or not primarily) the literary value of a dozen tours de force, but the diversity of satiric pos-sibilities and practices. Order-imposing assessments of a select canon have produced a misrepresentation of literary history: what actually exists is much more densely populated, much less logical in its change over time, and spectacularly multifarious.

IV. The Total Satire Canon and Its Economic Context

The canon of eighteenth-century satire has always been relatively small, and the works have been studied in formal or immediately topical and contextual ways. If we are trying to see satire as eighteenth-century readers and writers would have seen it, we need to look at more works and also to appreciate the realities of price and circulation. The first half of this section is an attempt to convey the magnitude and diversity of the primary material that falls under the heading of Satire in England, 1658–1770, and the second half of the section is devoted to a brief discussion of the price of satire and the implications of price for dissemination and audience.

The Production of Satire in England, 1658–1770

An astonishing amount of satire circulated in this period. Between 1689 and 1716, more than thirty collections of *State Poems* (or *Poems on Affairs of State*) appeared, including some twelve hundred verse satires. At least another twenty-five hundred exist only in manuscript form.[21] I have looked at over three thousand satiric works from the long eighteenth century in verse, prose, and dramatic forms, and despite my best efforts, what I have managed to get my hands on is nothing like the totality of what circulated in the period.[22] These works are many, and they come in all shapes and sizes. Verbal satire is found in anything from one-page, occasional squibs to five-hundred-page novels. Year in and year out throughout the long eighteenth century, in addition to the reprinting of classical and continental texts, new satires appeared in England, and quite a few were reprinted (frequently only once, some a small number of times, others more often and over longer periods). A considerable number of satires do not seem "literary." A lot of them are ephemeral, short, and cheap. Early in the period, many circulated in manuscript form, and only a small percentage of printed satires named an author on the title page. Subjects and targets are all over the map: satirists write on succession, revolution, and monarchy; on wine and brandy; on bad writers and on bad ministers of state; on marriage and satirists of marriage. Some works appear in neatly bound editions, handsomely presented and confidently at-tributed; many are broadsides sans publication information or date. In tone, format, and subject matter, virtually anything goes. We can find satirical ballads, lampoons, formal verse satires, narrative satire of various sorts, mock epics and burlesque satires, ballad operas, farce, mock journalism, cartoons and caricatures, and just about any other type of verbal or visual representation. Satire shows up everywhere, and it fol-lows no very rigid generic principles.

We need to have a sense of scope. One way of getting that is to look at the quantity and diversity of what happens in a single year, and any year will make the point. Different years reflect different patterns—the range in satiric types and targets is not the same in, say, 1660, 1715, and 1770—but at no time is there homogeneity or inactivity. One of the themes of this book is that looking only at canonical masterpieces gives us an incomplete picture of what goes on at any given moment, so I will use as my sample year one in which a major work is published. *Absalom and Achitophel* is only one of many 1681 satires and hardly a representative one. Table 1.2 is a list of satires associated with 1681, by which I mean satires published, performed, or apparently first circulated in manuscript in that year. Dating manuscript satires is obviously a thorny business, and no doubt many works were circulating in 1681 that cannot be dated with any certainty. I include only the ones for which, whether on the basis of internal or external evidence, we have some confidence about date.

The point is not only volume but variety. In some ways 1681 is an unusual year, as many writers are worrying about the same set of issues. Satirist after satirist decries Shaftesbury and Monmouth or tries to associate the Whigs with the sectarians of the 1640s, and a sizable portion of satire in the period 1679–1681 reflects marked authorial anxiety. The year 1681 was critical, and the crisis was very much on satirists' minds. That said, the thirty-five satires listed in table 1.2 do reflect appreciable range. College scorches the government (at the cost of his life), as does Ayloffe; both are primarily *offensive* satirists attacking the establishment. Dryden's sketches of Shaftesbury, Monmouth, Buckingham, and others are stinging, but his purposes are as much defensive as antagonistic; he is championing the Stuart monarchy and the status quo. Behn and the author of *Poor Robins Dream* both connect contemporary Whigs with the civil war radicals, but Behn's racy farce is quite different from the latter's anxious verse prophecy. Some of these works seem playful in their disparagement of targets (*The London Cuckolds*); some reflect irritation or disapprobation (*The Club of Royalists*); some are ferociously denunciatory (*Oceana and Britannia*). They consist of straight invective or ironic indirection; targets can be standard butts (*A Panegyric*) or hated rivals (*A New Ballad of London's Loyalty*). Satirists may either oppose or defend the status quo; they may revel in mockery (*The Ladies' March*) or defame for the sake of purposive negative propaganda (*The New Miracle*). These works do not represent manifestations of a unified satiric "mode," and neither are they typified in any way by Dryden's masterful biblical allegory.

Other "big" years are just as untidy. Swift's dizzying *A Tale of a Tub* appears in 1704. So does Maynwaring's (?) *An Address to Our Sovereign Lady*, a libelous attack on the Tory Commons; it has quite a lot of bounce and a good deal of venom, reflecting its author's bitter disenchantment. The anonymous *Tryal of Skill* is a universe apart from the fiery condemnation by Maynwaring and from Swift's mad *Tale*—it is a nonserious, high-spirited "session of the poets" piece whose writer does not pretend that anything is at stake. *The Devil Turn'd Limner* is a mixture of prose and verse, a

TABLE 1.2
Satires written or published in 1681

Author	Title	Published or MS	Length	Genre	Characterization
John Ayloffe	Oceana and Britannia	MS	201 lines	allegorical poem	high-heat execration of Charles II and monarchy; pro-republican
Aphra Behn	The Roundheads	perf. 1681; pub. 1682	58 pp.	parallel play	associates Whigs with Cromwell and civil war radicals
Henry Care	Towser the Second a Bull-Dog	pub.	2 pp.	personal lampoon	bilious Whig attack on L'Estrange and Dryden
Stephen College	Raree Show	pub.	2 pp.	ballad	violent libel against the government
College	A Satyr against Injustice, or, Sc[rog]gs upon Sc[rog]gs	pub.	48 lines	high-heat lampoon	one of several of College's libels on Lord Chief Justice Scroggs
Charles Sackville, Earl of Dorset	My Opinion	MS	20 lines	lively poetic squib	attack on both Monmouth and Duke of York; mildly pro-Whig
John Dryden	Absalom and Achitophel	pub.	38 pp.	verse biblical allegory	attack on Whigs and defense of king
Dryden	The Spanish Fryar	pub.	94 pp.	split-plot tragicomedy	ridicules priest; offers implicit political message
Thomas Durfey	The Progress of Honesty	pub.	23 pp.	narrative allegory in verse	Tory prevails over Whig with caricatures of Shadwell and Shaftesbury
Durfey	Sir Barnaby Whigg	pub.	63 pp.	intrigue comedy	topical political commentary
Andrew Marvell	Flecknoe, an English Priest at Rome	wr. 1646; pub. 1681	170 lines	defamatory poem	personal attack with religiopolitical point
Marvell	The Character of Holland	wr. 1653; pub. 1681	152 lines	harsh satiric poem	politically motivated attack on the Dutch
Charles Mordaunt, Earl of Monmouth	The Ladies' March	MS	97 lines	"procession" lampoon	ridicules 23 court ladies but with little real animosity; bawdy

Author	Title	Status	Length	Form	Description
Alexander Radcliffe	The Lawyers' Demurrer Argued	pub.	72 lines	ballad	anti-Whig expression of loyalty to the king; lighthearted
Edward Ravenscroft	The London Cuckolds	perf. and pub. 1683	63 pp.	sex farce	ridicules cits
Wentworth Dillon, Earl of Roscommon	The Ghost of the Old House of Commons	pub.	65 lines	"ghost"-scene poem	high-heat warning to king; detraction of Whigs
Anon.	Advice to the Painter . . . for Limning to the Life the Witnesses Against . . . Shaftesbury	pub.	112 lines	"advice to the painter" poem	topical attack on Irish witnesses against Shaftesbury; pro-Whig
Anon.	A Canto on the New Miracle Wrought by . . . Monmouth	MS	83 lines	lampoon	bawdy Tory derision of Monmouth; low heat
Anon.	The Club of Royalists	MS	44 lines	defamatory poem	Tory attack on (named) Whigs; relatively mild
Anon.	An Essay of Scandal	MS	84 lines	lampoon/advice poem	obscene attack on court ladies and King's whoremongering
Anon.	Grimalkin, or, the Rebel Cat	pub.	13 pp.	beast fable in prose	attacks Shaftesbury
Anon.	An Heroic Poem 1681	MS	140 lines	verse invective/libel	spiteful personal attack on Whig politicians; scatological
Anon.	A New Ballad of London's Loyalty	pub.	48 lines	ballad	stinging attack on (named) city Whigs; calls for loyalty to the king
Anon.	The Oxford Vision. April 1681	MS	37 lines	political "vision" poem	topical swipe at Irish informer against the Whigs
Anon.	A Panegyric	MS	85 lines	personal lampoon	bawdy political attack on Nell Gwyn
Anon.	A Panegyrick On the Author of Absolom and Achitophel . . .	pub.	98 lines	invective	attacks Dryden as a time server; politically and personally motivated

(continued)

TABLE 1.2 (continued)

Author	Title	Published or MS	Length	Genre	Characterization
Anon.	The Parliament Dissolved at Oxford	MS	36 lines	political libel	satire on Whigs in the Commons; defense of king
Anon.	Poor Robins Dream	pub.	6 pp.	dream vision	angry attack on Shaftesbury and Whig radicals
Anon.	The Quarrel between Frank and Nan	MS	171 lines	hudibrastics	indirect political commentary; topical
Anon.	Sir John Berkenhead Reviv'd	pub.	37 pp.	parallel history in verse	associates Whigs with civil war radicals; warns and defends Charles
Anon.	The Tune to the Devonshire Cant: Or, an Answer to the Parliament Dissolved at Oxford	pub.	36 lines	political poem	Whig defense of House of Commons
Anon.	Utile Dulce	MS	136 lines	shotgun libel	snarling attack on several named figures
Anon.	A Vision in the Tower to the Lord Howard . . .	pub.	100 lines	vision poem/ libel	politicized Tory attack on Lord Howard
Anon.	The Waking Vision	pub.	155 lines	vision/advice poem	high anxiety; warns king against Whigs and Catholics
Anon.	The Whiggs Lamentation For . . . their Dear Brother Colledge	pub.	72 lines	ironic elegy	bouncy, ironic derogation of Whigs with a "Whig" speaker

Note: Listed alphabetically by author when known, and alphabetically by title where authorship is unknown.

politicized lampoon blasting John Tutchin as a treacherous rogue. Nicholas Rowe's only comedy, *The Biter*, targets not a particular person but a recognizable type; the generalized "O tempora" satire called *A Hymn to Money* proves entirely toothless. These satires look nothing like Swift's *Tale*—how could they?—and they have little in common with each other. Writers like Maynwaring and Tom Brown pen religio-political invectives with conviction, whereas others are exuberantly general and un-troubled by what they describe. Defoe's *The Address* is the stuff of principled political commentary; the anonymous *The Folly of Industry* is clever for the sake of cleverness. The possibilities for and realities of satire—in 1681 and 1704, as throughout the long eighteenth century—were many.

A few more examples of what I mean: Swift wrote his abusive lampoon on Lord Cutts (*Description of a Salamander*) in 1705. Defoe's *The Consolidator*, a 364-page fantasy-narrative attack on the High Church position, appeared that year; so did Susanna Centlivre's lightweight reform comedy, *The Basset-Table*. In the same year, the anonymous *Korath: or the Danger of Schism* pessimistically complains about the Whigs, Occasional Conformists, and Presbyterians, while the chauvinistic author of *The D[utch] Deputies* excoriates the Dutch and hopes for their destruction. What these works have in common as *satires* is almost nothing. In 1706, Defoe publishes *Jure Divino*, a twelve-book verse satire of 374 pages advocating contractual government and targeting proponents of divine right, and John Dunton prints his *Whipping-Post*, an all-inclusive attack carried out on entirely personal grounds. Defoe's densely argu-mentative piece of political theorizing is a drastically different sort of satiric venture from Dunton's antagonistic lampooning of personal foes. In 1734, Pope's *Sober Advice from Horace* is published; on stage appear both Henry Carey's nonsensical *The Tragedy of Chrononhotonthologos* and Gay's *Distress'd Wife*, a cynical satiric comedy on Lon-don high life. Fielding is sour and shrill in *The Universal Gallant* (1735), and in the same year Robert Dodsley is lighthearted and affectionate in *The Toy-Shop*. No one would argue that Dryden is like Behn or Ravenscroft, that Swift's *Tale* represents the same kind of enterprise as Rowe's *The Biter*, or that Pope has much in common with Carey—but if we extract Dryden, Swift, and Pope from their contexts, then we tend to create the impression that, however much greater their works are, they somehow characterize the practice of their moments.

We cannot talk about eighteenth-century satire in terms of a single mode, or even two or three discrete modes. In any given decade or half decade, common themes and targets are apparent; trends come and go; controversial satires generate responses; the popularity of a particular satire (e.g., *Hudibras* or *Gulliver's Travels*) inspires imita-tions, allusions, or other forms of borrowing. Chapters 3 through 7 cover subperiods in which we find recognizable patterns and trends, but in each of those subperiods and in the long eighteenth century as a whole, we also discover considerable range.

Satires can be gloomy, solemn but not pessimistic, jolly, or anything in between. The subject can be global (*The Fatal Union of France and Spain*) or local (*A Satyr on Lincolnshire*), issues of monumental importance to both author and nation (*Absalom and Achitophel*), or matters purely trivial (*A Satyr against Coffee*). The satirist can be detached narrator, oppressive speech maker, or ironic commentator. His attitude toward his subject can range from delight to distaste, from laughter to sharp mockery or bitter denunciation. He may or may not believe that anything can change: Congreve's *The Way of the World* (1700) reflects glum acquiescence in an unalterable state of affairs, whereas Southerne's *The Wives' Excuse* (another hard-hitting social satire, staged nine years earlier) furiously denounces what the playwright cannot accept.

The satirist may rail angrily against a despised subject, or he may affectionately nudge a target with whom he mostly sympathizes, as in Fielding's mockery of Parson Adams. He may or may not be having fun. His purpose may be pure entertainment (Ward's *The Rambling Rakes*), abuse for the pleasure of abuse (Rochester's *My Lord All-pride*), or linguistic and formal play (Churchill's *The Ghost*). Satire can be plaintive (Tutchin's *A Pindarick Ode, in the Praise of Folly and Knavery*), defensive (Defoe's *The True-Born Englishman*), or preachy (Fielding's *Amelia*). Satirists write purposive defamation (Swift's *Fable of Midas*) and propaganda (Garth's *Dispensary*); they deflate their targets (*Tom Thumb*) or denounce them (*The Dunciad*). Many post-1682 satires on Shaftesbury are expressions of gleeful triumphalism; works like Richard Cumberland's *The West Indian* are exercises in satiric education. Rochester's *Upon Nothinge*, Mandeville's *The Fable of the Bees*, and Macklin's *The School for Husbands* are ultimately thought-provocative (though in quite distinct ways), and *Jure Divino* is a piece of sober ideological argumentation. Satirists sometimes invite laughter, as in George Colman the elder's *Polly Honeycombe*, and sometimes harsh judgment, as in *The Fall of Mortimer*. The point is diversity: even within a very short time span, "satire" can mean a wide range of things to writers, readers, and theatergoers. Satirists also write for different kinds of audiences. I deal with both explicit and implicit audiences for satire throughout this book, but here I want to look briefly at what price and format have to tell us about implied audience and circulation.

Price, Format, Dissemination, and Implied Audiences

Few students of satire have paid serious attention to its material contexts. The assumption often seems to be that the works we regard as great were widely read and celebrated and that any literate person had access to every published text. In fact, price and format make a great deal of difference to how extensively satires were circulated and to whom.

What did satire cost, and who could buy it? A systematic recovery of prices would have been all but impossible until very recently, and it remains a spotty and frustrating business. Some printed material carries its price on the title page, and publishers sometimes advertise prices in the newspapers or in lists appended to individual publications. Before 1702—and the advent of daily newspapers—prices are harder to come by than later in the eighteenth century. *The Term Catalogues* give some prices for the years from 1668 to 1709, but only occasionally; Narcissus Luttrell frequently records what he paid for pamphlets (1678–1730), but that is not necessarily the list price. The limits to our knowledge are real, but using the sources we do have (especially ECCO and the full-text-searchable digital Burney newspapers), we can now accumulate a substantial number of prices and get some notion of price norms.

Before particular prices can mean anything, we need to have a sense of the value of money in the period at issue. Appreciating the buying power of eighteenth-century money is difficult, largely because of a value-translation issue. The price of *Law is a Bottomless-Pit* (the first of Arbuthnot's 1712 "John Bull" pamphlets) is 3*d*, and Churchill's *The Prophecy of Famine* goes for 2*s* 6*d* in 1763—are these inexpensive or comparatively steep prices, and how significant is the difference between them? As Robert D. Hume has pointed out, converting eighteenth-century prices into modern terms is problematic: no single multiplier exists by which we may establish a present value for a sum of money. We cannot simply multiply a list price by a set number and arrive at the "right" figure.[23] Prices were relatively stable for most of the eighteenth century, but only relatively, and a multiplier that might work for some commodities at some dates gets us nowhere for other products or at other dates. In the realm of "culture," Hume suggests that a multiplier of two hundred to three hundred should usually give a reasonable indication of present-day value.[24] If we use those figures, Arbuthnot's pamphlet would have set buyers back somewhere between £2.40 and £3.60 by present-day standards. The 2*s* 6*d* that Churchill's poem went for in 1763 amounts to considerably more money, somewhere between £24 and £36 in today's terms—far from a meaningless sum for most consumers.

Affordability depends not only upon price but also upon income: who could without much difficulty afford to spend a shilling (or two, or three, or more) on a satire? What we have by way of primary material on income levels comes from a small number of well-known sources, the most famous of which is Gregory King's *Natural and Political Observations* (1696; concerning the year 1688). King offers estimated population statistics for late seventeenth-century England and describes demographic characteristics, including the numbers of people in different occupations, average incomes, and sizes of families.[25] Modern economic historians have tested and tweaked the figures given by King and others but have found these reports persuasive in their fundamentals.[26] The emended statistics indicate that, as of 1688, roughly 5 percent of the families in England grossed more than £100 per annum—suggesting, says Hume, that "no more than about 5 percent of the total population of England and Wales could have had the discretionary spending capacity to indulge significantly in the purchase of elite culture."[27] Laborers and outservants averaged £15 per annum—less than a shilling a day. How many of them could afford to spend a day's wages on a pamphlet or several weeks' income for a fancier edition? Those working in building trades grossed £25 per annum (under a shilling and a half per day) and those in manufacturing trades £38 (slightly more than two shillings per day). Would someone from those fields with a family of four to feed sacrifice a day's pay for *The Prophecy of Famine*? Probably not, and certainly not often. Obviously consumer behavior is somewhat unpredictable. Someone making £1,000 per annum will not necessarily spend a lot on culture, and someone earning a pittance might scrape and save to buy a particularly coveted book. That said, we can safely assume some correlation, on the whole, between income and consumption of culture, especially in its costlier forms. As William St Clair bluntly observes, "To trace readership, we need to trace access. To trace access, we need to trace price."[28]

What was the price of satire in the long eighteenth century? A representative list of titles sold at several standard price categories, from 1*d* to 15*s*, is given in the appendix. The point is not to be as exhaustive as the limited evidence would permit but to convey some sense of price norms for satire from 1658 to 1770. I include works across as broad a time span as is relevant for each price category. For example, 3*d* is a common price in 1700, but—in part because low-end works tend not to get advertised—that figure is rarely seen later in the period. Conversely, many works were sold at 6*d* and at 1*s* across the century, a fact this list should reflect. I include only printed texts. Little certain knowledge is to be had about the price of scribally circulated manuscripts, but such works are unlikely to have been cheap.[29] In the realm of print publication, I admit both the problem of piracy (making costly texts available at cut rates and presumably increasing circulation) and the importance of binding (a work sold in simple boards will be significantly less expensive than the same work in a fancy binding). Notwithstanding these issues and the gaps in our knowledge, looking at what a number of satires cost throughout this period should yield useful conclusions about circulation.

What do the prices listed in the appendix imply for the circulation of satire? One point is that the distance between low-end and high-end is vast: the high price category (15*s*) is 180 times the lowest one (1*d*). A broadside priced at a penny would have been a pretty easy acquisition, but for someone grossing less than £50 per annum, 6*d* would not have been a trivial sum. Likewise, a shilling does not sound like much, but it represents twelve times the price of 1*d* and is not an insignificant figure. Except in extraordinary cases, the circulation of anything priced over 2 or 3 shillings (roughly £20 to £45 in modern value) was probably going to be limited to the relatively elite. Ready access to a 4*d* pamphlet is very different from ready access to a fat novel priced at 5*s*: how many of the not-filthy-rich of 2012 would unhesitatingly drop £50 to £75 for a bit of light reading, even in the absence of television?

How much satire was sold at 1*d*, 6*d*, 1*s*, and so on is impossible to guess. Late seventeenth-century price information is scanty at best, and what is advertised at any point in this period are usually not the less expensive items. That said, some facts are clear. Shorter tends to be cheaper, and for good reason. Paper accounted for a staggering proportion of production costs: it was, says St Clair, "a commodity in its own right."[30] The correlation between length and price is inexact but considerable. The price of plays is more or less standardized: single titles tend to be 1*s* early in this period, and over time a price of 1*s* 6*d* becomes common. The price of novels is often, of course, extortionate. The four volumes of *Peregrine Pickle* in boards would set one back 10*s* 6*d*, and bound the price goes up to 12*s*. Works a third that price would have been painfully expensive for all but a tiny percentage of the population. The large sale of such books as *Robinson Crusoe* (5*s*) and *Gulliver's Travels* (8*s* 6*d*—roughly £80–£120 in modern terms) is testimony to a success even more phenomenal than most literary critics have realized.

Because price rises with length, most collections and miscellanies were quite expensive. In 1701, two volumes of Dryden's *Plays* in folio were advertised at £1 12*s*— upward of £300 in present-day money even by a conservative estimate. In March 1728, *The Monthly Catalogue* listed the "last Volume" of the Pope-Swift *Miscellanies* at 5*s* 6*d*; the two-volume *Miscellanies* had been advertised the previous summer at 8*s* 6*d*.[31] Whether one calculates the latter at a mere £85 or more like £125, this was a very pricey enterprise. Some of Dryden's, Pope's, and Swift's single titles sold fairly cheaply when originally published, but when reprinted in larger volumes they were fiendishly expensive. Even the writings of lesser satirists were often startlingly pricey: in 1733, Tom Brown's complete works were advertised in four volumes for 12*s* (£120–£180)— not exactly easy on the pocket. A 1719 ad puffs a five-volume set of Ward's *Works* for a dumbfounding £1 5*s*.[32] Obviously a good Englishman with cash to spare might feel compelled to own the writings of the preeminent authors of his isle, just as a patriotic Irishman might splurge on the famous Drapier's works in 1745, but bulky collections must have been largely out of the reach of the unwashed masses. At the very least, such a volume would represent a rare extravagance for most of the population, not a routine purchase.

Could a writer appeal to more than one market tranche simultaneously? Early in Pope's career, he sold his collected works exclusively to a very upper-end audience, but he came to resist the restrictions on readership imposed by steep prices. The first volume of his *Works* (1717) sold for a guinea in large folio, but the advertisement for the 1735 *Works II* lists three different prices, two distinctly high and one significantly lower. The large folio would set one back a guinea; a smaller folio could be had for

12*s*, and, we are told, the contents of the volume would "with all convenient Speed be published in Twelves at 5*s*."[33] For whatever reason, the cheaper version came out in two octavo volumes for 3*s* each—not a negligible sum by any means but less than a third the cost of the large folio. The print runs of the pricier versions, James McLaverty reports, were considerably smaller than had been the case for the earlier *Works*, suggesting that Pope "was starting to focus on the production of a popular edition."[34] The text and apparatus of the octavo volumes differed from the larger format version in important ways. The folio and quarto editions were "aimed at the 'subscribing' type of reader," and the 6*s* edition was aimed at more "casual" readers, those desirous only of "an up-to-date version of Pope's work that was accessible and comprehensible." McLaverty points out that Pope, energized by the possibility of a broader readership, followed *Works II* with octavo editions of his earlier poems.[35] Pope was perfectly clear on the effect of price on dissemination, and while the "cheap" editions still cost a goodly sum, their existence suggests the desire to reach an audience not limited to the ultra elite.

Defoe's satiric output nicely illustrates the importance of price. His many occasional satires had a sizable readership, and scholars have tended to see him as a "Merchant-Writer" addressing hoi polloi. That impression is incomplete and misleading. John Richetti describes *The True-Born Englishman* as "popular poetry, near-doggerel directed at untutored understandings, ready to be hawked in the streets like a tabloid newspaper,"[36] but this poem was reprinted in pricey collections that were successfully marketed to affluent readers. The dissemination history of Defoe's satires does not suggest that he wrote exclusively for a lower-end audience.[37] The first compilation was printed in 1703 under the title *A True Collection of the Writings of the . . . True Born English-man*, an anthology containing several early satires; it did sufficiently well to prompt another edition. The *Second Volume* was published in 1705; it sold for 6*s*—a substantial sum—but did well enough to justify further editions.

These two volumes were reprinted again in 1710, and subsequent editions were published in 1711, 1713, and 1714. Whatever the topicality of the individual satires contained therein, these books had a relatively long shelf life. *The Genuine Works of Mr. Daniel D'Foe* appeared in 1721; it included forty texts and went for an astounding 12*s*. Such was Defoe's confidence in marketing his work that his longest satire, *Jure Divino* (1706), was published by subscription for 15*s* (£150–£225).[38] Pirated versions appeared for a third of that price (still a hefty sum) and then in twelve parts at 1*d* each (totaling roughly £10–£15 in present-day terms). In his *Review*, Defoe complained bitterly about the "Robbery" represented by the "spurious" 5*s* edition; he appealed to "those Gentlemen" who had encouraged him to print *Jure Divino*, imploring them "to stand the Firmer by their Subscription."[39] Piracy notwithstanding, Defoe clearly imagined a different readership for *Jure Divino* than for his penny ballads, and that he made such a distinction is not shocking. A work like *Ye True-Born Englishmen Proceed* is stingingly direct in its denunciation of its targets; *Jure Divino* is a heavy-going argument about the competing theories of government. It is meant for a different kind of reader.

Price clearly matters to readership, and so does availability. Many of the satires produced in the long eighteenth century are topical and ephemeral—they appear just once or are reprinted only for a brief period. The great majority of the noncanonical satires are transitory, but not all of them simply vanish. Defoe's *Ye True-Born Englishmen Proceed* is reprinted seven times in 1701 and *The Mock Mourners* nine times a year later; *The Political History of the Devil* (1726) goes to a second edition in 1727 and a third in 1734 and is reprinted at least eleven more times in the century. Much the most popular of Defoe's satires is *The True-Born Englishman*, which appears again and again throughout the hundred years following its initial publication (1s is the standard price). Several of Ward's satires are regularly reprinted, including *A Trip to Jamaica* (published in 1698 and in its seventh edition by 1700) and *Female Policy Detected*, which comes out at least a dozen times between 1695 and 1788. Garth's *Dispensary* is popular (three 1699 editions; by 1768, it is in its eleventh). *Hudibras* is a particularly spectacular example of a topical satire with a long afterlife: new editions of Butler's poem appear every decade from the 1660s to the 1790s. Among the more heavily reprinted satires of the eighteenth century proper is Henry Carey's *Dragon of Wantley*, a lively parody of Italian opera, staged and published in 1737 and already in its fourteenth edition the next year.

Works now considered historically important were sometimes regularly reprinted—*Gulliver's Travels* and *The Dunciad* are prominent examples—but often not. *Absalom and Achitophel* is frequently reissued early in the period (the tenth edition comes out in 1701), but, except for a Latin edition in 1723, it does not appear separately in England after 1708. *Mac Flecknoe* is published by itself only three times (in 1682, 1692, and 1709). Of Dryden's satiric oeuvre, the works popular over the longest period of time are probably *The Spanish Fryar* and *Fables Ancient and Modern*. His now celebrated *Discourse concerning the Original and Progress of Satire* appears only in the fat volume of translations; to my knowledge it was never published alone.[40] Swift's *Modest Proposal* is printed singly only in 1729 and 1730. Johnson's *London* goes through four editions by 1739 and is reprinted in 1750, but *The Vanity of Human Wishes* appears separately in 1749 and not again. Much more widely visible is Churchill's *The Rosciad*, which runs through five editions in 1761 (at 1s 6d) and is in its ninth by 1765 (at 2s 6d). *The Memoirs of Scriblerus* is never printed in London by itself. It comes out in Dublin in 1741 and then in England that year as part of Pope's *Works*—in a vastly expensive volume, 10s 6d or a guinea depending on format. Students of eighteenth-century satire find Pope's *Epistle to Arbuthnot* very important, but it is published alone only in 1735. It is included in *Works II*, the cheapest version of which was 3*s*. That major works were widely available upon initial publication and forever accessible to all readers is by no means universally true.

The price of satire is interesting in two very different ways. (1) Collections and larger works (e.g., Christopher Anstey's *New Bath Guide*, at 5*s* for 132 pages) were punitively expensive for any but a small fraction of the population. (2) A remarkable number of satires were affordable. The most common prices of satiric poems and pamphlets are 6*d* and 1*s*—not trifling sums, but hardly out of reach for most potential buyers. A huge quantity of satires—mostly topical and timely—were fairly short, printed singly, and sold at a level that would allow for reasonably wide circulation. These works were meant to reach and influence readers, and while a lower-end price range does not guarantee broad distribution, it does at least create the potential for wide sale and real-world effect.

This study is an attempt to reconstruct the world of eighteenth-century satire, to understand insofar as possible what satire meant to authors and readers, and for whom and to what end particular works were written. Because a taxonomic survey of this scope and level of detail will necessarily be somewhat difficult to process, I will specify some of its features and claims before plunging into it. The next two sections are meant to prepare the reader for the kind of arguments that follow, and they anticipate, albeit in broad terms, some of the conclusions the study will yield.

V. Some Issues of Coverage and Organization

The title of this book invites two questions: why these dates and why "in England"? As my object is to test the conclusions drawn about "Augustan satire," I need naturally to include the years from (roughly speaking) the return of Charles II to the deaths of Pope and Swift. I begin in the late 1650s rather than 1660 because I wish to avoid giving the impression that the Restoration represents an abrupt turning point. The world of Cromwell is very different from the world of Charles II, in satiric as well as socio- and religiopolitical terms, but 1660 is better understood as a transitional year than as a beginning. I have carried the study a generation beyond the deaths of Pope and Swift in part out of my own curiosity: what happens to eighteenth-century satire after its two most famous practitioners cease to produce it? The critical attention given to the satire of the later eighteenth century has mostly been limited to verse, but treating the poetry alongside satire in other genres and placing all of it at the end of a fuller survey of satiric practice in the previous century are revelatory. The period covered in this book is the great age of satire not because Dryden, Swift, and Pope are the best satirists ever to have written satire but because the variety of satiric practice in these years is (I believe) not to be found anywhere else. The range we find in the 1670s or the reign of Queen Anne, for example, is considerably wider than what we find in the 1590s, 1640s, 1850s, or 1990s. Satire is not the same in all genres, times, and places. What makes the period from the late 1650s to 1770 so exceptional is the unparalleled number of modes emerging, developing, and sometimes disappearing.

What do I mean by satiric practice "in England"? I have for the most part limited the discussion to works belonging to London literary culture; only a small number of works printed elsewhere in England are cited. The decision is in part a matter of convenience: adding a systematic survey of Welsh, Scottish, and Irish satires would make this a bigger and more confusing book. Swift is the obvious exception: most of his works were printed or reprinted in England, and many of them are on English subjects, but this is not always true. Still, I include all of Swift's satires because of his importance to the canon of English literature; throwing out the Drapier's Letters or *The Legion Club* seems unwise. How eighteenth-century satiric practice in Wales, Scotland, and Ireland relates to that in England is an interesting question that warrants serious exploration but cannot be covered here.

A few further explanations about the coverage and method of this book are in order. The eleven satire studies discussed above in section III tend to offer detailed analyses of the works they treat. My enterprise is of a different sort: I cite roughly a thousand titles here, about a third of the works on which my conclusions are based. I read all the printed satires I could find (including both those originally printed and manuscript poems printed in modern sources), as well as some that survive only in manuscript form, and I have tried to demonstrate the differences among them and the prominent trends apparent at any given time. One of my aims throughout is to characterize the nature of the enterprise: what is the satirist trying to accomplish? Discussing authorial intention is a dubious business and its legitimacy has been hotly contested, but for most satires we can constructively and with reasonable certainty draw conclusions about what the satirist thought he was doing. I do not cite every example of a particular type (and I doubt readers will wish I had), but I have tried to represent the full spectrum of possibilities and to acknowledge outliers and oddities. I include some plot description where necessary to make the commentary on unfamiliar works comprehensible. I have kept such summaries brief, and I hope that where present they help rather than merely annoy the reader.

A crucial point is that this kind of survey cannot privilege the major satires as they are customarily privileged. Space is limited, satires are many, and my predecessors have produced sound interpretations of most of the canonical satires. I have made no attempt to do justice to the subtleties of, say, Pope's Moral Essays and Horatian imitations. In the few cases where I disagree with earlier critics about textual readings, I have said so at some length, as with *Hudibras* and *Gulliver's Travels*, but my focus is on the nature of satiric practice across a substantial span of time, and so I do not give special weight to the tours de force in my survey. I use as examples those works that seem most representative, illustrative, or significant without regard to familiarity, canonicity, or literary merit—even when this means devoting more space to Samuel Johnson of Cheshire than to the Samuel Johnson whose life was chronicled by Boswell. My object is not to challenge the superiority of *The Vanity of Human Wishes* to *Hurlothrumbo* but to suggest that the canon does not tell us how to read the period properly. For the headliners there has been adulation and explication aplenty, and while I agree that the great works are very great, my object is not to pay homage to that greatness. Still, the major authors are far from irrelevant to the survey: the point is to offer a set of contexts for them, and they loom large in my attempt to reconstruct the world around them.

One objection I anticipate is that I do not make a special effort to say more about female satirists. Although women did write satire in the long eighteenth century— Behn, Haywood, Sarah Fielding, and others—the clichés about satire being a male form are legitimate. Some feminist critics have argued for a female "tradition" of satire; others have faulted male scholars for not discussing more women. In a lukewarm review of Frank Palmeri's *Satire, History, Novel* (2003), Monika Fludernik takes the author to task for his "rather niggardly inclusion of women"—an objection both predictable and unfounded.[41] The fact is that the practice of satire was overwhelmingly a male enterprise. Griffin observes that "the organization of culture has made it difficult for women to write and publish satire" and speculates about the reasons for that difficulty. The small number of female satirists, he says, might be

> because women historically lacked access to a classical education (and thus to the conventions and traditions of satire); because women were long permitted little knowledge of the world outside their own domestic domain; because until recently women have been trained not to develop or display aggressiveness; because hostile images of gossip, nag, complainer, termagant, and virago may have discouraged women from cultivating in public a form that deals in grumbling and railing.[42]

All of these seem plausible to me. What is clear is that, leaving aside the fact that we cannot determine the authorship of anonymous satires, only a relatively tiny number of women tried their hands at satire in the eighteenth century.[43]

This is a study of English practice, and I regret not being able to devote space to systematic coverage of sources and influences. Classical imitations and translations were obviously important in the period at issue, but they mostly do not figure in the following chapters. The major Roman satires were of course widely known to educated Englishmen; they were available in Latin and in a number of significant translations; they mattered to writers' and readers' sense of satire. Imitations and translations by Pope and Johnson have been intensively studied, and William Kupersmith has done broader surveys of Roman satires in seventeenth- and early eighteenth-century England.[44] The ongoing tradition of composition in Latin, especially in the universities, has received good critical attention.[45] I cannot do justice to that material here. Particular imitations (not translations) come up along the way in this survey (Rochester's *Allusion to Horace*, Pope's Horatian imitations, Johnson's *London*). But my opinion is that the uses of classical satire often strongly display the circumstances of the adapter. Smart's 1767 verse translation of Horace, for example, is Christianized in a way that would no doubt have startled Horace considerably.[46] For my purposes, the crucial point is that Rochester's *Allusion to Horace* (for example) is very much a Carolean enterprise; Pope's Horace has little connection to Rochester's and is manifestly a product of the 1730s. Individual exemplars, in other words, tend to fit the particular milieus represented in the survey chapters—that is, they reflect their immediate contexts. Adding more examples and highlighting their classical sources, then, would not change my account of the trends described in this book.

The organization of this book needs a word of explanation. With the exception of chapter 2, the sequence of chapters is chronological but nondevelopmental. By way of introduction to the survey of practice, chapter 2 takes up the issue of contemporary commentary—what eighteenth-century critics and practitioners of satire had to say about it. Contrary to the conclusions drawn by P. K. Elkin in *The Augustan Defence of Satire* (1973), we will find that contemporary attitudes toward satire are scattered and inconsistent. The chronological survey of practice occupies chapters 3 through 7. Chapter 3 covers the reign of Charles II (1660–1685) and the years that immediately preceded it; chapter 4 focuses on satire at the end of the seventeenth century (roughly speaking, that produced under James II and William III); chapter 5 deals with the first quarter of the eighteenth century; chapter 6 features the "Scriblerian" heyday between the publication of *Gulliver's Travels* (1726) and the deaths of Pope and Swift in the mid-1740s; and chapter 7 surveys the period from 1745 to circa 1770. My reservations about the wisdom of periodization compel me to say that I do not imagine these subperiods as neatly discrete entities. Obviously no one rang a bell in 1725, heralding a transition from the old way of doing satire to a new dominant mode. The break points are only approximations; if works published a few years beyond a chapter's ostensible cutoff date are relevant to or clearly belong to the culture I am describing in that chapter, I include them there. The terminus a quo and terminus ad quem of each chapter are inexact—but the subperiods created by these divisions do represent the changing nature of satiric activity found within them, on which more shortly.

In the interest of clarity, let me say explicitly that each of the survey chapters attempts to accomplish two very different things, amid a variety of specific arguments about particular works and writers covered therein. The first aim is essentially negative: I am trying to show diversity and heterogeneity, to challenge the notion of, say, a "Restoration mode" or a "Scriblerian mode." But I am also demonstrating that each of the subperiods has its own particular markers by which it can be distinguished from the others—a constructive conclusion. I see no contradiction in this dual agenda: one can understand that no "Restoration mode" existed and also that what happens in the reign of Charles II is very different from what happens later. A few kinds of satire are, unsurprisingly, constant—invective, moral preachment, and mockery appear throughout the long eighteenth century—but each subperiod has a character all its own and, often, its own set of satiric purposes. Satiric prophecies and vision and dream poems are mostly a feature of Carolean satire; defense and triumphalism are more prominent in chapter 4 than elsewhere; monitory satire, impersonation, and provocation flourish in the reign of Anne; mixed-mode satire appears early in Bunyan and Shadwell but becomes increasingly conspicuous in the mid- and later eighteenth century; and so on.

Satire comprises many different kinds of enterprise, and we need to attend to those differences, while also appreciating the local identity of the subperiods. We should be aware, moreover, that just as practices shift from chapter to chapter, so do we often find distinct subperiods within chapters. To separate Carolean satire from what follows is important; so is recognizing that the late 1660s and early 1670s are significantly different, tonally speaking, from the late 1670s and early 1680s. Satire in the first quarter of the eighteenth century needs to be distinguished from that of the 1690s and the 1730s, but what we find in the reign of Anne does not even continue into the 1715–1725 period. The periods covered in chapters 4, 6, and 7, on the contrary, have less obvious subdivision within them. The bottom line that emerges from chronological investigation is that what actually gets written, when read year by year, looks radically different from the picture generated in an overview of masterpieces.

VI. The Uses of a Taxonomic Methodology

A taxonomic survey of the sort I am attempting demands a lot of its readers. It emphasizes discontinuity rather than continuity, variousness rather than uniformity, and it requires dealing briefly with a vast number of works, many of them unfamiliar. The resulting flood of endless differentiation is likely to seem overwhelming. Part of the problem is that the taxonomic categories that help with material in one subperiod are less useful, and sometimes irrelevant, in another. For that reason, each chapter has its own structure and logic and often a different set of groupings for readers to get accustomed to. The large number of noncongruent taxonomic categories issues not from a desire to abuse my readers but from a wish honestly to represent what is happening in the material surveyed. The point is diversity of practice and rapidity of change—though I am suggesting other patterns and new characterizations to replace the ones the survey challenges.

The Varieties of Satire

Up to this point, I have been trying to explain my rationale for and procedure in this book; I now offer some sense of what such a study can tell us. The object of any taxonomic survey is to improve our ability to characterize particular exemplars. My argument is that "satire" is not a single mode but many possible modes and that we need a better vocabulary by which to distinguish among (and within) those modes. Fowler explains, "We identify the genre to interpret the exemplar"—but invoking satire, whether we think of it as a genre or a mode, often helps interpretation only minimally.[47] If we want to cope adequately with particular satiric works, we need more categories and finer distinctions. The epilogue to this book includes a list of satiric modes—broadly speaking, reasons for writing—and subcategories of each, as well as examples that have appeared in the survey. This is not the place to give an exhaustive account of the variations we will find, but let me offer some brief illustrations of the nature of the distinctions that seem most important.

My taxonomy depends most broadly upon distinguishing among three fundamentally different types of satiric enterprise. (1) *Attack*. Here the element of critique is dominant, the satire essentially negative. (2) *Distributive justice*. This kind of satire presents positive as well as negative examples or includes exemplary critique. Classical satire theory allows for the possibility of recommendation of virtue as well as denunciation of vice, a position Dryden endorses in his *Discourse concerning Satire*. Some satire is basically positive in thrust; the critique is offset by the presentation of positives and is sometimes largely implicit. (3) *Provocation*. Some satirists do more than render judgment, instead aiming to provoke thought, issue a warning, or unsettle the reader. As a first step in dealing with particular works, we need to judge their essential nature, to classify them as negative, mixed to positive, or speculative and interrogatory. Beyond "type of enterprise," we need to consider important differences in the realms of *motive, nature of judgment*, and *intensity*. What follows is a brief sketch of the distinctive categories of satire that we will encounter in my survey. These are not mutually exclusive categories, but the distinctions are worth making because they help clarify the nature of particular works.

(1) *Motive*. For some satires "attack" is an irrelevant concept, and neither does "reform" seem helpful. Those satirists who do seem driven by reformative impulses are often addressing an audience they believe will be receptive to their critique. Defoe, as we will see, is looking neither to show up nor to rescue hardened sinners; he is centrally concerned to instruct like-minded readers. This kind of satire is positive

rather than negative, but even negative-mode satires cannot be usefully described in terms of attack. We need to differentiate between (1a) drubbing a target for reasons of personal hostility and (1b) bashing someone who is threatening something regarded by the satirist as important, sacred, and worthwhile. This is what separates *Mac Flecknoe* and *Absalom and Achitophel*. There is an equally important distinction to be made between (1c) satire that is vehemently protesting injustice and corruption as a way of demanding change (Southerne's *The Wives' Excuse*) and (1d) satire that laments a state of affairs perceived to be unchangeable (Congreve's *The Way of the World*). Other satires involve something more than rendering judgment. They (1e) issue warnings to readers they wish ultimately to help (Defoe's *The Shortest-Way*); (1f) explore a set of philosophical, political, or social principles (Mandeville's *The Fable of the Bees*); or (1g) provoke thought or doubt (Rochester's *Upon Nothinge*). One set of questions that we should bring to satires, then, involves motive—granting that many satires "do" more than one thing. Such questions might not always be answerable with confidence, but in most cases we can be reasonably clear about what the satirist is trying to accomplish.

(2) *Judgment.* A second set of distinctions have to do with the nature of the judgment being rendered. Again there are a variety of possibilities. (2a) Satiric judgment is often a matter of straight denunciation, however motivated (Swift does plenty of this). Sometimes we find (2b) a range of judgments, as in distributive satire, from condemnatory to mildly corrective to essentially positive (Sheridan's *The School for Scandal*). A less common phenomenon is (2c) actual exemplary judgment (Steele's *The Conscious Lovers*), where the recommendation of virtue is explicit and predominant, the criticism of vice secondary, even implicit. We need therefore to try to determine the satirist's relationship to and attitude(s) toward his or her target(s). Does he or she judge from a comfortably superior viewpoint, as Pope tends to, or are subjects treated sympathetically, as by Fielding and Sterne? Are distinctions made among targets, or—as for Gay—is the world "all alike"?

(3) *Intensity.* A third set of distinctions derive from differences in ferocity or lack of it. Satiric "attack" might be (3a) angry, violent, vitriolic (Smollett's *Adventures of an Atom*); (3b) sharp or tart, pointing out individual or social defects (Hogarth's *Gin Lane*); (3c) more cheerful, accepting the imperfections of human nature but mostly amused by them or hopeful for change (Fielding on Parson Adams, Tom Jones, Booth); or (3d) purely comic, past a certain point in which what we have is not satire but entertainment presented for the sake of amusement (Behn's *The Luckey Chance*). Evaluating tone and judging levels of heat is not always an easy matter. Irony is a problem, and so is the possibility of "performing" preachment. Juvenalian indignation can be deeply felt or feigned, and the example of *Absalom and Achitophel* makes plain that tonal restraint does not always signal absence of passion. Granting

these difficulties, we need to recognize that attack without animosity is remote from satire that denounces with real rancor.

Mingling various combinations of motive, judgment, and intensity easily yields more than a dozen fairly distinct varieties of satire, as I have just demonstrated. I am arguing that no umbrella definition can be of much practical utility in helping us understand what any one of them is trying to do. Taxonomy does much better. The bottom line is that identifying a work as "satire" is about as helpful as identifying a car as a car or an insect as an insect. Minis are not Hummers, and cockroaches are not mosquitoes. Beyond the broad label, we need to categorize individual specimens according to a variety of characteristics. Satires can be and have been classified according to genre, but that does not get us very far: how much do *Friendship in Fashion*, *The Beggar's Opera*, and *She Stoops to Conquer* have to do with each other? Satires on similar targets have been lumped together, as have works that use related techniques. *Mac Flecknoe*, *The Dispensary*, and *The Rape of the Lock* are all mock heroic, but (as we shall see) there are important distinctions to be made among them. Satire is a wildly variegated species. Taxonomy can help us differentiate (in more than one realm) and alert us to the purposiveness, features, and devices of individual satires. It does not tell us what to think of a particular specimen but instead gives us questions and discriminators that sensitize us to its features. Taxonomy serves as a warning against the simplistic reduction of "satire" to "attack," but it is also useful insofar as we want to describe the primary material with any precision.

Forecasting Some Conclusions

Some readers may wonder whether a taxonomic survey of the sort that follows will lead only to chaos. I do not believe so. Much of this book is admittedly devoted to demonstrating complexity and difference, and I am obviously concerned to desimplify dominant notions of "Augustan satire." The reality is a great deal more complicated and interesting. But the survey should yield a good many positive conclusions along the way, about how satire functions, about particular writers and groups of writers, and about subperiods and the period as a whole. Looking at a lot of satires changes one's sense of satiric practice. Detailed explanations of the conclusions and the evidence that bears them out will have to wait for the survey chapters, but I will mention here some of the large-scale findings and clarifications that emerge from the remainder of the book.

Satire is a principally *purposive* form of writing—and the purposes vary considerably. I distinguish above among satiric motives, an issue to which I will return at some length in the epilogue. For now, two particular conclusions are worth anticipating. The first is that "attack" can include enterprises as different as bitter complaint, particularized sociopolitical polemic, lampoon, defense of a cause, or abuse of an enemy for the enjoyment of friends. The second conclusion is that a lot of satire is not well explained as attack. That satire castigates the vicious is a critical commonplace, but a prominent mode of satire is sympathetic or even affectionate. As we see in chapter 6, one of the great proponents and practitioners of this kind of satiric writing is Fielding, too frequently regarded as a would-be follower of Pope and Swift. A related issue is audience. Most satire theory centers on attack and for obvious reasons features writer and target rather than the response of the reader (evidence for which is frequently purely inferential or nonexistent). For a number of kinds of satire, however, we need to think not in terms of writer and target but of audience. Satirists often do the equivalent of preaching to the choir, addressing like-minded readers or viewers rather than an antagonist they want to hurt. Some of Defoe's early satires are homiletic; the object is to compel better behavior but among an audience not best thought of as "victims." This kind of satire is principally educative rather than punitive.

The point of this book is neither to offer readings of the major works nor to "recuperate" the minor ones; it is instead to consider the canonical pieces alongside the rest of the satires that were being produced at the same time. To what end? This kind of contextual treatment changes the way we view individual writers, their relationship to the satiric milieu in which they operate, and their connection to one another. My conviction is that we should not regard Dryden and Rochester, for example, as the "Restoration" representatives in a selective literary history of satire but as two prominent writers functioning in a particular milieu that has its own distinctive features. Such a perspectival change naturally alters what we look for, what we find, what tendencies we emphasize in those writers. I have major reservations about treating Dryden as the beginning of the story of how Augustan satire came about, but in any case we can learn some things by restoring him to his original, local satiric contexts. Dryden has great range, reflected in works satire scholars rarely bother to read, including the smutty, farcical *Kind Keeper*, the cynical *Marriage A-la-Mode*, the sociopolitically instructive *Albion and Albanius*. We also discover that Dryden, one of the two major Carolean satirists, continues to write satire after Charles's demise and that his practice under James and especially under William is radically unlike his practice in the 1670s and early 1680s. What Dryden is capable of as a satirist we would never guess if we were going by what critics of "Augustan satire" have told us.

Some scholars have seemed to imagine that canonical works are somehow representative of the age, special because they are qualitatively superior, but typologically "like" the rest. In fact, a startling number of the much-studied works either turn out to be distinctly atypical or are typical only of a particular kind of satire practiced at a particular time. As we shall see in chapter 5, Pope's early output—before *The Dunciad* —has virtually nothing to do with the practice of his contemporaries. He is the most "of his moment" in the late 1720s and early 1730s, sneering at the dunces and denouncing Walpolean corruption. In subject matter, though not in tone or intensity, his satires are fairly typical—but only for about a decade. Swift, on the contrary, tends to fit very well within his satiric milieus. His output in the reign of Anne, for example, reflects many of the satiric aims and methods we find in works by Defoe, Tutchin, and Maynwaring. As different as Swift and Defoe are in almost all respects, they are much more similar satirists than are Swift and Pope. There are limits to Swift's typicality, of course: *A Tale of a Tub* and *Gulliver's Travels* resemble other contemporary works not at all. In fact, many of the works we pay particular attention to—*A Tale*, *Gulliver*, *The Rape of the Lock*, *The Beggar's Opera*, *Tristram Shandy*—are typologically highly abnormal. This matters.

If we look at the masterpieces alongside the "hell-broth," we also find that abstracting the canonical works and seeing them in relation to each other is a bad idea. The assumption that the works we have decided to privilege represent successive links in an evolutionary chain is fallacious. A simplistic point needs to be made: we do not have familial descent from Dryden to Swift and Pope to Fielding and Johnson. In terms of aims, technique, and genre, *The Dunciad* has very little to do with *A Tale of a Tub*. The critical temptation is often to seek evidence of influence and a high degree of connectivity among the major writers. If we are going to understand particular eighteenth-century satires, then we need to look not at their place within a broad, multifarious satiric phenomenon but at their connections to their immediate surrounds. If we limit our field of vision to big-name works, we might, for example, regard *The Shortest-Way with the Dissenters* (1702) as a botched precursor to *A Modest Proposal* (1729). What happens if we restore *The Shortest-Way* to its more immediate satiric milieu? As I argue in chapter 5, Defoe's pamphlet is one of a flock of impersonation-mode satires produced around 1702–1710. Defoe did not fail to do what Swift would later do; his venture is different in kind, and in fact he executed it superlatively well. *The Shortest-Way* exemplifies a short-lived phenomenon; so do *Mac Flecknoe* and *The Dunciad*, as well as most of the other major works. Obviously this book is not going to give the kind of big-picture map that lets one take in the totality at a glance; there is no simple definition with a few key examples. The map I am offering is highly detailed but, I believe, still helpful as we navigate among the particular works.

The most important conclusion of this study can be summed up in two words: chronology matters. Critics tend to jump rather casually from *Absalom and Achitophel* to *The Rape of the Lock* or to regard *Mac Flecknoe* and *Gulliver's Travels* as high points of an "Augustan" mode, paying little attention to precise chronological placement. Whatever the desire to understand great satire as transcending its moment, it is, as scholars routinely observe, a highly time-specific form. Usually what is meant by that is that satire is occasional, addressing issues of current and local interest. One of the conclusions of this book, however, is that external circumstances determine not only *content* but frequently *mode* as well. Extraliterary conditions often compel satirists to write a certain kind of satire: the small world of the Carolean court produces an essentially unique body of works, and the dissolution of the court (with the changes in modes of dissemination) terminates them. The phenomenon I call "monitory" satire is prominent in the reign of Anne and rarely found elsewhere; it is the response to a particular kind of issue. The dissenters' fear of High Church duplicity led, for reasons I do not claim fully to understand, to a boom in impersonation-style satire. In some subperiods we find considerable similarities in verse, prose, and dramatic satires being produced at the same time, but often the forms seem unrelated to each other. How do we account for that inconsistency? The answer would seem to be that sometimes a single issue or set of issues provides a conspicuous focal point, at which times we find generic overlap. This is true in the late 1670s and early 1680s, during the Exclusion Crisis, and again in the 1730s, when satirists were gunning for Walpole and for the mercenary hacks who defended him. The bottom line is that external circumstances supply more than grist for the satirist's mill, more than content alone. They sometimes significantly affect (or even determine?) the shape a group of satires take.

The fact that satire is tied to its point of origin is both obvious and in need of highlighting. Subject matter and mode are both closely connected to a relatively short span of time. If one looks at a great satire from 1681, another from 1704, a few from the late 1720s, and so on, that connection often disappears. I admit that when I began reading I saw little difference between a 1710 work and a 1730 one. Looking at a satire plucked from one decade and another plucked from a different decade does not tell us much, but reading a lot of works from any one decade often proves revelatory. If I were now given an anonymous and undated satire with topical references blacked out, I could in most cases place it within a decade, often within a half decade. Modes flourish—and then vanish. The most exciting result of this study is one I could not have predicted at the outset: close chronological survey shows that satiric practice changes radically and sometimes rapidly several times over the long eighteenth century.[48]

The change from one subperiod to another is not evolutionary, and of assured causal explanation the reader will find none here. At times I have some confidence in determining factors that would have contributed to manifest changes in satiric practice, and where that is true I offer a tentative explanation of those factors. At the end of the seventeenth century, for example, an extraordinary amount of generalized satire gets written—satires on greed, brandy, women—of a sort unprecedented in the Carolean period. The breakup of the court circle in the 1680s no doubt played a part in this transformation: the world got bigger, and before the advent of daily newspapers common knowledge was limited. A satirist writing for print in the 1690s (like Ward and Gould) is addressing a wide, disparate readership, not the close-knit court audience for whom Carolean lampoonists wrote. By the 1730s, the dissemination of news is such that satirists can count on a much higher level of familiarity with public figures and events, which was not the case in the late seventeenth century outside a narrow circle. Extrinsic circumstances clearly matter to the kind of satire that can be written. More often than not, however, the changes over time are partially or totally inexplicable. A writer is influenced, a work shaped, by all sorts of things—literary, political, social, economic, personal—and "evolution" is an acutely unhelpful concept in literary history.[49] The changes in satiric practice from subperiod to subperiod are major, and I have traced them here, but I frankly doubt that any tidy and logical explanation as to why they occur is to be found.

The Nature of the Enterprise

In some respects *The Practice of Satire* looks like a neotraditional project—a chronological study in contextual historicism of the sort theorized by critics from R. S. Crane in the mid-twentieth century to Hume in the last decade.[50] I would call it an exercise in "archaeo-historicism," not "old historicism" or "new historicism." I have profited from a flock of books and articles, some of them from more than a generation ago, that take up problems in historical interpretation and literary history.[51] In the last half century eighteenth-century scholars have become increasingly concerned with testing and trying to validate or challenge broad characterizations and definitions—as witness increasing discomfort with concepts like the "Age of Reason" and the "Augustan Age," the last unfortunately not yet dead. One of my underlying assumptions about this project was that it would provide a much-improved evidentiary basis on which to test the satire theories floated by Frye, Elliott, Paulson, Kernan, and other major critics from the 1950s and 1960s whose studies still largely dominate this field. The challenge that I am mounting against long-dominant ways of conceiving eighteenth-century satire is very much in line with twenty-first-century historicists' attempts to carry out more complete and rigorous contextualization of the works we study. What has changed only very recently are the means by which such research can be done. The release of the digitized Burney newspaper collection in 2007 adds immensely to the possibilities already opened up by EEBO and ECCO. The change has the potential to revolutionize the field: we can now test generalizations about this period, generalizations mostly made on the basis of very limited evidence.

Scholars in the field have been buzzing about where we go from here and how we conceptualize what amounts to a tectonic shift. The 2008 MLA meeting included a roundtable on "Reassembling the Cultural," set up in response to Bruno Latour's *Reassembling the Social* (2005), a clarion call for sociologists to get very specific about the particular objects and relations they observe. Latour proposes "redefining sociology not as the 'science of the social,' " in which the social is "a homogenous thing," but as "*the tracing of associations*" between many "heterogeneous elements."[52] This amounts to a reassembling of the "social" that is much more detailed and empirical than sociological work now tends to be. Latour argues that instead of relying on generalized or oversimplified theoretical concepts, we should be appealing to particularized evidence in bulk. Thanks to our new digital resources, eighteenth-century scholars are now uniquely positioned to do an English Department version of what Latour calls for; we suddenly have access to a great deal more "evidence." According to Latourean methodology, our aim is twofold: first, to supply deeply researched reconstructions that take all the evidence into account and, second, to use those reconstructions to reinterpret the complex networks that underlie the ways in which specific historical moments worked. Loosely speaking, I would associate what Latour is calling for with the Geertzian notion of "thick description,"[53] which works very well if you have a sufficiency of evidence and very badly if you do not. In the realm of satire, 1658–1770, there is quite a lot of evidence, much of it almost totally ignored—and now radically more accessible. I think we can understand both the general practice of satire and particular satires much the better in light of this sort of Latourean contextual description—which is precisely what I am trying to provide.

CHAPTER TWO

Contemporary Views on Satire, 1658–1770

Get Scraps of *Horace* from your Friends,
And have them at your Fingers Ends.
Learn *Aristotle's* Rules by Rote,
And at all Hazards boldly quote:
Judicious *Rymer* oft review:
Wise *Dennis*, and profound *Bossu*.
Read all the *Prefaces* of *Dryden*,
For these our Criticks much confide in,
(Tho' meerly writ at first for filling
To raise the Volume's Price, a Shilling.)
　　　　　—Swift, *On Poetry: A Rapsody*, ll. 245–254

What did eighteenth-century writers and critics have to say about satire? The relevant primary material is voluminous, including everything from Dryden's high-minded *Discourse* to sermons on ridicule, authors' self-promoting and formulaic prefaces, and innumerable passing strictures upon particular satires. The commentary is mostly patchy and occasional, and often intensely subjective and partisan. It tends either to focus exclusively on a single work (and so is not about "satire" but about a specific satire or satirist) or to operate in the realm of abstraction (and so offers no precise illustrations of its concepts). Only one serious attempt has been made to analyze critical pronouncements on satire written in this period—P. K. Elkin's *The Augustan Defence of Satire* (1973). Elkin argued that contemporary commentators mostly divided into two clearly defined camps: those "for" satire as morally useful and those "against" it as nasty and abusive. The object of this chapter is to test that conclusion.

　　A warning about structure is in order. The categories by which we might like to discuss these remarks are rarely, if ever, discrete in the seventeenth- and eighteenth-century imagination, and most commentators were clearly not trying to provide a coherent "theory" of satire. To make the material comprehensible one needs to establish loose groupings, but these are not well-defined "schools" of thought subscribed to by contemporaries and should not be taken as such. Because I believe that attempting to summarize the various contemporary remarks will only blunt the distinctions I hope to illuminate, I have tried to limit my interposition as much as possible. This means that I quote extensively in an effort to let the participants speak for themselves. What we will discover is that these commentators—readers, writers, politicians, philosophers, lexicographers, preachers—did not see satire as we see satire. In this chapter, I survey their often contradictory attitudes toward satire, beginning with mostly very general statements on the concept and purpose of satire, and then moving to more detailed commentary on the proper techniques and targets for satire and the character of the satirist. My principal aim is to demonstrate the absence of consensus, but that is not simply a negative conclusion. A number of particular arguments will be made in the course of this survey, but one of its broader implications is this: contemporaries would likely have had no idea that they were living in the great age of satire. The majority of them, whatever their positions, would undoubtedly be astonished to know that we celebrate such topical, ill-focused, incoherent, controversial, morally and ethically dubious ephemera. The importance we bestow on it is well deserved, but nothing in the eighteenth century suggests that *they* saw it as a significant mode.

I. Concepts of Satire

'Tis not a Song neither—it's a sort of an Epigram, or rather an Epigrammatick Sonnet; I don't know what to call it, but it's Satyr.—Sing it my Lord. (Congreve, *The Double-Dealer*, III.i)

Few eighteenth-century discussions of satire reflect a sharply defined "concept" of it. Those writers who offer an explicit notion of satire are often doing little more than echoing sweet-sounding platitudes. The satirist is society's moral custodian, and satire—Pope proclaims—is the "Sole Dread of Folly, Vice, and Insolence!"[1] Avowals to this effect are oft repeated but largely irrelevant to the actual writing of satires, a fact pointed out by Dustin Griffin and other twentieth-century scholars: a lot of satirists loudly broadcast valorous intentions, and precious few mean a word of it.[2] This discrepancy notwithstanding, we need to ask what sort of meanings commentators seem to attach to the term "satire."

"Satire": Etymology and Terminology

Twentieth-century critics have made much of the etymological debate over whether "satire" derives from the Roman *lanx satura* (full or mixed platter) or from the Greek *satyr* (a malcontent who is half human, half beast)?[3] Those contemporaries interested in classical satire and, like Dryden, in improving satire's reputation are fussed about etymology and keen to demonstrate satire's Roman provenance.[4] Griffin reminds us that Dryden's *Discourse* was written just after the first volumes of *Poems on Affairs of State* appeared in print: a Stuart apologist, Dryden "would have had a political motive for seeking to dismiss the importance of poems that promised to reveal the truth about 'Popery and Tyranny' at the English court." The *Discourse*, Griffin continues, "sought to efface the memory of the 'state poems' and to redirect the attention of English readers and would-be satirists to the Roman tradition of Persius, Juvenal, and Horace."[5] Whatever Dryden's agenda, he is the most aggressive proponent of redefining satire as a respectable literary form, and the *Discourse* is important insofar as it helps us appreciate the push toward gentrification of a disreputable mode of writing, though it tells us little about the satiric practice of Dryden or his contemporaries. Remarkably few commentators seem to share Dryden's concern over satire's etymological ambiguity, though eighteenth-century writers at least know that the term's origins are unsettled, and so—by extension—is its basic connotation.

Eighteenth-century commentators are uncertain about what "satire" means; neither do they agree about what satire is *like*. Terminology is an insoluble problem, as no clear-cut or consistent boundaries exist between related concepts (e.g., raillery, lampoon, libel). Some writers make distinctions without necessarily ranking the various forms—see Sir Thomas Pope Blount's *De Re Poetica* (1694), which includes sections on satire, burlesque, lampoon, and farce. More commonly, writers differentiate between and evaluate two or more kindred terms. Richard Flecknoe (1658) offers a spectrum of kinds of mockery, from raillery (the most good natured) to jesting to jeering to "satyr" (the most objectionable).[6] The author of *Some Critical and Politick Remarks On . . . Faction Display'd* (1704) stresses "the difference betwixt a fine Satyrist, and a blunt Railer" (12): the latter attacks personal defects, names individuals, or otherwise engages in slanderous defamation rather than "true" and "just" satire. Both of these writers separate satire from raillery, but they have exactly antonymous views of the two terms. Flecknoe sees raillery as the mildest and most innocuous form of ridicule and satire as vile calumny; the 1704 author argues the reverse, defining raillery as an abomination and satire as a praiseworthy corrective. In 1744, Corbyn Morris discusses the principles that should govern "wit, humour, raillery, satire, and ridicule," systematically expounding the considerable distinctions between them. For example:

> *Raillery*, and *Satire*, are extremely different; 1. *Raillery*, is a genteel poignant Attack of *slight* Foibles and Oddities; *Satire* a witty and severe Attack of *mischievous* Habits and Vices. 2. The *Intention* of *Raillery*, is to procure your *Pleasure*, by exposing the little Embarrassment of a Person; But the *Intention* of *Satire*, is to raise your *Detestation*, by exposing the real Deformity of his Vices. 3. If in *Raillery* the Sting be given too deep and severe, it will sink into Malice and Rudeness. . . . But *Satire*, the more deep and severe the Sting of it is, will be the more excellent; Its Intention being entirely to root out and destroy the Vice.[7]

Because satire should be biting, Juvenal is "greatly superior" to Horace. But this judgment is not entirely fair, Morris continues, because "many of the short Compositions of *Horace*, which are indiscriminately ranged together, under the general Name of *Satires*, are not properly such, but Pieces of *Raillery* or *Ridicule*" (51).[8] That Horace the satirist is often not actually writing satire might seem an odd contention, but the crux is that Morris seeks to demonstrate substantive differences between related types of writing.

Not everyone discriminates. A number of commentators appear indifferent to this sort of classification. The anonymous *A Discourse on Ridicule* and Richard Blackmore's "Upon Wit" (both 1716) treat satire, raillery, and ridicule as synonymous terms, as does the author of *Laugh upon Laugh, or Laughter Ridicul'd* (1740; 1s): "Mine is pure, honest, manly Satyre—/ Judge Those who know best of the Matter. / I own indeed 'tis Ridicule" (32). The point is inconsistency. These authors casually regard as comparable or even interchangeable terms that some critics view as crucially antonymous. Such nomenclatural discrepancies are frustrating, but they tell us something significant about contemporary attitudes: never in the long eighteenth century do writers employ a common vocabulary about satire, and neither does the vocabulary evolve in clear and distinct ways.

Definition by Contrast

Few writers specify what they understand satire to be, but a fair number do assert what satire is *not*. "Invectives," asserts the author of *The Law Corrupted* (1706), "are not to be allow'd the Title of *Satire*" (preface). In *The Tatler*, no. 92, Steele likewise emphasizes the disparity between "real" satire and libel. Although these terms have been "promiscuously joined together in the Notions of the Vulgar," he argues, "the Satyrist and Libeller differ as much as the Magistrate and the Murderer. In the Consideration of human Life, the Satyrist never falls upon Persons who are not glaringly faulty, and the Libeller on none but who are conspicuously commendable."[9] Along the same lines, the writer of *Ars Punica* (1721; 6d) insists that slanderous statements are not to be mistaken for satire: "*Satire* never attacks the Character or Reputation of any Man; to do this, is the Province of defamation, between which and Satire, there is as wide a difference, as between the Primitive Christians and the Modern inferior Clergy."[10] Implicit in these remarks is the belief that "real" satire involves more controlled and considered judgments than are found in crude insults.

Some critics are more specific about what satire is not, though their judgments often have less to do with general principle than with revulsion against particular works and writers. In *The Characters and Conduct of Sir John Edgar* (1720; 6d), John Dennis passionately contends that a string of now celebrated "satires" are only satiric impostures, complaining that we have had no just Satire in *England*, since the Author of *Hudibras* publish'd his, which seems to me, to be a very just one on Hypocrisy. . . . We have since had Libels which have pass'd for Satires, as *Absalom and Achitophel*, the *Medal*, *Mac Fleckno*, and the *Dispensary*. They are indeed, if you please, beautiful Libels, but they are every where full of Flattery or Slander, and a just Satire admits of neither. In the two first, how many were abus'd only for being true to the Religion and Liberties of their Country? And on the other side, some were extoll'd only for being false to both. The attempt to lessen *Shadwell* in *Mackfleckno*, is every whit as unworthy of Satire. . . . The business of Sir *Samuel Garth* in his *Dispensary* was to expose much better Physicians than himself, for no other reason but because they were not of his Opinion in the affair of the *Dispensary*. Now tho' these were Libels, and very injurious, yet the Authors justly thought it more creditable to suffer them to be publish'd without any Name, rather than to make use of false ones.[11]

Dennis admittedly has his own axe to grind, but his comment is interesting. He flatly denies the label of "satire," for example, to the three major verse satires written by Dryden, now regarded as one of the three most important "Augustan" satirists. Dennis sharply differentiates libel and satire, asserting—more heatedly than the authors of *The Law Corrupted* and *Ars Punica*—that the latter should be made of nobler stuff.[12]

Insofar as "concepts" of satire can be extracted from eighteenth-century commentary, what we find is often irrelevant to satiric practice and decidedly inconsistent. Much of what we now regard as satire and what was then labeled "satire" is—according to the attitudes and assertions of the writers I have been citing—illegitimate and unworthy of the title. By the standards of many writers, works like *Mac Flecknoe* and *The Dunciad* are hardly the satiric exemplars of the long eighteenth century: properly understood, they are not even satires. More important for my purposes is the fact that contemporary notions about satire are imprecise and contradictory. The opinions sometimes intersect, especially in the realm of bland abstractions, but they do not add up to uniformity. Although Fredric V. Bogel sees in the eighteenth century a "deep commitment to a particular idea of satire,"[13] contemporary commentary reflects nothing of the sort.

II. The Business of Satire

The Beggers Opera hath knockt down Gulliver, I hope to see Popes Dullness knock down the Beggers Opera, but not till it hath fully done its Jobb. (Swift to Gay, 28 March 1728)

Concepts of satire are hard to separate from its perceived objectives. When people discuss what they think satire is or is not, they almost always talk in terms of what satire can or cannot and should or should not do. Those who condemn satire outright maintain that it serves no legitimate purpose; those who approve of satire—with or without qualifications—believe that it has sociomoral utility. Concepts of satire, however, are almost always general and nebulous. Statements about the "business" or "job" of satire (the negative or positive results it produces) tend to be more explicitly particular. On what grounds do writers reject satire, and on what grounds do others sanction and even celebrate it?

The Opposition to Satire

As always, we need to recognize variation under all broad headings, but generally speaking, negative responses to satire take two different forms in the period under review: (1) attacks on satire as malicious and (2) worried objections to satire as a threat to sober reasoning.

(1) *Satire is mean-spirited attack.* Dictionary entries from the beginning to the end of the period call attention to satire's negative attributes. A number of lexicographers, including Samuel Johnson, define satire as libel, slander, or defamation. An especially good early example is from Josua Poole's guide to poetry writing, *The English Parnassus* (1657), which offers a colorful catalog of adjectives for "Satyre":

> Girding, biting, snarling, scourging, jerking, lashing, smarting, sharp, tart, rough, invective, censorious, currish, snappish, captious, barking, brawling, carping, fanged, sharp-tooth'd, quipping, jeering, flouting, sullen, rigid, impartial, whipping, thorny, pricking, stinging, sharp-fanged, injurious, reproachful, libellous, harsh, rough-hewne, odious, opprobrious, contumelious, defaming, calumnous.[14]

In *Enigmaticall Characters*, Flecknoe construes satire as "*rude Assault*" (30), and other later seventeenth-century writers also emphasize the satirist's tendency toward peevishness and derision.[15] Throughout the long eighteenth century, of course, those targeted by particular satires are perhaps readiest of all to object to satire's abusiveness. Responses to the various versions of *The Dunciad* are notoriously indignant about "King Pope's" pointless denunciation of undistinguished poets. His incensed dunces reply virtually en masse, decrying their attacker as a bad-tempered beast and at least implicitly rejecting the notion of satire as morally and socially constructive. Victims are not the only cavilers: a number of seemingly "neutral" critics complain about satire's malignity. But that objection has been overemphasized in modern scholarship. A comparatively small number of writers deprecate satire wholesale as vicious attack. Most either qualify their disapproval—claiming that while satire can be misused, it can also be of value—or oppose it on other grounds.

(2) *Satire threatens sober judgment.* Those who associate satire with malicious aggression often indict the satirist based on the treatment of particular targets, com-

plaining that he or she needlessly injures the innocent. Enemies of satire in this second category, however, tend to take it as a more general threat: satire is a type of laughter or wit or mirth that by its very nature endangers the core values of society. Some commentators bemoan and condemn the burgeoning vogue for "laughter." Joseph Glanvill's *A Blow at Modern Sadducism* (1668) includes "Reflections on Drollery, and Atheisme." To the modern reader, that section title suggests a curious association of ideas, but the relationship between humor and skepticism is at the heart of Glanvill's impassioned critique of both. The two terms intersect in the concept of "scoffing," which for someone like Glanvill implies both mockery and irreverence. Glanvill recounts a famed "disturbance"—a supernatural sighting—and then complains about the incredulity with which the story has been regarded. The reasons that men do not believe the truth, he explains, "are chiefly, I think, an *affected humour* of DROLLERY, and *Scoffing*, and a *worse* cause, ATHEISM." Describing the underlying problem, Glanvill explains that, in the humorist,

> *reason* becomes an obedient servant to his *fancy*. He makes himself *believe*, by those *arguments*, that at first were intended only to make him *laugh*, and in the end, concludes in *earnest*, that there is neither *Witch*, nor *Apparition*: and 'tis well if he stop there. Now these, Sir, are the WITS (if we will believe them) and their admirers take every *jest* for an *argument*, and a *loud laugh* upon an idle tale of a *Devil*, or a *Witch*, for a *demonstration* of the *non-existence* of such beings. And thus the *humour* propagates, And SADDUCISM is the *Fashion*. Nor is this all, but by the same method every thing that is *sacred*, or *serious* hath been exposed, and both *Government*, and *Religion* made the objects of idle, and phantastic *buffoonry*. (166–167)

By such "*darling entertainments*" as laughter encourages, "the mind is made incapable of *serious* and *deep reflections*" (168). This kind of sportive wit is to be feared, Glanvill gravely concludes, because, while "*Philosophy* can shame, and disable all the *reasons* that can be urged against it," the "*jests*, and *loud laughter* are not to be *confuted*" (175).

Satirical depreciation is hard to combat. Like Glanvill, the Anglican clergyman Clement Ellis is disturbed by ridicule's ability to shake the pillars of faith. *The Vanity of Scoffing* (1674) is a slashing critique of satirical wits, but it is also a dire warning to his coreligionists. Of the taunting blasphemers, Ellis says:

> The *bravery* of such men is to set their faces against the Heavens, and bid defiance to *him* that made them. . . . [T]hey are resolved to teach [the world] . . . that *there is no God, no Heaven, no Hell, no life after death, no Soul to be saved or damned, neither punishment nor reward to be expected in a future world*. Now if any man be so unmannerly as to require some *proof* of all this, some *probable* reasons at least why he should believe things so repugnant to the common opinions of the world; they

will *swear* it stoutly, *swagger* it out bravely, call all men *fools*, *talk* all, *hear* nothing, *scrible something*, ask *questions*, propound some *possibilities*; and when this is done, and some *Satyrical* strains of wit, to close all, lavished out on those, who dare *believe* the things which these men are most *afraid* of. (8–9)

Ellis adjures his devout readers "not to be *jeared* and *Hector'd* . . . out of our *old Faith* with some dazling *flashes* of this new-fashioned wit" (9). He urges them not to be browbeaten by "*Satyrical*" wits, but the virulence of his exhortation bespeaks anxiety about the threat mockery poses to belief.

Enthusiasm for laughter and ridicule undermines restrained moderation: society has to eschew the former in order to preserve the latter. Those who give in to this "smart *Itch* of *Writing* . . . in this *New Canting Drolling* Way," warns the author of *Raillerie a la mode Consider'd* (1673), have "licentiously let go the Rains of [their] *Sobriety*, *Reason*, and *Religion*, to play at Have at All" (7). He frowns upon the "*shameless incivility*" of calumnious mockery, but his disapproval is categorically different from those who censure the satirist as spiteful (19). This author's animated account of nefarious derogation is blistering. The detractor

> out-Huffs Hell, out-Hectors Beelzebub, and can dispence with the Name of *Atheist*, if he be not proud on't, and openly own and glory in it. This is one that with little *Fear*, and less *Wit*, will still be at his *Ludere cum Sacris*; that dare be impudent with Heaven, and sawcy with its most awful Majesty, to the Hearers astonishment, and his own shameful confusion; that, like an over-daring *Vaulter*, will . . . play at Hide and Seek with the *Devil* himself, till at last he catches him in his Clutches, as the Cat does her wanton Prey, and so spoiles his Sport on a suddain. (13–14)

Such a man "is Traytor to Truth," and a "*Monster* among *Men*, and hath a *double* Face, a *double* Heart, and a *cloven* Tongue" (55–56). Like Glanvill, this anonymous haranguer associates a certain species of mockery and mirth with the profane: to misuse humor is *ludere cum sacris*.

This association of mirth and drollery with blasphemy appears again and again in sermons and other religious discourse. Richard Allestree (*The Government of the Tongue*, 1667) and Isaac Barrow (*Several Sermons against Evil-Speaking*, 1678) both treat "Atheistical Discourses," "blasphemous Raillery," "prophane Swearing," and "Censoriousness, Detraction, and Slander" as equally offensive vices of the tongue.[16] Allestree explains malice as the primary motive of defamation, and he attributes human malevolence to diabolical inducement: "The Devil here plaies the Artist," he suggests, meaning literally that the detractor has been lured by demonic forces into wicked abuse of his fellow humans (54). Barrow emphatically deplores "profane Jesting, all speaking loosely and wantonly about Holy things," which is "an intolerably-vain and wicked practice" and "an infallible sign of a vain and light spirit, which considereth little, and cannot distinguish things" (61–62). Unrestrained revelry is at odds with due reverence. In *Mirth's Madness* (1702), a ponderous diatribe against excessive laughter, the Christian moralist Edward Grove cautions his coreligionists to "be on our Guard" against the "heinous" allurements of gaiety, and he defends the wholesome satisfactions of sobriety. Grove insists that he and his Christian readers should "not Delight in the vanity of . . . Laughter," but should "be serious and full of thought, Dedicated to Holy and Pious Speculations," cultivating the "sober Capacity for those most solid Pleasures at GOD's Right Hand provided for us."[17] Levity signifies at best daftness and at worst desecration.

Wholesale condemnation of laughter is far less common than more moderate warnings about its misapplication, its misuse on subjects worthy of serious treatment. In an oft-quoted passage from *The Spectator*, Addison observes that ridicule could be potentially useful but that unfortunately it is now "generally made use of to laugh Men out of Virtue and good Sense, by attacking everything that is Solemn and Serious, Decent and Praise-worthy in Human Life."[18] Addison shares something with earlier critics of misguided ridicule, though with the crucial difference that he would not—as they often did—associate mockery with evil speaking literally conceived. In "Upon Wit," Blackmore comes closer to recalling Glanvill and Barrow:

> In all the Errors and monstrous Productions of Nature, can any appear more deform'd than a Man of Parts, who employs his admirable Qualities in bringing Piety into Contempt, putting Vertue to the Blush, and making Sobriety of Manners the common Subject of his Mirth; while with Zeal and Industry, he propagates the malignant Contagion of Vice and Irreligion, poisons his Friends and Admirers, and promotes the destruction of his native Country? And if these foolish Wits and ingenious Madmen could reflect, they would soon be convinc'd, that while they are ingag'd against Religion they hurt themselves; and that Wit and Humour thus misapply'd, will prove but a wretched Compensation for their want of Vertue. (14–15)

Blackmore objects not to "wit" but to perversions of wit. Those who employ their talents for ridicule are deluded—incapable of reflection—and dangerous.

The disparagement of ridicule often includes at least an implicit defense of sobriety, which has (these critics lament) been rendered unfashionable by the popularity of wit. They worry about the dangers of sporting with serious subjects,[19] though they often disagree about what those subjects are or on what terms they can be mocked. A rudimentary spectrum of opinion might have at one end those who are untroubled by laughter and at the other those like Grove who are wholly intolerant of it. At intervals between the two would be the positions held by Blackmore (endorsing wit but cautioning against its abuse) and by Barrow (objecting to wit but admitting its occasional utility). Much of this material is clearly outside "literary" realms, but it does represent a substantial part of the negative response to satire. It signifies not aversion to spitefulness, but instead a broader social unease with satire.

The Case for Satire

Objections to satire and to particular satires in this period are many and sometimes forcibly expressed. As Elkin has demonstrated, eighteenth-century satirists often felt forced to justify their enterprises and issued boilerplate apologias with monotonous regularity. He highlights the defensive tone of such self-promotion, explaining the "core of the defense" to be the assurance of satire's moral function. The "orthodox viewpoint of the Augustan critics," Elkin decrees, "was that literature aims to instruct its readers at the same time as it delights them."[20] The conclusion is compelling, but also incomplete. Not all explanations of purpose are necessarily "defensive," though following Elkin modern scholars tend to read them as such. Far from illustrating a uniform and "orthodox" perspective, eighteenth-century commentators have very different notions about what satire is good for and equally dissimilar motivations for insisting on its utility.

(1) *The value of laughter*. Whereas writers like Glanvill, Barrow, and Blackmore warn about the hazards inherent in merriment and levity, others proclaim the pleasing necessity of laughter. The full title of *Mirth in Abundance* (1659) announces its author's hopes that the book will "relieve the Melancholy," "expell sorrow," and "advance Jollity." It also assures readers that the works included, despite their gaiety, are entirely "free from Rayling Baudery, Blasphemy, or Incivility"—clearly anticipating the accusations of mirth-as-profanity (à la Glanvill). Although laughter (satirical or otherwise) has its enemies in the long eighteenth century, not everyone is against it. Writers commend humor as an indispensable "antidote to melancholy" and as a requisite part of human society.[21] In *Sensus Communis* (1709), Shaftesbury endorses it not because it is a necessary corrective or *elixir vitae*, but because it is harmless.

> But let who will condemn *the Humour*. For my own part, I am in no such apprehension from this sceptical kind of Wit. . . . I can very well suppose Men may be frighted out of their Wits: But I have no apprehension they shou'd be laugh'd out of 'em. I can have no suspicion that in a pleasant way they shou'd be talk'd out of their Love for Society, or reason'd out of *common Sense*. A mannerly Wit can hurt no Cause that I am concern'd for. (53–54)

This is technically a "defense," but its tone is not really defensive.[22]

(2) *The value of attack*. Not all affirmations of satire's value are founded upon sodden pledges to advocate virtue and discountenance vice. Some commentators admit

that satire is in essence obloquy, but they do so sans Elkin's requisite apologia. In *The Muses Looking-Glass* (1706), Thomas Randolph maintains that punitive exposure of targets can be effective precisely because of its sting. The character "Satyre" speaks

> As one whose Whip of Steel can with a Lash
> Imprint the Characters of Shame so deep,
> Even in the brazen Forehead of proud Sin,
> That not Eternity shall wear it out.
> When I but frown'd in my Lucilius Brow,
> Each conscious Cheek grew Red, and a cold trembling
> Freez'd the chill Soul; while every guilty Breast
> Stood fearful of Dissection, as afraid
> To be anatomiz'd by that skilful Hand;
> And have each Artery, Nerve, and Vein of Sin
> By it laid open to the publick Scorn.
> I have untruss'd the proudest; greatest Tyrants
> Have quak'd below my powerful Whip, half dead
> With Expectation of the smarting Jerk,
> Whose Wound no Salve can cure: each blow doth leave
> A lasting Scar, that with a Poyson eats
> Into the Marrow of their Fames and Lives;
> Th' eternal Ulcer to their Memories! (9)

Randolph does not reiterate or recall Dryden's assertion of satire's noble aims: when he has "Satyre" describe how even the "greatest Tyrants" have to fear the lash and its attendant public humiliation, he is relishing the lasting effects of witty castigation.[23] A 1740 poet likewise celebrates satire's capacity to shame its targets: it is "that Rod / Men sometimes fear who fear not God" (*Laugh upon Laugh*, 32). These two poets commend satire, but not on moral grounds.

(3) *Ridicule as argumentative instrument.* Ridicule becomes a hotly disputed topic in the wake of Shaftesbury's famous assertion that it is an incomparably valuable test of truth. From the appearance of his *Letter Concerning Enthusiasm* (1708) and *Sensus Communis* through the midcentury, commentators of all stripes argue about the nature and utility of ridicule.[24] Although James Sutherland states confidently that "it was a favourite idea of the eighteenth century that ridicule is the test of truth,"[25] not all of Shaftesbury's contemporaries concurred with his assessment. Just as late seventeenth-century writers had execrated mirth as a menace to sobriety, many eighteenth-century commentators abominate ridicule. In a 1734 sermon, John Tottie grumbles that "nothing has done or can do our Religion greater harm" and that "an Inclination to *Ridicule* is apt to lead Men off from any Serious enquiries at all."[26] In

his painstaking response to Shaftesbury, John Brown concludes that reason trumps ridicule: "Reason alone is the *Detector of Falsehood*, and the Test of Truth," as well as "the superior and corrective Power."[27]

Ridicule, however, has its partisans. In 1731, William Asplin highlights the possibility for "the *Sober Use* of a *Rational Ridicule*"—words that, he says, will be taken by many "as a Contradiction, it being a Sort of Vulgar Error, that Reason and Ridicule are Things of a quite different nature, and inconsistent with each other." But, Asplin argues, "if duly consider'd, true and just *Ridicule* will appear to be one of the finest and politest Species of *Reasoning*, being no other than *Argumentum ex Absurdo*, a Topick which the greatest Logicians in all Ages have recommended to others, and had recourse to themselves."[28] Other writers go further, claiming ridicule to be an infinitely more effective tool than unmitigated reprimand. The author of *A Discourse on Ridicule* (1716) asserts its value, though not without qualification: "Ridicule if it be charitably designed, and seasonably and skillfully apply'd, may be allowed sometimes as a Means of reclaiming Men from their Vices, and their Sins, when serious Reproof, and grave Advice cannot attain that End" (11). The writer judiciously suggests that the careful exercise of mild humor (laughter "duly govern'd") is likelier to be heeded than is sober admonition. Ridicule is justified by its positive capabilities, but it is "useful" also, and never more so than

> when it is accompany'd with Facetiousness, and Wit: It may be useful for the Correction, or Prevention of those Follies of our Neighbors, which Nothing else perhaps can so effectually amend, or prevent. Nay, even the grosser Vices of Mankind, may sometimes be cured this Way, when grave Instructions, and severe Reproof, can make no Sort of Impression upon them. (7)

Despite the author's stated desire to "amend" human behavior, this is in fact far removed from the naïve or high-flown trumpeting of satire's consecrated powers. The writer does not simply assert reformative potentiality. Improvement is possible but not certain, and it requires a particular type of mockery, teasing amiability rather than sniping condescension.

(4) *The moral function*. The most "defensive" of the positive rationales for satire are the clichés about its moral utility. Dryden and the earl of Mulgrave's acclamation of satire as "the boldest way, if not the best, / To tell men freely of their foulest faults" and Pope's apostrophe to satire—"O sacred Weapon!"—are hardly representative of the period's satirical personae (much less the actual attitude), but neither are they anomalies.[29] The author of *The Law Corrupted* holds, "The Business of *Satire* . . . is to lash Vice to the Encouragement of Vertue" (preface). Morris also insists that the object of satire is "to scourge *Vice*, and to deliver it up to your just *Detestation*."[30] Primarily defensive in tone and purpose, these apologias are basically pro forma boilerplate.

If satire is defended on the grounds that it can do some good, then for whose good is it meant? Very few of even the staunchest supporters of satire express hope that the target will be reformed, and those who do suggest that possibility see the targets as only secondary beneficiaries. If the "victim" feels sufficiently bad—or embarrassed—to mend his or her ways, that is to the good, but the more realistic expectation is that the audience will be reformed or deterred from misbehavior. Defending himself against Jeremy Collier's attack (1698), William Congreve reasons that the satirical presentation of mistakes and misdeeds could have a positive effect on two different types of audience members: "as vicious People are made asham'd of their Follies or Faults, by seeing them expos'd in a ridiculous manner, so are good People at once both warn'd and diverted at their Expence."[31] Following a similar logic, the author of *A Grammar of the English Tongue* (2nd ed., 1712) likens satirists to doctors: both "propose themselves to the Health of the Patient," and the satirist's medicine can "correct the Perverse, and deter others from falling into Folly and Vice" (147). Satire is more likely to be an effective disincentive than an incentive; it will discourage potential offenders rather than reform those targeted by the attack.

A number of commentators seem wholly unconcerned with the target. Although Barrow worries mightily about the abuse of wit, he also insists that "Facetiousnesse" can serve as

> the most proper instrument of exposing apparently base and vile to due contempt. It is many times expedient, that things really ridiculous should appear such, that they may be sufficiently loathed and shunned; and to render them such is the part of a facetious wit, and usually can onely be compassed thereby. When to impugn them with down-right reason, or to check them by serious discourse, would signify nothing; then representing them in a shape strangely-ugly to the fancy . . . may effectually discountenance them. (49)

The point of ridicule, as Barrow understands it, is not the victim's mortification and subsequent amendment. In *De Re Poetica*—essentially a compilation of other thinkers—Blount recycles a number of platitudes about satire. He quotes Dryden frequently, and also Rapin, who proclaims "That the Principal End of *Satyr*, is to instruct the People by discrediting *Vice*" (42). "People" refers not to the butts of the satire but to potential butts of future satires, the audience who can yet save themselves from similar ignominy. A much later advocate of this kind of satire is Henry Fielding, whose stated preference for instruction by example rather than precept is well known. In the 10 June 1740 issue of *The Champion*, Fielding hails William Hogarth

> as one of the most useful Satyrists any Age hath produced. In his excellent Works you see the delusive Scene expos'd with all the Force of Humour, and on casting your Eyes on another Picture, you behold the dreadful and fatal Consequence. I

almost dare affirm that those two Works of his, which he calls the *Rake's* and the *Harlot's Progress*, are calculated more to serve the Cause of Virtue, and for the Preservation of Mankind, than all the *Folio's* of Morality which have been ever written. . . . Can there be a more instructive Lesson against that abominable and pernicious Vice, Ambition, than the Sight of a mean Man, rais'd by fortunate Accidents and execrable Vices to Power, imploying the basest Measures and the vilest Instruments to support himself; looked up to only by Sycophants and Slaves and sturdy Beggars, Wretches whom even he must in his Heart despise in all their Tinsel, looked down upon and scorned and shunned by every Man of Honour, nay, by every Man of Sense, and those whom his rotten rancorous Heart must in Spite of himself reluctantly admire; who knows that he is justly hated by his whole Country, who sees and feels his Danger; tottering, shaking, trembling; without Appetite for his Dainties, without Abilities for his Women, without Taste for his Elegancies, without Dignity in his Robes, without Honour from his Titles, without Authority from his Power, and without Ease in his Palace, or Repose in his Bed of Down. If such an Idea can make us nauseate Ambition, I believe if we turn over the Pages of our History we shall find such Examples.

The satirist, according to this account, should teach people to be "sensible of the Contempt a Man justly incurs" by his wrongdoing.[32] That satire can instruct or warn its audience through negative or positive examples is an oft-repeated maxim—what is surprising is that reformation of the target is, for most contemporary commentators, at best a peripheral concern.

(5) *Satire as persuasion or education of allies*. Not all satirists understood themselves to be addressing their enemies. Defoe uses satire to instruct and persuade, but not in the way modern scholars tend to think of satirical instruction and persuasion. "The End of *Satyr*," Defoe affirms in the preface to *A New Discovery of an Old Intreague* (1691), "*ought to be exposing Falshood*." In the preface to his *The True-Born Englishman* (1701), he issues a similar mission statement, asserting, "*The End of Satyr is Reformation*."[33] As clichéd sentiments often expressed by satirists, these declarations might sound merely self-righteous, but many of Defoe's satires seem to work toward precisely this stated end. The assumption that all expressed justifications for satire are just defensive apologias is part and parcel with Elkin's premise that all "satire is hostile by nature."[34] When the latter supposition does not hold—as in the case of Defoe—neither does the former. Despite appearances, Defoe's proclamations of satire's positive capabilities are not simply versions of the standard satiric defense Elkin describes. I have argued elsewhere that Defoe the satirist imagines readers who are receptive to the claims of conscience.[35] In *More Reformation* (1702), his poet explains to personified "Satyr" that he does not hope to reach those who are unreceptive to moral

reproach; satire, he suggests, can only "work" for the man who sins "like something of a Christian" (l. 636). Other writers also emphasize the importance of audience to satire, arguing (more broadly than Defoe) that readers and viewers of satire must be capable of feeling its sting. The author of *Vanelia: or, the Amours of the Great* (1732) has one character insist that "Satire loses its Force where Men have lost all Shame" (vii). Defoe's satire seems designed and carefully constructed to speak to readers capable of remorse and self-judgment.

Defoe's aims as a satirist have little to do with attacking or exposing those he disapproves of and much to do with educating a specific target audience. The readers he addresses in his satire are Christians—usually dissenting or Low Church Anglicans, in particular—who share his basic values. I discuss his concept and practice of satire in chapter 5, but here I must make a vital distinction. Defoe has plenty of antagonists, and he lashes them throughout his satiric career, but he writes for his allies, not his enemies. This represents a notion of satire remote from exposure and from reformation of target: to mount a soapbox and preach to your sociomoral enemies is one thing; to warn the group with whom you identify and sympathize about a mutual threat is quite another. Both are legitimate, if sanguine, conceptions of satire's positive functions, but they are worlds apart in practice and purpose.

What does this survey tell us? One conclusion seems especially significant: we should not be fooled by superficial resemblances into neglecting fundamental dissimilarities in viewpoint. The willingness of some—by no means all—satirists to utter high-flown mission statements does not represent an "orthodox" position. Not all of the writers who proclaimed satire's utility agreed about what it could or should do in practice or about how its objectives might be realized. We can identify woolly categories of support for and hostility toward satire (e.g., it can instruct the audience; it is unpleasant and unproductive), but we need also to admit peculiarities and divergences (e.g., satire is indecorous vs. satire is literally a form of devilry). In other words, we need to appreciate the correspondences—usually in the form of banalities irrelevant to the practice of satire—but also the often drastic discrepancies. Asserting that satire can reform its target is not the same thing as believing that it can deter potential malefactors, and both contrast markedly with seeing it as a means of enlightening like-minded readers about a shared enemy. All of these positions are "pro" satire, but they represent three essentially distinct concepts of methods and goals.

III. The Practice and Province of Satire

Statements about what satire *does* tend to be more specific than those about what satire *is*, and those about how satire *works* are often even more precise. Many writers express opinions about the operational particulars of satire, especially in the realm of method and target. What do contemporary commentators regard as legitimate and illegitimate (or appropriate and inappropriate) satiric techniques and targets? On what grounds do they make their arguments? My objectives in this section are two: (1) to demonstrate the widely discrepant attitudes about what should or should not be done in satire and (2) to suggest that morality and propriety, while no doubt important categories for many contemporaries, were not the only bases for approbation or condemnation of various methods and targets. A number of writers justified their positions by appeals to efficacy or charges of inefficacy. Contemporary commentary, then, reflects much disagreement about what satire could and should do—and how, and why, and to whom or what—and about how it might best "work."

Acceptable and Problematical Satiric Methods

A frequently stated "rule" of satire is that it must be true: sincere reportage constitutes the crucial difference between respectable satire and malicious slander. "Errant falsehood," contends one commentator, is "no just Satyr."[36] In his preface, the author of *The Law Corrupted* defends satire ("'tis an Action vertuous to make Examples of Vice") but demands honest representation ("Reputation is too tender a thing to be insulted by Surmise," etc.). In one of his many responses to Pope, Dennis admits that he is flaying Pope as personally as Pope flays his targets, but he distinguishes his own (truthful) satire from Pope's (fallacious) slander.[37] As Dennis explains elsewhere, "That only can be call'd a just Satyr, whose Censures are always true; but that which endeavors to decry true Merit, out of Malice, or Passion, or Interest, is in spight of popular Applause a Lampoon, and an infamous Libel."[38] But some writers challenge the dictum that satire should be faithful to fact. In *The Art of English Poetry* (1702), Edward Bysshe maintains that "Satire may be fine, and true Satire, tho' it be not directly and according to the Letter, true. 'Tis enough that it carry with it a probability or semblance of Truth" (preface).

Contemporaries also disagree about whether satire has to be kind. Unsurprisingly, a number of advocates of satire stipulate that it be delivered in as pleasant a manner as possible. In *De Re Poetica*, Blount paraphrases Rapin's discouragement of the satirist who lashes too directly, as Juvenal was thought to do: "*Satyr* that takes off the Mask, and reprehends *Vice* too openly, is not to be allow'd of" (43).[39] Amiable badinage is preferable to caustic aspersion—a judgment also asserted by the author of *A Grammar of the English Tongue*, who argues that the medicines of both doctors and satirists" are in themselves unsavory and disagreeable to the Palate of the Distemper'd on whom they make Incisions, whom they cauterize and spare not. The Physician gilds his Pill, that it may go down glibly, the Satiric Invectives must be sweeten'd with the mixture of Pleasantry and Wit, and agreeable Railery, till both the Medicines are swallow'd" (147).[40]

The statement implies a concern for efficacy as much as for morality or propriety: the "gilded" pills are likelier to be swallowed than more odious forms of medication.[41]

A considerable number of commentators think in terms of satiric efficacy. Despite the modern emphasis on "moral defenses," a lot of responses to ridicule and satire focus not on what is right or wrong but on what will or will not work (whatever that means). Barrow recognizes that sometimes "sarcastical twitches are needfull to pierce the thick skins of men, to correct their lethargick stupidity, to rouze them out of their drowzy negligence." "Facetiousness," to use his term, can be justly and gainfully applied "when plain declarations will not enlighten people, to discern the truth and weight of things, and blunt arguments will not penetrate, to convince or persuade them to their duty" (50). Although in Barrow's account the satirist must pass judgments heavier than "plain declarations," he must also take care when he does so:

> you must not chide them as their master, but you may gibe with them as their companion. . . . Most men are of that temper; and particularly the Genius of divers persons, whose opinions and practices we should strive to correct, doth require not a grave and severe, but a free and merry way of treating them . . . If we mean to be heard by them, we must talk in their own fashion, with humour and jollity: if we will instruct them, we must withall somewhat divert them: we must seem to play with them, if we think to convey any sober thoughts into them. They scorn to be formally advised or taught; but they may perhaps be slily laughed and lured into a better mind. (51–52)

Like Blount (or, rather, Blount's paraphrase of Rapin), Barrow disapproves of satire that is too direct, but whereas Blount opposes brusque candor on principle, Barrow does so on the grounds of prudence.

Barrow is not alone in suggesting that, if rightly managed, tempered ridicule can "work." Printed with the 1717 *Poems by the Earl of Roscomon* is "An Essay on Poetry, By the Earl of Mulgrave," in which the poet holds forth on the satirist's need for a soft touch. He acclaims the satirist's ability "To *mend* the Age, and *mortifie* Mankind" but advises those satirists who "think, if sharp enough, they cannot fail" to check their fury: "Rage you must hide, and Prejudice lay down." When he observes that "Satyr well-writ has most successful prov'd," "well-writ" is clearly not an aesthetic but a temperamental judgment (306, 307). William Whitehead offers much the same advice in his *Essay on Ridicule* (1743; 1st),[42] which concludes with a directive for those who wish to jeer (or sneer) men out of their follies:

> So let Goodnature o'er our Mirth preside,
> Divert, not check; without impelling, guide.
> Allur'd by this, the gath'ring Frown unbends,
> The Laugh grows gen'ral, and ev'n Wits are Friends.

Touch'd with this trickling Balm, fair Virtue wakes,
And gen'rous Satire heals the Wound it makes. (19)

The author of *A Treatise on Virtue and Happiness* (2nd ed., 1736) recites the standard line—satire can perhaps "put vice out of countenance"—but not without an important condition. "If it is rightly managed," the writer says, positive results might follow. Satirists should apply their ridicule "with *pleasantness* and *good humour* . . . and without any *sour aspects* or *magisterial airs*, to create offence, and render it disgustful." Like Barrow, this author is thinking in terms of practical human psychology: "*good company* and *polite conversation*, tend so much to refine mens manners, and to work off whatever is *indecent* and *immoral*. . . . [F]or there is nothing which men covet more than *esteem*, nor any thing they dread more than being despised, and exposed to *scorn* and *derision*" (180–181).[43] Or, as Whitehead more succinctly concludes in his *Essay on Ridicule*, "He feels the Lash, not listens to the Rein" (13). In his view, severity is not necessarily unethical or immoral but simply unproductive.

Some supporters of satire argue the opposite, insisting that to sweeten satire is to render it impotent. Effective correction requires a heavy hand. In "Upon Wit," Blackmore affirms that real satire must be biting, because the "inveterate Diseases of the Mind are as hard to be remov'd as those of the Body; and therefore their Cures requires as sharp and painful Applications" (xvi). The poet who uses milder forms of comedy "must have a very sanguine Complexion, that can hope with such feeble and unequal Weapons, to triumph over Vice and Immorality. . . . One may as well charge a Gyant with a Bull-rush, or play upon a Conflagration with a Syringe, as attempt to make a wise and vertuous Nation with pleasant Humor and facetious Fancies" (xix). In his *Essay Towards Fixing the True Standards of Wit*, Morris also encourages satirists to be rigorous in their attack. Whereas raillery is gentle, "*Satire*, the more deep and severe the Sting of it is, will be the more excellent." In sharp contrast to those like Whitehead, Addison, and Steele, Morris flatly rejects the notion that "Fear or Tenderness" has any place in satire (50).[44] In the preface to his imitations of Juvenal (1763), Edward Burnaby Greene likewise doubts the potency of mere persiflage: "the attempt to laugh people out of their vices" is "not a little deficient to answer the end proposed." Vice is a "violent disease" and "requires a more violent remedy" than laughing reproof.[45] Contemporary antagonists to and enthusiasts for satire wrangle over issues of morality and respectability, but expositors on either side do not always speak in perfect harmony. Satire's proponents prescribe markedly dissimilar methods for effective rebuke.

The point is simple. Writers who address issues of satiric technique have different reasons for approving or disapproving the methods they discuss. Some have in mind basic human decency, some propriety and morality, and some sheer pragmatism. These distinctions are equally pertinent to debates about legitimate or illegitimate and reasonable or unreasonable subjects for satire. Technique and target are naturally hard to separate. Most commentators acknowledge the fact that technique varies with, and to some extend depends upon, target: if human foibles should be met with a gentle laugh, then more contemptible iniquities deserve an iron fist. For my purposes, however, we can make some crude and imperfect distinctions between method and target. I now survey attitudes toward the latter.

Appropriate and Inappropriate Satiric Targets

The restriction of satire to follies (rather than vices) is something of a commonplace, and many writers of the long eighteenth century at least nominally espouse this position. Barrow claims in 1678 that the "proper objects of common mirth and sportfull divertisement are mean and petty matters" (63), and Blackmore issues a similar pronouncement in 1716, arguing that the "Object about which Wit is exercis'd, are the common and less important Actions of Life." The law should deal with greater crimes, he explains, and

> Where then the Legislature ends, the Comick Genius begins, and presides over the low and ordinary Affairs and Manners of Life. It extends its Power and Jurisdiction over the wide Field of inferior Faults and ridiculous Follies, over the Districts of Indiscretion, Indecency, and Impertinence, and is Visitor of the Regions void of Discipline, Politeness, and Civility. (10)

In the same year, the author of *A Discourse on Ridicule* also maintains that "there are some Crimes, and Sins of Men, of that Enormity, and Size of Guilt, that they . . . are therefore by no means proper Subjects of our Ridicule" (12). On the topic of illegitimate satiric concerns, this writer objects in particular to Lucian and especially his imitators, who are guilty of "mingling light Wit, and ludicrous Satyr with the Mention, and Description of Hell, and Judgment, which a good Christian cannot think of without Awe upon his Soul" (19). In the preface to *Joseph Andrews* (1742), Fielding cheerfully explains that the "Ridiculous only . . . falls within my Province," maintaining "the Absurdity of an Author, who should write *the Comedy of* Nero, *with the merry Incident of ripping up his Mother's Belly.*" Life's "blackest Villanies" and "most dreadful Calamities" cannot really be ridiculed (7). Although he has "introduced Vices, and of a very black Kind" into his writing, he says, those vices "are never set forth as the Objects of Ridicule but Detestation" (10). According to these writers, the satirist should apply his talents only to the trivial or should at least eschew *res severa*, those grave subjects that are not to be treated with laughter.[46]

A directly antithetical position is asserted by other authors, who contend that the satirist should target not petty failings but rather the most consequential offenses. Satire should be "concerned with *Vices* of *Persons*," Morris asserts, rather than with their foibles (52). More broadly, whereas Blackmore confines the satirist to those subjects "beneath" the legislature, others regard satire as a regulatory force comparable to the arm of law. The satirist "of true genius," suggests one commentator, "may be considered as a sort of supplement to the legislative authority of his country."[47] Another writer puts the satirist in charge of punishing those transgressions that, because not technically criminal, are outside the bench's jurisdiction: "There are Crimes of a very high Nature, which are not cognisable in the ordinary Courts of Justice, such as Ingratitude, the denying a Deposit, the betraying a Friend's Secrets; and among these I may reckon such Frauds, as for want of legal Evidence escape with Impunity. These and all other Evils . . . are surely the proper Objects of Satire."[48] The satirist, according to these accounts, has the right and even the responsibility to use his weapons to combat the weightiest infractions and failings.

Eighteenth-century writers disagree about the scale on which satire can operate and also about what particular types of targets should be exposed. What is beyond the purview of the satirist, and what is fair game? Commentators routinely condemn satire directed at irremediable defects. The author of *Some Critical and Politick Remarks On . . . Faction Display'd* claims, for example, that "we never see any body exposed in true Satyr, but for something that is their fault, and in their power to mend" (7). Or, as Swift would say of himself in *Verses on the Death* (wr. 1731; pub. 1739), "He spar'd a Hump or crooked Nose, / Whose Owners set not up for Beaux" (ll. 467–468). These assertions are manifestly false, of course, but then honesty is hardly the point of most satire theory. The objection to mocking unavoidable misfortunes is voiced repeatedly and angrily in the wake of the 1728 *Dunciad*. Ward's response, *Durgen*, is a marvelously nasty piece of vituperation on "the pigmy Bard," whose poem teaches readers "How to despise true Merit when it's poor" (4, 39). Another of Pope's aggrieved respondents bemoans more broadly the failure of modern satirists to follow their classical models:

> Satire was certainly of admirable Use among the Antients, and is of no less among the Moderns; but then they always chose for their Theme some reigning Vice, or growing Folly: But where can you find a *Persius*, a *Juvenal*, or *Horace*, lashing of Personal Defect, or Turns of Providence? These Pious *Heathens* well knew that Calamities were not Crimes; and always exempted such from being the Subject of Satire. They knew it was not in the Power of a Man to make his own Fortune, any more than he could make his own Person.[49]

Victims of satire are not the only writers who take exception to sporting with or sneering at unalterable deficiencies. In 1711, Addison announces decisively, "A Satyr should expose nothing but what is corrigible."[50]

Most commentators regard "natural" imperfections as exempt from satire. Blackmore specifies that

WIT is likewise misapply'd, when exercis'd to ridicule any unavoidable Defects and Deformities of Body or Mind; for since nothing is a moral Blemish, but as it is the Effect of our own Choice, nothing can be disgraceful but what is voluntary. . . . [I]t must be a Violence to Reason and Humanity, to reproach and expose for any Thing that was not in his Power to escape. (18)

At least in principle, Blackmore proscribes satiric attacks on either mental or physical imperfections. The author of *Some Critical and Politick Remarks On . . . Faction Display'd* had taken a slightly different view: real satire does not strike at unfixable deficiencies, and the only such defects are physical.

The civilest thing I can say of [a passage in *Faction Display'd*] is, that it puts me in mind of *Dryden's* broad way of abusing *Shadwell* in his *Mock Fleckno*. The Malice is too apparent, and the Epithets layed on too thick. Besides, *prov'd want of Sense*, is Nonsense, for a Negative cannot be proved. *Stammering and Fetter'd Tongue* point at natural Infirmities, which the Criticks will not allow to be Objects of Satyr. (7)

Both *Faction Display'd* and *Mac Flecknoe* exhibit "virulent-ill nature," he complains; the "business" of the real satirist, he says, "is with the maladies of the Mind," not of the body (7, 9). Whereas Blackmore refuses to condone attacks on either body or mind, this writer excludes only the former.

The author of *A Discourse on Ridicule* (1716) likewise insists that irremediable woes are illegitimate objects of satire, but that is not his only criterion.

We must exercise our Faculty of Laughter, and Talent of Ridicule upon due Objects; that is to say, upon proper Persons, and proper Things. Upon proper Persons: For there are some Persons, whom either their Dignity, or Authority, exempt from our Ridicule. . . . And as our Ridicule must be directed to proper Persons, so likewise to proper Things. We must not deride the Poverty and Calamity of our Neighbours. . . . Nor may we deride our own Misery: For this is to make a very irreligious Use of Afflictions. . . . Nor may we ridicule the Sins and Vices either of our Neighbour, or ourselves. (10)

An unspecified class of people is "above" mockery; anyone sensitive to ridicule should out of decency be spared; and several specified misfortunes cannot be rightly targeted. This directive wants particulars, but clearly the author is not merely supplying a standard catalog of impermissible satiric butts. Nothing of the sort exists to be invoked or recited.

A small number of authors protest that satirists—too often only ill-natured wits—abuse exactly that which should be applauded. In a 1718 sermon, Jasper How opines that "the brightest Virtue is liable to Censure, and cannot always escape the Slander of malicious Tongues. There are some who take delight in Satire, and are never employ'd more to their Satisfaction, than when reproaching and defaming the Innocent; such will make Virtue and Piety itself the Subject of their wicked Drollery."[51] How inveighs against the perversity inherent in condemning righteousness. His objection resembles Addison's complaint of the following year: the satire of a clever but petulant man will "chiefly fall upon those who ought to be the most exempt from it. Virtue, Merit, and every Thing that is Praise-worthy, will be made the Subject of Ridicule."[52] Addison repeatedly distinguishes between appropriate and inappropriate types of wit. In *The Spectator*, no. 23, he explains, "Lampoons and Satyrs, that are written with Wit and Spirit, are like poison'd Darts, which not only inflict a Wound, but make it incurable" (1:97; 27 March 1711). In *The Tatler*, no. 242, Steele had likewise emphasized the importance of benevolence to proper satire: good nature is "an essential Quality in a Satyrist," for "Good-Nature produces a Disdain of all Baseness, Vice, and Folly, which prompts them to express themselves with Smartness against the Errors of Men, without Bitterness towards their Persons. This Quality keeps the Mind in Equanimity, and never lets an Offence unseasonably throw a Man out of his Character" (3:241; 26 October 1710). Like Addison and Steele, How is troubled by the tendency of satirists to attack the innocent, but the correlation ends there. How's consternation resembles their controlled proprieties much less than it recalls Glanvill's fulmination against excessive mirth. Like Glanvill, if less fervently, How associates drollery not with bad manners but with impiety.

Should satire be general or particular? A frequently and vehemently asserted imperative is that the satirist should not specify individual targets: "real Names," says Ward, "turn Satyr to abuse."[53] At least in theory, many writers require that the satirical account be nonspecific—but not always because personal satire is unfair or indecent. A number of commentators appear just as concerned about efficacy as about moral or ethical appropriateness. In the 1711 *Essay upon the Publick Spirit* Dennis maintains, for example, that

> general Satyr is preferable to what is particular, not only because the Design is more generous, of obliging all, and offending none, but because there is a greater probability of its attaining the End to which it directs its Aim, which is the Reformation of the Reader: For the Pleasure which we find that the Generality of Mankind takes in particular Satyr, is a certain Sign that the Publick reaps little Benefit from it; for few are willing to apply those Faults to themselves. (27)

Attacks on individuals will not achieve the desired result (reform of audience, not target) because readers not specifically indicated will not admit the criticism's relevance to them. Swift's remark is only the most famous: "*Satyr is a sort of* Glass, *wherein Beholders do generally discover every body's Face but their Own*."[54] A 1717 writer likewise laments that the reformation through ridicule must "be made from general

Characters," because "where a particular Man is sneer'd at, every one is for throwing the Ridicule off from himself, and can find nothing in his own Conduct to correct from the Lesson."[55] Personal satire has plenty of enemies, but it is criticized for being inadequate as much as for being malicious.

Not everyone agrees that general satire is unable to get through to individual readers. Sir John Fielding argues that only in nonparticularized satire will a reader see his or her own faults described: "A general representation of an action, either ridiculous or enormous, may make those wince, who find too much similitude in the character with themselves."[56] Fielding is writing half a century after Dennis, of course, and his reversal of his predecessor's conclusion bespeaks a much more generous view of human nature. But back in 1677 Sir Carr Scroope had made a similar case, suggesting that satirical "wit, / Frightens a million where a few you hit."[57] Scroope is defending satire, and perhaps simply exaggerating claims about its potency—though he is underscoring its power to terrorize rather than to improve its targets.

Other commentators more solemnly denounce general satire. The author of the 1716 *Discourse on Ridicule* insinuates that too-general satire is not futile but blasphemous: to poke fun at common failings is to scorn human nature, and thus to deride the Creator. The proper targets of satire, he enjoins, are "acquired Follies, and Affectations." Because only those people "whom not GOD, but themselves have made Objects of Ridicule," the satirist is duty bound, to some extent at least, to particularize his attack (12). A late eighteenth-century critic of *Gulliver's Travels* indicts Swift's satire on the same grounds. James Beattie's 1783 judgment of Part IV of the *Travels* is filled with righteous indignation:

> this tale represents human nature itself as the object of contempt and abhorrence. Let the ridicule of wit be pointed at the follies, and let the scourge of satire be brandished at the crimes of mankind: all this is both pardonable, and praise-worthy. . . . But when a writer endeavours to make us dislike and despise, every one his neighbour, and be dissatisfied with that Providence, who has made us what we are . . . such a writer . . . proves himself the enemy, not of man only, but of goodness itself; and his work can never be allowed to be innocent, till impiety, malevolence, and misery, cease to be evils.[58]

Satire that tends toward the general rather than the particular, in this account, is taken as misanthropic and thus sacrilegious. Not all principled opposition to generalized satire is so stern. Henry Fielding frequently urges his readers not to pass judgment too soon or based on too little information. In *Tom Jones* (1749), he warns against passing "a severe Sentence upon the whole, merely on account of some vicious Part" (2:570). Fielding's disapproval of generalized satire is a long way from Beattie's solemn denunciation. A realist with a fair amount of sympathy (at least for non-Catholics) and a rich sense of humor, he is concerned not about irreligion but about impractical attitudes toward human behavior.

I will state the obvious: eighteenth-century writers did not agree about what was permissible (or not) and valuable (or not) in the realm of satiric practice. Writers worry about very different issues in radically disparate ways and for a wide range of reasons. Some commentators assert that satire must be true or else it is merely slander, but veracity is not universally regarded as requisite. Several people enthusiastically avow that satire should be "sweeten'd," but others contend just as emphatically that the best satire is that which uncompromisingly scorches its target. Even writers who advocate the same "type" of satire—razor-sharp ridicule or sugarcoated sallies, for example—have drastically dissimilar reasons for doing so. Participants in these discussions adopt fundamentally incompatible positions (e.g., the proper province of satire is the trivial or alternatively is everything but the trivial). The temptation is great to regard these disagreements as tidy binaries—Horatian amiability versus Juvenalian wrath, follies versus crimes, general versus particular satire, and so on. But to treat them as such is to smudge distinctions that we very much need. Even where we find at least apparent correspondences, we also find significant incongruity that cannot be ignored. As one eighteenth-century commentator astutely points out, "NEITHER is the Taste of Mankind less capricious with regard to the Methods of Ridicule, than the Objects of it."[59] As many other contemporaries no doubt understood, in the realm of satirical target and technique, observers then or now would be hard pressed to find *any* uncontested or uniform position.

IV. Characterizing the Satirist

How did satirists present themselves, and how was the satirist viewed by contemporaries? Elkin describes a straightforward phenomenon: a number of contemporaries vilified satirists as inhumane, and in response many satirists duly struck the moral pose, offering grandiloquent defenses of their work. The charges of malevolence and the countercries of sociomoral utility have been much quoted by modern scholars— but does that conflict fairly represent contemporary attitudes, pro or con, toward satirists?

Most positive representations of the *satirist* are actually affirmations of the value of *satire*. As I have already enumerated the various conceptions of satire's function, I will not rehearse them again here. I will only say that most positive characterizations of the satirist tend to be unremarkable. Not uncommon is the claim that the satirist is compelled by "generous Indignation"—by a resistance to wrongdoing that every good man should feel "when he reflects on the Insolence of Exalted Vice, which has a pernicious Effect on the Community."[60] The author of *The Repository, or General Re-*

view (1756) offers a judicious defense of the satirist, questioning those who "imagine that a satirist must be made up of spleen, envy, and ill-nature." That assumption, the writer dispassionately maintains, "is by no means certain and determinate: I know an author of a tragedy, who is the merriest man living; and one who has wrote a very witty comedy, though he will sit an hour in company without speaking a word."[61] Other supporters of the satirist operate on the principle that the best defense is a good offense: they accuse those who attack the satirist of having something to hide. A 1721 commentator alleges, "Whoever fears Ridicule, deserves Ridicule. He is conscious of a weak Side, and knows he cannot stand a Laugh."[62] Favorable attitudes toward the satirist are not as varied as the opinions about satiric practice surveyed above, but neither are they uniform. The satirist is alternately glorified (often in patently self-promoting ways), praised, and accepted by some writers, while others simply withhold judgment, refusing to malign his or her character on the basis of the work alone.

Negative representations of the satirist are wider ranging and usually more interesting. The accusation of meanness is as hackneyed as the moral defense, of course, though the degree of animosity varies. Giles Jacob maintains that the "chief Design" of satire is "to find fault," and that "A little Wit, and a great deal of Ill-Nature, will qualify a Man for a Satirist."[63] Half a century earlier, Walter Charleton had described the "malignant" satirical wits not just as excessively critical but as subhuman: they are "the ill-natured Disciples of *Momus, Derisores, Scoffers,* such who, like Beetles, seem hatch'd in dung, or Vermine bred out of Ulcers; perpetually feeding upon the frailties and imperfections of Human nature."[64] Ward's venomous castigation of Pope is just as vividly judgmental: the derisory brute "squirts down frothy Satyrs with contempt" (17). What is worse, for some critics, is that these writers seem to revel in contumelies. Describing the "satyrists," Blount maintains that "*Pleasure* [is] their Principle, and *Interest* their God," and a later commentator complains that modern poets have "deboched" satire, reprehensibly delighting in the expression of malice and in "the Joy of Spight."[65]

The satirist is not only accused of meanness but is also assumed to suffer a variety of psychological problems. Jasper How suggests that those satirists who abuse the innocent are not merely cranky but subconsciously aware of their own depravity. These writers have "secret Reasons" for their cruelty, "and more than every Man knows of, a conscious Sense of Guilt, which puts them upon this vile and abusive Practice, in hopes of composing their own rankled Spirits" (29).[66] If not remorse, then other forms of self-contempt compel satirists to apply the lash. In Dennis's *Remarks on Mr. Pope's Rape of the Lock* (1728), he explains Pope's nastiness as an unfortunate byproduct of his racking sense of inadequacy: "It was for no other Reason that he has libell'd Mr. *Theobald,* Mr. *Phillips,* and several others, than that they have surpass'd him." Feeling like less of a poet—so argues Dennis—this "little envious Creature" finds consolation in insulting those he perceives as his superiors (2:325). Charleton had put the point more broadly in 1669: "*the more imperfect men are in themselves, the more prone they are to defame . . . others.*"[67]

If the satirist is (as Charleton suggests) a "scoffer," then we are again in the realm not of incivility but of blasphemy. Detraction in the form of scurrility and mockery is inextricably linked, for those like Glanvill and Charleton, to the most heinous forms of disbelief. The author of *Raillerie a la mode Consider'd* provides perhaps the most eloquent of the objections to vicious wit. Before describing the detractor, he explains the difficulties of rendering such an execrable fiend: "I should find my Ink not Black enough to Paint so Foul a *Monster*; nor could a Man have Courage enough to Draw the Devil, without the Security of some Good Guardian by his side. But I'le venture on Him; for, as they say, if we can but draw the Bloud of *Witches*, their Envious Intents cease" (49). The detractor, he says,

> is a kind of *Camelion*, that lives upon the worst sort of Air; at first bred up and suckled with sour Sustenance from the lank and flaggy Dugs of his lean and meager Mother *Envy*, he afterwards feeds on Fame; his words are worse than *Poyson* of *Asps*, and are a kind of *Witchcraft*, so that the *Sufferer* may justly be said to be *under an Evil Tongue*. Like one of the *wayward* Sisters, he *spightfully* picks the foul and poysonous *Weeds* out of the fairest *Gardens* of Mens *fruitful* Labors, wherewith to work his wicked *Sorceries*; with *venomous* Breath endeavoring to *blast* the best and fragrant Flowers of Mens *Writings*, that they may *wither* in the *minds* and *memories* of the World. (51–52)

The detractor—the defamer, the malevolent wit—is not only ill mannered and impious but actually demented. His language is "a kind of *Witchcraft.*" Elkin quotes this passage at length, deeming the description of the satirist simply "unflattering" (53). To categorize this author's account with Addison's (55 in Elkin)—to combine them under the heading "unflattering"—is to misapprehend both. No mere bad-tempered bully or abuser of the innocent, the satirist this writer describes is dealing in diabolism.

Eighteenth-century commentary on "the satirist" is both mixed and surprisingly scant. A number of writers have opinions about the satirist, but most of their sentiments are voiced only indirectly, through statements about the utility or harmfulness of satire. Defenses of the satirist are usually defenses of satire, and those, as I have already suggested, take numerous forms. Attacks on the satirist are more often attacks on satire than systematic indictments of the motives of satirists. Observations explicitly concerned with the author of satire are rare and mostly noncongruent. Gilbert Highet has pointed to "two different types of satirist," distinct in every way: "One likes most people, but thinks they are rather blind and foolish. He tells the truth with a smile, so that he will not repel them but cure them of that ignorance which is their worst fault. Such is Horace. The other type hates most people, or despises them. . . . His aim therefore is not to cure, but to wound, to punish, to destroy. Such is Juvenal."[68] Highet rightly distinguishes between different notions of satire, but we cannot presume that eighteenth-century respondents would have shared our taxonomical schemes or recognized categories we now believe in. They do not appear to have in mind Leonard Feinberg's definitive notion of "the satirist"—a writer who "functions as an artist, not as a moralist," who "is never satisfied with an objective report," and who is motivated by the desire to earn "recognition and approbation."[69] Like Feinberg, Charles A. Knight tries to encapsulate and particularize "the satiric frame of mind." For Knight, the satirist is "a skeptical and bemused observer" but also "a trickster, an agent as well as an observer, proclaiming truths disguised as lies and directing the action to bring about the ends he has proclaimed."[70] To which satirists are Feinberg and Knight referring? Pope may be seeking "recognition and approbation," but the scores of anonymous writers can hardly be thought to have been so motivated. Neither Defoe nor Swift, two radically different satirists, can be justly explained as a "skeptical and bemused observer." Modern depictions of "the satirist" are badly out of sync with the actualities of eighteenth-century practice, and they do not reflect eighteenth-century notions, insofar as they exist, of "the satirist."

V. Perceptions of Eighteenth-Century Satire Then and Now

Did eighteenth-century commentators believe that they were living in the great and glorious Age of Satire? Apparently not. Satire was a contentious subject for many writers. Its opponents were clearly upset about it, considering it a significant enough problem that they needed to respond. Even those who approved of satire did not necessarily commend the works venerated by scholars (e.g., Dryden's *Mac Flecknoe*). Satire produced anxiety not only because of its moral and social consequences but also because of the sheer uncertainties of the form. What did it mean? How could it be used? What should be condemned? What should the models be? Who wrote it, why, and for whom? No consensus existed in the realms of definition, concept, terminology, objective, method, target, or characterizations of the satirist. Contemporary commentary is profuse but scrappy and sketchy, and attitudes toward satire are decidedly mixed. Modern scholars who have long thought of the years from the Restoration to the death of Pope as the "Augustan" period have also hailed it as the heyday of English satire, but however spectacular some of the works themselves, nothing suggests that contemporaries recognized satire as the crowning achievement of their age.

How did eighteenth-century writers view satire? The corpus of observations on the subject suggests an unsettled, variegated, and fundamentally dynamic state of affairs. The relevant primary material is unwieldy, a great number of often very patchy and imprecise bits. It comprises well-worn clichés, partisan swipes, blatant self-promotion, innumerable explications and expostulations, allusions en passant, and analyses interminable. The resultant conglomeration abounds with incompatible credos and amorphous concepts of satire. Writers quarrel with each other on a number of issues—see the debate about ridicule incited by Shaftesbury—but many appear indifferent to matters that others regard as vitally important, such as etymology. What the mass of contemporary commentary reflects is not a clear-cut dispute between advocates of satire and their adversaries but a mélange of values, interests, concerns, and convictions.

Elkin was the first scholar to try to describe theories of satire in this period at all systematically, and his study has been almost universally deferred to as the authoritative account of the subject. What is the nature of his description? Although he wisely warns against expecting "this formidable volume of critical writing to yield a 'theory' of satire," he also tries to illustrate what he calls "the orthodox viewpoint of the Augustan critics" (2, 71). His thesis, broadly, is that the "Augustans" said one thing and did another. Eighteenth-century defenders of satire trumpet its reformative powers, but the loudly asserted moral justification contrasts sharply with the predominantly abusive realities of satiric practice. For Elkin, the "Augustans" divided themselves neatly into two camps: those "for" satire and those "against." The battle lines are clearly drawn and ubiquitously articulated, suggests Elkin, who finds the combatants on either side part of a coherent and recognizable faction. The exception is Swift, whom he presents as the lone nonconformist in the realm of satire theory: the Dean delighted in satire's vindictiveness, making him "the only satirist of the age to look on his vocation with . . . honest discernment." The rest of "his fellow satirists," Elkin continues, "preferred to present themselves to the public as practical reformers" (88). He may be casually overstating his case, but the declaration of homogeny—with a single glitch in the form of Jonathan Swift—just does not square with the evidence.

Elkin read widely in a massive body of material, and he found the clear-cut categories that he evidently set out to find. He assumes the importance of a Drydenian/Popean position (defense of satire on high moral grounds) and of an Addisonian position (opposition to satire's meanness) and organizes the bulk of his material accordingly. The sorting of contemporary commentary into two clearly defined pigeonholes requires some problematic generalization, as here: "Contemporary satire, in the opinion of . . . Addison, Blackmore, Collier, Dennis, Shaftesbury, Steele, Whitehead, Wolseley, and countless others throughout the Augustan period, needed to be purged of malice and pettiness" (63). These writers no doubt agreed that satire was sometimes malicious and petty. To lump them together, however, is to enforce synchronicity on commentators who, even when they reach roughly similar conclusions, often make different sorts of arguments with varying levels of intensity.

Whence Elkin's apparent predisposition to find congruity and unity—to unearth an "orthodoxy"—in eighteenth-century attitudes toward satire? He wrote his account in the immediate aftermath of midcentury publications by major scholars such as Jack, Kernan, Mack, and Paulson. These critics, as Griffin has rightly observed, "had enough confidence and comprehensive vision to make large claims about satire as a genre."[71] Whatever its limitations, Elkin's study was timely. It provided the counterpart to—and even the theoretical justification for—the arguments made in the 1950s and 1960s about eighteenth-century satire. Modern scholars from the mid-twentieth century on have tended to think of satire as essentially pessimistic and ineffectual. As a result, they have also assumed (as Elkin does) that attitudes toward satire reflect its largely malicious nature. More specifically, they have made blanket assumptions about the nature of the opposition to and the defense of satire.

Both the "pro" and "con" positions have been badly oversimplified. (1) Satire's adversaries uniformly charged it with meanness and pointlessness. Is this true? Satirists are often accused of depravity, but I have demonstrated the substantial variations, in type and degree, of such charges. And for at least some of satire's detractors, its ineffectiveness would only have been a relief: a good many were alarmed by its potential to do real harm, either to an individual target or to society more broadly. (2) Satire's supporters were defensive and apologetic in their efforts to prove its moral utility, or so some modern critics assume, and in claiming its reformative powers were either innocent or hypocritical. Griffin is puzzled and unsettled by the fact that

> the moral defense of satire is presented in such crude terms, as if the satirist were offering elementary lessons in distinguishing good from evil, combating vice and regulating passion, to an audience of moral infants. Theorists devoted some attention to the *way* in which satire allegedly corrected its readers, but most were (by our lights, anyway) naïve and optimistic about satire's power to "banish Vice and Folly." (26)

The dismissal of contemporary considerations about the "way" in which satire works is too hasty. In fact, modern enthusiasm for drastic and bombastic defenses of satire (e.g., Pope's "O sacred Weapon!") has confused the issue. Critics are keen to see Dryden and Pope—loud proponents of high-minded satire but themselves capable of sordid lampoonery—as representative of the "Augustan Defense" described by Elkin. But a remarkable number of satire's advocates eschewed generalized declarations of its utility and instead asked fairly seriously just how it might work: *that* sort of technique will not reach *this* kind of audience, and so on. Yet others appear to have been uninterested in the "moral function" and instead unapologetically embraced the power and the glory of vituperation.

The division into "for" and "against" creates a false impression. Eighteenth-century attitudes toward satire do not reduce to a prosatire school and an antisatire school, each of which has its primary spokesmen (Dryden/Pope or Addison/Blackmore, respectively) and a legion of disciples of the same persuasion. Those who defend satire do not tend to quote Dryden, those who worry about satire's malice generally do not refer to Addison, and those who revel in satire's meanness do not mention Swift. What Elkin and others regard as central to the theory of satire was not very often cited, was not obviously familiar to contemporaries, and did not unite groups of commentators into "schools" of thought. Dryden and Pope are central to modern concepts of eighteenth-century satire theory, but few respondents evoked those writers to clarify their own positions. No single debate dominated, and no real consensus existed in the long eighteenth century on any issue related to the practice of satire.

At no point in this period does an orthodox position exist, and neither can we find a dichotomy of the sort promulgated by Elkin, but attitudes toward satire do change markedly over the course of the long eighteenth century. Harsh satire falls increasingly out of favor, "hard" comedy gives way to "soft," and instead of unsparing judgment writers are more inclined to sympathetic nudging. To the nature of this change I return in chapter 7; for the moment I simply point out that practice *does* shift, and so, to some extent, do responses to satire. No doubt for every trend there are exceptions and counterexamples. The debates about ridicule make manifest the existence of fundamental differences in opinion found among contemporaneous writers. And attitudes toward laughter in the middle of the eighteenth century, as Simon Dickie has convincingly argued, are by no means unequivocally sentimental. "Modern readers," he concludes, "will be struck by the callousness" of mid-eighteenth-century jokes and jestbooks, by "their frank delight in human misery. All take it for granted that one laughed at illness, disability, hunger, and domestic violence." While he grants that "politeness and sentimentality were powerful ideals," he also makes clear that "they had to compete with older freedoms," and he issues a potent reminder that the emergence of the humanitarian sensibility associated with the mid and late eighteenth century was slow and gradual.[72]

The striking tonal change from the late seventeenth century to the late eighteenth is a fact, but the differences between the world of 1660 and that of 1760 are not to be explained in terms of a traceable developmental pattern. One can document changes over time. The intensity with which mid- to late-seventeenth-century writers inveigh against wit as blasphemy is never matched later in the period. In the late seventeenth century, writers discuss "mirth" rather than "ridicule"; the latter becomes a noticeably more current term with Shaftesbury around 1708. That shift is a feature of, among other things, the general transformation in attitudes toward laughter. As Stuart M. Tave demonstrated in *The Amiable Humorist* (1960), the meaning of laughter changes noticeably over the long eighteenth century, becoming less disparaging—less a matter of Hobbes's joyful expression of superiority—and more sympathetic. A number of mid-seventeenth-century writers applaud laughter as an essential part of human society, and commentators a century later unashamedly endorse the castigatory powers of ridicule, but the shift in focus away from "mirth" and toward "ridicule" is one indication of a major climatic change. "Mirth" is a nonparticularized type of humor; "ridicule" is ridicule of a target. Writers worry less about "laughter" and more about "laughter *at*," about the (proper, legitimate, and fair) treatment of the satiric victim.

Eighteenth-century pronouncements on satire do not add up to a predominant mode practiced by "them." Most scholars have not wanted to deal with this evidence at all, and much of the modern sense of eighteenth-century satire theory derives from a small and unrepresentative sampling of favorite authors. Satire critics routinely feature Dryden's *Discourse* as both helpfully explanatory of satire in this period and as monumentally influential; they treat Pope's self-promotion as objective discourse, a reliable index to what authors believed satire ought to do; they cite Addison and Steele as tempering influences on contemporaries' concept of satire; they sometimes give a passing glance to Shaftesbury. Scholars after Elkin have understandably not felt compelled to read beyond Dryden, Pope, Addison, and Steele—in part because they have not been inclined to distrust Elkin's survey, which includes not only the big names but also many obscure texts and unknown writers. He read widely, but the results suggest that he began not by asking, "What sort of taxonomy makes sense, and how can these works best be discussed?" but "In which of my categories do these fit?" My survey is neither perfect nor complete, and other critics could organize the material differently, but a reasonably objective examination should reveal the heterogeneity of the culture of eighteenth-century satire.

At this point the exasperated reader might ask a couple of questions: why such disagreement about satire among eighteenth-century writers, and what can we usefully conclude from the differences of opinion? My answer is short, if not sweet. Classical, continental, and Renaissance predecessors in the practice of satire notwithstanding, "satire" was nothing like a settled form as of the later seventeenth century. It had both supporters and opponents, but as the supporters have no consistent notion of what the form is supposed to do, the debate started out unfocused and remained that way. Any attempt to formulate an ex post facto "Augustan" theory of satire (or whatever other term we choose) is necessarily doomed to failure. There is no underlying clarity and coherence of concept to be found in the writings of English critics of the late seventeenth and early eighteen centuries, and none emerges as we proceed past 1750. To acknowledge the full range of eighteenth-century satiric *theory*, in other words, is to anticipate and to accept the radical diversity in eighteenth-century satiric *practice*.

CHAPTER THREE

Satire in the Carolean Period

In the Isle of Brittain long since famous growne
For breeding the best C--ts in Christendome,
Not long since Reign'd (oh may he long survive)
The easiest King and best bred Man alive.
Him no Ambition mov'd to get Renowne
Like a French Foole still wandring up and downe,
Starving his People, hazarding his Crowne.
—Rochester, *In the Isle of Brittain*, ll. 1–7

But not one Lesson of the Ruling Art,
Cou'd this dull Blockhead ever get by heart.
Look over all the Universeal Frame,
There's not a thing the Will of Man can name,
In which this Ugly, perjur'd Rogue delights,
But Ducks, and loyt'ring, butter'd Bunns, and whites.
—Buckingham, *The Cabbin-Boy*, ll. 5–10

Henceforth a Series of new time began,
The mighty Years in long Procession ran:
Once more the Godlike *David* was Restor'd,
And willing Nations knew their Lawfull Lord.
—Dryden, *Absalom and Achitophel*, ll. 1028–1031

To make sense of satire in the reign of Charles II (1660–1685), we need to start with two basic questions. Why did Carolean satirists write satire, and what is the nature of the works they produced? Scholars have tended either to characterize late seventeenth-century satire in terms of post-1700 developments (as "pre-Augustan") or to formulate a "Restoration mode" of satire based on a small number of verse exemplars.[1] The first approach collapses important distinctions between Carolean and eighteenth-century practice; the second tends to obscure the differences to be found among "Restoration" practitioners. Critics invariably discuss *Mac Flecknoe* and *Absalom and Achitophel* and a few poems by Rochester; they sometimes include Marvell's

"Painter" poems and Oldham's *Satyrs upon the Jesuits*; they routinely mention but rarely discuss Butler's *Hudibras*. To get a better grasp of satire as it was written and read in the Carolean period, we will have to look at a lot more exemplars while resisting the temptations of teleology.

Two recent studies of satire in this period have sought, from different perspectives, to characterize Carolean satire less reductively than has been the norm. Harold Love's *English Clandestine Satire, 1660–1702* (2004) and Robert D. Hume's " 'Satire' in the Reign of Charles II" (2005) are useful accounts whose authors refuse to privilege the major writers and acknowledge the messy realities of scribal publication and uncertain attribution. I am indebted to both in my discussion here, though my focus differs from theirs. Love deals exclusively with scribally circulated satires, most of which were vituperative or subversive enough that print publication would have been imprudent—especially with an author's name attached. *English Clandestine Satire* surveys and analyzes a great deal of hitherto unstudied material in helpful and exciting ways, but it does not consider these works as part of Carolean satire more broadly conceived. Juxtaposing the lampoons Love covers with printed verse, prose, and dramatic satires will, I think, give us a yet fuller sense of what Carolean satire meant to its authors. Hume deals with satire across genres; he also attends to the various modes of circulation and to the availability of the works of earlier English, classical, and continental writers in Carolean England. He asks how contemporary readers and theatergoers would have understood "satire"; I ask more specifically how Carolean writers conceived of their enterprises—what satire meant to its practitioners and why they wrote it.

Reading this period either for evidence of an ascendant "Augustan" mode or for a common "spirit of the age" has led scholars to overemphasize similarities and to overlook inconsistencies in satiric practice. Marvell and Dryden are sometimes compared as "public poets"; Rochester and Butler both feature "low" subjects. Claude Rawson suggests that Oldham's *Satyrs upon the Jesuits* "to some extent anticipate *Absalom and Achitophel*."[2] Jeremy W. Webster refers casually to "the nature of Restoration political satire,"[3] though his discussion deals almost exclusively with Rochester. If we are to represent Carolean satire fairly, then we need to attend to its disparities as well as to its correspondences. We need also to look more fully at its authors and their works. "Carolean satire" includes hundreds upon hundreds of squibs, verse satires, character sketches, litanies, and broadsides (some of which are collected in the Yale *Poems on Affairs of State*) as well as the fiercely antimonarchical diatribes of John Ayloffe and the disgusted social satire of Thomas Otway, also the less studied works by canonical figures (e.g., Dryden's *The Kind Keeper*). We can wonder about "the degree and nature of 'satire' in Carolean comedy,"[4] but some plays unquestionably contain satirical elements, and these works have had little place in modern accounts of long eighteenth-century satire. Dryden's *The Spanish Fryar* belongs to a discussion of Carolean satire as surely as does *Mac Flecknoe*. A few scholars give a passing glance to Wycherley and Etherege, but *The Country-Wife* and *The Plain-Dealer* are no more relevant than Otway's *Friendship in Fashion* or Thomas Duffett's *The Mock-Tempest*.

The object of this chapter is twofold. I aim to demonstrate first that there is no "Restoration mode" of satire (a negative claim) *but also* that Carolean satire nevertheless has distinguishing features that separate it from what follows in the later decades of the long eighteenth century (a more positive argument). The bulk of the chapter is devoted to making distinctions among the major and minor authors and works of the Carolean years, and the final section explains what sets this period as a whole apart from the later seventeenth and eighteenth centuries. We should not come to this material looking for the underdeveloped antecedents of Pope and Swift. Critics have tended, crudely speaking, to look for the influence of Dryden and Rochester on later satirists—to stress Dryden's use of mock heroic, his cultural/moral arguments, his division between good and bad, and Rochester's obscenity, aggression, and irreverence. We should not read Dryden as pre-Pope and Rochester as pre-Swift. Both Dryden and Rochester belong to their particular historical moment and to a satiric milieu dominated by nasty personal attacks and by intense unhappiness about a political situation that ranges from unstable and unsatisfactory to dire.

A broader point about satire in the reign of Charles II is that, more than satire produced at any other time in the long eighteenth century, it has teeth. It is often fierce and only rarely funny. We do find considerable variation among these works, mostly in tone and intensity, but a large proportion of them tend toward the heated, angry, or alarmed. Carolean satire has often been seen as a negative enterprise, thanks in part to the boom in bawdy lampoonery, but one of the conclusions of this chapter is that many of these satirists are writing not only to demolish a target but to defend something or someone seen as under attack. Much of the negativity of this satire comes from the writers' fear or despair or outrage rather than from frivolous meanness, and we also find many satires penned from constructive impulses in the hopes of achieving positive results.

I. Some Preliminary Considerations:
Realities versus Assumptions

Carolean satiric practice has surprisingly little to do with "Augustan satire" as conceived by modern scholars. Carolean satires were, in the main, not composed at the desks of great poets and then published in nicely bound, well-annotated, definitively attributed volumes meant to be read in their moments by all and sundry and appreciated in the hereafter for their aesthetic value and transmundane moral utility.

The culture of satire in this period is strikingly incommensurable with the predispositions and constructs of most twentieth-century critics, but if we are to make sense of it—and it is like nothing else before or since—then we need to try to take it on its own terms.

Why and for whom was Carolean satire written? *Absalom and Achitophel* is an exemplar of highly polished literature, political satire cum biblical allegory written by a master craftsman. But equally part of this world is *A Litany* (wr. 1672), headed in manuscript, "These were writ in Lincoln's Inn Boghouse/1672"—the unknown author claims to have composed his unhappy plaint in a privy. The nature of the enterprise varies, and so does the audience for which satire is written. Dramatic satires were performed for a heterogeneous crowd; theatergoers did not possess identical values and assumptions then any more than they do now. Many satires were composed for the enjoyment of a small coterie and others to sway opinion among a broader readership; some authors are writing to members of their own party and some to the opposition; some printed material would have been taken differently by different readers. The rhetorical situation—the authorial stance vis-à-vis speaker, imagined audience, mode of transmission—varies from satire to satire, and we need to read with that in mind.

Many Carolean satires were evidently written for the moment. The majority of what appeared in print as "satyr" (or occasionally "satire") was produced not as a piece of culture for posterity but for immediate consumption. Scribal verse satires were not, as a rule, solidified into print by their authors, nor were most ever meant to be.[5] The notion of plays as literary enterprises evolved only in the late seventeenth century (no author's name appeared on a playbill until 1699),[6] and audience members would have been unlikely to think of dramatic satire in this period in those terms. Scholars in English departments tend to view satire as a "literary" mode, but that was hardly the point for many Carolean writers: "'satire' in the form of scribally circulated lampoons and false-imprint broadsides . . . is a very far cry from 'satire' in the rarefied world of Pope's Horatian imitations or Johnson's 'Vanity of Human Wishes.'"[7] Satire is assumed perforce to be connected to its moment, though critics are fond of praising its greatest exemplars for transcending particulars. "The richest satire," says George deForest Lord, "is that which transmutes concrete historical realities into universals."[8] This is a ringing assertion, and certainly it applies to some satires in the long eighteenth century (e.g., Edward Young's *Love of Fame* series), but it has little relevance for most Carolean satirists, who seem to care not a jot about posterity. These satires tend to be ephemeral and highly topical; they are emphatically present centered, local, circumstantial, particular, and pragmatic in terms of wishing for a negative outcome for the target. They represent a satiric enterprise different in kind from that which is generalized, abstract, sweeping in its coverage.

We need to be aware of the material realities of Carolean satiric culture. The vast majority of Carolean satires were circulated or printed anonymously.[9] Some satires appeared in printed books by single authors who were named on title pages, but many were published in miscellanies (whose contributors were often either unnamed or inaccurately named) or as anonymous broadsides or pamphlets. Others circulated only in manuscript form, whether individually or in anthologies that were never intended for print.[10] Rochester and Dryden are associated with satire by contemporaries—but so are Stephen College, Sir Carr Scroope, Sir Thomas Skipwith, Sir Fleetwood Sheppard, and Jack Howe. Marvell's satires would have been known among his cohort, but not beyond it until the 1680s; Butler's *Hudibras* was a spectacular hit but never appeared with his name on it in his lifetime; Rochester was recognized as a satirist, but what contemporaries meant by "Rochester" or "Cleveland" or "Marvell" was not what we mean by it, as those authors' names graced many works not written by them. The editors of the Yale *Poems on Affairs of State* provide critical accoutrements that were not there originally, including extensive notes to help us make sense of the dense topical allusions and often an attribution, whether confident or tentative. No doubt some contemporaries were confounded by less-than-obvious satires, and by the time *State Poems* began to appear in print in 1689, few readers could have "gotten" most of the works. Both Michael McKeon and Hume highlight the potential indecipherability of the satires even to contemporaries, but most Carolean scribal satire was designed for a fairly specific coterie.[11] I suspect that members of that audience often had a pretty good sense of what the satire was doing and to whom.

Another problem is that critics tend to look for humor, burlesque distortion, and literary imagination in satire—desiderata apparently not valued by most Carolean writers. Some of these works are funny (e.g., *The Sullen Lovers* and *Seigneur Dildoe*), but many are not leavened by wit, and plenty of satirists are not laughing at all. They are furious, disgusted, or terrified, and increasingly so in the 1670s and early 1680s. Scholars are inclined to see Carolean satire as either highly moral (following the Dryden of the *Discourse*) or as frivolously nasty (following Rochester at his dirtiest and most spiteful). Many of these satires are neither. Some express moral outrage (e.g., *On the Three Dukes Killing the Beadle*), but more reflect worry about practical politics—with varying degrees of flippancy, comedy, meanness, solemnity, pragmatic purpose, faith in the possibility for change, and personal commitment. Modern assumptions about "satire" turn out not to accord very well with the particularities of *this* satire.

II. Dryden, Rochester, Buckingham

Dryden and Rochester figure prominently in most studies of "Restoration satire," the one a happy precursor to the "Augustan" mode and the other a practitioner of the spiky personal lampoonery from which Dryden is at pains to dissociate proper satire in the *Discourse*. Rochester scholars now underscore the political and philosophical dimensions of his work, but in common critical imagination he remains a bawdy devil to Dryden's high-minded moralist. As the poet laureate, scholars suggest, Dryden defended his ideals about writing and addressed the monarchical succession in his satire, whereas Rochester, a misogynistic and misanthropic playboy, offered a colorful picture of Nell Gwyn laboring to arouse Charles II and a libertine's unrestrained invective directed at his own uncooperative member. Even more than Dryden and Rochester, George Villiers, second Duke of Buckingham, was in his day a celebrity. All three were public figures—two of them noblemen and the third a leading Tory playwright and poet—and their satire was read by and commented on by contemporaries. What sort of satirist was each of these writers?

Carolean Dryden: Lampoonist, Social Commentator, Propagandist

Two important facts are worth remembering at the outset. (1) Modern scholars often read Dryden's most famous verse satires in terms of the high moral dictates outlined in the *Discourse*, whether they invoke that essay directly or not. The *Discourse* is a product of the 1690s, however, and its dictates have little connection to Carolean satiric practices—including Dryden's.[12] (2) Our sense of Dryden as a satirist is derived largely from two poems, with occasional pro forma reference to *The Medall*.[13] Not one of his satiric plays is cited in major modern satire studies. If we look at the totality of Dryden's output as a Carolean satirist without trying to make him into a forebear of Pope, what do we find?

Of Dryden's works, satire scholars have dealt all but exclusively with *Mac Flecknoe* (wr. 1676–1677; 2*d**) and *Absalom and Achitophel* (1681; 1*s**). In order to establish Dryden as the auspicious prototype for "Augustanism," critics tend to deemphasize the crude lampoonery of the first poem and the partisan message of the latter. J. Paul Hunter glosses *Mac Flecknoe* in a grand manner. Dryden's satire

> draws on readers' traditional expectations of rational intelligence, orderly procedures, mentorship, monarchical succession, Judeo-Christian body-spirit dichotomies and England's (and London's) superiority over "northern," Irish and "barbarian" cultures to create a sense of displaced and perverted social and political order in contemporary literary taste and the reward system.[14]

This description is not untrue, but it is misleading. Literary critics who know something of Dryden's convictions can undoubtedly perceive such a noble aim in *Mac Flecknoe*, but how many contemporary readers would have thought that its author was drawing on their beliefs about "body-spirit dichotomies"? That Dryden was thinking in those terms is far from clear to me. We can appreciate the poem's subtleties and its political and philosophical implications, but we should not lose sight of Dryden's original intentions, which were apparently to do damage.

> From dusty shops neglected Authors come,
> Martyrs of Pies, and Reliques of the Bum.
> Much *Heywood*, *Shirly*, *Ogleby* there lay,
> But loads of *Sh*—— almost choakt the way. (ll. 100–103)

Scholars insist that in heaping derogation on Shadwell Dryden is making an object lesson of what he regards as a bad example. While James Winn is perhaps right to argue that *Mac Flecknoe* "measures its victim's inflated claims to literary excellence against the more permanent standards of the epic tradition," his contention that it "transcends the personal irritations that prompted it" seems overgenerous.[15] Dryden's ridicule of Shadwell clearly has more genuine animosity behind it than had Shadwell's portrait of Sir Robert Howard in *The Sullen Lovers*, but he is abusing a personal enemy and an author whose theory of writing he means to belittle.[16] If *Mac Flecknoe* had been written by Sir Carr Scroope, I daresay scholars would not exalt its author's creditable motives but would sneer at his dirty pool and even lament that he had not followed Dryden's model.

Absalom and Achitophel has a more obviously positive agenda than does *Mac Flecknoe*, and it also has more force. However controlled this poem is, its satire reflects considerable anxiety on Dryden's part. He is defending Tory patriarchalism and right order: "What Prudent men a setled Throne woud shake?" (l. 796). Narcissus Luttrell's inscription tells us that the poem is written both "agt ye Duke of Monmouth, Earl of Shaftesbury & that party" and also "in vindicacon of the King & his freinds [*sic*]."[17] It is not merely attack. Nevertheless, as in *Mac Flecknoe*, he goes after individuals here, and contemporaries would surely have understood *Absalom and Achitophel* as part of "the harsh world of political combat and personal abuse—anonymous, partisan expression of contempt and hostility intended to damage the target in the eye of the beholder."[18] Dryden's poem is propaganda, and his character sketches are invidious, facts sometimes lost in honeyed descriptions of the father of "Augustan" satire's preeminent work: "Its art everywhere mixes the comic and the grand; every corner, even its most wicked moment, is transformed by an incomparable style and by a perfect sense of timing . . . and by an irony that suffuses the whole."[19] Like Hunter's construal of *Mac Flecknoe*, this account of *Absalom and Achitophel* is textually legitimate but also somewhat misleading. The brilliance of Dryden's artistry is why we read the poem now, and original readers would certainly have appreciated its skill, but to privilege technique over substance is to underemphasize the viciousness of some parts of the satire.

Like *Absalom and Achitophel, The Medall* (1682; *6d**) is Tory propaganda, this time by way of frontal assault. Because it represents direct and unrestrained invective, most students of "Augustan satire" have disregarded it. Phillip Harth has maintained that the satire has a sophisticated agenda and has criticized those who read it as lacking poise—that is, as a reflection of its author's alarm at Shaftesbury's acquittal. As a satire, Harth explains, *The Medall* "seeks to discredit the Whigs and diminish their importance in order to forestall the revival of popular fears." Dryden wishes to suggest "that the Whigs have been crushed and scattered as an effective political force . . . by the king's actions of the previous year and by the revelations of their infamy that followed."[20] *Absalom and Achitophel* is purposely calm, and, as Harth convincingly argues, *The Medall*'s tone is no less a deliberate rhetorical maneuver closely tied to the satire's political agenda. Both satires are careful, well-crafted enterprises written out of real conviction by a master poet, but they are also partisan polemics meant to influence current events.[21] They are just as much meant to blacken individuals in political warfare as is something like the anonymous *Wiltshire Ballad* (1680), a snappy Tory broadside recounting the treachery of the radicals of the 1640s in order to indict the current Whigs and to raise the specter of civil war.

Dryden's satirical plays of the early 1680s have clear political resonance. In the subplot of *The Spanish Fryar* (perf. 1680; pub. 1681), Dryden pillories Friar Dominic, an unscrupulous Catholic priest. In the serious plot, he associates the Whigs with the radicals of the 1640s, suggesting the dangers of rebelling against proper authority by presenting us with "a fable about the evils of tampering with the legitimate succession." The caricature of Friar Dominic also has political import: Whigs loudly accused Tories of being Catholic sympathizers, and the Tory playwright here dissociates himself and his party from Catholic perfidy.[22] But, as Harth points out, Dryden is also eager to draw a crowd, and jeering at an easy target is one way to do so.[23] Unlike *The Spanish Fryar*, Dryden and Nat Lee's *The Duke of Guise* (banned in July 1682 but permitted in November) is a parallel play. Though ostensibly an innocent retelling of an episode from French history, its smokescreen is easy enough to penetrate. *The Duke of Guise* is an application satire insinuating that the Duke of Monmouth is a dangerous rogue who deserves to be killed—a touchy point to make about the king's favorite bastard. The Whigs screamed bloody murder, suggesting that they made the application; their response prompted Dryden to publish a sixty-page justification in which he claimed that the play is a piece of French history with no bearing on contemporary events.[24] The manifest disingenuousness of this defense might make us wonder how seriously we should take the high-minded pieties of the *Discourse*. Whatever Dryden's protests, *The Duke of Guise* represents overt political didacticism with brutally clear application.

Two of Dryden's Carolean satirical plays are not party pieces but social commentaries. The comic plot of *Marriage A-la-Mode* (perf. 1671; pub. 1673) presents an unhappy image of married life: the imminent union of Palamede and Melantha, arranged by parents for economic reasons, is dreaded by both parties; the already-wed Rhodophil and Doralice are mutually dissatisfied. Conjugal bliss appears impossible for these couples, but the possessive instinct prevents the men accepting an "open" relationship (both women available to both men, and vice versa). "The clear implication," Hume argues, "is that marriage is unsatisfactory but that people must make the best of what they cannot change. This is more than merely 'cynical': it is sad, serious, and wry, a skeptical and unhappy comment on the human condition." The play's gloomier undercurrents are undeniable, but most contemporary audience members ignored them, content to enjoy the show.[25] In *The Reformation* (perf. 1672; pub. 1673), Joseph Arrowsmith criticized Dryden's spicy comedy, raising moral objections to the picture of sexual freedom presented in *Marriage A-la-Mode*. Dryden also addresses social issues in *The Kind Keeper; or, Mr. Limberham* (perf. 1678; pub. 1680), which in its dedication he called "an honest Satyre against our crying sin of *Keeping*" (14:5). Unlike *Marriage A-la-Mode*, this play is a romp. In the earlier play, Dryden's judgment is clear enough, but righteous anger is hard to find in the exuberantly lewd *Kind Keeper*. *Marriage A-la-Mode* is not trying to influence current events and is not, as far as I can tell, earnestly urging moral or social reform, but it has substance; *The Kind Keeper* is a salacious farce.

Scholars tend to take Dryden very seriously as a straitlaced theorist of satire. They privilege *Mac Flecknoe* (assumed to have transcended the realm of personal abuse) and *Absalom and Achitophel* (hailed as a poised defense of monarchical succession). But the former—whatever its concern with theory of writing—is a lampoon, and a vulgar one at that. The latter was written in support of something Dryden strongly believed in, but it contains enough personal invective that John Dennis denied its status as "satire"; he described both *Mac Flecknoe* and *Absalom and Achitophel* as "Libels which have pass'd for Satires."[26] These two poems, moreover, do not complete Dryden's satiric corpus. While Harth is probably right to underscore the purposiveness of Dryden's indignation in *The Medall*, it is ultimately a partisan invective. *The Spanish Fryar* trashes an obvious butt, albeit for religiopolitical reasons. *The Kind Keeper* is smut, plain and simple, as Dryden well knew. He explicitly acknowledged the influence on it of Durfey's *A Fond Husband*, a roistering, farcical sex comedy staged in May 1677.[27] It is in a different universe from *Absalom and Achitophel*, and if scholars admit the poem but exclude the play in their discussions of Dryden as satirist, then the results are necessarily skewed. The author of the *Discourse* might be able to justify a solemn biblical allegory written in defense of king and country, but how would he have defended *The Kind Keeper*? I doubt that he could have made any of his Carolean satires, even the verse, conform to the grandiose dictates he set forth with such magisterial confidence in 1693. Dryden as Carolean satirist is not the venerable father of a moralizing "Augustan" mode: he is prepared to attack standard targets to increase the popularity of his plays, he is a polemical combatant, and he is willing to smear individuals without any apparent reformative objectives.

Rochester: Skeptical, Provocative, Negative

Rochester's satires are difficult to characterize. They tend to be defined by what he disapproves of and objects to, rather than by what he is supporting; he is "better at attacking than proposing an ideal,"[28] though the nature of attack is not uniform. He is frequently disgusted, often violent, sometimes playful, and his satire ranges from vigorous abuse (*On Poet Ninny*) to incisive self-parody (*To the Post Boy*) to politicized personal defamation (*In the Isle of Brittain*) to sharp articulation of misanthropy (*A Satyre against Reason and Mankind*) to aggressively thought-provocative expression of epistemological uncertainty (*Upon Nothinge*). A word of warning: for my purposes, classification of Rochester's satiric enterprises is what matters, and so what follows is not at attempt to resolve (or exhaustively to represent) critical disagreement about complex and challenging poems. Such a survey cannot do justice to the subtleties of the primary works or to the fullness of comment on them; the point is to appreciate where Rochester fits vis-à-vis his contemporary satirists.

Some of Rochester's satires are straightforward. His account of contemporary authors in *An Allusion to Horace 10 Sat: 1ˢᵗ Book* (1675–1676?) distinguishes decisively between the commendable (including, among others, Shadwell, Wycherley, Butler, and Buckingham) and the obnoxious (Dryden, Crowne, Settle, Otway, and others). In his lampoons on individual writers, he likewise leaves little doubt as to the verdict being passed.[29] In *On The Suppos'd Author of A late Poem in Defence of Satyr* and *On Poet Ninny*, he bludgeons Sir Carr Scroope as a vain but ugly and untalented writer.[30] In *My Lord All-pride*, he does the same to Mulgrave, calling into question that author's talent, intelligence, sexual prowess, and masculinity.[31] Mulgrave is the self-exposing speaker of *A very heroical epistle in answer to Ephelia* and in *An Epistolary Essay, from M.G. to O.B.*, an egoist who admits, "In my dear self, I center every thing" (*A very heroical epistle*, l. 7). Marianne Thormählen is right to highlight the contrast between the clear-cut diatribe of *My Lord All-pride* and "the carefully wrought ironies of the two 'epistles,'"[32] but these are withering condemnations delivered with bold assurance.

Just as acerbic are Rochester's cutting impromptus on the Duchess of Cleveland, Etherege, and other court personages, including the king:

> God bless our good and gracious King
> > Whose promise none relyes on,
> > Who never said A foolish thing
> > > Nor ever did A wise one.[33]

The epitaph stings, but not so much as the critically renowned "scepter lampoon," the earl's ruthless attack on Charles II and travesty of kingship more broadly. The tirade is manifestly personal (Rochester clearly loathes the man he is describing) but also political.[34] The sexual adventures of the "merry Monarch" endanger the state. To abuse this "easiest" of kings is to challenge his administrative competence, and Rochester obviously associates Charles's promiscuity with major governmental failings. Not content merely to jeer at Nell Gwyn's "Imploying Hands, Armes, Fingers, Mouth and Thighs / To raise the Limb which shee each Night enjoyes," he concludes, "I hate all Monarchs and the Thrones they sitt on."[35] The verdict is devastatingly clear.

Rochester does not always pronounce with the same confident clarity. Critics have wrangled over the meaning of *The Disabled Debauchee*, in which the libertine speaker gaily affirms his own debauchery. How are we to interpret the speaker's values, and how much do they share with the poet's? What (if anything) is being satirized here, and with how much conviction? Thormählen asserts that scholars who read ambiguity into this text do so because they "naturally expect any poem by the notorious Rochester to defend debauchery" but argues that "judged on its own terms," this satire "paints a forbidding picture of the pursuit, and the consequences, of riotous living."[36] She takes this poem and *To the Post Boy* as evidence that the earl was no hypocrite, that he could admit the ethical dubiety and other limits of libertinism and denounce it.[37] Critical discord suggests, however, that the satiric argument of these works is far from transparent.

Some of Rochester's other satires are likewise complex, and though the targets are clear, the poems have generated conflicting readings. The speaker contemptuously describes a rotten state of affairs in *A Ramble in St. James's Park*, which ends with his imagining getting his vengeance on the false Corinna by ruining her future marriage. In the *Letter from Artemiza in the Towne to Chloe in the Countrey*, Artemiza complains to her correspondent that love no longer exists in the world.[38] *Tunbridge Wells* attacks various types of individuals and vices, "The Rendevous of fooles, Buffoons, and Praters, / Cuckolds, whores, Citizens, their wives and daughters" (ll. 4–5). The speaker surveys the corruption and folly all around him—but he does not pretend to be better than his targets.

These works are plenty negative, as are *A Satyre against Reason and Mankind* and *Upon Nothinge*. At the end of the former, Rochester admits the hypothetical possibility of men leading decent, rational lives ("If upon Earth there dwell such God-like men"), but the poem's finale is grim. There is a definite sting in the tail: "If such there be," he concludes, then "Man differs more from Man, than Man from Beast" (ll. 220, 224, 225). In *Upon Nothinge*, Rochester ridicules human pretensions and the vanity of attempts to understand the world. He satirizes ex nihilo theories of creation and derides "the wise," those speculative philosophers who arrogantly "Enquire, defyne, distinguish, teach, devise," attempting to explain such a process (ll. 28–29). Whereas the *Satyre against Reason* "criticizes certain notions and doctrines," Thormählen says, *Upon Nothinge* "asserts that there is no foundation for any doctrine at all."[39] That sounds heavy—but late eighteenth- and nineteenth-century commentators referred to *Upon Nothinge* as they might a trifle. Rochester's "little poem" shows "admirable fertility of invention," consists of "a tissue of clever conceits," reflects "novelty of thought," is alternately "grave" and "playful."[40] Most scholars have found bitter pessimism in the *Satyre against Reason*, but A. D. Cousins suggests conversely that it "might well be, in effect, Rochester's attempt to locate, within the world of Charles's failed rule, a basis for a genuine restoration of order to the individual and society."[41] Is the *Satyre* grimly hopeless or (as Cousins implies) tentatively affirmative? Is *Upon Nothinge* playfully skeptical or despairing? Is Artemiza a satiric butt or spokeswoman? Does she constitute a moral norm? That Rochester is passing judgment is obvious, and his targets are usually readily discernible, but in these satires he is doing more than rendering a verdict.

What does all of this indicate about Rochester's concept of satire? I offer three conclusions as a partial answer to that question. (1) His output is best discussed not as a uniform whole but from exemplar to exemplar. The works differ not only in subject matter but in tone, intensity, and purpose. (2) We tend to think of strong satire as written from the conviction that the author knows and distinguishes right from wrong. This is what we find in *On Poet Ninny* and other lampoons, but the provocative nature of works like *Upon Nothinge* and *A Ramble* differentiates them from direct attack.[42] Cocksure rubbishing of Sir Carr Scroope's literary merit and appearance is one thing; evaluating the morality of libertinism in a corrupt society is quite another. (3) The interpretation of some of Rochester's works depends upon the expectations a reader brings to them. A moralizer would likely abominate in *The Imperfect Enjoyment* what an unabashed roué would only find amusing; *Upon Nothinge* can be read either as unsettling and upsetting or as teasingly clever. Rochester appears, at least some of the time, to be writing for very different types of readers: those who will be shocked, for either aesthetic or ethical reasons; those who can and will be entertained by it; those who might agree with the grim picture presented; and so on.[43] Authorial contexts can help modern critics make surer guesses about the attitude of the satirist, but a contemporary reader would probably have reacted according to his or her own disposition. Readers of *Absalom and Achitophel* might respond differently depending on their political leanings, but there can be little question about Dryden's central thrust or the commitment behind it. Rochester's more provocative satires are another matter; they seem, as Umberto Eco would say, partially "open" rather than entirely "closed."[44] Rochester quite often leaves us asking questions.

Buckingham's Purposive Satire

Satire scholars who mention Buckingham usually have only *The Rehearsal* (perf. 1671; pub. 1672) in mind. The most conspicuous satiric butt, at least in the 1671 version, is Dryden, though the duke also parodies a number of recognizable scenes from contemporary plays and from plays staged as early as 1663, when Buckingham evidently began to work on *The Rehearsal*.[45] How serious was Buckingham in his attack? "Many scholars have assumed that *The Rehearsal* was written out of genuine indignation and in the hope of driving heroic drama off the London stage," Hume and Love point out—but they express well-founded doubt that Buckingham was trying anything of the sort. His play was produced by the King's Company; Dryden was its leading playwright and a shareholder; *Tyrannick Love* and *The Conquest of Granada*, exemplars of the heroic drama satirized in *The Rehearsal*, had been major successes. The King's Company managers are extremely unlikely to have presented a satire intended to destroy the popularity of their principal playwright or of their stock plays.[46]

The dramatic burlesques of Thomas Duffett make a useful contrast to Buckingham's most famous satire. *The Mock-Tempest* (perf. 1674; pub. 1675) and *Psyche Debauch'd* (perf. 1675; pub. 1678) are terrific single-play parodies produced by the King's Company—spoofing Shadwell's revision of the Dryden-Davenant operatic *Tempest* and his *Psyche*, both staged by the Duke's Company. Relocating the original plots in a world of bawds and prostitutes, Duffett's plays are funny and lewd, as well as hostile.[47] Buckingham's burlesque of heroic drama is not sympathetic, but it is different in kind from Duffett's slashing travesties of Shadwell. There is a fair chance that the King's Company wanted to do real harm to the Duke's Company, even as they capitalized on their rivals' successes. That Buckingham had anything like this objective in mind for *The Rehearsal* is highly improbable.

Buckingham's satire is often at least as political as it is personal. The literary ridicule of *The Rehearsal* needs to be appreciated in its own right, but it should also be seen as a camouflage for political satire on Arlington.[48] Arlington is savagely satirized in *Aduice to a Paynter, to draw the Delineaments of a Statesman, and his Vnderlings*. The physical description of the "arrant Fopp" is acid:

> Giue him a meane proud Garbe, a dapper pace,
> A pert dull Grinn, a black Patch crosse his Face,
> Two goggle Eyes soe cleare, though very dead,
> That one may see through them quite through his Head.
> Let eu'ry Nod of his, and little winke
> Declare, the Foole would speake, but cannot thinke.
> Let him all other Fooles soe farre surpasse,
> That Fooles themselues poynt at him for an Asse. (ll. 1, 3–10)

This is character assassination with no pretense of fairness, but it is aimed at a political figure who mattered. In *Upon the Installment, of Sir [Thomas] Os[bor]n, and the Late Duke of New-castle*, as well as in *A Song on Thomas Earl of Danby*, Buckingham excoriates a former protégé turned rival. The description of Danby is vicious—"You're such a scurvy, stinking, Errant Knight, / That when you speak a Man would swear you S[hi]te" —but to detract from the man Thomas Osborne is to damage the reputation of the Earl of Danby, with whom Buckingham fought fiercely over issues of dissent and toleration.[49] This is a radically different enterprise from a work like *An Heroic Poem* (wr. 1681), in which the satirist's enmity is directed at Whig politicians rather than at their principles. The anonymous author of that poem, John Harold Wilson observes, was "motivated more by spite than by moral or political indignation."[50] The same cannot be said of these attacks on Danby, vindictively mean-spirited though they are.

Although Buckingham's *The Cabbin-Boy* and *The Ducks* are only brief snapshots, they convey quite an unflattering picture of the king. I quote the latter in full:

Whilst in the State all things look smooth and Fair,
Ile dabble up and down and take the Ayr.
But the first appearance of foul Weather,
I and my Ducks will quack away together. (2:34)

Charles's attitude toward governing is not what it should be, and, as in *The Cabbin-Boy*, the implication is that the leader of the country might have had better things to do with his time. Buckingham is manifestly prepared to thrash individuals in his political satires, but his motives are rarely only personal.

Although scholars are inclined to define satire in negative terms, most of Buckingham's satires are written as much *for* a cause as they are *against* a person. His main contribution to his and Sir Robert Howard's *The Country Gentleman* (scheduled for production in 1669 but stopped) is the table scene obviously meant to demean well-known political figures, especially Sir William Coventry. It succeeded brilliantly. Coventry tried and failed to get the play suppressed but managed to prevent its being staged by threatening to have someone cut the nose of the actor representing him. Incensed by gossip, he challenged the duke to a duel; Buckingham tattled to the king, who promptly dismissed Coventry from his Treasury job, to Buckingham's and Howard's immense satisfaction.[51] In addition to its political satire, *The Country Gentleman* also goes after businessmen, fops, and Francophilia in England, but it is simultaneously an ideological, pro-Country-party play with an explicit set of positives.[52]

Some of the duke's less well-known works are likewise affirmative as well as destructive.[53] In a short dialogue skit called *The Militant Couple*, he argues that certain kinds of mistreatment will lead to domestic discord and even to justifiable cuckolding. While the piece includes some comic bits, it is no droll portrayal of marital friction;

the satire advocates a standard of civility and courtesy. *The French Generall* (a skit written in 1685) is another exercise in purposive detraction, this time of the Earl of Feversham, whom James imprudently put in charge of the royalist army at the time of Monmouth's invasion and who nearly managed to lose the Battle of Sedgemoor. The general is justly lambasted as pompous, incompetent, and uncomprehending, but this is not idle lampoonery: Buckingham is making a critical point about James's ability to govern the country. In a dialogue entitled *An Account of a Conference between His Grace George, late Duke of Buckingham, and Father Fitzgerald an Irish Priest,* "Buckingham" guns for Catholic sympathizers, including the king. He ridicules transubstantiation in a way that calls the whole Catholic religion into question. The piece is a tall tale with a fair amount of humor and a stinging critique of intolerant religions that rely on blind faith and belief in miracles. It is also a hard-edged argument for toleration probably written just after James II's accession, a time of contentious debate about the official attitude toward religion. These satires uphold, and were perhaps primarily designed to uphold, the positive principles that Buckingham consistently champions.

Among the satiric works "associated with" Buckingham, the oddity is *Sir Politick Would-be* (wr. ca. 1662–1665), a play written in French in collaboration with Saint-Évremond and d'Aubigny. *Sir Politick* is set in Venice, where two scheming foreign travelers (the English Sir Politick and Monsieur de Riche-Source) are mistaken for conspirators against the Venetian Republic, arrested, identified as harmless lunatics whose venture is strictly fantastic, and released. Meanwhile, their wives—roundly mocked for their social pretensions and self-importance—resolve to rescue the Venetian women from their captivity by showing them a good time. They plan a ball for the dogesse and the senators' wives, but the mischievous *railleur* (Tancred) and his friend instead bring "a madam and a few of her girls" who impersonate the honored guests.[54] Sir Politick, Monsieur de Riche-Source, and their wives all have grand notions of themselves and singularly little grip on reality.

Sir Politick is markedly unlike much early- to mid-1660s satire. It has debts to a small number of English plays (including *Volpone*), but as H. Gaston Hall and Wallace Kirsop point out, it is very much in line with seventeenth-century French comedy as practiced by Jean Desmarets, Molière, and Corneille.[55] The French influence on English satire is clearest in the realm of farce—see *The London Cuckolds*—but *Sir Politick* represents a direction in which English satire could have gone. Its mockery of presumptuous gentlemen is unusual in the midsixties; slightly later, Buckingham and Howard would return to this theme in *The Country Gentleman*, but such satire was uncommon in this decade. This play's commentary on political and economic philosophy is also strange in the context of early Carolean satiric drama. *Sir Politick* is full of "would-bes"—almost everyone is vain, assuming, and self-congratulatory—

and totally lacks a positive plotline. The *raisonneur*, Tancred, is a sensible chap and the play's voice of reason, but he is also a detached observer, a bored and supercilious commentator on the action. The last lines of the play are his (*solus*), and his summation well captures the impression *Sir Politick* leaves us with: "They are entertaining for a while, but in the end become boring; and thank God I am now rid of them" (399).

To state the obvious: Dryden, Rochester, and Buckingham do very different things in satire. Dryden is a defender of the status quo. He supports the extant power structure and ridicules what he perceives to be threats to that order: people with subversive social views, Catholic priests (at least prior to his conversion), scabby men who keep mistresses they cannot satisfy in bed, writers unworthy of the honors bestowed on them. Rochester, in sharp contradistinction, is not supportive but contemptuous of the power structure in place, and he is profoundly skeptical of the epistemological basis on which that structure claims to rest. Buckingham's satire almost always has a political dimension; Dryden's satire sometimes does; Rochester is hardly as "apolitical" as he has sometimes been called,[56] but he does not address current affairs in anything like the same way as Dryden, Buckingham, or Marvell. Rochester and Buckingham are noblemen, close friends, and political allies; both support religious toleration for Protestant dissenters, criticize Charles II as a negligent monarch, sneer at Dryden as a fatuous and arrogant blowhard, and lead outrageous personal lives. Similar satirists, they are not. Both Rochester and Buckingham can be nastily abusive of their targets, but on the whole the earl is a much more negative, much more skeptical, satirist than the duke. Dryden has implicit positives; many of Buckingham's satires seem better understood in terms of what they are for rather than what they are against; Rochester usually denies us even the faintest hope for something worth defending.

Critics have largely ignored Buckingham, and they have rightly been inclined to stress radical incongruities between Rochester and Dryden. The two are often presented as a tidy binary, the one crude and rough, the other serious and respectable: "Dryden reflects the heroic impulses of the age," Griffin has asserted, "and Rochester the anti-heroic."[57] But just where do we locate the heroic impulses of *The Kind Keeper*? Rochester is capable of pointed philosophical critique, and Dryden can be vulgar and unfair. They are neither satiric bedfellows nor foils for one another. Dryden, Rochester, and Buckingham are surely three of the most brilliant satirists of the later seventeenth century, but if we are looking for commonalities in targets, motives, positives, or technique, we discover little to point to. I have grouped them to underscore their individual range and the striking degree of their collective differences. No "Restoration mode" is to be found here.

III. Marvell, Ayloffe, Oldham

Marvell, Ayloffe, and Oldham, unlike Dryden, Rochester, and Buckingham, were hardly celebrities with high visibility and public reputations.[58] Neither Marvell nor Oldham printed his satires in his lifetime; both Ayloffe's and Marvell's canons remain at least partially uncertain. Love uses "Marvellian" to refer (tentatively) to "state satire that was either attributed to Marvell at the time, written under his influence, or reflects views with which he probably concurred."[59] Although Ayloffe was a political ally and personal associate of Marvell's—and while Marvell "probably concurred," at least after a fashion, with the views Ayloffe expressed in his satire—the two represent significantly different kinds of hard-core political commentators. Oldham is another patriotic Protestant, but his satires rarely treat affairs of state directly, and he departs from Marvell and Ayloffe in almost every respect.

Marvell as Polemical Satirist

Marvell's satires have received comparatively little critical attention. Attribution problems have made some scholars reluctant to deal with them, but as Love explains, that accounts for only a small part of the neglect. Even *The Last Instructions*, always accepted as Marvell's, has had little discussion, "perhaps because its views are regarded as too patent and outspoken for a poet otherwise admired for his 'ambivalently suspended meanings.'"[60] Marvell's satirical verses are not as lyrical as his lyrics; the elusive poet of *An Horatian Ode* gives everything away in the satires.[61] He is a not very subtle political writer whose aims are basically pragmatic.

Marvell does not write purely "personal" satire. *Flecknoe, an English Priest at Rome* (wr. 1646?; pub. 1681) is perhaps his most defamatory attack on an individual (the titular character has "gouty fingers," "hungry guts," and a "gristly tongue" [ll. 41, 43, 50]), but the man is not really the point. Flecknoe depended heavily upon English aristocrats for patrons, and, Nigel Smith suggests, he would have recognized Marvell's utility as a path to Buckingham.[62] The "light-hearted" *Flecknoe* "avoids the kind of direct denunciation of Catholicism that one might have expected from a militantly Puritan poet," David Norbrook observes, but it "does offer Villiers a warning about the kinds of company he should avoid keeping."[63] Marvell's other satires are even more clearly written with political motives. Annabel Patterson notes that *The Character of Holland* (wr. 1653; first complete version pub. in 1681) was written "in a mood of unabashed jingoism" and demonstrates "the lowest forms of the kind of insult that is based on stereotypes of national character."[64] Composed during a period of intense economic and ideological rivalry with Holland, however, this satire is not well explained as chauvinistic deprecation. *Clarendon's Housewarming* (1667),[65] *The Loyal*

Scot (wr. 1667–1673; pub. 1690s), and *The Statue in Stocks-Market* (wr. 1672–1674; pub. 1689) all feature attacks on individuals without being merely smear jobs. The criticism of Lauderdale in *The Loyal Scot* is strategic, meant to reduce the influence of Clarendon and other political enemies. Occasioned by the unveiling of a statue of Charles II, *The Statue in Stocks-Market* is meant to expose governmental failings; the poet expresses support for Charles but only because the people would "better by far have him than his brother" (l. 60).

Marvell's positives and negatives are usually explicit. His "Painter" poems certainly indict and demean public figures, but that cannot be the last word in characterizing them. *The Second Advice* (1667) treats English blunders following the victory over the Dutch in the Battle of Lowestoft; the handling of the affair is presented as evidence of dangerous mismanagement. These poems are not the stuff of social raillery but of serious political criticism. *The Last Instructions to a Painter* was composed in 1667, after the Dutch had burned the English fleet at Chatham in the Battle of the Medway. Marvell's intentions were, Patterson suggests, "to shift the blame from the Commons to the Cabal," to damage Clarendon's reputation and increase the chance of his impeachment, and to exonerate military administrators who were being blamed for the Chatham disaster.[66] The satiric point is as much positive as negative. The same could be said of *The Rehearsal Transpros'd*, in which Marvell wants not simply to trash Samuel Parker but also to discredit the antitolerationist principles loudly championed by Parker.[67] Marvell's satires are sober and judgmental; however personal he can be, and however caustic some of his denunciations, they make controlled arguments rather than express uninhibited anger.

If we compare Marvell with Dryden, another Carolean writer known for satire on affairs of state, we naturally find major disparities stemming from their vastly different political positions. More surprising are the differences between Marvell's satire and that of his religiopolitical ally Buckingham. He and the duke have the same enemies and are committed to some of the same causes, but they share little in tone and technique. Marvell is verbally clever, especially in a work like *The Character of Holland*, and sometimes lighthearted, but he is not really a "funny" satirist. His is not Buckingham's wit, and neither does he mean it to be. Unlike Buckingham and Rochester, Marvell never assumes the role of lampoonist. The duke's skewering of Arlington in the *Advice to a Paynter* is no less politicized than Marvell's attack on Clarendon, and Buckingham's motives are political, but the results are gleefully and sometimes gratuitously vindictive in ways Marvell's personation is not. More than any of his well-known contemporaries, Marvell is first and foremost a polemical satirist.

Ayloffe's Antimonarchical Diatribes

John Ayloffe has had few modern readers. The one piece of scholarship devoted solely to his work is a quasi-biographical essay published by Lord in 1966.[68] The critical component of Lord's article is an argument cautiously but plausibly attributing to Ayloffe a number of satires, including *Britannia and Raleigh* (wr. 1674–1675), once ascribed to Marvell but now accepted as Ayloffe's. In the *Oxford Dictionary of National Biography* entry for Ayloffe, Warren Chernaik explains that he and Marvell were leading members "in a clandestine organization . . . working in the interests of William of Orange against France." Ayloffe was also closely associated with Shaftesbury, was a member of the Green Ribbon Club, and was tried for treason for his participation in the 1683 Rye House Plot, at which point he fled to Holland and continued to conspire against the Stuarts. A radical Whig and a classical republican, Ayloffe used satire to execrate the Stuart monarchy with exceptional ferocity.

Ayloffe is an angry and pessimistic satirist, longing for a return to republicanism but aware that such a solution is impracticable. Unlike most of Charles's detractors, Ayloffe actually envisions an alternative to monarchy. As vehemently as Rochester claims to "hate all Monarchs," there is nothing to suggest that he really imagined other possibilities. Of the Carolean satirists, Marvell perhaps comes the closest to Ayloffe's extreme position, reminding his readers in *The Last Instructions* that the royal neck has a joint in it: "And ghastly Charles, turning his collar low, / The purple thread about his neck does show" (ll. 921–922). Yet at the end of *The Statue in Stocks-Market*, Marvell also wryly admits that the prospect of James makes Charles seem a good deal more acceptable. Ayloffe is never moderate or cautious. *Nostradamus' Prophecy* (wr. 1672), tentatively ascribed by Lord to Ayloffe, is passionately antimonarchical, as is *Marvell's Ghost* (wr. 1678). The latter regrets both the accession of James I and the Restoration ("curse the days that first gave birth / To a Cecil or a Monck on earth") and accuses Charles II and his government of having "laid waste the commonweal" (ll. 35–36, 24). *Oceana and Britannia* (wr. 1681) foretells a return of republicanism and abuses Charles and his circle. The king is a "lewd ravisher," and "Rapes, burnings, murders are his royal sport; / These modish monsters haunt his perjur'd Court" (ll. 16, 17–18). Discussing his rationale for ascribing this poem to Ayloffe, Lord concludes, "Here is the histrionic—if not hysterical—tone which appears" in the more certain attributions, and here too is "the attack on the Stuart as a Neronian tyrant . . . delighting in murder (an allusion to Sir Edmund Berry Godfrey?) and rape, the servile imitator of France."[69] Ayloffe's frenzy sets him apart from Marvell, who, though capable of impassioned critique and invective, is never "hysterical."

Ayloffe's *Britannia and Raleigh* is one of many Carolean "vision" satires.[70] The force of the poem is the more obvious if we compare it with another "prophecy," *An*

Historical Poem (wr. 1680), whose author disapprovingly recounts the reign of Charles II from the Restoration to the present. Grousing that "the poor Priapus King" has led the country "to Popery and shame," the anonymous poet foretells a worse fate for England when James ascends the throne. "If a king's brother can such mischief bring," the poet asks, "Then how much greater mischief as a king?" (ll. 64, 58, 181–182). Like Ayloffe, this author indicts Charles in particular and expresses suspicion of the Stuarts more generally, and both writers grumble that England is in a very bad way. But the satirist of *An Historical Poem* is merely discontented; Ayloffe is desperate. In *Britannia and Raleigh*, he complains about the French influence at the English court, where "Pimps, priests, buffoons" are "slimy monsters" who endanger the state by corrupting the monarch, and, finally, "fairy-like the King they steal away, / And in his place a Louis changeling lay" (ll. 26, 27, 33–34). Raleigh encourages Britannia to try to save Charles by bringing him back to the English mode of governing, but Charles says that he has no hope of such recovery: "too long in vain I've tri'd / The Stuart from the tyrant to divide" (ll. 141–142). The author of *An Historical Poem* is grumbling about a bad situation; Ayloffe is damning Stuart monarchy.[71]

Ayloffe and Marvell were friends and political allies, but Lord is right to contend that the two have patently distinct satiric voices. Marvell's "treatment of Charles and James is humorous and rueful, but not bitter," and his satires "are marked by irony and ridicule, but not by hatred." Lord is correct, too, to underscore the "uncompromisingly individualistic" nature of Ayloffe's satire and to insist that it "be distinguished sharply" from the work of Dryden as well as Marvell, "both moderates in their own ways."[72] Ayloffe's satire is tonally different from either of those writers, and so are his purposes. He probably hopes to deepen the frustration of those likewise discontented, but he is not trying to change minds or otherwise to achieve anything constructive. In life Ayloffe is a plotter, conspiring to overthrow the monarchy in favor of republicanism; in satire he is not a would-be political reformer but a bitterly unhappy firebrand.

Oldham's Juvenalian Performances

Oldham's reputation among modern scholars is as the English Juvenal, as the Clevelandesque railer of the post-Restoration years, sharp tongued, immoderate, and overpowering. He is known primarily for his *Satyrs upon the Jesuits* (1679–1681), penned by someone, says Paul Hammond, "who mistook violence for strength, and abuse for wit."[73] These poems are grimly vehement, but they are also sensational, even theatrical.[74] The speaker of the first is Henry Garnett, Jesuit and superior of the English province at the time of his execution for complicity in the Gunpowder Plot. Reprimanding the Catholics for being too cowardly to kill Charles in order to make James king, Garnett recounts Catholic glories of the past—the atrocities committed against Protestants—with gruesome vividness. He laments that Bloody Mary's reign was not bloody enough (ll. 155–156) and revels in the macabre details of the 1572 St. Bartholomew's Day massacre of the French Huguenots (ll. 203–230). Finally, he enthusiastically envisions an English Catholic uprising:

> Rip teeming Wombs, tear out the hated Brood
> From thence, and drown 'em in their Mothers bloud.
> Pity not Virgins, nor their tender cries,
> Though prostrate at your feet with melting eyes
> All drown'd in tears; strike home as 'twere in lust,
> And force their begging hands to guide the thrust.
> Ravish at th' Altar, kill when you have done,
> Make them your Rapes, and Victims too in one. (ll. 290–297)

The second satire is equally lurid. Garnett cries that he would gladly "stride o're Crowns, swim through a Flood, / Made up of slaughter'd Monarch's Brains and Blood" (ll. 177–178). The particulars of past and (Garnett hopes) future bloodbaths are grisly, and Harold F. Brooks suggests that not until the *Satyrs upon the Jesuits* did Oldham bring real passion to satire. But, as Love says of some of the "quasi-theatrical" anti-Catholic satires of this period, their weakness "lay in an intertextual playfulness that makes it hard to take their ingenious recyclings of libertine fantasies of violent destruction seriously."[75] Oldham's satires have been described as exercises in "rhetorical exaggeration," expressed by "a dramatically-distanced and unreliable persona."[76] Oldham's anti-Catholicism is evidently sincere, but given the rest of his satiric output, we have reason to suspect that there is at least an element of hyperbole at work in the thunderous Jesuit poems.

Oldham's other satires do not suggest much real conviction. *The Careless Good Fellow* (1680) has to do with the Popish Plot, but its author is far from outraged. The poem was written when Tories were starting "to shrug off the Terror [of the Popish Plot] as a ploy of the Whigs," as Brooks points out, and "Oldham changed with the nation," treating the horrid plot "with a humorous detachment of which no Shaftesbury Whig would have been capable."[77] The speaker of the poem casually laments that the silly intrigue has created a fuss, and he claims to be indifferent to England's political crisis ("I mind not grave asses who idly debate / About right and succession, the trifles of state") and to Louis (ll. 19–20). He worries only about enjoying good claret. This satire expresses none of the venom of the *Satyrs upon the Jesuits*, and neither is it an exemplar of the Juvenalian rage with which Oldham is associated. His "curse" satires—*Upon a Woman*, *Upon a Bookseller*, and *Upon the Author of the Play call'd Sodom*—are wrathful, but they appear to be performances of righteous anger rather than expressions of real fury.

Sardanapalus, A Dithyrambique on Drinking, and other poems are in Brooks's phrasing *"vers d'occasion"* composed without passion.[78] *Sardanapalus,* like Rochester's "scepter lampoon," depicts a libidinous and irresponsible monarch whose promiscuity is a liability to the country he rules. A brief comparison between the two satires illustrates something fundamental about both. Griffin rejects the political reading of *Sardanapalus,* explaining the poem as "little more than gross obscenity and a choreographed orgiastic extravaganza."[79] Like Rochester, Oldham conspicuously uses images of statecraft along with those of sexual incontinence—with "Love's great Scepter in [his] hand," the monarch never does "withhold [his] Liberality, / Nor ever drain the vast Exchequer of [his] Lechery" (ll. 37, 69–70). The poem has, however, neither the directness nor the visceral disgust of Rochester's invective.[80] Oldham's bawdy 182-line romp is clear enough in its presentation of the monarch's misdeeds, and the irony of his "Ode" to the profligate "Great Prince" is manifest (l. 1). But his discursive blame-by-praise of an ancient Assyrian king—divided into formal stanzas and delivered in past tense—is a universe apart from the earl's apparently impromptu tirade, a short, forceful, direct attack on *this* king, the monarch of *this* country (as the opening lines make plain).

Oldham's rendition of social (as of political) evils is usually distinctly unimpassioned. In *A Satyr Against Virtue* (wr. 1676?; pub. 1679), he ironically decries goodness, maintaining that virtue can only thrive where there are no people. Morality is "unfashionable," conscience is a "giddy airy Dream," and only "dull unbred Fools" would "discredit Vice" (ll. 100, 143, 161). Otway makes a useful contrast. On the surface, Oldham says what Otway implies in his darker social satires like *Friendship in Fashion*: people behave badly and nothing can be done about it. Otway surveys a bleak state of affairs and is revolted; Oldham's attitude is more difficult to determine.[81] Griffin usefully suggests that "imitation" is a crucial part of Oldham's satire, in which he "typically speaks not in his 'own' voice, but sets out to 'imitate' or to 'impersonate' a Juvenalian declaimer, a Jesuit conspirator, a Rochesterian rake."[82] A satirist who mimics Rochesterian satire is not the same kind of satirist as Rochester, just as feigning moral outrage is not the same as expressing real ire. Oldham the satirist is ultimately a dynamic and sometimes dazzling performer.

Unlike Marvell, Buckingham, and Dryden, Oldham is not an overtly political satirist. He prefers Protestantism to Catholicism and is a good English patriot on that score, but his satires do not reflect a positive agenda. Neither do they express the vitriol and negativity of Marvell and Ayloffe. Marvell is the most restrained of this trio, but his tonal moderation hardly signals absence of conviction, and Oldham's blustery satirical curses do not necessarily indicate deeply felt hostility. Marvell makes arguments in hope of influencing the present course of action. Ayloffe articulates his hatred of a king and government that has failed him and England, though without practical positive objectives. Unlike Marvell and Ayloffe, *all* of whose satires are topical and occasional, Oldham comes across as one conscious of writing in a tradition or a form, not as one deeply immersed in crises of the moment. The *Satyrs upon the Jesuits* are at least superficially impassioned and, in the late 1670s, probably manifest real anxiety, but his other satires seem largely fireworks, full of sound and fury but signifying little.

IV. *Hudibras* and Other Camouflage Satires

I have been dealing with contrasts found in individual satirists and their works. I now look at a particular case, one that presents us with a fundamentally different concept of how satire might function. Samuel Butler's *Hudibras* (1662–1678 [for 1677]) was one of the most popular satires of the Carolean period and was frequently reprinted throughout the eighteenth century, a widely known and influential text.[83] The customary reading of the poem explains it as a straightforward attack on the king's enemies in the English civil wars. The ridicule of Puritan folly has been taken as the satire's sole political agenda, and scholars generally assume that *Hudibras* can be tidily categorized as a "mega-lampoon pinned up over the defeated Puritans."[84] Echoing the scholarly consensus, Griffin flatly asserts that "Butler in the 1660s writes *against* the defeated and discredited Puritan party. Of that much there is no dispute. But critics of Butler have found it very difficult to define what it is that Butler is *for*."[85] As I have argued elsewhere, however, Butler is writing for a cause in *Hudibras*, not just against an easy target.[86]

Why would Butler expend such time and energy debunking a defeated enemy? *Hudibras* is generally read as a triumphant condemnation of the radicals, but its author never celebrates the king's return. The poem was apparently composed after the Restoration, but the narrative is not one of royalist power and order. Hudibras is not captured and tamed at the poem's end; indeed, by the end of part III, his troublemaking is matched by the rioting of the rabble. My argument is that the issues that precipitated the civil war did not disappear in 1660 and that Butler's seemingly retrospective satire should be read with that in mind. In parts I and II, he writes a blistering denunciation of Presbyterians and Independents. What are the contexts and implications, in the early 1660s, of such a satire?

In 1660 moderate Presbyterians had been considered acceptable, at least by some Anglicans. The Act of Uniformity in 1662 did less to *exclude* them because they were nonconformists than it did to *redefine* them as such. The exclusion of Presbyterians from the Church of England in part required and in part resulted in their being linked with more radical Independents as a homogeneous sectarian threat. Butler's poem reinforces this gesture of consolidation, uniting Presbyterian Knight and Independent Squire as a rabble-rousing, peace-disturbing duo. This union is not merely a casual attempt at a blanket dismissal of nonconformity, or at least it would not have been read as such in the early 1660s. Presbyterians had opposed the regicide, supported the Restoration, and pressed for a moderate church; to lump them with extreme separatists would have had obvious connotations for readers with any knowledge of English politics in the immediate aftermath of Charles's return. Butler's poem appears to support the move by Anglican royalists to redefine Presbyterianism as nonconformist, as beyond the pale. He is on the side of those opposed to toleration, and the first two parts of *Hudibras* join in the public debate about what the official policy toward dissent should be. Butler implicitly argues for the practicality of a hard-line approach, for the denial of liberty of conscience and the rigorous enforcement of uniformity.

Parts I and II of *Hudibras* expose the perfidy of the dissenters. Early in the poem, the Knight and Squire tussle with a group of bear-baiters who eventually withdraw to regroup. The party's female combatant, Trulla, returns and trounces Hudibras and Ralpho, and the first part ends with the blundering antiheroes appropriately imprisoned in the stocks. The two protagonists, representing the Presbyterians and Independents specifically and the dissenters more generally, are doubtless the most conspicuous targets of the satire in this first part. Hudibras is especially ridiculous, fancying himself a glorious hero but finding himself urine soaked (after giving way to terror during a skirmish) and then bested by a woman. The title page identifies this poem as "The First Part," so Butler expected to produce a sequel. Although the incendiaries are duly detained at the end of part I, then, the impending second part promises the continuation of Hudibras's troublemaking. A widow visits the pair in the prison at the start of part II and bails them out on the condition that Hudibras whip himself and reform. With Ralpho's help, the Knight talks himself out of self-flagellation and proceeds to the lady's house to court her and to swear that he has kept his word.

Butler's fanatics are laughingstocks as well as cheats, but the first two parts of *Hudibras* do not represent a gratuitous thumping of defeated radicals. They are instead a timely warning about Carolean governmental policies. Hudibras and Ralpho are hardly the satire's only dupes: the Knight successfully gulls almost everyone in the world of the poem, and though he does not always win, he is never stopped. The ungainly Presbyterian is never coerced into more suitable behavior but instead makes fools of his captors and contrives to be released from jail. The central message of *Hudibras* is that, impassioned oath taking notwithstanding, the nonconformists are not to be trusted. *Hudibras* is a polemical contribution to a contemporary debate about how dissenters of all stripes should be treated in the years following the Restoration, and Butler belongs to the group of royalists made uneasy by Charles's tolerationist leanings.

The narrative of *Hudibras* resumed in 1677, but the third part is noticeably different from, and more complex than, the first two. Part III is a commentary on a constitutional crisis, and one of its villains is—anticipating Dryden's later satire—the treacherous "Achitophel." From Butler's point of view, Shaftesbury represents a two-fold menace: he seeks to undermine royal prerogative while serving as "patron of the dissenters,"[87] and he has manipulated a large body of supporters by sensationalizing the Catholic threat. From a Tory perspective, the Whigs' cry of counterreformation is overblown, merely scandalmongers' hearsay offered up to a gullible populace whose manic responses endanger civil order. Butler would agree with Dryden's characterization of Achitophel as the proponent of "Weak Arguments! which yet he knew ful well,/Were strong with People easie to Rebell" (ll. 214–215). Like a number of Tory writers in the late 1670s, Butler attempts to associate Shaftesburyian Whigs with the radicals of the 1640s; he was not the only Tory who worried that "the '41" had come again. The message in part III is not unlike that of its predecessors: to be lenient toward the dissenters is to court disaster. The link among the three parts of *Hudibras*, and the real target of Butler's satire, is not just nonconformist folly but hazardous changes in the operation of English government.

In the 1660s, Butler showed the danger of granting clemency to those who had attempted to topple the monarchy and warned against granting formal toleration to the dissenters. In the 1670s, he attacks the popular control of government and the diminishing inviolability of monarchical authority, targeting Shaftesbury as the voice of the opposition. In parts I and II, Butler was critical of the nonconformists and suspicious of Charles's policies; in part III, he is equally scornful of dissent and toleration, but such a position requires him to defend the administration against its opposition. Though Butler seems to have had little interest in either celebrating or maligning the character of any particular monarch, he does appear to defend monarchy as the most effective and practical form of government—so long as it is unmoved by popular influence. The alternative is the world of *Hudibras*, a mad world in which bilkers and knaves are unrestrained and authority is unasserted.

Butler, no less than Dryden, wants monarchy and patriarchal authority to work. He does not share Dryden's nostalgia for mystical politics; he is interested not in divine right but in the exercise of sovereign control over the state. In *Absalom and Achitophel*, Dryden's primary positive agenda is succinctly delivered in a question: "What Prudent men a setled Throne woud shake?" (l. 796). However willing Dryden is to denounce Shaftesbury and Monmouth, and Butler to defame the radicals, neither *Absalom and Achitophel* nor *Hudibras* can be adequately explained in terms of those attacks.[88] They are written in defense of monarchy by satirists intensely apprehensive about the internal and external threats to that ruling structure.[89] Although Butler is sometimes associated with Rochester—both are "low" and coarse[90]—in satiric terms he has more in common with Dryden. He and Dryden both use satire to revile what they find repulsive (like Rochester), but they also write in defense of something they see threatened and wish to preserve. Butler's return to the narrative of the civil war should not prevent us from reading his poem as a Carolean satire in the most literal sense: *Hudibras* represents the civil war period but largely as a way of commenting on the radically changing political climate of the 1660s and 1670s. Though superficial and one-sided readings of *Hudibras* have held sway to the present day, Butler was writing a far more immediately topical and political satire than he has ever been given credit for.

Hudibras has been read as the foremost example of what Love calls "a predictable early [Restoration] vogue for anti-Puritan satire."[91] But like Butler, a number of other apparent participants in this fad have other motives; many of the satires that conspicuously trash nonconformists have contemporary applications. In *The Presbyterian Lash. or, Noctroff's Maid Whipt* (an anonymous closet comedy printed in 1661), the central character and most obvious butt is the Presbyterian priest Noctroffe, whose duplicity causes chaos and does considerable damage. In Noctroffe's triumphant closing address, however, he explains how much his success owes to a gullible society. His Independent and Cavalier counterparts do not see that he has "contrived every minutes circumstance," and because of their laxity he is left in a dangerously powerful position (30). Even as the Presbyterians are exposed as treacherous, the Cavaliers are revealed as naïve and negligent. This, we should remember, is *not* an attack on radicals: in 1660–1661, most Presbyterians were royalists seeking to dissociate themselves from more extreme dissenters and hoping to be incorporated into an established church.

Satires on the late and unlamented Puritan regime frequently have more practical relevance than their most obvious targets might suggest. Sir Robert Howard's *The Committee* (perf. 1662; pub. 1665 in Howard's *Four New Plays*) explicitly derides the Commonwealth government, but it also implies problems with the new administration. In the final scenes, the parliamentarian committee men realize that they must "cozen those that cozen all the World" (133) and pledge allegiance to the group now in power. One character offers shrewd counsel to another: "If you will have good luck in every thing, / Turn Cavalier, and cry, God bless the King" (134). The play's Puritans are knaves, but the monarch looks foolish for seeking the help of his enemies and accepting their cheaply purchased loyalty as sincere. Abraham Cowley was accused of attacking the Cavalier party in his *Cutter of Coleman-Street* (perf. 1661; pub. 1663), a charge he denied in the preface to the printed version. Nevertheless, contemporary audiences were probably right to sense that the play does more than lampoon the radicals: the themes of pretended loyalty and political opportunism had clear application. Cutter and Worm are cunning rebels disguised as Cavalier officers, so that professed loyalism becomes dubious. When the two impostors reunite after a quarrel, they shake hands and agree to forget the fuss, all the while crooning songs in celebration of his majesty's happy return. The king's champions, that is, are not his own men but dissenting charlatans, and their superficial reconciliation is linked directly to the formal Stuart reinstatement. The Restoration, as Cowley presents it, seems both unsatisfactory and unstable.

The Puritans were safe targets and convenient camouflage for riskier criticisms in the 1660s, and illustrating their menace made for a nice warning, still painfully relevant after Charles's return. John Wilson's *The Cheats* (1663), a coarse city comedy satirizing the Puritans, also points to widespread deception. As the astrologer-physician Mopus observes in the play, "[T]here are but 2 Sorts of people in the world—Aut qui Captant aut qui Captantur" (196 [IV.ii.124–125]). Wilson's play concludes, says Derek Hughes, "with the fanatic cynically surviving and prospering within the restored order."[92] As in *Hudibras*, the implication is that no one is to be trusted—and disloyal dissidents least of all. Hughes calls John Lacy's *The Old Troop* (perf. 1664; pub. 1672) yet "more irreverent" than *The Cheats*. Lacy's satire is directed primarily at the roundheads, but

> we are also shown the milder, but still considerable, flaws of the plundering Cavaliers, and . . . Lacy reiterates and discredits the moral and social vocabulary associated with idealizing representations of restoration: trust, honour, honesty, truth, troth, faith, service, and friendship. . . . Not surprisingly, this play does not promise restoration of Astraea-like absolutes of order.[93]

The Old Troop is more openly impertinent in its treatment of the restored monarchy and its supporters than are the other pieces with which I have been dealing—but none of these satires should be airily dismissed as a retrospective thumping of defeated enemies.

Because scholars define satire principally in terms of writer and target, there is a marked tendency to believe that once a clear satiric object has been identified, the work has been deciphered. *Hudibras* serves as a salutary warning against that way of reading, as does *The Rehearsal*, where Buckingham is almost certainly smudging his satiric targets. Bayes is manifestly a parody of Dryden, and Buckingham's disapproval is genuine. But Bayes is a composite figure, representing both Dryden and Arlington—just as Marvell's mockery of Bayes in his *Rehearsal Transpros'd* is at once an attack on Samuel Parker, Dryden, and Davenant.[94] Camouflaged attack is a possibility and—in a world where Stephen College is executed for a seditious libel and Dryden clubbed for saying unpleasant things about powerful people—even a necessity.[95] Butler and Buckingham in particular appear to be consciously, and prudently, obscuring their targets. Dryden creates distance through allegory in *Absalom and Achitophel*, but allegorical displacement is not the same thing as camouflaging one target under another. *Hudibras* and *The Rehearsal* present ostensibly real objects of ridicule, whereas

Absalom and Achitophel does not, unless one could believe that Dryden was actually just retelling a biblical episode. The presence of obvious contemporary targets in But-ler's and Buckingham's satires is "safe" from the sort of decoding that Dryden invites the reader to carry out in his allegory. While both Butler and Buckingham give the audience some signals (e.g., the use of Quixote in *Hudibras* and the nose patch in *The Rehearsal*), "proving" the camouflaged attacks is impossible. The lesson of *Hudibras* and *The Rehearsal*—two of the most popular satires of the Carolean period—is that the most obvious butt is not always the only or even the most significant target.

V. Personal and Social Satire: From Lampoons to Otway and Lee

Satiric "attack" can take a variety of forms, and we need to make distinctions regard-ing tone and intensity, among other things. In the realm of personal and generalized social satire, we might usefully ask questions about the *nature* of the attack, insofar as that can be guessed at. How seriously does the writer take the offender/offense, or how serious is the perceived threat? How much does the satirist care, and is judgment being rendered? Idle abuse is different in kind from principled criticism. Drubbing easy targets for the sake of pleasing an audience is one thing; expressing genuine disapproval of someone or of a situation is quite another. Likewise, walloping a per-sonal rival merely to vent frustration is not the same enterprise, in satiric terms, as attempting to malign someone in defense of a position or set of principles to which the author is deeply committed.

Not all attacks on individuals seem personally motivated.[96] Shadwell's stingingly funny depiction of Sir Robert Howard as Sir Positive At-all in *The Sullen Lovers* (1668) evidently does not reflect strong authorial animosity. "We are not to suppose," says Montague Summers, "that Shadwell had any particular grievance against . . . Howard," who was "conspicuous as a butt for irresistible satire."[97] Shadwell's goal was more prob-ably "to amuse an audience prepared to revel in mockery of a pompous and pretentious playwright and man of affairs,"[98] and he seems to be enjoying himself in that effort.

Some of the lampoons on court ladies are gleefully disparaging, but they too are exercises in thrashing oft-thrashed targets. *On the Ladies of the Court* (wr. ca. 1663) moves briskly from victim to victim, providing bawdy snapshots of each woman's sexual adventures and misadventures in turn. The pictures are not flattering, but the poem is a pageant of insults rather than a high-heat denunciation. Charles, Viscount Mordaunt's *The Ladies' March* (1681) is another spectacle of contumelies, a sequence of quasi-epigrammatic derogations. Mordaunt describes a procession of twenty-three court ladies (in fewer than one hundred lines), and he does so with "kinaesthetic force."[99] The sketches are deprecatory but in very standard ways. The *Ballad on Betty*

Felton (wr. 1680), unusual in aiming at only a single and rather insignificant court lady,[100] is likewise jauntily insulting. Felton is an easy target, not a threat or problem; the author is enjoying saying dirty things, not making a moral, social, or political argument. *Lampoon* (wr. 1676) is a vulgar put-down of the Countess of Castlemaine, and it, like the bawdy, fast-paced *On Several Women about Town* (wr. 1680), reflects no real malevolence. Personal rubbishing of this sort is common in Carolean satirical writing, much of it just good fun (if unwelcome to its targets).

Satires on the court ladies are not always purely frivolous, written sans genuine authorial conviction or concern. Compare the lampoon on Betty Felton to *An Essay of Scandal* (wr. 1681), a satire on various court ladies. Nell Gwyn is described as a "hare-brained, wrinkled, stopped-up whore, / Daily struck, stabbed, by half the pricks in town" (ll. 43–44), and the denigration bears some resemblance to that of Felton—but the satires are drastically different in tone and purpose. The deriding of the women in *An Essay of Scandal* is not the point: the satirist is entreating Charles to replace these costly harlots with cheaper and less treacherous courtesans. As Love rightly insists, "We have to read past this sexual narrative for its political core."[101] The subject is not a particular mistress or set of mistresses but the insolvency of king and state. The image of Nell in *A Panegyric* (wr. 1681) is similar in combining personal scorn with an expression of political anxiety: the "imperial whore" finds herself "dangling scepters in her dirty hand" (ll. 15, 21).[102] This is both mean and amusing, but the political implications of the monarch's promiscuity prevent it from being only entertaining. The author of *The Royal Buss* (wr. 1675) is worried not about the king's sexual antics per se but about the ways in which wantonness affects his prerogative. "Carwell" is a bad influence, and Charles rules—as he lives—with wild abandon: "red hot with wine and whore, / He kick'd the Parliament out of door" (ll. 69–70). The animosity toward the king's mistresses reflects the author's sense that they are not only strumpets but also tempting distractions and power mongers, and Charles, whores' cully and merry monarch, is a political liability.[103]

Many Carolean satires are personally vicious for political reasons. Not much could be done about the easy king and his many women, but conspicuous governmental figures could often be ridiculed to some practical effect. Buckingham's vilifications of Arlington and Danby, and Marvell's of Clarendon, are purposive attempts to blacken the personal reputations of public men.[104] So are the attacks on Clarendon ("Old fatguts"), Arlington, Clifford, and Castlemaine (the "prerogative quean") in *A Ballad* (wr. 1667)—not idle expressions of malice but biting articulations of practical frustration with the current state of affairs in England (ll. 13, 44). Likewise, the author of *Upon his Majesty's being made Free of the City* (wr. 1674) decries both Charles's personal lasciviousness and his political failings, related manifestations of his unrestraint. The poet judges the king's misconduct harshly—as does Rochester in the venomous "scepter lampoon," a satire penned by a man much closer to the king and more intensely disgusted than the anonymous poet appears to be.

The ten-line squib *A Character of the Church of Chichester* (wr. 1673) targets the bishop of Chichester for his tolerance of non-Anglicans. *Strange's Case, Strangly Altered* (1680) censures Roger L'Estrange as a Yorkist and as an enemy to Protestantism; L'Estrange is also attacked in the scurrilous *Crack upon Crack: or Crack-Fart Whipt with his own Rod* (1680) and Shadwell's (?) *The Protestant Satire* (wr. 1684). The author of *The Cabal* (1680) hotly accuses the Green Ribbon Club members of sedition, and his satiric portraits of Buckingham, Monmouth, Shaftesbury, and Halifax give vent to solemn hostility. *The D: of B: Letany* (1679) includes a good bit of plain meanness, but the satirist is clearly upset by Buckingham's power and influence:

> From beginning an Execrable Traitors health
> To destroy this Parliment, King, and himself,
> To be made Dukeall, -Peere of a new common Wealth.
> Libera nos etc. (ll. 65–68).[105]

A number of attacks on Monmouth and Shaftesbury are likewise primarily political rather than personal, though they vary in length, format, technique, tone, and level and type of aggression.[106]

What divides these satires from Shadwell's caricature of Howard or the anonymous lampoon on Betty Felton is their level of intensity, a feature by which we can also differentiate generalized social satires. Ridiculing standard butts and bantering generalized targets is amusing and often very popular, but the level of authorial commitment tends to be low. In *The London Cuckolds* (perf. 1681; pub. 1683), Edward Ravenscroft portrays the cuckolding of three imprudent cits, each of whom has married a woman he thinks will not or cannot cuckold him (i.e., one takes a witty, one a foolish, and one a godly wife). The play is a romp; Ravenscroft seems untroubled by the scenes he is describing. Nothing is at stake: the intrigues are comical, and we are meant to laugh at them without judgment. The cits were evidently not offended: *The London Cuckolds* was staged annually on the Lord Mayor's Day until 1751, largely for their entertainment.[107] Although *The Country-Wife* (1675) and *The Man of Mode* (1676) are formulaic and do not present a coherent moral program, there is a fair amount of rueful irony underlying the contemplation of libertinism in their satire.[108] The contrast between gentlemen Tories and citizen Whigs in Ravenscroft's play has implicit sociopolitical significance, particularly in 1681, but I have trouble seeing why most viewers would have taken it at all seriously.[109] It seems essentially a lighter, brighter, more frivolous enterprise.

Thomas Otway's social satires, on the contrary, exhibit unmitigated contempt. The world of *Friendship in Fashion* (1678) is a place of vile inanity. Infidelity and betrayal are inevitable (they are "in fashion"). The protagonist, Goodvile, is bored with his wife and tries to seduce his friend Valentine's fiancée; meanwhile, he is pursued by his cast-mistress, whom he tries to marry off to another friend, Truman. Mrs. Goodvile feigns ignorance of her husband's disloyalty while fooling around with Truman. Goodvile's attempts to bed Valentine's betrothed fail, though he unwittingly has sex with an undesirable woman thinking her to be his targeted prey (she is just as surprised, having taken him for Truman). In the end, Goodvile finds out about his wife's intrigues but cannot catch her in the act; he is stuck with the spouse he does not want, the knowledge of his friend's betrayal, and the cuckold's horns. He is far and away the most monstrous of the lot, but none of the characters represents a positive norm. All are cold-bloodedly self-seeking, capable of deception, and entirely willing to deceive. The implications are bleak: "We are shown a brutally unappetizing world—and that is exactly the point of the play."[110]

Both *The London Cuckolds* and *Friendship in Fashion* involve unsatisfying marriages, sexual intrigues, and adultery, and the message of the latter play shares something with Oldham's in the *Satyr Against Vertue*, but in Otway we are a world away from Ravenscroft and Oldham. *Friendship in Fashion* is a strongly moral satire; its author is passing judgment. Hughes suggests that *The London Cuckolds* shows "no interest whatsoever in analyzing or evaluating sexual conduct,"[111] and the absence of such reckoning is important. And whereas Dryden is not amused by the scenes he describes in the comic plot of *Marriage A-la-Mode*, Otway is thoroughly sickened. Both satirists are engaged in ways that Ravenscroft is not; both plays have clear-cut morals that *The Man of Mode* does not. Dryden voices disapproval, Otway voices disgust—and they mean it.

So does Nat Lee, whose *The Princess of Cleve* (perf. December 1682?; pub. 1689) is a grim social satire, as well as a vastly underappreciated play. The titular female confesses her love for Duke Nemours, a swinish and cynical whoremonger, and her doting prince, overcome by unrequited love and jealousy, expires. Nemours is never punished for his wickedness, and at the play's end he remains as powerful and as alluring as ever. The real-life model for Nemours was Rochester, and Lee's villain is a wholly unromanticized image of the libertine code. But when Nemours says that he is no worse than those around him, we are inclined to accept his verdict: "Why 'tis the way of ye all, only you sneak with it under your Cloaks like Taylors and Barbers; and I, as a Gentleman shou'd do, walk with it in my hand" (2:178). Lee does not offer much to balance the negative picture. Certainly the driveling prince and the uncomprehending princess do not represent ideals. Lee blasts the upper classes, court life in general, and Rochester in particular. He attacks the ethos of both libertine comedy and heroic drama, bringing "the two value systems together and let[ting] each expose the hollowness and inadequacy of the other." *The Princess of Cleve* "is more a despairing than an angry satire: we are not given a comfortable sermon from a superior vantage point, but rather a brutal exposé whose author can find *no* meaningful positive norm. . . . The result is a dizzying and deliberately sickening view into a moral abyss."[112] Like Otway in *Friendship in Fashion* and *The Souldiers Fortune* (1680), Lee can find no clear-cut positives to present.

VI. Chronological Change, 1658–1685

Carolean satire comprises very different sorts of works. Uniformity is not to be found at any given moment, and we need also to attend to variation over time. Satire in the reign of Charles II tends to be time specific and local, and an account of it or of its component bits should take into consideration the external realities of the world in which it was written.

Did the return of Charles II produce a change in the nature of English satiric practice? Most scholars who discuss Carolean satire begin in 1660 and look forward, assuming 1660 to be a tidy dividing line. The few who have studied pre- and post-Restoration satire together have sensibly argued for continuity across that period.[113] These critics emphasize the debts of writers like Butler, Marvell, Oldham, and Dryden to midcentury satirists like Cleveland, whose works were reprinted regularly in the 1660s and in the later 1670s.[114] Brooks points out, moreover, that individual satires of the midcentury are reprinted in miscellanies after the Restoration and that the popular satiric genres of the civil war and interregnum remain current in the reign of Charles II (e.g., parodies, litanies, dream visions).[115] The two-volume *Rump Songs* (1662) made more than two hundred earlier seventeenth-century poems available; a high proportion of those collected in volume 1 are royalist, anti-Puritan satires of the forties and fifties. Obviously the satirists of the 1660s did not emerge ex nihilo when Charles claimed crown and miter: Marvell, Butler, and Dryden were active under Cromwell, and the minor Cavalier satirist Alexander Brome (among others) published from the early 1640s to the early 1660s.[116] Some Carolean satirists had to have been influenced by the works circulating in the decade before the Restoration.

The reestablishment of Stuart monarchy did not mark a sudden and complete transformation of satiric practice, but some things changed. Satire is almost always tied to external particulars: even when it has general application, it tends to be topical and circumstantial. The replacement of one regime with another necessarily affected writers' sense of their world, for better or worse depending on their outlook. The Restoration was a public event of major—if uncertain—import, and the resultant settlement influenced at least some satirists. Proud loyalists drubbed dissenters, and disgruntled Cavaliers complained about the conspicuous absence of rewards for their loyalty. The political transition and concomitant social changes created new situations and thus new material for satire. In the early 1660s, as I have shown, a number of royalist writers heaped scorn upon the radicals while also expressing distrust, unease, and sometimes unconcealed disapproval of their own party. The first years of Charles's reign were particularly conducive to such camouflaged attacks, in part because so much of the settlement was decidedly *un*settled (would this regime last, and on what terms?) and in part because the ill treatment of Cavaliers deflated their triumphalism.[117] As happy as most writers were to see the last of Cromwell and company, these were not—as Lord has deemed them—the "halcyon" days. Lord blithely claims that, with the exception of "one or two inferior squibs on the plight of the Cavaliers," criticism of the restored monarchy did not begin until late in the 1660s.[118] The mode and intensity of the attacks change, but even some adamantly promonarchy satirists were discontented with and anxious about Charles's management of the state in the early 1660s.

The situation worsens considerably in the second half of the decade. The five years following the Restoration saw overt and sometimes covert disparagement of the government, but what those critics were voicing was not disgust but annoyance and disappointment. That the state of affairs would deteriorate rather than improve was not yet clear, and for a while at least some of Charles's detractors could be hopeful even in their disgruntlement. But the plague, the fire, the Second Dutch War, the impeachment of Clarendon, and the increasing problem of the king's licentiousness fostered a noticeable tonal shift in satire. As the mismanagement of the state became ever clearer, satire grew gloomier and more expressive of distress. The first two parts of *Hudibras* differ from the third not only in targets but in intensity; appearing some fifteen years later, the last part is neither so comical nor so indirect in its political message as its predecessors. *The Presbyterian Lash* (1661) and Richard Brathwaite's *The Chimneys Scuffle* (1662) issue warnings, showing us a world in which the threat has been or threatens to be realized. But prophetic satires later in the period (e.g., *Hodge* [wr. 1679] and *A Satyr against Satyrs: or, St. Peter's Vision Transubstantiated* [1680]) tend to be not monitory but minatory, heavy-handedly sinister. *Hodge* ends portentously. The titular English rustic tensely surveys the state of affairs, has a vision of James and Kate slaying Charles, cries out ("Plots, Papists, murders, massacres, and fire! / Poor Protestants"), and then falls over dead (ll. 166–167). This is not a brilliant satire, but it does sharply communicate its author's fears.[119]

Satires are distinctly more sour in the 1670s. Satirists in the late 1660s targeted Clarendon and other government officials for incompetence and treachery; in the next decade, personal slurs directed at figures close to the king and at the monarch himself are more widespread and nastier. Satire after culpatory satire lashes Charles, his brother, and his mistresses. Satirists vilify his ministers (*The Dream of the Cabal* [wr. 1672]) and his favorite *filius nullius*, Monmouth (*A Ballad called the Haymarket Hectors, On the Three Dukes Killing the Beadle*, and *Upon the Beadle* [all wr. 1671]). The aggrieved satirist of *The History of Insipids* (wr. 1674) scorches the monarch and the too-obliging

Parliament; reviews the myriad instances of governmental misconduct since the Restoration; and, reflecting on Thomas Blood's earning favor at court after attempting to thieve the crown, proposes, "Since loyalty doth no man good, / Let's seize the King and outdo Blood" (ll. 47–48). From the early 1670s come Nevil Payne's ferocious *Siege of Constantinople* (1674), most of Rochester's verse satires, the enraged *A Dialogue between the Two Horses* (wr. 1676),[120] and Ayloffe's wrathful *Britannia and Raleigh*.

With the Popish Plot and the Exclusion Crisis came much greater cause for alarm, and, unsurprisingly, satire of this period often reflects panic as much as indignation. To grumble about government ineptitude during the Third Dutch War is one thing; when Charles sprinkles bastards all over the land but cannot sire a legitimate Protestant heir, frustration gives way to sick anxiety. Stephen College's notoriously declamatory satires were produced in this period, including *Truth Brought to Light Or Murder Will Out* (wr. 1679), *Justice in Masquerade* (wr. 1679; pub. 1680), and *Raree Show* (1681), the last of which contributed to his being executed for treason.[121] A number of satirists responded apprehensively to the slaying of Godfrey (e.g., *On the Murder of Sir Edmund Berry Godfrey* [wr. 1678] and *Sir Edmund Berry Godfrey's Ghost* [wr. 1679]). Another angst-ridden satire is *A Tale of the Tubs, or Rome's Masterpiece Defeated* (wr. 1679), in which the Jesuits vow to "make all England stagger ere't be long" and to "strike the stroke may ruin Christendom" (ll. 90, 92).

In *Naboth's Vineyard* (1679), John Caryll (a Catholic who spent time in the Tower during the Popish Plot) objects to the persecution of his coreligionists.[122] As Dryden would do in *Absalom and Achitophel*, Caryll reviles Shaftesbury for provoking the "giddy rabble" with sham accusations (l. 37). The satire concludes with poetic justice of a sort. Shaftesbury and his wife are left, at the poem's end, dreading the "fate to come" (l. 497). Nevertheless, the plight of Naboth—the predictability with which the innocent man is "exposed" and found guilty by a perverse justice system—is appalling, and that the principal agitators are punished does nothing to right that wrong. Political satire produced in this period is essentially different in kind from that which would be directed at Walpole and the "Robinocracy" in the 1730s. The screenmaster general's power was, until late in his reign, fairly secure. Satires directed at the government during a volatile situation, as in the autumn of 1681, have more urgency and more potential significance than those written in times of relative stability.

Satires from late 1682 through the end of Charles's reign are mostly rather different from those of the earlier Carolean period. Attacks on Shaftesbury and Monmouth continue well after the former had fled England and even after his death, but the Whigs were no longer the threat that they had been, as both parties understood. John Dean's *Iter Boreale* (1682) is a piece of mock mourning written after Slingsby Bethel's departure from London, an event that represented "the first real evidence that the Whig control was beginning to break."[123] Dean's satire is an exultant piece of Tory triumphalism, and others of his party struck the same note. The author of *Satire, or Song* (wr. 1682) surveys the political landscape, observing that the Whigs are gone, the Tories jubilant, and "The *Raree Show* will be sung no more" (l. 29). Whigs were not silent, of course. The Whig satirist of *To the Loyal Londoners* (wr. 1682) features as his speaker an ominously jeering Tory whose newfound supremacy (the author implies) will have dire consequences, the prospect of which is meant to make "loyal" Englishmen shudder. *A New Ballad To the tune of The Irish Jig* (wr. 1684) is a later and more caustic piece of opposition satire. Sharp rebukes of the government can be found (e.g., *A Merry New Ballad: In Answer to Old Rowley the King* [wr. 1683]), but little of the political satire has bite.

My intention here is not to define satiric practice at any particular moment but to suggest the importance of contextual changes to the kind of satire produced. Again, I return to the example of *Hudibras*. Treating that work as a "Restoration satire" badly obscures the degree to which the individual parts belong to their respective moments; 1662 and 1663 are significantly different in religiopolitical terms, and 1677–1678 is another world altogether. Attitudes and levels of trepidation or outrage obviously differ from satirist to satirist. Not all or even most Second Dutch War or Exclusion Crisis satires are alike in tone, intensity, or purpose. And things can change drastically even over a very brief span of time, as we well understand: American political culture was not on 12 September 2001 what it had been forty-eight hours earlier. We can find similar works produced in different decades, especially in the realm of moral and social satire—but the overall, predominant character changes across this period. The targets and the nature of the satire alter within half decades or more frequently, and the practice at any given moment is far from uniform.[124] These works are not much like earlier or later satires, but they should not be explained simply as part of a well-defined and consistently applicable concept of "Carolean satire."

VII. Issues: Satiric Intensity, Tone, Positives—and the Problem of Application

If we are looking not at particular Carolean authors and works or at chronological subsections but at more general characteristics, what distinctions are to be found in satiric practice?

Intensity

We need to see the full range of satiric intensity—from frivolity (*The London Cuckolds*) and snide recitation of popular attacks (as in some of the court lampoons) to hostility (*Clarendon's Housewarming*) and unmitigated disgust (John Phillips's *A Satyr Against Hypocrites*). The level of authorial commitment matters. Interpretation of tone, like interpretation of content, can of course differ from reader to reader. Some satires that I take as articulations of genuine disapproval or anxiety might imaginably have been written as ironic romps, and some that I read as fireworks produced with gusto but little conviction could be wholly in earnest. Determining commitment is impossible to do with certitude, but satire is an exceptionally purposive form of writing, and in a fair number of cases we can make reasonable guesses about motive and intensity. In the *Satyr Against Vertue*, Oldham presents a lot of bad news; he is, at least on the surface, complaining about a debauched world. But I suspect that the recounting of ills is to some extent pro forma. Reading Otway's social satire alongside Oldham does much to accentuate the depth and ferocity of the playwright's revulsion. Scholars tend to think of satire as attack, which in many cases of course it is; attack without animosity is, however, quite different from satire that denounces with real rancor. *The Sullen Lovers*, *The Rehearsal*, *Upon Nothinge*, and *The Medall* are all instances of or include satiric attack—but they hardly represent kindred ventures. We need to make distinctions.

Tone

Little attention has been paid to tonal variations in satire, in part because the best satires are assumed to be either admirably sober (because highly moral) or savagely funny (if unsporting). Irony is a problem. If we know enough about an author, then we have some chance at recognizing the presence of irony in his or her text. The assertions made in, say, Swift's *Modest Proposal* are sufficiently extreme that we think to look for irony. But if we do not have confidence in our comprehension of what the authorial meaning must be, and if the text's argument does not give itself away, then we are in muddy waters. Oldham is sometimes described as the post-Restoration inheritor of Cleveland's furious scurrility, but, as Selden rightly suggests, he "outdoes" Cleveland with his use of "satiric hyperbole."[125] Cleveland composed *The Rebell Scot* just after the Scots joined the war on the side of Parliament, and he damns them wholesale as a brood of traitorous devils. Here and in *The Scots Apostacy*, his execration of a political enemy is vindictive, probably giving vent to visceral hatred, whereas there is some chance that Oldham's fiery declamations are enhanced by hyperbole. And if Oldham's "curses" suggest that smoke does not necessarily signal fire, then the example of *Absalom and Achitophel* makes plain that tonal restraint need not denote lack of passion. Tone is not a perfect indicator of intensity, but it is often a vital key to the nature of the enterprise and the effect desired.

What sort of tonal range does Carolean satire exhibit? Satires like *Seigneur Dildoe* and *The London Cuckolds* are jolly,[126] though we need to remember that not all superficially merry satires are actually funny. An author can be witty and clever without being amused. In *The King's Vows* (wr. 1670), Charles recites the charges made against him in the 1660s, and rollicking as the monarch's enumeration of disturbing intentions is, the account is not cheerful. Charles merrily details how things will go, pledging to follow his prerogative without restraint, popular sentiment be damned: "If this please not, I'll reign upon any condition" (l. 46). Or take *The King's Farewell to Danby* (wr. 1679), a poem written in the wake of Danby's impeachment. A buoyant Charles breezily exposes himself as just as guilty as his fallen minister, reveling in the fact that Danby has taken the blame. The pardon the king promised Danby signified nothing. It does not matter at all,

> like all the oaths we've sworn to defend
> The Protestant cause, which we ne'er did intend;
> Or like all the tricks we've play'd since we came
> To ride on the necks of a people so tame. (ll. 21–24)

As in *The King's Vows*, Charles swears here to "rule by my will"—or to "follow my father once more to Edgehill" (33–34). The lampoon has bounce, but the recollection of the clash between parliamentary privilege and royal prerogative (and the ensuing civil war) is no laughing matter. In *A New Ballad, to an Old Tune, Call'd, I Am the Duke of Norfolk, etc.* (wr. 1679), Charles just as gaily exposes himself: "I am a senseless thing, with a hey, with a hey," he sings,

> I corrupted the age, with a ho;
> The nation once were men
> But now are slaves again,
> With a hey tronny nonny nonny no. (ll. 1, 12–15)

Some Carolean satires are genuinely fun, and some acerbically humorous, but others are remarkably unpleasant in their cheerlessness. In Otway's *Friendship in Fashion*, we are given nothing to laugh at, only shown one revolting event and objectionable character after another. Rochester is capable of the same degree of negativity, though his energy and his obscenities give his works a verve lacking in Otway. Most verse satires do not achieve the depth of gloom that *Friendship in Fashion* presents, but some are plenty somber.[127] *A Ballad called the Haymarket Hectors* (wr. 1671) is a response to the attack on Sir John Coventry. Coventry's punishment for making a snide remark about Charles and his mistresses was a beating by twenty Life Guards. Monmouth was evidently not among them, but as captain of the King's Life Guard he almost certainly gave the orders.[128] The poet criticizes Charles and Nell Gwyn, and the final lines express concern that at Nell's command a war could be started: "Should you but name the prerogative whore, / How the bullets would whistle, the cannon would roar!"

Two other satires from the same year—*On the Three Dukes Killing the Beadle* and *Upon the Beadle*—address the murder of a beadle by Monmouth and other members of the nobility, all of whom were pardoned.[129] *Upon the Beadle* ends with an image of "one poor old man" having been "subdued" by the dukes, but the other poem is yet more tragic, its author's denunciation of the "bastard dukes" even more chillingly unfunny: "See these men dance, all daub'd with lace and blood" (ll. 12, 36). The appalling pathos of these satires is a world away from something like *A Ballad Called Perkin's Figary* (wr. 1679), a vigorous Tory attack on Monmouth:

> He aims at a crown for his noddle unfit
> As Howe for a duchess, or he for a wit.
> > He danceth, he skippeth,
> > He frisketh, he leapeth,
> To trumpet and drums he manfully trippeth—
> But his Highness, God bless him, is safely come back
> To the shame and confusion of Perkin Warbeck. (ll. 12–17)

The satire has serious implications—the author is worried about the succession and the fate of England—but Monmouth is an unimpressive booby, not (as in the Coventry and Beadle poems) a sadistic thug.

These satires are not mere flippant diatribes, and they are not diverting or droll. *Friendship in Fashion* and the Beadle poems are not sober in the way Pope's *Moral Essays* are sober; they seem to indicate intense unhappiness, apprehension, loathing, and sometimes terror. So do the anonymous *A Summons from a True Protestant Conjurer to Cethegus' Ghost* and its sequel, *Cethegus' Apology for Non-Appearance upon his Conjurer's Summons* (1682), both darkly humorless. In the former, the Tory author has a radical nonconformist speak so as to expose his own treachery. The current Whigs are associated with the sectarians of the 1640s as king-killing conspirators: "Rise Peters, Nol, Scroop, Scott, Hell's modern furies; / Meet Satan, fire and brimstone, and Whig juries" (ll. 38–39). "Restoration satire" is usually regarded as crude and coarse, but its abrasiveness has perhaps more to do with Carolean satirists' propensity for unrestrained personal venom than with the degree of real hostility found in these works. The articulation of outrage, fear, and disgust—often apparently not delivered for the sake of the performance, and not leavened by wit—can be overwhelming. This satire is sometimes simply about venting, sometimes about warning readers, sometimes about producing real anxiety as a way of provoking agitation against the target or subject, and sometimes about spreading gloom. It is neither play nor display and is being used not simply to attack and certainly not to reform its targets.

Presentation of Positives

Antagonism can be expressed in jingoistic high jinks, in disgruntled objections, or in blistering invective, but Carolean satire cannot be explained adequately just in terms of aggression. In 1963 Ruth Nevo suggested, "Satire is not the only channel for the political impulse, since there is always a cause, or a personality, to be fought for, as well as against."[130] Hers is a standard assumption: satire's purposes are negative rather than positive, the latter being the province of panegyric. Griffin downplays the role of "ideology" in satire, concluding, "The satirist's primary goal *as writer* is not to declare political principles but to respond to a particular occasion and to write a good satire." He substantiates this claim with reference to Butler (suggesting that *Hudibras* has no positive values), Rochester (whom he describes as largely apolitical), Dryden (who "appeals at last not to principle but to pragmatism"), and Swift and Pope.[131] Griffin's contention does not hold for all or even most Carolean satires: like *The Country Gentleman* and *Hudibras*, many of these works are written in defense of something the writer strongly believes in.

Some satires in this period are better understood in terms of what they support than of what they attack. Christopher Wase's *Divination* (1666), a response to the *Second Advice*, is an attempt to refute the author of that poem, but his primary aim is to defend the government. Robert Wild's *Iter Boreale* (1660) lampoons the radicals and exults in the king's return. The speaker of *The Banished Priests' Farewell to the House of Commons* (wr. 1673) addresses the Parliament that has just ordered Charles to cancel the Declaration of Indulgence (1672) and assent to the Test Act, in exchange for which they will supply funding for the Dutch War. The satirist blasts the antitolerant parliamentarians as "sots" and "high-shod clowns" (ll. 1, 4). In a vehemently pro-Catholic and pro-Indulgence satire, he savages his foes:

> Go, get you home, you rustics! *You* dictate
> T' his Majesty the great intrigues of state?
> Must your hodge-podge, piss'd upon religion be
> The standard of all worship, and must we
> To that bald bawdy stuff submit, who name
> The codpiece can, and cause from whence it came? (ll. 97–102)

The author is livid, and one can understand why: he is a Catholic, or at least a Catholic sympathizer, and his targets are "bumpkins" pressing the king to revoke toleration and enforce religious conformity (l. 105). His lashing of the parliamentarians is ferocious, but "they" are not the point. Lord likens this satire to *A Charge to the Grand Inquest of England* (wr. 1674), which he describes as "a rare piece of pro-government propaganda."[132] That poet denounces Charles's parliamentary opponents and defends royal prerogative, as does the anonymous author of *The Character* (wr. 1679) and Matthew Taubman in *Philander* (1680). Other satires with at least implicit positive agendas include *A Pulpit to be Let* (1665), Wild's *The Loyal Nonconformist* (1666), Dorset's *On the Young Statesmen* (wr. 1680), *Popish Politics Unmasked* (wr. 1680), and Thomas Thompson's *Midsummer Moon* (1682).

A markedly different sort of positive satire is that of John Bunyan, whose Christian allegories are a universe away from, say, Rochester's bawdy diatribes but who does belong to the Carolean satiric milieu. *Pilgrim's Progress* came out in the same year (1678) that *The Kind Keeper* was produced and Oldham's *Satyrs upon the Jesuits* began to appear, and *The Life and Death of Mr. Badman* (1680) was published in the year that *The Spanish Fryar* was staged. What kind of satire is featured in Bunyan's allegories? Brainerd P. Stranahan suggests that what is so remarkable about the satire of *The Pilgrim's Progress* "is that its premises are so firmly on the Lord's side rather than on the devil's." Bunyan is a true believer, "using the Bible to roast the complacent foes of Christianity" and "to laugh away the fears of the faint-hearted faithful."[133] His satire is homiletic, addressing not his enemies but his friends, those who share his moral and theological convictions. The eponymous character of *The Life and Death of Mr. Badman* is, of course, a bad man, one who commits all the sins proscribed in Puritan conduct manuals. Badman has some material success, but what Bunyan emphasizes is "the ugliness and sheer uncomfortableness of his way of life." He is a thoroughly negative example, "a model not to be emulated if indeed we wish to escape hell."[134] This is vice made ridiculous for the sake of the virtuous. It is precisely the sort of instructive derision for which in 1740 Henry Fielding would extol Hogarth "as one of the most useful Satyrists any Age hath produced."[135] *Pilgrim's Progress* and *Badman* include caustic social satire,[136] but they are didactic rather than punitive, strongly positive enterprises such as we will later find in Defoe.

Carolean satires vary in force and passion, in degree of levity and sobriety, in purpose and in method. Many of them have at least an implicit positive agenda and so are better understood in terms of what they are defending than of what they are decrying or whom they are abusing. Insofar as modern critics discuss the "positive" in satire, they usually have in mind the sweet-sounding vows of reformative intentions rather than any practical agendas in the works themselves. Few Carolean satires promise moral reform or exhibit buoyant Pollyannaism, but several of these writers clearly believed that satire could be productive, if in very local and specific ways. The extent to which Carolean satire is a positive as well as a negative enterprise has been vastly underestimated.

The Problem of Application

Carolean satirists are often devastatingly blunt in their judgments, blasting their targets in words of one syllable, but satiric meaning is often a matter of application and implication rather than explicit attack.[137] Did Sir Robert Howard mean *The Great Favourite, or the Duke of Lerma* (1668) to be a "parallel" satire on current events and on Charles II? Pepys believed so and expressed discomfort: "The play designed to reproach our King with his mistress; that I was troubled for it, and expected it should be interrupted; but it ended all well, which salved all. The play a well-writ and good play; only, its design I did not like, of reproaching the King."[138] Hughes describes the play as an anti-Clarendon satire, in which "a weak, manipulable, and amorous king is reformed and the ambitious and evil Duke of Lerma is finally neutralized," though remaining "in triumphant impunity because of his rank as cardinal."[139] Such a reading is plausible, but Pepys's entry is all we have to substantiate it. Whether Howard conceived of his play as an indirect satire on Charles and contemporary politics we have no way of determining. Such "application" depends upon the eye of the beholder.

Edward Howard's *The Change of Crownes* (perf. 1667; not pub. until the twentieth century) was also taken as obnoxious satire, not by Pepys but by the king, who personally suppressed the play. The high plot is heavy on the theme of heroic love, but the low plot is funny, ridiculing influence peddlers at court and pursuers of government posts. Pepys gave *The Change of Crownes* a rave review ("the best play that I ever saw at that House") but complained that "only, Lacy did act the country gentleman come up to Court, who doth abuse the Court with all the imaginable wit and plainness, about selling of places and doing everything for money."[140] Lacy played Asinello, an avid if simple-minded place seeker, and however much even the loyal Pepys delighted in the performance, Charles was not amused. Lacy was promptly arrested, leading to a row between him and the playwright.[141]

In the one case we have an apparent application for which we have no evidence of either authorial intention or audience comprehension beyond Pepys. In the other, we can only guess what the playwright meant but have indisputable evidence that strong exception was taken. I have mentioned Dryden and Lee's *The Duke of Guise* (1682), where the targeting of Monmouth cannot sanely be denied. Aphra Behn's *The Roundheads* (1681), based on John Tatham's *The Rump* (1660), is another such instance: Roundheads equal Whigs. Less specifically pointed satires were sometimes allowed on stage and sometimes not. Otway's *Venice Preserv'd* (1682) bashes "plotters" but is hard to tie explicitly into London particulars. Nahum Tate's touchier *The History of King Richard the Second* was initially banned (December 1680) but then performed the next month disguised under the title *The Sicilian Usurper*—with the result that the theater was shut down for ten days. Tate protested his innocence, but why he thought a play featuring the deposition of an English king would be permitted in the midst of the Exclusion Crisis is hard to figure.[142] One may fairly say that some of the most effective satire is applicative (witness *Absalom and Achitophel*)—*if* it got by the authorities, and *if* the reader or viewer duly made the connection.

VIII. The Discontinuous World of Carolean Satire

An obvious point needs to be made: Carolean satirists had not read Dryden's *Discourse*, Swift's *Tale of a Tub*, or Pope's Horatian imitations. They did not foresee the happy advent of an "Augustan" mode; they had no inkling whither eighteenth-century satire would be tending. The notion that somehow Swift's and Pope's origins are to be found in Rochester and Dryden is misguided; so is the idea that the chaotic multiplicity of Carolean satire somehow evolved into what Pope or Swift practiced. Later satirists read some of the work of their predecessors and perhaps even borrowed from or otherwise followed them, but Pope is not an advanced form of Dryden any more than Rochester is an earlier Swift. Carolean satire has been considered as the primitive beginning of what would become a great age of satire; it has been characterized on the basis of a few favorite texts; it has been misrepresented and apologized for. One recent satire scholar, Fredric Bogel, skips this period entirely, bounding directly from Jonson to Swift.

Carolean satire is sui generis, and it obviously does not reduce to a single mode. If we attend to motive, level of commitment, tone, intensity, presentation of positives, hope for change, apparent desired effect, and so on, then we see quite clearly that Dryden is not Buckingham and Marvell is not Ayloffe. Scholars have not exactly asserted that Dryden and Buckingham are identical, but most studies of late seventeenth-century satire have emphasized continuity and commonality. As recently as 2007, Griffin could lament that "the canon of Restoration satire remains fairly small," and that "the range and vigor" of satiric practice in this period "are not fully recognized."[143] Range is hard to appreciate if one is seeking cohesion among a small body of works. Selden has claimed, for example, that "the leading satirists of the Restoration period (Butler, Rochester, Oldham and Dryden) all ridicule deviations from a strongly held rational norm in the spheres of philosophy, religion, politics or literature."[144] Literary critics in all realms usually seek to define the spirit of the age, and attempts to characterize this period are no exception, but the whole idea of a "Restoration mode" is methodologically indefensible and acutely unhelpful.[145] The features that differentiate texts and authors from each other can be either superficial or fundamental, but if literary history is to have any real utility, then we cannot afford to ignore them.

Attempting to identify or enforce uniformity among disparate works written for a wide variety of reasons across a twenty-five-year period is unlikely to yield accurate results. Selden links Butler, Rochester, Oldham, and Dryden—but if we are not looking for kinship, what do we find? Butler defends monarchy entirely on pragmatic grounds, and his most famous work is an entertaining burlesque and a camouflaged satire. Rochester is an aggressively skeptical author, whose satires' moral positions are sometimes open to multiple interpretations. Oldham is a comparatively apolitical anti-Catholic poet whose satires might be expressions of conviction but tend to seem more like spectacular performances composed without a positive agenda. Carolean Dryden is a High Anglican, a believer in mystical politics, and Charles II's poet laureate; his most celebrated satire is a biblical allegory motivated by alarm and anxiety, written in defense of the status quo and meant to sway public opinion. Butler and Dryden both satirize Shaftesbury as Achitophel and denounce the Whigs as threats to monarchical order, but Dryden would not write even part III of *Hudibras* any more than Butler would write *Absalom and Achitophel*. If we lump these authors together under a generalized heading (they all "ridicule deviations from a strongly held rational norm"), then we obliterate distinctions that we very much need. These four satirists do not a "mode" make—and Buckingham, Marvell, Ayloffe, Ravenscroft, Behn, Otway, and the countless other Carolean satirists differ variously from these writers and from each other.

Granting this heterogeneity, however, we need also to realize that Carolean satire is unlike satire in the subperiods covered in the following chapters. Misleading though I find the idea of a "Restoration mode," the fact is that satires in the reign of Charles II mostly do belong together. What sets them apart is largely a matter of the particularities of Carolean court culture and politics and the world of scribal publication. A high percentage of these works are personal, heated, and abusive; most are concerned, directly or indirectly, with political issues, though some address social and/or literary subjects. Exclusively "moral" satires there are few, and not many writers offer moral justification for their work. Bunyan's overt Christian didacticism makes him something of an oddity. This satire is closely connected to its contextual circumstances: its meaning mostly does not "transcend" the moment for which it was written. Never again in England would there be so much personal satire; never again would satire contribute in the same way to a decisive political choice during a national crisis. No later satirist is "like" John Ayloffe; Andrew Marvell does not come again. Attempts to explain this material by reference to a few unrepresentative exemplars or to post-1700 developments deprives us of an exciting set of responses to a tumultuous historical moment. Carolean satire comprises many diverse enterprises, but much of it has energy and fierce commitment. Later seventeenth-century satire is tamer, blander, and exceedingly unlike what we find in the reign of Charles II. The reasons for the difference are now to seek.

CHAPTER FOUR

Beyond Carolean

Satire at the End of the Seventeenth Century

◇◇◇◇◇◇◇◇◇◇◇◇◇◇◇◇◇◇◇◇◇◇◇◇

> Ho, brother Teague, dost hear de decree,
>> Lilli burlero, bullen a-la;
> Dat we shall have a new debittie,
>> Lilli burlero bullen a-la,
>> Lero lero, lero lero, lilli burlero, bullen a-la;
>> Lero lero, lero lero, lilli burlero, bullen a-la.
>> —Wharton, *Lilli burlero*, ll. 1–6

Satire at the end of the seventeenth century differs markedly from Carolean satire, and scholars have found singularly little in it to admire. Many satires were written in these years, and some (like Garth's *Dispensary*) were much read and often reprinted. Critics routinely cite Dryden's *Discourse* of 1693 and the accompanying translation of Juvenal and Persius, but for the most part the years between *Absalom and Achitophel* (1681) and *A Tale of a Tub* (1704) are assumed to constitute a black hole in which nothing of import or interest happens.

Writers well known as satirists in their day—the likes of Ned Ward and Sir Samuel Garth—are rarely mentioned in satire studies and then only briefly and apologetically. Hardly any major authors have been associated with these years, although both Dryden and Defoe were practicing satirists in the 1690s. Dryden's titanic modern reputation as a satirist derives largely from two Carolean poems; his substantial post-Carolean satiric output, including the brilliant *Amphitryon* (1690), has been almost totally ignored by students of satire. Defoe's career began not with *Robinson Crusoe* but with a series of political verse satires in the 1690s; his *True-Born Englishman* (1701) was a huge and lasting success, and throughout much of his writing life his reputation depended heavily on his satire.[1] Few satire theorists have had anything to say about drama, but a number of first-rate satiric plays premiered on the London stage during William's reign—including hard-hitting social commentaries by the still underappreciated Thomas Southerne, his protégé William Congreve, and John Vanbrugh. These playwrights are not (or not only) *attacking*; they are calling attention to serious wrongs and inequities. Given present-day critical concern with women's rights and gender issues, continued lack of attention to these plays is surprising.

Sociopolitical circumstances change in the last decade and a half of the seventeenth century, and the practice of satire changes with them. The works in this roughly fifteen-year period have little in common either with the types dominant in the Carolean era or with the later masterpieces beloved by modern scholars. If we approach this material looking for *Absalom and Achitophel*, the early Swift, or the mature Pope, we can only be disappointed; neither do we find the blistering bawdiness of Rochester or the ribaldry of the Carolean court lampoonists. Our distaste for much of what we do find—works by Sir Richard Blackmore, Robert Gould, and company—should not deter us, however, from trying to make sense of the change that late-century satires illustrate.

By comparison with Carolean satire, the verse satires of the 1690s mostly seem bland and uninteresting. This is not astonishing. Section I of this chapter is an attempt to explain the causes and nature of the shift, but I will make two points here. First, Carolean satire is remarkable in part because many writers were alarmed by religious conflict and political instability that brought the country to the brink of another civil war. Discontent with James generated comparatively little public fuss, and the 1688 revolution that toppled him was important but (in England) bloodless. William's domestic politics and expensive wars bred considerable rancor, but there was no real possibility of drastic change. Under neither king did the country face the kind of crisis it had under Charles II. The second point is that extraliterary forces necessitated changes in satiric practice. The breakup of the Carolean court circle and the shift from scribal to print publication coincided to transform the possibilities for satire; satirists found themselves addressing a broader audience among whom they could not count on much common knowledge about topical events and personalities. This state of affairs changes rapidly with the rise of daily newspapers after 1702. I treat both of these issues at some length in what follows, but we need to realize that what happens at the end of the century represents a short-lived phenomenon, one that has been expunged from the history of satire in the long eighteenth century.

I begin by addressing the radically altered circumstances in which satire was practiced in the last decade and a half of the seventeenth century. Beyond that, I make arguments in three realms. (1) The preeminent satirist of the late seventeenth century is Dryden, whose late-life satiric oeuvre gives us a very different sense of him and of this period. If we want to characterize Dryden's satiric practice and his role in "long eighteenth-century satire" broadly conceived, we need to attend to what he produces in the last decade or so of his life. His example illustrates a fundamental principle: satire written for a positive end is a different enterprise from satire that is simply grousing. (2) Late-century satiric poets are not doing what their Carolean predecessors had done—and for good reasons. The satiric verse of this period goes in several directions because poets respond differently to changes in sociopolitical circumstances, target audience, and print culture. However we judge the results, the poems reflect attempts to adapt to a broader readership and a new world. (3) Some high-quality satiric drama is produced in the last decade of the century; if one is looking for the most interesting, important, substantive satiric arguments at the end of the seventeenth century, one must look to the stage.

I. Altered Circumstances

Satire at the end of the late seventeenth century is almost entirely unlike that produced in the reign of Charles II. Nothing like a Marvell or a Buckingham exists in this period; there is no Gould or Ward or Blackmore in the world described in the preceding chapter. The snappy personal lampoons, the acid demolitions of public figures, the obscene court libels, and the mordant antigovernment satires—the works that give Carolean verse satire its energy and force—are not to be found in the reigns of James and William. Whence the transformation?

One cause of change is clear: satire is closely bound, in the second half of the seventeenth century, both to the character of the monarch and to the nature of the troubles of his reign. From Charles's rule to James's and then William's, times changed—and so did the type and intensity of political controversy. The decade following the Restoration had been increasingly tense, satire darkened yet further in the 1670s, and by the early 1680s the country faced a major crisis. The likes of Butler and Rochester were saying—not in generalized abstractions but in specific topical commentary—that circumstances were terrible and getting worse all the time. The Exclusion Crisis created a dire political situation. In somber terms, writers asked whether England should emend its political foundation to deal with a particular problem. Both those who wanted to exclude James from the succession and those like Dryden who asked "What Prudent men a setled Throne woud shake?" could support their positions; on either side there was legitimate anxiety. This was a practical issue, not a hypothetical or theoretical concern. Someone was going to assume the throne, and who and on what basis had to be decided. The satiric contributions to this debate mattered to their authors in utterly serious ways. Satirists in the later eighties and nineties had plenty to complain about, but there was nothing like the same severe division of opinion, nothing like the same sense of urgent uncertainty at a time of acute national crisis.

Many Carolean satires had focused on Charles II, and—to state the obvious—James was not like his brother. However much derogation was heaped upon him as the Duke of York, in his short tenure as monarch he appears to have suffered less scabrous personal abuse than Charles had or William would, but he was scorned as a fool, loathed as a tyrant, and ridiculed as a coward. He was never popular; his popery caused dubiety at best and hostile apprehension at worst; his staunch belief in the royal prerogative and his relentless pursuit of his agendas made him terrifying. Particular issues were disputed in his reign, but he did create relative consensus. The majority of his subjects accepted his accession but disliked and distrusted him: "James's policies succeeded in alienating nearly every segment of the political nation," and when trouble came, "he was deserted on every side."[2] William did not match Charles in brazen carelessness or profligacy any more than James had. He was disparaged not for being a "merry Monarch" but for being a foreign bisexual who stole the throne from his father-in-law, rewarded his (foreign) buddies with lucrative positions, and promptly got England bogged down in a long, costly, unpopular continental war.[3] Whatever the antagonism toward William, however, his subjects were mostly prepared to accept his authority. What fundamental, future-altering issues could satirists write about in the reigns of James and William? What concerns would have anything like the urgency of those central to much of Carolean satire?

A transformed political climate produces differences in satire—but other changes are if anything more important. The significant decrease in lampoon production after Charles's death has less to do with politics or with an increasingly refined collective sensibility than with a change in the circumstances in which satire was composed and disseminated. Few literary scholars or satire theorists have been concerned about such matters, and of course modern critical awareness of scribal publication is a recent development. Harold Love's groundbreaking *Scribal Publication in Seventeenth-Century England* did not appear until 1993, and until then even those who dealt with manuscripts paid little attention to dissemination. The editors of the Yale *Poems on Affairs of State* made much material readily available and provided useful annotation and explication, but they were pretty casual about the distinction between what was printed and what was not, and they had little to say about why or how that distinction might matter. In fact, the dispersal of the court wits in James's and especially William's reign—and the concurrent rise of print culture—dramatically alter the possibilities for verse satire in this period.

A great deal of Carolean satiric verse was written by insiders for insiders. The poems were sometimes printed and sometimes attributed, rightly or wrongly, but as both Love and Hume have emphasized, most of the touchier works circulated scribally and anonymously. Rochester's wickedly unsparing "scepter lampoon," Marvell's critical responses to the Second Dutch War, the antimonarchical diatribes of Ayloffe, the smear jobs on political powerhouses, and the colorful billingsgate directed at court ladies—these were not usually meant for print or for widespread consumption, even if such material sometimes got published. Publication would often have been imprudent, but it was also largely unnecessary. These satirists were writing for coterie audiences who could be reached by manuscript circulation. Hume explains that

London was a city of about four hundred thousand at the time of the plague in 1665 (which killed about a quarter of that population), and the overlapping groups of nobility, gentry, government officials, members of Parliament, and great merchants and their families cannot have constituted more than a small fraction of the whole. We are in the world of Samuel Pepys's *Diary*, a place in which those who are part of one network know virtually everyone in it and recognize many in other networks. This was a self-contained little universe that revolved round the court and thrived on gossip. Like Hollywood in its heyday, the court world was conspicuous, scandalous, and inevitably the focus for floods of gossip.[4]

The importance of in-group mentality to the nature of Carolean satire is difficult to overestimate. Michael McKeon and Hume both underscore the potential indecipherability of such materials, which were circulated without helpful annotation, but I suspect that the target audience often had a good idea of how to interpret the satire.[5] This was a small and often extremely closely connected court world.

When that changes, so does satire. James filled his court with Catholics, and by the summer of 1686, John Harold Wilson observes, "Many of the Protestant courtiers who had made the libertine Court of Charles II so brilliantly sinful retired to their country estates."[6] The implication for satiric practice is at least twofold: the reduction in blatant licentiousness gives lampoonists less to talk about, and the surviving Carolean court satirists cease to write court satire. William and Mary's court is yet more remote from that of Charles; the tone and indeed most of the personnel change. In the 1690s, the government got bigger, the court world got smaller, and, argues Love, "Pure court satire became increasingly rare . . . because the court itself had largely surrendered its cultural supremacy and distinctiveness."[7] The phenomenon is simple: the disintegration of the Carolean court circle means that the scribal satirists largely disappear. After 1688, few satirists are court wits writing for a small, specific audience with inside knowledge; they are a socially mixed lot writing for print for a wider, more disparate readership. Some poets are commercial drudges keen to make a living off their pens, representing a category nonexistent in Carolean verse satire, but in any case the diminution of the viability of scribal publication fundamentally alters the type of satire that will work.

Readers are not likely to appreciate—buy, read, enjoy—satire that does not communicate anything to them. That many Londoners would care about the indecencies of a minor court lady who was not even a name to them is highly unlikely. What could members of a disparate reading public be assumed to know? In the world of the 1690s, common knowledge was limited. Before the founding of the first daily newspaper—*The Daily Courant* in 1702—the distribution of printed news and gossip was scrappy and minimal. Newsbooks circulated throughout much of the seventeenth century, offering detailed accounts of particular events, but coverage was erratic. Coffeehouses provided access of various sorts to some information, though they tended to be expensive and the discussions far from uniform.[8] Satirists writing for print could not safely assume that a broad readership would "get" highly topical references. The audience for satire changed after the death of Charles II, and satirists needed new material.

The best-known and perhaps the most influential satire of this period worked precisely because it did not depend upon the particularities of its content. Thomas Wharton's anti-Catholic ballad, *Lilli burlero*, was spectacularly popular and had considerable practical effect. Initially written in response to Richard Talbot's administration in Ireland in 1687, *Lilli burlero* was set to a lively tune by Henry Purcell and circulated in broadside form in October 1688. Wharton himself reportedly bragged that his doggerel—evidently read by all and sundry as James fled England—had "sung a deluded Prince out of Three Kingdoms."[9] In his *History*, Bishop Burnet would marvel at this squib's success: the satire "made an impression . . . that cannot be well imagined by those who saw it not. The whole Army, and at last all people both in city and country, were singing it perpetually. And perhaps never had so slight a thing so great an effect."[10] *Lilli burlero*'s words are not always intelligible: its opening lines are "Ho, brother Teague, dost hear de decree,/Lilli burlero, bullen a-la." But the poem was all the rage, so effective at rousing anti-Jacobite sentiment that James's government attempted (to no avail) to counter by having its balladists compose a parallel version against the Dutch.[11] *Lilli burlero* and other celebrations of William's campaign, such as *The Plowman* and Matthew Prior's *The Orange*, reflected and were evidently meant to bolster popular support of James's removal. As late as *Tristram Shandy*, in which Uncle Toby famously whistles *Lilli burlero*, the import of Wharton's satire was clear to English readers, but the song's notoriety and public impact owed as much to its associations as to its actual content.

At the other extreme is Dorset's *A Faithful Catalogue of Our Most Eminent Ninnies* (wr. 1688), a topical court satire meant not for wide print distribution but for manuscript circulation among a court circle. An oddity in the late eighties, the *Faithful Catalogue* would have seemed commonplace a decade earlier, and it illustrates the change I am trying to describe. It represents one of the most "Carolean" of the post-Carolean satires, written for those among the gentry who would understand the topical allusions to court scandals. The lampoon is insulting, but it is, as Galbraith M. Crump explains, "more than a display of gross abuse. Written sometime early in 1688, it appeared when James still remained awesome enough to dismay all who opposed him. The poem rehearses . . . all that by nature would tend to reduce James and his courtiers to the level of buffoons acting out an absurd low comedy."[12] Dorset's attack on James recalls Carolean satirists' ridicule of Monmouth and others: "Oh, sacred James! may thy dread noddle be / As free from danger as from wit 'tis free."[13] The catalog of offenders sounds familiar to readers of Carolean court satire: "Pimp-statesmen, bug'ring priests, court bawds, and whores" (l. 14). The difference between this satire and something like Gould's antifeminist diatribes or Ward's attack on vintners is enormous—and unsurprising, given the difference in mode of circulation and intended audience. The *Faithful Catalogue* is satire written for a small world.

If one was writing for print in the 1690s, what could one do? What kind of satire would work for an increasingly wide audience among whom no very substantial shared knowledge base could be assumed? At least two possibilities exist: a satirist could provide, in the text itself, everything a reader needed, as in the case of very general satires, or he or she could address topics sufficiently well known, as in the case of Gould's attack on popular actors and actresses or Garth's contribution to the dispensary debate. The generalized verse satire in this period is largely unprecedented in Charles's reign: Carolean satirists were not taking up their pens against greed or brandy, but such works are legion at the end of the century. The many satires on women produced by Gould, Richard Ames, and others probably represent not only a sudden upsurge in bitter misogyny but also another means of reaching a broad readership. In section III, I will return to these categories and offer particular illustrations of them. For now, the crucial point is that verse satires by the likes of Ward, Gould, Garth, and others represent different ways of dealing with a set of contextual circumstances unique to the late seventeenth and very early eighteenth centuries. If verse satires at the end of the century seem a universe away from their earlier counterparts, that is because in many ways they are. A lot had changed, and much of what had given Carolean satire its remarkable scurrility and energy had disappeared.

Because of the changing audiences for satire, modes of transmission, and assumed satiric literacy, what happens in satire under James and William could not have happened sooner, and it soon ceased to happen. For a variety of reasons, post-Carolean satire represents another world altogether, a fact well illustrated by the late career of John Dryden. *Mac Flecknoe* aside, Dryden was always a print rather than a scribal writer. Alterations in transmission of satire would simply not have mattered to him, but he was unquestionably drastically influenced, in his work and his life, by regnal changes.

II. Dryden as Satirist, 1685–1700

Dryden's twentieth-century reputation as a satirist rests almost entirely upon two poems and his *Discourse concerning the Original and Progress of Satire*. He is usually seen as a commanding moral and political satirist, delivering his judgment with conviction and trying to make things happen—whether discrediting a literary rival or defending king and country in a time of crisis. Dryden scholars have done excellent work on the individual pieces, but no one has looked systematically at his entire satiric output.[14] What kind of satirist was he? We need to remember two things to answer that question properly: the theory he promulgates in the *Discourse* is almost totally unrelated to his satiric practice, even in verse, and he has considerable range as a satirist and does not do the same things in any one phase of his career or over time. I want to survey Dryden's satires for the period at issue and also to think more broadly about how to characterize his long and varied career as a satirist.

Dryden's Carolean satires, as I argue in the preceding chapter, cannot be satisfactorily explained as practical illustrations of the high moral theory he would later outline in the *Discourse*. *Marriage A-la-Mode* and *The Kind Keeper* include social satire, albeit of very different sorts. *Mac Flecknoe* is often exalted as a statement of Dryden's deeply held literary principles, though it is essentially a well-crafted and destructive lampoon. *The Medall* slashes at the Whigs in general and Shaftesbury in particular, and like *Absalom and Achitophel*, it is a party document, skilled and principled but also ferocious. *The Spanish Fryar* warns against challenging rightful authority (in the serious plot) and savages an easy target in the crooked friar Dominic (in the subplot). *The Duke of Guise*, written in collaboration with Nat Lee, is a more strictly political satire, a straight parallel play implying that the Duke of Monmouth is a traitorous malefactor who ought to be killed. Dryden as Carolean satirist is aggressive, self-assured, and usually politically minded. He sometimes plays dirty, but he is at his best when he defends a cause in which he believes, and his satires around the Exclusion Crisis are impassioned, clear cut, and uncompromising.

What sort of satirist is Dryden under James? He remained poet laureate and a favorite of the king; he was loyal to the authorities and a champion of the status quo. His conversion to Catholicism in 1685 allowed him to be James's poet as much as he had been Charles's, though it also earned him much abuse from fellow satirists, who heaped scorn upon him as an unscrupulous opportunist and flagrant timeserver. "More Libels have been written against me," he complains in his *Discourse*, "than almost any Man now living" (4:59).[15] Assaults on his character notwithstanding, Dryden was in a good spot under the new king, and his satires from this period evince his relative security. Few satire scholars include *Albion and Albanius* (1685) and *The Hind and the Panther* (1687) in their purview, but both of these works pass judgment while also providing positive commentary—according to the criteria established by Dryden in the *Discourse*, that is, these pieces count as satirical enterprises.[16]

Albion and Albanius is an allegorical masque recounting the history of the reign of Charles II and commenting on the politics of England from the eve of Restoration to the present.[17] It begins with the city of London (personified in "Augusta") in chaos.

Augusta regrets having been swayed by faction and recognizes that the restoration of peace requires the reinstallation of the rightful king (Charles II as "Albion"). Albion's return is widely celebrated, but "Democracy" and "Zelota" ("Feign'd Zeal") conspire to destroy him and to rule again: Achitophel-like, Zelota vows to "Inspire the Crowd / With Clamours loud / T'involve his Brother and his Wife" (15:54, 33). As in *Absalom and Achitophel*, the sovereign's mercy only invites sedition, but the mutineers (Whigs) cannot carry out their plot, and Albion attributes his salvation to divine intervention. In the epilogue, Dryden urges allegiance to the rightful monarch, and the work as a whole is a piece of didactic political commentary whose message is crystal clear: Dryden indicts those who are or would be disloyal to the king as menaces, suggesting that Providence is against them, and he implicitly defends the legitimacy and the future of the Stuart monarchy. An elaborately staged opera, *Albion and Albanius* may seem a strange inclusion in a study of satire, but in basic concept and purpose it is not so very remote from *Absalom and Achitophel*, regardless of their tonal and generic differences. In both, Dryden defends a monarchy he believes in by debunking those who threaten it. He stresses the allegorical nature of *Albion and Albanius* in the preface, and in the epilogue he calls the opera "our Æsop's Fable"—naming a type long recognized as a satiric vehicle for social, moral, and political instruction (54; italics reversed).

The Hind and the Panther (1687) is more clearly and combatively satiric: Dryden calls it a "Satyr" in his address "To the Reader," and contemporaries branded "Bayes" a "*Satyrist*" for this performance.[18] Dryden ridicules the various groups of dissenters in turn—the "the bloudy *Bear*" (Independent), "the *Quaking Hare*" (Quaker), the "bristl'd *Baptist Boar*"—but the Anglicans are his primary targets, and toward them he is defensively antagonistic (ll. 35, 35, 43). In the theological debate between the spotless Catholic Hind and the beautiful but dangerous Anglican Panther (part II), Dryden attacks the church that he had upheld in *Religio Laici* (1682). In part III, he goes after individual Anglicans, especially Edward Stillingfleet and Gilbert Burnet (a "Brawny" Buzzard). The poem celebrates Catholicism and denigrates the Church of England, but it is not for the Catholic king what *Absalom and Achitophel* had been for his brother. As Winn points out, Dryden had initially "designed the poem . . . as an argument to persuade the Established Church to agree to a cancellation of the Test Act," but in issuing a Declaration of Indulgence "James made a bid to ally Catholics and Dissenters against the Establishment"[19]—an alliance Dryden is absolutely not seeking to forge in this poem. His mockery of the dissenters suggests, says David Bywaters, that he is more interested in aggression than in persuasion. Whatever the propagandistic value of a pro-Catholic piece published two months after the Catholic king's Declaration of Indulgence, Dryden is not merely serving James's cause.[20]

The Hind and the Panther is as personal as it is broadly political, and like *Albion and Albanius* it is a strongly positive satire. That they both lack the urgent intensity of *Absalom and Achitophel* is hardly astonishing: in 1685, James's crown seemed safe. Monmouth's rebellion in July had been effectively suppressed without more widespread mutiny, and the Anglican hierarchy had supported the king. James could have ruled until his death had he ruled with more prudence and restraint. *Albion and Albanius* at least implicitly discourages would-be malcontents from making trouble; it does no more and needed to do no more than that. *The Hind and the Panther* is not remote from contemporary policy issues (especially Indulgence), but it is not a defense of a beleaguered monarch or an attempt to influence the outcome of a current crisis. Writing under James, Dryden is less fiery than he had been in Charles's reign, in part because of external circumstances and in part because his interests and concerns had shifted.

Dryden's satire in the reign of William is so far removed from his earlier work that it might have been written by a different man. To some extent it was: gone is the imposing poet laureate and self-assured believer in the status quo. Dryden in Williamite England is embittered and financially stressed; he is a Catholic in a violently (and, as of 1689, officially) anti-Catholic country. He can no longer afford to execrate his enemies in direct invectives—his enemies are in power.[21] Dryden scholars have convincingly demonstrated the presence of veiled anti-William, even Jacobite, sentiment in his late works. He recognized, observes Kirk Combe, that "Frank, laureate declarations . . . were no longer his prerogative."[22] If we measure *King Arthur* by the standards of *Absalom and Achitophel*, then we miss the mark by a very great distance. Dryden's position changed in 1688, and so—necessarily—did his motives and methods as a satirist.

Several of Dryden's post-Revolution works include quasi-covert satire, though the type and degree of indirectness and ambiguity varies. *Eleonora* (1692; 6d*) has been taken as an indictment of Williamite England, but the vehicle for Dryden's complaint about a fallen world is a richly poetic elegy praising the recently deceased Countess of Abingdon. His commendation of the countess is, Winn suggests, "the satire that he dares not write."[23] *Cleomenes* (1692) indisputably expresses sympathy for James II: an exiled king plots from afar to reclaim his throne, but his attempted revolution fails, making the piece a tragedy. Queen Mary initially forbade the staging of *Cleomenes* but relented within a week. In the preface to the printed version, which takes its epigraph from Juvenal, Dryden disingenuously denies the play's political application: "I dare assure you, that here is no Parallel to be found: 'Tis neither Compliment, nor Satyr; but a plain Story."[24] The political message must have been clear to theatergoers and welcome to some of them, but Dryden did not make it explicit. His 1693 translations include much anti-Williamite satire; his modernization of the original works and his added details made contemporary application unmistakable.[25] *Alexander's Feast* (1697), the translation of Virgil's *Aeneid* (1697), and *Fables Ancient and Modern* (1700) have likewise been read for surreptitious Jacobite sentiments.[26] In the reign of William, Dryden writes a number of works that are—sometimes definitely, sometimes arguably or plausibly—satiric, but he is in no position to issue thundering denunciations.

Much of Dryden's Williamite satire depends upon the perception of the audience: he wishes not to offend the authorities, but he does want to communicate a negative point of view to that part of the audience whose assumptions allow them to identify and comprehend it. In the *Fables*, for example, his satire really only reaches those who sufficiently share his outlook to understand what he does not make explicit. The late-life Dryden shares something with Defoe in the realm of satiric practice: neither writes in order to change minds or to persuade opponents to see reason, but instead they (sometimes) design their arguments primarily for like-minded readers or viewers. Dryden adds cover or lightens the tone to avoid alienating or enraging the rest of his audience. The point is elementary but needs to be made: Dryden cannot afford to go after his enemies directly, and nothing would be gained if he did. Those whom he wants to perceive his concealed satire will presumably perceive it, and those whom he wants to miss it will miss it or will at least be unable to prove it. The results lack the punch of satire written from a position of authority, but they are no less skillfully crafted and can be remarkably forceful.

Amphitryon (1690) is a great play and a tremendous satire with brutally clear implications about the abuse of power. The basic plotline is as follows: Zeus (an imperious tyrant) assumes Amphitryon's shape in order to bed his wife; when the deceit is revealed to the victims, the omnipotent adulterer's response is essentially "What are you going to do about it?" The finale resolves nothing. Amphitryon is outraged, his wife has been abused, and whether they will stay together or separate is uncertain. Despite the seriousness of the plot, *Amphitryon* has comic gusto. Mercury inquires of Zeus, preparing for another intrigue, "whether you wou'd recreate your self in Feathers, or in Leather?"[27] The combination of mordant political commentary and racy farce is peculiar but effective. The play is darkly cynical and its author disillusioned, but the sexual humor and the slapstick make it, in Winn's phrasing, "one of Dryden's funniest comedies."[28] Dryden does not force-feed his audience scathing political satire: Zeus's victims are not terribly sympathetic, the supernatural plot and remote setting work against topical application, and the lively tone means that those resistant to the play's harsh message could ignore it.[29]

Amphitryon is undoubtedly satirical, but would audience members have applied its argument to a specific person or situation—namely, to William or Williamite England?[30] The identification of William with Zeus (wanton monarchical playboy) is a stretch; the fit with Charles II is closer but implausible coming from Dryden. I would argue that the satire makes a general statement about power and justice. Rather than depicting the current king on the stage, Dryden seems interested in inculcating a specific viewpoint in those members of his audience who can be receptive to it. The point is not that viewers see the play and think of William but that perhaps some of them will remember the play—and its ideological position—when they think of William and will judge accordingly. This kind of satire is a far cry from *Mac Flecknoe* and remote from *Cleomenes*, which is indirect but clearly targets real-world particulars. *Amphitryon* represents more ideological satire: Dryden is trying to instill certain patterns of thought.

Dryden and Henry Purcell's *King Arthur* (1691) is a yet more problematical case. Given Dryden's acute disgruntlement in the 1690s, scholars have been inclined to see this work as another expression of hostility toward William, and it can, after a fashion, be read that way. But we have no evidence that contemporaries understood *King Arthur* as emphatically anti-Williamite, and some modern critics have promulgated reverse readings, arguing that Oswald (the invader) represents Charles/James or that the identification shifts from Charles to James to William over the course of the opera.[31] The text itself does not sustain either allegorical reading. Probably, Dryden deliberately crafted an ambiguous piece. The play's nationalism would have pleased devoted Whigs and Williamites, but for disaffected Jacobites "the story must have rung hollow, and there are a variety of sour ironies to be found along the way."[32] Oppositional audience members might have perceived a welcome attack on the new monarch, and Dryden might have wanted them to do so, but that reading is not provable from the text.

Dryden's satiric practices in the last decade of his life differ markedly from what he did in the reign of Charles, and his *Discourse concerning Satire* has precious little to do with any of it. In the *Discourse*, printed with his translations of Juvenal and Persius, Dryden attempts to make what had become in England a rather disreputable form of writing into a creditable artistic mode. Following Casaubon, Dacier, and others, he defines satire in terms of a respectable classical tradition, emphasizing moral purpose and artistic refinement and insisting that good satire presents positives as well as negatives, virtue as well as vice. He renounces the lampoon as "a dangerous sort of Weapon, and for the most part Unlawful": the satirist should not damage a man's reputation unless that man is "a Publick Nuisance" (4:59, 60). The *Discourse* is not an attempt to codify past and present practices, and neither do Dryden's contemporaries produce works that seem to exemplify his theory. He projects an idealized concept, "not so much what satire was and had been as what Dryden and his followers wanted it to be."[33] The *Discourse* was designed to illumine Roman formal verse satire, so its irrelevance to what Dryden does in drama is not surprising. But even *Mac Flecknoe* and *Absalom and Achitophel*, or the more explicitly positive *Albion and Albanius*, are far from being practical illustrations of his satiric theory.

The *Discourse* is not, however, merely an abstract statement of theory. The commendation of Juvenal has pronounced satiric edge. Comparing Juvenal to Persius and the "Mild" Horace, Dryden concludes that

> *Juvenal* was as proper for his Times, as they for theirs. His was an Age that deserv'd
> a more severe Chastisement. Vices were more gross and open, more flagitious, more
> encourag'd by the Example of a Tyrant; and more protected by his Authority. There-
> fore, wheresover *Juvenal* mentions *Nero*, he means *Domitian*, whom he dares not
> attack in his own Person, but Scourges him by Proxy. (4:69)

Dryden does not mention William, but he identifies himself with Juvenal and so makes manifest his opinion of the usurper now on the throne. If the grander precepts loudly trumpeted in the *Discourse* do not explain Dryden's practices, the praise of Juvenal supplies a not-very-subtle signal that he is perfectly aware of the possibilities for indirect satire. Author of *Amphitryon* and the *Fables*, translator of Juvenal, the Dryden of the 1690s knows how (and why) to scourge the king by proxy.

Dryden's satiric output changes with his circumstances. As a Carolean satirist, he delivered judgments; he made a case, often for a specific audience; the authorial position was readily discernible. The satires belonging to the reign of James are likewise straightforward, if less vehement. In his post-Revolution satires, he is alert to multiple audiences (in particular, people of his own mind and Williamites) and more evasive. Winn says of late-life Dryden that his "cause was indeed lost, but he was willing to be a 'patient Sufferer,' supporting himself by his pen, and he did not regard the occasional political jibes in his plays and prologues as threatening any real disturbance to the government."[34] In the satires for which he is most famous, Dryden assumed that his argument would carry weight. Here, he has no hope of real influence, and that, in satire, changes everything. The Dryden discussed by satire scholars is the "pen for a party," a propagandist, a self-assured activist. The author of *Absalom and Achitophel* and *The Duke of Guise* had an agenda, and his political satires are largely defined by what they are defending. But what is *Amphitryon* written *for*? What imaginable practical effect could *Eleonora* have?

Dryden's late-life satires depend almost completely upon application by readers,[35] and this bespeaks a radically different satiric purpose from anything he wrote in Charles's or James's reign. His argument in *Amphitryon* and the *Fables* is sufficiently guarded that his opponents do not have to be offended, and those contemporaries inclined to agree with him can discern the critical commentary. In other words, Dryden has no practical object for writing. In his Carolean satire, he had defended the status quo, taking up his pen against change; during James's tenure, he had advocated discreet amendments in line with the monarch's preferences and sympathies; under William, he is out of favor and grumbling, directing his complaints not at those whom he hopes to influence but at those who share his unhappiness. Post-Revolution Dryden is a disaffected Catholic needing to make a living off his writing without pledging loyalty to a king whose accession he perceived as usurpation. No pen for his party, he is essentially powerless—a satirist without a viable cause.

What kind of satirist is Dryden? The question is not answerable with a single characterization. At no point is his output uniform—the 1670s and early 1680s satiric writings are especially varied—and as I have been arguing, there is little connection between the Carolean and later phases of his career. In satiric terms, how much does *The Kind Keeper* have in common with *Amphitryon*? What relates *Alexander's Feast* to *Mac Flecknoe*? Dryden is capable of smut and viciousness and heartfelt defense; he is often powerfully assertive (*Absalom and Achitophel*), occasionally wryly resigned to a reality he cannot change (*Marriage A-la-Mode*), sometimes grumpy (his *Juvenal*). He has often been touted as the dignified forebear of moralizing "Augustan" satire, and critic after critic has looked to him for evidence in support of high-minded claims about satire's reformative potential and socioethical utility. Taking *Absalom and Achitophel* and the *Discourse* alone, one can (with some coercive reading) conclude that Dryden was a straitlaced satiric moralizer; looking at his entire satiric oeuvre yields a different picture. The notion that he was a satirist of lofty moral aims strikes me as simply wrong. He was a master craftsman of enormous literary talent and ambition, and he was a celebrity, but his concerns were often grittily political and circumstantial. He played dirty when he was so inclined, he took the hard line when he could afford to do so, and he limited himself to grousing, painfully aware of his own ineffectuality, when he was no longer a government man.

III. Poetic Satire

Accounts of eighteenth-century satiric poetry often jump from *Mac Flecknoe* and *Absalom and Achitophel* to *The Rape of the Lock* or *The Dunciad*, effectively skipping the decades in between. My objective here is in part to map a territory that has never hitherto been charted, but we need also to understand these works as responses to the changing world described in section I. Modern satire scholars dismiss this material in toto, regarding the likes of Defoe, Tutchin, Ward, Brown, Garth, Blackmore, and Gould as minor-league hack poets. And so they mostly are: Ward is an often clumsy versifier, Gould has no restraint whatever, and Blackmore is something of a blowhard, but qualitative evaluation is not the point. What is at issue is characterizing the natures of their enterprises.

What we find in post-Carolean satiric verse is varied experimentation, necessitated by changes in target audience and print culture. Not all of the experimentation is successful, but it does reflect different authors' attempts to reach a broadening readership. No tidy subgeneric divisions are to be found, and I see no object in pretending otherwise. The organization that I have adopted reflects my conviction that what is most important and interesting about this material is its shift away from Carolean norms. I therefore begin with types of verse satire that seem to carry over in some way from the reign of Charles II—in particular, political and defamatory satire. I then survey kinds of writing that are drastically unlike anything in the 1660s and 1670s, including works by Garth and Blackmore, as well as satires definitely intended for print, often with commercial motives and aimed at a general audience.

Tutchin, Defoe, and Political Satire

As in the reign of Charles II, scores of satires address politics, monarchs, and the state of the country. Unlike Carolean political satire, however, much of the verse produced in this period is, for reasons I have already discussed, relatively small scale. Not all but many satirists in the 1670s and early 1680s addressed order and monarchy, imagined and feared major changes, and worried about social and political instability. In the late seventeenth century, political satires are much more constrained by the particular circumstances and much less burningly important. They fall into three broad categories: triumphalism, complaint, and defense.

(1) *Triumphalism.* Pointless triumphalism in Carolean satire was atypical but not unheard of—see the cheerful Tory satires following Shaftesbury's departure from London. Exultant derogation is not at all common under William, but some exemplars can be found in James's short reign. The conviction of Titus Oates for perjury in May 1685 inspired celebratory pieces like *The Salamanca Doctor's Farewel* and *The Tragick-Comedy of Titus Oates*, playful works penned by writers delighted to see Oates—persona non grata but not a threat—get his comeuppance. A less lively but equally aimless set of poems appeared after Monmouth's defeat at Sedgemoor: *The Western Rebel, Monmouth Degraded*, and Prior's *Advice to the Painter. On the happy defeat of the Rebels in the West* denigrate the vanquished insurgents. They could imaginably have been intended also to bolster James's regime, though in the late summer of 1685 he did not really need such reinforcement. Some of the satires following the king's flight three years later are likewise gleeful but have more significant implications. *The Scamperers*, Henry Mildmay's (?) *The Progress*, and *A Hue and Cry* mock the recently fled monarch, the first giddily observing that "the coming of Orange has quite spoil'd the jest" (l. 27). To celebrate the "abdication" is de facto to acquiesce in the new regime, but for the most part satiric triumphalism is pointless revelry.

(2) *Complaint*. Political satire is often simply complaint, with no more practical purpose than triumphalism. While some such works were imaginably intended to reinforce or challenge the legitimacy of the current regime, most seem merely to vent unhappiness or record grievances. The author of *The Humble Address* (wr. 1685) takes a gloomy view of James's accession, grimly foretelling that the English will "become slaves to the French" (l. 9); his tone reflects not hostility as much as resignation. The Revolution did not quiet querulous satirists. Those who ultimately approved of William's takeover were not necessarily upbeat about the new king's preferment policies, his push for a comprehensive Church of England, his foreign underlings, or his entangling England in a long and costly war in aid of the much-reviled Dutch. *A Pindarick Ode, in the Praise of Folly and Knavery* (1696; 6*d*), written by the violently anti-Stuart John Tutchin, voices real personal acrimony. Having been dismissed from a minor government post, Tutchin inveighs against a corrupt society in which the loyal are punished.[36] He is especially sour, but many supporters of the Revolution objected to particular episodes in William's reign. When the king went to Ireland in 1690, he left Mary and nine counselors to govern England; the prompt embarrassment of the navy at the battle off Beachy Head shook national pride and roused much antagonism toward the regency. The acting administration is excoriated in Mulgrave's (?) *The Nine*, the Earl of Monmouth's *The Female Nine*, and the anonymous *Reflections on the Council of Nine*. Like Tutchin, these satirists are expressing frustration—not trying to agitate against the monarch, whose practices they dislike but whose reign they support.

More thoroughly anti-Williamite and Jacobite satires are legion, but few reflect serious hope for another Stuart restoration. The early Jacobite works are trenchant but glum. Poems like Arthur Maynwaring's *Tarquin and Tullia* (wr. 1689) and *The Reflection* (wr. 1689) "leave the reader with the unmistakable impression that the author is writing for a lost cause."[37] The author of *Advice to a Painter* (wr. 1697) is pessimistic in his response to the Treaty of Ryswick, the end of the war, and William's homecoming. He assumes the impossibility of improvement, encouraging the painter to leave some "vacant Room" on the canvas "For Knaves in Embrio, and Rogues to come; / Who undiscover'd, yet will us betray, / And sell their Country in a closer way" (ll. 143–146).[38] Satirists for William, against William, and for James articulate much discontent—varying in kind and intensity—but are often reacting negatively to something already determined, bemoaning what cannot be changed.

(3) *Defense*. In the reigns of James and especially William, a number of satirists comment on issues of policy, apparently hoping for a desired present-day outcome, not griping or generalizing or retrospectively bashing an enemy. Many such satires, moreover, are as defensive as they are offensive. The possibility of satiric "defense" has not been much considered, as scholars tend to understand satire principally as an

offensive instrument; *Absalom and Achitophel* is the only defensive satire that gets much attention from modern critics. But Defoe, one of the best-known political satirists in the reign of William, often writes defensive satire, and so do his contemporaries. *The Man of Honor* (wr. 1687; pub. 1689) extols those who, uncompelled by "the threats or favors of a crown" (l. 1), refused to convert to serve James; the satirist (Charles Montagu?) devotes most of his poem to praise, becoming explicitly negative only at the end. The trial of the seven bishops (1688)—one of the great mistakes of James's reign—produced a number of satiric responses. *The Dissenters' Thanksgiving for the Late Declaration* is an occasional poem written without a clear-cut authorial position, and *The Clerical Cabal* and *The Sentiments* are both sharply anticlerical. Other satiric responses are much more positive. *A New Catch in Praise of the Reverend Bishops* loudly sings the bishops' praises, and *The Church of England's Glory* blasts them for sedition and champions James.

The Church of England and ecclesiastical policy loom large in the political satire of William's reign. Attacks on the nonjurors are also defenses of the new monarch, as in *Marvell's Ghost* (wr. 1691), whose author deprecates the nonswearers for defying the king and weakening the country. William's push for religious comprehension produced a flurry of satiric responses. Maynwaring's (?) *Suum Cuique* (wr. 1689) defends the High Anglican position, contesting the proposed liturgy reform that would reconcile moderate dissenters to the church, and the author of *Vox Clero, Lilli burlero* (wr. 1689) advocates comprehension. William and Mary's policies of ecclesiastical preferment—nonjurors were stripped of their positions and replaced by oath takers—were heatedly objected to.[39] *On the Promoted Bishops* (wr. 1691) denounces this patronage system and the elevated clergy; so do *The Divorce* and *A Litany for the Monthly Fast* (both wr. 1692), which also implicitly back the nonjurors and the system disrupted by the new regime. Many satires of the decade are passionately anticlerical, including Tutchin's *The Tribe of Levi* (1691; 2*d**), but the clergy had their partisans. One response to Tutchin, the anonymous *Rabshakeh Vapulans* (1691; 6*d**), is as defensive of priests as it is antagonistic toward Tutchin and other satirists. Luttrell's gloss emphasizes this satire's positive agenda: "A poem in vindicacon of ye Clergy."[40] Writers and readers of political verse clearly understood "defense" as a legitimate and worthy motive for satire.

Defoe's early verse satires are written against William's enemies in staunch support of England's Protestant savior. In *A New Discovery of an Old Intreague* (1691), he lampoons a group of Jacobite petitioners creating unrest under the hero-king and recalls the nightmare of absolutism under James II. In the first decade of his satiric career, Defoe repeatedly claims that England has been delivered from the Catholic threat by William. In *The Mock Mourners* (1702, nine editions in that year; 6*d**), he lambastes the English ingrates who rejoice in the king's death (the satirical "elegies" for William were indeed rancorous).[41] Defoe's poem was written, says Luttrell, "in great Commendation" of the late sovereign.[42] But his most celebrated verse satire, *The True-Born Englishman*, had appeared while the king still reigned, and it illustrates a fundamental change between Carolean and Williamite satire.

The True-Born Englishman is a response to Tutchin's *The Foreigners* (1700).[43] Because of this pair of poems, Tutchin and Defoe are sometimes associated with each other, but the similarity is only in subject matter. Tutchin's satires are complaints, vitriolic expressions of disapproval and disgruntlement; he almost always writes against, Defoe almost always for, the cause at issue. *The Foreigners* could imaginably have had a practical purpose—unlike the strictly grumpy *A Pindarick Ode* and *The British Muse: or Tyranny Expos'd. A Satyr* (1702)—but it has nothing like the positive thrust evident in Defoe's most famous poem. *The Foreigners* was inspired by xenophobia, but Tutchin is perhaps hoping also to rally public opinion yet more intensely against foreign-born men in power. He does not impugn William, instead blaming Israel's (i.e., England's) problems on "crafty Knaves at home" (the Whig junto) and "a Foreign Brood" (ll. 48, 49). Whatever Tutchin's intentions, the government was not amused; he was arrested for libel, though his strategy of covert naming—Bentir for Bentick—prevented his prosecution.[44]

Defoe likewise perceived in *The Foreigners* an attack not only on the Dutch but on the king himself. His response is a thoroughgoing defense of William, the heaven-sent alternative to James, in which he accuses the malcontents of ingratitude toward their Protestant hero-king and toward Providence, whence salvation had come, and so indicts them as "Rebels to God, and to Good Nature too" (l. 960). Like *Absalom and Achitophel*, *The True-Born Englishman* is a defense of the current monarchy and a satire on the king's enemies. Dryden and Defoe are both championing their sovereign and sniping at his attackers. That the results are different is not just a matter of poetic talent. The striking discrepancy between *Absalom and Achitophel* and *The True-Born Englishman* has to do with the position of the authors—Dryden is a loyal "insider" and Defoe a dissenting "outsider"—and also with a shift in the nature of political satire from Carolean England to the late century. That Dryden is an abler poet than Defoe is not in question, though Defoe has his moments. Perhaps he could not have written anything like *Absalom and Achitophel*, but the point is that he had no need to do so.

Gould and Defamatory Satire

Like political satire, nonpolitical defamatory satire was written in the reigns of Charles, James, and William, but again there is a fundamental change from the Carolean to the post-Carolean period. For reasons I have already explained, defamatory satire at the end of the century is increasingly generalized. With the shift from scribal circulation to print, moreover, touchy satire became a riskier prospect. Subject to libel charges, publishers were understandably resistant to issuing the sort of vulgar, slanderous fare that had thrived in a world of manuscript transmission. Derogatory satire is not, in these years, what it had been for Rochester, Butler, and their contemporaries. We need to ask, therefore, what sort of satires in this mode are written in this period, by whom, and why.

The best-known and perhaps the most prolific defamatory satirist was Robert Gould. Gould produced quite a lot of scabrous verse in this period, penning obscenities worthy of Rochester and railing with a ferocity worthy of Oldham. Although his often-reprinted *Love given o're* originally appeared in 1682, most of his satires date from the reigns of James and William, and what he writes is much more typical of satire in the late 1680s and 1690s than of Carolean satire. Few satirists in the seventies and early eighties had professed a moral basis for their condemnation. Gould does precisely that, slashing individuals and groups and all of humanity in what Susan M. Martin describes as "fiercely moral" and "viciously negative" satire.[45] In the prologue to the "Satyrs and Epistles" section of *Poems Chiefly consisting of Satyrs and Satyrical Epistles* (1689), Gould insists that "Mankind is Criminal, their Acts, their Thoughts;/ 'Tis Charity to tell 'em of their Fau'ts" and that satire "is our truest Friend,/ For none before they know their Faults can mend" (132, 134). But despite his loud trumpeting of reformative intentions, his aim is not to correct but to abuse and punish.

Because Gould writes for print rather than for a small coterie, he either deprecates general types or people with considerable public reputations. In *The Laureat* (1687), he ravages Dryden as a turncoat, as villainous as his Achitophel and less "stedfast" than his Zimri (1, 2). Dryden is but one of Gould's targets in *A Satyr against the Playhouse* (in the 1689 *Poems*), where he scorns a degenerate playhouse, the playwrights, the actors and actresses, and the audience. Gould's account of the stage's dissipation is damning, Martin points out, but "he makes no attempt whatsoever to propose a remedy for the ills which he perceives."[46] The negativity is familiar enough, but the severity of Gould's moral fervor is unusual, distinguishing him from Oldham and other Carolean predecessors. How much readership he would have enjoyed in Charles's reign I have to wonder. The overt moral imperative behind his verse reflects the changing assumptions of writers and readers vis-à-vis certain kinds of damaging satire.

A high percentage of the defamatory verse in this period is exceedingly general.[47] Gould's most famous satire is *Love given o're: or, a Satyr against the Pride, Lust, Inconstancy, &c. of Woman*, a violent attack that inspired many antifemale satires and generated feminist counterattacks. No doubt Gould was a misogynist—he seems to have been a thoroughgoing misanthrope—but few of the other participants in the antifeminist versus feminist satiric war have much venom. The first response to Gould was Sarah Fyge Egerton's *The Female Advocate* (1686; 4*d**), which Felicity A. Nussbaum hails as "a prototype of defenses of the sex."[48] Egerton's retaliation predictably insists upon man's inconstancy and woman's rationality and devotedness. To the battle of the sexes Richard Ames contributed *Sylvia's Revenge, or, a Satyr against Man* (1688; 4*d**) and *The Folly of Love* (1691; 4*d**). The last piece is witty but biting, among the best of the she-satires, though it was evidently meant mostly to amuse and entertain.[49] For the most part, these works are primarily exercises in a highly popular form of generalized defamation.

These satires are varyingly incisive or playful, belligerent, or restrained, but their authors tend to recite standard charges in largely formulaic ways. Ames's *Sylvia's Revenge*—a "Satyr against Man"—is far tamer than, say, Rochester's *Satyre against Reason and Mankind*, and the blistering diatribe directed against the faithless Corinna in *A Ramble in St. James's Park* is acid and despairing in ways Gould's contemporaries never match. Rochester's rambler observes a horde of drunken libertines pursuing "The sav'ry scent of Salt-swolne *Cunt*" and watches in horror as his beloved welcomes their advances. Had his darling strumpet been more discriminating, the rambler explains, he would not be so disgusted—but she is "A Passive *Pot* for *Fools* to spend in," and he vows to ruin her life (ll. 86, 102). Rochester does not communicate a clear-cut positive or provide an indisputable moral norm. Gould, Ames, Egerton, and others are much sharper in their distinctions of good and bad, and also much less fiery. Beside Rochester, lines like these seem pale and abstract: "Woman, there's Ropes and Daggers in the Name; / The *Dregs* of the Creation, Nature's *Shame*" (*The Restor'd Maiden-head*, 5). These works are meant for wider consumption (and sold at prices cheap enough to make that possible), and the nature of the satire reflects that expectation. Given the popularity and success of Gould's *Love given o're*, we have to entertain the possibility that some contributors to this battle of the sexes simply had an eye to the main chance and were peddling spirited misogyny on the grounds that it would sell.

What is not debatable is that, however "moral" the attacks on female or male inconstancy, lust, and immodesty claim to be, they were not meant to reform their targets. And though they are plenty abusive, their potential to do real damage is limited. Denigratory satire in the reign of Charles II was abundant and often brutal. Like political satire of that period, it tended to be present centered, local, particularized, and ultimately pragmatic in terms of wishing for a negative outcome for the target. Satirists named names and flayed individuals with gruesome clarity and verve, and, for the most part, they could count on their readers to "get" (and to relish) the abuse. Because of the changes in court culture, attacks on individuals become much less viable after 1688, and there are a lot fewer of them. James's court was not his brother's. Unlike Charles, he cultivated an "image of frugality, sobriety, and more refined ceremony," and insofar as possible, scandal was kept "out of sight." William and Mary's court was yet more rigidly moralistic: the character of neither monarch "was conducive to the active social side of the court that could attract much 'wit.' "[50] In James's reign, and especially in William's, grist for the gossip mill and material for lampoonists was much harder to come by than it had been under Charles.

Such satire as did get directed at court figures is considerably less cutting than it had been in the quarter century after the Restoration. *The Compleat Fop* (wr. 1685) mildly mocks a common court type; *The Two Tom Lucys* (wr. 1686) tamely recounts the recent misdeeds of a couple of courtiers; *Madam Le Croix* (wr. 1686) is a lifeless summary of recent court scandals; *Julian's Farewell to the Coquets* (wr. 1687) targets an insignificant family. Among the liveliest court satires is *The Session of Ladies* (wr. 1688), whose graphic coarseness sets it apart from other examples from James's reign: the satirist describes "pockey lewd Hinton," the "chestnut-maned Boutell, whom all the Town fucks," and "chaste Mrs. Barry," who makes a lover "a present of chancre and pox" (ll. 29, 33, 35–36). With few exceptions, however, the court satires of the late seventeenth century are without real bite, and they target figures of marginal importance. The decline of nasty personal satire is disappointing for those who revel in derisive Carolean scurrility, but the falling off of lampoonery was made all but inevitable by radically altered extraliterary circumstances.

Garth and Blackmore

Sir Samuel Garth and Sir Richard Blackmore were celebrities in their day, though of a very different sort. Garth was a physician of some stature but was scarcely known outside his profession before the publication of *The Dispensary* in 1699. With that poem, Richard I. Cook explains, he "was elevated almost overnight to a position of eminence among the wits of the literary world."[51] Blackmore was much reviled: he was, in Richard Terry's phrasing, "perhaps the most roundly and routinely vilified of all English poets."[52] Neither Garth nor Blackmore wrote to make a living, and we have nothing to suggest that Garth sought a literary reputation. Their satire was public and signed, but it was neither chiefly defamatory (like Gould's) nor principally commercial (like Ward's). Both Blackmore and Garth are decidedly non-Carolean authors: nothing quite like Garth's poem is found in the reign of Charles II, and one can imagine what the likes of Rochester and Butler would have said about Blackmore's moralizing. And yet neither do Garth and Blackmore seem "like" most of their contemporary verse satirists. Given the originality, atypicality, and popularity of *The Dispensary*, the relative paucity of modern critical comment on that poem is surprising.

What sort of satire did Garth and Blackmore produce, and why was Garth's in particular so successful?

The Dispensary is a mock epic in six cantos describing a wrangle between physicians and dispensarians, a battle that had been raging throughout the 1690s. Garth and his allies (physicians) wanted to establish a dispensary where lower-class patients could buy medicine cheaply; their opponents (mostly apothecaries, though also some physicians) resisted mightily, eager to protect their profits. In 1696, the Committee on Medicines passed a resolution requiring all members to contribute money toward "the furnishing [of] a Repository of Medicines, out of wch the poor shall be supplied."[53] Garth was one of the first to sign. Two years later the dispensary was open for business, though the apothecaries and their supporters continued to voice opposition.

Garth's poem belongs to this debate, narrating in mock-heroic fashion the skirmish between the physicians on one side and, on the other, the druggist Horoscope, the greedy Querpo, the pretentious and untalented Bard (Blackmore), and the rest of the antidispensarians. Although *The Dispensary* does not end with the physicians triumphant, the poem clearly supports them. Garth ridicules the druggists, comically but thoroughly and caustically. When Horoscope faints in the second canto, he is revived by his assistant ("Officious *Squirt*"), who applies "Steam" from a urinal; when he decides in canto III to take action, he invokes the goddess Disease, promising that in return for her help, the apothecaries will "fix [her] Empire"—that is, the druggists will work against good health (17, 22).[54] The dispensarians are not exactly glorified, but they are only lightly mocked, and alongside their enemies they appear much more sympathetic. And though Garth lampoons the antidispensarians, the title of the poem names that which the poet supports, not what he condemns, and his satiric agenda is positive as much as negative.

The Dispensary has been described in blandly general terms—Garth's "purpose is moral reformation"—and as a bridge between the mock heroics of Dryden and Pope.[55] But Garth's poem has little in common with Dryden's lampooning of a literary rival, and neither does it have much to do with Pope's battering of the dunces—or, for that matter, his eloquent and well-crafted account of Lord Petre's cutting of a lovelock from Arabella Fermor. Neither, finally, is it adequately characterized as a poem concerned about the "danger to traditional institutions from the chaos of individual interests" or as an attempt "to transform the contemporary conflict between London physicians and druggists into an Homeric *agon*."[56] For one thing, Garth is having a lot of fun. And while he may have wanted his poem to transcend its moment, his main objective appears to have been to influence a particular issue at a particular time. In the preface to the poem's second edition, he insists that he wrote *The Dispensary* in an "endeavor to Rally some of our disaffected Members [of the Royal College of Physicians, e.g., Blackmore] into a Sense of their Duty." And Garth's satire was taken in that manner. "So well-received was the poem," Cook explains, "that two historians of the Society of Apothecaries credit Garth with having all but chased the opposition from the field," though, as Cook also points out, antidispensarian counterblasts attested to a still-vocal opposition.[57]

Blackmore's *Satyr against Wit* is at once a hostile reply to Garth's attack on him and a continuation of his own moralistic literary program. Blackmore led the "Apothecaries Physicians" against the building of the dispensary, and he is part of the opposition caricatured in Garth's poem, an ally of the ridiculous Horoscope and the avaricious Querpo. As commentators on the Garth-Blackmore battle have recognized, however, Garth sneers at his enemy's verses, not his position on the drug repository. One suspects that Garth knew enough of Blackmore to understand that derision of his literary principles and talents would have especial sting: Samuel Johnson reflected that Blackmore "wrote not for a livelihood but for fame; or, if he may tell his own motives, for a nobler purpose, to engage poetry in the cause of Virtue."[58] However righteous his stated aims, Blackmore was the butt of many wits' jokes, and he gave as much—if rarely as good—as he got. He perceived social evil in some of his contemporaries (especially Dryden, Congreve, Garth, and Southerne), and he pointed this out in no uncertain terms in *Prince Arthur* and *King Arthur*.[59]

In *A Satyr against Wit*, he again champions a reformation of literary manners, rebuking many of the wits for their contribution to the degeneracy of the times. Blackmore charges the "Insect-Wits" (l. 8) with threatening to ruin the country, and however overblown the indictment, he evidently means it. The wits whom Blackmore targets are, from his perspective, obscene blasphemers; he calls for higher standards, urging readers to recognize the profanity of these writers' works. Blackmore claims a dignified moral basis for his denunciation of immoral wits, but he also slings a fair amount of dirt. He names names, and he includes his share of crudity even as he declaims against obscene wit: the poets he describes "strain / Always to say fine Things, but strive in vain / Urg'd with a dry *Tenesmus* of the Brain" (ll. 39–41).

I have argued that the prominence of generalized satire in this period is one response to changes in audience and assumed bases of knowledge; *The Dispensary* and the *Satyr against Wit* represent another possibility. Garth's satire is highly topical, but it could afford to be. Garth is addressing an issue well and widely known, a public controversy of considerable social import and apparently of interest to many readers. Blackmore's poem is loosely connected to the same debate; its title page describes it as a response to *The Dispensary*, and Blackmore undoubtedly hoped to capitalize on the popularity of his rival's blockbuster. His *Satyr* is at once social commentary on a conspicuous issue, a response to Garth penned by a piqued victim, and a piece of spiteful defamation made intelligible by the public status of its targets. *The Dispensary* and the *Satyr against Wit* resemble Ward's generalized entertainments or Gould's unconstructive grumblings not at all. Garth and Blackmore found a readership by other means.

Brown, Ward, and Commercial Satire

In the reign of Charles II, many gentlemen had written satire, though rarely for print. After 1688, a noticeably smaller percentage of satire was produced by the gentry. There were some exceptions: Garth wrote for a cause, Blackmore for a reputation, Prior in the hopes of patronage. The likes of Sir Fleetwood Sheppard and the Earl of Dorset wrote but did not publish satire. The commercial satirist is a category without parallel in the Carolean period, and on average the social level of verse satirists is distinctly lower in the 1690s than it had been two decades earlier. Neither Tom Brown nor Ned Ward is producing gutter journalism, but their work is essentially popular and commercial; their satires, at least initially, are not printed in great books or sold at high prices.[60] They pay little attention to literary quality or philosophical profundity. Ward and Brown are often lumped together with Gould, Defoe, and hack poets of this period, but they share little with those writers. And although they both lived by the pen, writing for bread and writing a lot, in satiric practice they also differ significantly from each other.

Brown is sui generis—he does not fit any single category well. Although he is chiefly remembered as a "facetious" hack poet who led a rowdy personal life, there is more to him than that. Many of his prose and verse pieces are neither playful nor frivolous. He is influenced by the classics; his most famous collection, *Amusements Serious and Comical* (1700), is largely a translation of a 1699 French work of that title; and he is surprisingly learned and bookish, proudly erudite in a way Ward is not. Brown is capable of lighthearted and mischievous banter, as in some of his contributions to the *Commendatory Verses* written against Blackmore, and equally capable of blistering personal abuse and biting political commentary. His attack on Dryden in *The Reasons of Mr. Bays Changing his Religion* (1688) has nothing to do with religious issues in general or *The Hind and the Panther* in particular; it is simply vindictive detraction. His 1707 *Works* include a concentrated version of this satire, *To Mr. Dryden, on his Conversion*, where he rebukes Dryden as "Traytor to God, and Rebel to thy Pen" (1:17). Brown pokes fun at Thomas Durfey's stutter and derides his principles in *To the Author of Gloriana* (wr. 1695), and he writes cutting epigrams on Blackmore: "Thine is the only muse in British ground, / Whose *satire* tickles and whose *praises* wound."[61]

Brown bludgeons individuals with conspicuous energy, and his tongue is just as sharp in his political satires.[62] His *Advice To the Kentish Long-Tails* (1701) is accusatory, but his most trenchant sociopolitical satire is *A Satyr upon the French King* (1697; 1d*). In this response to the Treaty of Ryswick, Brown curses Louis and ruthlessly mocks the plight of the Jacobites. A High Tory—but no Catholic—he asks,

Who cou'd have e're believ'd, unless in Spite,
Lewis le Grand wou'd turn rank *Williamite*?
Thou, that hast Look'd so fierce, and Talk'd so bigg,
In thy Old Age to dwindle to a *Whigg*! (ll. 14–17)

The persona is admittedly an unsympathetic figure, but, as Frank H. Ellis points out, his catalog of personal losses constitutes "the emotional center of the poem. . . . Since 1689 the speaker has lived in London on pawn tickets, credit, and the hope of a second Stuart restoration."[63] The government took offense, and Brown was arrested.[64] As a satirist, Brown is by turns good humored and sneering. He writes some general sketches of London lowlife but many highly particularized attacks, and he addresses current events like Sherlock's conversion and the Kent petition, but he rarely appears to be seeking a practical positive effect.[65] He does, however, pass judgment, with varying degrees of intensity and sharpness. The penetratingly judgmental quality of his satire, his propensity for piercing sarcasm, and his frequent targeting of specific individuals all distinguish him from his contemporary and fellow commercial hack Ned Ward.

Most of Ward's early satires are generalized and apparently meant to amuse, though some of his later efforts (covered in the next chapter) are more politicized. In *Sot's Paradise: or, The Humours of a Derby-Ale-House* (1698), he criticizes cheating vintners and alehouse keepers in rollicking hudibrastics. The speaker, "Loaded with Sorrow" (5), heads for the alehouse to find solace but, frustrated by the drunken fools he meets, he crawls home disappointed. *Labour in Vain: or, What Signifies Little or Nothing* (1700; *6d*) and *A Journey to Hell* (in three parts, 1700–1705) are both essentially funny pieces. In *A Journey to Hell*, Ward attacks dissenting ministers, physicians, apothecaries, vintners, wits, lawyers, careless printers, and roguish publishers. Some representatives of targeted groups issued counterattacks,[66] but whatever the social barbs present in his satire, Ward's purpose was evidently diversion, not reformation or even punitive attack. His comic narratives usually supply everything a reader needs to comprehend the satire. His first known work and one of his most famous pieces—*The Poet's Ramble after Riches* (1691)—is a jaunty romp, an exercise in mildly satirical storytelling. One episode in particular has some political zing: the speaker reports to a friend that James has been dethroned, and William is described not as Protestant savior but as barbaric usurper. But the speaker finishes his account of the coup and promptly asks for supper, unfazed by the news he has delivered. Ward occasionally raises serious issues in passing, but at least early in his career they are not the point. They serve to locate the satire, to make the story all the more relevant to English readers of the 1690s. *A Trip to Jamaica* (1698; *6d*) relates a real-life journey, no doubt with poetic license: Ward was sorely disappointed when he went seeking his fortune in Jamaica, and here he voices disgust with the island and its people. His vituperative travelogue was evidently popular.[67]

Ward used the "journey" motif again and again as a vehicle for lightweight satirical reportage, often employing local settings that would have had special appeal for English readers.[68] *A Walk to Islington: with a Description of New Tunbridge-Wells, and Sadler's Musick-House* (1699; 2*d*) recounts the poet's brief sojourn in Islington with a woman from London, and presumably different readers would have responded differently to the satire. Those who belonged to the world described are likelier to have taken pleasure in recognition, in the familiarity of the account, than to have been offended, while outsiders could sneer at the neat putdown of rackety suburban London life. *The Rambling Rakes* (1700; 6*d*) and *Three Nights Adventures* (1701) are spicy tales of merrymaking, full of women and wine and nocturnal pleasures. In *The Rambling Rakes*, a prose piece, the speaker describes his visit to "the floating Seraglio," where he and his companions are greeted by "a Brace of Harlots," who tender "an invitation to Dance: The Countenance of the Whores, was an Antidote against Carnality to us; not but we were willing to be Lew'd, tho' not with such Common-Strumpets" (8). These two satires represent, in Troyer's phrasing, "Ward's most slavish attempts at catering to the baser tastes of his public."[69] This is not the stuff of solemn moralizing. We are not invited to judge the speaker. Like Ward's other works, these lack the "moral purpose" that satire theorists often emphasize as requisite to the form.[70]

Satire is neither a political weapon nor a moral instrument for Ward, at least early in his career. He is not trying to denounce, provoke thought, or make a case; his object is not to influence present-day circumstances, denigrate an enemy, or defend a cause, and the results are neither propaganda nor social commentary. Satire is Ward's trade, and he tells stories that will entice and entertain readers, cranking out waggish pop journalism keen to market his wares. Ward and Defoe are both usually regarded as mercenary drudges making their livings off of their pens, but they have little in common. I deal further with Defoe in chapter 5, but even the example of *The True-Born Englishman* suggests a major disparity between these two hack poets. Defoe's satire is an angry response to a perceived attack on the king whom he regarded as England's savior; his anti-Catholicism is deeply felt and crucially important to him and his view of the world. Here and elsewhere, Defoe's satire is, among other things, principled argumentation. Ward's commercial entertainments represent an entirely distinct concept of satire. J. Paul Hunter likens Ward not to Defoe but to Gould. They "announce their quarry with flailing bluster and claim huge consequence, but usually end up at best with superficial observation on insignificant matters," he says, and their "charges are often trivial, and the satire is bland, toothless and pretty insignificant."[71] The comparison has some utility: both Gould and Ward are responding to conditions that will not allow for much more than what they do. But as general as Gould's attacks are, they are also fulminatory and at least putatively driven by moral judgment. Ward does not claim for himself much consequence, and neither does he work up much steam. He is not a moral, sociopolitical, or defamatory satirist but a *commercial* one who produces a type of generalized satire common in the late seventeenth century but entirely without Carolean precedent.

Carolean poets did not commit much energy to satirizing abstractions. We find few attacks on money or alcohol or inconstancy in the period from 1660 to 1685. What gives the verse covered in chapter 3 much of its intensity is its specificity. Most of the political satire in the reigns of James and William is likewise topical, but at the end of the century a new category of verse satire appears: a number of writers hold forth against very general vices (e.g., love of money) or inanimate objects (e.g., wine). The lethal spirits are a favorite target of late seventeenth-century satirists: an anonymous poet rails against the "damn'd *Stygian* Juyce, that dost bewitch" in *A Satyr against Brandy* (1683), and other satirists pen comic poems on drinking and the geniality associated with inebriation (l. 1).[72] Writers complain about the universal pursuit of wealth, as do Gould in *The Corruption of the Times by Money* (1693) and Ward in *Bribery and Simony; or, a Satyr Against the Corrupt Use of Money* (1703). Others satirize "Painting" (1697), "Ingratitude" (1699), and even "Confinement" (1702). In 1704, Wycherley (?) publishes the clever and playful *The Folly of Industry: or, the Busy Man Expos'd*. These bland declamations have been found unworthy of modern critical attention, and unexciting they certainly are, but they are best understood as experimental responses to a changing world. Like Ward's journey satires, these works are self-conveying: they do not depend for their effects on knowledge extrinsic to the text. Such satire does not always work well as printed verse—but it can be extremely effective on stage.

IV. Dramatic Satire

Studies of satire in the long eighteenth century usually privilege verse, treat a small number of prose works at some length, and have little to say about drama. A few well-known dramatic satires are frequently cited if not much discussed—the major examples are *The Rehearsal*, *The Beggar's Opera*, and *Tom Thumb*—but from the period under review here only *The Way of the World* figures at all, and it only in passing. Jean I. Marsden's 2007 "Dramatic Satire in the Restoration and Eighteenth Century" deals briefly with a number of mostly Carolean plays but essentially skips from *The Rehearsal* to Gay and Fielding.[73] The scant attention paid to end-of-century dramatic satire is unfortunate: in these years, much of the best, liveliest, and most forceful satire is found on stage.

Nineties drama differs greatly from that of the seventies, a fact pointed out—surprisingly late in the twentieth century—by A. H. Scouten, whose differentiation has been borne out by Hume, Hughes, and others.[74] But Carolean norms do not abruptly vanish upon the death of Charles II. The most successful attempted continuations of Carolean comedy are those of Dryden (*Amphitryon*), Southerne (*Sir Anthony Love* [1690]), and Congreve (*The Old Batchelour* [1693]). Dryden's message is dark and his satire sharp, and the play is much less vulgar than *The Kind Keeper*, but its farcical spiciness is undeniable. Congreve's high-spirited play, which Henry Higden snidely dubbed "the Baudy Batchelour,"[75] is cynical in its attitude toward love and matrimony, but the sex, deception, seduction, and cuckolding are energetically presented, substantially lightening the tone. Congreve's next play, *The Double-Dealer* (1693), is harsher and more negative; its moral seriousness makes it heavy. In the villain Maskwell, Congreve presents genuine evil with cold realism. *The Double-Dealer* did not do well: the times and values were changing.

Excepting the Carolean carryovers and some experimentation,[76] what we find in dramatic satire at the end of the century (and just beyond) are three quite different satiric enterprises: (1) exemplary and distributive justice satire, the principal exponent of which is Shadwell; (2) social satire sugarcoated with improbably happy endings or otherwise mitigated; and (3) hard-core harsh satire as practiced by Southerne and Congreve.

Shadwell and Exemplary Comedy

Shadwell's stock has never been high with modern scholars, and in satire studies he gets no mention whatever, except of course as Dryden's target. In fact he writes several satirical or partly satirical works—a number of plays and a few poems—both in the Carolean period and later in the century. His satiric plays of the 1660s and 1670s are varied, but none of them is really like what he does in the late eighties and early nineties. In plays like *The Squire of Alsatia* (1688) and *The Scowrers* (1690), he goes in a different direction, writing overtly exemplary satire for a new audience.

What kind of satire did Shadwell produce in the reign of Charles II? *The Sullen Lovers* (1668) includes stingingly funny caricatures of Sir Robert and Edward Howard (Sir Positive At-all and Poet Ninny). Shadwell also targets the freewheeling gentry, but the satiric thrust of the play is its humorous representation of particular characters and its lively action.[77] This personation notwithstanding, even in his early career he tends toward moralistic judgment—though he recognizes the need to pander to an audience not inclined to welcome a dressing-down. His sex comedies of the seventies, *Epsom-Wells* (1672) and *The Virtuoso* (1676), are boisterous romps filled with intrigue, copulation, and discovery. *The Virtuoso*—whose title character is the ridiculous Sir Nicholas Gimcrack—is most often studied for its satire on science and on the experiments of the Royal Society in particular.[78] The play does indeed have a moral:

Shadwell's "earnest emphasis on the proper ends of knowledge" is (says Hughes) very far "from Etherege's open-minded relativism and Wycherley's labyrinthine skepticism,"[79] and his attitude toward the ruses presented is indisputably negative. In his satirical tragedies, *The Libertine* (1675) and *The History of Timon of Athens* (1678), he likewise attacks the moral code of Carolean comedy. Shadwell was prepared to minimize his preachment in order to popularize his plays, but his impulse was clearly toward moral judgment.

In *A True Widow* (1678), Shadwell's moralizing is dominant, and for it the play was summarily damned. The highlight of the piece, and evidently among the only parts to which viewers warmed, is its play-within-a-play scene in act IV. Like Dryden, Shadwell was displeased by the success of Durfey's *A Fond Husband*, and here he condemns the vogue for farce and caricatures Durfey as Young Maggot. "The playhouse scene presents a Durfeyesque cuckolding intrigue," Richard Bevis explains, "while fractious spectators roar for even lower stuff."[80] *A True Widow* failed, and Shadwell knew why: "For some, I believe, wish'd all the Play like that part of a Farce in it; others knew not my intention in it, which was to expose the Style and Plot of Farce-Writers, to the utter confusion of damnable Farce, and all its wicked and foolish Adherents" (3:288). Shadwell's satire in *A True Widow* is substantively similar to that in *The Virtuoso*, though his approach differs. In the earlier play, he had attacked the sex comedy boom from within; here he denounces as an outsider. As usual, he responded to failure by revising his methods. *The Woman-Captain* (perf. 1679) is straight farce, and in its epilogue he irritably acknowledges that he is catering to the tastes of an unrefined crowd: "Remembring how you used that last he writ, / He made this Low, so to your Level fit; / Plenty of Noise, and scarcity of wit" (4:17).

Shadwell as a Carolean satiric playwright is variously farcical and straitlaced, tending toward moralism but aware of audience preferences and willing to moderate his tone. He well comprehends the enthusiasm for sex comedy, and a year after denouncing such lewd amusements in the preface to *The Humorists*, he delivers one with great success in *Epsom-Wells*. He is prepared to be bawdy, though he consoles himself (as in *The Virtuoso*) by passing judgment on the genre even as he stages an energetic exemplar. Shadwell's focus on sympathetic characters in his later plays—*The Squire of Alsatia* and beyond—is a return, as Hume has argued, "to the quasi-exemplary method he had touted" twenty years earlier.[81] Nevertheless, these later works tend to be preachier, their central point more strongly didactic.

In exemplary satiric comedy like *The Squire of Alsatia* the emphasis is upon representation of positive models, though negative ones are bluntly presented. In the prologue to *Squire*, Shadwell praises his predecessor, "Master *Ben*," a signal that he regards the play as a satiric comedy, and he insists that his aim is "to correct, and to inform," as well as to entertain (4:204; italics reversed). The basis of *The Squire of*

Alsatia is the contrast of town and country educations and of the morality (or not) of their products, in this case two brothers. Shadwell's preferences are made plain from the start. Belfond senior is described as "abominably vicious," having been reared by his "sordidly covetous, clownish, obstinate, positive and froward" father in the country; the younger brother has been brought up in town by his upstanding merchant uncle, and he is mischievous but also "a man of Honour and of excellent disposition and temper" (4:206). The country education has turned the elder brother into an obnoxious swine; toward the younger brother we are meant to be sympathetic, whatever his failings. When we meet Belfond junior, he has just seduced a kindhearted virgin, whom he later dumps, and he is being aggressively pursued by his cast-mistress, who is raising his child and cursing his cruelty. His harsh dismissal of her—"if a man lies once with a Woman is he bound to do it for ever?" (4:228)—should be cause for satire. We expect Shadwell to be targeting both systems of education, revealing both the town and country guardians as failed mentors who have been sorely deceived by their errant charges.

But this is not what Shadwell does. Belfond junior turns out to be the hero of the play. His uncle shells out huge sums of money to the cast-mistresses, thereby setting the situation aright, and Belfond Junior is at last compelled to reformation by his love for the rich and virtuous Isabella, to whom he swears a solemn oath in the final scene: "*I* call to Heav'n to witness, *I* will hereafter be entirely yours. *I* look on Marriage as the most solemn Vow a Man can make; and 'tis by consequence, the basest Perjury to break it" (4:279). A rakehell he most definitely has been, but the point of the play is his *reclaimability*, presumably made possible by his town upbringing. Shadwell upholds both Belfond junior and his guardian as overtly exemplary figures—the picture of fine gentility—and he does so with strong moral conviction. What makes the play's conclusion so remarkable is the seriousness with which he means us to take his protagonist's transformation. In *Squire*, as in *The Scowrers* and *The Volunteers* (1692), Shadwell's emphasis is on the capacity for reform. Converted by the love of good women, sowers of wild oats mature into the upstanding gentlemen that they have been, in their essences, all along.

Shadwell is not Steele: the latter would never feature a hero who dishonestly seduces, promptly ditches, and shamelessly pays off a sweet middle-class girl. But *Squire*, *Bury-Fair*, *The Scowrers*, and *The Volunteers* present us with models of probity and morality, contrasted with a wide array of fools and cads. Shadwell clearly conceived of the latter three plays as satiric enterprises, claiming in the prologues to be exposing vice justly and humorously. *The Volunteers* appeared posthumously with a second prologue, written by Durfey, insisting that the play would please "all you that can good *Satyr* bear." The epilogue is a sort of elegy for Shadwell, hailed as a comic satirist of the stage, "Born to expose the Follies of the Age: / To whip prevailing Vices, and unite / *Mirth* with *Instruction, Profit* with *Delight*" (5:159, 161; italics reversed). Shadwell definitely saw himself and was seen as a satirist—despite also being a moralist and a dramatist. Other playwrights of the early nineties likewise combine satire with ethical preachment, satiric butts with moral exemplars—Crowne in *The English Frier* (1690) and Durfey in *Love for Money* (1691) and *The Campaigners* (1698).[82] Such satire, basically positive in thrust, is far removed from the attack-based modes privileged by scholars.

Exemplary comedy was on the rise in this period, but the truly successful satiric drama of the 1690s is "hard" rather than "soft" comedy. Much of the weighty satire focuses on marriage. The inadequacies of romance comedy—in which boy gets girl and the play ends on the expectation of everlasting bliss—become increasingly clear at the end of the century, as evidenced in Durfey's *The Richmond Heiress* (1693). The central action of the plot is the attempted courtship of the heiress, Fulvia, by a number of suitors looking to score a fortune. When she discovers that even the hero apparent courts her for purely mercenary reasons, she renounces marriage altogether: "Since such a general defect of honesty corrupts the Age," she proclaims definitively in the final act, "I'll no more trust Mankind" (63). While such a resolution is hardly cheery, one must admit that in the circumstances Fulvia's judgment is sound. John McVeagh suggests that the ending is "a dramatic rather than a moralistic stroke," that Durfey's motive is "to engineer a theatrical coup, not to expound a reformist programme."[83] Possibly so, but the satire does attest to a rising awareness of just how unattractive matrimony is for women. Indeed most of the truly first-rate drama in the 1690s and early 1700s confronts and sometimes sharply criticizes the economic bases for matrimony, the nearly total subjugation of women in marriage, and the social and legal realities that deny them a way out. Such works tend to fall into "happy"-ending plays, in which the author mitigates his satire, and harder-hitting satires that do nothing to diminish the force of the negative commentary. These are not tidy categories, but they do represent distinct satiric enterprises.

Mitigated Satire: Cibber, Vanbrugh, Farquhar

Mitigation can be achieved in a variety of ways and to different extents. I include in this category works in which the satire is implied rather than overt (Colley Cibber's *Love's Last Shift*); the implications of the plot resolution are neatly evaded (John Vanbrugh's *The Relapse*); the playwright admits the negatives but counterbalances them with something positive (Vanbrugh's *The Provok'd Wife*); or the author departs from reality altogether, offering a thoroughly fantastic conclusion (George Farquhar's *The Beaux Stratagem*).

Cibber's *Love's Last Shift* (1696) is an oddity, treated here in part because of its connection to *The Relapse*. In the "romantic" plot of Cibber's play, the dissolute Loveless returns to London, convinced that the wife he abandoned a decade earlier has died. In his absence, the virtuous Amanda has remained loyal to her husband, presumed dead; she has also inherited a pot of money. When Amanda learns of his homecoming, she contrives to "court and conquer him, as a mistress" (72), and after they sleep together, she upbraids him for his past misdeeds and reveals her true identity. In a moment he is a changed man: "Oh! thou hast roused me from my deep lethargy of vice!" and so on (106). All tenderness and mercy, Amanda forgives him—and then informs him that she has been left a sizable fortune, of which he is now "the undisputed master" (107). The sudden and total conversion of the seemingly unprincipled Loveless constitutes a splendidly moral piece of feel-goodism, and for it *Love's Last Shift* was long regarded by twentieth-century critics as the first sentimental comedy. If, however, one calls to mind the raffish author's biography, one is likely to see the piece as an over-the-top burlesque of reform comedies. That a libertine realist like Cibber penned this improbable conversion with a straight face seems inconceivable. Original viewers and readers presumably responded according to their own predilections, and no doubt some were pleased to believe the sincerity of Loveless's transformation. Probably Cibber enjoyed laughing at sniveling sentimentalists who accepted the volte-face as true and took comfort in it.

The satire in *The Relapse* (1696), Vanbrugh's sequel to *Love's Last Shift*, functions very differently. The story begins with the newly reunited Lovelesses gushingly discussing their reunion,[84] but the scene is hardly sweetness and light. Amanda distrusts Loveless's conversion, and rightly so. He cheats on her again in short order, this time with her confidante; she herself is propositioned by the fine young gentleman Worthy but turns him down, and we see no more of that plot. The "romance" of the secondary plot is distinctly sour. Young Fashion marries the rustic Hoyden, the intended bride of his obnoxious older brother, Lord Foppington (Sir Novelty Fashion from *Love's Last Shift*), getting her attendant fortune as well. Thus Young Fashion cops the loot, but Lord Foppington's ironic congratulation suggests that Hoyden is a high price to pay for the money: "you have Marry'd a Woman Beautiful in her Person, Charming in her Ayrs, Prudent in her Canduct, Canstant in her Inclinations, and of a nice Marality, split my Wind-pipe" (99–100). Vanbrugh is dryly skeptical about Loveless's alleged reform, and he deflates the rapture of winning a great heiress. The satire is wry, mitigated by Vanbrugh's not calling attention to either couple's bleak future. Amanda is trapped in a thoroughly depressing situation, but we are not forced to think much about it. As a piece of social commentary, *The Relapse* is dark without being heavy handed. Vanbrugh softens his satire by refusing to make the implications of his plot explicit.

In *The Provok'd Wife* (1697), Vanbrugh's satiric presentation of marital discord is again mitigated, but not by evasion. In the main plot, Sir John Brute behaves abominably to his wife, and neither is contented with their union. Lady Brute fantasizes about cuckolding her barbarous mate; she flirts with and almost succumbs to Constant, who sincerely loves her, and who eventually threatens Sir John into a promise to reform. In the other plot, Lady Brute's niece Bellinda falls for Heartfree, whom she resolves to marry although he does not have much money. For them, the ending is presumably happy. Unlike Southerne in *The Wives' Excuse*, Vanbrugh suggests that a satisfying marriage is possible. He counterbalances his picture of gross marital discord with the presentation of a pair of sober, decent, well-matched lovers and so prevents *The Provok'd Wife* from being as intensely unpleasant as *The Wives' Excuse*—though the fact remains that for Lady Brute there can be no good future.

Farquhar's *The Beaux Stratagem* (1707), like *The Relapse*, includes potentially serious social satire that is implicit rather than explicit. Again we are shown a gruesomely unhappy married couple, but in the end Farquhar offers a fairy-tale plot resolution to a very real social problem. The Sullens are mismatched—"we are," laments Mrs. Sullen, "united Contradictions" (1:176)—and each is displeased by the other. Cast as he was in the original performance, Sullen was evidently not meant to be a dim yokel but a scary menace.[85] The beaux are Archer and Aimwell, respectively attempting to seduce Mrs. Sullen and woo the wealthy Dorinda. In the final act, Farquhar merrily unites one couple and splits another, courtesy of an improbable conversion and a handsome piece of illegality. Aimwell confesses his mercenary stratagem to Dorinda, wins her with his belated honesty, and is then promptly rewarded with news of his brother's death, giving him the title to which he had been pretending. In the other plot, Sullen is blackmailed out of his wife's fortune and resolves that they will "divorce."

Viewers would have recognized the implausibility of the tidy resolution. Divorce was not only uncommon; it was all but unheard of and legal only in special circumstances at vast expense.[86] Farquhar waves a magic wand, giving us a satire that would not trouble those in the audience who wished to enjoy the happy ending. Perhaps he is simply backing off to make his critique more palatable, wishing to highlight the nastiness of the social and legal realities of marriage and to underscore (indirectly and sans moralistic tub-thumping) the need for a solution. For someone willing to reflect upon the absurdity of the illegal "divorce," however, Farquhar's magic could not have been very convincing.[87] For an unhappily wedded woman it could only have been a bitter mockery. In these instances, the illegality of the plot's "solution" serves as a crunching reminder that in the real world Mrs. Sullen's problem is just not soluble.

Harsh Social Satire: Congreve and Southerne

Cibber, Vanbrugh, and Farquhar produce very different satires, and the "meaning" of *Love's Last Shift*, *The Relapse*, *The Beaux Stratagem*, and *The Provok'd Wife* has much to do with production choices and audience viewpoint. In all cases, a theatergoer so inclined might manage to ignore the implications of what the playwright is presenting. This is not the case with Congreve and Southerne, whose romance and marital discord plays are forceful expositions of incontrovertible social problems.

Congreve's *The Way of the World* (1700) is a dourly critical presentation of the upper-class, leisured part of the London world in which people do not behave decently. The satire on Lady Wishfort is savage, but Congreve does not take a cheerful view of any of the characters. The two male leads (Mirabell and Fainall) are not collaborators and confidantes but enemies; they feign friendship but are rival plotters in a series of stratagems. Mirabell is in love with and wants to wed Millamant, niece of Lady Wishfort, but he also covets her fortune, half of which (£6,000) she gets only if her aunt consents to her marriage. But (of course) Lady Wishfort loathes Mirabell and refuses to sanction the union. Meanwhile, Fainall and his paramour seek to thwart Mirabell's plans and to see that the £6,000 is transferred not to Millamant but to Arabella—at which point Fainall would control it. The subsequent schemes are many and complicated, but ultimately Mirabell is triumphant, winning the girl and her fortune. The point of the play, however, is not the happily-ever-after that the right union ought, in a romance comedy, to produce.

The Way of the World is not at all sentimental in its attitude toward love and marriage. The action of the play is driven almost entirely by the £6,000, and the proviso scene (IV.i) suggests nothing if not that matrimonial felicity requires more than love. Millamant names her conditions ("Good *Mirabell* don't let us be familiar or fond, nor kiss before folks") and assures him that, if he meets her demands, she "may by degrees dwindle into a Wife" (450).[88] He agrees to her terms and is quick to offer his own: "*Imprimis* then, I Covenant that your acquaintance be General; that you admit no sworn Confident, or Intimate of your own Sex" and so on (451). Millamant disdains the "Odious proviso's" (452), but the two have clearly come to an agreement, suggesting, Bevis says, that "intelligent people will approach marriage pragmatically, seeking a *modus vivendi*." The seriousness with which Congreve takes "marital, legal, and financial issues is characteristic of the 1690s," he continues, but nowhere else "do they receive such a frank premarital airing."[89] The lovers achieve the union they jointly seek, but any satisfaction in the prospect of wedded bliss is muted by the icy realism with which the whole affair is presented. The sympathy with which Congreve had treated the lovers in *Love for Love* is noticeably absent here; the detachment with which he had surveyed human weaknesses in *The Old Batchelour* is gone. Congreve was never a sunny optimist, but *The Way of the World*, as the title suggests, reflects deep pessimism. Self-interested dissimulation is a fact of life; the high-life society he renders is "a selfish, combative one, in which personal survival depends on skill in deception."[90] Congreve's romance comedy is patently dubious and anxious, and he does not allow for even a partially positive interpretation of a glumly cynical play.

Southerne's *The Wives' Excuse* (1691) is less gloomily pessimistic than violently angry, depicting not an unromantic courtship but a gruesomely unpleasant marriage.[91] John Harrington Smith rightly calls *The Wives' Excuse* "one of the five most considerable" plays of the late seventeenth century.[92] A theatrical failure in 1691, it is a sour, complicated, and sober piece of satiric commentary, dwelling harshly on the wretched lot of unhappily married women. Friendall is a contemptible oaf who married his honorable, well-meaning wife to get her money and to seduce her friends. She is abused, neglected, and despondent but also determined not to think the worst of her spouse: "He does many things, he shou'd not do," she admits early on, "but I think he loves me, and that excuses him to me" (1:284). She is tenaciously pursued by the rake Lovemore but resists his advances, pledging virtue and loyalty to her loutish husband. In the play's finale, she catches Friendall in flagrante delicto with one of her friends, but he does not exactly wax remorseful. Unabashed, he observes that both parties have been badly disappointed—the marriage "is not the condition you expected; nor has it the advantages I propos'd"—and he decrees that they will separate (1:339). He will be even freer to philander, but her position is dismal and she knows it: "I must be still your Wife, and still unhappy" (1:340).

The Wives' Excuse is a thoroughly negative play. Matrimony pleases no one, but for women it is a nightmare. Not for nothing does one character suggest that "the Woman shou'd cheat the Man, as much as she can, before Marriage, because, after it, he has a Title of cheating her, as long as he lives" (1:297). Southerne does not seem to believe that a good marriage is possible: humans are by nature predatory, and the characters who "try to believe in rules . . . look foolish for doing so."[93] Like Otway before him, Southerne depicts a debased society in which insensitivity and disloyalty are the norms. We are not meant to sympathize with Mrs. Friendall any more than we are with Mrs. Sullen—Southerne's satire, like Vanbrugh's, is provocative, not pathetic or sentimental—but the fact remains that neither wife has much to look forward to. The representation of marriage is depressing; the indictment of the libertine code that permits men to mistreat their wives, and of the social and legal reality that denies women any recourse, is severe. Even more vigorously than Congreve, Southerne rubs his viewers' and readers' noses in the nastiness of the world he renders.[94]

Both Congreve and Southerne coldly survey the ways of the world and find them wanting, but the author of *The Way of the World* is resigned to a reality that Southerne forcibly exposes as unacceptable. Congreve laments but acquiesces in a world that is what it is; he distinguishes right from wrong, but he is not trying to make anything happen. Southerne recognizes that change is unlikely: "Our Author does not set up for reforming," the epilogue to *The Wives' Excuse* tells us. But he denounces the status quo with ferocity not present in *The Way of the World*, and his rage at least raises the possibility that he wanted to provoke change, though the disgust could just as easily signal his awareness that nothing can be done to ameliorate a deplorable state of affairs. Congreve is glum, Southerne angry, and the tonal disparity of their plays indicates two distinct satiric enterprises.

The "happy"-ending satires of Cibber, Vanbrugh, and Farquhar share some plot features with each other and with those of Congreve and Southerne. All of them present varyingly ugly situations, but offering chimerical solutions to real problems, or ignoring the mess altogether and ending cheerily, is quite different from force-feeding cynicism to the audience. Audience members of dissimilar values and expectations can derive from *Love's Last Shift* disparate and even incompatible conclusions. Likewise a theatergoer might respond to *The Relapse* with "That was fun," or "That's disgusting," depending upon his or her own attitude or position. *The Beaux Stratagem* can be done as a farce; *The Wives' Excuse* cannot, and neither Southerne nor Congreve leaves the viewer much room for alternative interpretations.

The end of the century represents a period of intense experimentation in dramatic as in poetic satire, and the ventures go in different directions. Shadwell had tried a version of exemplary satire in the Carolean period, but what he does in plays like *The Squire of Alsatia* and *The Scowrers* really is a new pattern, more educational and preacherly than anything found in the reign of Charles II. The more serious social satires do not represent a "type" as much as a spectrum from dissatisfied to disgusted, from tentatively hopeful to unremittingly pessimistic, but none of them has many precedents. Southerne's angry denunciation shares something with the furious social satires of Otway, but he is also addressing a specific issue uniquely central to the satiric drama of the 1690s. Few plays have figured in modern satire studies, but much of the most interesting and innovative satire of this period was written for the stage.

V. The State of Satire ca. 1700

The possibilities for satire change after the death of Charles II. The dispersal of the court circle represents a particular problem: in a world in which daily newspapers full of juicy gossip do not yet exist, a reading public is far less likely to be able to comprehend highly individuated, personally directed satire. Carolean satire had been a largely scribal venture. In the later 1680s and 1690s, satire is increasingly commercial, written and published for wider consumption and for profit. That material change significantly influences—one may safely say revolutionizes—the practice of satire.

Carryovers from the Carolean period exist, and every trend has exceptions, but the overall level of fervor and ferocity in satiric verse drops considerably in the later 1680s and 1690s. Many Carolean satirists evidently hoped to affect the world around them.

Far fewer late-century satirists seem to have such pragmatic aims. Post-Carolean writers, on the whole, deal with smaller-scale religio- and sociopolitical issues; they are more inclined to vent than their predecessors had been, and they often seem to believe that nothing much can change. They tend to write less purposive satire and tamer denigration. Gould and company do not match Rochester's militant skepticism or his acerbity. Garth, clever and successful and committed as he was, does not write with the same urgent intensity as Butler, and *The Dispensary* has neither the sting of *Hudibras* nor the bite of Dryden's *Mac Flecknoe*. Late-century satirists are not without passion—Defoe is passionately devoted to William and to Protestantism, and some of the best plays of this period treat marital issues with great seriousness—but the climatic change from the 1670s to the 1690s is unmistakable.

Extraliterary forces necessitated adjustment and alteration, and late-century writers conceive and use satire differently than had their Carolean counterparts. Scholars have been unenthusiastic about the results, regretting the demise of Carolean lampoonery and discontentedly awaiting the emergence of Pope. These satires, however, should not be dismissed as poor examples of what is done well by a few earlier and later writers. Some of the material is splendid, but for my purposes what is more important is that the kind of satire practiced in this short period has only tenuous connections to what precedes or follows it chronologically. Satirists of the eighteenth century proper do not emerge directly from the Carolean milieu, but neither do they evolve out of the 1690s. The circumstances that produced post-Carolean satire were to prove short lived, and so was the kind of work they generated. The radically altered sociopolitical and print culture conditions of the reign of Queen Anne were to open up a whole new world for satire.

CHAPTER FIVE

Defoe, Swift, and New Varieties of Satire, 1700–1725

The End of Satyr is Reformation: And the Author, tho he doubts the Work of Conversion is at a general Stop, has put his Hand to the Plow.
                              —Defoe, Preface to *The True-Born Englishman*

Satyr being levelled at all, is never resented for an Offence by any.
                              —Swift, Preface to *A Tale of a Tub*

Characterizations of "early eighteenth-century satire" almost invariably derive from *Gulliver's Travels* (1726), *The Beggar's Opera* (1728), the first *Dunciad* (1728), and a few other works, mostly by Pope and Swift—which is precisely what I want to avoid in this chapter. Insofar as scholars focus on the first quarter of the century, they usually regard the satire produced then as a promising antecedent to what would happen in the late 1720s and 1730s, a "Scriblerian" trial run. The period 1700–1725 needs to be distinguished, however, both from what precedes and what follows it: the norms of the 1690s rapidly gave way to different types of satire, and the works produced in these twenty-five years bear little resemblance to those of the next twenty. My terminus ad quem is not arbitrary. I am deliberately cutting off my survey before the appearance of the later-twenties blockbusters. To read backward from those much-studied and easily remembered satires is a mistake. We need to understand what satiric practice would have looked like to an informed observer who did not know what was about to happen. What we will discover is an upsurge in experimentation and great diversity in satiric practice. This quarter century is harder to characterize than the subperiods covered in the preceding two chapters, but it nevertheless has its own distinctive markers and surprisingly little connection to the twenty years that follow.

Satire in the first quarter of the eighteenth century moves fairly abruptly in new directions and takes on different forms than those common in the latter half of the seventeenth. In the reign of Charles II, satire is dominated by personal lampoons, usually scribally circulated, and by contributions to fierce political debate. In the years 1685 to 1700, we find some topical political commentary but a great deal of relatively tame social and moral satire—nonparticularized diatribes against women, jesting tirades against ale, toothless denunciations of greed, and so on. Satire on the 1690s stage is not predominantly political as it was in the Carolean period; most of the satiric plays include exposés of social problems, whether hard hitting (Southerne) or mitigated (Vanbrugh). In the first quarter of the eighteenth century, little of the drama has any bite. "Attack" and "defense" remain standard categories after 1700 and are therefore useful in this chapter as in the preceding two. Beyond that, we find little continuity from the late seventeenth century. Changes in sociopolitical conditions and in print circumstances contribute to the morphing of old types; new kinds of satire develop for particular reasons around particular events.

The satire produced in the first quarter of the eighteenth century reflects a broader range of satiric purposes than does the satire covered in chapters 3 and 4 and is therefore messier to deal with. To make this material more comprehensible, I will briefly characterize the seven different types of satiric enterprise covered in this chapter. These categories are not mutually exclusive: "attack" is varyingly prominent in warning-mode satires, ideological argumentation, generalized and topical social satire, and so on. On the whole, however, the seven groupings reflect significantly distinct central motives. These categories do *not* correspond with the five sections of the chapter. The surveys of Defoe's and Swift's outputs necessarily cover several of these categories; the section on religiopolitical satire features exemplars of attack, defense, warning, and ideological argumentation; the discussion of social and moral satire includes illustrations of generalized and topical satire, didacticism, and argument/inquiry. The oddity is the section on the Scriblerians, which shows how little the work of those writers (excepting Swift) fits the satiric milieu described in the rest of this chapter.

(1) *Attack and defense.* Religiopolitical satirists attack their enemies, defend their friends, or complain about state affairs. Swift's satire in this period is often antagonistically and grittily political, whether gratuitously destructive (the *Satirical Elegy* on Marlborough [wr. 1722]) or practically purposive (*The Fable of Midas* [1711]).

(2) *Warning.* A less straightforward type of religiopolitical satire is monitory, written not to humiliate or punish adversaries but to warn like-minded readers. The object of Defoe's *The Shortest-Way with the Dissenters* (1702) is not to ridicule the High Church position but to school his fellow dissenters about the dangers concealed in that position. Much of the cautionary satire in these years deals with issues of dissent and toleration.

(3) *Ideological argumentation.* Religiopolitical commentators in this period sometimes use satire as a form of argumentation or investigation. Defoe's *Jure Divino* (1706) is a poetic analysis of monarchical government and a satirical exposition of his political philosophy. He raises questions about subjects'

rights, the bounds of royal prerogative, the viability of the doctrine of passive obedience—and though he sharply divides right from wrong, the point of this satire is its argument as much as its final judgment.

(4) *Generalized social satire.* Early in this quarter century, social satirists pen numerous generalized plaints, whether lively and witty (Ward's *The London Terrae-filius* [1707–1708]) or preachily castigatory and moralistic (the anonymous *The Merchants Advocate* [1708]).

(5) *Didacticism.* The preceding category includes negative moralistic satire that is heavy-handedly preachy; moralistic satire can also be more positively didactic. Addison and Steele promote sympathetic satire in the *Tatler* and *Spectator* essays; Steele's *The Conscious Lovers* (1722) is the major exemplary comedy, an attempt to instruct the audience in sociomoral propriety.

(6) *Topical social satire.* Social satire—usually generalized in the late seventeenth century—becomes increasingly topical in this period; its practitioners target well-known figures (like Pope) and current events (e.g., the South Sea crisis).

(7) *Social argument and inquiry.* Some social and moral satirists—like some political satirists—write not straight condemnation but argument and inquiry. Matthew Prior's *Alma* (1718) is a burlesque that explores the reigning philosophies of mind/body dualism; Bernard Mandeville's *The Fable of the Bees* (first version 1714) asks provocative questions about social structure. Neither is simply delivering judgment.

Some of the satires in these categories are relatively clear-cut demolitions of specified targets, but in many works ridicule or abuse is not the point. The "job" of satire, for a surprising number of its early eighteenth-century practitioners, is not merely clear transmission of negative judgment.

A few key points about the material covered in this chapter ought to be made up front. First, we need to be aware that there are distinct subperiods within the quarter century. Some kinds of satire are uniquely prominent in the reign of Queen Anne, mostly disappearing by 1715.[1] Nowhere else in this survey do we find such *difficult* satire. *A Tale of a Tub* is the famous example, but dense, argumentative, interpretively problematic satires are numerous in the first fifteen years of the century and virtually nonexistent elsewhere. We also find more provocative satire in this subperiod, especially during Anne's reign, than in any other. Quite aside from its subject matter, Defoe's *Jure Divino* simply would not have been written a decade sooner or a decade later. Satiric impersonation (see *The Shortest-Way* and Swift's *An Excellent New Song, being the Intended Speech of a famous Orator against Peace*) flourishes during Anne's reign. Students of eighteenth-century satire have tended to see irony as central to the entire period, but (leaving aside *A Modest Proposal*) much of the most interesting ironic satire appears over the course of about ten years at the beginning of the century. This is not an age but a decade of irony, or of satiric indirection we associate with irony. Satire in the reign of Anne is much more distinctive than what we find in the years 1715–1725, when there is less coherence among the works, which exhibit fewer unique characteristics.

The two principal satirists of this period, from the modern vantage point, are Defoe and Swift, both prolific sociopolitical commentators throughout the entire quarter century. (*The Rape of the Lock* has gotten plenty of ink, but Pope was not much of a satirist until the later 1720s.) Swift and Defoe are far from politically or socially simpatico, and they write different types of satire for different reasons, but they both produce straightforward attack, indirect and ironic critique, and the more complex, thought-provocative satires mentioned above. They both "fit" the particular satiric milieu of Anne's reign in a way that Pope and Gay do not. To seek and overstress pre-Scriblerianism in the early eighteenth century is to misrepresent it: especially in the first fifteen years of the century, what dominates is religiopolitical controversy as engaged in by the two major polemicists named in this chapter's title.

My organization in this chapter is conceptual rather than chronological. I treat the material in five sections. I begin with Defoe, whose satiric aims and techniques are jarringly unlike those of, say, Pope—but who would probably have been regarded by his contemporaries as the preeminent living satirist. The second section surveys the religiopolitical satire of Arthur Maynwaring, William Shippen, John Dunton, and others. These works are characterized by formal experimentation—technical innovations, new modes of critique—and by several different concepts of satiric purpose (comprising the first four of the seven enterprises described above). The third section covers the less experimental moral and social satires by Ned Ward, Susanna Centlivre, Mandeville, and others. Much of the drama produced in these years fits here. Section four focuses on the satires produced by the alleged "Scriblerians," especially Pope, Gay, and Arbuthnot. The fifth section is an attempt to understand Swift's place in early eighteenth-century satire, with particular attention to the range of his output and its distance from what we think of as "Scriblerian" satire.

I. Defoe as Satirist

Scholars tend to think of Defoe primarily as a novelist, secondarily as a journalist and a topical commentator on politics and economics—but he clearly conceived of himself as a satirist. He signed a number of his works "The True-Born Englishman" after his most popular satire, had much to say about satire, and wrote some fifty satirical or partly satirical texts over a period of almost four decades.[2] Despite his output and reputation as a satirist, he is lucky to get even a passing mention from modern satire scholars in their discussions of the period. The neglect is unfortunate but unsurprising: Defoe's reputation as a mercenary hack and occasional writer, often dealing with nonliterary subjects, has led to his exclusion from literary histories of satire. He is not part of the "Scriblerian" cohort, and whatever one imagines "Augustan satire" to mean, his works are a far cry from it. If one is looking for a heavily published, often-reprinted, widely known satirist in the early eighteenth century, however, Defoe's name ought to be the first to come to mind.

What did Defoe imagine himself accomplishing as a satirist? I have addressed this question at length elsewhere, arguing (among other things) for the remarkable consistency of his concerns and positions throughout his long career as a satirist.[3] He repeatedly returns to the same themes—anti-Catholicism, dissent and toleration, and English manners—though the three cannot really be separated. For Defoe, the events of daily life are connected to the political events of the nation, which are linked with the broader international stage, and all are in turn united to the right order of a Christian cosmos. His vision is undoubtedly social and his judgments often moral, but in subject matter his satires are almost always religiopolitical. His techniques are not as consistent as his concerns: he is sometimes direct and sometimes (as in *The Shortest-Way*) indirect. Especially in his indirect satires, his aim is evidently not to condemn or support a cause but to expose those he perceives as obnoxious or threatening and to warn those readers with whom he sympathizes against their religiopolitical enemies.

Attack and Defense

Defoe is capable of direct invective, though few of his satires can be well explained in terms of attack. His denunciation is almost always part of a defense of a commitment or a cause he believes in. In chapter 4, I deal with his vindications of William—especially *The True-Born Englishman* (1701) and *The Mock Mourners* (1702; 6d*), where he scorches his hero-king's detractors in no uncertain terms. He champions William, but his broader cause is the preservation of Protestantism in England. His rejection of Catholicism, absolute in both political and theological terms, pervades his satirical and nonsatirical works, as do his concomitant fears of the possibility of Catholic control of England. In *Ye True-Born Englishmen Proceed* (1701; sometimes called "A New Satyr on the Parliament"), Defoe reviles Parliament for failing to support the Dutch and to restrain Louis XIV, and in *The Address* (1704) he reproaches the Tory-dominated House of Commons, not least for "their flirtations with the Pretender."[4] Defoe condemns France for political error, to be sure, but the graver charge is doctrinal. In *The Spanish Descent* (1702) he inveighs against the French, who "mock their Maker with Religious Lyes" (l. 362). He champions the Protestant cause and decries Catholicism throughout his career, as in a 1713 set of ironical pamphlets on the Hanoverian succession.[5]

Defoe's satires on English manners are castigatory, but they are also strongly positive enterprises. His most generalized satires, *Reformation of Manners* (1702) and *More
Reformation* (1703; 1s†), include sweeping indictments of English incivility, the former
seeking to expose the "Shams of Reformation," the charade of public moderation
that only thinly disguises private indulgences (l. 2). In *The Conduct of Christians made
the Sport of Infidels* (1717)—only a probable attribution—the Turkish letter writer
similarly disparages the British Christians who profess religion but lack the moral
restraint to practice it in any meaningful way. The scathing attack on the indecency
of nominal Christians is wide ranging, but these seemingly general satires on English
manners have "urgently topical preoccupations,"[6] as well as religiopolitical import.
Defoe criticizes a society he perceives as irreverent. He recognizes the degree to which
society at large has lost its sense of the sacred, making possible (for example) the rise of
deism and atheism. These positions, with Socinianism, recur as bugbears throughout
Defoe's satiric canon, and though he devotes no entire satire to attacking them, their
advocates frequently appear as objects of his contempt. He specifically rebukes John
Toland in several poems, including *Ye True-Born Englishmen Proceed* and *Reformation
of Manners*, where Toland is described as "poyson[ing] Souls with his infected Breath"
(l. 416).[7] Throughout his career Defoe satirizes those who disbelieve the supernatural,
as in his late-life *The Political History of the Devil* (1726; 5s†).[8] His satires on anti-Wil-
liamites, Catholics, hypocrites, and other offenders are condemnatory, but they were
evidently written in defense of causes or convictions that Defoe takes direly seriously.

Instruction and Direct Warning (Aimed at the Audience)

Defoe's satiric object rarely seems to be simple ridicule or the humiliation of his
targets. His direct satires suggest that he is uninterested in making his victims look
bad just to amuse or please his readers. He publicly exposes only such individuals as Henry Sacheverell and Charles Leslie who practice deception on the public.
Except in those particular circumstances, he focuses not on public image but on the
guilty conscience. In *The Spanish Descent*, he invites the offenders to feel the pangs
of their "secret Guilts" (l. 208), and there and elsewhere Defoe—an often homiletic
satirist—repeatedly emphasizes "shame," appealing to private scruples and neither
relishing his targets' degradation nor trying to reform the morally reprehensible. The
distinction is crucial: Defoe writes satire not primarily to denigrate or reform his
enemies but to school like-minded readers, both in their own ways and in the ways of
their adversaries. Most readers, of course, appreciate satire only insofar as it exposes
the sins of others. The guilty reader (as Swift recognized) almost never sees his own
guilt being described. But Defoe has a particular sense of audience: he imagines a
properly attuned reader, something like Milton's "fit audience" (*Paradise Lost*, 7.31).

His reader is not impervious to moral reproof, as he explains to personified "Satyr" in *More Reformation*:

> For when to Beasts and Devils men descend,
> Reforming's past, and Satyr's at an end.
> No decent Language can their crimes rehearse,
> They lye below *the Dignity of Verse*.
> But if among thy Lines he would have place,
> Petition him to *Counterfeit some Grace*,
> Let him like something of a Christian sin,
> Then thou't ha' some pretence to bring him in. (ll. 630–637)

For Defoe the satirist, the right reader is one who sins "like something of a Christian"—who is, in other words, capable of self-reproach.

From the beginning to the end of his satiric career, Defoe worries about the danger of dishonesty,[9] and he often uses satire to expose what he perceives to be the most pernicious enemy of true Christians: the wolf in sheep's clothing. He recognizes that the too-innocent reader can be misled by a seemingly harmless speaker—or worse, a seemingly benevolent one. Deception is for Defoe a political issue: the obscurity of the High Church intentions toward nonconformists made this "an Age of Plot and Deceit" in which one cannot always know "Friends" from "Enemies."[10] Defoe often seems concerned that "his" people (sometimes the English, sometimes the Whigs, sometimes the Protestants, and sometimes the dissenters) will not recognize "their" adversaries. His direct satires are not designed to deride his victims but rather to educate his allies in moral, social, and political terms; his indirect satires are not straightforwardly instructive but monitory, deliberately provocative of unease.

Indirect Exposure and Discomfiture

In Defoe's indirect satires, he seems to mislead his readers, articulating a position in such a way as to expose it. *The Shortest-Way with the Dissenters* (1702) is the best-known instance of his satiric indirection, and I concentrate on that text in my analysis of this technique.

Much ink has been spilled on the supposed blunder of *The Shortest-Way*. Almost universally regarded as the work of a failed ironist or a too-successful impersonator, the pamphlet is Defoe's mimicry of the "incendiary rhetoric of the . . . notorious Anglican firebrands," Sacheverell and Leslie.[11] Modern scholars have been so distracted by the uproar caused by *The Shortest-Way* that we now have a hard time imagining that work without thinking of its consequences for its author. Immediately after its publication, Robert Harley had Sidney Godolphin investigate the text's authorship, at which point Defoe was not a suspect; Godolphin delegated the job to the Earl of Nottingham, who arrested Edward Bellamy, and Bellamy in turn confessed that he had taken the manuscript to the printer, George Croome. Defoe was named as the author in the *Observator* for 30 December–2 January 1702/3.[12] When the writer of *The Shortest-Way* was identified as a dissenter, the situation became dire. The church felt it had been parodied, the government worried that the author was trying to incite a nonconformist uprising, and the dissenters themselves were unsure what to believe or whom to trust.

Because of this fiasco, critics tend to assume that Defoe botched the construction, that he tried to signal irony but failed to tip his hand, and that the work was (against his wishes) taken straight. In my understanding, this take on the text is, given what we know of Defoe and his commitments, highly implausible.[13] *The Shortest-Way* is not author-centered satire and should be approached not with the aim of identifying the "real" position behind the persona but rather in terms of judgment of content. What the reader is meant to find in the pamphlet is not a dissenter's ironic attack on the High Church, but instead the threat inherent in the High Church position. My presumption is that he did *not* expect readers to find irony in this piece: he meant it to be accepted as a genuine high-flying screed. He wanted to anger and horrify the dissenters and to unite resistance among them, as well as to alarm moderates in the House of Lords to prevent the passage of an Occasional Conformity bill.[14] If the High Churchmen were willing to endorse *The Shortest-Way* loudly and enthusiastically, then the greater fools they. I read *The Shortest-Way* not as insufficiently ironic but as *counterfeit*, an intentional fake not meant to be decoded. As Defoe insisted in his defense of *The Shortest-Way*, his "real design" had been to make "other People's thoughts speak in his Words."[15] He said much the same thing in *The Present State of the Parties in Great Britain* (1712), claiming that his intent in *The Shortest-Way* had been to "speak [the high Tories'] Language," and also to "make them acknowledge it to be theirs" (24). When Defoe engages in satiric lying, he is not trying to deceive his enemies but rather to undeceive those with whom he identifies. His indirect satires deal almost exclusively with either dissent (*The Shortest-Way*, *The Consolidator*) or Jacobitism (*And What if the Pretender should come?*), and this is not coincidental. Defoe sees in the arguments around these issues the most dangerous sort of deception. His direct satires provide an ongoing tutorial on gullibility, duplicity, and feigned benevolence. His indirect satires seem meant to supplement those lessons.

Defoe passes judgment, sometimes shrilly or venomously, but his concept of satire is largely audience rather than target based. His output is not well explained in terms of aggression and ridicule. He experiments quite a lot with technique—irony, indirection, and counterfeit—and often addresses a specific audience in an effort to expose his enemies and to provoke unsettledness or anxiety on the part of like-minded readers. As peculiar as this type of satire may seem to lovers of the Carolean Dryden or the mature Pope, Defoe is not exactly an anomaly. Audience-oriented satire has a great deal of currency in the early eighteenth century, especially in the realm of religiopolitical controversy. None of Defoe's contemporaries do everything he does, but they variously replicate some of his rather distinct satiric motives—particular forms of attack, defense, exposure, and provocation. The wide range of satiric objectives makes early eighteenth-century religious and political satire strikingly heterogeneous.

II. Religious and Political Satire

Many of the "political" satires in the early eighteenth century are, in some fashion, religiopolitical; satirists have much to say for and against occasional conformity, the power and security of the Church of England, and the trial of Sacheverell. The commentary on these and other issues takes a variety of forms. I have organized the material according to its apparently dominant satiric motive, though we should remember that satirists were not choosing off a menu of half a dozen available satiric aims. Few of the relevant works appear to be doing one thing and only one thing, but the religiopolitical satires of this quarter century take different shapes and reveal demonstrably distinct satiric agendas.

Topical Controversy

Only a small percentage of early eighteenth-century satires can be defined as attack, but one possibility for satire is straight derogation, whether personally or politically motivated. Most of Swift's satires in this quarter century are grubbily political—the stuff of anonymous party warfare, sometimes propagandistic and sometimes simply destructive. His *Description of a Salamander*, *The Virtues of Sid Hamet the Magician's Rod*, and *A Satirical Elegy On the Death of a late Famous General* (discussed below) have little practical point but much destructive energy. They are viciously personal, respectively targeting Lord Cutts (commander in chief in Ireland), Sidney Godolphin, and the late Duke of Marlborough. The last is particularly stinging, a mock elegy defiling the general's reputation for martial heroism. More clearly than the others, it has broad implications about human wishes and values, but all of these works get their force from personal assault on well-known political figures.

Many of Swift's contemporaries deal in politically motivated personal abuse. The anonymous *The Seven Wise Men* (1704) and Shippen's (?) *The Junto* (1710) are character assassinations of several prominent Whigs, pillorying their subjects in turn.[16] Defoe and Tutchin are slammed with monotonous regularity—as in *The Republican Bullies* (1705; 2*d*), *The Monster: Or, The World turn'd Topsy Turvy* (1705; 6*d*), and *The Country*

Parson's Advice to Those Little Scriblers Who Pretend to Write Better Sense Than Great Secretaries (1706). A 1711 engraving by George Bickham, *The Three False Brethren*, features Defoe—cross-eyed in the pillory—with Benjamin Hoadly and Oliver Cromwell. Both Defoe and Tutchin were easy targets, and their assailants often delivered their body blows with sadistic glee. The anonymous poet of *The Monster* indicts the two hacks as enemies of the state who "on their Country's vital Honours prey" (3). In ubiquity and intensity, the scorn heaped upon Defoe and Tutchin rivals that with which Dryden met in the wake of his conversion to Catholicism; they were widely disliked and resented pens of the Whig party. Just as the Duke of Buckingham's blistering mockery of the Earl of Danby was more than a personal lampoon, so published attacks against politicians and their journalistic mouthpieces have political edge and can discredit the position for which the targets stand.

Denunciatory political satire in this period, as in the late seventeenth century, is often a form of complaint.[17] *Korath: or the Danger of Schism* (1705; 2*d*) is a dour poem written against Occasional Conformity, Presbyterians, and the "Spurious, Unbred, Mongrel Whigs" (8). The satirist responds to the issues of the day with sadness rather than anger: "*England*, unhappy *England*! Scene of Woes!" and so on (5). The satirist grumpily itemizes problems, impugning factions that are presumably both incorrigible and ineradicable. Satiric complaint can be petulantly mournful like *Korath* or, as in *The D[utch] Deputies* (1705), very high heat. The author of that poem rails against the Dutch—"Sprung out of *Mire* and *Slime*" (6)—and, whether motivated by visceral prejudice or by political animosity, he fantasizes about their destruction. Writers like this one found much to grouse about in the reigns of Anne and George I, but on the whole, satire as lamentation is far less common in this period than it was in the late 1680s and 1690s.[18]

Much early eighteenth-century religiopolitical satire is propagandistic, often combining offensive and defensive impulses. Some of the works are specifically pragmatic, as are *A Health to the Tackers* and Charles Darby's (?) *The Oxfordshire Nine* (both 1705), both meant to influence local elections. Character assassination is often propagandistically defensive. Swift's desecration of Marlborough in the 1722 elegy is politically pointless, but his 1712 castigation of the duke had a practical purpose. Marlborough had just been stripped of his position by the queen in a move that might have caused trouble for the Oxford ministry—chucking a popular hero was a risky maneuver. Swift's *Fable of Midas* is an unsparing smear job on a political opponent and almost certainly an attempt to secure the ministry that Swift supported. Broader in subject is the anonymous *The Tacking-Club: or, a Satyr on Doctor S[achevere]ll, and his Bulleys* (1710), a fierce assault on the high church position. The satirist leaves nothing to the imagination, attacking the "*High Lyers*" as the "Vermin of *England*'s Apostolick Church" (3). Defoe-like, the satirist rages against the duplicity of Sacheverell and his allies in a rancorous diatribe, but to malign the High Church in 1710 is to take a stance on current debates and controversies. These authors clearly wrote with defensive conviction.

Ward is a much more aggressively topical satirist in this quarter century than he had been in the 1690s, continuing to write lightweight entertainment pieces but also producing religiopolitical satire from a High Church position. Howard William Troyer argues that, while Ward was not the sort of pen for his party that Defoe and Tutchin were, he did have a political function: he "disseminated the policies of the growing Tory faction among the lower classes, heaped prejudice and odium upon the opposition, stimulating the rabble to an open expression of their hatreds."[19] Ward returns again and again to the dissenters and Whigs, to whom he gives a sound scourging, as in *The Secret History of the Calves-Head Clubb* (1703) and *All Men Mad* (1704). The title page of the former explains that the purpose of the piece is "To demonstrate the Restless, Implacable Spirit of a certain Party still among us, who are never to be satisfied till the present Establishment in Church and State is subverted." In his satire *The Dissenting Hypocrite* (1704; 1s) he fulminates against Occasional Conformity as "a *Modern Policy of Republicans* and *Dissenters*, to strengthen their own Factious *Interest* by weakening the *QUEEN's Party, Power,* and *Prerogative*" (To the Reader, A3r). Ward is lashing much-lashed targets, but he is also expressing hostility at a level of heat unprecedented in his early satires—and presumably trying to influence popular opinion against his political rivals.

Some satires are more overtly positive, manifestly written in defense of a position. Defoe's *True-Born Englishman* represents this kind of enterprise. So do some of Swift's personal attacks, which are at least potentially pragmatic; his responses to Steele's *The Crisis* (discussed below) are excoriations of Steele and defenses of the Tory ministry. The same combination of motives is evident in several anonymous pro-Sacheverell poems from 1710, including *The Old Pack, The Westminster Combat, The History of Seven,* and *The Save-Alls.* The author of the last condemns the men who voted against Sacheverell, but, as the title suggests, he is more concerned to celebrate the bishops who voted not guilty. Luttrell's annotation calls attention to the positive thrust of that satire: "Upon ye Bishops yt were for Dr. Sacheverel, for them."[20] The much-maligned Marlborough has a satiric advocate in the closet dramatist of *The General Cashier'd* (1712; 1s 6d), who depicts a popular general ousted by the duke during a hard-fought war. The rabble clamors in support of the general, his soldiers refuse to fight without him, and disaster seems imminent until the Duke and the general reconcile and the war is won. Marlborough is not named in the play, but this satirist's point would have been obvious enough to readers in 1712. Supporters of the Oxford ministry had tried to demonize Marlborough in the public imagination. *The General Cashier'd* is a counter to that anti-Marlborough propaganda, and its political moral is crystal clear:

to remove beloved and effective military leaders is to invite disaster. The function of these propagandistic satires is to uphold a position, not to defame a target.

Monitory Satire in the Manner of Defoe

In many early eighteenth-century religiopolitical satires, attack/defense is but an incidental feature, and the principal audience includes those the satirist wants to help rather than those he wants to harm. Defoe seeks to educate like-minded readers directly (*Reformation of Manners*) and indirectly (*The Shortest-Way*), and his contemporaries likewise produce both straightforward and not so straightforward satires. Some Carolean and post-Carolean satirists had written for their friends, whether cheerleading or trying to persuade moderates; in the late 1670s, a few writers used satire as a form of warning. In this quarter century, however, monitory satire is a much more conspicuous and variegated phenomenon.

Monitory satires in these years tend to deal with a few particular religiopolitical rather than social or moral issues. Most examples date from the Queen Anne period (1702–1714), and almost all of them address subjects related to church affairs. Debates over Occasional Conformity in particular incite impassioned paper wars, and the satiric commentary on the issue is often aimed at fostering distrust of the dissenters, or alternatively at inspiring hostile skepticism about the intolerant High Church position. As Howard D. Weinbrot has observed, dissenters were genuinely frightened that the church "would use the strong secular arm of the state" against those "with whom it disagreed"—including them.[21] Sacheverell's incendiary sermons notwithstanding, perhaps the most inflammatory event of Anne's reign was the failure of the Tack in 1704. Frustrated by the defeat of two earlier bills against Occasional Conformity, a group of Tories tried to force a similar bill through the House of Lords by tacking it to a piece of land tax legislation. Frank H. Ellis explains that "the Lords could neither alter nor amend a money bill, but could only pass or reject it outright" and "rejection seemed unthinkable since this would sacrifice the single most important source of revenue for the war against France." To the country Tories' dismay, however, the bill *did* fail, marking "the momentary triumph of moderation over high church extremism."[22] The Whigs exulted in the Tack's defeat, but fears of High Church extremism ran high. Defoe's unease at living in "an Age of Plot and Deceit" is plain in his satires,[23] and he associates the high-fliers with deception. The vast majority of this quarter century's monitory satires deal with these issues.

Direct admonition—in which the satirist says, more or less outright, "Don't do X" or "You can't trust Y"—is common in these years, though its exemplars take different forms. Each tale in Thomas Yalden's *Æsop at Court. Or, State Fables* (1702) is followed by a short moral, either scolding the English or warning them about a particular political miscreant or group of miscreants. Attack is part of the enterprise, but the satiric thrust comes from the cautionary messages like the one at the end of fable 13, where Yalden foretells that "the Regicidal Breed / Will swarm again, by them thy land shall bleed" (35).[24] The accused, never explicitly named or defined, are unlikely to feel stung—but their mortification is hardly Yalden's point. *The Tale of a Nettle* (1710), a High Church broadside written in response to the Sacheverell trial, is more preachily monitory. Its author uses not a fable but a straightforward parable to depict the growth of dissent (as nettle beds) eventually overtaking the once healthy church. Those already worried that the church was in danger were horrified to find that Sacheverell was being tried for having said as much, and this satirist writes with marked anxiety, ominously predicting in his conclusion, "Thus one NETTLE uncropt, encreas'd to such store, / That 'twas nothing but Weeds, what was Garden before" (ll. 53–54). Luttrell's inscription on his copy calls attention not to the satirist's censure but to his solemn counsel: "Showing the dangers of the Church by the Dissenters."[25]

A number of religiopolitical satirists in these years explicitly warn their readers not to believe everything they are told. *The Lawyers Answer to the Country Parson's good Advice to My Lord Keeper* (1706) is not so much a comment on a particular issue as (in Ellis's phrasing) "a poem about Tory rhetoric."[26] As the pro-Sacheverell speaker would do in *A Letter to Mr. Bisset* (1709; 1d; probably by Defoe),[27] this poet ironically insists that listeners admire the parson's "*High-Church* Eloquence" (l. 4). This satirist clearly shares Defoe's suspicion of Sacheverellite silver-tongued proclamations, of the good doctor's dangerous "Subtilty."[28] *On the Queen's Speech* is a response to Anne's proroguing speech in April 1710, an address written by her Whig ministers, who put in her mouth the expression of "unqualified satisfaction at the outcome of the Sacheverell trial."[29] Although her subsequent actions demonstrated that she did not in fact share her Whig counselors' enthusiasm, the damage of the speech was, this poet suggests, already done. That the queen's language is not to be trusted—she speaks "Words not her own"—is painfully clear (l. 10).

Monitory satirists often let their targets expose themselves—not saying "X is not to be trusted" but letting X reveal his or her own treachery. This kind of mock self-exposure is not unprecedented, though it is much less common before 1700 than in the quarter century after it.[30] The irony in these indirect satires is often readily perceptible. Swift's *An Excellent New Song, being the Intended Speech of a famous Orator against Peace* (1711; discussed below) has the Earl of Nottingham implicate himself as a crooked opportunist. An earlier example, and a more strongly cautionary satire, is Maynwaring's (?) *An Address to Our Sovereign Lady* (1704; 1d*), a zippy piece with an important point. The satirist puts treason in the mouth of the Tory majority's speaker, who addresses the queen with an unabashed acknowledgement of his party's perfidy:

We are forc'd to Invent, in this Dangerous Crisis,
Some pretty New Whim to Confound their Devices:
Why Madam, You're Ravisht, Your Queenshipp's Invaded,
And we must Squeal out till of this You are perswaded. (ll. 13–16)

Maynwaring's (?) *The Humble Address of the Clergy of London and Westminster, Paraphras'd* (1710) features a high-flying speaker who cheerfully details the duplicity of his position:

Thus the Church Bacon's sav'd, come Whig or come Tory,
We've a Meaning reserv'd, to prove we are for ye;
We have taken the Oaths and our Livings secur'd,
Yet ne'er heard of his Claim, whose Claim we've abjur'd.
Sometimes Right divine by Descent's our Expression,
Sometimes we cry up the establish'd Succession.
So that catch as catch can, we've engage'd the Caresses
Of one or the other by our two-fac'd Addresses. (ll. 19–26)

The high-flyer of *The Age of Wonders* (also 1710) just as nonchalantly calls attention to his party's dirty work, as had the brazen Whig persona of Shippen's (?) *Faction Display'd* (1704). In the controversy surrounding the High Church and the dissenters, satirists of the latter group in particular devoted much energy to exposing the falsity of their religiopolitical enemies and would-be persecutors.[31] *A New Ballad Writ by Jacob Tonson and Sung at the Kit Kat Clubb* (wr. 1705) represents, says Ellis, "a kind of verse counterpart" to Defoe's *Shortest-Way*, ironically recommending a way to get rid of Tories once and for all.[32] In this satire, as in *A Great Noise About Nothing: Or The Church's Danger* (1705), irony is to some extent discernible, and the nature of the threat exposed by these authors is essentially plain.[33]

Elsewhere irony is much harder to read. Ellis describes *The Tack* (wr. 1705) as a "Tory coolant": its author exalts the Tackers as loyal English churchmen in order to counter the Whigs' overblown charges of the Tackers' deceit.[34] The satirist surveys the many positive connotations of "tacking": "The Parsons Work is Taylor like,/To Tack the Soul to Heaven" and so on (ll. 5–6). Even the Crown and the church are "Tack'd" together, and so, the poet wonders, "[W]hy about one honest Tack,/Do Fools keep such a Pother?" (ll. 21–22, 27–28). Ellis might be correct in interpreting this as a straight-faced (if innocent) defense of the Tories, but we could just as easily take this as a piece of anti-Tack Whig irony, a mock defense that only further belittles the Tories. Is this a Tory writer deliberately downplaying the seriousness of the issue or a Whig satirist exposing the vacuity of the Tories' defense?[35] *A Welcome to the Medal* (1711) is another tricky case: Ellis understands it as an anti-Jacobite poem, but he also observes that some contemporaries took it for Jacobite propaganda.[36] In both instances, much depends on how we read tone and irony.

Swift uses irony and impersonation in yet more complicated ways. His *Argument against Abolishing Christianity* (wr. 1708; pub. 1711) and *Mr. C[olli]ns's Discourse of Free-Thinking, Put into plain English* (1713) are, like Defoe's *Shortest-Way*, fundamentally difficult, nonstraightforward satires. I discuss both at length below, but for now the point is that Swift uses monitory satire in a fashion similar to his less well-known contemporaries and on related subjects. As Defoe and Maynwaring mimic or translate the High Church position, Swift "paraphrases" the freethinking Collins in ways meant, ultimately, to compel the audience to more critical habits of reading and interpreting. Just as purposefully problematic are the Bickerstaff pamphlets (1708–1709), the satire of which is retaliatory against the quack Partridge, defender of the dissenters and antagonist of the High Church. However funny Swift's hoax, it does at least implicitly demonstrate the possibility of seemingly authentic lies, the untrustworthiness of print and speech, and the need for the percipient deconstruction of what one reads and hears.

Directly or indirectly, these satirists suggest that readers would do well not to believe everything they are told. The advocacy of healthy skepticism is not merely an abstract moral lesson; it has considerable topical relevance to the hottest debates of these years and applies to contested subjects of real practical importance to everyday life. The preoccupation of dissenting satirists with High Church eloquence (and their concern that the queen's "Words" are "not her own") gives us reason to believe that they were genuinely frightened that the Anglicans would proceed to extreme measures. They might not go to the hyperbolic lengths recommended in the *Declaration without Doors* (1705)—once thought to be Defoe's, but deattributed by Furbank and Owens—in which a High Churchman swears that if the nonconformists press for moderation, "We will cut all their Throats" (l. 119).[37] But from a dissenter's point of view, the danger of violent persecution was real. These satirists, like Defoe in *The Shortest-Way*, are exposing enemies (for the sake of like-minded readers) rather than simply mocking or rebuking them. What makes *The Shortest-Way* so much more upsetting is the completeness of the impersonation; the piece is not ironic, and the distinction between authorial position and words on the page is never really established. Literary critics have tended to see *The Shortest-Way* as an anomalous misfire, an aberration in its author's career and a bungled precursor to *A Modest Proposal*. Defoe's pamphlet is not well explained, however, as an injudicious deviation from early eighteenth-century satiric norms—it is in fact an example of a kind of satire common from about 1702 to about 1714.

How do the works I am labeling "monitory" function as satire? Ridicule is sometimes a conspicuous component of such works (as in Swift's *Excellent New Song* on

"Dismal") and sometimes entirely beside the point. Straightforward satiric admonitions are either explicit (see *The Tale of a Nettle*) or use obvious and stable irony (*Address to Our Sovereign Lady*); their authorial positions can be determined with some confidence, and the object of suspicion is particularized and made plain. In other words, readers of straightforward monitory satire ought to know of whom to be afraid. Sometimes irony is unstable and the line between truth and fiction blurred (as in Swift's reply to Collins)—representing, among other things, a warning against taking words at face value. More complete simulation without irony can be equally upsetting (see Defoe's presentation of barefaced extremism in *The Shortest-Way*). Whether the irony is made plain or the satire is less obviously "fictional," the cumulative effect of these works is much the same: the point is the productive disorientation of like-minded readers, not the humiliation of enemies. Monitory satire of this sort fits very badly the "attack" and "reform" categories employed by modern satire scholars, but it also represents one of the most exciting developments of satire in this quarter century.

Ideological Argumentation: Dunton, Defoe, and Others

Political satirists from the mid-seventeenth century through the early eighteenth century and beyond lampoon their enemies, seek to discredit the opposition, defend their own causes, propagandize on their party's behalf, and complain about any number of issues or about the general state of affairs. Another type of satire in this period is different from straightforward attack, defense, or admonition, though sometimes comprising all three. It is primarily investigative, raising important questions or expressing fundamental concerns about the organization of society or government. Dustin Griffin's categories of "inquiry" and "provocation" are useful here, if not perfectly applicable. He defines satirical inquiry as that which is either genuinely or ostensibly inconclusive: "the satirist writes in order to discover, to explore, to survey, to attempt to clarify." Satirical provocation is for him essentially negative, a form of "critique of false understanding."[38] The satires I am talking about here are neither apparently open ended (most do clearly convey a judgment) nor purely negative.

Early eighteenth-century satirists reflect on the nature and basis of power, not in terms of philosophical abstractions but as topical responses to ongoing debates of the day. Issues of toleration and dissent were a source of stormy disagreement throughout Anne's reign, but religious controversialists like Sacheverell, Leslie, and Hoadly were just as concerned with broader questions about obedience and allegiance. When Leslie launched his periodical *The Rehearsal* (1704–1709), he did so expressly to challenge Tutchin, Defoe, Hoadly, and the other Whigs who disavowed divine right and argued that monarchical injustice could be lawfully resisted. High-flyers like Leslie and Sacheverell promoted patriarchy, passive obedience, unblinking allegiance to the divinely ordained sovereign. Sacheverell captured the attention of the masses when he at least implicitly assailed the principles underlying the Revolution of 1688 in inflammatory pamphlets (such as the collaborative *The Rights of the Church of England Asserted and Proved*) and sermons like "In perils amongst false brethren" (1705). His trial in 1710 was a cause célèbre. The meaning and legitimacy of 1688 continued to be hotly contested long after the death of William, and the imminent Hanoverian succession was hardly unproblematic, especially with the Pretender alive and well across the English Channel. The questions addressed by Sacheverell, Hoadly, and others were very much a part of the public imagination. Defoe and Tutchin, arguably the best-known political satirists of this quarter century, were embroiled in these disputes, as were many of their contemporaries.

The anonymous *Leviathan, or, a Hymn to Poor Brother Ben* (1710) belongs to the world of religiopolitical defamation—but to challenge Hoadly is to slur a leading proponent of contractual theories of kingship. In 1709, Hoadly was involved in a back-and-forth exchange with the bishop of Exeter, a loud advocate of divine right and passive obedience. Like most Whigs, Hoadly maintained that Anne was " 'a good behaviour Queen' . . . appointed by parliament *durante bene placite.*"[39] *Leviathan* ironically refutes those "who blind Obedience pay / To royal Monarchs' Princely Sway" and praises the mob as "our Sov'reign Lord" (ll. 20–21). To this ruling mass, the poet sings:

Thou giv'st the sacred Rule to Kings;
And at thy Nod they're useless Things.
What, tho' they stile themselves divine,
And would succeed by Right of Line,
There is no Law on Earth, but thine. (ll. 32–36)[40]

The poet is unquestionably taking a position, and of the satiric judgment against Hoadly readers can be in no doubt, but this piece is very poorly explained as simply a put-down of Hoadly and his supporters.[41]

Prose satirists like Dunton likewise combine politically motivated invective with argumentation about the structure of current politics and the nature and basis of authority. Dunton's *King-Abigail: or, The Secret Reign of the She-Favourite* (1715; *6d*) targets Abigail Masham, a prominent court favorite under Anne. In this opaque mock sermon, Dunton opposes the involvement of women in governing, grumbles mightily about court favorites, and suggests that divines like Sacheverell have no business meddling in state affairs. Dunton's main concern seems to be with the principles underlying party politics, prerogative, and the management of the state. Here he reflects on ancient notions of order and authority:

> Nor can I think that they were perplexed with the *Roar of the Church's Danger*, or
> bully'd into a Belief, that Kings are in Possession of the Crown *By a Divine Right and
> Commission, which place 'em above the Reach of all Laws and Power upon Earth.* . . .
> That they are invested with an absolute and *Arbitrary Power*, over the Lives, Lib-
> erties and Fortunes of their Subjects. . . . That an unconditional, slavish, Passive
> Obedience in all cases, without Exception, to all the Commands of such Princes,
> are to be observ'd upon *Pain of Damnation.* . . . No, *those were Doctrines unknown
> to former Ages.* (6)

This is hard going, a universe apart from spirited drubbing of a target. Like the authors of *Rome, or Geneva: or, the True Church of England Without Either* (1717) and
Rightful Monarchy: or, Revolution Tyranny (1722), Dunton is soberly exploring questions about political power, not just passing judgment.

Defoe's *Jure Divino* (1706; 15s by subscription, 5s pirated) is perhaps the best illustration of satiric argumentation. Defoe takes aim at high-flyers, Tories, and anti-Wil-
liamites, but, as Furbank points out, "this poem, with its footnotes, constitutes the
fullest account of his political philosophy" (2:28).[42] Defoe's contention is straightforward: divine right and patriarchal theories of monarchy are dangerously misguided,
subjects have the right to defy the commands of tyrants, and passive obedience is not
only a mistake but a sin. At the end of his introduction, Defoe encourages "Satyr"
personified to begin "the Grand Inquiry" (75), and critical inquiry is crucial to the
spirit of the poem. In the prose preface, he raises questions he perceives to be devastating to his adversaries' position.

> Kings, *say our Champions of Absolute Power*, have their Authority from God, *and
> from him only*; of such Gentlemen it would be well to ask some such Questions as
> these; When they receive this Power? And what Kings are they have it? If all Kings
> have it, then the Usurper who murthers the Right Heir has it, and Crookback *Rich-
> ard* had it, and was King *Jure Divino*; and what was *Henry* VII. then? . . . If Usurpers
> have not this Divine Right, Where then will you find it? (39–40)

Jure Divino's twelve books delve into various related themes—universal self-interest,
allegiance, tyranny, justice, power—sometimes inquisitively and sometimes with
sharp hostility. Defoe's footnotes are substantive, argumentative, and ponderous:
"Passive Obedience is a Contradiction in Terms; for, if they suffer, it must be for first
disobeying; if they obey'd, there could be no Penalty inflicted; if they first merited
the Penalty, How could they Obey?" (150n).[43] Defoe's satire is a weighty exploration
of the role of subjects in a monarchy and of the basis and nature of kingly power.
Satire of this sort is less a punitive or didactic tool than a form of "Grand Inquiry."
A modern critic might object that only the denunciatory parts of the poem are sa-

tiric, that the inquiry and argumentation are separate, but Defoe evidently made no such distinction, titling *Jure Divino* "a satyr" rather than "a satyrical poem." Remote though it is from twentieth-century notions of "Augustan satire," it is very much a part of what readers in the early eighteenth century assumed satire could and should do.

III. Social and Moral Satire

Social and moral satire is much less experimental than religiopolitical satire in this quarter century. As in the late seventeenth century, we find a considerable amount of all-inclusive satire or satire on types. Some exemplars are evidently lightweight efforts at entertainment (in the fashion of Ward's apolitical satires), and others are sober and pompously moral. In dramatic satire in particular, we see more distributive justice, didacticism, and exemplary satire, the last a category familiar from works like Shadwell's *The Squire of Alsatia* and *The Scowrers*. Compared to the late seventeenth century, more particularized social satire is written in this period, ranging from relatively mild to very harsh. Finally, just as early eighteenth-century religiopolitical writers use satire as a form of sometimes dense argumentation, so a number of satirists write substantive social commentary that is explorative as much as or more than it is heatedly judgmental.

Generalized Satire

Generalized satire continues from the late seventeenth century, though the abstract "attacks" on concepts (e.g., confinement) and inanimate objects (e.g., wine) have radically diminished by 1705 or thereabout. Thomas Baker's *An Act at Oxford* (1704) includes satire directed at the university—pointed enough that offense was taken and the play banned—but the piece is basically a spicy intrigue comedy.[44] Some early eighteenth-century satirists produce comic or satiric descriptions of "types," as in Ward's *The Wooden World Dissected* and *Mars Stript of his Armour*, humorous pamphlets respectively published in 1707 and 1708, the first attacking the navy, the other targeting the army.[45] Ward's best-known example is probably *The London Terrae-filius: or the Satyrical Reformer* (issued in six parts in 1707 and 1708), a playful catalog of London pedestrians. He takes the passersby in turn: "Here comes a *She-Devil* of a *Prattle-Box*, who is so very full of the spirit of *Contradiction*," he says, "that she never agreed with her husband in any one thing, except in *Child-getting*" (no. 2, p. 33). Ward's commentary is sometimes sharp or bawdy, but the tone is uniformly bantering.[46] As in *A Journey to Hell*, Ward's object in these generalized pieces is to divert, not to punish or instruct and certainly not to correct.

Generalized satires in this period are sometimes flippantly entertaining but more often somber and dull, sonorously moralistic versions of the satiric journalism Ward practiced in the 1690s. The author of *A Net for the D[evi]l: or, the Town Display'd* (1705), a work of the "reformation of manners" variety, thunders against widespread impiety ("Yet let God's House be empty as it will, / You'l see the *Taverns*, and the *Play-House* fill") and then denounces his readers for hypocrisy: "in Humility your Sins disguise. / Which, in *Plain English*, is but just to say, / Be very *Wicked*, in a Godly way" (9, 11). He concludes with an uncompromising judgment on his reprobate targets, suggesting that moral reclamation is beyond the power of satire. This is heavy-going, generalized satiric moralism, as is *The Merchants Advocate, A Poem, In an Imitation of Juvenals XIII. Satyr* (1708), whose author's supplications are plodding and pedantic: "Hear next almighty Reason. Thus she cries, / That Man, who best ill fortune bears, is wise" (3). The satirist describes a variety of sins, gravely reminding his readers that a vengeful God is noting their transgressions and concluding with a sermonic promise of final justice: "Only God can *See*, and *Hear*, and *Punish* too at last" (20). These and similar social satires, like those by Gould covered in the preceding chapter, are mostly generalized and sometimes fiery.[47] Their authors are rendering moral judgment.

Didactic Satire in the Manner of Steele

Not all satiric moralists are punitive. "Soft" satire—aimed at moral education rather than castigation—has had scant critical attention from those who associate satire primarily with aggression. The exemplary plays of Shadwell are not popular among modern satire scholars, and Swift is a more fashionable subject than Addison. The rigidly "pejorative" definition of satire has been rightly challenged by Matthew J. Kinservik, who points out, for example, that Cibber's *The Careless Husband* (1704) was regarded by its author as a satire but, because it emphasizes correction rather than punishment, is not usually treated that way by critics.[48]

The loudest early eighteenth-century proponents of reformative satire are, of course, Steele and Addison.[49] In *The Tatler* (1709–1711) and *The Spectator* (1711–1712; resumed June–December 1714), they advocate satire written from a position not of judgment but of sympathy.[50] "I am very much troubled," Addison says in *The Spectator* no. 23, "when I see the Talents of Humour and Ridicule in the Possession of an ill-natured Man." In *The Tatler* no. 242, Steele likewise stresses the importance of compassion and generosity to true satire. Benevolence is "an essential Quality in a Satyrist," for "Good-Nature produces a Disdain of all Baseness, Vice, and Folly, which prompts them to express themselves with Smartness against the Errors of Men, without Bitterness towards their Persons. This Quality keeps the Mind in Equanimity, and never lets an Offence unseasonably throw a Man out of his Character."[51] To pass harsh judgment from a position of superiority is to do little more than libel or lampoon. The proper satirist is not judge but fallible teacher—amiable, ultimately sympathetic, and himself not beyond moral reproach. Satire's tone should be sober but forgiving, the objective not reproof but improvement.

Addison and Steele are not the only early eighteenth-century advocates of benevolent satire. Charles Johnson's *The Wife's Relief: or, The Husband's Cure* (1711) is a slow-going reform comedy—like Centlivre's *The Basset-Table* (1705), though Johnson is more somberly preachy than Centlivre.[52] *The Wife's Relief* centers on the imperfect union of the unfaithful Riot and the devoted Cynthia, who hopes to "mend" her wayward husband (28). Little interested in being mended, Riot is raring to have sex with Cynthia's cousin Arabella, who is actually in love with his confidante Volatil. Cynthia and Arabella plot against Riot but after tormenting him confess their jest—and (hey presto) the errant husband becomes his better self, vowing to Cynthia that "my future Life shall pay the mighty Debt I owe thy Virtue" (86). Like Belfond junior's conversion in *The Squire of Alsatia*, but unlike Loveless's in *Love's Last Shift*, we are clearly meant to take this seriously. In the epilogue, Johnson spells out the moral: he urges "Ye *Riots* in the Pit" to "Reflect, Reform: Go to your several Houses, / And from this very Moment—Love your Spouses" (87). The prologue stresses the author's empathy: "he laughs and mourns," and "*Feels* the very Characters he Paints." The virtuous (like Cynthia) are very virtuous, and even the badly behaved Riot is, above all, reclaimable. Johnson is not simply judging the naughty male lead and, by implication, his real-life counterparts; he is educating them in their capacities for decency.

The famous exemplary comedy is Steele's *The Conscious Lovers* (1722), his most thoroughgoing attempt to instruct the audience in proper social mores. In the prologue, Steele employs language drawn from the terminology of the satiric theory of the day (language picked up by twentieth-century critics like Mack). He announces that he wishes to "please by Wit that scorns the Aids of Vice" (303) so that he may function as "the Champion of . . . Virtues" (304). The point of the play, as one contemporary put it, was "to move the Audience to the Suppression of Vice, by presenting 'em with such a Worthy Noble Character as *Bevil*."[53] Bevil junior, and his eventual bride, Indiana, are Steele's models of polite respectability; draft titles for the play included "The Gentleman" and "The Fine Gentleman."[54] In the most famous scene, this well-mannered youth nobly refuses to duel with his friend, after which the two reconcile, becoming "Dearer Friends than ever" (357). Theatergoers reportedly burst into tears, presumably benefiting from the moral lesson.

The social and ideological division in *The Conscious Lovers* is represented by Sir John Bevil (a Tory gentleman) and Mr. Sealand (a Whig merchant). Following John Loftis, scholars long believed Steele to be celebrating the latter at the expense of the former, though he in fact commends and criticizes both groups, and the hero of the play is a country heir rather than a city merchant.[55] Ideological interpretation of Steele's comedy is not an altogether simple matter. Mark S. Dawson—a historian, not a literary critic—has challenged the reading of *The Conscious Lovers* as a "moralistic drama which . . . presented upper-middling Londoners with an uncompromisingly positive representation of themselves and their social position."[56] Dawson encourages a more nuanced understanding of attitudes toward and dramatic representations of class:

> Even if a new type of sentimental comedy did come to chide "aristocratic" or "gen-
> teel" standards of behaviour and offer something more improving in its place, we
> must not assume either an equally straightforward, parallel rejection of aristocracy
> or gentility as *social* concepts or, conversely, that any improvement correlates with
> a clearly defined and alternate social group (i.e. a bourgeoisie) becoming newly
> prominent as both theatrical producers and spectators. (44)

Dawson is rightly skeptical about the value of simplistic ideological explanations of *The Conscious Lovers*, but that Steele's play is strongly ideological is not in question. Steele is making a social argument; he has definite views on gentility and propriety; and he presents his audience with unequivocal models. A much preachier play than his *The Funeral* (1701), *The Conscious Lovers* is an overtly didactic satire. What Steele offers is not mere platitudes or a pro forma representation of reform; he is trying to educate viewers and readers in admirable social behavior.

Particularized and Topical Satire

Topical social satire in this period is more conspicuous than it was toward the end of the seventeenth century. The anonymous author of *The Female Wits: or, the Triumvirate of Poets At Rehearsal* (wr. 1696; pub. 1704) targets the female playwrights Delarivier Manley, Mary Pix, and Catherine Trotter. *The Lunatick* (1705; perhaps by William Taverner?) satirizes Elizabeth Barry, Anne Bracegirdle, and Thomas Betterton. Opera is chirpily mocked in Richard Estcourt's *Prunella* (1708) and Mrs. Aubert's *Harlequin-Hydaspes: or, The Greshamite* (1719). The anonymous poet of *The Dancing-Master* (1722; 4*d*) rails against Italian opera and other forms of imported culture, contemptuously branding its producers and consumers "the Dregs and Scum of all the Earth" (4).[57] How much of this is earnest and how much rhetorical performance is anybody's guess.

Particularized satire tends to have or at least to claim broader implication and application. Defoe's indictments of English civility in *Reformation of Manners*, *More Reformation*, and *The Conduct of Christians made the Sport of Infidels* are sweeping, but they too are highly particularized, targeting Toland, freethinkers, Occasional

Conformists, and so on. In *The South Sea Scheme* (1721), William Hogarth satirizes a topical event as a symptom of widespread social malady. From a distinctly moral viewpoint, Hogarth illustrates "Monys magick power" to blight a society (as he writes in the verse that appears on the print).[58] *News from Hell: or, A Match for the Directors* (1721; 1s) is both a generalized plaint on acquisitiveness and an angry attack on a specific manifestation of widespread avarice: "How goes the Stock, becomes the gen'ral Cry," encouraged by the "Villain *Crew*" of directors, and England is "Bought and Sold, / By the damn'd thirst of curst delusive Gold" (6, 7, 8). Particularized social satires vary in intensity of moral judgment, tone, and ferocity, but together they represent an increasingly common type of enterprise.

Argument and Inquiry: Mandeville and Prior

Social and moral satire in the early eighteenth century can be all-inclusive or individuated. Like religiopolitical satire in this period, it can also be more a matter of Defoe's "Grand Inquiry" than simple denunciation. Mandeville and Prior both produce inquisitive, argumentative satires in this period, and though they are not the only practitioners of this type of satire, I focus my discussion on them.[59]

Mandeville's *The Fable of the Bees: or, Private Vices Publick Benefits* (1714) comprises rigorous, if often playful, social commentary. The *Fable* includes an earlier version of the satire (*The Grumbling Hive* [1705]), twenty prose "Remarks" on that work, and "An Enquiry into the Origin of Moral Virtue." The satire was reprinted in 1723 (5s†) with expanded "Remarks" and two new essays, "A Search into the Nature of Society" and "An Essay on Charity and Charity-Schools," in which Mandeville contends that charity schools are detrimental to a flourishing society. Such institutions inculcate their pupils with a sense of ambition, rendering them unfit for the dog's work that is theirs to do in a hierarchical society. The argument, says Richard I. Cook, is that "economic expediency . . . justifies keeping the lower orders in a perpetual state of poverty and ignorance."[60] In the other 1723 addition, "A Search into the Nature of Society," Mandeville sharply opposes the third Earl of Shaftesbury, who "calls every Action perform'd with Regard to the Publick Good, Virtuous; and all Selfishness, wholly excluding such a Regard, Vice" (372). Witheringly personal as passages of the "Enquiry" are, the satirical thrust of the essay is not mere derogation of Shaftesbury. Mandeville is exploring, arguing, scrutinizing. Like the rest of the *Fable*, this represents, in Phillip Harth's phrase, a kind of "intellectual satire."[61]

The Fable of the Bees is investigation and revelation of paradoxes as well as negative critique. The central paradox is famous: individual vices like greed and vanity are necessary to a prosperous society. In a world in which "reformation of manners" movements have succeeded, the standard of living would become intolerable. Mandeville ridicules those who claim "virtue" for themselves, observing that they live happily in a society whose affluence requires the very vice they deprecate. The point is that society can have *either* morality *or* prosperity, and Mandeville insists that "having decided in favor of one alternative," the people "ought not to lament the absence of the other."[62] The tone of the piece is less harshly condemnatory than coolly logical; the *Fable* is short on savage indignation. This is the work of a realistic social philosopher, not a malcontent or a misanthrope. That some of the responses it elicited were substantive, engaged attempts to refute his arguments is unsurprising. Lampoonists often generate lampoonery in return, and bluster is commonly met with bluster, but *The Fable of the Bees* was answered by Christian moralists and Anglican scholars eager to defend human virtue, and it belongs to a discussion of social and theological controversy in this period as well as to one about satire.

Another mocking piece of satiric inquiry is Matthew Prior's *Alma: or, The Progress of the Mind* (1718), a burlesque poem with a weighty philosophical point. Prior's subject, Monroe K. Spears observes, "is the problem of the mind's relation to, and situation within, the body—a problem given a new urgency by the dualism implied by scientific method and formulated . . . by Descartes." Spears concludes that the "system" of *Alma* is an illustration, against Cartesian dualism, "of the intimate union between mind and body."[63] Prior also rejects the Aristotelian argument that the mind or soul is everywhere in the body, a position he ridicules in the poem's opening:

> ALMA in Verse; in Prose, the MIND,
> By ARISTOTLE's Pen defin'd,
> Throughout the Body squat or tall,
> Is, *bonâ fide*, All in All.
> And yet, slap dash, is All again
> In every Sinew, Nerve, and Vein. (ll. 14–19)

This is the stuff of philosophy, but its tone is that of a hudibrastic romp, and neither the denseness of the argument nor the liveliness of the satire should be neglected. As a compromise between Aristotelian and Cartesian notions, Prior sarcastically advocates "a system in which the mind progresses from the feet to the head as the man ages."[64] *Alma* is both ponderous and playful, an overtly mocking piece of philosophical argumentation.

The religiopolitical, social, and moral satires surveyed in sections II and III have received scant critical attention: they are mostly nonliterary in subject and conspicuously short on artistic trappings. An informed reader in the 1710s and early 1720s, however, would almost certainly have pointed to these pieces to illustrate contemporary English satiric practice. These works are what early eighteenth-century satire looked like, little though they figure in our histories of eighteenth-century satire. What modern scholars do discuss from these years is the practice of the so-called Scriblerians, and I now consider where those satirists fit in the world I have been surveying.

IV. The Alleged "Scriblerians"

Scholars rarely discuss eighteenth-century satire without invoking the Scriblerians.[65] Because the "Club" met in this period (the known gatherings occurred in 1714), and because Pope, Swift, and Gay loom so large in the later 1720s, critics have tended to see the early eighteenth century as dominated by these writers. Implicitly or explicitly, the works of Pope, Swift, Gay, and Arbuthnot are understood to constitute a mode of satire—variously practiced by each of them throughout his career and widely influential among their contemporaries. Two basic but vital questions are how similar are the works of the men we call the Scriblerians, and how predominant is what they do in the satiric culture of the early eighteenth century?

I will begin with Pope, not because he is the star satirist in the quarter century before *The Dunciad*, but because, unlike the others, he is barely a satirist at all. "Although Swift was a lifelong satirist," Leopold Damrosch observes, "Pope was not. Of the three great poems of his twenties—*An Essay on Criticism*, *Windsor-Forest*, and *The Rape of the Lock*—only the last is satiric, and it is as much a comedy as a satire."[66] Griffin and others have regarded *An Essay on Criticism* (1711; 1s†) as at least quasi-satirical, and Weinbrot has recently defined the work as a "Menippean satire" of sorts.[67] Pope's program for moral criticism no doubt contains satirical jibes, but that contemporaries would have recognized it as a satire, or that Pope imagined himself as a satirist in writing it, seems unlikely.

The Rape of the Lock (1714 edition; 1s†) is universally included in the canon of eighteenth-century satiric masterpieces and hailed as the culmination of the mock epic in English satire. But, as George Sherburn accurately remarked in 1934, "The *Rape of the Lock* one almost forgets to call satire."[68] What is it a satire *on*? The social squabble behind it is well known. Pope claimed to intend no offense to anyone; he wanted simply to effect reconciliation between quarreling families by way of a pleasantly comic depiction of the cutting of the lock. That Pope is mocking the vanities and pretensions of the beau monde is clear, but his criticism is gentle and sympathetic, aware of both the triviality and the beauty of the world he describes. Ian Jack sensibly distinguishes the *Rape* from Dryden's more abrasive and judgmental lampoon against Shadwell. He argues that, insofar as Pope's poem is a satire, "it opposes not a person but a moral fault: immoderate female pride." Whereas *Mac Flecknoe* is a thoroughgoing "annihilation" of Shadwell, Pope's agenda is not defamation but potentially productive amusement.[69] *The Dunciad* is the work of a self-appointed cultural custodian, and the Epistles the compositions of a high-minded moral guardian, but *The Rape of the Lock* is a brilliantly crafted diversion, the effort of an artist rather than a social reformer.

What negative satire Pope writes in his early career is small scale and mostly unpleasant. A version of his memorable portrait of Addison ("Atticus" in the *Epistle to Arbuthnot*) was evidently drafted in 1715; it was published in 1722, possibly without Pope's consent, and expanded in *Fragment of a Satire* for the 1727 *Works*.[70] In 1716, he attacked Edmund Curll in *A Full and True Account of a Horrid and Barbarous Revenge by Poison, On the Body of Mr. Edmund Curll, Bookseller* (3d†), the publication of which was "stupid," says Mack, because Curll was sure to retaliate. He got his hands on a jeu d'esprit in which Pope ironically praises a quack physician, and he printed it in 1716 under the title "Worms," clearly attributed to Pope. This little pasquil, Mack argues, "was to haunt Pope for life" as an example of his spitefulness.[71] Curll also published another of Pope's poems that year, a burlesque of the sixteenth-century version of the first psalm done by Thomas Sternhold. Mack contends that Pope meant to ridicule "the sixth-grade singsong of Sternhold" but that Curll and other enemies used the satire to underscore his Catholicism—that is, his irreligion.[72] The lines against Addison are retaliatory, unkind, and personal; "Worms" is mean spirited but essentially frivolous; the burlesque of the psalm is teasingly derisive. Sherburn is correct to describe these works as "firecracker squibs such as a clever schoolboy might produce."[73] Pope's early satire has little to do with our image of him as a high-toned moralizer and a denunciatory cultural warrior.

Gay is definitely writing satire in the early eighteenth century. He is a master of burlesque: he travesties epic in *The Fan* (1713), tragedy and comedy and pastoral in *The What d'ye Call It* (1715), classical epics and georgics in *Trivia* (1716), and intrigue comedy in *Three Hours after Marriage*, written in collaboration with Pope and Arbuthnot in 1717. In *Wine* (1708) and *The Shepherd's Week* (1714) he parodies the prurience of John Philips. He makes a hobby out of lampooning John Dennis, whose *Appius and Virginia* he burlesques in *The Mohocks* (1712); the preface to *The What d'ye Call It* parodies the critic's ponderous style; the caricature in *Three Hours after Marriage* of Dennis as Sir Tremendous Longinus is brilliantly funny, as is the representation of John Woodward as Dr. Fossile. Gay mocks people and ideas and genres to wonderful effect, but the satiric thrust of his early pieces is by no means always obvious.

Some of Gay's targets are easily identifiable, though not all of them and not all the time, and even where the objects of ridicule are discernible, the satirist's position is not necessarily evident. *Wine* is his earliest satiric piece, a parody of Philips's *Cyder* (1708) and a burlesque drinking georgic that ends with a series of encomiums to the queen and four politicians. David Nokes concludes that "*Wine* is a youthful exercise, ostentatious and sometimes uncertain in its parodic effects, and ambiguous in both its literary and political affiliations."[74] Scholars have worried about the irony of the encomiums, but no reading has been conclusive. Nokes says the "political significance . . . is far from clear"; Downie asks if Gay "is applying his encomiums 'directly wrong'"; Juan Christian Pellicer argues that the passages "are neither ambiguous nor subverted by the ironies of parody, and since they represent a shrewd and timely bid for [Whig] patronage they need not seem confusing."[75] What Gay thinks he is doing in these verses is probably now unknowable, but the crux is their essential ambiguity, their openness to multiple interpretations. Whether the satiric object of *Wine* is anything more than a spirited burlesque of Philips is hard to guess. Gay's next satire, *The Mohocks*, a highly topical piece that was never acted is a satirical representation of the gang of London rakehells that has sometimes been read in very sober terms. As Peter Lewis points out, "The hooligans paradoxically acquire some of the dignity of the heroic world, and the result is a disquieting indeterminacy. If hooligans can sound like heroes, might it not be the case that heroes actually behave like hooligans?"[76] I grant the implication, but I have a hard time taking this piece as anything but a cream puff.

The more problematic satires are those in which Gay's tone is sunnily buoyant despite the dark ramifications of what he describes. The alarming disparity between despairing conclusion and bouncy delivery is not unique to *The Beggar's Opera* (discussed in the next chapter). In *The Fan*, Gay describes the titular high-society accessory in the elevated style of the mock heroic: "I sing that graceful Toy," the poem opens, "whose waving Play / With gentle Gales relieves the sultry Day." Nokes is probably right to suggest that Gay is exposing unpleasant social realities,[77] but what are we to make of the comic frivolity of the poem? The same lack of correspondence between tone and subject is found in *Trivia: Or, The Art of Walking the Streets of London*, which has been read as everything from a celebratory topographical poem to a profound sociomoral satire.[78] The Walker describes the sights, sounds, perks, and dangers of strolling the city; much of what goes on is grubby and sordid, but the Walker is cool and unperturbed rather than disgusted and judgmental of the waste he describes. Stephen Copley and Ian Haywood highlight Gay's "ironic circumlocutions" and his "evasions of the implications of the subject-matter."[79] The interpretive difficulties arise from the fundamental ambiguities of the Walker himself: what is his status, vis-à-vis the world in which he traffics, and what exactly is his perspective on what he describes? The elusive ironies of this poem have yielded no consensus. *The Fan* and *Trivia* both reflect Gay's discontentment with existing social structures, but they are also jolly. *The What d'ye Call It* is similarly unsettling, its potentially trenchant social satire diffused by its appearance in a nonsensical plot.

Gay has a disconcerting tendency to present unhappy social truths with merry exuberance. He is undoubtedly conscious of the social issues he raises in his early satires, but the literary contexts in which he presents them are such, generically or tonally, as significantly to undercut them. The critique, in *Trivia* and elsewhere, is abated. One interpretation is that Gay is genuinely concerned but has no conviction that positive change can occur, so he makes his social points as throwaways. Another possibility is that he raises these issues in some seriousness but leaves their interpretation strictly up to the reader or viewer, who can admit and worry about the social commentary if so inclined or ignore the criticisms and let the tone rule. Other plausible explanations no doubt exist, but Gay is not making a systematic, strenuous effort to communicate a sociopolitical satiric point.

Arbuthnot's reputation as a satirist depends largely on *The History of John Bull*, published under that title in 1727 but comprising four parts, which appeared in 1712.[80] The John Bull pamphlets are straightforward political allegory concerned with foreign and domestic affairs of Anne's reign—the War of the Spanish Succession, Sacheverell's trial, arguments for war or peace, the personalities of the major political players of the day. The basic plot outline is as follows: John Bull (England) and Nicholas Frog (the Dutch) are engaged in a lawsuit (the War of the Spanish Succession) against Philip Baboon (the Duke of Anjou), who has acceded to the estate of Lord Strutt (Philip V) courtesy of Lewis Baboon (Louis XIV). In chapter 5 of *Law is a Bottomless-Pit*, Arbuthnot provides sketches of Bull, Frog, and Humphrey Hocus, their chief attorney (Marlborough). Bull is "an honest plain-dealing Fellow" who "was very apt to quarrel with his best Friends, especially if they pretended to govern him: If you flatter'd him, you might lead him like a Child" and so on, forming the now-famous composite of British characteristics that Bull has been taken to represent. Frog is portrayed as "a cunning fly Whoreson" willing to "pine his Belly to save his Pocket"—a caricature of the much-reviled Dutch (10). Led by the self-seeking Hocus, lawyers convince Bull and Frog that the suit can be settled quickly, but the affair drags on, draining their resources and accomplishing nothing. Bull's wife (the Whig ministry) dies, leaving him with three daughters (war, faction, and penury); he takes another wife (the Tory ministry of Oxford and Bolingbroke), who wisely advises him to abandon the legal wrangle and get back to work. When he discovers that the attorneys are swindling him, he calls upon Sir Roger Bold (Harley) for aid in escaping the lawsuit. Hocus and others scheme to prevent peace at all costs. At the end of *John Bull Still In His Senses*, Bull, Frog, and Lewis meet to resolve their differences at a conference at Salutation Tavern (Utrecht). After much difficulty, they decide upon an acceptable treaty, and the fourth and fifth pamphlets describe the financial settlement between Bull and Frog, the uproar in Bull's family upon his return from Salutation Tavern, and other aftereffects of the peace agreement.

What did Arbuthnot think he was doing in these pamphlets? He mocks individuals, political factions, religious sects, and institutions in ways that would have been clear to his readers, but he does so without much animus. The allegory is high spirited, written by a politically minded humorist who was obviously enjoying himself. Had Arbuthnot foreseen the fall of the Tory ministry two years later, Robert C. Steensma points out, the satire would certainly have been noticeably more sour and gloomy.[81] Written during a period of Tory dominance, however, these pamphlets were evidently meant not to influence the course of current events (e.g., war and peace) but to show up the Whigs and to gratify the Tories.

The Art of Political Lying (1712; 3d†) is a much different—and considerably more difficult—satire. The definition of the "art of political lying" it provides is, like the piece as a whole, ponderous:

> *The Art of convincing the People of* Salutary Falsehoods, *for some good End.* [The author] calls it an *Art* to distinguish it from that of telling Truth, which does not seem to want *Art*; but then he would have this understood only as to the Invention, because there is indeed more Art necessary to convince the People of a *Salutary* Truth, than a *Salutary* Falsehood. (8)

What follows is not a theory of this art but a proposal for a theoretical examination of it.[82] The Proposer projects chapters that will cover the nature of political lying and lies, the lawfulness of the practice, the characteristics of the lies and liars, the question of which party is most skilled at the art, "the Celerity and Duration of Lyes" (20), and so on. A later chapter purports to classify various species of political lies: the detractory, including simple libel and gossip; the additory, which "gives to a Great Man a greater share of Reputation than belongs to him"; and the translatory, "a Lye that transfers the Merit of a Man's good Action to another who is in himself more deserving; or transfers the Demerit of a bad Action from the true Author, to a Person who is in himself less deserving" (11).

The Art of Political Lying is oblique, ironic, and dense, a piece of at least implicitly judgmental probing, not invective or comic ridicule. It belongs to the world I described in section II much more than do any of Pope's or Gay's satiric writings. In Conal Condren's illuminating study of this satire, he describes it as "a somewhat disingenuous commentary on contemporary and party generated accusations of dishonesty," as a "parody of views of theoretical knowledge," as "a satire of Machiavellian and post-Machiavellian political theories," and as "a comment on contemporary changes in the lexicon of English political values, on the fraught and refracted relationships between the terms of public virtue and private worth."[83] The piece is full of mocking ironies. Condren underscores Arbuthnot's two different uses of indirection: the author distances himself from the satiric persona, and "the force of the satire itself is indirect or ambivalently focused" (29). On the apparent satiric object of *The Art of Political Lying* I again quote Condren:

Through a non-confrontational approach and encoded invitations to skepticism, Arbuthnot can . . . inveigle the reader into a tacit and critical participation as the account unfolds. If perchance the fiction is swallowed, the presupposition that politics is a fundamentally dishonest business is taken down as well. If we merely appreciate the joke, say as Tory sympathizers, we are nevertheless nudged toward a critical perspective on the political world of which we are a part. (31)

The satire's effect depends heavily upon the reader's disposition and political sensibilities. Arbuthnot's motives are hard to discern. At a guess, he is calling attention to treachery in contemporary English politics and (inconsistently) ridiculing the speaker, the author of the phantom proposals. *The Art of Political Lying* is a product of the decade and a half of cautionary irony and dissimulation I discussed above. Arbuthnot seems to be raising questions about the language of politics, and its potential for deception, in a frustratingly indirect satire.

Clichés about the "Scriblerians" and longstanding assumptions about their interconnections have made scholars assume more commonality than actually exists. Pope, Gay, and Arbuthnot (with Swift) spent some time together in 1714; they were friends and sometime allies; at different times and to varying degrees, they were in touch with each other and occasionally made suggestions about each other's work. In the advertisement to *Three Hours after Marriage*, Gay acknowledges having received help "from two of my Friends" (unnamed, but almost certainly Pope and Arbuthnot). Pope and Gay both have some fun at Dennis's expense; Arbuthnot and Gay employ irony, though not in the same way. If we look for incongruities as well as correspondences, without trying to make these men into a "Scriblerian" cohort, what do we find?

Pope is a master technician who produces very little satire in these years. What satire he does write is either pure fluff or personal lampoon. Not much is at stake for him in *The Rape of the Lock*; he implicitly exposes the vacuity and triviality of the beau monde, but the degree to which he objects to what he describes seems limited. Gay also uses mock epic in *The Fan*, though his is a much chillier poem than Pope's. Neither Pope nor Gay does straightforward allegory of the sort Arbuthnot practices in the John Bull pamphlets. Insofar as Pope has deeply felt satiric concerns in this quarter century, they are predominantly cultural. Gay has a great deal of fun travestying literary forms, and most of his early pieces include criticism of social structures, though the complaint is usually obscured or neutralized by tone and contexts. Gay definitely does not force-feed negativity to his audience, but unlike Pope he seems bothered by the unhappy realities he perceives. Arbuthnot's preoccupations are largely political. The conflict between the sobriety of Gay's allegations and the joviality with which they are presented is jarring, but the effect is not at all like the difficulty posed by Arbuthnot's ambiguities in *The Art of Political Lying*. Neither is it like Swift's vexing irony. Gay can come across as flippant and hands off; Swift's satire cannot be read that way. Arbuthnot and Gay deal with different subjects, and their methods and satiric styles have nothing in common. And, as Condren points out, the doctor's satire is radically dissimilar from Pope's and Swift's, whose "aggressive and socially driven satiric impulse" he does not exhibit.[84]

The notion that Pope, Arbuthnot, and Gay are three of the four chief practitioners of a "Scriblerian mode" of satire is a critical delusion. Another much-cherished fancy is that this "mode" is somehow central to and illustrative of the world of early eighteenth-century satire. Except in very loose terms, the satires of these writers do not really "belong" to the categories discussed in sections II and III; attack, defense, warning, ideological argumentation, and didacticism are not what we find in Pope and Gay. Gay's *The Fan* and *Trivia* include what could be trenchant social satire, but the lightness and brightness of their tone differentiate them from frivolous generalized satire (e.g., *The London Terrae-filius*), heavy-handed social preachment (e.g., *The Merchants Advocate*), and more pointedly topical satires (e.g., *The Dissenting Hypocrite*). Arbuthnot comes closer to his contemporaries: the John Bull pamphlets mock recognizable political figures, and *The Art of Political Lying* is dense and disconcerting, very much a part of the decade and a half of ironic satire described in section II. Pope is particularly out of sync with what is going on around him. His squibs are antagonistic, but his better-known works are remote in kind from the satire of his contemporaries. That *The Rape of the Lock* typifies satiric practice in this quarter century is a conclusion that can be drawn only if one ignores the vast majority of the satires produced and circulating at the time. The idea of a single mode practiced by the "Club" members is equally difficult to credit. For all their personal interaction, Pope, Gay, and Arbuthnot produce utterly different types of satire—and Swift is another beast altogether.

V. Swift before *Gulliver*

Swift writes a lot of satire in this quarter century, and his practice is far from uniform. From this period, only *A Tale of a Tub* (with *The Battle of the Books* and *The Mechanical Operation of the Spirit*) has received much attention from satire scholars. Critics discuss the Bickerstaff hoax, *An Argument against Abolishing Christianity*, the Drapier's Letters, and a few of the poems, but our sense of Swift's early satiric practice derives largely from *A Tale* and from its author's (later) association with the so-called Scriblerians. In this section I attempt to answer a simple question: what does "Swiftian satire" in this quarter century comprise? I will say flatly at the outset that Swift as early eighteenth-century satirist belongs not to the world of the Scriblerians but to that of Defoe, Tutchin, Maynwaring, and the other religiopolitical satirists discussed in section II.[85] If we look beyond *A Tale*, not reading for evidence of latent Scriblerianism, what sort of satirist do we find Swift to be?

Jokiness and Play

The playfulness of Swift's satire has been frequently commented on, especially in discussions of *Gulliver's Travels*. He doubtless had fun savaging some of his foes, though the tonal difficulties posed by some of his works make determining his mood difficult. A rollicking delivery does not always signal levity, and, as Claude Rawson points out, Swift tended to use light verse as a "vehicle of serious commentary."[86] How many of his early satires are simply amusements? I consider *Mrs. Harris's Petition* (wr. 1701; pub. 1709) and *Mary the Cook-Maid's Letter to Dr. Sheridan* (1718) primarily entertaining pieces, both mimicking servant-speak. Swift wrote the first while staying at Berkeley Castle; the speaker is the chattering waiting maid of the countess. His one-page *A Meditation upon a Broom-stick* (wr. 1703; pub. 1710; *2d*) is a jauntily irreverent parody of Boyle's *Meditations* (devotedly read by the countess). Swift slipped his parody into the *Meditations* when he was asked to read aloud from them; his delivery was sober, and the lady, not realizing that she was getting a burlesque rather than a bona fide piece of moralizing, guilelessly commended Boyle for his ability to offer edifying lessons even when treating the most trivial subjects. The satire is a practical joke.

Swift's early satiric output includes rather a lot of genially mocking playthings and jeux d'esprit; taken together they represent a counterbalance to the aggressive anger we associate with him. The object of *A Ballad on the Game of Traffick* (wr. 1702; pub. 1746), also dating from his stay at Berkeley Castle and depicting part of domestic life there, is principally to amuse Lady Betty. *Apollo Outwitted* (wr. 1709; pub. 1711) teasingly celebrates another lady friend, the Countess of Winchelsea, with whom Swift played cards and whom he liked to entertain with comic rhymes. In several lightweight squibs, he teases friends with affectionate banter. *On the Little House by the Church Yard of Castleknock* (wr. 1710; pub. 1746) pokes gentle fun at the smallness of the vestry of Archdeacon Wells's church; the "Epigram" beginning "As Thomas was cudgelld one day by his Wife" (wr. 1723?; pub. 1727) lightly ridicules Swift's close friend and fellow clergyman Thomas Sheridan for suffering the torments of a shrewish wife; and several poems mock Stella and Rebecca Dingley.[87] The point is that, important though Swift's ferocious hostilities are, he often wrote in the capacity of mischievous friend, cheerful debunker, and amused rhymester—a fact that remains true across his writing life.

Destruction and Negativity

Swift's indignation is notoriously savage, and in his early satires the devaluative impulse features prominently. I focus here on those satires in which he is destructive or plaintive for the sake of destruction or complaint, before turning to his more propagandistic satires, in which he defames individuals or groups with apparent practical purpose.

Several of Swift's early satires are essentially nonparticularized negative commentary. They are sometimes melancholy, sometimes disgusted or angry, but largely purposeless—except insofar as they reveal to humankind the pathetic smallness of the race or the squalor of its surroundings. For *Baucis and Philemon* (1709), he borrows Ovid's tale, in which Jupiter and Apollo (in Swift's version, two unnamed saints) wander the earth to test the hospitality of its inhabitants. They are uniformly mistreated, except by the singularly poor Baucis and Philemon, who invite the saints inside to share their meager rations. Virtue gets its reward: the couple's home is turned into a church, and at the end of their lives, they become intertwining trees. Swift's version, however, does not end there. Generations pass, and a parson cuts down Baucis for wood to repair his barn; a grief-stricken Philemon deteriorates and is "stub'd and burnt" by the next parson (l. 178). This conclusion obviously subverts Ovid's image of natural prosperity and immortality; *Baucis and Philemon* is a statement of general pessimism. *A Description of a City Shower* (1710) is a humorous but hardly jolly mock georgic, surveying a scene of grubbiness and malodorous filth. The memorable last lines point up the soiled reality of the city: "Sweepings from Butchers Stalls, Dung, Guts, and Blood, / Drown'd Puppies, stinking Sprats, all drench'd in Mud, / Dead Cats and Turnip-Tops come tumbling down the Flood" (ll. 61–63).[88] In *Phillis, Or, the Progress of Love* and *The Progress of Beauty* (both wr. 1719), Swift once again offers negative description, rendering the full unpleasantness of human relationships and the human body. *The Progress of Beauty*, the first of the Strephon-Celia poems, describes Celia's ghastly appearance ("Crackt Lips, foul Teeth, and gummy Eyes") before she creates a softer facade by means of "Pencil, Paint, and Brush" (ll. 15, 46). Too close a view will reveal the characteristic ugliness of the body—a familiar point in Swift's satire, and a thoroughly unpleasant one.

In more particularized satires, Swift is less doleful than destructive, reveling in gratuitous vituperation. His vilification of individuals often seems to have broad implications about society and humanity, making these works both personally nasty and more generally negative. His *Description of a Salamander* (wr. 1705; pub. 1711) "depicts Lord Cutts, appointed commander-in-chief in Ireland in 1705, as a repulsive lecher who has infected the country with venereal disease."[89] The devaluation of the man is undeniable, and Swift also undercuts modern notions of valor, as he does even more witheringly in *A Satirical Elegy On the Death of a late Famous General* (wr. 1722). That poem opens with ironic lamentation on the demise of Marlborough, who has expired in a totally unheroic way: "His Grace! impossible! what dead! / Of old age too, and in his bed!" (ll. 1–2).[90] The man and his legacy are defiled: "He left behind *so great a stink*," we are told, and heroism and heroes become "empty things" (ll. 16, 25). Swift tromps on the duke's grave with visceral pleasure, though his perception of the vacuity of human grandeur cannot have been happy-making.

The same cynicism marks *The Virtues of Sid Hamet the Magician's Rod* (1710), Swift's "revenge" poem on Sidney Godolphin.[91] Written upon Godolphin's fall from power, the satire could have had little practical point: Swift is lampooning a political enemy as a dastardly louse who buys off potential opposition. A personalized complaint of another sort is *Whitshed's Motto On His Coach* (wr. 1724), blasting not a shady politician but a crooked judge.[92] In the wake of the Wood's halfpence controversy, William Whitshed had presided over trials in Dublin involving Swift's printers, bullying jurors until they produced the desired verdict. Swift pulls no punches: "Libertas & *natale Solum*; / Fine Words; I wonder where you stole 'um" (ll. 1–2). As Herbert Davis rightly concludes, in Swift's angriest satires "a fierce indignation burns within him, fed by his outraged sense of justice, his bitterness at the hollow mockery of so much human greatness."[93]

Purposive Defamation and Defense

The condemnations of Marlborough and Whitshed are acid, but some of Swift's best deprecation is propagandistic and even defensive. Like many political satirists, he uses personal attack as a form of pragmatic defamation of his enemies. *An Excellent New Song, being the Intended Speech of a famous Orator against Peace* (1711) is a response to Nottingham's defection to the Whigs, whom he joined in order "to bring down the ministry on the question of peace without Spain." Swift reports in his *Journal to Stella* that Oxford "was hinting as if he wished a ballad was made" on Nottingham.[94] The *Excellent New Song* ridicules the speechmaking of the turncoat ("Dismal") and reveals his defection as the unscrupulous machination of an unscrupulous man. Using a technique current among his fellow political satirists, Swift lets his target expose himself. The text, as the title suggests, is Dismal's "Intended Speech."

> But, some will cry, *Turn-Coat*, and rip up old Stories,
> How I always pretended to be for the *Tories*:
> I answer; the Tories were in my good Graces,
> Till all my *Relations* were put into *Places*. (ll. 21–24)

Swift satirizes Nottingham again in a prose lampoon called *A Hue and cry after Dismal* and in *T[o]l[a]nd's Invitation to Dismal, to Dine with the Calves-Head Club* (both 1712;

both 1d*†), the latter a piece of political exultation disparaging a number of leading Whigs by name.[95]

In 1711, the Oxford ministry seemed vulnerable—but Marlborough had *not* managed to bring the ministry down, and Nottingham's defection had *not* converted other Tories to the Whig cause.[96] By the time Swift wrote this poem, the ministry was much more secure. *T[o]l[a]nd's Invitation* is snidely exultant, but it is not just a piece of merry triumphalism. The satire is also a familiar denigration of the Whigs as radicals. The freethinking Toland invites Dismal to join him and his fellow Whigs/traitors, and again the treachery is put in the mouth of the target: "At Monarchy we nobly shew our Spight, / And talk *what Fools call Treason* all the Night" (ll. 15–16). Swift is smearing Nottingham and his new political brethren, but he is also writing as *chef de propagande* of the Oxford ministry and at least implicitly upholding the political status quo.

One of the threats to the Oxford ministry in 1711 had been Marlborough, and Swift's execration of him in *The Fable of Midas* (1711; 1d†) is more defensive propaganda than malicious lampoonery. Marlborough returned from a victorious campaign in 1711 and promptly began agitating against the Tory ministry. In particular, he pushed for the continuation of the war, challenging Oxford's promotion of peace; after he voted against the peace preliminaries in December 1711, Anne summarily dismissed him from his offices.[97] Marlborough's disgrace was not unproblematic for the Tory ministry. He was a popular war hero, and he had been effective as a diplomat; his public shame risked weakening the support for peace. That the ministry did not greatly suffer from his sacking, Ellis argues, owes something "to a careful plan of propaganda" against Marlborough—the campaign to which *The Fable of Midas* belongs.[98] Swift retells the story of Midas and then identifies his descendent in "a certain *Leader.*"

> That Virtue in the Fingers ends:
> What else by *Perquisites* are meant,
> By *Pensions, Bribes,* and *three per Cent?*
> By *Places* and *Commissions* sold,
> And turning *Dung* it self to *Gold?* (ll. 42, 44–48)

The "*British Midas*" has, Swift insists, both "*Asses Ears,* and *dirty Hands*" (ll. 70, 82). This is personal, to be sure, but Swift is also attempting to besmirch a political rival whose popularity threatened to undermine the ministry and the cause in which he seriously believed. Similarly purposive is *The W[in]ds[o]r Prophecy* (1711), a mock prophecy warning the queen to dismiss the Duchess of Somerset. In Hermann J. Real's fine analysis of the controversy surrounding this poem, he emphasizes Swift's serious aims: "Whoever wants to get to grips with *The Windsor Prophecy* had better work from the assumption that Swift was not playing a wantonly (self-) destructive game out of sarcasm, malice, and spite. On the contrary, there is evidence that he sincerely wished to serve his country at a time of acute political crisis when, he felt, nothing less than England's future was at stake."[99]

Swift's best-known piece of propaganda is *The Conduct of the Allies* (1711; 1s), a pamphlet promoting peace—that is, advocating what was negotiated two years later as the Treaty of Utrecht.[100] Evidently Swift's argument had practical effect. In the *Journal to Stella*, he boasts that "the Resolutions printed t'other day in the Votes, are almost quotations from it; and would never have passed, if that book had not been written" (2:482). The substance of *Conduct* is persuasive polemic, no less a weighty argument than Dunton's *King-Abigail* or Defoe's *Jure Divino*. Like those authors, Swift is passing judgment. He ferociously denounces the warmongering Whig opposition, the Allies, and the entire war effort.[101] I doubt that Swift thought of this essay as satire, but it deserves mention as an example of the sort of polemical aggression that he practiced in his early career.

Swift's responses to Steele in 1713–1714 are just as politically argumentative as *Conduct* and more sharply satirical. In *The Crisis*, Steele had defended Revolution principles and the Protestant succession; on the eve of Anne's death, he loudly claimed that the church was in danger from the Pretender and argued for the legality of a Hanoverian monarch. Calhoun Winton describes Steele's sort of propaganda as "the hortatory, the viewing-with-alarm, the call for a return to first principles," and, he points out, the "pomposity was too much for Swift." The Protestant succession, Winton observes, was an issue "which the Tories could not comfortably dispute. The obvious course, then, was to discredit the author of the offending publication,"[102] and so Swift does in *The First Ode of the Second Book of Horace Paraphras'd* (1713; 3d). Published before the appearance of *The Crisis*, the *First Ode* is a response to the advertising campaign that preceded Steele's pamphlet.[103] Swift does not challenge the argument of *The Crisis* but mocks its author, who "pompously wilt let us know / What all the World knew long ago"—that is, "That we a *German* Prince must own / When A[N]N for Heav'n resigns Her Throne" (ll. 7–8, 11–12). He then banteringly advises Steele to return to Drury Lane after he has "settled *Europe's Grand* Affairs" (l. 40). The object of the *First Ode* is to deflate the credibility of a political antagonist, in this case before the publication of his argument. *The Publick Spirit of the Whigs* (1714; 1s) is a point-by-point refutation of *The Crisis*, alternately teasing, parodying, and savaging its author. Ehrenpreis describes the pamphlet as Swift's "final defense of the Oxford ministry" and as a remarkably un-Swiftian satire. "There are no hoaxes here, no impersonation, no self-ridicule, no elaborate, satirical fantasies. The voice throughout is the true author's. . . . So far from playing clever games with Steele's propositions or willfully misunderstanding them, Swift's regular . . . procedure is to cut down the implications and innuendos to simple language and then refute them as squarely and openly as he can."[104] *The Publick Spirit of the Whigs* is straightforward, defensive, argumentative, and purposively defamatory.[105]

Swift's Irish tracts are aggressive, castigatory calls for political action—but are they satires? Several satire scholars have at least mentioned the Drapier's Letters (1724–1725), written to strengthen Irish resistance to Wood's halfpence, but Griffin is probably correct in suggesting that "we should read them not as satire but as polemic that makes local use of satire."[106] *A Proposal for the Universal Use of Irish Manufacture* (1720) is another borderline case. The essay calls for an Irish boycott of all English goods: Swift exhorts the Irish "never to appear with one single *Shred* that comes from *England*," but instead to be "*universally* clad in their own Manufacture" (9:16). This is a call for action, laced with bitter ridicule, but it is not really satirical. Swift's verse follow-up to the proposal, *An Excellent new Song on a seditious Pamphlet* (1720), is more mockingly satiric. The Irish have ignored his entreaty: "We'll buy *English* Silks for our Wives and our Daughters, / In Spight of his Deanship and Journeyman *Waters*" (ll. 8–9). In the poem's last lines, the imprudent Irish anticipate the worst for their would-be liberator. If the printer betrays him, he will be arrested, leaving them to buy English silks without recrimination. The *Excellent new Song* expresses Swift's usual outrage at English treatment of Ireland, just as it reflects his angry exasperation with the Irish.

Swift's satiric objects in the works hitherto surveyed—both the nastily destructive satires and the more purposive pieces of defamation—are relatively clear. He refutes, decries, defends, mocks, and propagandizes. Swift is easy to find in these works, his authorial position not obscured to the point at which readers can no longer be certain where they are or why. He is varyingly ironic and straightforward, explicit and implicit, but neither the target nor the nature of the satire is particularly elusive. Other satires—*A Tale of a Tub* is the major example—are much less clear cut and require more of the reader.

Indirection and Difficult Satire

Swift's most famous satire of this period is also his most disorienting—*A Tale of a Tub* (1704; 4s‡) is dizzying, much more than merely an "attack." If it were that, it would be better explained by analyses of Swift's satire on abuses in religion and learning. The speaker is a modern hack dissenter who sometimes speaks Swift's truth but more often reveals himself as untrustworthy, illogical, unreasonable, and even mad. The parable of the three brothers is easy enough to follow, and the ridicule of Peter (Roman Catholicism) and Jack (Calvinism) is undeniable. But is Swift defending or deriding the Anglican Church? Modern scholars, aided by authorial contexts, have not been able to agree on an answer to that question.[107] Contemporary readers of the anonymous text would have been on even shakier ground; most of them must have been thoroughly befuddled. In much of Swift's satire, his position is comprehensible; the force of the satiric argument depends upon clear rendering of judgment. That *A Tale* is doing something different is thumpingly obvious—though no one has ever been able to say with any certainty what that something is. Rosenheim's verdict of 1963 seems useful: "the identification of particular satiric victims is a piecemeal procedure, during which, if anything, whatever satiric 'unity' the work may claim tends to disappear." The "umbrella-terms under which we try to subsume" the multiple targets, he continues, quickly "become inadequate or meaningless."[108] One important point is that interpretation of the satire depends heavily upon how it is read and by whom. This is not straightforward transmission of satiric judgment.[109] Much of the effect comes from the technique and from the experience of reading.

Are Swift's Bickerstaff pamphlets (1708–1709) a practical joke, a humorous burlesque, or a biting satire on Partridge and astrology? No doubt Swift enjoyed the prank, but as several critics have pointed out, Partridge was not simply a nonsensical quack. He championed everything that Swift despised and decried all that Swift supported: he abused the High Church, vigorously protested the bill against Occasional Conformity, and defended the dissenters.[110] Swift's satire is not a social entertainment but a "defense of established authority," a pointed attempt to discredit a loud proponent of the unorthodoxy that Swift abominated.[111] Moreover, as Ronald Paulson rightly concludes, the satire is also "on the crowd, the reader who accepted the news of Partridge's death," and more broadly on "the tendency of people to take whatever appears in print . . . as gospel truth."[112] Again, Swift's purposes are not only punitive but also instructive: the satires on Partridge expose the potential for printed untruths and (therefore) the dangers of being an uncritical reader. "The Bickerstaff controversy," Robert Phiddian contends, "is not about truth. It is about plausibility and about verification."[113] Did Swift—like Defoe and others—hope that his satire would provoke thought and even discomfiture? That seems possible, even in such a playful set of satires as the Bickerstaff pieces.

How seriously are we meant to take *A Tale* and the Bickerstaff papers? Both pieces are in some ways very funny works, though Weinbrot has recently issued a salutary reminder of "the *Tale's* deep sadness."[114] One point is worth remembering. The author of *A Tale* was essentially an obscure nonentity who had no practice at managing complicated satiric writing. Samuel Johnson was right to reflect that nothing in Swift's later writing is "like" *A Tale*.[115] That Swift simply failed to control his satiric argument (or effect) is somewhere between a strong possibility and a safe bet. Another explanation might be that the "strategy of mystification" is a deliberate attempt to unsettle or even unnerve readers.[116] Or perhaps *A Tale* is merely a game played by a technical experimentalist—doubtful, given what we know about Swift, but not unthinkable.

Conceiving of Swift's Bickerstaff satires as part of a spirited jest is more plausible, but Partridge was no mere joke. He was a political enemy. *A Tale* and the Bickerstaff works are showpieces of Swiftian irony, and they both have bite. In these satires, Swift might very well be trying to make a point about the possibilities for deception, about the untrustworthiness of even those speakers who are sometimes (somewhat) right, and about the need for readers to cultivate perspicacity.[117] Swift's other difficult satires of this period are the answer to Anthony Collins and the *Argument against Abolishing Christianity*, both striking displays of his irony but quite unlike either *A Tale* or the Bickerstaff pamphlets.

Swift responds (anonymously) to Collins in *Mr. C[olli]ns's Discourse of Free-Thinking, Put into plain English* (1713; 4*d*), but he does not do what he was to do to Steele in *The Publick Spirit of the Whigs*. He does not rebut. His strategy is paraphrase, a form of impersonation practiced by Defoe, Maynwaring, and other religiopolitical satirists in this quarter century. Swift restates Collins's views—with distortion, tactical omissions, and amplifications—and translates the freethinker's careful reasoning into canting drivel. The garbled paraphrase presumably serves to reveal the illogic of the original. The piece is (says Phiddian) "a virtuoso deconstruction" in which readers "are taken inside Collins' discursive world and shown it without the window-dressing and concealments that hide its 'true' implications from public view."[118] What is Swift doing? Obviously, Collins is the principal butt of the joke, but like some of the self-exposure satires discussed in section II, this piece does more than ridicule its target. Translating a text "into plain English" inevitably calls into question the true meaning of the original. Swift's paraphrase of Collins makes plain the potential for inauthenticity, duplicity, and misleading eloquence. Part of the lesson—for those inclined to see it—is the necessity of critical reading, the need to apply reason to the arguments with which one is presented.

Swift's indirection in *An Argument against Abolishing Christianity* (wr. 1708; pub. 1711) is if anything more problematic. The piece was occasioned by the agitation for the repeal of the Test Act in Ireland, a move that Swift felt would be tantamount to abolishing Christianity—though the connection that was obvious to him would have been anything but clear to his readers. Even if Swift had published the piece in 1708, says Ellis, "the argument against repealing the test clause in Ireland would have been so deeply buried in anonymity and allegory that his powerful Whig friends would not have been able to penetrate the disguise."[119] The degree and completeness of the piece's irony is hard to determine, and Swift's relationship to his speaker is complicated and unstable. The narrator is manifestly untrustworthy. Edward A. and Lillian D. Bloom have pointed out that, as the antiabolitionist moves through his argument, "he unconsciously proves his reliability suspect, his propositions specious, and his religious motives reducible to hypocritical self-seeking."[120] As in *A Tale*, Swift's speaker is a modern. He is part of the problem rather than the voice of reason and resolution, though he is not systematically and consistently satirized.

The narrator of the *Argument* seeks to rebut a proposal for abolishing Christianity, though he also emphasizes that what he wishes to retain is not real but nominal Christianity—that is, the hypocrisy Swift ironically advocates in the *Project for the Advancement of Religion.*

> I hope, no Reader imagines me so weak as to stand up in the Defence of *real* Christianity; such as used in primitive Times . . . to have an Influence upon Mens Belief and Actions: To offer at the Restoring of that, would indeed be a wild Project; it would be to dig up Foundations; to destroy at one Blow *all* the Wit, and *half* the Learning of the Kingdom; to break the entire Frame and Constitution of Things. (2:27)

The antiabolitionist defends nominal Christianity on purely pragmatic grounds: its removal will hurt society. "Read superficially," Nokes argues, "the *Argument* attacks hypocrisy by . . . 'defending' the residual utilitarian functions of religious institutions in a society whose ethos and impetus are to be found elsewhere."[121] Swift describes a world in which hypocrisy is customary; he proposes and ridicules the retention of Christianity in name only. Knowing Swift, we may be certain that he is not really championing the merely nominal preservation of Christianity, but that he believed a return to "real" Christian practice was possible is highly unlikely. What is he advocating? What are his purposes, beyond an oblique and obscure defense of the Test Act? He is, of course, also seeking to undercut those who from his point of view represent threats to the established church, including deists, atheists, and dissenters. Another target, as Ian Higgins has convincingly demonstrated, are the Socinians, the most prominent anti-Trinitarians in late seventeenth- and early eighteenth-century England.[122] The polemical intention behind Swift's parody is not in doubt—but, as in the case of his response to Collins, he is doing more than simply conveying an opinion or passing judgment.

Why does Swift use indirection in his early satire? The question no doubt seems a strange one to ask of someone celebrated for impenetrable ironies and insoluble difficulties. *A Tale* still leaves readers mystified, and *Gulliver's Travels* has inspired an evidently irresolvable critical tangle. The majority of his early satires, however, are relatively easy to cope with. The exceptions are *A Tale*, the Bickerstaff pamphlets, *Mr. C[olli]ns's Discourse*, and the *Argument*—all published within a span of nine years, during the decade and a half of irony discussed above, and all definitely not straightforward. On what issues does Swift employ indirection? As I argue in section II, religiopolitical satirists of the day tend to use impersonation and self-exposure in responses to subjects concerning High Church versus Low Church controversies, dissent and Occasional Conformity. Dissenters warn their brethren not to believe in High Church eloquence; High Church advocates try to demonstrate that the non-conformists' cant is a cover for treasonous schemes.

Swift's most difficult satires all deal, after a fashion, with religious controversy. This is probably not a coincidence. Michael F. Suarez has suggested that "wisdom and critical discernment" are "the allied goals of Swift's satires," and that Swift's "moral purpose" is to equip "readers to see through the world's deceits."[123] I doubt the applicability of this description to all of Swift's output, but for the indirect satires in particular, Suarez's conclusion seems fruitful. Swift's object, in these works, is similar to Defoe's in some of his satires, however different the aims and allegiances of those writers. Like Defoe and other contemporaries, Swift uses indirection to demonstrate the possibilities of deception and the problems of credulity. I suspect that he is (to some extent) trying to educate readers in these satires, though he evidently had a great deal less faith than Defoe in his ability to do so—or, rather, in his readers' ability to appreciate, comprehend, or benefit from the education.

I am less interested here in generating new and improved readings of particular texts than in suggesting that Swift has been miscontextualized in modern satire studies as an "Augustan" and "Scriblerian" writer. The culture of satire in this quarter century includes satiric impersonation, ironic self-exposure, technical experimentation, and deliberately disorienting satire. Swift is much the most brilliant practitioner of this sort of satire, but he is far from anomalous. This is the world to which he belongs; these are his satiric contexts. *A Tale* is usually regarded as a "pre-Scriblerian" enterprise; it gets twinned with *Gulliver's Travels* as pinnacles of achievement; its author is viewed as a great literary satirist and a devoted confrere of Pope, Gay, and Arbuthnot. Like them, he has literary and cultural concerns, though his religious concerns separate him from those writers. His friendship with Pope and company notwithstanding, what they are doing in the early eighteenth century is ultimately irrelevant to what he is doing. Forcing Swift into a "Scriblerian" pigeonhole badly misrepresents his early career as a satirist.

In the early eighteenth century, Swift writes a great deal of both verse and prose, uses different techniques, is varyingly direct and indirect. He sometimes writes to protect the status quo, as in *The Fable of Midas*, and sometimes vehemently to oppose it, as in *An Excellent new Song on a seditious Pamphlet*. Swiftian satire tends to be associated with negativity, but several of these works have clear positives, whether or not they are overtly expressed; the degree to which Swift writes *defensive* satire has been underestimated. He is certainly capable of gratuitous nastiness or of grumpy and plaintive commentary on a sad state of affairs; he is also a tenacious activist, concerned to influence the present and productively to discredit those he finds threatening to what he supports. Swift can be funny, abusive, anxious. He is by modern standards a religious bigot, and he is a superbly effective propagandist. Sometimes both a preacher and a clown, he cries for reform and mocks himself for doing so.[124] In technical range, he shares much with Defoe and other religiopolitical satirists of this quarter century—he denounces, propagandizes, complains, defends various causes, and allows his targets to expose themselves. Playful dedications to "Prince Poster- ity" notwithstanding, Swift's early satires are grittily political and his hands are often dirty; he goes after individuals at Oxford's nod. His politics and friendships are more respectable than Defoe's, and his skepticism more welcome to modern scholars than Defoe's Puritanism; unlike Defoe, he did not have to write for bread. Nevertheless, Swift belongs to the world of *Poems on Affairs of State*—a culture of largely anony- mous lampoonists, propagandists, and muckrakers, of party men whose satiric mo- tives and concerns are extremely remote from the ill-defined preoccupations of the "Scriblerus Club."

VI. Characterizing the Early Eighteenth Century

Among the most recent attempts to characterize early eighteenth-century satire is that of Ruben Quintero, who argues that these years represent

> an especially innovative time for satire in both prose and poetry, as satiric authors openly experiment within all genres for more effective ways to instruct savvy readers about folly and human nature. When normative values are not clearly understood, satiric art will be loud, divisive, and combative, for it is only upon accepted values that recognition of the ridiculous is premised. We cannot know what is absurd un- less we know, or believe we know, what is . . . reasonable, and this period developed a firm sense of what it considered ethically reasonable. It is this common ground of perceived understanding that makes the eighteenth century one of the richest periods of satire in any language.[125]

Quintero is absolutely right to emphasize satiric innovation in this period, though his analysis does little to demonstrate the new directions of English satire. That eighteenth-century writers and readers shared a "common ground of perceived un- derstanding" is a hypothesis hard to test, but my main reservation about Quintero's account is that, though alluring in its neatness and eloquence, it is functionally ir- relevant to what actually goes on in most early eighteenth-century satires. Modern critical approbation of (alleged) eighteenth-century ethical consensus does nothing to describe the dynamic satiric culture of the period. To what works does this description apply? Pope had a strong sense of what was ethically reasonable, and he is Quintero's centerpiece, but if we are going to do any justice to early eighteenth-century satire, then we need to be talking about particulars.

Those particulars do not reduce to tidy verities. The quantity of satiric output in this quarter century is considerable—I found some five hundred satires, roughly comparable to the number in the subperiods covered in the next two chapters. Beyond the sheer number of works written and published, we need also to recognize the satirists' bravura technical experimentation and their diversity in method, conceived audience, and apparent purpose for writing. Some satirists are denunciatory and some didactic, but the material cannot be divided into Swift and Pope versus Addison and Steele. "Attack" includes wanton punishment of enemies, calculated campaigns against political powerhouses, and moralistic blanket scoldings of English society. Some fifty monitory satires appear in a span of less than a decade and a half (most of them from the period 1704–1711), and together they represent a phenomenon I had not foreseen at the outset of this investigation. Satirists as different as Swift and Defoe attempt to instill capability as well as to convey knowledge; others use satire as a form of philosophical inquiry and social critique; yet others raise questions about the structure of government and the legitimacy of political authority.

What makes early eighteenth-century satire so spectacular is not, or not only, the genius of its best loved practitioners or the supposed ethical consensus of its readers and writers. The most conspicuous feature of these years is the multiplicity of satiric practices. That multiplicity means that this subperiod is more resistant to characterization than were the reigns of Charles, James, and William. What distinguishes this subperiod from the others covered in this book is precisely that diversity of satiric purposes—that sort of spread is not to be found anywhere else. Other distinctive markers of Anne's reign in particular are the high number of dense, soberly argumentative, and heavy-going texts and the equally conspicuous body of monitory satires. Twentieth-century notions of satire-as-attack are never very satisfactory when applied to the long eighteenth century, but for the first quarter of the eighteenth century they are especially misleading. A great many of the satires in this subperiod simply do not do what modern critics expect them to do.

Scholars have tended to assume the inevitability of *Gulliver's Travels*, *The Dunciad*, and *The Beggar's Opera* and so have too often mined this quarter century for happy harbingers of the "Scriblerian" heyday, ignoring the many other satires that fit the "Scriblerian" model not at all. The satiric productions of Pope, Gay, and Arbuthnot are a long way from representative of the culture in which they were written. Pope's and Gay's works jar especially badly against that which is, if not predominant, at least prominent in this period—namely, the religiopolitical satires produced by Defoe, Swift, and the satirists surveyed in section II. Granting the peculiarity of *A Tale*, Swift is much more a part of his milieu than Pope or Gay, who are basically misfits. We have a problem of perspective: Defoe is all but unmentioned in accounts of early eighteenth-century satire, and the Scriblerians represent a putatively unified titanic force. An informed English reader in 1725, however, would probably have regarded Defoe as a long-standing major player, Swift as a brilliant and politically toxic oddball now in the obscurity of exile, and the other so-called Scriblerians as only peripherally relevant to satiric practice. The truth is that such a reader, asked to forecast the near future of English satire, could not have guessed what was about to happen. The canonical masterpieces of the late 1720s and 1730s were by no means obvious, necessary, or an inevitable development from the work of the previous two decades. From the vantage point of contemporaries, they were neither predictable nor even probable.

CHAPTER SIX

Harsh and Sympathetic Satire, 1726–1745

The World is all alike.

—Gay, *The Beggar's Opera*, III.xiv.5

If he makes *Mankind* bad as *Elves*,
I answer, they may thank themselves;
If *Vice* can ever be abash'd,
It must be *Ridicul'd*, or *Lash'd*.
But, if I chance to make a *slip*,
What right had he to hold the *Whip*?
—Swift, *The Life and Genuine Character of Dr. Swift*, ll. 115–120

The Man of Candour and of true Understanding is never hasty to condemn.

—Fielding, *Tom Jones*, 1:329

Let *Sporus* tremble—"What, that Thing of silk,
Sporus, that mere white Curd of Ass's milk?
Satire or Sense, alas! can *Sporus* feel?
Who breaks a Butterfly upon a Wheel?"
—Pope, *Epistle to Arbuthnot*, ll. 305–308)

The years between the publication of *Gulliver's Travels* and the deaths of Pope and Swift are usually hailed as the high moment of eighteenth-century satire, and not without reason. *Gulliver* and *A Modest Proposal*; the *Dunciad*s, Moral Essays, and Horatian imitations; *The Beggar's Opera*; Fielding's plays, *Shamela*, and *Jonathan Wild*; Johnson's *London*—this is a prodigious period in the history of English satire. Here we arrive at the span of years from which most modern notions of eighteenth-century satire are derived; the themes that have been emphasized by satire scholars (e.g., vilification of Walpole, bitter complaint about burgeoning Grub Street culture, denunciation of cultural decay) deserve the notice they have received. The big-time satires have mostly been dealt with often and competently, and I see no reason to quarrel with my predecessors over interpretations of most of those works, but I do think some crucial issues need to be addressed concerning satire in this period and its most studied practitioners.

Amid the nitty-gritty clutter of this chapter covering quite a lot of disparate material, I argue four cases that I want to make explicit at the outset. (1) In terms of satiric practice, scholars tend not to distinguish much between the first and second quarters of the eighteenth century. In fact there is little continuity from the first quarter of the eighteenth century to the 1726–1745 period, and we need to take these years on their own terms. (2) Pope, Swift, and Gay are often treated as a satiric triumvirate who share a life-changing commitment to the "Scriblerian" mission and who devote their satiric energies to attacking a common enemy. Granting some shared targets and occasional collaboration, these three writers are significantly different satirists, and to lump them together is to misrepresent them and to mischaracterize the subperiod at issue here. (3) *Gulliver's Travels* is the best-known and most widely read satire of the eighteenth century, and it has received much critical attention, but precious little consensus has been reached on some very fundamental issues of interpretation. In section III I offer my own interpretation of the *Travels*, but one conclusion is that Swift's satire is a one-off, both brilliant and largely unconnected to the culture of satire in this period. (4) Henry Fielding is usually seen as a would-be "Scriblerian," tenaciously striving to emulate his betters, whatever his temperamental differences from those writers. He writes a lot of satire throughout the second quarter of the eighteenth century, and I argue that his concepts of satire are remote from those of any of the Scriblerians. He is capable of preachment and hostility, but on the whole he tends to be a good deal more playful, and in the fiction much more sympathetic, than Pope, Swift, or Gay.

Taking the production of these twenty years as a whole, one can only say that it was a fabulous time for satire. No doubt a reason for this is that the late 1720s and 1730s mark a return to intense political controversy of a sort we have seen in the reigns of Charles II and of Anne. Satire in this period has mostly to do with a fairly limited set of issues, and it appears in a narrower spectrum of forms than we encounter in chapter 5. This material is much less dizzying, the subperiod more coherent, than was true in the previous quarter century. That is not to say that we find uniformity, but some of the more important conclusions have to do with the subperiod as a whole. My chapter title highlights the two directions in which satire goes during these years. A crucial point is that, although some of the most remarkable punitive satires of the century date from this period, this is also a time in which sympathetic satire is on the rise, as witness some of the works of Fielding, Robert Dodsley, and others. Another conclusion is that the major works often seen as exemplary (in kind, if not in quality) of eighteenth-century practice turn out to be either atypical or part of a short-lived phenomenon.

I. Pope and Swift among Their Contemporaries

In chapter 5, I survey the period from roughly 1700 to 1725, deliberately stopping just prior to what J. Paul Hunter has called "the peak of the Augustan moment," that three-year span in which three of the most celebrated satires of the long eighteenth century appeared.[1] *Gulliver's Travels*, *The Beggar's Opera*, and the first *Dunciad* are—as should be clear from the previous chapter—without precedent in the earlier eighteenth century. Far from representing the inevitable culmination of an evolving tradition, they come, in many respects, virtually out of nowhere.

The discontinuity in this period is not just a matter of a few innovative headliners bursting forth ex nihilo: the culture of satire alters in major and not wholly explicable ways. Some connection exists between these two periods—satirists complain, mock, denounce—but the carryover from the first to the second quarter of this century is startlingly limited. Trying to put the material of the late twenties and thirties into the pigeonholes appropriate for the works of the previous twenty-five years would produce ludicrous results. (Whether that is because the satirists of the 1730s are trying to write *Gulliver*, *The Dunciad*, and *The Beggar's Opera* will have to be determined.) Some prominent satirists are active in both periods, as Swift is, but their practice shifts noticeably. No one in this quarter century does anything, in satiric terms, "like" Defoe, Maynwaring, or Dunton, and one of the most exciting developments of the 1700–1725 period—monitory satire—has effectively disappeared well before the mid-twenties. Satirists of the late 1720s and 1730s do not practice the kind of dense ideological argumentation that was a conspicuous part of religiopolitical satire. Something changes. The reasons for that change are not obvious, probably not simple, and ultimately beyond the responsibility—or at least the powers—of the humble student of the history of satire. What I can say is that people write different kinds of satire in the second quarter of the century than they had in the first. This marked discontinuity raises an important question: can satire be traced in generic fashion (supposing that authors are consciously operating in a particular genre with rules and norms), or does one need to go from work to work without assuming the sequential connectives whose existence critics have often taken for granted?

Satiric objectives are much less diverse in these years than in the previous quarter century; instead, what is remarkable about this material is tonal fluctuation, the varying intensities with which writers respond to a relatively small and contained set of issues. I have subdivided the survey into thematic categories—political, cultural, and social satire—and within each I highlight the range in tone, intensity, and level of apparent authorial conviction to be found. Political satirists are sometimes amusing themselves and their like-minded readers, sometimes plaintive or antagonistic, and sometimes despairing. Some cultural satirists cheerfully deflate or parody their enemies (as Fielding does in *The Tragedy of Tragedies*), others sharply deride (Pope in the first *Dunciad*), and yet others solemnly denounce cultural collapse (Pope in the last *Dunciad*). Social satirists tease their targets, express not uncritical sympathy, lament human folly, or revile society and its members. These distinctions are simple-minded and uncontroversial—few people would suggest that *The Tragedy of Tragedies* is tonally "like" the last *Dunciad*—but satire scholars have tended to privilege form and content with little sensitivity to tone and intensity. The interpretation of tone is admittedly to some extent subjective, but the point is not that a particular work is "extremely harsh" or "mildly gloomy." The point is the wide degree of variation.

A word of warning is in order. With the exception of *Gulliver's Travels*, the canonical satires of this period have been pretty well understood. Pope's major works in particular have been carefully studied, and I see no point to repeating agreed-upon readings in any detail. This means that I do not give special weight to Pope's Moral Essays or Horatian imitations. Instead I refer to his works—along with those of Swift, Gay, Fielding, and Johnson—in much the same fashion that I refer to the satires of Henry Carey, Paul Whitehead, Dodsley, and others. The first group comprises great and important examples, but they are treated here as only examples. Another awkward problem: Pope, Swift, and Gay are substantially different both from what goes on around them and from each other. That uniqueness confounds even crude efforts at categorization. To try to force their satires into pigeonholes that do not satisfactorily accommodate them risks misrepresenting them; to treat this "Scriblerian" trio entirely separately from the broader culture of satire implies a likeness among them that is yet more distortive. My aims in this section are to demonstrate the range of satiric practice in this period and to show where Pope, Swift, and Gay belong in their contemporary contexts. To do so, I deal with their works in the categories that seem the most appropriate—or the least inappropriate—and attempt to be as clear as possible about the nature and limitations of the fit.

Political Commentary and Combat

The Walpole era is famous for its divisiveness. In the early 1720s, satirist after unhappy satirist disparaged the "Skreenmaster" for shielding the ministry from investigation into the disaster of the South Sea Bubble. Disapproval turned to abhorrence in 1727: when George I died and Walpole managed to stay in power, his detractors were surprised and infuriated. The Great Man grew ever greater and looked as though he would preside until he dropped. Oppositional satirists became louder and more irascible throughout the 1730s and up to the minister's fall in 1742. They heaped scorn upon Walpole and objected to the unscrupulous machinations—Fielding's "*Pollitricks*"—associated with his regime. No doubt alert to the prospect of patronage,

Walpole's supporters duly rebuked the "false patriots" as ungrateful malcontents and disappointed placemongers.[2] The political warfare of the Robinocracy has been much studied,[3] and my aim here is to characterize tone and type of satiric enterprise rather than to analyze political content.

Lightweight political satire. Few political satirists in the Walpole era find humor in state affairs, but some satires are more the stuff of entertainment than of partisan abuse. Scholars of political satire have been more inclined to overestimate than to underestimate the political import of the works they have studied. Fielding's plays were long ago mined for systematic antiministerial satire, most of which turned out to be imaginary; subsequent critics have usefully labored to counter overpoliticized readings.[4] *Tom Thumb* is no longer taken as a slashing attack on the Great Man; that the topicality of *The Author's Farce* does not add up to a political position is now more or less understood. On those plays, more in due course. The example I will mention here is *The Welsh Opera* (1731), a lively little entertainment full of slapstick and good-humored lèse-majesté. Fielding presents us with the affable Welsh squire Ap-Shinken (King George), his wife and son, Robin the Butler (Walpole), and William the Groom (Pulteney). The plot is slight and the happy resolution thoroughly far fetched. The exchanges between Squire and Madam Ap-Shinken are funny; however impudent Fielding's personation of the royal family, it has no real bite. The only political substance is William's criticism of Robin as a thief and a liar, but when the rivals start to spar, their back-and-forth is quickly silenced by another servant, who bids the men make nice. *The Welsh Opera* is unquestionably political, but it is just as certainly nonpartisan. This is burlesque for fun, a universe apart from the coarser political satires of the 1730s.[5]

Harsh political satire. Most political satirists during the Walpole regime take its problems more seriously than Fielding does in *The Welsh Opera*, and their works tend heavily toward complaint. No doubt some of these writers would have liked to have a practical effect, but the notion of toppling Walpole must have appeared to the opposition a remote possibility at best, which probably accounts for some of the sourness of the antiministerial screeds. At crisis points, such as before and after the failure of the Excise in 1733, satirists probably hoped to undermine Walpole's security, but for the most part his attackers are simply venting frustration and enmity, and like-minded readers surely consumed the negativity with satisfaction. However much these works tell us about the political controversy surrounding the Walpole regime, they are not terribly effective as satire. The seriousness with which their writers take themselves and their charges is not itself a problem: a work like *Absalom and Achitophel* is both reflective of deeply held belief and also satirically powerful. Walpole's assailants mostly lack Dryden's restraint; they are sufficiently upset that they lose their self-control, temper, and perspective, and as a result they produce satire so one-sided as to be mere abuse. These antiministerial philippics provide an object lesson in the dreary, trivial nature of certain kinds of negative propaganda—no doubt welcome to oppositional fellow travelers, but little more than crude defamation.

Walpole's detractors stridently enunciate familiar complaints: the minister is a corrupt usurper of royal power whose peculation knows no bounds, votes are bought, places are bestowed on incompetent yes-men, merit is irrelevant, and so on. The satires range from petulant to abusively scabrous, but the nature of the attack is fairly consistent. *The Honest Electors; or, the Courtiers sent back with their Bribes* (pub. 1733; not perf.; 1s) is a ballad opera composed after the failure of the Excise scheme and featuring Sir Positive Screenall, "a conceited, foolish, blundering M[iniste]r" (as he is described in the dramatis personae). *The City Triumphant: or, the Burning of the Excise-Monster* (1733) and *Lord Blunder's Confession* (another unperformed 1733 ballad opera; 1s 6d) more rancorously impugn the Great Man, the latter denigrating Walpole (Lord Blunder), his scheming henchmen, and his unscrupulous hired pens. The author of *The Lion and Fox, or, the Matchievelian* (1735; 1s) depicts Walpole as the sycophantic Reynard, whose "lurking Wiles" and "cringing Flattery" allow him to get in the good graces of the Royal Lion. The sly fox's "pious Maxims"—patriotism, fidelity, sincerity—disguise his base designs (6, 12). Such allegations are repeated in scores of opposition satires, including Haywood's *Adventures of Eovaai* (1736; 2s†), *The Craftsman*, and much of the antiministerial visual satire,[6] with varying degrees of heat and ferocity. The satiric epithets for Walpole—the Great Man, Bob, Robin—rapidly became synonymous with hypocrisy and political chicanery.[7]

Many of the antiministerial complaints have little to recommend them, but some attacks are direct or sharp enough to have considerable shock value.[8] The two most prominent dramatic examples of nasty political application satire are Gay's *Polly* (pub. 1729) and *The Fall of Mortimer* (staged at the Little Haymarket in the spring of 1731), both of which riled the authorities.[9] Walpole was none too pleased to be represented as a pirate who gets hanged: *Polly* was not staged in Gay's lifetime.[10] *The Fall of Mortimer* begins with a group of loyal men bemoaning the power of a tyrant (a liar and would-be rapist) who misleads the benevolent and much-adored King Edward.[11] Just before the faithful Englishmen make their overtures to the king, he has a vision of his father's ghost warning him to beware Mortimer, leaving him receptive to their charges, and the play ends with orders for Mortimer's richly deserved execution. In the epilogue, the author reflects on ministerial corruption, rejoicing that "No MORTIMER wants now to rule alone"—a bitterly ironic indictment of the Great Man. The contemporary application was glaringly obvious, and Sir Robert did not approve. The authorities attempted to arrest the Little Haymarket performers, who took to their heels; the theater was raided and de facto silenced, and the raids were publicized as warnings to other playwrights, pointed reminders of the government's sensitivity to certain kinds of criticism. A work expressing the ideology of the opposition was within bounds, but as *The Fall of Mortimer* demonstrated, too direct an indictment of the minister himself was likely to lead to trouble.

Swift's truculent invectives against Walpole are among the most interesting of the nondramatic satires—and almost got the Dean into hot water.[12] *On Mr. P[ultene]y being put out of the Council* (wr. 1731), a short verse fable, concludes with an admonition to "honest *R[obi]n*": "Thy *Turns* and *Doublings* cannot save thee long" (ll. 39, 44). Equally jaunty but much more withering is *The Character of Sir Robert Walpole* (wr. 1731; not pub. in Swift's lifetime), an undisguised lampoon on the "bully & briber," "the Cur dog of Brittain & spaniel of Spain" (ll. 12, 14). More blistering yet is *To Mr. Gay on his being Steward to the Duke of Queensberry* (wr. 1731), where the description of the Great Man is acid:

> I place a St[atesm]an full before my Sight.
> A bloated *M[iniste]r* in all his Geer,
> With shameless Visage, and perfidious Leer,
> Two Rows of Teeth arm each devouring Jaw;
> And, *Ostrich*-like, his all-digesting Maw (ll. 32–36)

The directness and indecorousness with which Swift savages Walpole makes his vilifications considerably more toxic than most antiministerial calumny of the thirties.

Few of Swift's contemporaries match his vituperative energy, but Paul Whitehead comes close in *Manners* (1739; *6d*), a satire sufficiently scandalous to rouse the government to order the arrest of both author and publisher.[13] The thrust of Whitehead's satire is familiar enough—manners make the man, and the higher-ups are acutely short on worthy conduct—but the brazen ferocity of his delivery gives to the satire especial sting. "Whence have St. *Stephen*'s Walls so hallow'd been?" he asks irreverently, observing that neither church nor state has preserved a trace of the requisite decency (6). Whitehead then turns his attention to the Great Man himself, explaining that while monarchs can be mocked without fear of reprisal, ministers must be spared the chastising pen:

> I name not *W[alpol]e*; You the Reason guess;
> Mark yon fell Harpy hov'ring o'er the Press.
> Secure the Muse may sport with Names of Kings,
> But Ministers, my Friend, are dang'rous Things. (13)[14]

The attack is devastatingly particularized and also more generally cynical. Whitehead is not only lamenting the rise and reign of Walpole but denouncing an ever-worsening society.

Gloomy political satire. Other satirists perceive political collapse, sharing what I take to be Whitehead's profound disillusionment but often seeming more glum than angry. Pope's *Dunciad, in Four Books* is an apocalyptic comment on the cultural and political state of England. Even a decade earlier, by the time of *The First Satire of the Second Book of Horace Imitated* (Fortescue) (1733), says Howard D. Weinbrot, Pope is responding to a world apparently "rotten at its political core." The poem's "dark tones" are undeniable, though it is not utterly pessimistic.[15] Five years later, hope no longer springs eternal in the papal breast: the *Epilogue to the Satires* (1738) presents corruption as securely entrenched.[16] Like *An Excursory View of the Present State of Men and Things* and *The State of Rome, under Nero and Domitian* (both 1739), Pope's satires are usually broadly political, dealing with widespread moral turpitude, a state of affairs encouraged by governmental failings and ministerial jobbery. Pope, like the authors of *An Excursory View* and *The State of Rome*, is perhaps voicing genuine despair—though there is also a possibility that, just as indignation à la Oldham could be a performance, so might "gloom" be a pose struck to render the satire more potent. In Johnson's telling, Pope "frequently professes contempt of the world, and represents himself as looking on mankind, sometimes with gay indifference . . . and sometimes with gloomy indignation." These "dispositions," Johnson concludes matter-of-factly, were "apparently counterfeited."[17] In any case, Pope seems concerned not only with political rot but also with the role of the artist within society and with the province of the satirist in attempting to combat the wrongs he sees around him.[18]

The Culture Wars

The political satires I have been discussing range from primarily comic to harsh to despairing. Cultural satires vary in similar ways. By "cultural" I mean something specifically concerning arts and letters, not something related more broadly to behavioral patterns or manners—this category includes *The Dunciad*, in other words, but not *The Modern Husband*. Most of the pertinent satires in this period are responses to what the writers perceived as the proliferation of low culture,[19] to the purveyors of bad art, or to the debauched patronage system in which sycophantic hacks are the darlings of the ministry and semicompetent artists have to debase themselves to win favor. Some of these works have explicit political implications—Pope's dunces are repeatedly described as Walpole's venal hirelings—and these more comprehensive satires tend to be among the angrier, more despairing of the responses to perceived cultural decay. As in the survey of political satire, I begin with exemplars of lower-heat satire and move on to those pieces that express more outrage or general despondency.

Lightweight cultural satire and entertainment. Burlesques and other forms of low culture fared well in the late 1720s and early 1730s. Samuel Johnson of Cheshire's *Hurlothrumbo* (1729), one of many successful burlesques and unquestionably the zaniest, ran up thirty-three performances in its first season at the Little Haymarket.

The epigraph offers mischievously confounding counsel: "Ye Sons of Fire, read my *Hurlothrumbo,*/Turn it betwixt your Finger and your Thumbo,/And being quite outdone, be quite struck dumbo." The piece is straight nonsense, full of dizzying action snippets, prophecies, intrigues, high-flown speeches, and demented characters, one of whom states flatly, midplay, "I rent my Brain" (17). Fielding's *Tom Thumb* (added to *The Author's Farce* as an afterpiece in April 1730; 6*d*) is another snappy burlesque of heroic tragedy, without reference to particular exemplars, past or present.[20] In the play's memorable ending, Tom is swallowed by "A Cow, of larger than the usual Size," after which his ghost is slain by Grizzle, Grizzle by Huncamunca, Huncamunca by Doodle, and so on until the king slays Mustacha and himself and the curtain falls on a pile of bodies (1:403–404). *Tom Thumb* is much less disorienting than *Hurlothrumbo*, but, the critical quest of yesteryear to detect systematic political satire notwithstanding, it is just as silly.[21] Henry Carey's *The Tragedy of Chrononhotonthologos* (1734; 6*d*), an imitation of *Tom Thumb*, opens with impenetrable gibberish: "*Aldiborontiphoscophornio!* Where left you *Chrononhotonthologos?*" This is a patently good-tempered debunking of tragic and operatic bombast.

More substantial is Fielding's *The Author's Farce* (1730; rev. 1734), a boisterous deflation of popular entertainment forms (John Henley's oratory, John Rich's pantomimes, Eliza Haywood's novels) and a satire with more bite than *Tom Thumb*.[22] Fielding was unhappy about the rejection of his plays at Drury Lane and aggravated by Cibber; his personal irritation combined with a more general disapproval of the cultural tastes of the town to produce an inspired piece of parody. Witmore voices his creator's exasperation when he enjoins the impecunious playwright Luckless to abandon wit and learning in his compositions: "If you must write, write Nonsense, write Opera's, write Entertainments, write *Hurlo-thrumbo's*—Set up an *Oratory* and preach Nonsense; and you may meet with Encouragement enough" (1:234–235). Granting the animosity behind the play, however, Fielding does not condemn but instead mockingly reproduces cultural nonsense. This is a chirpy caricature, tonally a long way from *The Dunciad* or even the toothless *Peri Bathous*. Closer to Fielding in tone are Gabriel Odingsells's *Bays's Opera* and James Ralph's *The Fashionable Lady; or Harlequin's Opera* (both 1730). All three are amusing satiric parodies of low culture, as is Henry Carey's *The Dragon of Wantley* (1737), an especially exuberant takeoff of Italian opera.[23] In a fabulous anticlimax, the valiant knight slays the dragon "by a kick on the Backside," and the dying dragon cries out, "Oh! oh! oh!/The Devil take your Toe" (17). These satirists travesty undesirable cultural forms with disapprobation but also with comical gusto.[24]

Harsh cultural satire. A great deal of the cultural satire in this period is more soberly derogatory. Fielding parodies rather than damns the tastes of the town, but other disapproving traditionalists are readier to rail, often in high moral terms. In *A*

Satyr on the Times: And some of the Modern Plays (1730), the Anglican minister John Loyd cheerlessly bemoans the "pleasing Poison" of nonsensical entertainments, condemning various contemporary plays in turn. He finds fault with *The Beggar's Opera* ("Whose Characters throughout are all so loose"), *Timoleon* ("the best Character in all his Play's a Whore"), *The Humours of Oxford* ("insolently dull!"), and *Hurlothrumbo* ("Which without either Head or Tail appears!")—all of which point to a culture in decline (5, 11–12). Loyd, like the author of *A Satyrical Poem: or, the Beggar's-Opera Dissected* (1729; 6*d*), thumps a tub grumpily, lecturing both the producers and the consumers of nonsense.

The best-known exemplar from the culture wars of this period is, of course, Pope's *Dunciad*.[25] While the 1728 version (1*s*†) is considerably lighter than the 1743 *Dunciad, in Four Books*, the satire in both is primarily punitive—not for nothing does Leopold Damrosch describe *The Dunciad*'s "sprawling fertility of defamation."[26] Pope's satire is defensive,[27] but it is also harshly *offensive*, a serious and troubled protest against foes, the Grub Street drudges, and the peddlers of low culture. Pope writes from a position of superiority but not from one of much comfort. The indignant duncen struck back, for their own parts nettled but also taking furious exception to Pope's self-appointed role as cultural guardian. In *Durgen. Or, a Plain Satyr upon a Pompous Satyrist* (1729; 1*s*), Ned Ward thrashes "the pigmy Bard" (4) and then denies the right of any man to play custodian of the arts, deprecating the notion that a poet's or a critic's composition needs to be "stamp'd with some fam'd Poet's seal, / Who proudly thinks, in his imperious Breast, / Is lodg'd the pow'r of damning all the rest" (14). This is satiric vengeance, to be sure, but Ward clearly resents Pope's presumption that he could and should regulate culture.[28] In any case, *The Dunciad* made "dullness" a buzzword for cultural degeneration, but the majority of Pope's duncen were ministerial supporters, making dullness a political problem as well as a cultural one.

Many satires in this period link political misrule to cultural degradation. The opposition's charges are familiar enough: the government shows an obnoxious partiality toward those authors who will toe the party line, unskilled scribblers prepared to play toadies can find patronage, talent is immaterial, and true artists have either to prostitute themselves or starve.[29] In the *Epistle to Arbuthnot* (1735; 1*s*), Pope sneers at kowtowing hacks and their benefactors: "May ev'ry *Bavius* have his *Bufo* still!" (l. 250). The minister's role in the perceived cultural collapse is notorious: Walpole "was putting an exponentially increasing network of opportunity at the disposal of writers whose only qualification was that they would write on his side of any question."[30] Swift notoriously dubbed the Great Man "*B[ob]*, the Poet's Foe" in *To Mr. Gay* (l. 4), and in *A Libel on D[r] D[elany]* (1730), he excoriates the ministry for its shabby treatment of true wits like Congreve, Gay, and Addison. The *Libel* is a provocatively sharp satire on Walpole and the entire Walpolean system, concluding with a scorcher:

For, no imaginable things

Can differ more than GOD and [Kings]

And, *Statesmen* by ten thousand odds

Are ANGELS, just as [Kings] are GODS. (ll. 195–198)

Walpole was inextricably connected, in the opposition's imagination, to the sort of scribblers immortalized in *The Dunciad.* In *The State Dunces* (1733; 1s), Whitehead inveighs against the tyrant Appius (Walpole) and his penmen.[31] His main concern is political, but he swipes at Cibber, Welsted, Dennis, and the lot of mercenary drudges who "Unlade their Dullness, and for *Appius* bawl" (16). Swift's *Directions for a Birthday Song* (wr. 1729) is a cleverer piece of politicized anti-duncery, a poem of ironic counsel to the hacks (and Laurence Eusden in particular) on how to cajole the royal family:

Thus your Encomiums, to be strong,

Must be apply'd directly wrong:

A Tyrant for his Mercy praise,

And crown a Royal Dunce with Bays:

A squinting Monkey load with charms;

And paint a Coward fierce in arms. (ll. 117–122)[32]

Like scores of his contemporaries, Swift exposes corruption and unmerited rank, but the irony and control of this poem gives it verve hard to find in the late twenties and thirties.

Gloomy cultural satire. The perception of political and cultural collapse causes some satirists to write not particularized invectives but solemn denunciation on a much bigger scale. The most celebrated of these works is Pope's *Dunciad, in Four Books* (1743), considerably broader in focus than the primarily literary 1728 *Dunciad.* Cibber replaces Theobald as the central dunce, and Pope's victims here are not scribbling hacks but ministerial penmen. The problem is not bad art but a "generally collapsing world," and the satirist is not self-righteously annoyed but disgusted, despairing, and apprehensive about "the increasing violence of Dulness's ever-growing forces."[33] The apocalyptic ending ("Universal Darkness buries All") is often cited. In the world of Pope's fourth book, something has been irretrievably lost. In the previous decade, a few satirists had issued similar plaints. The author of *The Connoisseur* (1735; 1s) laments that the crowd sleeps through Shakespeare and applauds "the Mimic *Harlequin,*" pronouncing, Pope-like, that "despotic *Folly* governs *All*" (12, 6). That work, like *The Modern Englishman* (1738; 1s), connects failures of taste and the decline of cultural standards with degeneracy writ large.

Three points need to be made. (1) Only a small number of cultural satires are apocalyptic in the manner of Pope's 1743 *Dunciad.* Much of this satire is either jolly (see *Hurlothrumbo*), however genuine the author's disapprobation, or pointed and particularized (*The Author's Farce*). *The Dunciad* is brilliant, and not an isolated example of gloomy cultural commentary, but it hardly typifies the attitude toward the state of letters in this period. (2) Tonal differences matter. Fielding and Pope both disdain "low" culture, but Fielding stages lively, popular, highly effective nonsense pieces by way of parody, whereas Pope denounces purveyors of bad art root and branch. Weinbrot has rightly rejected the idea that, in *The Tragedy of Tragedies* in particular, Fielding is "battling the legions of Night" hand in hand with Pope. He points out that "such dark language makes heavy weather" out of a rather peppy play and that "Fielding's contemporaries sometimes regarded his burlesques as exemplums of the dangerous dulness that Pope satirized."[34] The notion that *The Tragedy of Tragedies*, *Peri Bathous*, and the last *Dunciad* somehow represent a "mode" of Scriblerian cultural criticism can be compelling only to the hopelessly tone deaf. Adding *Directions for a Birth-day Song*, the 1728 *Dunciad*, *Tom Thumb*, and the rest makes for an even messier picture. (3) The third observation is actually a question. How confident can we be that the "gloom" of some of the political and cultural satires of this period is sincere? Obviously tone is not a failsafe indicator of authorial feelings; what one reader takes as indignation another could interpret as hyperbolic performance. In some cases, authorial anxiety seems hard to deny, but we need to understand that cynicism and despair can also be useful rhetorical devices. Objecting to Walpole's failure to support England's ablest pens is obviously a common practice in these years, but it is unlikely to win the sympathy of all and sundry. If one wants to demonize the Great Man in popular imagination or to demonstrate his cultural negligence, then a picture of omnipresent stink makes for a stronger piece of persuasion than a cantankerous plaint by an aggrieved poet.

Social Satire

Like political and cultural satires, social satires range in tone and intensity. Lightweight social satire such as we find in Robert Dodsley's *The Toy-Shop* tends to be mild in its critique, generalized in its subject, and primarily—if not exclusively—entertaining. Harsh social satirists denounce society or express sharp disapproval of an unacceptable state of affairs. Despairing social satire (Swift's scatological poems?) has some affinities with harsh condemnation, but its practitioners tend to be resigned to that which their angry counterparts (however vainly) refuse to endure.

Lightweight social satire. This sort of social satire becomes an increasingly conspicuous phenomenon after the reign of Charles II, in part because of the need for generalized satires in the 1690s and early 1700s. While satire on abstract concepts all but disappears a decade into the eighteenth century, those on particular groups or parts of society do not. These works are usually amusing and lack much specific application or topical relevance.[35] An anonymous ballad opera satirizing high life, *The Humours of the Court* (1732; 1s 6d) is filled with court intrigues, superficial pleasures, the desire for novelty, and so on. The spirit of the satire is well captured in an observation made by the character Modish: "Virtue, Modesty, and Honour, I must own, are pretty Things to talk on, and sound very well in one's Mouth; but for the Practice of them, 'tis almost as much out of Fashion as Sincerity amongst Courtiers, and altogether as unprofitable" (17). Though not without satiric point, this is an entertainment piece. So is the first of Young's *Universal Passion* satires (1725). Satires II through VII are heavier handed, not very effectively mingling Horatian calm with Juvenalian anger, but satire I's generalized critique of the human desire for fame is mild and amused. The same could be said of Dodsley's *The Toy-Shop* (1735; 1s), in which the toy-shop owner good-naturedly moralizes over the trifles in his store. In one scene he merrily expounds on the utility of an impossibly tiny box: "would you think it, in this same little Box, a Courtier may deposite his Sincerity, a Lawyer may screw up his Honesty, and a Poet may—hoard his Money" (15). The owner delivers his jibes without heat; *The Toy-Shop* is genially witty rather than abrasive.

Harsh social satire. Harder-hitting social satire is less common than lightweight exemplars, but there are examples. In 1730, Fielding wrote to his cousin Lady Mary Wortley Montagu about a play draft that he describes as "written on a Model I never yet attempted" and distinguishes from his "lighter Productions."[36] The play was *The Modern Husband* (staged at Drury Lane in 1732), one of Fielding's few attempts at hard-hitting social satire. Mr. and Mrs. Modern's union is far from holy: he is a "contented Cuckold" who allows his wife to sell herself to Lord Richly, a sleazy womanizer; she markets her favors, and her husband blackmails her lovers (2:223).[37] "The play exudes adultery," Hunter observes, "and there is no attempt to pretend that it is all jolly fun and games."[38] Fielding sharply satirizes the Moderns and Lord Richly, truly contemptible characters, and implies throughout that "It is a Stock-jobbing Age" in which "ev'ry thing has its Price" (2:237). *The Modern Husband* is reminiscent of Otway's *Friendship in Fashion* in its bleak depiction of society. Fielding tried straight denunciation again in *The Universal Gallant* (1735), a long and oppressively serious social satire. Unlike *The Modern Husband*, it failed immediately. Fielding is a master of indirection, brio, and comic irony: that way lies his satiric genius. When he tries to be a soapbox satirist, decrying social ills without anything to mitigate his disgust, he quickly becomes strident and dull.

Harsh satiric deprecation is not limited to the stage.[39] An illustrative verse satire exemplar is Thomas Newcomb's *Blasphemy As Old as the Creation* (1730), signed "By a Gentleman and a Christian" and full of fire and brimstone.[40] Newcomb's central target is irreligion—namely that sponsored by the freethinking Matthew Tindal, author of *Christianity as Old as the Creation*, and by Mandeville, who (in Newcomb's tell-ing) argues "That *Damning*, must promote a Nation's Good" (4). Newcomb's scope is broad: blasphemy is everywhere, leaders are beloved for bad behavior, irreverence is blithely tolerated, and so on. This is moral topsy-turvydom, and Newcomb is ap-palled and indignant. He condemns society in similar terms in *The Manners of the Age* (1733), but that work is more resigned than angry. There he laments the human condition, and he does not exclude himself: "The little fame we boast, we give our-selves" (23). He also concedes the ineffectuality of satire: "folly sprouts as fast as satire kills" (2). In *Blasphemy As Old as the Creation*, unlike in *The Manners of the Age*, he had declaimed with enough ferocity to suggest that he hopes his outraged homily will reach *someone*.

Gloomy social satire. Anger and despondency sometimes coexist, and distinguish-ing between the two is often difficult to do with any confidence, but the distinction is nevertheless worth attending to. A satire written with purposive fury is not the same thing as one written in sad acquiescence with no hope for change. In *A Satyr. In the Manner of Persius* (1730), John, Lord Hervey reflects dolefully that all existence is pointless—an "empty Show"—and that humans are basically not very good (5). Pope, of course, proclaims widespread degeneracy in the *Epilogue to the Satires* (1738). In *The Second Satire of the Second Book of Horace Paraphrased* (*Bethel*) four years ear-lier, he had portrayed, says Weinbrot, "a vision of mankind too brutal to be found in the epistles. In this poem the main object of attack is Man, who is 'all . . . one intestine war.'"[41] The degree to which Pope is expressing genuine despair rather than assuming a rhetorical pose is difficult to determine, but the content of these satires reflects a grim indictment of a thoroughly distasteful society. The same might be said of the *Sober Advice from Horace* (1734; 1s). Pope, however, passes judgment from a high moral position, suggesting that standards *do* exist, that right and wrong can be distinguished.

More convincingly despairing is the satiric message, if not the tone, of Gay's *The Beggar's Opera*, an oddity. Some of its targets are readily comprehensible—Walpole, Italian opera, and other literary forms and conventions. The political and cultural satire is undeniable, though the central thrust of the satire is social. Not for nothing does Macheath airily announce that "Money well tim'd, and properly apply'd, will do any thing" (II.xii [2:39]). The moral, ultimately, is that "the World is all alike"—but, as in some of Gay's previous satires, this bad news comes in a thoroughly zippy work. "Government, professions, and aristocracy are cheerfully savaged," says Hume, "but it is *cheerfully*, and any 'vehement' satire is strictly by implication."[42] As I argue in chapter 5, Gay might very well be offering his social critique fully aware that noth-ing can come of it—and so feels little need to rant—or he might be counting on the reader or viewer to grasp his meaning and worry about it if so inclined. Whatever

Gay thinks he is doing, we can be pretty clear on what he is not doing. His satire does not represent a systematic attempt to force-feed an uncompromising sociopolitical argument to his audience.[43] *The Beggar's Opera* is not really "like" any other satire in this period. To ignore the nihilism of its apparent moral would be misrepresentative; to call it simply "harsh" or "cynical" is to privilege the implications of its content over the sunny buoyancy of its tone.

Equally hard to place in any pigeonhole are Swift's scatological poems. *The Lady's Dressing Room* (wr. 1730; pub. 1732; *6d*), *Strephon and Chloe*, *Cassinus and Peter*, and *A Beautiful Young Nymph Going to Bed* (all three wr. 1731; pub. together in 1734; *1s*) forcefully communicate a satiric point, but the tone is elusive. As J. A. Downie observes, these works are written out of "a desire to strip man of his pretensions and to remind him of his own mortality and the vanity of human wishes."[44] In *The Lady's Dressing Room*, the besotted Strephon is revolted by what he finds in his darling's "Chamber":

> But oh! it turn'd poor *Strephon's* Bowels,
> When he beheld and smelt the Towels,
> Begumm'd, bematter'd, and beslim'd
> With Dirt, and Sweat, and Ear-Wax grim'd. (ll. 3, 43–47)

Swift conveys a visceral disgust with the human body, but the serious implications jar badly against the tone. *A Beautiful Young Nymph* in particular is marked by what Claude Rawson calls "horrific jauntiness."[45] About "the facts of squalor and filth, lust and physical ugliness,"[46] Swift is shockingly explicit without being preachy.

What does this survey tell us? I reserve some of my conclusions for the end of the chapter, but I offer two observations at this point. The first is that the world I have been describing looks almost nothing like the world covered in chapter 5. Attack- and complaint-mode satire continues, albeit in slightly different forms and in response to ever-changing issues, and so does lightweight social satire. Beyond that, little stays the same. The most interesting forms of satire practiced in the first quarter of the eighteenth century (monitory satire, ideological argumentation) do not continue into the later twenties and thirties. This period should not be casually combined with the quarter century that preceded it. Second, the satires of Pope, Swift, and Gay fit to some degree in several different categories, often imperfectly, but they do not form the beginning and end of the culture of satire even in the years the "Scriblerians" supposedly ruled. Scholars have derived their conclusions about eighteenth-century satire largely from the major works of these writers. I flatly deny that this trio of writers typifies satiric practice in this period, and we need now to consider the extent to which they "go" together at all.

II. Pope, Swift, Gay

That Pope and Swift are satiric twins—walking hand in hand to posterity—is a critical truism whose verity few have doubted.[47] Many thesis-driven books on eighteenth-century satire follow a Swift chapter with a Pope chapter, or they cite examples from Swift's and Pope's corpora to "prove" something about satiric practice. Scholars do not so much argue similitude as assume it, sometimes with alarming nonchalance. One of the preeminent living critics of eighteenth-century satire defines "Scriblerian," in passing, as "Popean, Swiftean"—suggesting that the meanings of "Popean" and "Swiftean" are obvious and uncomplicated (a dubious proposition) and implying that they are equivalent terms.[48] Gay is usually seen not as identical to them but rather as the devoted junior member of the Scriblerian enterprise. The late 1720s and 1730s are now regarded as the glory days of eighteenth-century satire, dominated by the "Scriblerian mode." We need therefore to ask what sort of satire each man was writing in these years and whether such a "mode" ever existed.

Pope

Pope's satiric output before the first *Dunciad* is limited and basically remote from our conception of him as moral guardian and cultural custodian. The mature Pope writes a great deal of satire, the concerns of which are variously moral, political, and cultural. His range is not as wide as Swift's or Fielding's, but his practice is not uniform. Weinbrot has distinguished between Pope's satiric and epistolary works: "In the epistles," he argues, "man is often sad, often silly, and generally not a danger to anyone but himself," and the satires "are harsher in tone, more apocalyptic in scope, more biting in attack, and less affirmative in vision." The *Essay on Man* (1733–1734)—a reaffirming rather than destructive satire on man—is epistolary. Only in the satires, as Weinbrot notes, does Pope "deny that whatever is is right."[49] For my purposes, this division offers a useful way of dealing with Pope's satirical poems.

The *Epistles to Several Persons* (1731–1735) are less punitive than moralizing, an attempt to provide "a system of Ethics in the Horatian way."[50] In *Cobham*, Pope suggests that the characters of men are all but inscrutable, that the ruling passion of an individual is impossible to discern with confidence in his lifetime, and that man himself is perverse and contradictory. *To a Lady* illustrates the changeability of the softer sex, though it is not just another misogynistic diatribe: Pope "attempts to educate rather than to lash woman," urging her "to improve so that she in turn can improve man's life."[51] The theme of the sermonic *Epistle III (To Bathurst)* is the use and misuse of riches, the effect of wealth on society and the social implications of its abuse.[52] Pope satirizes individuals by name (e.g., Ward, Waters, Chartres) and expresses anxiety about the vagaries of Fortune and "the World's respect for Gold" (l. 125). He also tries to illuminate, in Miriam Leranbaum's phrasing, "the centrality of virtue as the essential basis for individual happiness and eternal salvation."[53] In *Burlington*, he returns to themes of taste and expenditure, vanity and ostentation: Timon's villa, that site of indulgence and extravagance, "is part of the downward antisocial progress in which architect and client cut themselves off from man, nature, and God."[54] The epistles are negative, ridiculing vice in the form of deviations from Pope's ideal order of things, often typified by named personages such as Chartres in *Bathurst* and George Bubb Doddington in *Burlington*. They are also positive, praising living exemplars of virtue (e.g., "brave COBHAM" in the last lines of his epistle) and normative social order.

Elsewhere Pope is more aggressively harsh, increasingly so late in his career. Weinbrot observes, "The direction of Pope's career as a formal verse satirist is from an essentially Horatian ethic [*sic*] epistle like *Burlington* (1731), to mingled satire with a variety of Horatian, Juvenalian, and Persian emphases, to the overwhelmingly Juvenalian-Persian elevation and gloom of the *Epilogue to the Satires* (1738)."[55] The first *Dunciad* is about as playful as Pope will ever be; his vision grows ever darker, culminating in the 1743 *Dunciad*, his apocalyptic last word on political-cum-cultural collapse. Between the first and final versions of his satire on the dunces, he produces his Horatian imitations, beginning with *Fortescue* (1733), in which he condemns the current ministry and surveys the corruption for which it is to blame. *Bethel* (1734; Sat. II.ii.; 1s) combines generalized satire on the folly of greed and gluttony—offset by praise for restraint and moderation—with particularized Juvenalian castigation of named individuals. Pope locates vice "not in the human situation or the rich . . . but in the court that mirrors Sir Robert—who was known for his generous appetite, girth, and, the opposition claimed, wealth used tastelessly and for selfish ends."[56] He returns again and again to this theme in his imitations, deploring the fallen world around him from a position of isolated superiority and impugning Walpole and the dubious morality of the Hanoverian court. By the *Epilogue to the Satires* (1738), the poet is embattled and outnumbered, forced to confront vice triumphant and to admit that issuing sage counsel about the path to virtue is only whistling in the dark.

Pope's satires have antagonism aplenty, and the imitations are clearly oppositional insofar as they are political. They are increasingly combative and cynical or despairing, though at least until Walpole's fall in 1742 Pope seems to imagine that a governmental change might ameliorate the sociocultural problems he perceives. In his epistolary satire, he discourses on vice and virtue, satirizing aberrations from the high road but ultimately preaching the ethical life to his readers as one who lives beyond reproof. The satirist is well trained in this rigorous sociomoral code and sermonizes on that code for the benefit (he hopes) of an educable audience. That reformation is the sole objective is unlikely: how many readers enthusiastically heed the obiter dicta of a preacher expounding upon good and evil? In his moral and political satires, Pope is always both judge *and* artist. At once rendering a verdict on society and insisting on his own remoteness from it, he is at least as concerned with determining and reaffirming his position as cultural custodian as he is on having an effect on the world around him.

Swift

Swift's most celebrated satire from this period is, of course, *Gulliver's Travels*, which I deal with at length in the next section. For now, what needs to be said is that *Gulliver* is not representative of his output, and neither does it share much, excepting a few particular targets, with the practice of Swift's fellow "Scriblerians" or his less well-known contemporaries. It is a sometimes funny, sometimes corrosive, and undeniably brilliant satire, and it is also singularly peculiar. In addition to *Gulliver*, in this period Swift writes *A Modest Proposal* (1729), *Polite Conversation* (pub. 1738), *Directions to Servants* (pub. 1745; 1s 6d), and a fairly varied bunch of satiric poems.

Most satire scholars (as opposed to Swiftians) too often forget that, for the better part of this heyday of English "Augustan" satire, Swift—the Drapier and the Dean—lived in Ireland and thought Irish thoughts. *A Modest Proposal* is only the best known of his Irish satires of this period. The argument of this mock scheme for economic stability through cannibalism has been pretty well understood: he lashes English oppression, but he also indicts the Irish, both ruling and ruled. Swift takes Ireland's dire plight seriously. In a 1730 broadside called *An Excellent New Ballad: or, The true En[gli] sh D[ea]n to be hang'd for a R[a]pe*, he explores the "sexual dimension of England's oppressive behavior" toward Ireland.[57] The last word of every stanza in this high-heat satire is "R[a]pe." The incendiary *Libel on D[r] D[elany]* (1730; 6d) satirizes Walpole, but it is also a vitriolic commentary on England's mistreatment of Ireland: the Irish lord lieutenant Carteret "comes to *drain* a *Beggar's Purse*: / He comes to tye our Chains on faster, / And shew us, E[ngland] is our Master" (ll. 124–126). A dangerous work, the *Libel* "indicted the King's representative in Ireland of corruption, and openly suggested that he was merely following orders from England."[58]

In the late twenties and thirties, Swift writes invective after blistering invective against Irish dignitaries who are now not even names to most students of satire—versus Lord Allen, who tried to force the prosecution of the printer and author of *A Libel on D[r] D[elany]*, in *Traulus* (two parts; 1730); versus a group of Irish bishops, and in defense of the lower clergy, in *On the Irish Bishops* (1732) and *Judas* (wr. 1731/2; pub. 1735); versus Sir Thomas Prendergast, whom Swift regarded "as an inveterate enemy of the clergy," in *On Noisy Tom* (wr. 1736).[59] He drubs Prendergast (and others) again in *A Character, Panegyric, and Description of the Legion Club* (1736), a diatribe against the Irish parliament. This poem is one of Swift's few genuine excursions into Juvenalian satire, its tone boiling from start to finish: "Let them dabble in their Dung" and so on at length (l.52). The targets of these topical squibs include both notables and small fry. For Swift, fair game includes anyone on the wrong side of a policy issue or debate. His Irish fulminations tend to be stingingly personal, hostile, present centered and issue based—and very little concerned with the particulars of English politics or letters.[60]

Swift does on occasion commit his satiric energies to English affairs. I have already dealt with his attacks on Walpole in *On Mr. P[ultene]y being put out of the Council, The Character of Sir Robert Walpole, To Mr. Gay, An Epistle to a Lady*, and most ferociously in *A Libel on D[r] D[elany]*.[61] The *Libel* defends Swift's English writer friends and is audaciously aggressive in its denunciation of the Great Man. *On Poetry: A Rapsody* (1733; 1s) connects bad literature and crooked politics: "The vilest Verse thrives best at Court," Swift seethes, for "A Pamphlet in Sir *Rob's* Defence / Will never fail to bring in Pence" (186, 187–188). A less explicitly sour but related satire is his *Directions for a Birth-day Song*, which denigrates ministerial pens and undercuts the personages whom they so obsequiously flatter. These poems—together with the political hits in *Gulliver's Travels*—represent the totality of the Dean's substantive satiric commentary on matters strictly English. Swift's animus toward Walpole is obviously strong, but most of his complaints about English politics have their basis in the plight of Ireland—and in his personal grievance against the prime minister, who responded with indifference when during a 1726 private meeting Swift entreated him to change Irish policy. Swift spent the vast majority of these years on Irish soil, and his satiric focus in the second half of his life is almost entirely on Ireland.

Not all of Swift's satires are limited to a single country or group of people. The scatological poems discussed above—*The Lady's Dressing Room, Strephon and Chloe, Cassinus and Peter*, and *A Beautiful Young Nymph Going to Bed*—are grossly physical statements on the whole human condition. Swift's political satires are painfully unambiguous exercises in destructive defamation: judgment is being rendered. The scatological poems communicate unpleasant realities, but they are also at least potentially more complex. In *Strephon and Chloe*, the eponymous newlyweds immediately lose their bashfulness once alone together, becoming mutually comfortable to the point (Swift suggests) of arrant indecency:

> They learn to call a Spade, a Spade.
> They soon from all Constraint are freed;
> Can see each other *do their Need*.
> On Box of Cedar sits the Wife,
> And makes it warm for *Dearest Life*. (ll. 204–208)

The couple sheds all pretence of delicate purity (a good thing), but in so doing they also abandon decency (not so good). "'Decency' itself is a mere social fiction," Rawson argues, but "Swift would nevertheless not do without it. . . . Between the civilised lie and the beastly truth, the middle way is hard to find. The poem may seem to warn the Strephons against poetic fictions which impute aethereality to the fair sex. But the moral is not quite so cozy as the commonsense critics would have it."[62] Swift's political satires have an implicit set of positives, even if they are unattainable; the positives in the scatological poems are much harder to discern.

Swift's other satires of this period do not fall into tidy categories. *Polite Conversation* is a send-up of London (not Irish) society, obviously reflecting Swift's erstwhile immersion in that world. Although the piece was not published until 1738, he had been collecting material for upward of thirty years before its completion.[63] Swift's concern in *Polite Conversation* is with linguistic abuse. He ridicules the clichéd speech and laughable affectation of haut monde, transforming the list of hackneyed expressions into a comedy of manners that is lightweight but tediously protracted. A companion piece of sorts is *Directions to Servants* (pub. 1745; incomplete),[64] which sardonically records the speech of society below stairs. These works are obviously related to *Mrs. Harris's Petition* (1701) and *Mary the Cook-Maid's Letter to Dr. Sheridan* (wr. 1718; pub. 1732), lively satiric mimicries of servant-speak. They are sportive, a world away from the acidity of his political verse and the bitter ironies of *A Modest Proposal*.

The other oddity in Swift's late-life satiric oeuvre is the difficult *Verses on the Death of Dr. S[wift], D. S. P. D.* (wr. 1731; pub. 1739; 15†), which comprises imagined responses to his demise and a sort of apologia pro vita sua.[65] The tones and ironies of the poem fluctuate from self-abuse to self-defense and self-praise, and Swift's attitude toward his accomplishments is not at all straightforward.[66] In the final section, one respondent to the Dean's death waxes eulogistic, and the poem becomes a memorial to Swift's life ("Fair LIBERTY was all his Cry" [l. 347], etc.). This panegyric has caused problems for critics.[67] It is ironic, but not entirely ironic. Self-mocking Swift may be, but he is cataloging deeds of which he is sincerely proud. In what remains the best discussion of the *Verses*, Scouten and Hume describe the Dean's exercise as a teasingly provocative "half-genuine apologia."[68] The poem is extraordinary, and it deserves the appreciation it has had, but as a satire it is like nothing else in Swift's canon and like nothing done by his contemporaries.

Even *The Life and Genuine Character of Doctor Swift* (pub. 1733)—which also invokes La Rochefoucault at the outset—is remarkably different from *Verses*.[69] *Life* was long regarded as a trial run for *Verses*, one with which Swift was dissatisfied; now it is more often regarded as a parodic redaction of the longer apologia or, more specifically, as an April Fool's joke directed principally at Pope.[70] My own sense is that lumping *Life* and *Verses* together produces misleading results: *Life* represents neither a misfire nor a hoax but (among other things) a response to the early 1730s attacks on the Test Act in Ireland.[71] The emotional center of the poem—a lengthy warning that the

Presbyterians will destroy both the church and monarchy (ll. 146–179)—has received almost no comment. Ehrenpreis observed a generation ago that *Verses* is an English and *Life* an Irish work,[72] but this is a much more important point than has been appreciated, one obscured by Pope-centric readings. In *Verses* Swift presents himself as connected with Pope, Bolingbroke, and others; his audience seems to consist largely of politically minded, informed English readers, including the authorities. In *Life* he is focused almost entirely on the superficial gossip of "the people," and the setting is Hibernia. The "Swift" in *Life* is first and foremost an Irish dean—not so in *Verses*. The emphases and motives of *Life* are quite different from those of *Verses*, though they share a dual mode of self-defense and aggression directed at Swift's current (political) enemies.

Swift's satiric practice in the first quarter of the century included derisive mockery, abuse, defensive propaganda, argumentation, and anxiously monitory satire. His targets and objectives were sometimes brutally clear and sometimes bewilderingly indeterminate. In the roughly two decades at issue here, his output is assorted but not in the same way. He writes a great deal of bloody-minded invective against targets of whose identity there can be little doubt. His attacks on ministerial mistreatment of poets are defensive, though that defensiveness is as much of his friends as it is of his political commitments. His responses to Ireland's plight—his indictment of English oppression and Irish folly—are vehement, and while Swift might not have thought anything could change, he certainly wrote with the conviction that something *should*. His nonstraightforward satires in this period, *Gulliver* and the *Verses*, are very little "like" his difficult satires in the previous quarter century. The Bickerstaff pamphlets are witty enough, but they and the others (especially *A Tale of a Tub* and the *Argument against Abolishing Christianity*) are disconcerting, raising questions about deceptiveness and the hazards of credulity. *Gulliver*'s difficulties are of another sort, and the *Verses*—whatever its mystifying passages—is hardly *unsettling*. The monitory satire that he practiced early in the century does not reappear in his late-life output. What is consistent in Swift's satiric writing is the occasional nature of particular pieces and the fierce energy of his judgment.

Gay

In his earlier works, Gay mostly worried about social and cultural issues. In the late twenties and early thirties, his primary concerns are sociopolitical. His importance to satire in this period has much to do with the success of *The Beggar's Opera*, a wonderfully high-spirited play despite its bleak implications. In *The Fan, Trivia,* and *The What d'ye Call It*, he had also leavened potentially trenchant satire by means of generic or tonal lightness. *Polly*, the sequel to *The Beggar's Opera*, is a not-very-innocent political application satire that was immediately suppressed and not staged in Gay's lifetime. Like its predecessor, *Polly* comprises incisive sociopolitical criticism diffused by its cheerful ballad opera form: "The familiar objects are . . . lambasted," Richard W. Bevis concludes, "until a jingle dissipates the gloom."[73]

Gay's other late-life satires are variously political.[74] The first series of *Fables* (1727), ostensibly written for the edification of the young Prince William, was part of Gay's struggle to find patronage. The favorite themes of opposition satirists are omnipresent—the animal tales involve corruption, treachery, flattery—but this is not partisan satire. Gay's commentary is highly generalized, not more applicable to dishonest politicians than to wayward nobodies: the 1727 *Fables'* morality, political or otherwise, is not to be taken all that seriously.[75] The second series of *Fables* (pub. posthumously in 1738) is more topical: "the Morals of most of 'em are of the political kind," Gay wrote to Swift.[76] The author of the 1727 *Fables* had been amiable, self-mocking, and ironic; the satirist of the later series is judgmental and angry. "In almost all these new fables," Nokes explains, "the corrupt minister . . . is finally exposed and defeated by the valiant voice of honesty and virtue."[77] Also published posthumously was *The Rehearsal at Goatham* (wr. ca. 1730; pub. 1754; 1s†), a one-act comedy mocking the governmental paranoia that leads to censorship: an author's puppet show is mined by the officials for nonexistent political innuendos. The satire indicates real frustration on Gay's part, as does *The Distress'd Wife*, a satiric comedy on the London bon ton staged in 1734 (eighteenth months after Gay's death). The play is not terribly interesting as drama, but it does reveal "the unusual intensity of Gay's feelings of disillusionment."[78] The tone is one of moral indignation and disgust; the picture of dissolute court life is unrelievedly negative, and Gay makes his hostility toward place-hunting very clear. The second series of *Fables*, *Rehearsal at Goatham*, and *The Distress'd Wife*, all belonging to the post-*Polly* period in Gay's life, reflect acute personal disappointment and animosity.

How much do the writers I have just described have in common as satirists? Pope, Swift, and Gay are almost always understood as a "Scriblerian" trio banded together against the forces of dullness and evil.[79] I have just covered their late-life satiric canons more or less in toto. What is the common ground?

One might observe that the Pope-Swift *Miscellanies* and *The Memoirs of Scriblerus* represent joint enterprises, making individual treatments of the Scriblerians more problematic. That is basically true. One difficulty is that the nature of the collaboration is hard to judge. Critics tend to assume that in about 1714 the group conceived the *Memoirs* and were mutually devoted to it. In fact the authorship is far from clear. Pope seems to have been most committed to the work and was responsible for its publication, though many scholars now think Arbuthnot wrote much of it. Charles Kerby-Miller claims outright that Swift's contributions to the *Memoirs* became, "by evolutionary process," *Gulliver's Travels*—but his lengthy commentary on the relationship between the travels chapter of the *Memoirs* and Swift's *Travels* rests wholly upon supposition.[80] Whether Swift in particular had anything to do with the composition of this key "Scriblerian" text is anybody's guess.

What of the 1727–1732 *Miscellanies*? Pope's enthusiasm for the project, as expressed in a letter to Swift, is often cited: "methinks we look like friends, side by side, serious and merry by turns, conversing interchangeably, and walking down hand in hand to posterity."[81] The *Miscellanies* brought together works from multiple Scriblerians, but just how collaborative was it? The first volume essentially reprinted the contents of Swift's 1711 *Miscellanies*; the second included some of Pope's very minor works and Arbuthnot's John Bull pamphlets; the third consisted of poetry, five-sixths of which was Swift's, and some of his best verse at that. As James McLaverty has explained, Swift was none too pleased when the *Miscellanies* "became a repository for Pope's least impressive pieces, but a collection of some of Swift's most impressive works, especially in verse."[82] The contents of the *Miscellanies* do not, on the whole, reflect a shared satiric agenda; the volumes collect a range of not very related works produced by quite dissimilar men. Camaraderie and a desire for a joint memorial do not prove much, especially when we consider that, whatever help and encouragement they provided each other, our "Scriblerians" wrote very different kinds of work.

Gay is something of a distraction, so I will deal with him only briefly before focusing on Pope and Swift. With the exception of the *Fables*, Gay's satires are plays, and the *Fables* are sufficiently unlike the works of his friends that even scholars keen to enlarge the "Scriblerus" canon do not canonize them. He is only alive for six of the years covered in this chapter, dying in 1732—a year (we should remember) before the publication of Pope's first Horatian imitation. Gay's place in this triumvirate depends largely on *The Beggar's Opera*, one of the three late-twenties tours de force of the "Scriblerian" enterprise. Conventional wisdom tells us that *Gulliver's Travels*, *The Beggar's Opera*, and the first *Dunciad* exemplify a cohesive and widely influential mode of eighteenth-century satire. These works are masterpieces penned by friends and sometime allies, but they are not the same sort of satire. *Gulliver's Travels* is a scattershot attack on any number of targets, some readily comprehensible and some not. Little consensus has been reached about what Swift was actually trying to do in this work. Gay's satire is bouncy, but his conclusion—"the World is all alike"—obliterates the distance between good and bad so fundamental to the major satires of Pope and Swift. Whereas Gay implies that the satirist is no better than his targets, Pope blasts the loathsome dunces and energetically separates himself from them. In technique, tone, targets, and aim, these works share little. Gay is almost always regarded as the lesser practitioner of the satiric mode perfected by Pope and Swift. In point of fact, he looks nothing like either of them (and what he does, he does quite well). More important than Gay's position vis-à-vis his "Scriblerian" comrades, however, is their position vis-à-vis each other.

Pope and Swift scholars of course recognize the significant differences between what those writers do, but in accounts of eighteenth-century satire, they tend to become the premier practitioners of a satiric mode ("Augustan," "Scriblerian"). The focus is all too much on their similarities. Phillip Harth was the first critic systematically to challenge the interconnectedness of Pope's and Swift's practices.[83] His discussion of their relations in the 1730s is sound and refreshingly commonsensical in its admission of disparities between those two writers. I am much indebted to his study, but he does not emphasize some of the more powerful implications of his argument. I want to add to Harth's analysis and, more explicitly, to dispute the enduring notion that Pope and Swift are Siamese satirists.

The early satiric careers of Pope and Swift connect remarkably little. Most critics associate them in the first quarter of the eighteenth century because of the "Scriblerus Club" meetings (1714), but the *Memoirs of Martinus Scriblerus* did not come out until 1741 (in Dublin),[84] and if Swift's interest in that project lasted beyond 1714, we have no evidence of it. Swift's satires in the first quarter of the eighteenth century are almost invariably the stuff of politics and propaganda—they belong to the world of *Poems on Affairs of State*, and in that regard their author shares more with Defoe or Maynwaring than with Pope. They are grittily partisan, often belligerently and vindictively personal, and there are a lot of them. Pope's early satires are few. *The Rape of the Lock* and the *Essay on Criticism* are only barely satirical; "Worms," the lines on Addison, and the burlesque of the first psalm (all discussed in chapter 5) are, in George Sherburn's phrasing, "firecracker squibs such as a clever schoolboy might produce."[85] Swift is thirty-six years old when *Tale* appears, Pope not quite sixteen. They would become friends, sometime political allies, and coproducers (after a fashion) of the *Miscellanies*, but they are of different generations, different religions, and different classes and backgrounds. They share some satiric targets: the Great Man, the injustices of patronage, bad poets, and so on. Both believe that society is mostly getting worse; their visions darken over the course of the 1730s. They have mutual friends, and they discuss their work together. Similarities in satiric practice are, however, decidedly limited.

The most crucial difference between Swift and Pope as satirists is one that both men fully recognized: one thrived on involvement in the world, the other wanted isolation from it. Writing Pope in June 1728, Swift highlights the distinctions between them:

[W]hat I do is owing to perfect rage and resentment, and the mortifying sight of slavery, folly, and baseness about me, among which I am forc'd to live. And I will take my oath that you have more Virtue in an hour, than I in seven years; for you despise the follies, and hate the vices of mankind, without the least ill effect on your temper; and with regard to particular men, you are inclin'd always rather to think the better, whereas with me it is always directly contrary. (*Correspondence*, 3:184)

As Harth points out, Swift "is not confessing his moral inferiority to his friend so much as he is defining himself in response . . . to a theme that had been growing increasingly prominent" in Pope's letters—the latter's ever more insistent celebration of "the virtues of retirement, indifference to the world, and calmness of temper."[86] While Pope was commending the glories of isolation, Swift was growing ever more resentful about the plight of Ireland: "These evils [e.g., importing too much from England] operate more every day, and the kingdom is absolutely undone," he writes to Pope in 1729. After another such communiqué, Pope's tolerance wanes: "Your continual deplorings of Ireland, make me wish, you were here long enough to forget those scenes that so afflict you."[87] Harth translates Pope's response as his urging Swift "to acquire some much-needed indifference, like Pope himself."[88] Pope is equally clear on the distinctions between him and his friend: "I have not the courage however to be such a Satyrist as you, but I would be as much, or more, a Philosopher. You call your satires, Libels; I would rather call my satires, Epistles: They will consist more of morality than wit, and grow graver, which you will call duller" (20 April 1733; *Correspondence*, 3:631). Pope, says Harth, was "bored by what he preferred to call 'Hibernian Politicks'"—that is, by what was central to Swift's late-life satiric career.[89] Swift was in Ireland unwilling and unable to retreat from the dire realities of his country; Pope was in England entreating his friend to join him above the fray. Johnson later recounted Swift's response to Pope's tendency to affect world-weariness: Swift would inform his friend, writes Johnson, that he "had not yet either acted or suffered enough in the world to have become weary of it."[90]

These letters only reinforce what ought to be glaringly obvious from their works: Pope is first and foremost an artist, Swift a sociopolitical warrior. Pope works from and to general propositions, and though he sometimes produces specific examples to illustrate the broader philosophical points of his satires, his concern is not for the particular. "Pope's . . . vision comprehends the entire world in one sweeping glance," Fabricant justly concludes, and "Swift had little to do with the exalted status . . . of this kind of God-like spectator. . . . Swift . . . portrays himself as a figure *in*, rather than overlooking, the landscape."[91] Pope depicts himself in specific settings like Twickenham or Timon's villa, but he issues his commentary from a pulpit; he is well above the muck and mire he criticizes, and he knows it. This is not to say that Pope never deals in grunge (see *The Dunciad*), or that he cannot be personally nasty; his attack on Hervey and others in the *Epistle to Arbuthnot* is highly individuated abuse.

But in that poem, he is ultimately concerned with defending himself ("Whom have I hurt?" [l. 95]) and with presenting himself to posterity. In a 1743 letter to Warburton, he looks forward to the appearance of Warburton's elaborately annotated edition of "the *Epistles* & *Essay on Crit.* &c.": "I know it is there I shall be seen most to advantage."[92] Pope is worried about the well-being of his person and his reputation, both now and hereafter. Such an issue is not Swift's driving force. Pope broadens out; Swift zeroes in. Pope defines himself as a highly literary, moral verse satirist; Swift is a patriotic activist fiercely and sometimes rashly committed to specific causes. Pope is a master versifier of astounding technical skill. In great poetry, general thought, and high morality, few could rival him in his age or any other. Pope out-artists and out-philosophizes Swift every time. The Dean's métier is not high-flown moral sentiment. As a poet he is mostly undistinguished, and his subjects are often nonliterary—but he is a passionate topical interventionist and a fiendishly effective commentator on the particular. I would not claim that Swift had no artistic ambition, but in the bulk of his satiric output he seems to want primarily to maim people, not to dazzle them with erudition and technical proficiency.

Pope scholars have wanted to see him as politically combative, but Swift is the satirist who participates in actual fights in the real world throughout his career. Swift is deep into everyday political issues—the proposed repeal of the Test Act, the Irish bishops' policies, Wood's halfpence, Irish imports from England. On what particular issues does Pope actually engage in combat? He grumbles mightily about Walpole, and he is plenty unhappy about the rewards system in place. But with the exception of the *Epilogue to the Satires* poems, he tends to perch well above the battleground. Pope's late-life satires are politicized—they rehearse all the opposition charges against Walpole's England—but next to Swift's imprecations they look tame. Swift has the capacity for rage, even when rage is imprudent; again and again, he finds himself a hunted man. Pope's political commentary is usually delivered at a high level of moral sobriety and aimed at an upper-end niche audience of cultured, philosophically interested readers; much of his critique would have been diffused by the grandiosity of the presentation. A modern reader of Swift's political verse satires might want footnotes, but the satiric thrust rarely needs much exposition. When he slams the Great Man, he does so in words of one syllable—minus allusive frosting—for anyone willing to glance at the passage.

The exception in Pope's output is a pair of 1738 satires, *One Thousand Seven Hundred and Thirty-Eight* and its sequel, the two poems printed together as *Epilogue to the Satires*. Here Pope's protest against Walpolean corruption is more direct than it had ever been. "His political partiality was too plainly shewn," Johnson said: "he forgot the prudence with which he passed, in his earlier years, uninjured and unoffending through much more violent conflicts of faction." The explicitness of his satire attracted the government's attention, and Pope got scared. He never again "attempted to join the patriot with the poet, nor drew his pen upon statesmen."[93] The *Epilogue* poems notwithstanding, Pope was (in Harth's phrasing) much "less willing than Swift to jeopardize his safety,"[94] and he himself admits to lacking the "courage" for Swiftian satire. In 1738 he tried to assume a hard-line position; two years later he wrote another virulent, politicized satire, a fragment called *One Thousand Seven Hundred and Forty*, where he expresses fear of physical and legal reprisal for saying touchy things about the Great Man. But Pope evidently lost his nerve, and the later poem was not published in his lifetime. Swift and Pope share some political principles, but the Dean is involved and defiant, while Pope is for the most part much more general and risk averse.

Scholars tend to emphasize correspondences among their favorite writers, and both Pope and Swift have suffered from this inclination. The long-standing association of these two (and, to a lesser extent, Gay) has relied too much on generalization: a "Scriblerian" satire is "a parody of serious forms of art" or one that participates in the "crusade against modern dullness."[95] If we want to put Swift and Pope into the same pigeonhole, then that pigeonhole needs to be more than expansive. Neither of them is unitary and consistent—the *Essay on Man* is not *The Dunciad*, and *A Libel on D[r] D[elany]* is not *A Tale of a Tub*—and they "do" very different things from each other. I suspect that Pope would be scandalized to find himself considered "like" the Hibernian Patriot in satiric terms, and Swift would almost certainly be piqued by that identification. In level of intensity, form, priorities, practice, and purpose, they were radically dissimilar satirists—and they well knew it.

III. The Problem of Meaning in *Gulliver's Travels*

Gulliver's Travels . . . filled the reader with a mingled emotion of merriment and amazement. . . . Criticism was for a while lost in wonder. (Johnson, "Swift," *The Lives of the Poets*)

Gulliver's Travels (1726) is the best-known, most often read, and most frequently republished satire of the eighteenth century, and a vast amount has been written about it, but what it "means" remains an unsettled issue. Or perhaps I should say that numerous critics have pronounced confidently on its meaning but without managing to arrive at anything like consensus. Many specifics of Swift's satire are pretty well understood, such as the attack on Walpole and the parody of travel literature. What remains contested are the larger issues of the overall object of the satire and what it tells us about Swift's values and his view of the world. Given the long-standing disagreement over this text, we need to ask why an entertaining and seemingly comprehensible four-part tale has proved so intractably resistant to our achieving a basic critical position. Two obvious questions need to be addressed: what are Swift's satiric targets? and how are we to take the Houyhnhnms and the Yahoos?

If *Gulliver's Travels* is a satire, then what exactly is it a satire on? Most scholars might be prepared to agree that it is a Menippean satire, but that label does not get us very far.[96] Swift strikes at multiple, sometimes unconnected targets—and what are we to make of that? Critics acknowledge the scattershot nature of the attack, but many argue as if they believe that a central message is to be uncovered, one that confers some sort of coherence on the *Travels*. Various hypotheses have been offered as to where this underlying unity might be found. Some scholars describe Swift's central thrust in terms sufficiently broad to explain the sundry hits—the *Travels* is about order and chaos, reason and unreason, truth and mendacity, and so on—but such overly general conclusions do not help a great deal, and few critics have found these descriptions satisfactory explanations of the text. More numerous are particularized readings of the *Travels*, proposals toward identifying an organizing principle behind the *Travels*.

A great many such readings have been published in the last seventy-five years or so. Several critics have argued that the unity comes from the book's political satire. Charles Firth put forward (1938) and Arthur E. Case further developed (1945) the thesis that the *Travels* is a sustained political allegory, a claim disputed by Phillip Harth (1976) and F. P. Lock (1980) and subsequently defended by Irvin Ehrenpreis (1989).[97] Lock has asserted more loosely that "the political purpose of *Gulliver's Travels* was . . . to attack not particular Whigs or Whig policies, nor even Whiggism, but the perennial disease of which Whiggery was only a contemporary manifestation."[98] Similar in kind to the allegorical readings are the analogical interpretations sponsored, for example, by Simon Varey and J. A. Downie. The latter contends that Swift's "method is one of analogy. . . . There is no need for him to present a consistent allegory to score his political point."[99]

Other critics have been yet more specific in explicating a perceived central thrust of Swift's satiric argument. Charles A. Knight defines the text as "the great proto-nationalist satire on nationality."[100] According to Clement Hawes, "The satiric effect of *Gulliver's Travels* depends on Swift's ironizing, and, above all, reversing of the commonplaces of eighteenth-century British colonial discourse."[101] After emphasizing the text's elusiveness, Donoghue pronounces that "*Gulliver's Travels* is only superficially about big men and little men: it is really about entrapment."[102] Fabricant reaches a similar conclusion, suggesting that the *Travels* is "explicitly and pervasively concerned with the theme of confinement."[103] Boyle contends, "The satiric charge is ultimately straightforward. Individual narcissism . . . leads to moments when the frustration of the narcissistic will detaches us from a sense of human sympathy."[104] For Patrick

Reilly, the Dean is obsessed with the past; for Alan D. Chalmers, the governing anxiety of his work is his apprehension of the future.[105] However rich and provocative these and many other readings are, they cannot *all* explicate the exclusive center of Swift's satiric argument. They depend on the assumptions and point of view of a particular kind of reader and are often derived from a relatively small percentage of the text. Not all readers would or should have been interested in Whiggery, confinement, colonization, nationalism, or any one of the many "principal" targets critics have identified as defining the central thrust of the *Travels*.

The great debate about *Gulliver's Travels* has of course had to do with Swift's attitude toward a particular target: the human race. That argument has centered on part IV. Soft-liners and hard-liners alike suppose that Swift is delivering a verdict here, passionately though they disagree about the nature of that judgment. For Thackeray and the Victorians, the author of the *Travels* was a nasty, half-mad misanthrope, a view that remained strong into the 1920s. In 1923, William A. Eddy grumbled that "the fires of misanthropy" had "obscured [Swift's] judgment."[106] Three years later, T. O. Wedel mounted an early challenge to the misanthropic argument, and Quintana's Swift (1936) was quite a different fellow from Thackeray's: he is a believer in "the universality of reason," a well-meaning moral reformer hoping to chastise human pride.[107] The soft reading, stressing the comic elements of part IV and identifying Gulliverian misanthropy as Swift's target, was in ascendance from the late twenties through the late fifties and sixties, when George Sherburn initiated and R. S. Crane developed the hard-line approach.[108] They insisted upon the seriousness of Gulliver's final reaction to the Yahoos, contending that Swift wanted to shock readers into recognition of human depravity and the inadequacy of human reason. Crane's judgment of the soft reading was stern: "however appealing this interpretation may be to those who want to think well of Swift . . . it is not merely obvious exegesis [of part IV] . . . or one that most common readers . . . have spontaneously arrived at."[109] In the last half century, the soft interpretation has mostly been regarded as the invention of tenderhearted critics keen to salvage Swift's image.

Can we conclude on the basis of the *Travels* that Swift was a violently pessimistic misanthrope? In the last half century this has been the prevailing opinion. Rosenheim claimed that "Swift's attitude is, indeed, beyond despair—an icy compound of resignation and cynicism," and Ehrenpreis has suggested, "According to Swift, human nature, impartially examined, shows itself to be radically vicious."[110] Rawson argues that from part IV we can determine "not (of course) that Swift would enact the killing if he could, but that the Yahoos, like mankind in Genesis, deserve the punishment." In Swift's satire, Rawson continues, "the death-dealing curse . . . is extended to whole classes of men . . . and indeed to the human race itself."[111] Explicitly or implicitly, critics in both camps have claimed that they are expounding what "Swift says." But this is not really true. *Gulliver's Travels*, whether we like the fact or not, is essentially opaque, and scholars tend to find in it what they are predisposed to find. Granting the wisdom of Rawson's more recent observation—"you are equally 'bit' if you believe literally what Gulliver says in Book IV, and if you think you can discount it because in a formal sense he is not Swift"—the text does not *say* what either school of interpreters find in it.[112] As of 2013, some positivistic hard-liners seem unwavering in their faith that they know what Swift thought and felt and wished to convey. The implicit attitude seems to be that any dissenters from Crane's view are simply bad readers. Without subscribing myself a latter-day soft-liner, I would like to suggest that there are some problems with the hard interpretation—or at least that it is no more demonstrable from the text than the alternatives.

If Swift intended the *Travels*, or even its final voyage, to be a vehicle for expressing bitter misanthropy, he made some odd decisions. Why have Gulliver meet decent people along the way, including the honorable, generous Portuguese captain (and why have the Houyhnhnms, far from ideal, conspicuously lack the compassion that we are to admire in Pedro de Mendez)?[113] Rawson has maintained that the occasional positive examples do not offset the harshly negative judgment of humanity. "The Captain is a rarity, who appears only briefly," he concludes, and who serves only to illustrate Gulliver's alienation.[114] One can just as well argue, I think, that Gulliver's response to him serves only to alienate us from Gulliver and to make us resistant to his outlook. The captain, moreover, seems much more human than the exaggerated and unreasonable Yahoos. Why would the average reader identify with them or recognize him- or herself in them? They represent not human nature but an extreme distortion of the worst features of human nature. In any case, how one reads part IV has much to do with the assumptions one brings to it: we can emphasize the bad and dismiss the good or vice versa, depending on the predilections we bring to the text and our sense of Swift's mind and character.

The hard reading depends upon our taking Gulliver's final judgment seriously—but Swift manifestly does not ask us to sympathize with his protagonist. Our lack of empathy for him creates an interpretative problem, which Rawson most prominently has attempted to solve. He admits that the *Travels* ends "with Gulliver a monomaniac and his last outburst a defiant, and silly, petulance," granting that we are not "invited to share his attitudes literally." But, Rawson continues, the ridiculousness of Gulliver's attitude is "appropriate," "dissociating Swift from the taint of excess, without really undermining the attack from Swift that the rant stands for." I admit to having difficulty understanding how this works. Why would the obvious silliness of the position not undercut the "attack" behind it? Rawson goes on to concede that perhaps "Swift is making a more moderate attack on mankind than Gulliver"—but he insists that "Gulliver's view hovers damagingly over it all."[115] Why "damagingly," if his stance is patently extreme or preposterous? Believing that we are not meant to take Gulliver's desire to live among his horses seriously but that his outlook is somehow preeminent is tantamount to wanting to have our cake and eat it too. Rawson's interpretation of the fourth voyage—and his conclusions about the authorial judgment it reflects—depends upon suggestive but sometimes dizzying argumentation. In his reading, Gulliver both is and is not Swift, and when Gulliver imagines the extermination of the Yahoos, "Swift doesn't 'mean it,' though he doesn't *not* mean it either."[116] If the aggressively misanthropic position is simultaneously meant and not meant, where does that leave the interpreter—except to be guided by his or her own assumptions and predilections?

Part IV has been responded to in exactly contrary ways, and that has to do in part with its openness to interpretation. Someone inclined toward cynicism can find a harsh judgment, but what in the text prohibits a cheerier reader from finding Gulliver's extreme reaction nonsensical? The book that Swift's friend Arbuthnot found "merry" is now more commonly understood as one whose "comical foundation . . . dissolves under the acid of Swift's rage."[117] I would say that parts of the final voyage seem more whimsical than brutal, including the Houyhnhnms threading needles with their hooves and the worldly-wise voyager coming to prefer the smell of his horses. Ultimately, the *Travels'* disconcerting end strikes me as provocative rather than conclusive: Swift propounds an unanswerable question and then exits gracefully, leaving us to contemplate Gulliver living "in great Amity" with his two young stone-horses but beginning to permit his wife to sit at dinner with him (11:290). Readers may feel rebuffed by this, stung by Gulliver's unsocial behavior, or we might simply laugh at him.

The absurdity of some of what we are shown in the last voyage, taken in conjunction with the presence of generous, well-meaning individuals, seems to undercut the hard-line reading—or at least that has to be admitted as a reasonable response to the text. We can conclude with Rawson that the *Travels'* last passage, where Gulliver enjoins the English Yahoos never again "to presume to appear in my Sight," is "quarrelsome and disorientating," yet another assault on the reader.[118] That the *Travels* unsettles the reader, leaving him or her uncertain and uncomfortable, is now a widely held conviction. But some readers, even in this post-Crane era, manage to read part IV without feeling harassed and disconcerted. The worst parts of human nature are forcefully represented at numerous points in the *Travels*—notably the political quarrels of part I and the war passage in part II (the latter hardly testimony to Gulliver's good judgment), not to mention the Yahoos. I admit that my own readerly tendencies incline me toward the hard-line response to the final voyage—though the closing lines do seem to make Gulliver look mad—and I confess to not caring whether he had used me more civilly. Reactions to the Yahoos aside, only a reader who takes Gulliver awfully seriously and (like the horrified Victorians) wants to identify narrator with author could take the misanthropy of part IV as the message of the whole book.

What can we safely deduce or presume about Swift's primary "point" in the *Travels*? The answer seems to be very little. One credible explanation might be that Swift, gifted as he was, lost control of the text and did not give the necessary clues to interpret its central satiric argument, whatever he may have intended it to be.[119] Another is that he deliberately constructed the indeterminacy as a way of tackling fundamental questions about human reason, in which case the response to the *Travels* is evidence of humanity's desire—and inability—to answer such questions. A third is that he was having such fun attacking multiple targets that he did not much worry about consistency or resolution. That Swift has several agendas in the *Travels* is a real possibility, as is a variable level of commitment on his part to those many concerns. Such multiplicity limits our ability to define his satiric purposes precisely, let alone to privilege any one of them as the sine qua non of his argument. We can agree that war and the decrepitude of old age are ghastly and that human pride is preposterous, but beyond such particularities critical certitude is hard to validate.

My position is that *Gulliver's Travels* is an eminently readable text, dazzling but not especially mystifying (or mystifying only if we seek what is not there). If we expect a single dominant meaning to explain a complex, far-flung work, then we are bound to be puzzled. Perhaps Swift meant us to be able to detect the foundational meaning behind it all but failed to provide the proper signals; he might also be tantalizing us by withholding what we need to make sense of the whole. The *Travels* could represent a profound piece of hermeneutic education or a joke. Whatever Swift meant or felt or thought he wished to accomplish, we are left with a text that seems not to have a cohesive point. The *Travels* is probably best understood not as *a* satire but as a vehicle for a mélange of satiric hits. If Swift intended it to communicate a focused satiric-cum-didactic moral, then his book has to be seen as a failure. As a provocative scattershot attack on several mostly identifiable targets, the *Travels* is satirically both comprehensible and effective. Swift had a lot to say about a lot of subjects, from the trivial to the appalling, but that he attempted to convey a central message I am inclined to doubt. The hard-line reading, like others, depends largely on the presumption that we understand Swift's mind—a dangerous supposition. Even Vanessa, after all, felt that she could not know Swift's thoughts, "which no humane creature is capable of geussing [*sic*] at because never any one liveing thought like you."[120]

Gulliver's Travels is intriguing, brilliant, and strange; it has been described both as a by-product of Scriblerianism and as the grimmest satire on the human condition of all time. Nothing else in Swift's output looks quite like it; certainly none of Pope's satires comes close. Swift is an extraordinary satirist, among the most prolific of his lifetime; his satiric oeuvre shows tremendous range and includes a number of deeply felt, admirably forceful works. Many of his works belong very much to their "moments"—that is, they have clear affinities with satires produced by other writers at the time. Not so *Gulliver's Travels*.[121] The best-known satire of the most celebrated eighteenth-century satirist is essentially without precedent in the early eighteenth century, inimitable by contemporaries, and confounding to modern critics—a freak phenomenon in the history of satiric practice.

IV. Fielding and the Move toward Sympathetic Satire

Most scholars take for granted Fielding's connections and debts to Pope and Swift, regarding him as a would-be "Scriblerian." The fact that his disposition is quite different from those writers has compelled critics to combine their assertions of Scriblerian influence with a disclaimer about tonal discrepancies. They tend to see him as Scriblerian with a difference—an awkward combination of Swiftian rage and Addisonian benevolence that leaves him torn between satire and sentiment, pessimism and optimism. His work reflects, in Hunter's phrasing, "the perilous balance of values in a mind divided."[122] In Paulson's recent biography of Fielding (2000), he argues that the writer learned "almost everything about writing from the great trio of Pope, Swift, and Gay, together with their antagonists in the *Spectator*."[123] But Fielding does not say anywhere in his extant letters or writings that he sought inclusion in Pope's circle or even that he recognized such a coterie; how familiar he was with the work of these writers is unclear, but he does not appear to have been very directly influenced by them.[124]

Fielding signed six plays "Scriblerus Secundus" in 1730 and 1731, on the basis of which many scholars have presumed that he was declaring himself a follower of the Scriblerians. To what extent do those plays reveal "Scriblerian" preoccupations? At least in its print form, *The Tragedy of Tragedies* spoofs the bombastic pedantry and critical jargon at which Pope sometimes takes aim, and *Peri Bathous* and the *Dunciad Variorum* were no doubt part of the contextual background of that play. As I have argued, however, we need to recognize the importance of the tonal differences between Fielding's satire and Pope's. And while *The Tragedy of Tragedies*, *The Author's Farce*, and *Tom Thumb* are hailed as "Scriblerian" send-ups of popular culture, when Fielding later returns to the game of mocking popular forms of entertainment—as in *Tumble-Down Dick* (perf. and pub. 1736)—he does not think to signal his lasting Scriblerian commitment by ascribing his efforts to H. Scriblerus. His other "Scriblerus" works share little with *Peri Bathous* and the *Dunciad* (as of 1730–1731, the only works of the club members signed by "Scriblerus"). *The Letter-Writers* (1731), a three-act contretemps-farce spoof of sex comedy, has nothing at all to do with the favorite

"Scriblerian" targets, and neither does *The Welsh Opera* (discussed above). I see no reason for believing that Fielding recognized a Scriblerian cohort or that he realized that the pseudonym signaled a particular kind of satire. If we do not assume that Fielding is a happy cross between Addison/Steele and the "Scriblerians," what sort of satirist do we find him to be?

Playful Satire and Entertainment

In several works, Fielding's primary goal is evidently to make his audience laugh: they may or may not be invited to feel superior, but they are being entertained. *Tom Thumb* is an enjoyable burlesque written with farcical gusto. The ridicule of Colley Cibber and others in *The Author's Farce* has bite, but the play is basically a romp. *The Welsh Opera* likewise seems to have little serious point, whatever the desire of some critics to read political import into it. *An Old Man taught Wisdom* (1735) is a slight ballad-farce, the substance of which is Old Goodwill's attempt to marry off Lucy, his fifteen-year-old daughter. The ditsy ingénue accepts the offers of three of her five suitors; while they puzzle over the mix-up, she ties the knot with someone else. Old Goodwill approves of the match, happily agreeing that the chosen mate is a more attractive son-in-law than any of the "Booby Relations" with whom he had tried to pair her (2:33). *The Lottery* (1732), a high-spirited ballad opera afterpiece, is a more topical satire targeting the annual lotteries Parliament approved in order to reduce the national debt. Fielding ridicules the avarice of speculators and stockjobbers associated with these lotteries, and he scoffs at the romantic hopes and unrealistic wishes of those who buy tickets. The satire in these plays is jokey, nonparticularized banter written by a master of comic amusements for the stage.

Provocation and Preachment

Some of Fielding's works are more substantial in satiric terms. Many of his plays include sharp critique, raise questions, and push readers and viewers to think, though they vary in acerbity and intensity. Where *Tom Thumb* had been a general travesty, in *The Tragedy of Tragedies* Fielding goes after a number of specific exemplars among heroic plays (many of which were more than forty years old), including Dryden's *Conquest of Granada, Don Sebastian, Aureng-Zebe,* and *The Indian Emperour.* He also targets plays by Lee, Banks, Dennis, and others and, more broadly, false scholarship.[125] A reader could have detected the bite in Fielding's burlesque of the genre, its bombastic language, and instances of same from recognizable plays—though, as Hume points out, in performance *The Tragedy of Tragedies* would have come across in ways similar to its fluffier predecessor. Like *Tom Thumb,* this would probably have been taken by theatergoers as "a travesty of heroic drama to be enjoyed for its sheer silliness."[126] In *The Covent-Garden Tragedy* (1732), Fielding returns to parody, this time not of heroic but of pseudoclassic tragedy.[127] Unlike *The Tragedy of Tragedies, The Covent-Garden Tragedy* is a severely unsympathetic play that shows clear distaste for its subject. In *Eurydice* (perf. 1737; pub. 1743), Fielding tartly mocks the mores of London high society, a world of domineering wives, henpecked husbands, and devotees of the imported culture he despises. No less than *The Covent-Garden Tragedy*, this piece reflects Fielding's offended disapproval, in this case of Italian opera and its consumers.

Fielding's topical satiric plays often include clear sociopolitical criticism. *The Old Debauchees* (1732) combines farce with severe invective, the latter directed at the Catholic Church. Fielding's plot features the depraved Father Martin's attempt to seduce the world-wise Isabel, but—no helpless innocent—she orchestrates the wicked Jesuit's self-exposure, and the play ends with his mortification. Fielding's scathing abuse of the Catholic priests in this play is sincere, but his unremitting defamation is not terribly funny and would have been palatable only to a committed anti-Catholic. The principal satiric target of *Rape upon Rape* (1730) is the corrupt Justice Squeezum. A number of critics have argued that Fielding was explicitly alluding to Colonel Francis Charteris, notorious for raping his maidservant and getting off with a fine. Charteris was a friend of the ministry, and opposition satirists pointed to his relative impunity as an egregious example of Walpolean improbity. *Rape upon Rape* indubitably alludes to Charteris, but, like *Don Quixote in England* (wr. 1729; perf. and pub. 1734), this play is topical without being overtly partisan.

Fielding's explicitly political plays are *Pasquin* (1736), *The Historical Register, For the Year 1736* (1737), and *Eurydice Hiss'd* (1737). The first includes mock rehearsals of two plays, "The Election" (satirizing the sleaziness and duplicity of both the Court and Country factions) and "The Life and Death of Common-Sense" (anti-Walpole). The oblique antiministerial satire of the latter is very different from the frontal attack of *The Fall of Mortimer*; it has political bite without being a party document. *The Historical Register* attacks a long list of theatrical and political targets including Cibber, the ministry's taxation policy, and high society's nonsensical infatuation with the castrato "*Farinello*" (3:423). The play is plotless. In the auction scene, Hen tries in vain to peddle unfashionable items: "Lot, 2, a most delicate Piece of Patriotism, Gentlemen, who bids?" he asks, but after dropping the price several times he gives up (427). Modesty, courage, and wit all meet the same fate; Hen cannot move "the Cardinal Virtues," but for "a very considerable Quantity of Interest at Court" the participants are prepared to bid a fortune (429–430). Fielding's satire is biting, high spirited, and effective.

Eurydice Hiss'd, an afterpiece to *The Historical Register*, is bolder. Fielding here associates Walpole with a failed farce-writer named Pillage, and *Eurydice Hiss'd* becomes an allegorical rendition of one of the Great Man's most outstanding failures. Just as Fielding had been booed when he staged *Eurydice* (the occasion recalled by the title of this new play), "so had Walpole and his ministers been soundly humiliated . . . for trying to act out their little public farce known as the Excise Bill."[128] *Eurydice Hiss'd* is an example of Fielding's skill at superimposing one target on another—a potent form of camouflage, in this case both glaringly obvious and unprovable. In this provocative afterpiece, Fielding escalated hostilities, and the ministry was not amused. The Great Mogul was not long for the theater, but these plays represent some of his most successful satiric ventures on stage.

Satires like *The Historical Register* and *Eurydice Hiss'd* are trenchant without being oppressive, their effectiveness greatly improved by Fielding's restraint. In a small number of works, however, he abandons the indirection that works so well for him, heavy-handedly delivering a solemn moral. The antiministerial satires of 1737 are hard hitting but indirect; a work like *The Modern Husband* is infinitely harsher, and *The Universal Gallant* is likewise shrill in its preachment. "Never before," says Wilbur L. Cross, "had Fielding been so dull."[129] The principal example of Fielding's harsher social satire in fiction is of course *Amelia* (1751).

Distributive Justice: Joseph Andrews *and* Tom Jones

Fielding's works have been pretty well understood, and none have been so closely studied as *Joseph Andrews* (1742; 2 vols.; 6*s*†) and *Tom Jones* (1749; 4 vols.; 12*s*†)—but those novels have never really been regarded as part of the satiric culture of the mid-century. Individual critics have described parts of both books as satirical, and recently Joseph F. Bartolomeo has included them in an account of eighteenth-century satiric fiction,[130] but satire scholars have not devoted much attention to these works in their surveys. Even Paulson, in his widely influential *Satire and the Novel in Eighteenth-Century England*, has little to say about the way satire functions in these novels. He sets out to prove that "the novel" and "satire" represent two fundamentally different ventures: "The novel, as the name implies, represents new values, and satire, usually a conservative genre, represents old." Crucially important to the novel and to novelistic attitudes toward character, he argues, is the "growing acceptance of the assumption . . . that man is basically good" and "the belief in progress"—suppositions, says Paulson, "with which the satirist could never agree." Fielding is portrayed as an ambitious writer who begins as a satirist ("grasping the coattails" of Pope, Swift, and Gay) and then—increasingly committed to the idea of positive values—abandons satire to write *Joseph Andrews* and *Tom Jones*.[131] This compartmentalization is misleading, distorting our sense of Fielding as a satirist and of midcentury satire. *Joseph Andrews* and *Tom Jones* are not "satires," but they do contain plenty of satire.

Joseph Andrews is always regarded as a comic epic poem in prose and *Tom Jones* as the cheery history of the eponymous foundling. But Fielding undeniably regards satire as a form of moral and social instruction, and a significant part of *Joseph Andrews* and *Tom Jones* is education carried out by means of satire. That satire operates distributively: Fielding shows us positive and sometimes very negative examples. He affectionately mocks but ultimately rewards the mostly good, ridicules the less good, and punishes the truly depraved—see Blifil, who is "a parody of Tom, a negation of Tom's natural vigor and goodness, which is real and substantial." Tom, Paulson reminds us, "survives and thrives," whereas "Blifil's plots, like Satan's or the flimsy webs of Swift's spider, collapse, and he is exiled to the north, where the Devil is supposed to have resided."[132]

Fielding is committed to the idea that a positive model can also be foolish, misguided, and inconsistent. Parson Adams, satirized as a man but never as a clergyman, is a well-intentioned but ineffectual hero who tries instinctively though often injudiciously to do the right thing. He is described as "a Man of good Sense, good Parts, and good Nature," one who is "as entirely ignorant of the Ways of this World, as an Infant just entered into it could possibly be" (23), and his innocent wholesomeness makes him the dupe of lesser but shrewder men. Some scholars have been uncomfortable about the decision to make such a decent man appear ridiculous, but the use of "mixed" characters is fundamental to Fielding's satire.[133] He repeatedly presents us with scrupulous men of weak resolve or other limitations, with whom we are meant to sympathize and in whom we are meant to see ourselves. Discussing characters who "raise our Compassion rather than our Abhorrence," Fielding says in *Tom Jones*:

> nothing can be of more moral Use than the Imperfections which are seen in Examples of this Kind; since such form a Kind of Surprize, more apt to affect and dwell upon our Minds, than the Faults of very vicious and wicked Persons. The Foibles and Vices of Men in whom there is a great Mixture of the Good, become more glaring Objects, from the Virtues which contrast them, and shew their Deformity; and when we find such Vices attended with their evil Consequence to our favourite Characters, we are not only taught to shun them for our own Sake, but to hate them for the Mischiefs they have already brought on those we love. (2:527)

Adams's benevolence ought to inspire benevolence, and his mistakes ought to be recognized, assessed sympathetically rather than harshly, and if possible avoided. Tom's faults have been extensively commented upon, but he is not only decent and well meaning (like Adams) but also educable. His history is a progression, his enthusiasm for life and his essential humanity never diminish, his capacities for judgment improve, and his final good fortune is to be applauded by the reader. Fielding understands the difficulty of behaving well: in *Amelia*, he has the irresponsible, often thoughtless Booth cry in earnest, "Why can I not imitate what I so much admire?"[134] Perfection is an impossible standard, and condemnation based on minor human shortcomings is therefore unreasonable and even perverse. Fielding's main concern here is *educability*, in his good characters and in the readers for whose entertainment and edification they were created.

Fielding scholars understand these novels' incidental satire pretty well, but satire scholars (Paulson excepted) have not worried much about fiction. Of course satire in novels tends to be very different from satire in verse: the presence of plot and characters usually tempers or dilutes the satire, and fictional works are often satiric but are rarely "satires." That said, broad conclusions about "eighteenth-century satire" ought to take into account the various ways and places in which satire appeared. Satire scholars sometimes mention the novels of Fielding, Sterne, and Smollett, but their conclusions come largely from (part of) the practice of Dryden, Pope, Swift, and a few other non-novelists. Adding *Joseph Andrews* and *Tom Jones* to our satiric pantheon naturally makes for a messier picture but provides a more balanced view of what satire meant and how it was used in the mid-eighteenth century.

Fielding's Concept of Satire

Scholars have long observed Fielding's temperamental differences from the "Augustans," but they have almost entirely failed to acknowledge the degree to which "temperament" matters, especially in satire. Critics tend to agree that Fielding, as Brian McCrea says, "gives us a sense of human nature that, in its fullness and tolerance, we think of as Fieldingesque."[135] Hunter's description is as tenderhearted as the man he seeks to render: Fielding "is genial and pleasantly garrulous; he sees the humor in everything including himself; he loves life and savors its every moment; he is tolerant of others without compromising his strong beliefs; he is uncommonly decent and fair."[136] Fielding is not entirely lighthearted and optimistic, of course, as pieces like *The Modern Husband* and *Amelia* make clear. He can be unkind and unfair, angry and rude; he has dark moments, and he features a few irredeemable characters (e.g., Lord Richly, the Moderns, and Blifil), but for the most part his attitude toward the world and its inhabitants is positive.

Even Fielding's more punitive satire has little in common with that of Swift or Pope. For one thing, he rarely moves from particularized derogation to sweeping complaint. In the satirical "elegy" for Marlborough, Swift savages the man and implies the meaninglessness of human notions of heroism and grandeur; like many of his personal satires, the mock elegy is manifestly cynical. And when Pope lashes the dunces, he is undoubtedly complaining about more than a Welsted here or a Ward there—this is cultural collapse writ large. Fielding's expressions of contempt or hatred rarely work that way. Even *Amelia* includes pronounced positives that do not cancel out but do mitigate the darkness of the world described. Rawson has emphasized Swift's tendency to make satiric lists that "convey the notion that they may be extended to include everyone," and he goes on to distinguish that "exhaustiveness" from the effect created by Fielding's satire. "Fielding mocks specifiable types," Rawson shrewdly observes, and "the satire leaves out other types by definition." Unlike Swift, that is, Fielding does not leave one with the impression that the follies or vices under attack are going "to overwhelm the whole fabric of life."[137]

When Fielding does denounce the worst specimens of the human race, he does not do it very convincingly. The condemnation of Lord Richly is unpleasant and unsuccessful because Fielding cannot rant with Pope's confident solemnity and cannot rage with the intoxicating fury that fuels Swift's libels. Swift can hate, Pope can despise, and Gay can conclude that the world is all alike without losing his edge. When Fielding tries to convey anger, as in *The Modern Husband*, it comes across as stiff and contrived. Unlike Swift or Pope, Fielding seems unable to exult in the contempt he occasionally expresses. When he loses restraint, he has no fun and neither do we.

Fielding usually displays a joie de vivre that neither Pope nor Swift seems to possess. After his death, Lady Mary reflected that "no Man enjoy'd life more than he did," describing her cousin as a devil-may-care chap enraptured of food and drink, women, gambling, good fellowship, any and every thing in life.[138] Swift has a sense of humor, but at least as a satirist he often tends toward fiery hot, and his humor stings; he can be playful, low key, charmingly intimate and personal—as in his birthday poems to Stella—but much of the time he is an angry man. Pope is assured and judgmental. Fielding has a great deal more zest and joy and good fun. His "optimistic drift," John Richetti observes, is that "modern disorder is really a form of comic recurrence; what else can you expect from human nature?"[139] Pope and Swift have little tolerance for that which departs from their standards—which is what gives such force to their satire. Fielding knows that young men are going to sow their wild oats; he knows that people are going to be silly or vain or spiteful. He is prepared to mock such failings, but he is not greatly troubled by them. Of some things—extreme dishonesty, Catholicism—he is not at all tolerant, but even his most bitter satire would never end with universal darkness covering all.

A discussion of Fielding as satirist needs to specify which Fielding, in which works. His use of satire changes from the 1730s to the 1740s and early 1750s, and while the shift is not a radical reversal, it is significant. As a playwright in the 1730s, his satire includes the exuberant, the biting, and the heavy-handedly harsh; as a novelist and author of miscellaneous prose in the 1740s and 1750s, he is more didactic and sympathetic. Some of the change has to do with the shift from plays to fiction, but a novelist like Smollett manages to be judgmental and intolerant. Fielding's use of satire in his novels is instructive rather than punitive: "it is much easier to make good Men wise," he observes in the dedication to *Tom Jones*, "than to make bad Men good" (1:8). To rebuke the morally reprehensible who do not want to improve is pointless; to rail at those who do want to be better is futile, inhumane, and unjust. Fielding recognizes that, for those sinners who can be reformed, guilt is a stronger instrument than shame. He is closer to Defoe, in satiric terms, than to Pope or Swift, though he is much less earnest than Defoe.

Fielding features mixed characters in his fiction, those neither blameless nor wholly evil, and he encourages his readers to refrain from passing judgment too early or too rigidly.[140] The "Man of Candour, and of true Understanding," he observes in *Tom Jones*, "is never hasty to condemn" (1:329). As critics have uniformly acknowledged, Fielding seeks to improve his readers' capacities for reading and judging. We should base our opinions on motives but often have access only to actions, so we must train ourselves to judge with sensitivity and caution. In the late forties and fifties, Fielding defines his satiric method in direct contradistinction to that of those who "pass a severe Sentence upon the whole, merely on account of some vicious Part" (*Tom Jones*, 2:570). On this basis, he disapproves of generalized satire, arguing in *An Essay on Conversation* (1743) that "such general Satire is not founded on Truth" (147). The "Opinion of our Superiority is commonly very erroneous," he observes, because "we are apt to over-rate our own Perfections, and undervalue the Qualifications of our Neighbours" (138). Fielding's is a spectrum of rightness and wrongness—not, as for Pope and Swift, a black-and-white division between acceptable and objectionable.

Fielding's concept and practice of satire is radically unlike Swift's or Gay's, but the clearest example of the contrast between Fielding and his "Scriblerian" forebears is Pope. In verses written in 1729 but first printed by Isobel M. Grundy in 1972, Fielding chastises "Codrus" (Pope), the "Lilliputian Bard" who writes out of "Ignorance and Malice."[141] From Fielding's point of view, the author of *The Dunciad* typifies the "sour, morose, ill-natured, censorious Sanctity" that he later criticizes in *An Essay on the Knowledge of the Characters of Men* (1743). The judgment of someone who writes from such a position, Fielding explains, "will neither do Good itself, nor suffer others to do it" (169). The poet of *The Dunciad* decries what he finds repulsive without offering much in the way of explicit positive values, angering and alienating his targets. Was Fielding any happier with Pope's Horatian satires? Probably not, judging from "An Epistle to Mr Lyttelton" (wr. 1733), also printed by Grundy, which is the only evidence we have of Fielding's thoughts on the subject. In the "Epistle" he holds forth on the nature and proper purposes of satire, and he excoriates Pope: "Go on," the poet encourages the malevolent satirist, "enjoy the Triumphs of thy Spite, / And curse thy Self, and curse the World, and write" (245; ll. 158–159). The poem's closing image depicts Pope as a "little Curr" barking at all passersby, overwhelmed by self-loathing, unprovoked by those he attacks, and as impotent as he is unkind (l. 166). Fielding may be loyally taking up the cudgel on behalf of Lady Mary here, but he is not cringingly reverential of Pope, and the attitude he expresses toward satire is consistent with his later views on its legitimate functions.

If we approach Fielding without trying to make him into a would-be "Scriblerian," we find him to be an experimentalist who takes great pride in his originality and, mostly, a rather cheerful writer—at least until *Amelia*, which despite its positives reflects its author's darkening outlook.[142] Fielding's frivolous satire has no parallel in the works of Pope and Swift, and his derogation is of a very different sort from theirs. In the forties and early fifties, he produces *tempered* satire—drastically remote from the satiric practice of his most renowned contemporaries, but not without significant currency in this period, celebrated "heyday" of harsh satire though it is now considered.

Sympathetic Satire

The period between the publication of *Gulliver's Travels* and that of Pope's last *Dunciad* is with reason regarded as the high moment in punitive satire. Scholars have tended to valorize the combative satirists of the 1730s, those who savagely abuse Walpole and his dunces and describe politicocultural collapse with marked cynicism. But not all satires from this period are punitive. Sympathetic satire is increasingly prominent by the late thirties and forties; it features not denunciation or ridicule but milder, more tolerant critique. This is not the same as exemplary satire, which provides positive models meant to represent ideals for the audience. It involves the amiable and generous representation of those characters who are not paragons but "real" human beings, complete with foibles and flaws.

Sympathetic satire is less common in verse than in other forms, but there are some instances. The author of *Human Passions* (1726; *6d*) deals at length with human unreason, but this "satire on man" is far from harshly judgmental. The satirist clearly differentiates between exceptional misconduct and more ordinary, harmless folly—this is not the breezy nihilism of Gay's "the World is all alike"—but toward the less grave failings he is sympathetic. He registers human affliction not with scorn or despair but with sympathy, somberly bidding his readers to "mark what various Ways has Fate to vex / Poor Mortals, and their best laid Schemes perplex" (5). James Miller's *Seasonable Reproof* (1735; *1s*) is likewise sympathetic. Although he attacks such individuals as Henry Carey and Aaron Hill with real indignation, on humanity more generally he waxes compassionate: "We *all* our *Frailties* share" (19).

Sympathetic satire is more effective when readers and viewers are presented with characters, "real" individuals living in the world. This type of satire is, unsurprisingly, more common in drama and fiction than in verse. The best fictional examples are *Joseph Andrews* and *Tom Jones*. Drama has remained almost entirely outside the purview of satire scholars, but there is a lot of satire on the stage, and as Matthew J. Kinservik has conclusively demonstrated, the pejorative definition of satire applies rather badly to many of the popular plays in the first half of the century.[143]

The Beggar's Opera was one of two great theatrical successes of 1728; the other was *The Provok'd Husband*, Cibber's completion of Vanbrugh's *A Journey to London*. Like Vanbrugh's *The Provok'd Wife*, *The Provok'd Husband* is a vivid illustration of marital discord, this time between a decent husband and a wayward wife. Lady Townly is sexually faithful but spendthrift, "Immoderate in her Pursuits of Pleasures" (3:184). Aggrieved by her excesses, Lord Townly laments in the play's opening lines: "Why did I marry?—Was it not evident, my plain, rational Scheme of Life was impracticable, with a Woman of so different a way of Thinking?" (3:185). When his well-meant pleas for her better behavior come to naught, he settles on legal separation; she tearfully vows reformation, he forgives her, and they will presumably live happily ever after. As Lady Townly must accept "The Husband's Right to Rule," so (in the subplot) Lady Grace must accommodate to Mr. Manly's "Doctrine" of marriage or let him find someone who will (3:252, 192). The final message of the play is "a very conservative statement about the proper nature of marriage—an obnoxious one by present-day standards. . . . Cibber's response to disharmony is to assert a traditional solution: submission to duly constituted authority."[144] *The Provok'd Husband* includes some sharp satire—as on the country "gentry"—but the play is mostly positive. In sharp contradistinction to *Love's Last Shift*, the emphasis is on seriously presented reform. Cibber's play makes good on the principle advocated in his prologue: "Plays should let you see / Not only, What you Are, but Ought to be" (3:183). This is not a platitudinous expression of human goodness but an admission of human imperfection, a representation of misbehavior that is critical without being unsympathetic.

A number of dramatic satirists in this period adopt sympathetic stances. Miller's *The Man of Taste* (1735), concocted from Molière's *L'Ecole des Maris* and *Les Précieuses Ridicules*,[145] is a London comedy of a distinctly humane sort. Miller mocks the pretensions of those who aspire to social high life; he critiques the manners of fashionable society and laments the absence of decency in the "polite" world. The tone is light. Dodsley's *The King and the Miller of Mansfield* (1737) is more sentimental and moralizing. The play begins with King Henry II lost in Sherwood Forest, having been separated from his courtiers; he is given shelter by honest John Cockle, the eponymous miller. Meanwhile, the miller's son (Richard) and his former sweetheart (Peggy) fantasize about exposing the king's iniquitous courtier, Lurewell, who wrongly persuaded Peggy of her lover's infidelity so that he could win her for himself. When the king arrives incognito at the miller's house, he learns of Lurewell's villainy and resolves to punish the miscreant and help the young lovers. The resolution is a happy piece of distributive justice: the beneficent monarch bestows a knighthood on the upstanding John Cockle (with a handsome sum attached), Lurewell is reprimanded and forced to pay Peggy £300 per annum (45), Richard forgives all, and the euphoric lovebirds reunite. The center of the play, however, is the king himself, who rejects the code in which aristocratic privilege negates charitable obligation. When he metes out punishment to the offending courtier, he insists that Lurewell's title does not license inhumanity: "My Lord, you see how low the greatest Nobleman may be reduced by ungenerous Actions" (45). Wickedness is punished and goodwill rewarded. *The King and the Miller of Mansfield* is an overtly didactic play, advocating social morality that applies to people of all ranks.

A more complicated example is Hogarth's *A Rake's Progress* (1735), a sequence of eight plates offering an intricate mixture of punitive and sympathetic satire. The rake is Tom Rakewell, a young innocent who aspires to social standing beyond his means and comes to a bad end. Rakewell, Jenny Uglow argues, "is no Lovelace, no dashing blade . . . decoying women and terrorizing the town with nonchalant, demonic arrogance. He is a young bourgeois, first seen as a trembling youth with a fresh face haloed in curls, attractive, open, innocent—and weak."[146] The "progress" portrays Tom living beyond his means, impregnating and abandoning the unworldly Sarah Young, being arrested for debt, buying his release by marrying a wealthy woman whose fortune he soon exhausts, finally being imprisoned and then sent to Bedlam. In the madhouse he is shown with a bandage on his breast, suggesting attempted suicide, and his despair is evident. "The reverse of the spiritual autobiography," Paulson explains, Hogarth's "progress" sequence "shows the closing off of awareness," as the Rake's model leads "not to conversion but to self-annihilation."[147]

A Rake's Progress is hardly an uncritical representation of Tom, but it is a morally instructive picture of a sort of human weakness to which most of us may be presumed susceptible. But Hogarth's notion of satiric didacticism is more complex than Fielding's, often though the two are coupled.[148] As Fielding explains in the preface to *Joseph Andrews*, "The only Source of the true Ridiculous (as it appears to me) is Affectation" (7), and both he and Hogarth (says Paulson) "are concerned with those ordinary people who act according to inappropriate ideas of themselves." But, Paulson continues, the two satirists have very different opinions about punishment for misbehavior: "The most important difference between Fielding and Hogarth is in the matter of rigorous consequences: Hogarth's Tom Jones would have died of tertiary syphilis or at the very least suffered a clap."[149] This distinction is right, and crucial. Fielding forgives and rewards his fallible protagonist; he exposes his villains, but he is not pitiless in subjecting even Blifil or the Moderns in *The Modern Husband* to vindictive punishment.

V. Alive and Well: The State of Satire at Midcentury

Satiric practice in the first half of the eighteenth century—from the publication of *A Tale of a Tub* to the deaths of Pope and Swift—is far from uniform. The most exciting developments of the first quarter of the century do not continue into the later twenties and thirties; the most interesting satires of the second quarter of the century cannot be organized into the categories described in chapter 5. The 1730s are not the 1710s—the entire culture of satire undergoes a transformation, whose causes are not wholly clear but whose importance is not to be underestimated. The great successes at the beginning of this period appear without warning and could not have been anticipated by readers in 1725, but they do not usher in a new mode of satire. The practice of Pope, Swift, and Gay is neither representative of a "type" nor a particularly useful guide to what goes on in this period. A more productive way of looking at the subject is to widen our consideration and try to reckon with the diversity of the famous works seen amid the rapidly changing satiric output of the time.

What do we gain from broadening our perspective? One point is that this survey calls into question a still common characterization: the period from the late twenties through the early forties is widely touted as the heyday of "Augustan" satire, and Augustan satire is usually understood as a largely negative enterprise. Antiquated as Louis I. Bredvold's 1949 "Gloom of the Tory Satirists" now seems, his description of the satiric temperament remains standard in its essentials. He asserts of the Augustan satirist, "The darkness of his gloom is the measure of the depth of his indignation, and a sense of isolation is inevitable in his calling."[150] To what extent do gloom, indignation, and isolation typify the practice of satire in this period? Some satirists are indeed gloomy and some indignant, but a great many have a jolly good time. And gloom is not outrage: incriminatory derogation of a much-reviled minister is not the same thing as all-inclusive pessimism about a world gone to pot. Privileging content over tone is therefore misguided. Thematically, the satire of this period is more coherent than that of the first quarter of the century, but the utility of a category that includes both *The Dunciad* and *The Tragedy of Tragedies* is functionally nil. A great deal of less harsh and indignant satire is written in this period by satirists who are not gloomy and not isolated. This is at once a great age of abusive and cynical political satire *and* a period of transition toward increasingly sympathetic and humane satire as described by Stuart M. Tave in *The Amiable Humorist* (1960), which traces a shift from judgmental to compassionate laughter.

Attitudes toward human nature are changing by the middle of the eighteenth century. Fielding's comic didacticism in the forties is much more in line with the directions in which satire is moving. He is no would-be Swift; by the Dean's standards, Fielding is a mighty soft touch. The anti-Catholic satire of *The Old Debauchees* and the preachment of *The Modern Husband* are not exactly "sympathetic," but Fielding does not much go in for angry, hurtful satire, and he clearly has the capacity for sympathetic critique. He understands the potentiality for evil but also for good. Swift pays relatively little attention to the good in his satires. Pope is sometimes convincingly positive, as in the Martha Blount passages of *To a Lady* and in various bits of the *Epistle to Arbuthnot*. The apostrophes to virtue and the virtuous throughout the Moral Essays represent "good," though many of the positives come across at least to this reader as formulaic, abstract, and impersonal. At bottom Pope remains a profoundly judgmental writer, drawing hard lines between what is acceptable and what is not. I have difficulty imagining either Pope or Swift indulging in the kind of affectionate ridicule of a positive example we find in Fielding's handling of Parson Adams. *The Rape of the Lock* is light in tone, but the lightness is more a matter of performance of burlesque than in the presentation of Belinda, who, though not sharply criticized, is not sympathetic. Readers are not asked or expected to relate to her. Swift does some affectionate personal joking, but neither in his nor in Pope's satiric oeuvre do we see much "mixed" satire. Neither of them would give us a Parson Adams or a Tom Jones, and this is no mere technical differentiation. The distinction between "harsh" and "sympathetic" satire is fundamental, indicative of two strongly contrasting views of human nature and attitudes toward the operation of satire.

Again and again in this survey we have found that satire is a highly time-specific form, not only in its targets but in its dominant modes and patterns, and this period is no exception. The destructive energies directed at the Walpole ministry are undeniable, as are the anxious grumblings about cultural decline, but they are closely tied to a particular moment in the eighteenth century. Scholars have tended to generalize about satiric practice in the long eighteenth century on the basis of a very small number of examples, and those works not called *Absalom and Achitophel* or *A Tale of a Tub* tend to come from the 1726–1745 period. In fact the major works of this period are far from exemplary of the century as a whole. Pope's *Dunciad* is "like" some of the cultural-cum-political verse satires written in the late 1720s and 1730s, but that is one of many kinds of satire being produced at that time, and it is also a relatively short-lived phenomenon. Harsh cultural satires—no less than Carolean court lampoons, generalized verses denouncing abstractions, and monitory satires in the reign of Queen Anne—are the product of a particular moment. The second quarter of the century is neither representative of the whole century nor the evolutionary culmination of what precedes it. *Gulliver's Travels, Verses on the Death of Dr. Swift, On Poetry: A Rapsody, The Beggar's Opera*, the *Dunciad*s, *Tom Thumb*, Pope's Horatian satires, and *Eurydice Hiss'd* are an astonishing efflorescence of satiric brilliance. They are also wildly variegated, unrepresentative of their own time, unprecedented, and (as we are about to see) bearing surprisingly little connection to satiric practice in the next quarter century.

CHAPTER SEVEN

Churchill, Foote, Macklin, Garrick, Smollett, Sterne, and Others, 1745–1770

◇◇◇◇◇◇◇◇◇◇◇◇◇◇◇◇◇◇◇◇◇◇◇◇◇◇◇◇

> The first half of the eighteenth century concluded the Augustan
> Age—the great age—of English satire. But in the same decade that
> saw the death of Swift and Pope, the novel . . . began to produce a
> series of masterpieces that contributed importantly to the eclipse of
> satire for the greater part of the next one hundred and fifty years.
> —Ronald Paulson, *Satire and the Novel in
> Eighteenth-Century England*, 3

That the golden age of satire ended with the deaths of Pope and Swift is a well-established critical truism. Not for nothing does Thomas Lockwood explain his enterprise in *Post-Augustan Satire* (1979) as "something in the way of an autopsy."[1] In *The Amiable Humorist* (1960), Stuart M. Tave argued for a transition, over the course of the century, from harsh to sympathetic laughter. Counterexamples can be cited, and the change is gradual, hazy, and incomplete, but it is also indisputable. As we move into the second half of the eighteenth century, good nature and benevolence are increasingly celebrated, while severity in judgment is increasingly scorned. Such circumstances are not propitious for a satirist moved by Swiftian indignation, and scholars have in the main been content to accept Paulson's conclusion that satire qua satire does not really survive the deaths of its most famous practitioners. The principal exception is Charles Churchill, who has been well studied by Lockwood and Lance Bertelsen.[2] Smollett is often cited as a quasi-satiric writer of this period (and Paulson's readings of his major novels are excellent); critics dub *Tristram Shandy* "satirical," or sometimes even a "satire." But because later eighteenth-century satire is so remote from what scholars tend to privilege, the attention it gets is usually tepid and dismissive. The one true satirist of this period has been dealt with carefully and thoroughly—what more need be said about an otherwise moribund genre?

The presence of this chapter is in itself a denial of the accepted wisdom about satire in the third quarter of the century. Obviously I do not believe that satire dies in the mid-1740s, and neither do I agree with Paulson that the energies of "real" satire are transformed beyond recognition and subsumed by a fundamentally distinct genre. The tendency to define satire, at least implicitly, as that which Pope and Swift practice is a bad idea. If we conclude that "all true satirists are pessimists" who think "that the world is exceedingly ugly and vicious, and that nothing is likely to change it,"[3] then the great age of satire includes precious few satirists. In fact, hundreds of works are called satires by their authors in the third quarter of the eighteenth century. Contemporaries routinely describe Samuel Foote's onstage personations as satire, some appreciatively and some disapprovingly. Charles Macklin's *The Man of the World* was refused a license on two separate occasions (1770 and 1779) for its trenchant political satire before a heavily revised version was finally staged in 1781. The primary material does not bear out the modern critical notion that satire was somehow in extremis by midcentury.

The organization of this chapter is generic, because the shifts in satiric practice differ from genre to genre. The ways in which verse satire changes are not the ways in which dramatic satire changes, and satire in fiction is something else again. In the opening section, I survey the largely undistinguished types of verse satire, with some speculation as to what changes and why, including the nonpolitical satire of Charles Churchill. Section II focuses on the political situation of the early 1760s, and particularly on John Wilkes, *The North Briton*, and Churchill's Wilkesite poetry. I argue that, for reasons probably having to do with Pope's posthumous influence on poetry and with relative sociopolitical stability, much of the verse in this period is not very effective *as satire* and that there is an important distinction between satiric poetry written for a cause and that which is not. Section III surveys the most common types of dramatic satire, produced for a commercial theatre. These works are driven as much by well-tried popular formulas as by authorial conviction or deeply felt moral indignation. I also cover Macklin and Foote, from a modern vantage point the two most important satiric playwrights of this quarter century, and David Garrick, the period's most eminent theatrical personality. An elementary but important point: we find quite a lot of positive-mode satire (contra standard critical notions of satire) and also much negative-mode satire (contra characterizations of the "Age of Sensibility"). Section IV covers satire in fiction, in particular in the works of Smollett, Henry and Sarah Fielding, Sterne, Charlotte Lennox, and Oliver Goldsmith. These writers evidently understood their enterprises as satirical (if not as "satires"), though they are far from uniform in their practice. I argue that the presence of plot and characters, in fiction as in drama, can mitigate the force of the satire, and I seek to demonstrate the limitations of a single theory of how narrative satire functions. One object of the chapter as a whole is to challenge the standard cliché about the dearth, let alone the death, of satire in the third quarter of the eighteenth century.

Satire neither dies nor disappears in the later eighteenth century—it fragments. In the periods covered in the preceding chapters, extrinsic circumstances either made some kinds of satire impossible (as discussed in chapter 4) or provided focal points for satirists (chapters 3, 5, and 6). Carolean satirists are preoccupied with political issues and court figures; many satires in the reign of Anne concern debates about political power and religious toleration; in the 1730s, most satirists target Walpole, the opposition, hack writers, and a variety of cultural forms. Especially in chapters 3 and 6, we saw a significant degree of connection between genres; playwrights and poets during the Exclusion Crisis and during the 1730s produce related satiric works. There is much less generic overlap in the second half of the eighteenth century, in part because of censorship imposed by the Licensing Act of 1737.[4] Polemicists, cartoonists, and some poets blast Bute's ministry, but hard-hitting political commentary could be kept off the stage. For a variety of reasons, we do not find conspicuous focal points for satire like the ones we saw in earlier subperiods. In practice, what this means is that satire appears in many forms and deals with many subjects, and no one target or technique is particularly prominent. The culture of satire in this period is much more polyvalent and pluralistic than what we have previously encountered; it is, as the title of this chapter suggests, rich but uniquely scattered and disconnected.

I. The Rise of "Poetic" Satire

Insofar as critics have discussed verse satire in this period, Churchill's is usually the first and last name mentioned. He is the foremost satiric poet in the generation after Pope's death, but a substantial amount of satiric poetry is produced in these years. I have read some two hundred separate pieces of various lengths plus single-author collections (e.g., by Lennox, Mary Leapor, Robert Lloyd) and miscellanies (e.g., *The Theatre of Wit* [1746]). The problem, as Lockwood wryly acknowledges at the beginning of *Post-Augustan Satire*, is that they are not very good. Rather than plodding through hundreds of examples of fairly straightforward and largely uninteresting pieces, what I wish to do here is characterize the predominant types of verse satire found in these years.

By way of generalization, I suggest that part of the insipidity of these works has to do with the fact that they are intended principally as works of art. This is not a phrase that would have been used by eighteenth-century writers, but what I mean is that in a high proportion of the satires the skill exhibited by the artificer seems more important than the work's practical object (if any). Some of the satires are simply jeux d'esprit, but much of this material is self-consciously and self-indulgently poetic. These pieces give the impression of having been written for the appreciation of their style rather than for the communication of content. Some of the major canonical satires are purposive as well as brilliant, but trying first and foremost to craft a piece of art tends to produce radically different results than does attempting to offer serious commentary on something the author believes is important. I return to this subject in due course, but the survey of satiric poetry should be read with this basic fact in mind. I have organized the poems into three loose groupings: (1) lightweight entertainment pieces, usually containing insubstantial social satire; (2) socioethical preachment, including complaints about political venality, mostly generalized and made from a moral perspective; and (3) particularized satire and more focused attacks, whether political, social, or literary in subject.

Frivolity and Entertainment

Many satires in this period make no pretense to moral judgment: they are divertissements, bouncy narratives (sanitized versions of early Ned Ward), or playful depictions of social scenes and characters. *The Important Triflers* (1748; 1s) is a verse "journal," in which the poet describes his comings and goings among the court: "At *Breakfast* sometimes we to *Ranelagh* go, / And find Fault, as usual, with—more than We know" (11). The pastimes of high society are exposed as senseless and hollow, and the principal types (the wit, the beau, the coquet) all seem duly silly, but the breezy diary contains not a jot of moral reproach. Satirical entertainment pieces of this sort tend to be insubstantial. The author of *Garrick's Vagary: or, England Run Mad* (1769) justly describes his poem as "a miscellaneous Production," intended to serve the public as "a laughable What d'ye call it, some Thing or other" (preface).

Other satirical diversions are more actively good natured, including Christopher Anstey's extremely popular *New Bath Guide* (1766), a warm, featherlight social satire (and very expensive at 5s†). Anstey's work comprises a series of verse letters written by members of the Blunderhead family during their visit to Bath, describing the manners and fashions of the English spa town, a place of "Fine Walks, and fine Views, and a Thousand fine Things" (43). Here Simkin Blunderhead marvels at his visit to "a Place where the Ladies undress":

> Oh 'twas pretty to see them all put on their Flannels,
> And then take the Water like so many Spaniels,
> And tho' all the while it grew hotter and hotter,
> They swam, just as if they were hunting an Otter;
> 'Twas a glorious Sight to behold the Fair Sex
> All wading with Gentlemen up to their Necks. (37, 38)

Anstey's send-up of Bath living is genial—Howard D. Weinbrot calls attention to its "amiable satiric flaccidity"[5]—and representative of the kind of limpness that critics have pointed to as evidence of satire's demise. This kind of "wholesome Satyr" (7) is admittedly less interesting than lampoonery or sharp critique, but it represents a type of satire alive and well in this quarter century. Anstey's satire is benevolent, though it is not of a piece with, say, the heartier, tempered satire of Henry Fielding, which is tolerant but also vigorously didactic. Fielding is trying, among other things, to teach his readers a lesson about judgment; Anstey is content to be amusing.

Moral Preachment

The authors of the lightweight social satires do not even feign moral indignation, but most nonparticularized verse satires in this period at least claim moral purpose. Many of these works are fairly focused theme satires. Common targets are political corruption (e.g., *Bribery A Satire* [1750]), women of fashion (e.g., *Advice to the Ladies* [1754]), and modern taste and manners (e.g., William Kenrick's *The Town. A Satire* [1748]). The author of *Advice to the Ladies* laments the softer sex's infatuation with makeup, and in *The Town*, Kenrick grumbles that "All seek intent for what is new To-day, / And Noise and Nonsense bear them all away" (4). Works such as *The School of Man* (1753; 3s†), *The Devil upon Crutches in England* (1755; 1s 6d†), and *Folly, A Satire on the Times* (1763?; 2s) are more comprehensive in their social critique. The authenticity of the indignation expressed is impossible to determine, but clearly these authors conceive of satire as something that ought at least nominally to ridicule generalized vice and folly.

The claim that the satirist is society's custodian and moral scourge represents what P. K. Elkin describes as the "core" of the standard eighteenth-century "defense of satire." In 1973, Elkin argued that this apologia was a widespread phenomenon, part of the "orthodox viewpoint" of the eighteenth-century defenders of satire: satirist after satirist in the long "Augustan" period loudly asserted his noble intentions, maintaining that he told the hard truth because, as disinterested guardian of virtue, he had no choice.[6] In fact, defensiveness of this sort is relatively infrequent until the second quarter of the eighteenth century. Carolean lampoonists, entertainers like Ward, and the satirical propagandists of the 1710s evidently felt little need to apologize for their offerings. Dryden's *Discourse* is a much-celebrated piece of satire theory, but it does not represent the mood or practice of the 1690s or any other decade in the long eighteenth century. Pope, Young, and others make high-flown claims for their satire in the late twenties and thirties, but such moral assurances are most conspicuous in the 1740s and 1750s.

Midcentury satirists have much to say about why they feel they must write satire. Smollett's *Advice* (1746; 1s) and *Reproof* (1747; 1s) are largely the stuff of Juvenalian indignation, and in them he is concerned not only to lash individuals and deplore the rotten state of society but also to consider "the question of how the satirist should conduct himself in an unreceptive, largely unworthy world." The subject of both works, Lockwood concludes, "is not 'the world' but 'the-satirist-and-the-world,' or perhaps 'the-satirist-versus-the-world.'"[7] The author of *Plain Truth: A Satire* (1747) opens in grand defensive manner: "Yes, I will write. And let them laugh who will, / 'Tis Honour, Virtue, guides the honest Quill" (3). He proceeds to mock the female sex, their male counterparts, and a host of named politicians, ending as high-handedly as he began, asserting his desire to "humanise Mankind," and to "poise the World aright" (23, 24). Both *Modern Virtue: A Satire* (1746) and Charles O'Brien's *A Dialogue between the Poet and his Friend* (1755) consist of conversations in which a well-meaning companion counsels the satirist to hold his tongue. The subject of these poems is the satiric impulse and enterprise, the poet's role in the epic battle between virtue and vice.

The low-heat surveys of social ills, like the satires about satire, tend to read more like performances of preachment than like expressions of actual indignation, especially alongside their higher-heat counterparts. (Smollett's satires are exceptions: in *Advice* and *Reproof*, as elsewhere, he damns with passion.) As I say in chapter 3 with regard to Oldham's rants, we cannot always distinguish with certitude between genuine and performed righteous anger, but differences in intensity—sermonic vehemence versus recitation of defensive boilerplate—are fairly easy to detect. John Taperell's *Swearing, A Satire* (1751; 6*d*), a heavy-handed condemnation of the titular sin, warns the swearer: "You are already in the Suburbs of Hell, learning the infernal Language, sending out your Oaths like Arrows against Heaven, which will rebound and bring double Vengeance on the Heads of those that shot them" (iv). *Swearing* is a homiletic satire, evidently meant to deter Taperell's fallible fellow Christians rather than to reform hardened blasphemers.[8]

Particularized Attack

Most of the comprehensive, social survey satires include incidental swipes and topical allusions, but the number of verse satirists in this period whose principal object is to convey judgment on a person or a group of people is strikingly small. The major exception is Churchill, of whose political satires I say more in the next section. Most of the verse in this period consists of trifles and generalized moral preachment; only a small fraction of the total output is centrally concerned to denigrate particular people.

Much of the satirical commentary on individuals involves actors and writers. The most notorious example is Churchill's *The Rosciad* (1761; 1*s* 6*d*†), in which a group of named players vie for the coveted chair of the just-deceased Roscius. The succession of performers—a standard gimmick in "session" satires—allows Churchill to offer mocking commentary on Macklin, James Quin, Spranger Barry, and others before naming Garrick the victor. A year earlier, Robert Lloyd had offered an anatomy of onstage infelicities in *The Actor*—cracking, for example, that "none emphatic can that Actor call, / Who lays an equal emphasis on *all*" (10)—but Churchill's satire was personal enough that it generated a paper war.[9] Wounded, Arthur Murphy responded with his *Ode to the Naiads of Fleet-Ditch* (1761), charging Churchill with plagiarism and lambasting his comrades, Lloyd, George Colman, and William Shirley. The Bruiser met outrage with outrage, redoubling his attack on Murphy in later editions of *The Rosciad*.[10] Both men and several others are chided by the anonymous author of *The Scrubs of Parnassus* (1761; 1*s* 6*d*†), who describes the paper war as the dirty play of malicious men:

> Now flew the mud about like fury,
> And authors swore like brims of *Drury*;
> Some here and there with dirt did *faddle*,
> Others with excrement did *paddle*;
> And *splashing, dashing, dibbling, dabbling*,
> Were almost choaked with *squibbling squabbling*;
> Till *bawling, squalling, railing hissing*,
> They fell to spewing, *sh———g, p———g*. (28)

The satire might well spring from deeply felt disapprobation, but it might just as easily be an attempt to capitalize on a highly visible public squabble.[11]

Literary infighting is ubiquitous in this period: a great many topical satires involve self-contained warfare between individual writers and actors. The satirical journalism of the Nonsense Club members well illustrates the vogue for this sort of mockery. Bertelsen's coverage of the group is thorough and sharp.[12] He focuses at some length on Bonnell Thornton's *Have At You All: or, The Drury-Lane Journal* (16 January to 9 April 1752), which burlesqued several periodical writers, including Johnson and Smollett, but most roundly derided Fielding's "Sir Alexander Drawcansir." The mission of *The Drury-Lane Journal*, Bertelsen concludes, was "purely and simply . . . to ridicule and absurdly imitate the works of others."[13] With *The Covent-Garden Journal*, Fielding had "provoked a literary free-for-all by declaring . . . war on all of Grub Street and particularly on John Hill."[14] Thornton's *Journal* belongs to this battle. A more personal satire is Christopher Smart's *The Hilliad* (1753; 2*s*†), written after Hill criticized Smart's *Poems*. In a vivacious *Dunciad*-style mock epic, Smart presents his enemy as the Arch-Dunce Hillario, whose "cavalcade" includes "Pert Petulance," "drowsy Dulness," "neutral Nonsense," and so on (ll. 79, 80, 81, 83). The deflation no doubt stung—Hill retorted with *The Smartiad*—but Smart seems to be enjoying himself. Murphy's (?) *The Spouter* (not perf.; pub. 1756) is meaner and more comprehensive, though often quite funny. The satirist complains about the vanity of the leading actors and the need to pander to audience tastes, disparages theatrical personalities such as Theophilus Cibber and John Rich, and scorches Hill and especially Foote with venom. This sort of cultural caterwauling is conspicuous in this period. Motives differ—the satire can be a matter of personal rivalry, gratuitous abuse, self-defense, expression of jealousy, a desire for publicity, or whatever—but the bickering of writers, critics, and actors accounts for much of the personal satire in this quarter century.[15] The rise in satire on players probably owes something to the beginnings of a celebrity culture: increasing newspaper publicity means readers more receptive to and hungry for satiric commentary on cultural icons.

The rest of the particularized verse satire in this period is exceedingly miscellaneous. The author of *A Letter from a Gentleman in London, to his Friend in Pensylvania* (1756; *6d*) solemnly denounces the Quakers, who vainly presume that "To them alone, the Favourites of Heav'n; / This happy Inspiration first was giv'n" (12). A handful of satires target Kitty Fisher, an aspiring actress notorious for her liaisons with wealthy men. *Kitty's Stream: or, the Noblemen turned Fisher-Men* (1759) depicts the promiscuous courtesan as a "pamper'd Strumpet" who is not worth her price (9). Edward Thompson's *The Meretriciad* (1761; *2s*) gripes about loose women more broadly, treating Kitty as an outstanding example: "Fisher thou'rt young,—but in the rolls of fame," he asks, "Who can, or dare eclipse a Kitty's name?" (10). These topical satires are unfriendly, but not nearly as stingingly personal as what we have seen earlier in this survey, and far fewer in number.

Poeticized Satire

What topical thrust this verse possesses is often obscured by overt poeticizing, as in Lloyd's *The Progress of Envy* (1751; *1s*). The subject of the poem is William Lauder's accusation that Milton plagiarized large passages in *Paradise Lost* from several sources.[16] Lloyd describes Envy being aided by Malice and Lauder ("Son of Darkness," vi) in her attempt to cast gloom upon the Parnassian scene (i.e., to ruin Milton's reputation):

> Impatient Envy, thro' the aetherial Waste,
> With inward Venom fraught, and deadly Spite,
> Unto this Cavern steer'd her panting Haste,
> Enshrouded in a darksome Veil of Night.
> Her inmost Heart burnt with impetuous Ire,
> And fell Destruction sparkled in her Look. (9)

In the end, of course, Parnassus is restored, and deserved Fame triumphs over Envy and Lauder. The use of Spenserian stanzas and the rich personification, as Lockwood observes, relegates Lauder to a very minor role: "The intended victim . . . is completely swallowed up in the picture of Envy's progress," as "the pictorial qualities of the allegory obscure its meaning."[17] The satiric thrust is clear if one is looking for it—Lauder is motivated by jealousy and must not be listened to—but the punitive force of *The Progress of Envy* is essentially nil.[18]

Lloyd's poetry is illustrative of the literary and performative qualities that are characteristic of much of the verse satire in this quarter century. With the exception of the scrappy, lightweight "trifles" and a few plainspoken Juvenalian denunciations, a staggering amount of this material "sounds," tonally and stylistically, much the same. In *New-Market* (1751; 2s†), Thomas Warton describes the imprudent life of a wastrel heir, whose inheritance of a fortune immediately turns him into a spendthrift adept in the art of "fashionable shame" (4). The satire on gaming, promiscuity, and horse racing is light, but the language and tone are grand: "Ye rival Youths, your golden hopes how vain, / Your dreams of thousands on the lifted plain!" (8). The satiric target is lost amid the ostentatious poetic allegory:

> How are th' advent'rers of the *British* race,
> Chang'd from the chosen chiefs of ancient days;
> Who warm'd with genuine glory's honest thirst,
> Divinely labour'd in the *Pythian* dust. (15)

The epic language is not the stuff of deflationary mock heroic, the elevated tone not part of the joke (much of this verse has little sense of humor). Lockwood points out, moreover, that *New-Market* includes quite a lot of visual detail that "has little or nothing to do with the poem as satire. . . . This kind of description is 'pure' in the sense that it seems to have no moral implications."[19] That Warton is exposing social folly is manifest, but "New-Market" seems more a poetic subject than a satiric target.

In this quarter century, verse satirists seem to become increasingly self-conscious about form and aesthetics. They are trying to produce what we would call "art," works to be enjoyed as much for their skill as for the content. The results represent a largely, though not absolutely, unprecedented phenomenon in the long eighteenth century. For most of the satirists covered in chapters 3 through 6, the central object usually appears to be something other than creating poetry. They produce satire for the joy of defamation, to entertain their friends, to agitate for change, to complain—but with relatively few exceptions, the satiric argument is of crucial importance. The likes of Young and Pope are indisputably keen to compose fine verse to be appreciated by present and future readers for its craft, but this kind of conspicuously "poetic" satire does not become predominant until the midcentury. Granting the greatness of *Absalom and Achitophel* or the brilliance of *A Modest Proposal*, Dryden and Swift seem to me *primarily* concerned with achieving an effect and making a point. Dryden exercises his talents in the service of a cause; he is not using the Exclusion Crisis as material for a masterpiece. I return to this vexed issue in the epilogue, but at present I only suggest that the verse satires of the 1750s and 1760s seem much more artistic in motivation—meaning the style and craft is not a feature but an end in itself—than most of what we have seen in earlier chapters. This tendency does not seem odd if one is thinking in terms of Pope, but alongside the hundreds upon hundreds of satires produced from the Restoration through the 1740s, this spate of poeticized satires is disconcerting. The distinction between "satirical" poetry written for its own sake and practical, present-centered satire written to make things happen is fundamental—a difference evident in the satiric canon of Charles Churchill.

Churchill's Nonpolitical Satire

Churchill before Wilkes is a prominent satirist—*The Rosciad* made him a household name—but he is also doing what most of his contemporaries do. He is a poet, obsessively hung up on the poet's role in society, adamant about his independence as an author, and not terribly interested in making things happen. Throughout *Post-Augustan Satire*, Lockwood emphasizes the self-absorption of much of the satiric poetry in this period, rightly observing that "Churchill . . . often shows himself . . . as concerned with protecting his individual integrity and asserting his own genius in a world that cannot care for such things."[20] Churchill's nonpolitical output reflects the major trends in verse satire of this quarter century: it is sometimes aggressively self-defensive about the writer's province (as in *The Apology*), sometimes a performance of preachment (as in *The Times*), and sometimes a literary display (as in *The Ghost*).

Like Pope, Churchill warmly defends the satirist's right to pass judgment; like Smollett in *Advice* and *Reproof* and the authors of the "dialogues" between the poet and a friend, he writes satire about the role of the satirist. *The Apology* (1761; 1s) is a contentious response to the displeasure with which *The Rosciad* had been met in the *Critical Review*. He plays the injured poet, lamenting that the critics, "With partial rage rush forth,—Oh! shame to tell!—/To crush a bard just bursting from the shell" (ll. 13–14). Churchill, says Lockwood, "translates his quarrel with the critics into a profounder opposition between freedom and slavery."[21] He again champions the independent spirit—his idée fixe—in *Night* (1761; 1s), the frank libertine's defense of his modus vivendi. Churchill sets up a contrast between the happy, independent, reasonable "sons of NIGHT" and the prudent majority, "slaves to business" whose way of life is not to be admired or emulated (ll. 18, 7). Brazenly asserting his independence, opinion of the masses be damned, the poet proclaims, "I would not be *that* THING, *that* PRUDENT MAN," who "err[s] with millions on [his] side" (ll. 344, 382).[22] *Night* is not a purposive satire—what would he be trying to accomplish?—but a boisterously indignant display of Churchillian audacity.

Churchill, like Pope, is preoccupied by the satirist's role and willing to mount a pulpit. One of the oddities in his career is *The Times* (1764), the only nonpolitical satire he produced after allying himself with Wilkes. In this rancorous denunciation on the theme of "*o tempora, o mores*," Churchill surveys his world with solemn disapprobation: "Time was, e'er Temperance had fled the realm," he reflects, and "Time was, that Men had conscience" and so on (ll. 13, 33). The fractious Juvenalian deplores corruption, duplicity, unkindness, and other general sins, and he bitterly criticizes the abuse of privilege. *The Times* is best known for its forceful attack on homosexuality; John Sainsbury calls it the "most sustained literary assault on sodomy."[23] Like a number of his contemporaries, Churchill performs the part of indignant moralist and righteous social guardian, satiric champion of virtue over vice.

Churchill's least purposive satire is perhaps *The Ghost* (1762–1763), which is not self-defensive but self-consciously poetic. Scholars who mention this meandering poem usually highlight its "Shandean" element of playful digressiveness, a connection likewise made by contemporaries.[24] Churchill's ostensible subject is the Cock Lane Ghost affair, and that incident is precisely what he does not focus on. Churchill covers a broad range of sociopolitical and literary topics, but insofar as *The Ghost* has a central satiric point, it lies in his mocking exposure of "collective popular fancy," the widespread tendency of people to abandon reason and be led astray by superstition and credulity.[25] Bertelsen argues that the Nonsense Club writers believed in "free" writing, emphasizing "the importance of the poet's mental process and the spontaneous manipulation of his materials. The poet does not plan his work in relationship to a set of literary laws or purposes." And, he continues, Churchill practiced the spontaneity he preached,[26] especially in a work like *The Ghost*, a jauntily bantering, freewheeling, fast-moving poem upon nothing (a nonexistent ghost). The author of *The Ghost* is a mischievous, defiantly unconventional artist at play.

These works do not amount to a coherent program of satire, but they do reflect what Lockwood calls the "increasing self-absorption and inwardness of satire."[27] Churchill as a nonpolitical satirist is primarily a poet, worrying about the poet's role, playing moral custodian, and exercising his imaginative powers. These satires are personal and literary, looking inward rather than outward. If we did not know who wrote them, they would simply be categorized among most of the other verse satires produced in this quarter century; granting their higher quality, they represent nothing unusual in midcentury satiric practice. When Churchill meets Wilkes, however, his personal and literary obsession with independence becomes political. While he never wholly abandons his concern with his own role as a poet, in aid of Wilkes he does turn his attention and his satire outward. Churchill becomes unrepresentative of later eighteenth-century verse satire when he is given a cause.

II. Wilkes, Churchill, and Political Controversy in the 1760s

Midcentury verse satire reflects a huge change in satiric practice. The world of *Poems on Affairs of State* has all but disappeared; verse satire has become an essentially literary performance rather than a practical enterprise. Satire and partisan propaganda are not discrete enterprises for the likes of Dryden, Defoe, Brown, Maynwaring, Tutchin, and Swift. In the world of the 1750s and 1760s, however, verse satirists tend not to use their works to voice serious critique of sociopolitical circumstances—so much so that Churchill's use of poetry in Wilkes's antiministerial campaign makes him exceptional among his contemporaries. Writing as a poet-patriot, Churchill is both versifier and propagandist.

When Churchill met Wilkes is unclear,[28] but by the summer of 1762 they were coauthoring London's most outspoken opposition journal, *The North Briton*. Theirs was a union of twin souls: both were pleasure-seeking, independence-preaching, self-proclaimed social rebels who reveled in the celebrity that their scandalous personal lives brought them. Both were champions of autonomy and free expression. Each man proudly asserted his patriotism, and both perceived in the Earl of Bute a triple threat to England (a Scotsman, a Stuart, and a peacemonger bent on ending the Seven Years' War that had been so effectively managed by Pitt). How much Churchill worried about politics before he allied himself to Wilkes is anyone's guess, but—whether inspired by newfound political activism or just taking up the cudgel for his friend—he enthusiastically joined Wilkes in a vitriolic antiministerial campaign.

The North Briton

The North Briton was launched on 5 June 1762 as a counterattack to Smollett's pro-ministerial *Briton*.[29] Wilkes had originally imagined a three-issue project, specifically meant to undercut the *Briton*, but that plan was abandoned when the journal's "irreverent appeal for 'liberty of the press' caught the mood of the town."[30] The essays were scurrilously antiministerial, praising Pitt and abusing the Scots in general and Bute in particular, though often by way of historical allegory or other forms of indirection. Churchill was evidently responsible for five complete issues,[31] whose anti-Bute implications are crystal clear. In no. 10 (7 August 1762), Churchill's speaker ("Presbyter") foretells future Scottish supremacy in Great Britain, an admonitory satiric tactic to which he would return the next year in *The Prophecy of Famine*. I doubt that Wilkes thought of himself as a satirist, though *The North Briton* has its fair share of ridicule and ironic attack.[32] Its essays are, in any case, politically combative, swaggering, and brashly subversive.

Opposition became treason in the incendiary no. 45, published 23 April 1763. This fearless and forthright (nonsatirical) essay is a response the king's speech to Parliament delivered by George Grenville, who had succeeded Bute as prime minister after his resignation earlier in the month. About Grenville's speech, which had commended the Peace of Paris, Wilkes is unambiguously hostile. It represents "the most abandoned instance of ministerial effrontery ever attempted to be imposed on mankind," and Wilkes wonders how a king "of so many great and amiable qualities . . . can be brought to give the sanction of his sacred name to the most odious measures, and to the most unjustifiable, public declarations, from a throne ever renowned for truth, honour, and unsullied virtue" (*North Briton*, 2:230–231). Wilkes's target is clearly Grenville rather than George III, but the authorities took it otherwise. The king was annoyed, and the administration glad of the chance to silence a persistent gadfly.[33] The story of Wilkes's arrest, the ministry's mistake in issuing a general warrant without naming an individual, and Wilkes's release needs no repeating. His oppositional journalism and his dogged insistence on freedom turned Wilkes into a hero, and Churchill devoted his verse to support of the patriot cause.[34]

Churchill's Political Satire

Churchill's first major political effort in verse is *The Prophecy of Famine* (1763; 2s 6d†), inscribed to Wilkes and including a lengthy tribute to him (ll. 149–178). The poem begins with ironic praise of Scotland, proceeds to ridicule the Scots as "poor, mean, despis'd, insulted" (l. 180), and then introduces two Scottish shepherds, Sawney and Jockey, whose conversation reveals the barrenness of their homeland and the despair of its people. Their exchange is interrupted by the arrival of Famine, whose prophetic counsel serves as Churchill's satiric warning to his English readers: "The pow'r of mischief lost," she encourages the shepherds, "retain the will." Though the Scots have long "borne this mighty weight of ill," happier times are coming: she foretells the Scots' takeover of England, not by force but by patient cunning. The goddess predicts that the English ministry will abandon the principles of 1688 and endanger their country to appease the Scots (ll. 434, 444). Churchill's message is clear: Bute's rise to power is but the first concession, and England needs to be aware of the threat posed by its northern neighbor. The satiric point is not its derisive anti-Scot sentiment, genuine though that is. As in *The North Briton* no. 10, Churchill puts treachery into the mouth of a pro-Scot speaker, looking to capitalize on English prejudices in order to heighten popular resistance to Bute's ascendancy.

Churchill's other political satires appeared after Wilkes's arrest (30 April 1763) and subsequent release (6 May). These works have both positive and negative propagandistic effect: Churchill speaks *for* personal and political freedom, and *against* Wilkes's particular antagonists. *The Author* (December 1763), *The Duellist* (1764; 2s 6d†), and *The Candidate* (1764; 2s 6d) are not exclusively political ventures—they comment on the poet in society, virtue and vice, and so on—but they were occasioned by incidents concerning Wilkes, and they scorch his enemies. In *The Author*, Churchill blasts progovernment hacks like John Shebbeare, whose *History of the Excellence and Decline . . . of the Sumatrans* (1760) had concluded with a panegyric on Bute and George III. He also satirizes John Kidgell and the Earl of Sandwich, both of whom had been involved in the controversy surrounding Wilkes's *Essay on Woman*. *The Duellist* is a response to Samuel Martin's challenge to Churchill's patriot friend; its object is "to support the opinion that the duel was an attempt by the administration to assassinate Wilkes."[35] The poet reproachfully describes the duel as a dark "contrivance," whose engineers wanted to "tear up Freedom by the root, / Destroy a WILKES, and fix a BUTE" (ll. 148, 152–153). In *The Candidate*, he goes after Sandwich again. In each of these satires, Churchill fashions himself an impartial arbiter and a devoted champion of liberty and patriotism.[36] He also earns his reputation as the Bruiser, excoriating those on the wrong side of his political cause.

Nowhere is Churchill more cutthroat than in *An Epistle to William Hogarth* (1763; 2s 6d), in part a vehement defense of his right to produce satire and in part a bludgeoning of a political enemy. He devotes a good deal of time and energy to self-defense (Hogarth does not enter until line 309 of a 654-line poem), but Churchill's vilification of his target is savage. Garrick called the *Epistle* the "most bloody performance that has been publish'd in my time."[37] Churchill's satire is retaliation, a personally abusive contribution to an ongoing war between Wilkes and Hogarth. The battle began after the appearance of plate 1 of *The Times* (7 September 1762), where Hogarth criticized Newcastle and Pitt and supported Bute. Hogarth, says Paulson, "had apparently changed sides." From his perspective, "the Whig crowd has gotten out of hand . . . a positive has turned negative, festivity into fire and destruction, and riot into uprising; liberty from restraint has been pushed over the edge, becoming a threat to law and order."[38] Wilkes was piqued by his old friend's entrance into politics and his support of Bute, and in a letter to Churchill he suggested that they go after him: "Hogarth has begun the attack to-day—I shall attack him in hobbling prose, you will I hope in smooth-pac'd verse."[39] Wilkes accused Hogarth of vanity and spite in *The North Briton* no. 17 (25 September 1762),[40] and the painter responded by representing Wilkes in the pillory with *The North Briton* around his neck in plate 2 of *The Times*. Just after Wilkes's arrest, Hogarth's famous satirical portrait appeared, depicting the notoriously unattractive patriot as squint eyed and deviously leering.

Wilkes did not counter, but Churchill did on his behalf. He reiterates Wilkes's charges against the painter—envy, malice, egotism, and so on. He then intensifies his attack, ruthlessly mocking Hogarth's physical "decay": "The Body shrivell'd up, thy dim eyes sunk / Within their sockets deep" (ll. 419, 423–424). The poem concludes with a piece of cruel counsel:

Hence, Dotard, to thy closet, shut thee in,

By deep repentance wash away thy sin,

From haunts of men to shame and sorrow fly,

And, on the verge of death, learn how to die. (ll. 431–434)

This is Churchill at his most punitive. Hogarth would retort with *The Bruiser*, his memorable sketch of Churchill, a tame response by the standards of the *Epistle*. In a decade hardly known for its harshly castigatory satire, Churchill's invective is exceptional—and he meant it to be. While composing the *Epistle*, he wrote to Wilkes, "My Head is full of Hogarth, and as I like not his Company I believe I shall get him on Paper, not so much to please the Public, not so much for the sake of Justice, as for my own ease. . . . I have laid in a great stock of gall, and I do not intend to spare it on this occasion—he shall be welcome to every drop of it" (*Correspondence*, 48). He is manifestly reveling in his own powers of defamation, but this is also propaganda, championing Wilkesite notions of independence, smearing antagonists, and rousing popular support for the cause.

Visual Satire

The political controversy of the 1760s inspired Churchill to develop a more purposive form of satire than that practiced by his fellow poets, and likewise the political visual satire of the decade has little to do with the trends reflected in verse. Later eighteenth-century political caricature and graphic satire exists in vast quantities; this material has been well studied from various angles, and I will not attempt anything like an exhaustive survey.[41] These prints represent a "popular" form of satire, widely accessible even to those with little education or political knowledge.[42] Vincent Carretta emphasizes the degree to which the increase in caricature and visual satire accompanies a "great rise in political interest and information outside of Parliament's walls."[43] The oppositional and ministerial graphic satire of the early 1760s is part of the battle for public opinion; its creators operate on the assumption that such opinion matters. This is not art for art's sake, whatever the fun of mashing prominent people, and neither is it angling for reformation. Like Churchill in his propagandistic invectives, many of these satirists are trying to besmirch their targets, whether directly or by way of allegorical representation.

The satire is both political and personal. Bute's supporters represent Pitt as a false patriot, as in *Sic Transit Gloria Mundi* (1762). Or, like Hogarth, they depict Wilkes as a self-interested charlatan, misleading the people he claims to represent. Bute's detractors rehearse standard charges: he bribes unscrupulous writers to support the ministry (*The Hungry Mob of Scriblers and Etchers*), he is usurping royal power (*The Highland Seer, or The Political Vision*), and so on.[44] Like Churchill's *The Prophecy of Famine*, the

1763 print *Scotch Paradice a View of the Bute[eye]full Garden of Edenborough* insinuates that a Scottish takeover of England is occurring. In the 1762 *John Bull's House sett in Flames*, a "bare-assed Bute fans the flames engulfing St. James's Palace." This is the print that incited Hogarth to publish *The Times*, where George III plays city-saving fireman and a union of Scottish and English men lend support, working against the incendiary efforts of the opponents of the Peace of Paris.[45] Such satire ranges from the quite crude to the relatively sophisticated. Carretta is excellent on the changing attitudes toward George III as reflected in the visual representations of the 1760s and 1770s, and he also traces differences in the iconographic patterns found in this quarter century and those common a generation earlier.[46] I cannot do justice here to the various trends and methods of graphic satire, but a basic point can be made. Literature scholars do not tend to include visual satire in their accounts, and in this case that omission is especially problematic. This material represents a very different kind of enterprise from what goes on in poetry, fiction, and drama. Like Churchill's atypically purposive satire, caricature and graphic satire tend to be deflationary, defamatory, and propagandistic—a form of invective rarely found in verbal satire during this quarter century, and a long way from the sympathetic slush associated with this period.[47]

Wilkes's Essay on Woman

Although the *Essay on Woman* is an insubstantial and nonpolitical venture, it frequently gets mentioned in discussions of *The North Briton*, and as a satire of sorts it needs at least summary analysis here. After Wilkes's release in the summer of 1763, the ministry got hold of the *Essay* (now known to have been written with Thomas Potter) and tried to prosecute its author for libel of Bishop Warburton. The details of the *Essay's* discovery remain vague, and the subsequent sequence of events is complicated—involving ministerial contrivances to find copies, debates about what charges to bring, witnesses, duels, Wilkes's failure to appear for sentencing, and his eventual flight to Paris.[48] The controversy was serious, the work itself decidedly not. It is a bawdy parody of Pope's *Essay on Man*, with notes allegedly by Warburton, who had edited the *Essay on Man* after Pope's death. Potter hated Warburton, as Arthur H. Cash explains, but for Wilkes "the writing of the *Essay* was a game, a sort of sophomoric literary exercise."[49] The dirty humor is indeed sophomoric, but the parody is clever enough, and imagining Pope's irritation at having his pieties transformed into a Rochesterian celebration of sexual promiscuity is amusing. Pope's "Laugh where we must, be candid where we can" passage becomes, in the Potter/Wilkes version, a warning against premature ejaculation:

> Observe how Nature works, and if it rise
> Too quick and rapid, check it ere it flies;

Spend when we must, but keep it while we can:
Thus Godlike will be deem'd the Ways of Man. (ll. 13–16)

Wilkes travesties Pope, rewriting *The Dying Christian to His Soul* as *The Dying Lover to His Prick*, and throughout the *Essay* he combines uninhibited libertinism with cheerful blasphemy. The piece is plenty irreverent, but it is strictly playful.

I conclude the first two sections with three observations. (1) The death-of-satire cliché is based largely on the marked shift from "satire" to "sentiment," but the feebleness of verse satire in this quarter century probably has little to do with softening attitudes toward human nature. Satirists have less to be livid about, writing in a world whose sociopolitical circumstances seemed less immediately dire, if far from idyllic, and this seems a likelier cause of change than does an upsurge in finer feelings. (2) A sharp division exists, in the 1760s, between "satire" and "propaganda." Whereas earlier verse satirists evidently understood political commentary as part of their province, much of the strongly propagandistic commentary in this period appears in newspapers and pamphlets. Satiric poetry becomes a largely literary exercise. (3) Churchill is (sometimes) an exception to that generalization. His divided career, with its two different modes of satire, helps highlight the distinction I draw in chapter 6 between Pope's and Swift's satiric practices. Churchill's nonpolitical poetry is inward looking and reflective; his politicized satire is outward looking and purposively combative. *The Apology* is a self-defensive poem about poetry; the *Epistle to Hogarth* is a bloody-minded demolition of a political antagonist. The two represent not simply a change in subject matter or tone; they are entirely different enterprises.

III. Satire in the Commercial Theater

Studies of eighteenth-century English satire rarely have much to say about drama, especially after the Licensing Act of 1737. The usual assumption seems to be that after the imposition of censorship, satire in the plays all but disappears. Consequently, little is said even about Foote and Macklin, let alone the likes of Hugh Kelly, Arthur Murphy, and Oliver Goldsmith. Contrariwise, students of the drama tend to focus on the laughing/sentimental dichotomy and are more interested in assessing the degree of humor versus the degree of emotional slop than in analyzing the nature of the satire that can be found in the plays. The supposition on both sides seems to be that "satire" and "drama," especially increasingly sentimentalized drama, are unrelated ventures, and that such satire as may be found in these plays is of little or no significance.

In this section I attempt to demonstrate that satiric drama does not come to an end when Walpole silences the yappy Henry Fielding, though it does differ considerably from that of the 1730s and earlier. Some of the best dramatic satire in the period covered by the preceding chapter was done at the Little Haymarket during a time of intense competition among theaters, no censorship, and tremendous political turbulence. *The Beggar's Opera* and *The Historical Register* would not have been written or staged a generation later. The Licensing Act not only enforced censorship, but (worse) it also put a stop to experimentation by closing fringe theatres and effectively ending competition between the two patent theatres, Drury Lane and Covent Garden.[50] Most of the plays that do get staged are designed at least in part as vehicles for the companies' favorite actors and actresses, and playwrights and theater managers like David Garrick and John Rich are acutely aware of what audiences want and will pay for. The imposition of censorship, the absence of competition, the need for commercially viable vehicles for actors, and the essentially stable (if querulous) state of domestic politics have major implications for satiric practice, changing what is possible and practical for playwrights, but this by no means renders satire extinct. It simply means that our understanding of dramatic satire in the third quarter of the eighteenth century will be badly skewed if our definition privileges harsh judgment and political targets.[51]

What sort of satire do we find on the later eighteenth-century stage? Dramatic satire occurs in two conspicuous and distinct varieties. (1) Social comedy, almost always in mainpiece form. These plays are usually generalized and good humored, either pleasantly moral or satire/sentiment hybrids whose critique is very mild indeed. (2) Lightweight entertainment, generally in afterpiece form, sometimes topical and sometimes not, varyingly condemnatory or punitive but rarely substantial. Here I survey the common trends in these two forms of satire and then go on to deal in separate subsections with three prominent playwrights of the third quarter of the century—Foote, Macklin, and Garrick.

Social Comedy

Satire in later eighteenth-century social comedies tends to be humane, reform oriented, and strongly positive in its authors' assumptions about human nature. Some of these plays are weightier than others, and the emphasis on sympathy or pathos varies from playwright to playwright, but the motifs and patterns are pretty standard. These comedies often include exemplary characters, offer tidy solutions to problems that are never very worrying, and operate on the basis of distributive justice. This is not the comedy of ridicule, abuse, and punishment; its satire is a long way from the attack mode admired by most modern scholars. These works were definitely conceived of as satiric by their authors or by contemporaries, however, and the satire they contain is in line with the exemplary and instructional satiric modes that we have encountered in earlier parts of this survey.

Consider, for example, Benjamin Hoadly's immensely popular *The Suspicious Husband* (1747). By present-day critical standards it is a sentimental play, but contemporaries understood it as an exercise in satiric instruction. "The whole piece," says one reviewer, "is admirably adapted to shew the folly of *suspicion*, which seems to be the author's chief design."[52] *The Suspicious Husband* has a moral without being drearily moralistic, and its combination of benevolence and ridicule is effective. It is pseudo-libertine comedy, full of nocturnal intrigues and attempted-seduction scenes carried out by people who are ultimately shown to be decent and well meaning. What looks like betrayal never is; the happy ending is not in doubt; the men like each other, the women like each other, and the rake performs the most selfless action in the play. Strictland (the title character) unfairly charges his wife with infidelity after he finds a man's hat in her room—that of Ranger, the play's winsome "rake" (played by Garrick). In the end, of course, Strictland is duly repentant for his jealousy and reconciles with his exemplary wife. Ranger with his tomcat ways is no model, as he himself recognizes, but Hoadly has no interest in punishing his likable playboy. His satire is directed at Strictland, in whose character, Foote explains, "the Author has designed to ridicule the Folly and Absurdity of Suspicion."[53] The audience members are invited to apply the lesson to themselves. The medicine is mild, presented with plenty of sugarcoating.

The tidy division between satire and sentiment works badly for many of these plays, whose authors tend to indulge in sentiment even where they also (gently) mock its excesses. Goldsmith's mistaken-identity farce, *She Stoops to Conquer* (1773), centers upon the havoc caused when the mischievous Tony Lumpkin tricks two travelers (Marlow and Hastings) into believing that his stepfather's house is really an inn. Eventually the prank is exposed, Marlow and Hastings win the girls they came to court, and Tony learns that he is of age. The principal satiric target is Mrs. Hardcastle, Tony's overindulgent mother—but in the all-is-forgiven atmosphere of the play's ending, she is brought back within the family circle, unpunished for her bad judgment. *She Stoops to Conquer* ridicules sentimental absurdities, especially in Hastings's courtship of Kate Hardcastle, but Goldsmith heavily emphasizes the importance of good nature. He is, as Hume points out, "glad to have his cake and eat it too."[54] So is Hugh Kelly, whose *False Delicacy* (1768) makes plain the folly of excessive sentimentalism: the problems of the play are brought about by the reticence and restraint caused by the characters' "delicacy." Nevertheless, the tone of *False Delicacy* is patently sentimental, and Kelly clearly appreciates finer feelings. His have-it-both-ways attitude is captured nicely by one of the play's voices of reason: "Well, the devil take this delicacy; I don't know any thing it does besides making people miserable:—And yet some how, foolish as it is, one can't help liking it" (20). Goldsmith's *The Good-Natur'd Man* (1768), like *False Delicacy*, mocks a virtue taken to such extremes that it becomes a liability. Whereas

Kelly ridicules *behavior*, however, Goldsmith's sights are on *character*. Young Honeywood's indiscriminate charity—he gives to all who ask—gets him into trouble, and earns him a rather severe chastisement at the play's end. Too severe, in fact: Honeywood is so decent and likable that the satire does not work terribly well.[55]

The satire in most of these plays focuses on the minor failings of ultimately benevolent characters, and the object is usually some combination of pleasing entertainment and instruction. We are closer to the world of *Tom Jones* than to that of *The Modern Husband*; targets are well meaning and the scolding is light. The central character of Richard Cumberland's phenomenally successful *The West Indian* (1771) is the hot-headed and imprudent but compassionate Belcour, who like Young Honeywood is simply too good for this world. *The West Indian* is a distributive justice satire (à la *Tom Jones*) and a strongly moral play, as well as a funny one. Like Fielding's foundling, Cumberland's scapegrace is impetuous and foolhardy but also a positive model. He is also educable, and capable of self-reproach: "I know I'm tainted with a thousand faults," he reflects, "sick of a thousand follies" (92). If his imperfections are affectionately satirized, they are also distinguished from the very real vice of the maleficent Fulmers and Lady Rusport. Cumberland's attitude toward his protagonist is more than lenient; he *likes* Belcour. And Belcour is not simply another Young Honeywood: he is a nonnative, born of English stock but raised as a West Indian, and yet nevertheless an essentially exemplary character. The Irishman O'Flaherty is just as favorably presented. Cumberland is not only giving us more examples of tenderhearted scapegraces; he is extending the parameters of the distributive-justice satiric form by asking us to feel empathy and admiration for figures who are not "English."

Like *The West Indian*, Richard Brinsley Sheridan's *The School for Scandal* (perf. 1777; pub. 1780) features a benevolent hero (Charles Surface), a guardian pretending not to be (Sir Oliver), a virtuous young lady (Maria), and villains who attempt to use the hero's goodness against him (Joseph Surface, Lady Sneerwell, and Snake). As in *The West Indian*, bad is punished (Joseph's hypocrisy exposed) and merit rewarded (Charles and Maria get together). The other characters, Sir Peter and Lady Teazle, are decent but fallible people whose marriage is in difficulties until he relaxes his rigid treatment of his young wife and she abandons her naïve efforts to emulate the world of fashion. Sheridan's satire on scandalmongering is pointed, and he does not pretend that Joseph and company will change their ugly ways. His high-spirited comedy is more negative than Cumberland's, focusing more on the machinations of the villains than the psychology of the virtuous hero. For the present-day reader, Charles's goodness and reclamation are a bit too pat, the Teazles' reconciliation too easy. The unflinching negativity of the presentation of the depraved characters, however, gives the play an edge that few comedies of the time have. Sheridan's positive exemplars are essentially commonplaces of this quarter century, but the refusal to reform the malefactors gives *The School for Scandal* a genuinely wide range of distributive-justice results.

The satire in these social comedies is *educative* rather than *punitive*. The level of moral gravity varies—*The Suspicious Husband* is not *The West Indian*—but the satire tends to work by combining character critique and a spectrum of positive and sometimes negative examples. That said, there are important distinctions to be made. *The Suspicious Husband*'s psychological and moral depth is slight; *False Delicacy* and *She Stoops to Conquer* are exemplary and reform oriented, chastising folly without depicting serious vice; *The Good-Natur'd Man* presents the possibility of goodness taken advantage of, but *The West Indian* and *The School for Scandal* show real depravity. Joseph is not a scamp but a monster, and Sheridan makes no pretense of his reclaimability. The satiric point is educability. The bad characters are those who are willfully malevolent and beyond redemption, and the good characters represent not paragons but flawed human beings with whom the audience can identify. In dealing with these works, we have to assume audience receptivity to teaching and example that is remote from modern patterns: eighteenth-century playgoers evidently did, at least sometimes, understand that they were being taught a lesson as well as being entertained.

Lightweight Afterpiece Entertainment

The afterpieces, farces, and short comedies are more overtly satirical than the mainpiece social comedies; they do not educate or correct but mock and expose. They tend to offer little in the way of character or plot development, instead featuring humours figures and situational comedy. With the exceptions of Foote's and Macklin's afterpieces (of which more in due course), most of these plays are either fluffy topical entertainments or slightly more substantial social satires.

The satire in these afterpieces is often scant. Garrick's highly popular *Miss in Her Teens* (1747) is a rollicking two-act farce with much zip but no sting whatever. Miss Biddy is in love with Captain Loveit but has been promised to his father (Simon) by her aunt. While the captain is away in the wars, Biddy amuses herself by letting the blustering Flash and the dandyish Fribble court her (the latter played by Garrick). That Captain Loveit and Miss Biddy will attain their happily-ever-after ending is never in doubt; the enjoyment of the play comes entirely from the comical discomfiture of its "vap'ring bully" and "frib'ling fop," chased off by the captain upon his return (1:72). Garrick's three-scene *Lilliput* (1756), like his earlier *Lethe* (perf. 1740; pub. 1745), is a gentle send-up of English manners and mores, this time set in fantasyland. In *The Guardian* (1759), he does a sort of two-act comic preview of *False Delicacy*, exposing the folly of sentimentalism. *A Peep Behind the Curtain* (1767) ridicules the taste of the town for machines, burlettas, and other nontraditional forms. Garrick may have been cross at having to prostitute his talents with such entertainments, and his attitude toward the "town" is often tart, but his satiric afterpieces are unquestionably meant to be crowd-pleasers.

Some of the liveliest satiric afterpieces of the midcentury are travesties of sentimentalism. The most popular comic afterpiece of the sixties was George Colman the elder's *Polly Honeycombe* (1760), which mocks the vogue for sentiment in novels and plays. An antecedent to Sheridan's Lydia Languish, Polly translates the commonplace events of her love life into the stuff of novelistic melodrama. Meeting the accountant to whom her parents intend to marry her, she affects distress ("I am now . . . just in the situation of poor Clarissa" [13]). Rejecting the accountant as an insufficiently romantic suitor, she congratulates herself: "This would make an excellent chapter in a new Novel.—But here comes Papa—In a violent passion, no doubt.—No matter—It will only furnish materials for the next chapter" (18). *Polly Honeycombe* is light and bright, chirpily ridiculing Polly, her parents, the suitor, and Scribble (her true inamorato). This is a comic debunking of a popular craze, without judgment or bite. Colman scored another hit in *The Deuce is in Him* (1763), a two-act farce satirizing platonic love. The self-proclaimed sentimentalist Colonel Tamper decides to test the devotion of his dearest by pretending to have lost a leg and an eye in battle; she discovers his plot and shames him, and he is duly mortified. Like *Polly Honeycombe*, the show is full of joie de vivre and without stringent critique. In these afterpieces—as in Foote's *The Devil Upon Two Sticks* (perf. 1768; pub. 1778) and William Whitehead's *A Trip to Scotland* (1770)—the audience can laugh at the people whose silliness is shown up. Insofar as this is "satire," it is designed to make viewers and readers feel comfortably superior to characters they need not dislike.

The afterpieces of Arthur Murphy include more topical satire, and, while his métier is farce, he seems to want to use his afterpieces as vehicles for varyingly sharp social commentary. Most of these works target standard types or social follies. *The Upholsterer, or, What News?* (1758) mocks the foibles of the ridiculous but amiable Quidnunc, who ignores his domestic life in his zealous pursuit of political news, and those of the humours characters who surround him (e.g., Pamphlet, Razor, Termagant). *The Old Maid* (1761) harshly ridicules its eponymous target, who dismisses her betrothed when she fancies herself desired by a younger man. *The Citizen* (also 1761) is an equally abrasive attack on the merchant class, but in both plays the severity of the satire is mitigated by the roistering tone. A more intense satire is *What we must All come to* (1764),[56] which disparages the pretensions of middle-class social climbers as well as the haut monde. As part of his criticism of the high life, he exposes the emptiness of mercenary marriage: the social-climbing Druggets marry off one daughter to the wealthy Sir Charles Rackett, and only their discovery of how unhappy the Racketts are changes their plan to unite their other daughter to an aristocrat. Granting the sometimes farcical tone of the play, its social commentary has some bite. Pride, vanity, and the endless strife among people of fashion is, the servant Dimity wryly observes, "the way of the world now" (2). Murphy's afterpieces present a type of social critique far removed from Garrick's toothless entertainments and Colman's sunny presentation of basically likable people.

The afterpiece form does not allow for much character development, and neither Murphy nor his contemporaries use these works for moral instruction or reformation—making afterpiece satire markedly different from that found in full-length social comedy. As in social comedies, we find among the afterpieces a considerable spectrum of possibilities. *Lilliput* is not *Polly Honeycombe*, and neither has much to do with *What we must All come to*. That said, afterpiece writers mostly invite easy laughter at an obvious, nonthreatening target, or they are content to provide frivolous entertainment that requires no serious judgment from the audience. The principal midcentury writers of afterpieces are Foote and Macklin, who differ from their contemporaries and from each other.

Samuel Foote

The foremost dramatic satirist of this quarter century is Samuel Foote, who touted himself as the "English Aristophanes" and whose contemporaries regarded him—reverentially or resentfully—as the most fearsome "satyrist" of his time. His reputation is for boldness and controversy. He mimicked recognizable individuals and feuded with literary celebrities; he lost his leg in a horse-riding accident and then wrote parts for himself to accommodate the injury (e.g., Sir Luke Limp); his onstage antics inspired Dr. Johnson to threaten that impersonation of him would meet reprisal; and in the last years of his life he was wrongly tried for sodomy.[57] Some satire scholars allude to the "English Aristophanes" in their accounts, but the plays themselves get scant attention. Foote is often regarded as an anomaly, a punitive satirist in a period awash with sentiment and sympathy. The atypicality is true enough, but the conception of Foote as scurrilous Aristophanic scourge has little to do with most of his output.

Foote is always an entertainer, whatever else he does. One of his earliest ventures, *Taste* (1751), is a brisk-moving satire on the antiquarian craze, the egotistic aristocratic dilettanti, and the inanity of the fashionable world's pursuit of "taste." The plot is slight. Puff the auctioneer and Carmine the painter are gulling the town, peddling rubbish as antiques to a credulous crowd. Foote ridicules Lord Dupe and Novice (among others), who fancy themselves connoisseurs without caring about art or knowing how to appreciate it, but *Taste* is not a moralizing play. Foote knows that nothing is going to change the world he describes, and he does not invite much concern about that fact. As in *The Patron* (1764), his exposé is the stuff of lightweight entertainment, not preachment.

Foote never goes in for sermonizing, but elsewhere he eschews generalized commentary for more pointed ridicule. *The Minor* (1760) is his most famous play, a biting attack on Methodists and on George Whitefield in particular. The plot functions mostly as a vehicle for Foote's mimicry and satire. Sir William Wealthy conspires to cheat his wayward son George of his fortune in order (he claims) to teach him prudence; Sir William's brother Richard has disowned his daughter Lucy following her refusal to marry the man he chose for her. In his scheme against George, Sir William enlists the aid of a fast-talking mimic, Samuel Shift—a role meant both as a jibe at Tate Wilkinson (an actor gifted at impersonation) and as a spectacular vehicle for Foote, who as Shift imitates a lawyer, a linkboy, an auctioneer, a usurer, and finally Squintum (the Whitefield figure) in the course of a short play. The bathetic romantic denouement smacks of sentimentalism, but the characters are undeveloped and their story of little consequence. The point of *The Minor* is its satire, especially its ridicule of the bawd Mother Cole, a Methodist convert who sees no conflict between her new-found zeal and her dissolute way of life. The harlot (also played by Foote) reveals the superficiality of the "saving grace" offered by Squintum's doctrine, and in the epilogue Foote contemptuously mocks Whitefield as a fraud and a bigot. But does the play represent an Aristophanic scourge at the height of his powers?

The Methodists no doubt felt "scourged," but the majority of Foote's audience would have seen *The Minor*'s satire as essentially noncontroversial. As Kinservik has argued, the play illustrates the discrepancy between Foote's self-presentation and the actual content of his satire. In the introductory dialogue with Canker and Smart, Foote has Canker warn him against deriding the itinerant preachers of this religion ("Have a care. Dangerous ground. Ludere cum sacris, you know"), in response to which he flaunts his satiric intrepidity: "I must beg leave to assert, that ridicule is the only antidote against this pernicious poison" (8, 9). Foote claims a devil-may-care attitude, but the satire of the play seems not risky enough to warrant such declarations: "Ridiculing Methodists in 1760 was neither dangerous nor original. By suggesting it was, Foote is not appearing as himself; instead, he is trying to make himself appear a certain way."[58] This is not to say that Foote's satire went uncontested. *The Minor* was hotly condemned in a number of pamphlets, but, as L. W. Conolly concludes, Foote's anti-Methodist satire "reflected the prevailing mood of the government in 1760, and so received the backing of the Lord Chamberlain."[59] Foote did have to make concessions to the opposition, including a substantial revision of the epilogue, but the point of the censorship was evidently to diminish the personal attack on Whitefield rather than to weaken the anti-Methodism. What *The Minor* gave contemporary theatergoers was an impressive display of Foote's talents as a mimic and a spirited assault on a widely disliked group.[60]

Whatever his self-projected image as fearless Aristophanic satirist, Foote devotes a lot of energy to ridiculing standard butts—that is, safe targets. *The Englishman in Paris* (1753) mocks both English Francophilia and the churlish Buck's unreflective hostility to all things French; the play ends with his being told he cannot wed the virtuous Lucinda until he abandons his errant ways. In a sequel, *The Englishman return'd from Paris* (1756), Buck returns home beastlier than ever, still loudmouthed and now a confirmed Francophile who disdains English customs, pals around with his imported cohort of French fops, and proposes to keep Lucinda as a mistress rather than marry her. She convinces him that she has poisoned his tea; in return for the "antidote," he agrees to relinquish part of his deceased father's fortune to her, leaving her rid of a self-loving swine. The play advocates English patriotism, and Foote dispenses poetic justice—but the "Englishman" works are very much in line with popular themes and motifs of the midcentury. In *The Lyar* (perf. 1762; pub. 1764), Foote takes passing shots at Methodists, Grub Street hacks, theatrical players, and Francophiles. The piece is featherlight, as is *The Mayor of Garratt* (perf. 1763; pub. 1769), which ridicules Methodists again, as well as country politics, soldiers, the trials of marriage, and the fickleness and credulity of the mob. Based on an actual mock election held annually in Garratt, the play is a farce about a farce, buoyantly insubstantial. None of these afterpieces includes a challenge to the status quo, and neither do they do much sharp-tongued scourging.

The liveliest satiric venture in Foote's varied output is *The Handsome Housemaid, or, Piety in Pattens* (perf. 1773; not pub. until 1973),[61] a high-energy playlet debunking sentimentalism. Foote parodies Isaac Bickerstaff's *The Maid of the Mill* (1765), a dramatic version of Richardson's *Pamela*. Channeling the irreverence of *Shamela*, he narrates the trial of Polly Pattens's "vartue." Polly is the "handsome housemaid" pressed by Squire Turniptop to accompany him to London. When Thomas the butler warns her that Turniptop means to assail her virtue, she rejects the squire's offer, at which point he—convinced of her piety—pledges his love and vows to marry her. Polly rejoices ("& shall Vartue be rewarded at last? it shall"), but remembers that Thomas is responsible for this fortunate turn and resolves to wed him instead. Ever the gallant, he refuses: "you desarve the Squire for presarving your Vartue, & he desarves you by knowing how to reward it" (34–35). Turniptop too proves himself noble, encouraging the union of Polly and Thomas and promising to settle ten pounds a year on them. Not to be outdone in delicacy, Polly forswears them both: "I cannot purfur one without afflicting the other. Justice & Gratitude therefore demand as I must not have both, to take—neither" (35). By August 1773 *Piety in Pattens* was being put on by living players,[62] but in its original form it was part of *The Primitive Puppet-Shew*, done with hand puppets to underscore the unreality of the sentimentalism. Foote's theme is familiar enough, but his wit and concision give especial energy to this fizzy demolition.

Foote's eighteenth-century and modern reputation as the English Aristophanes has to do not with his sociocultural satire but with his onstage mimicry of recognizable people. Foote's game was not to feature these figures as characters in the plays but to create roles for himself that he could perform *as* the person he meant to mimic. This is improvisation for the pleasure of the audience and not at all evident from the text itself; the satiric thrust is exclusively part of the production. In *The Author* (1757), a long-absent father returns to London and discovers that his son (an impecunious writer), is a man of virtue; he reveals his paternity and his fortune, making the son's marriage possible. In performance, the satiric bite came from Foote's acting the part of Cadwallader, mimicking the real-life John Apreece, a well-known eccentric. The play was suppressed in 1758, probably because of pressure from Apreece, though he had reportedly encouraged Foote and even loaned him a conspicuous suit of his own clothes. Conolly ventures a tentative explanation: Apreece "had no objections . . . until he realized that he had become a public laughingstock," widely associated with the clown Cadwallader.[63] In *The Orators* (1762), Foote mocks Thomas Sheridan's London oratory, the Dublin publisher George Faulkner, the Cock Lane Ghost affair, the amateur debating club known as the Robin-Hood Society, Methodists, and a number of other well-known episodes and stock butts. Faulkner took offense and sued Foote for libel. What gave edge to this ephemeral, topical, plotless revue was again the onstage mimicry.[64] The victims of Foote's impersonations, unnamed in the plays, would have been perfectly obvious to some of the audience members, who no doubt promptly enlightened their friends. This kind of mimicry represents a type of personal satire very different from the standard-pattern social comedy or toothless divertissements done by many of his contemporaries.

Foote's satires also tend to reflect a much less sunny view of human nature than is common in this quarter century. Actively positive characters are rare and not very convincing when present; George Wealthy and Lucy in *The Minor* are cardboard conveniences. Foote is never a jolly optimist, but his vision darkens markedly late in his career. *The Nabob* (perf. 1772; pub. 1778) is a severe satiric portrait of the nabob (Sir Matthew Mite) "in his various roles as vulgar materialist, *nouveau riche* antiquarian and unprincipled destroyer of families."[65] At the start of the play, Sir Matthew has contrived to get the decent Sir John Oldham into his debt for roughly £10,000 and has demanded that Oldham either give him Sophy Oldham's hand in marriage or lose his estate. In the end, Sir John's brother pays off the debt and saves the day, a satisfactory enough resolution for the Oldhams, but the nefarious Sir Matthew is not punished, and his preying on defenseless families will clearly continue. Foote does not pretend that the social evil he represents—an increasingly visible group of nabobs in late eighteenth-century England—is anything but real. In this play, as in *The Maid of Bath* (perf. 1771; pub. 1775?) and *The Bankrupt* (perf. 1773; pub. 1776), the imposition of a too-easy resolution only serves "to reveal the powerlessness of Foote's 'good' characters,"[66] and the villains are incapable of shame.

Foote's output is not well explained as the audacious attacks of "the English Aristophanes." He is sometimes lightweight, and the degree to which the audience cares about the satiric punishment of, say, Lord Dupe in *Taste* or Buck in *The Englishman return'd from Paris* is minimal. His more pointedly antagonistic satires are hardly the work of a defiantly transgressive scourge: he knocks Methodists, Francophiles, social upstarts, and other common targets. Foote has great range. *Taste* is an entertaining spoof, *Piety in Pattens* is stingingly funny, the zing in *The Author* derives largely from recognizable personation, *The Orators* is a scattershot satirical revue without plot, and the harsh social satire of *The Nabob* makes that play much darker than Foote's earlier ventures. What is consistent in his oeuvre is the absence of a desire to change things. When what Foote is poking fun at are social foibles or personal eccentricities, he seems neither to expect amendment nor to be seriously upset by its improbability. In his later plays, he satirizes not folly but vice, and he is manifestly more troubled by his own sense that vice is the way of the world. Like Gay, the late Foote is philosophically sour even when he manages to be tonally light. He is an entertainer, a commercial playwright eager and able to please the crowd, but his view of human nature makes his satire much less positive than that of most of his contemporaries.

Charles Macklin

Macklin's interests and impulses are very different from Foote's, but, like Foote, he is a commercial comic playwright with little faith in the innate goodness of humankind. Macklin is prepared to punish and to provoke thought; his comedies are hard-nosed and unsentimental.

Macklin's early plays are caustically satiric afterpieces. The first of these, *A Will and No Will: or, A Bone for the Lawyers* (perf. 1746; not pub. until the twentieth century), is a condensed version of Regnard's five-act *Le Legataire universel* (1708); Macklin tightens the plot and adds significant satiric edge in his revision.[67] Sir Isaac Skinflint is an elderly valetudinarian who wants to disinherit his nephew Bellair and to take Bellair's fiancée, Harriet Lovewealth, for himself. Sir Isaac's servant, Shark, contrives to foil his scheme, motivated by sheer self-interest. Impersonating a dying Sir Isaac, Shark has the lawyer draw up a will in which Bellair and Harriet can marry and he (Shark) is rewarded with a princely cut of the fortune. Sir Isaac discovers the scam and sets up a squawk but the will is legally binding, and he is left unreconciled to the others. Skinflint is sufficiently slimy that we are not much bothered by his distress, but the conniving Bellair and his gold-digging betrothed are not exactly the sympathetic lovers of romance comedy, and Shark is altogether lacking in charm. *A Will and No Will* is a racy farce with a lot of humor, but the satire is cutting and the world it reflects mostly bad. *The Fortune Hunters* (1748) is sharper yet—a "biter bit" play in which two knavish fortune-seekers make what they believe to be lucrative matches only to discover that their wives are whores; the women are just as deceived, having taken the beaux for men of status.[68] The play ends with all four under lock and key. Unlike most of his playwright contemporaries, Macklin is not amused by what he describes. His satire is not affectionate critique of a fallible exemplar; his world is populated by cheats and rogues and short of shining models.

Macklin's most successful afterpiece was *Love à la Mode* (perf. 1759; pub. 1779), a less wholly negative play. Charlotte Goodchild's four suitors are a proud and censorious Scotsman (Sir Archy Macsarcasm), a narcissistic Jew (Beau Mordecai), an improvident English squire (Squire Groom), and a bashful Irish soldier (Sir Callaghan O'Brallaghan).[69] The first three are interested only in Charlotte's money, and when she and her father feign bankruptcy, they all find reasons to decamp, disinclined to wed a penniless girl. Callaghan reaffirms his love and is handsomely rewarded with Charlotte and her fortune. The play ends with the impenitent scoundrels disappointed, aware that they have been duped, and the noble Sir Callaghan exultant: *Love à la Mode* is distributive justice satire of a highly entertaining sort, tailor made for the midcentury London crowd. As in Foote's *The Minor*, however, Macklin's point is not plot (which verges on sentimentalism) but satiric deflation of the mercenary suitors.[70]

Macklin's two full-length comedies represent very different types of serious satire. *The School for Husbands* (perf. 1761; not pub. in the eighteenth century) is an errant-husband reform play featuring Lord Belville, a philanderer governed by his passions rather than by his conscience: "wives and moralists may preach up what they will," he coolly remarks, "but variety is nature's prime bliss" (137). Pretending to be an upstanding Staffordshire gentleman named Jackson, he attempts to seduce Harriet, who, smelling a rat, pretends to be Miss Margery Packington, "a raw, ignorant, unexperienced, country thing" (144). Harriet, Lady Belville, and others plot not only to expose Lord Belville but to make him suffer. Belville is bound, gagged, roughed up, told that he is being hauled off to America to fight with Cherokees, and made to think that his wife has cuckolded him. In the final act, Belville begs for mercy and—mirabile dictu—even blesses his tormenters (193), thus earning forgiveness.

Macklin's plot has all the sentimental devices, but *The School for Husbands* is not a sentimental play. Kinservik argues that it represents a transition in Macklin's career, a move from punitive to disciplinary satire. Whereas earlier pieces—like *A Will and No Will*—featured undeveloped characters and did not try to elicit sympathy, *The School for Husbands* includes more psychological realism and character development.[71] I disagree. Comparing a full-length play to a two-act afterpiece in terms of character depth is a tricky matter, but I have a hard time imagining Belville eliciting much sympathy from audience members, even on his knees. As Kinservik points out, Belville's self-awareness of wrongdoing makes him all the more disturbing, and the extent of punishment he has to suffer before his volte face is in itself telling. The protagonists of rake-reform plays often wax remorseful when their ladies say "for shame"—but Belville's contrition comes only after a night of abuse. Macklin's stated desire "to mend a vicious age" notwithstanding, the conversion of Belville does not convince (127). A good-hearted scapegrace brought back in line by the love of a virtuous woman or by his own conscience is one thing; an unscrupulous libertine terrorized into promising reformation is quite another. Macklin does not ask us to sympathize with this rogue; he invites us to enjoy his richly deserved punishment.

Macklin's most trenchant satire is *The Man of the World* (perf. 1781; pub. 1785), an acid attack on political venality. The gist of the action is this: Sir Hector Mackcrafty, a nasty-tempered, power-seeking Scot, has disowned one son because of liberal tendencies and wants to marry the other one to Lady Rodolpha, in the hopes that such a union will raise his own social and political status. An earlier version of Macklin's play (now lost) was performed in Dublin as *The True-born Scotchman* in 1764. His attempt to stage it in London met with official resistance; the play was refused a license in 1770 and again in 1779. The objections are not surprising. As Findlay explains, in the original Macklin's satiric thrust was directed at "the numerous Scottish politicians and place-seekers who thronged to London in the 1760s under the patronage of the Scottish Earl of Bute. . . . The play is fraught with satiric slaps at Parliament, the Ministry, and the Court Party."[72] Macklin made substantial revisions after both denials, and the play as we know it premiered in 1781. Sir Hector became Sir Pertinax Macsycophant, "no longer merely a topical sketch of a self-seeking follower of Bute, but a perennial portrait of a greedy and hypocritical politician." Macklin also toned down the topical satire on the Scotch, the court party, and political corruption.[73]

Whatever Macklin's modifications, the satire is unrelentingly harsh and the tone icily cynical. The central conflict is between the perfidious Sir Pertinax and Egerton, his incorruptible son. A violently anti-English bigot, Sir Pertinax upbraids his Briton-at-heart son for being "nai true Scot" (218).[74] He presses Egerton to speak publicly for a measure Sir Pertinax supports, but Egerton's refusal is principled and accusatory: "you . . . would make me a devoted slave to selfish leaders, who have no friendship but in faction—no merit but in corruption—no interest in any measure, but their own—and to such men I cannot submit." His appeal to conscience shocks his father, who schools him in the ways of the political world: "Conscience, quotha? I hai been in Parliament these three and thratty years, and never heard the tarm made use of before—sir, it is an unparliamentary word, and ye wull be laughed at for it" (250). Egerton stands his ground, and in the end he wins his true love, as does Lady Rodolpha (whose beau turns out to be Sir Pertinax's other son). The play is not entirely without positives, but the obtrusive presence of the unregenerate Sir Pertinax (played by Macklin) is mood darkening. The stridency of Macklin's political satire is exceptional in this quarter century, and he makes perfectly clear the fact that the villain is beyond redemption, the corruption he represents irremediable. *The Man of the World* is a strikingly unsentimental and unfunny play.

The oddity in Macklin's dramatic career is *The Spoild Child*, an incomplete play probably drafted in the very late 1770s or early 1780s and printed for the first time by Kinservik.[75] The manuscript is not a coherent scene-by-scene draft but a set of working notes and plans, which sketch a fairly straightforward plot. The protagonist is the spoiled child of the title; his father is a soldier in the East Indies, his mother overindulgent and largely to blame for the child's extravagant ways. The father's servant in India returns to England, falsely claiming that the father has died in battle and that the son now owns the estate. The son, a gaming addict and a spendthrift, promptly loses the family fortune at the hands of two professional sharpers (Vermin and Lord Fleecum), at which point he talks his mother into selling her jointure. The father miraculously appears in the end, the child repents, the villains are exposed, and all is set right.

What is interesting about the manuscript, as Kinservik points out, is that it includes detailed remarks about the responses Macklin wanted his characters to elicit from the audience. These notes give us rare insight into the process of creation, showing us a playwright thinking about how to create effect. Macklin's directives for the characterization of the spoiled child are particularly illustrative:

> He must be drawn with Parts, good Sense, and good Nature, otherwise he
>   will not excite Pity in his adversity which he must do.
> He must encourage the Arts, merit wherever he finds it.—No; I think this
>   gravity is too amiable.—He must be rather witty, thoughtless, avaricious
>   except where his vanity is concernd. (225–226)

The spoiled child is undoubtedly a satiric target—his imprudence causes the problems in the play—but Macklin clearly wants the audience to identify with him, at least up to a point. Macklin did not want his protagonist to be "too amiable," but neither should he be irredeemable. Vermin, we are told, "must be a man of Fortune, a Lord who was ruined as an honest man & a gentleman" (221). The audience was not to dismiss either the child or even Vermin as a reprobate. *The Spoild Child* manuscript is a salutary reminder that playwrights do think in terms of audience reaction; Macklin is clearly trying to ensure that his satiric point comes across as he means it to.

Insistence on sympathetic response notwithstanding, *The Spoild Child* has much of Macklin's usual darkness. The eponymous figure's uncle is the satiric spokesman, who is aware of his own ineffectuality as a satirist: Macklin stipulates that he is to be "peevish,—ironical—with now and then a Strong vein of gravity & Severity.—his

Mirth and laughing Satir must be the Consequence of an assured Resignation" (226). The uncle is convinced that the child is incorrigible—he "does not want for good nature," but he has been ruined by his upbringing and by the depravity of the age (240). What reactions a final version of the play would have elicited is impossible to guess, but Macklin seems prepared both to grant potential human goodness and to take a less than sunny view of human behavior. Nowhere does Macklin approach the softness of the popular reform-oriented social comedies; his view of society is decidedly jaundiced, his exposure of human failings never particularly affectionate or amused.

David Garrick

To conclude a section on dramatic satire with Garrick may seem strange. Insofar as scholars think of mid- to late-eighteenth century satiric drama, they mostly have in mind Foote and Macklin and sometimes Goldsmith and Sheridan. But Garrick acted satiric roles, staged satiric plays as comanager of Drury Lane (1747–1776), and wrote quite a lot of satire in his own right, in the form of plays, prologues, epilogues, and poems. Garrick scholars venerate their subject, hailing him as the great eighteenth-century champion of Shakespeare, the high-minded enemy of pantomime and other "low" forms, and a smooth, witty, charming man about town. About his wide range of satire, neither his own students nor satire critics have had much to say.

Garrick's plays are fairly standard-pattern stuff: lightweight, mildly satiric entertainment. His afterpieces, as we have seen, vary in tone from flip (*Miss in Her Teens*) to tart (*A Peep Behind the Curtain*). Whatever his disdain for the taste of the town, and whatever the grand claims his twentieth-century admirers make for his single-handed reformation of the stage, he does pander to the crowd. Richard W. Bevis explains Garrick's relationship to his audience as an odd mixture of "flattering accommodation and barely concealed hostility,"[76] and that seems about right. When he mocks the morals and manners of "the town" in *A Peep*, he does so with a faint but distinct sourness. Nowhere is the conflict between high-minded artist and hard-headed businessman clearer than in *Harlequin's Invasion* (perf. 1759; not pub. until the twentieth century). Garrick's satire on pantomime takes the form of a pantomime; the champion of high culture simultaneously mocks and capitalizes on the popularity of theatrical *illegitimi*. Garrick would no doubt have liked loftily to ignore pantomime, but Covent Garden Theatre had made huge sums with the genre. His rival manager, John Rich, was the principal contriver (and until 1752 had been the principal performer) of pantomime, and even Garrick admitted that in his own line Rich was a genius. Rich, he granted, could "with matchless art and whim" give "the pow'r of speech to ev'ry limb," but Drury Lane's Harlequin "Requires a tongue" if he is to be "understood."[77] Nonsensical pantomime might be, but Garrick's theater was forced to fight fire with fire and did so (much to his frustration) with only limited success. Garrick hardly celebrates the form. His Harlequin is a French interloper who needs to be expelled from England,[78] and a stage direction in the final scene reflects the playwright's wishful thinking: "*Shakespear rises: Harlequin sinks*" (1:224). Whistling in the dark, yes, but Garrick is no fool. He is commercially minded, notorious among his contemporaries for his desire for wealth and fame, and prepared to supply what audiences demanded.

Garrick's revision of Wycherley's *The Country-Wife* is some indication of his desire to suit the crowd—and of the radical shift in preferences from hard to humane comic satire. In the "Advertisement" to *The Country Girl* (1766), Garrick explains that he wished "to preserve as much of the original as could be presented to an audience of these times without offence," but stresses the "absolute necessity for reforming" such plays (7:199). Cleaning up Wycherley required considerable revision: Pinchwife becomes Moody, not yet married to Peggy Thrift (Margery); the Fidgets and Squeamishes disappear; instead of Horner we have Belville, who wants not to bed and abandon the country girl but to marry her and live happily ever after, even if that means losing her fortune. Everything is for the best and all is forgiven. The result, in Hume's phrasing, is a "gutted corpse."[79] Wycherley's play is a cynical critique of London life; Garrick's emasculated version is emphatically humane, offering a traditional romance plot in which youth and love triumph.[80] Isaac Bickerstaff's revision of *The Plain Dealer* (staged at Drury Lane in 1765) reflects the same moralizing impulse. The basic plot remains unchanged, but, the author tells us, "several things . . . called very much for correction" (vi). Bickerstaff's modification of the discovery scene—in which Vernish realizes that Fidelia is a woman—is a nice example of what would not do. In Wycherley's play, Vernish "Pulls off her Peruke, and feels her breasts,"[81] but Bickerstaff's Fidelia reveals herself as a woman and remains untouched (78). This is Carolean comedy turned to mush.

Garrick and Colman's *The Clandestine Marriage* (1766), which invokes Hogarth's *Marriage A-la-mode* in its prologue, is very much in line with the full-length social comedies described at the start of this section. The eponymous union is that between Fanny Sterling and the clerk Lovewell; they have been married for four months and she is pregnant, and neither of them has wanted to inform Fanny's mercenary father of the match. The plot thickens when two visitors—Lord Ogleby and Sir John Melvil, the latter come to marry Fanny's older sister, Miss Sterling—both fall head over heels for Fanny. They separately announce their desires to her and to her father, and Sir John even offers to knock £30,000 off the demanded dowry if he can swap Miss Sterling for Fanny (1:295). Marriage will out, however: Lovewell is discovered in Fanny's room in the middle of the night, and Mr. Sterling is violently angry, but finer feelings naturally supervene, and all ends happily. *The Clandestine Marriage* combines trenchant social satire against the greedy Mr. Sterling with gentle mockery of sensibility, but Garrick and Colman cheerfully celebrate benevolence and right-doing.

Garrick as manager of Drury Lane and commercial playwright is a public entertainer, but he is also on occasion a private entertainer capable of a very different type of satire. In 1981, Harry William Pedicord printed for the first time Garrick's bawdy Shakespearean parody, *Ragandjaw*, done for a small group of friends in 1746.[82] This skit is a travesty of IV.iii of *Julius Caesar*, in which Brutus quarrels with Cassius and is then visited by the ghost of Caesar. In *Ragandjaw*, the Roman generals become English officers, Brutarse (played by Garrick's host, John Hoadly) and Cassiarse (played by Garrick), and instead of Caesar's ghost the paranormal visitor is the Devil's Cook (played by Hogarth, another of Hoadly's guests). This is "tent travesty," Pedicord explains, and "serves as a heady sample of the taste of these gentlemen and their friends in private" (198).

That taste is categorically obscene. The 186-line skit is playfully ribald, closer in tone to Carolean lampoonery than to the decorous innocence promised in *The Country Girl*'s advertisement. Cassiarse objects to Brutarse's turning out of camp a woman he fancied for himself; Brutarse sneers at him for risking his health on such a strumpet ("I smell the brimstone and see the scabs" [200]). After an animated exchange of excremental insults, Cassiarse exits, and Brutarse is accosted by the Devil's Cook:

> I am Old Nick's cook—and hither am I come
> To slick some steaks from off thy brawny bum!
> Make sausage of thy guts, and candles of thy fat,
> And cut thy cock off to regale his cat. (202)

When the cook departs, Brutarse realizes that he has shat himself, and the parody ends with Garrick (as Brutarse) delivering up a piece of nonwisdom: "Trust not your breeches too far—Our moral teaches, / That turds were made for pots and not for breeches" (203). As satire, *Ragandjaw* provides little more than sophomoric humor and coarse entertainment, but it does illustrate the fact that the sainted Garrick could spin anything from high-toned humane comedy to scatological travesty.

Garrick is better known as a playwright and a performer than as a poet, but his miscellaneous verse is at least quasi-satirical. These works represent an affable socialite's slightly acid acknowledgment of the way of the world. The epilogue to *The Lying Valet* (1741) is spoken by the title character: "That I'm a lying rogue, you all agree; / And yet look round the world and you will see / How many more my betters lye as fast as me."[83] Garrick's disapproval of the manners and taste of the town is a recurrent theme. In his epilogue to James Ralph's *The Astrologer* (1744), he grumbles that "nought but *Alamode de France* goes down," and in his 1763 "Address to the Town" he sarcastically hits at the fickleness of the crowd (1:89, 192–193). The 1785 edition of

Garrick's *Poetical Works* includes some sixty pages of epitaphs and epigrams, the satire in which consists of cheerily insubstantial put-downs, such as the "*Epigram*, written soon after *Dr. Hill's* Farce, called *The Rout*, was acted" and "A *Recipe* for a *Modern Critic.*" The latter offers a predictable ironic formula for success: the best criticism is composed "Of sarcasms two hundred from any old book;/Of candour a grain, and of scandal a ton" and so on (2:510). In these verses, Garrick is captious without being harsh, clearly enjoying hitting people with a peashooter. The prologues and epilogues have buzz with no sting; the epigrams and miscellaneous poems have bite without teeth.

Garrick can issue mild rebuke, but he can also play nasty. Like Foote, he had a flair for onstage mimicry—so much that Theophilus Cibber charged him with starting the vogue on which Foote capitalized.[84] In Garrick's 1741 performance of Bayes in *The Rehearsal*, Kinservik explains, "He changed the nature of the satire . . . from a burlesque of authors to an attack on acting styles," unkindly aping "the exaggerated performances of Denis Delane, Sacheveral Hale, and Lacy Ryan."[85] Garrick's biographers insist that he "soon abandoned the personal mimickry in order clearly to attack the concept" of ostentatious acting,[86] but disapproving contemporaries do not let him off quite so easily. In *A Letter to David Garrick, Esq.* (1772), David Williams rebukes Garrick, repeating a myth much repeated in the late eighteenth century—namely, that Garrick's mean-spirited impersonations contributed to the alcoholism and death of Delane (11). William Kenrick, admittedly a personal antagonist of Garrick's, similarly upbraids Roscius for his cruel and unjustified onstage lampoons.[87] In his adulatory *Memoirs* of Garrick, Thomas Davies distinguishes between his subject's satiric practices and those of Foote: "to insure a laugh," the English Aristophanes "would deal in scandal, obscenity, and profaneness," but Garrick "always paid a proper respect to himself and his company."[88] This encomium is typical of the rapture with which Garrick scholars regard him, but the contemporary protests against Roscius's hurtful impersonations suggest that his personal ridicule was not always taken in good fun.

Much of the topical satire of this quarter century, as I have suggested, has to do with literary and theatrical squabbles like the ones between Garrick and some of his contemporaries.[89] Garrick is a common target and generally a cheerful combatant in these paper wars, but on one occasion he took serious offence. Kenrick had disagreed with Garrick about the distribution of proceeds from the final night of *Falstaff's Wedding* in 1771, and he had been frustrated by delays in staging his plays. In 1772, looking for vengeance, he published *Love in the Suds*, in which the desolate Roscius laments the absence of Nyky (Bickerstaff, who had fled the country to escape a sodomy charge): "why should NYKY thus be blam'd?/Of manly love ah! why are men, asham'd?" (6). Kenrick's explicit satiric point is that Garrick has been homosexually involved with the disgraced Bickerstaff. Garrick was outraged. Afraid of prosecution for libel, Kenrick published an apology of sorts, though his *Letter to David Garrick* (1772) is full of barbs. He asks why Roscius can dish out abuse but cannot take it and mocks the "parasitical servility" with which Bickerstaff "clung round the heels" of Garrick (7). Literary history remembers Kenrick as the loser of this battle, and rightly so: his irritation and jealousy provoked him to write a libelous personal lampoon, and the result was public embarrassment. Garrick and his contemporaries wrote abusive personal satire and were themselves satirized in turn, but there was clearly a limit to how far such attacks could go.

What kind of satirist is Garrick? His comic afterpieces and miscellaneous poems have edge, but they are never abrasive; he does not go for the jugular, and does not upset his audience. Like Foote, he is an entertainer, a performer as well as a satirist. His view of human nature seems neither particularly dark nor particularly sunny. A work like *The Clandestine Marriage* presents benevolence and decency, but his feelings toward his audience are mixed at best. Garrick is a socialite trying to get on in the world. Does he write satire? Absolutely. Is it significant satire, trying to make things happen or to do damage? No. In many ways his output is some indication of how satire was being used in the third quarter of the century. Few satirists in either verse or drama seem to be trying to bring about change; for the most part, they do not challenge the status quo. Generic differences notwithstanding, we will find that much the same can be said of mid- to late eighteenth-century novelists.

IV. Satire in the Mid-Eighteenth-Century Novel

What is the relationship between "satire" and "the novel" in the mid- to late eighteenth century? Paulson was the first scholar to try systematically to answer that question, and what he describes is an awkward and imprecise union of two fundamentally distinct kinds of writing. In his view, the novel "was by no means uninfluenced by satire, and yet was no longer what a critic could safely call satire." He contends that satire "infiltrated" the novel, that it "entered" the novel, that the novel "accommodated" satire, and that we find "satire adjusting to, rather than being submerged by" the assumptions made by novelists.[90] Frank Palmeri's explanation of changes in satiric practice after Pope and Swift is an attempt to complement Paulson's. Palmeri concludes, "Despite being discredited and suppressed, satiric form continued to be appropriated, reinterpreted, and reshaped by . . . novels throughout the eighteenth century."[91] Paulson and Palmeri are right that reference to Swiftian satire does not help us much with the second half of the century, but they conceive of what happens to satire in very narrow and negative terms.

The ways in which narrative utilizes satire and the difference between verse and prose narrative satire remain underexplored and undertheorized subjects. One of the principal contributions in this realm is Palmeri's *Satire in Narrative* (1990). Palmeri offers a bold and basic differentiation: verse satire "almost always expresses a conservative view of the world in language that approaches a purely dogmatic, monological state," but narrative satire by contrast "usually expresses a more subversive line of attack, making a more dialogical use of language."[92] Whatever the utility of the Bakhtinian viewpoint and terminology, the ideological differences between verse and narrative satire seem to me overstated. Obviously one can find satiric poets with "subversive" outlooks (Ayloffe and Rochester come immediately to mind), and plenty of novelists seem fairly conservative in their satire, including most of the writers relevant to this chapter as well as, say, Evelyn Waugh, one of the major satiric novelists of the twentieth century. Smollett uses satire in both poetry and prose, and the authorial position reflected in *Peregrine Pickle* is not so unlike that reflected in his verse satires. The novels are longer and their satire somewhat mitigated by plot and character, but Smollett's concept of satire does not shift markedly as he moves from genre to genre.

A broadly based attempt to theorize what happens to satire when it is practiced in narrative forms is a genuine desideratum. How much such a theory would help us with eighteenth-century English novels is another matter. There are not a great many satiric novels in this period, and there does not seem to be enough consistency in target, method, or authorial outlook to generate an implicit theoretical position. I have therefore limited myself to a basic question: what forms of satire are found in mid to late eighteenth-century English fiction? Surveying Smollett, Fielding, Sterne, and others, we find considerable differences in the way satire is used. One of the most obvious factors to consider here might be termed "dilution." Some novels contain a relatively high proportion of satiric material; in others it is more occasional or incidental. Proportion of satiric content aside, what I have found suggests a significant degree of taxonomic parallelism between fiction and other genres. Some novels stress negative presentation (Smollett), some portray both positive and negative models (Fielding), some pass judgment (Lennox), and some seem designed to provoke thought (Sterne). Real differences are created by the relative prominence of plot and character and by the dilution of satiric impact caused by those elements, but what the novelists do with satire seems to me generally similar to the kinds of satire practiced in poetry and drama.

Smollett's Dark Satire

Of the eighteenth-century novelists, Smollett is considered the most satirical. A notoriously fiery Scotsman, he lashed a corrupt society in his two verse satires, *Advice* and *Reproof*; ridiculed French cowardice in his dreadful patriotic farce, *The Reprisal: or, the Tars of Old England* (1757); and attacked Newcastle and then the opposition to

Bute in his polemical *Briton* (29 May 1762–12 February 1763).[93] Smollett is outspoken, politically and personally combative; his critics always underscore his moral intention. What he thought his satire would accomplish is impossible to guess, but his novels undoubtedly have moral seriousness, as well as a satiric edge not often found in this period.

Both *Roderick Random* (1748; 2 vols.; 6*s*†) and *Peregrine Pickle* (1751; 4 vols.; 12*s*†) recount the adventures of a wayfaring protagonist whose exploits allow the author to satirize a number of character types, institutions, follies, and so on. In the preface to *Roderick Random*, Smollett champions satire that is both *dulce* and *utile*: "Of all kinds of satire, there is none so entertaining, and universally improving, as that which is introduced . . . occasionally, in the course of an interesting story." He also suggests that the reader ought to be "prepossessed" in favor of the hero in distress and to appreciate "the contrast between dejected virtue, and insulting vice" so that "the heart improves by the example" (3). Roderick is an essentially well-meaning but far from exemplary innocent, and the people he meets—excepting a few truly virtuous individuals—behave abominably. The satire in *Peregrine Pickle* works similarly, though its protagonist is a less sympathetic figure than Roderick. In these novels, as throughout his oeuvre, Smollett takes passing shots at doctors, lawyers, politicians, and other writers, presenting a panoramic picture of inanity, injustice, cruelty, and vanity. The romantic denouements—Roderick marries his Narcissa, and Peregrine reforms to win his beloved—are overly facile, probably deliberately so.[94] Smollett is no optimist, and the imposition of the fairy-tale ending only calls attention to its own implausibility. Distributive justice seems an idealist's fancy: this is not the way the world works.

The epistolary *Humphry Clinker* (1771) is, of course, the most genial of Smollett's novels. The two principal letter writers are Matthew Bramble (cantankerous but secretly philanthropic) and his easygoing nephew Jery Melford. The two men are surrounded by a comic cast, including Tabitha (a prudish but sex-starved elderly maiden), the Cervantean Caledonian, Lismahago, and the eponymous Humphry, a good-hearted simpleton. Unlike the earlier novels, *Humphry Clinker* does not just present a succession of abuses or a string of episodes revelatory of human treachery. Whether it reflects Smollett's concession of the futility of indignation (as Beasley suggests) or simply his mellowing, *Humphry Clinker*'s satiric edge is blunted and its tone significantly less dark than the earlier works.[95]

Smollett's other two novels, less well known, are different from each other in plot and tone, but as satires both have unpleasant implications. Like *Roderick Random* and *Peregrine Pickle*, both *Ferdinand Count Fathom* (1753; 2 vols.; 6*s*†) and *Sir Launcelot Greaves* (pub. serially, 1760–1761) narrate the adventures of wandering protagonists. Fathom is no mere rogue but a criminal and a sexual predator whose charm and evil make him terrifying. The novel is packed with villains, sharpers, murderers, and thieves, and although Smollett shows us virtue in Renaldo and Monimia, the world he describes is oppressively negative. Fathom's eventual repentance makes a satiric point by its very impossibility. If Fathom is the picture of evil, Sir Launcelot is the picture of goodness. Zealously pursuing ways to help his fellows (while fitted out in full armor), the quixotic Sir Launcelot is regarded as a lunatic. Although the knight wins small battles and triumphs over particular foes, the values and the ways of human society cannot be transformed. Neither chivalry nor satire can make much difference. Sir Launcelot is Smollett's most idealistic figure, but *Sir Launcelot Greaves* is in many ways his darkest novel.

The History and Adventures of an Atom (1769; 2 vols.; 55†) is a political rather than social or moral satire and Smollett's angriest prose piece. The *Atom* is a lengthy allegory, ancient Japanese political history as told to a London haberdasher by an atom that has lived inside the bodies of several leaders of state. In this hate-filled screed, Smollett issues a blanket denunciation of midcentury political life—the handling of war, ministers, parliamentary venality, the aristocracy, the ignorant mob, George II and George III, and both parties. Smollett rebukes both the Whigs and the Tories, but his most savage energy is directed at Newcastle, named "Fika-kaka" in the scatological *Atom* in what is undoubtedly a pun on the Italian words *fica* and *caca*—"cunt-shit."[96] Smollett shows contempt for the importance of sycophancy and the irrelevance of merit; his attitude toward the higher-ups is deflationary and irreverent. To become the sovereign's favorite, Fika-kaka "not only devoted himself intirely to the gratification of his master's prejudices and rapacity, even when they interfered . . . with the interest . . . of Japan; but he also . . . presented his posteriors to be kicked as regularly as the day revolved; and presented them not barely with submission, but with all the appearance of fond desire" (14–15). The *Atom* represents Smollett at his most irascible, obscene, and ferocious, and it is livid satire of a kind uncommon in this quarter century. Smollett does not just criticize the status quo but damns it wholesale. His diatribe received mixed reviews, some commentators admitting its cleverness but most censuring its indelicacy; several respondents objected on political grounds. As Day notes, publishing the *Atom* in 1765 would probably have gotten Smollett in trouble, but by 1769, the key personages scorched in the satire were either dead or had become politically insignificant.[97] Smollett's political opponents caviled at his bilious invective, but the *Atom* is no more than that. Neither a Juvenalian performance nor a piece of propaganda, it is a bitter, hopeless expression of unmitigated disgust.

The Late Career of Fielding

The Fielding described in chapter 6 tends toward satiric indirection and parody, sometimes sharp but only rarely heavy handed. *Tom Thumb* is great fun; *Pasquin* and *The Historical Register* are stinging but lively; *Joseph Andrews* and *Tom Jones* reflect Fielding's hearty sense of humor. His early career is not without gloomy moments—*The Modern Husband* and *The Universal Gallant* are both shrill—but in his last years he is, as his students observe, a more somber commentator on human life and society. The major ventures of this period are *Amelia* (1751; 4 vols.; 12s†) and *The Covent-Garden Journal* (1752), both of which reflect the increasing social-mindedness of Fielding, Bow Street magistrate. They also represent the author at his darkest, writing as a would-be moral and social reformer and as someone dubious about the possibility of change.

Amelia is a hard book to like: Fielding is a master of comic indirection, but here his hand is heavy. In narrating the domestic problems of the virtuous Amelia Booth and her improvident husband, Fielding satirizes innumerable moral and social ills— self-interest, self-delusion, deceptiveness, adultery, official indifference to individual suffering, the injustice of the legal system, and so on. Not for nothing are the two principal images the masquerade and the prison: this is a novel of duplicity and iniquity. *Amelia* is a book of social realism and grave Christian didacticism, and its satire is a dreary mixture of dour indictment and melancholic preachment. Booth matter-of-factly remarks upon the "malicious Disposition of Mankind" and "the cruel Pleasure which they take in destroying the Reputations of others" (1:173). The narrator sermonizes on the nature of mankind: "Wantonness, Vanity, Avarice and Ambition are every Day rioting and triumphing in the Follies and Weakness, the Ruin and Desolation of Mankind" and so on, ever more strident (2:40). The innocent Amelia eventually renounces her faith in humanity, crying out at the end of book VII, "Well then, there is an End of all Goodness in the World" (3:105). The happy ending supplied for the Booths does nothing to dispel the gloom of the novel. Fielding's satire on particular groups (e.g., clergymen in book IX) is acerbic; his didacticism is harsh. That he conceived his novel as a vehicle for social protest is undeniable. As J. Paul Hunter concludes, however, Fielding abandons both his amiable tolerance and his belief in the efficacy of didacticism: "This is no longer the method of the patient, bemused, benevolent teacher, nor of the less jovial, many-faced satirist; it is more like that of a humorless policeman."[98] *Amelia* is as cynical as Smollett's works in its implications, but Fielding's last novel has a sadness Smollett never exhibits. The hotheaded Scotsman can thunder with conviction; Fielding seems acutely uncomfortable with his own pessimism.

The Covent-Garden Journal (4 January–25 November 1752), like *Amelia*, reflects the gravity of Fielding's late-life concerns. As in *The Champion* and *The Jacobite's Journal*, he adopts "the role of Censor on the Roman model, the overseer and judge of the nation's moral health, charged with examining into the lives and manners of its citizens."[99] Here his focus is on the morals, manners, and taste of English society, including a wide range of problems from discourtesy to impiety. He covers the "PEOPLE OF FASHION" (no. 37), pornography (no. 51), prostitution (no. 57), and adultery (no. 67), critics and editors, bad writers and false learning, the vain and the proud, scandalmongering and calumny, the disturbing "Rise and Progress" of the mob (no. 49), and numerous public and private vices. His stated goals are to serve "the noble Interests of Religion, Virtue, and good Sense" and "to restore that true and manly Taste, which hath . . . degenerated in these Kingdoms" (nos. 5, 43). The Battestins explain Fielding's *Journal* as an attempt to supplement his role as magistrate, to expose the evils he could not combat with the law. Although his litany of social ills is often delivered with "wit and a sort of sad good humor," they observe, "the sheer scope of the indictment is a measure of Fielding's pessimism as he contemplated society during these last years of his life."[100] His essays are frequently ironic rather than directly denunciatory, and they are sometimes lighthearted, but they exhibit neither the tolerance nor the optimism of his earlier satire. As in *Amelia*, Fielding is both would-be reformer and glum skeptic.

To read *The Covent-Garden Journal* simply as the solemn moralizing of a disinterested satirist, however, would be misleading. Bertrand A. Goldgar and others have underscored the *Journal*'s utility as a publicity medium for the Universal Register Office,[101] and Bertelsen rightly argues that Fielding's Bow Street reports were meant to have entertainment value. "The dialectic of humane and exploitative . . . that informs Fielding's descriptions of prostitutes . . . recurs with remarkable vigor in his reporting of domestic violence and rape cases," most of which are presented "in great detail and include such literary amenities as first-person dialogue, twists and turns of plot, and surprise endings." Legal depositions presented in a commercial paper also served as racy amusements, Bertelsen points out, as Fielding's detractors hastened to observe. They described his *Journal* as a sensationalist venture designed to promote its author's personal and business interests.[102] *The Covent-Garden Journal* is an oddity—a mixture of levity and cynicism, of literary ridicule, social criticism, moral preachment, self-publicity, and sensationalism.[103]

Tristram Shandy *and the Singularity of Sterne*

Almost all critics would agree that *Tristram Shandy* (pub. serially, 1759–1767) is a satiric novel—but if it is a satire, what is it a satire on? To attempt to discuss *Tristram* in the contexts of standard definitions of satire achieves little beyond illustrating the limits of those definitions. Putting Sterne in a sequence of satirists merely makes him seem as weird as he is; placing him in a sequence of early English novelists fails to demonstrate "the rise of the novel." Some satire scholars have wanted to see Sterne as a sentimentalized successor of Pope and Swift, an inheritor and modifier of the "Scriblerian" mode. Others view him more broadly as a follower of Rabelais and Burton in the tradition of "learned wit." Most critics, however, have acknowledged the disconcerting fact that *Tristram Shandy* must be taken on its own terms. For the purposes of the present investigation, I want briefly to address three questions. First, how did Sterne's contemporaries understand the nature of his enterprise? Second, what sorts of views of Sterne as satirist do we find in the criticism of the last half century? And third, what sorts of satiric functions do we find in the text itself?

That *Tristram Shandy*'s first readers did not respond uniformly is hardly surprising. Some readers, as Thomas Keymer points out, "either ignored or consciously refused the interpretive challenge of the text," enjoying the book as "a source of comic pleasure or obscene wit" or "dismiss[ing] it as an impudent hoax, a farrago of nonsensical shocks."[104] The gist of many reactions is bewilderment. A 1760 reviewer begins his discussion with a caveat: "This is a humorous performance, of which we are unable to convey any distinct idea to our readers."[105] Other commentators treat *Tristram*'s incomprehensibility with obvious delight: "Oh rare Tristram Shandy!—Thou very sensible—humorous—pathetick—humane—unaccountable!—what shall we call thee?—Rabelais, Cervantes, What?" (*CH*, 52). One of Sterne's critics observed crossly that the public had been taken by *Tristram*, even though "they did not understand the joke." At length, he says, they "began to see clearly that . . . [Sterne's] work was a *riddle*, without an *object*."[106] The author of *An Admonitary Letter to the Rev. Mr. S[terne]* (1761) addresses Sterne directly: "I should be glad to know, from your own Mouth, what it is you drive at" (7).

Not everyone threw in the towel: some respondents attempted to define Sterne's satiric aims and targets. One reviewer confidently assured his readers that he had the key to *Tristram*, a work he described as a "compleat system of modern politics," in which the 1690s wars were meant to represent the Seven Years' War. By the Siege of Namur, Sterne meant the 1756 Siege of Fort St. Philip; by Toby's wound, he meant "the distress the nation was thrown into" by that siege's failure; and so on. *Tristram*, he concludes, "is a master piece of allegory" (*CH*, 66–67). Another expositor just as positively insisted that *Tristram Shandy* was a general satire on humankind and on the softer sex in particular: "I am entirely convinced 'tis a smart satyrical piece on the vices of the age, particularly of that part of the Creation, which were designed for the pleasure and happiness of man" (*CH*, 85). Others identify religion as Sterne's principal target, some of them charging him with blasphemy. An enthusiastic advocate of *Tristram* says cheerfully, "[H]e makes such a joke of religion!—What do you think of his introducing a sermon in the midst of a smutty tale, and making the preacher curse and swear by way of parenthesis?" Sterne's attackers, he continues, are "stupid drones . . . who do not enter into the spirit of the thing" (*CH*, 64). How many of the responses are ironic is hard to guess.

Most of the commentators on *Tristram Shandy* as satire tended to speak in broad terms. Sterne was "ridiculing the ruling passions, or hobby horses, as well as the vices and follies of mankind," and his novel "contains much good satire on the follies of life" (*CH*, 105, 139). Less enthusiastic readers balanced praise of Sterne's general satire with disapprobation of his indecency and indelicacy. Many contemporaries rebuked the clergyman's bawdiness or were irritated by his self-indulgence and unintelligibility, but some took him much less seriously. In a letter to a friend, Thomas Gray said simply, "[T]here is much good fun in it, & humour sometimes hit & sometimes mist" (*CH*, 89). What does not get a lot of mention is the philosophical import of *Tristram Shandy*, which few contemporaries seem to have appreciated; they apparently did not think of Locke when they read Sterne.[107] Sterne was undoubtedly making a significant epistemological point, but his contemporaries were mostly exasperated, appalled, moved, or amused.

Twentieth-century critics tend to agree that the novel is satirical—if not a "satire"—but exactly how the work should be characterized and what Sterne is targeting remain open questions. In "Satire and *Tristram Shandy*" (1961), J. M. Stedmond represents Sterne as a friendlier "Scriblerian." He contends that "*Tristram Shandy* is one more engagement in the perpetual war between wits and 'dunces'" but that Sterne's "approach is much more tentative, his attack much less bitter" than Pope's or Swift's—"presumably because his positive beliefs are much less surely held."[108] The only book-length study devoted exclusively to Sterne's satire is Melvyn New's *Laurence Sterne as Satirist* (1969). New offers a reinterpretation of *Tristram Shandy* that places it "in the mainstream of the conservative, moralistic Augustan tradition." Sterne's masterpiece, New usefully argues, should be read "through the intentions and conventions of the dominant literary form of that tradition, satire." He bases his investigation on the premise that "*Tristram Shandy* joins works like *A Tale of a Tub* and *The Dunciad* as one further effort to stem the eighteenth century's ever increasing enthusiasm for human self-sufficiency" and to counter this enthusiasm Sterne tries to expose man's limitations.[109] The problem with New's argument, at least in *Laurence Sterne as Satirist*, is that it exaggerates the degree to which Sterne is Swiftian, representing *Tristram Shandy* as centrally an attack on pride and obscuring the book's amiability and humor.

The question of Sterne's Scriblerianism continues to worry critics, and how one answers it obviously matters to the interpretation of *Tristram Shandy*. Scholars in the last generation have for the most part been prepared to admit huge temperamental and tonal differences between Sterne and his canonical predecessors, though they naturally tend to emphasize his most "Swiftian" or "Popean" targets: bad writing, false learning, critical jargon, the Royal Society scientists, the inanity of public taste, and so on. J. T. Parnell proposes that "Scriblerian and Sternean satire" belongs in the "tradition of skeptical, anti-dogmatic arguments of the sixteenth and seventeenth centuries" and that Sterne—like Swift—is principally concerned to satirize "system builders."[110] Keymer rejects the notion of Sterne as a "Scriblerian throwback," though he too understands *Tristram Shandy* "as heavily conditioned by satirical traditions that culminate with Swift." He argues, "If *Tristram Shandy* is a satire . . . it is above all a satire on the novel, and in this respect it cleverly capitalizes on a potentiality that *A Tale of a Tub* had intimated but been unable to fulfil." Sterne's "primary interest," Keymer concludes, "is with large questions about the novel and its mechanisms."[111] That *Tristram Shandy* reveals the limitations of novel writing and parodies generic conventions is beyond question, and Sterne just as clearly mocks false pedants and scientific arrogance. But none of these represents a central satiric target—each is only a small part of what the novel "does," and his satire shares little with Pope or Swift in technique, tone, or principal object. What they denounced in their different ways, Sterne makes playful fun of in the midst of a multifocused and exceptionally jumbled book. He is doing something different.

Sterne claimed a constructive purpose for his novel, insisting that he wrote *Tristram Shandy* in "the hopes of doing the world good by ridiculing what I thought deserving of it." To his publisher, he explained that the novel's "Plan" was "a most extensive one,—taking in, not only, the Weak part of the Sciences, in wch the true point of Ridicule lies—but every Thing else, which I find Laugh-at-able in my way—."[112] What he found "Laugh-at-able" mostly involves egotism and epistemological overconfidence: he illustrates the unknowability of people, the limitations of language, and the insufficiency of reason and sentiment to help us organize the chaos of life and cope with it. As a response to those constrictions, however, he offers amused acceptance as an alternative to despair.[113] Peter M. Briggs argues that "*Tristram Shandy* is . . . about man's attempt to give a reasonable and definitive form to his experience of the world—and about the inevitable tendency of experience to run counter to man's formulations."[114] This seems about right. The satiric message of *Tristram Shandy*, underlying a lot of scattershot ridicule, is philosophically skeptical.[115] The skeptical thrust of the satire, however, is presented with good cheer, a sense of humor, and manifest warmth toward humankind. (How often do the targets of satire feel that the satirist likes them and wishes them well?) Sterne, in Weinbrot's phrasing, is "having too much fun to be gloomy."[116] Sterne's emphasis on human limitations has a positive upshot: "*Because* man lives in this world amongst riddles and mysteries, *because* he cannot gain a consistent grasp upon his own experiences and upon the values and perceptions of others, he should be generous, patient, honest, and good-humored."[117]

What Sterne achieved in *Tristram Shandy* is, among other things, a brilliant and complicated interplay between satire and sentiment. His novel includes positive and negative forms of "satire," as critics have recognized. He mocks novelistic conventions, pedants, legalese, the Royal Society scientists, and the sort of intellectualism reflected in Walter Shandy, a comic virtuoso both benign and ridiculous. Walter is "a philosopher in grain,—speculative,—systematical,"[118] and Sterne invites readers to laugh at him, both as a natural philosopher determined to regulate life and as an orator unable to communicate with those around him. Sterne approves of deep feeling, and "many of the hallmarks of literary sentimentalism," Keymer concludes, are "on display in *Tristram Shandy*." The book is replete with

> vignettes of felt benevolence and emotionally fragmented syntax; wordless recognitions of sympathetic mutuality and consolatory exchanges of tears; a pathology of nervous response and disorder, debilitating in the face of grief; above all, an understanding of virtue, and of personal identity and human society, that places the capacity for exquisite feeling at the very centre.[119]

But Sterne is known for regarding sentiment with both praise and skepticism, for worrying that too much indulgence in altruistic fine feeling leads to self-congratulation. In *Tristram Shandy*, he admiringly presents the tenderhearted Uncle Toby—"This world surely is wide enough to hold both thee and me," says Toby to the fly whose life he is sparing—but he can revel in bathetic sentiment while teasing it (1:131). The joke of *Tristram Shandy* is often on the reader, whom Sterne jestingly taunts throughout.

Tristram Shandy is peculiar, brilliant but frustratingly hard to cope with in a taxonomic survey. It is a work of great fun and of real sadness. It includes many kinds of satire, from clear-cut ridicule to critical scrutiny of our epistemological pretensions that has serious import for anyone who wants to read beyond the flip story and dirty jokes. But all of this satire comes in one of the liveliest, friendliest books in the language. Unlike Pope and Swift and many other satirists, Sterne is not really passing judgment. Jonathan Lamb rightly argues that Sterne's "engagement with the public sphere" is not done in terms of "the satirist's monitory guardianship of society's rules and norms"—that Sterne as satirist functions in a very different way.[120] New's conclusion in a reassessment of 1994 seems to me spot on: Sterne "rarely seeks 'orthodoxy' or adherence to dogma," instead trying to "demonstrate the inevitable errors of the human mind in relation to the world."[121]

My aim is not—cannot be—to do justice to the complexity of Sterne's satire, but a few conclusions need to be drawn. For my purposes, what is important about *Tristram Shandy* is that Sterne is not decrying evil in the fashion of the "Scriblerians," and neither is he offering commercial entertainment or superficial social mockery. This is an altogether heartier kind of satire. In 1994, New issued a salutary reminder about the dangers of defining satire too negatively. Because modern critics think of satire as "fundamentally *judgmental* rather than *tolerant* . . . , *discriminating* rather than *open-minded*" and so on, he concluded, they "*cannot tolerate* the notion of Sterne as a satirist—or indeed, of satire as a healthy literary mode."[122] *Tristram Shandy* contains straightforward negative-mode satire but also lively satiric provocation and clear positives. Another point is that to ignore Sterne's ridicule of pedantry (etc.) is foolish, but to place him in a Scriblerian tradition requires quite a lot of special pleading, and in the end the Scriblerian tag does not seem much to advance our understanding of what Sterne is doing. *Tristram Shandy* is not well explained in terms of pre-1750 satiric targets and thrusts. Neither does it fit any midcentury category. For a satire, this is strange. One of the lessons of my survey in this book is that a work's particular place in chronology tends to be of crucial importance. Sterne's parody of novel writing, the sympathetic nature of his satire, and his mockery of sentimental excess all make *Tristram Shandy* of its moment, but as several critics have rightly concluded, it is essentially a one-off.[123]

Sterne's other satirical ventures share little with *Tristram Shandy*. *A Sentimental Journey through France and Italy* (1768; 5s†) satirizes travel writing, particularly Smollett's *Travels through France and Italy* (1766; 10s†), which Sterne condemns as the censorious production of "the learned Smelfungus" (1:86). The problem for critics has been how we are meant to feel about the sentimental narrator, Parson Yorick. He is a man of sensibility (good), but he is also self-interested—following charitable acts with telltale self-congratulation—and his carnality makes *A Sentimental Journey* a book of double entendres and bawdy humor. Sterne uses Yorick to satirize a variety of targets, but he also invites satiric judgment of the narrator. Sterne's digs at Smollett and at false charity are undoubtedly sincerely meant, as is his appreciation of benevolence and finer feelings, but how seriously we are to take it as satire remains a vexed question. More straightforward in its satiric purposes is *A Political Romance* (1759), a burlesque squib written against ecclesiastical chicanery in York. The allegory now seems opaque, but to those in the know the satire was clear enough: *A Political Romance* "scathingly . . . exposed the rapaciousness of several easily identified members of the Minster clergy," and upon its publication "the archbishop of York hastily intervened to save the blushes of the Church and peremptorily ordered the entire edition to be burned."[124]

Charlotte Lennox, Oliver Goldsmith, Sarah Fielding: Satire and Sentiment

Lennox, Goldsmith, and Sarah Fielding are names not often associated with satire, but what they do in their major prose works has much in common with the kinds of satire practiced in the third quarter of the eighteenth century, especially in the social comedies covered in section III. Differences in satiric objects notwithstanding, *The Female Quixote*, *The Vicar of Wakefield*, and *David Simple* all expose the folly or ill effects of excessive sentimentality.

The eponymous protagonist of Lennox's *The Female Quixote* (1752; 2 vols.; 6s†) is Arabella, raised in isolation by her widowed father and deluded into believing that her cherished romances are fact rather than fiction. Convinced that life follows the heroic code of romance novels, Arabella fancies herself an exalted heroine.[125] Her suitor's "Happiness," we are told, depends "upon curing her of her romantic Notions"—and in the end this "cure" is effected by an elderly clergyman, who disabuses Arabella of her fantasies (117). When he insists that romance writers have created a world very different from reality, her reply is sadly acquiescent but also judgmental: "I am afraid . . . that the Difference is not in Favour of the present World" (380). Having exchanged her romantic pretensions for realistic modesty, she and Glanville unite. Arabella is a satiric mouthpiece who reveals the folly of most of the men she meets and pointedly criticizes the trivial interests of high society. She is also a target who needs to be satirically educated: "She is ready to be a wife because she has learned that what romance teaches is false: men do not exist to serve women."[126] The satire is not simply a matter of humiliating a few male types (a fop, a pedant), mocking romance conventions, and correcting the clever but misguided heroine. Arabella needs to be brought back in line with a patriarchal society, but Lennox's endorsement of that society is far from unequivocal.[127]

The Vicar of Wakefield (1766; 2 vols.; 6s†) is in some ways a more difficult case. Whether Goldsmith is producing straight sentimental slush or (lightly) parodying same has been debated. In 1969 Robert H. Hopkins went so far as to argue that Goldsmith belongs to the "tough-minded Augustan tradition" of satire as practiced by Pope and Swift,[128] a claim difficult to credit. What one can say is that *The Vicar of Wakefield*—published two years before *The Good-Natur'd Man* premiered—reveals the folly of overmuch trust in people, chastising the decent but credulous country parson, Dr. Primrose, and exposing the depraved ways of the world.[129] The vicar's naïveté and pride in his daughters leads to a series of disasters, but they sustain their devout optimism, and fortune finally smiles on them. The conclusion finds the vicar in a state of reflective contentment: "I had nothing now on this side of the grave to wish for, all my cares were over," and so on (4:184). How satirical a reader finds *The Vicar of Wakefield* depends largely on one's response to Primrose. He was long hailed as an unambiguously exemplary figure and Goldsmith's work viewed as a sentimental parable, but most critics now regard the good parson as a well-meaning dupe rather than a paragon. As Ricardo Quintana concluded in 1967, simpleminded faith in human goodness becomes a problem: "in the presence of experience," innocence is foolish, "and in the presence of evil it ceases to be wholly admirable."[130] The "satire" in *The Vicar of Wakefield* is both educative (innocence is schooled) and condemnatory (of the knaves who take advantage of innocence).

The satire of Sarah Fielding's *The Adventures of David Simple* (1744) and its sequel, *Volume the Last* (1753; 2s 6d†), works in much the same way, though Fielding is much darker than Goldsmith. In *David Simple*, the eponymous ingenue travels to London in search of true friendship. Instead (of course) he finds only false friends whose bad behavior allows Fielding to satirize the hypocrisy and corruption of London life and manners. The novel ends with a double marriage (David and his brother both take wives). *Volume the Last* begins several years later, with the family now living in the country, enjoying health and good fortune. The tone of the sequel is considerably gloomier—and the satire sharper—than that of *David Simple*, though the theme is the same. The altruistic, tenderhearted David is deceived by men who take advantage of his artlessness and manage to cheat him of all his money while pretending to be his benefactors. David and his family bear their sufferings in a spirit worthy of Job, but unlike Goldsmith Fielding does not relieve her hero's distress by a highly implausible improvement in material fortune. David's niece dies, and then his brother, and then all but one of his children, his wife, and himself. Like Young Honeywood and Belcour, David is too good for this world, and Fielding's indictment of that world is severe:

> if any of my Readers chuse to drag *David Simple* from the Grave, to struggle again in this World, and to reflect, every Day, on the Vanity of its utmost Enjoyments, they may use their own Imaginations, and fancy *David Simple* still bustling about on this Earth. But I chuse to think he is escaped from the Possibility of falling into any future Afflictions, and that neither the Malice of his pretended Friends, nor the Sufferings of his real ones, can ever again rend and torment his honest Heart. (432)

Like her brother's *Amelia*, Fielding's *Volume the Last* suggests not that virtue does not exist but that it does not always get its reward.

As in *The Female Quixote* and *The Vicar of Wakefield*—and *The Good-Natur'd Man* and other plays—Sarah Fielding's decent protagonist needs an education in the indecent ways of the world. If the scolding of Young Honeywood seems a bit hard, David's fate seems an excruciatingly excessive punishment for his simplicity. Sara Gadeken rightly suggests that *David Simple* is more "Horatian" and *Volume the Last* more "Juvenalian," though Fielding's condemnation of society is revealed less through direct denunciation than through the affecting account of the victim's suffering. Gadeken sees this form of satire as definitively "female," postulating that midcentury female satirists had to "negotiate the difficult course of producing morally forceful satire while avoiding manly vigor" and that *David Simple* and the sequel show "both the restrictions on female satire and the ways in which Fielding manipulates those restrictions."[131] I have difficulty believing that Sarah Fielding was trying to avoid "manly vigor" in these works. The type of satire practiced in these novels is current at the midcentury among satirists of both sexes. If she is responding to pressure to produce a certain kind of satire, that pressure is not brought because of her gender. *Volume the Last* includes, moreover, much more vigorous satire than does Sarah's brother's *Tom Jones*. In any case, *David Simple* and *Volume the Last*, like *The Female Quixote*, include at least two different kinds of satire: (1) The self-deluded or overly sentimental and credulous hero is a sympathetic character who is satirically educated in his or her own folly. (2) The satirist calls into question the social codes against which the protagonist's ideals are contrasted, or exposes the deplorable ways of the world and the untrustworthiness of most of its inhabitants.

V. Satire for a Stable Era

Satire is alive and well in the third quarter of the eighteenth century. Again and again I have insisted on the folly of rigidly narrow definitions: one needs to appreciate what is done at any given time, and a lesson of this book is that satiric practice changes in response to external circumstances. What we find in the midcentury is neither the sudden and near-total disappearance of satire nor an anemic attempt to carry on the traditions of potent "Scriblerian" satire. This chapter's title is designedly strange—a roll call rather than a conceptual focus—but it is meant to point the reader toward the scrappy, disconnected set of practices the chapter describes.

Satire in the third quarter of the century does not reduce to a single descriptor or explanatory concept, or even to a relatively limited number of groupings such as we have found in the preceding chapters. Churchill, Foote, Macklin, Garrick, Smollett, and Sterne are all prominent satirists of this period, but they have little in common, and adding Lloyd, Colman, Smart, Sarah Fielding and others does not simplify the picture. By 1750, satiric practice has become much more fragmented than in the previous hundred years, and the change does not issue solely from one cause (e.g., the death of Pope or the rise of sensibility). The marked transformation of satiric poetry has much to do with the increase in self-styled English poets; a high percentage of the verse satire is elaborately poeticized, its content often secondary to its form and style. In drama, the changes come in part from the reimposition of censorship, and they also reflect enlarged theaters designed to appeal to a middle-of-the-road audience. Theatergoers, as Garrick says in the preface to *The Country Girl* (1766), wanted something nice. In drama and fiction, satire is necessarily diluted: the use of semiplausible characterization and "realistic" plot in most novels and plays tends to set satire in a context that is not purely satiric.

Satire's supposed demise has, in common critical imagination, long been linked to the upsurge of finer feelings. Later eighteenth-century satiric poetry includes little crude lampoonery, playwrights focus as much on reform as on ridicule, and the most famous fictional character is Tristram's gentle Uncle Toby. More than half a century ago, Northrop Frye published a little piece with a big claim. The second half of the century had "suffered from not having a clear historical or functional label applied to it," he argued, and the label that should be bestowed on the period is the "Age of Sensibility."[132] Frye was frustrated by the attitude that the second half of the century is simply "pre-Romantic," without its own defining features, and rightly so, but as Weinbrot decisively demonstrated, Frye overstated the elements he identified with the rise of sensibility. [133] In any case, whatever terminology we use ("Augustan" or "Scriblerian" on the one side, "Sensibility" or "Sentimentalism" on the other) the premise has long been that "real" satire gives way to drippy sympathy. We are in the world of *The Good-Natur'd Man* and *The Man of Feeling*, not *Gulliver's Travels* and *The Dunciad*, and the golden days of satire are over. One problem with this way of thinking is that it tends to invite selective attention: those attempting to describe the age of sensibility are wont to overlook the likes of Foote, Macklin, and Smollett. *The Adventures of an Atom*, *The Nabob*, and *The Man of the World*—and, say, the *Epistle to William Hogarth*—are not the stuff of affectionate pathos.[134] One can agree that more "soft" satire is produced in the second half of the century than in the first, but the years 1745–1770 also feature much more negativity and bite than tends to be acknowledged.

The changes reflected in later eighteenth-century satire cannot be explained simply as the unfortunate consequence of softening attitudes toward human nature. Punitive satire does not disappear—see Foote and Smollett, among others—but on the whole the techniques and tones of satire change markedly during the eighteenth century. I would not undertake to offer a complete explanation of why this happens, but one major contributory factor is surely the relative stability of the 1750s and 1760s. Jeremy Black explains that, despite the seeming implausibility of describing Wilkesite Britain as "fundamentally stable," given "the difficulty of forming a lasting ministry and the extent of extra-parliamentary political action," in fact

> the radicalism of the period scarcely prefigured that of the 1790s. All politicians, and the majority of those who thought about politics and society, wished to make the existing system work better . . . rather than to introduce change. This shared objective did not prevent discord, in part because of the absence of general agreement over several major constitutional issues, but largely because discord was and is compatible with a stable political system.[135]

Black rightly distinguishes between discontent with a monarch and a sense that his rule was illegitimate, underscoring the "broad popular acceptance of the Hanoverian regime" by the 1750s. Whatever the annoyances and discontents to which satirists responded, they were not of the scale or the direness that generated harsh satiric commentary on earlier issues and problems. Satirists react with anxiety, disgust, and angry conviction to the Exclusion Crisis, King William's long and expensive war, and the much-reviled Robinocracy—and a surprising amount of the time, they are not just kvetching. They want to make something happen, or at least they sorely wish something could. Midcentury satirists are sometimes splenetic, but on the whole they are *not* fiercely committed to demanding change.

The relative political stability of the 1750s and 1760s, along with Pope's posthumous influence on poetry, seem powerfully to affect the practice of verse satire. With few exceptions, what we find in this material is much less heat and urgency than we have seen before, and a great deal more obvious concern with poetic craft. This shift is much easier to identify at the end of a wide-ranging survey of satiric practice across time than it is after reading the canonical heavyweights in relative isolation. If we view the satires of the 1760s by the standards of Dryden and Pope, they seem inferior but not generically odd. Viewed in the light of a more comprehensive satiric canon, however, the self-consciously literary satire of the midcentury seems jarringly atypical. Art trumps occasion. Admittedly, the occasions are mostly contrived or trivial, but the art is not great art. As poets, the writers of the 1760s are a long way from matching Pope's technical skill; as satirists, they have neither the purposiveness of *Absalom and Achitophel* nor the *saeva indignatio* of the Dean.

This is the satire of relative quiescence, negligible as *satire* but accurately reflecting the sociopolitical conditions in which it was written, and the dispiriting nature of these works does suggest something fundamental about satiric practice. What makes satire so exciting in the eighty years between the Restoration and the fall of Walpole is its writers' passionate desire to do damage, to effect change, or at least to protest the defeat of their causes—a desire that is almost entirely lacking after 1745. Satire written in the third quarter of the eighteenth century is often witty or instructive or provocative of thought, but the results do tend to seem rather tame. They serve to remind us, however, that great satire usually springs from crisis or profound discontent or bitter hostility—and that these were the generative forces that produced the many brilliant satires that make the century between the era of Cromwell and the fall of Walpole the historical acme of this astonishingly varied and multifarious form.

Toward a New History of English Satire, 1658–1770

◇◇◇◇◇◇◇◇◇◇◇◇◇◇◇◇◇◇◇◇◇◇

History-writing is not story-telling but problem solving.
—David Hackett Fischer, *Historians' Fallacies*, xii

The preceding survey of satiric practices in England from (roughly) 1658 to 1770 is meant to challenge the "story" of eighteenth-century satire as put forth by Ian Jack half a century ago and still largely dominant. Jack is hardly the only promulgator of the myth of "Augustan satire," but his treatment of this material exemplifies some common patterns. His *Augustan Satire: Intention and Idiom in English Poetry, 1660–1750* (1952) stresses literary technique and style rather than content and virtually eliminates all background, reducing "satire" to a small number of works by four poets. Butler, Dryden, Pope, and Johnson were the authors, we are told in the book's opening sentence, "of the most representative poems written in England between the Restoration and the middle of the eighteenth century." The question, of course, is representative *of what*? Does reading Pope's Horatian imitations give us an accurate sense of what 1730s satire was like? Can we assume that Dryden significantly influenced Pope's practice and that Johnson was conscious of following Pope? I think not. The bottom line is that accounts of eighteenth-century satire have presumed the typicality and the connectedness of the major works. I have tried to demonstrate that neither presumption is well founded.

The present study offers the history of a large, complex phenomenon that does not reduce to a tidy story. The literary historian should not be seeking—and certainly should not be finding—anything like a coherent narrative. Implicit in most accounts of eighteenth-century satire is the conviction that the canonical works are the most brilliant examples of a unified mode and that studying them can tell us what we need to know about satiric practice. This is not true. If we want to write a history of eighteenth-century satire, we have to avoid treating the masterpieces as though they were produced in immediate succession; we have to realize just how far from chronologically proximate the worlds of 1681 and 1704 and 1728 really are, and we have to focus on smaller spans of time. My "history," then, is really a composite comprising at least five smaller histories, each of which is individually more susceptible of characterization than is the totality of the period 1658–1770. The epilogue to this study is divided into two parts, and they point respectively to "chaos" and "order." If we try to explain eighteenth-century satire as a whole in ways that do justice to all the complexities and disparities, what we get is a muddled mass of contradictory detail. Narrowing our field of vision to each of the five subperiods makes the situation a lot more manageable and the material more comprehensible. The history of eighteenth-century English satire as offered in this book depends upon the recognition both of the diversity of the works themselves and of the presence of distinct subperiods.

I. Motives and Modes

> Satire can be described as the literary art of diminishing or derogating a subject by making it ridiculous and evoking toward it attitudes of amusement, contempt, scorn, or indignation. It differs from the *comic* in that comedy evokes laughter mainly as an end in itself, while satire derides; that is, it uses laughter as a weapon, and against a butt that exists outside the work itself. (M. H. Abrams, *Glossary of Literary Terms*, 284–285)

This definition is unlikely to evoke surprise from many readers. Abrams's *Glossary* is a widely used teaching tool and an authoritative source of conventional wisdom; essentially similar views of satire can be found in many other reference sources. To anyone who received an Anglo-American university education in the last sixty years and has been teaching Dryden, Swift, Pope, and company, such a definition probably seems reasonable. It presumes that satire is a *literary* art; that it *attacks* its targets, with varying degrees of seriousness or intensity; and that the targets are *real*. These definitional principles work passably well when applied to most of the eighteenth-century satires commonly studied by literary critics. For many of the satires surveyed in chapters 3 through 7, however, they are varyingly irrelevant. A huge number of satirists seem less concerned with form and aesthetics than with content and immediate impact, and "attack" is a crude oversimplification at best, simply wrong for many works. "Satire" turns out to be a multifarious phenomenon that does not reduce to a neat formula, and much of the diversity stems from the radically different motives that drive satirists. To the question of motive, therefore, we need now to turn. What exactly are satirists attempting to accomplish, and for whom?

One of the more fundamental distinctions to be made in the realm of motive is between satire written primarily as an *aesthetic performance* and that chiefly motivated by *practical concerns*. Satire is an occasional and circumstantial form, but the difference is whether the "occasion" provides material for a work of art or represents a cause in the service of which a writer can exercise his or her talents. The issue is the primary impetus behind the enterprise, not the "literariness" or unliterariness of the results. I would not deny for a moment that Dryden and Swift, for example, have great literary talent and a considerable degree of literary aspiration, but being deeply committed to a cause can inspire a talented writer to an even greater performance. Take *Absalom and Achitophel*. That Dryden's principal ambition in penning this satire was to craft a lasting work of art seems unlikely to me. He wrote in passionate support of the king in the midst of a dangerous political crisis; he did a brilliant job of turning the biblical characters into present-day politicians, and *Absalom and Achitophel* is the product of inspired genius. The fact remains that what gives it such force is the political occasion and Dryden's fierce conviction as to what is right. The same could be said of *A Modest Proposal*. Swift's mounting frustration with the situation in Ireland produced a state of disgust in which he could conceive a devastatingly biting, double-edged satire that that could shock and grip his readers.

Three hundred years on, we can fully relish language, form, and structure, but I suspect that original readers of *Absalom and Achitophel* and *A Modest Proposal* were focused mostly on the content, on the succession crisis and Ireland's economic plight. Dennis's take on Dryden's verse satires is telling. He described *Absalom and Achitophel*, *Mac Flecknoe*, and *The Medall* as abusive partisan libels, admitting their skill—they "are indeed, if you please, beautiful Libels"—but only as an incidental feature.[1] The modern critical appreciation of literary form and execution is entirely legitimate, but, like most of their contemporary satirists, Dryden and Swift probably wished readers to respond first and foremost to their arguments. As Edward Said observes of Swift's occasional writings, they were conceived "not as art in our sense of the word or as craftsmanship for its own sake," but instead were "stimulated by a specific occasion and planned in some way to change it"—to shape historical events.[2] This is true of the vast majority of the satire produced from the late seventeenth century to the middle of the eighteenth.

Satire in which the essential point is "the performance" is a different animal. Pope had little at stake in the social contretemps that inspired *The Rape of the Lock*; it provided him an occasion for an artistic tour de force. He wrote with a strong sense that he was a great English writer in a tradition descended from the classics, and he shows off his skills with verve. Swift represents a sharp contrast: the intense topicality of most of his output suggests that he is principally motivated by (usually sociopolitical) purposiveness. Swift might well be pessimistic about the possibility of reforming the human race, but he writes to do damage, to expose limitations, to deliver judgment. In his life and career he does more than propagandize, but in satiric terms he is above all a propagandist. Of course Swift thought of himself as a writer of some importance, but he did not work in settled genres in ways that would proclaim him a distinguished author in a classical tradition à la Pope, and when he boasts of his work, he seems proudest of impact. Though Pope often has a serious satiric message to convey, he is manifestly concerned with posterity and desirous of readers beyond the occasion for his satire. He is ever aware of his own artistry, and so are we. This is not common among verse satirists prior to the 1730s, but by the mid-eighteenth century many satiric poets have no very potent cause and seem hyperconscious of their status as writers. Determining motive is at best an uncertain business, but I would argue that the conspicuously conscious artistry of something like *The Rape of the Lock* or Lloyd's *The Progress of Envy* (1751) sets them apart from the satiric verse of Marvell, Ayloffe, and Rochester in the late seventeenth century or Defoe, Tutchin, and Maynwaring in the early eighteenth.

Most of the satires covered in this study are occasional. The nature of the resulting satires, as this survey demonstrates, is enormously varied. Plenty of satirists write to attack and punish their targets—but "attack" is a broad category and not always a useful one. Not all satiric attacks are motivated by authorial hostility: Shadwell's caricature of Sir Robert Howard as Sir Positive At-all in *The Sullen Lovers* (1668) is funny but not particularly damaging. Charles Viscount Mordaunt's *The Ladies' March* (wr. 1681) mocks a string of court women, but his lampoon comprises a catalog of standard charges, probably meant to amuse readers more than to wound the targets. Fielding in *Tom Thumb* (1730) and Samuel Johnson of Cheshire in *Hurlothrumbo* (1729) are chirpily deflating the conventions of heroic tragedy; these burlesques are wonderfully entertaining, but they are not attempts to do harm. Drubbing easy targets to please a crowd is very different from high-heat denunciation. Ayloffe's anti-Stuart diatribes are rants, meant to vent disgust rather than to produce change. Fielding's *The Old Debauchees* (1732) is the satiric equivalent of preaching to the choir, purveying harsh anti-Catholic satire for the enjoyment of those already opposed to priests and the Catholic Church. Satirists sometimes slash individuals out of sheer malice or for the pleasure of abuse—see Rochester's bludgeonings of Scroope or Foote's hostile caricature of Whitefield in *The Minor* (1760). Mockery can also be merely a matter of triumphalism, gleeful stomping on a no longer threatening target, as in anti-Shaftesbury satire produced after his departure from London in 1682.

A surprising amount of defamatory satire, however, is propagandistic rather than gratuitously malicious. Butler's exposure of the radicals in *Hudibras* is a contribution to current debates about what the official policy toward dissenters should be; Garth's *Dispensary* is a satiric response to a battle between dispensarians and physicians over the availability of cheaper medicine for lower-class patients. Detraction, in these instances, is emphatically polemical. The same is true of Buckingham's character assassinations of his rivals (Arlington and Danby), Dryden's *The Medall* (1682), Swift's *Publick Spirit of the Whigs* (1714), and Churchill's *Epistle to William Hogarth* (1763)—as well as a considerable number of other works throughout the upward of a century at issue. These satires undeniably include ridicule, but they are not wanton derogation.

Marvell's *Clarendon's Housewarming* (1667) and Swift's *The Fable of Midas* (1712) have immediate practical objects; Rochester's *On Poet Ninny* (wr. 1677) and the Dean's "elegy" for Marlborough (wr. 1722) do not. A number of satires include mockery but are *defensive* rather than *offensive* in their essential nature, though satiric defense is not a category to which critics have paid much attention. In *True-Born Englishman*, Defoe targets William's enemies but champions the king he perceives as the Protestant savior of England. Works designed to endorse and support the status quo, however vigorously they denounce its opponents, are different in kind from those merely intended to diminish, derogate, or expose the satiric targets.

Other possibilities exist beyond malicious abuse, propaganda, and defense. Satirists often write less to ridicule a target than to vent spleen—see Tutchin's *Pindarick Ode, in the Praise of Folly and Knavery* (1696) and other querulous responses to William and his expensive wars. The same could be said of Gay's censorious second series of *Fables* (pub. posthumously in 1738) and Smollett's *Adventures of an Atom* (1769). Some social and political satirists agitate for change (Southerne's *The Wives' Excuse*), while others glumly survey a rotten society (Congreve's *The Way of the World*). Satirists are not always trying to accomplish anything beyond provocation or complaint. Some invite audience members to contemplate serious problems if they are so inclined, as in Vanbrugh's *The Relapse* (1696) or *The Provok'd Wife* a year later. Social satire can be toothless entertainment. Something like Ward's *A Walk to Islington* (1701) would almost certainly have worked differently for different audiences: those who belong to the world being mocked could enjoy the familiarity of the account without taking serious offense; outsiders are likely to have snickered at the satiric depiction of rackety London life. Alternatively, social criticism can be sober or shrill or heavy handed (as in Fielding's *Amelia*). *A Walk to Islington* seems designed to please readers, *Amelia* to provoke and disturb them. Any useful system of taxonomy must be polyvalent. In terms of motive, Rochester's "scepter" lampoon, Ward's *The London Spy*, Swift's responses to Steele, Fielding's *The Historical Register, For the Year 1736*, and Churchill's *The Times* (for example) have virtually nothing in common.

A remarkable number of satires are primarily positive rather than negative in their apparent agendas. Shadwell and Steele produce didactic plays whose purpose is less to condemn the bad than to uphold the good. In *Joseph Andrews* and *Tom Jones*, Fielding affectionately satirizes essentially decent characters; Tom is a full-blooded young man capable of folly and imprudence, but he is also a positive model. So is Belcour in Cumberland's *The West Indian* (1771), a play that stresses the educability of its tenderhearted scapegrace. In these works, the aim of satiric critique is decidedly not punitive. Authors of distributive justice satire gently correct targets with whom they sympathize, and they assume an audience receptive to instruction by example: readers and viewers can identify with the good-natured but fallible protagonists, and they are invited to apply the lessons to themselves. Defoe is capable of direct denunciation, but he too mostly conceives of satire as an educative business, meant more for the benefit of the audience than for the punishment of the target. Like a number of satirists in the first fifteen years of the eighteenth century, Defoe writes a lot of monitory satire, evidently designed to heighten awareness among readers whom he wants to help. His *The Shortest-Way with the Dissenters* (1702), several of Maynwaring's verse satires, Arbuthnot's *The Art of Political Lying* (1712), and Swift's *Mr. C[olli]ns's Discourse of Free-Thinking, Put into plain English* (1713) all issue warnings of one sort or another and make a point about the dangers of credulity. A surprising number of satires in the long eighteenth century are better defined by what they support than by what they defame. Howard and Buckingham's *The Country Gentleman* (banned in 1669) ridicules real-life individuals and types, but it also takes a fervently positive pro-Country position in both lifestyle and politics. Though Marvell goes after Samuel Parker in *The Rehearsal Transpros'd* (1672), his principal concern is to defend religious toleration and to put down a prominent opponent of same. This is satiric advocacy rather than condemnation, written *for* a cause as much as *against* a variety of targets. The degree to which satire can be a *positive* enterprise has been greatly underestimated.

One needs to appreciate just how various this material is, in terms of tone, presentation of positives, and degree of authorial animus. Critics have usually been content to define the aims of satire as either punitive or reformative, but satiric motives differ quite dizzyingly. Table E.1 is an attempt to display some of this heterogeneity. This list of satiric modes is by no means exhaustive, but it does suggest the range and diversity of possibilities in the realm of motive. Purposive detraction and routine mockery of sitting ducks are disparate enterprises; we need to make distinctions.

I must emphasize that there are limits to what motive tells us. Many of the works surveyed in this book could be satisfactorily categorized under the headings and subheadings I have listed here, but quite a lot of satires "do" more than one thing or can be taken differently by different readers or viewers. Where does *The Country-Wife* (1675) belong in this grid? Critics have read the play as a harsh satire on violations of sociomoral codes, as a distributive justice satire, as a celebration of libertinism, and as mere Cloud Cuckooland entertainment without any moral point at all. What one finds in Wycherley's satire and how one labels it depend very heavily on the assumptions one brings to it.[3] Satirists sometimes write for entirely personal reasons, and the results are unlikely to fit at all well in pigeonholes generated from even a very broad survey— see *The Rape of the Lock* and *Verses on the Death of Dr. S[wift]*. Under what single heading would *A Tale of a Tub*, *Gulliver's Travels*, *Trivia*, and *The Beggar's Opera* fall? Gay's much-celebrated ballad opera evidently provided simple entertainment for the many people prepared to ignore its cynical message; for those who are not, it might function as a seriously thought-provocative piece of social and political commentary.

The many modes of satire

Harsh Derogation
morally outraged (Brome, *The Satyr of Money*; Otway, *Friendship in Fashion*)
splenetic (Tutchin, *The British Muse*; Smollett, *The Adventures of an Atom*)
abusive (Cleveland, *The Rebell Scot*; Swift, *The Virtues of Sid Hamet the Magician's Rod*)
general political commentary (Macklin, *The Man of the World*)
specific political commentary (*The Fall of Mortimer*)
purposive attack on an individual (Buckingham, *Aduice to a Paynter*)
defense of the status quo (Dryden, *Absalom and Achitophel*; Samuel Johnson, *The False Alarm*)

Mockery and Ridicule
triumphalism (various *Rump Songs*)
negative cheerleading (Arbuthnot, *History of John Bull*)
personal derision (Shadwell, *The Sullen Lovers*)
mean-spirited entertainment (Pope, the 1728 *Dunciad*; Foote's personations)

Preachment
moral denunciation (Shadwell, *A True Widow*; Smollett, *Advice*)
performance of preachment (Churchill, *The Times?*)
ethical sermonizing (Pope, *Epistles to Several Persons*)

Entertainment (little or no authorial animus)
literary performance (Churchill, *The Ghost*)
drollery/lightweight social commentary (*Musarum Deliciae*)
comic narrative (Ward, *The Rambling Rakes*)
burlesque (Carey, *The Dragon of Wantley*; Garrick, *Ragandjaw*)
humorous presentation of standard butts (Ravenscroft, *The London Cuckolds*)

Polemic/Ideological Critique
political propaganda (Swift, *The Publick Spirit of the Whigs*)
religiopolitical argumentation (Defoe, *Jure Divino*)
social (Mandeville, *The Fable of the Bees*)

Provocation of Thought (undercutting readers' or viewers' confidence in what they know or
    believe)
social (Farquhar, *The Beaux Stratagem*)
epistemological (Rochester, *Upon Nothinge*; Sterne, *Tristram Shandy*)
philosophical (Prior, *Alma*)
monitory (Defoe, *The Shortest-Way*; Arbuthnot, *The Art of Political Lying*)

Exemplary Satire and Sympathy
presentation of an ideal (Steele, *The Conscious Lovers*)
didactic (Dodsley, *The King and the Miller of Mansfield*)
affectionate critique (Fielding, *Joseph Andrews*)
distributive justice (Fielding, *Tom Jones*; Sheridan, *The School for Scandal*)
cautionary (Bunyan, *The Life and Death of Mr. Badman*)

Another problem is that similarly motivated works can have quite different effects. "Provocation" more or less describes Rochester's motive in *Upon Nothinge* and the *Satyre against Reason and Mankind*, but it applies just as well to the distinctly cheerful *Tristram Shandy*. Provocative works such as Defoe's *The Shortest-Way*, Mandeville's *The Fable of the Bees*, Swift's *The Lady's Dressing Room*, and Hogarth's *Marriage A-la-Mode* (to name just a few) need to be distinguished from punitive, judgment-passing satires—but they hardly represent kindred ventures. Emphasizing a single factor in attempting to categorize eighteenth-century satire proves distortive and dangerously reductive in a large number of cases. If we privilege content above all else, then we can imagine that *The Tragedy of Tragedies*, *Peri Bathous*, and the last *Dunciad* somehow go together as high-minded cultural satires in a "Scriblerian" mode, but their strikingly different tones should tell us otherwise. Overmuch focus on form leads to the conclusion that *The Dispensary* serves as a bridge from *Mac Flecknoe* to *The Rape of the Lock*. Favoring motive at the expense of other factors is just as unwise: *The Dragon of Wantley* (1737) is not really "like" *Ragandjaw* (privately perf. 1746), whatever the similarities in the deflationary impulses behind them, and Shadwell's moralizing *A True Widow* (1678) likewise has little in common with Smollett's Juvenalian *Advice* (1746). Investigating authorial motive is clearly no panacea in trying to categorize satires, but we need to realize that these works are variously motivated and often variously executed. The audience being appealed to differs, as does the nature of the appeal.

Some readers might wonder at this point whether any cohesion is to be found in "Tory" or "Whig" modes of eighteenth-century satire. Following Bredvold's "The Gloom of the Tory Satirists" (1949) students of eighteenth-century satire have often spoken in terms of a "Tory mode" dominated by Dryden, Pope, Swift, Gay, and Johnson. Tory satire as posited by Bredvold is marked by gloom—though the gloom is not profoundly philosophical or religious but is instead "a mundane darkness conjured up by human folly and knavery." Bredvold also stressed "the practical intent" of the Tory satire, written by men who "were in the mêlée, not above it, and who wrote with the conviction that they were dealing battle-blows to save from extinction the virtue and glory of England."[4] I see a number of problems with this argument. For one thing, Pope (unlike Swift) mostly does *not* seem eager to enter the fray. For another, Swift's political identity has been much debated (was he an Old Whig? a moderate Tory? a Jacobite?); unless one wishes simply to brand him a Tory by association, his case has to be treated with care. A third reservation: one can grant that Pope and Swift were unhappy about Walpole and about directions in which English society was moving, but that is hardly a unique feature of their satire. The long eighteenth century is full of occasions in which a particular group reacts to changes in the socio- or religio-political situation with alarm, frustration, or despair. The dissenters were terrified about what might become of them under Anne; Defoe routinely gives voice to his awareness (and fear) of human knavery. Dryden's Williamite satire reflects Bredvold's Tory characteristics, but what of the Dryden responsible for *Absalom and Achitophel*? Carolean Dryden is as politically conservative as they come—but also a great believer in progress. Bredvold does not say much about Dryden, though most literary critics see him as the major precursor to the Bredvoldian Tory satire so dominant in our account of the eighteenth century.

What of the Whig tradition in satire? The strongest advocate of paying more attention to Whig writers in our accounts of the late seventeenth and early eighteenth centuries is Abigail Williams, who complains, not without justice, that critical preference for Swift, Pope, Gay, Goldsmith, and Johnson has meant that Whig poets prominent in their day have been vastly underappreciated in ours.[5] My own view is that the Whig "culture" is an identifiable phenomenon but that it is broadly ideological and does not equate tidily with satiric practice. Assuming an absolute division between Whigs and Tories in the realm of sociocultural controversy does not tend to work: "'Whigs' and 'Tories' had so interpenetrated both artistically and socially that their political identities hardly mattered when faced with what they mutually perceived to be vulgar upstarts and terrible poetry."[6] If one is looking to draw thematic parallels, then of course like-minded satirists tend to write about similar subjects and from broadly consonant points of view. My concern has been to characterize and categorize the nature of the satiric enterprises, but no very good correlation is to be found among the writers we think of as Whigs or Tories. Party affiliation, important though it is to content, does not seem to generate responses belonging to a particular mode. A larger question is whether satire is in its nature essentially conservative or subversive. The answer, from my point of view, is neither: at any moment in the long eighteenth century, we can find both defenses and fierce denunciations of the status quo.

Satiric motives and modes vary in dauntingly messy ways, and for that reason we should resist demands for a totalized characterization of "eighteenth-century satire" in its entirety. I grant that one can apply a label ("Augustan," "Scriblerian") without insisting on total homogeneity and that my predecessors do not—would not—claim that Dryden *is* Swift or that Pope *is* Johnson. But conclusions about how satire operates and about the features of eighteenth-century satire tend to be overly simplistic and reductive. The fact is that trying to grasp satire in England from 1658 to 1770 while also appreciating the large and small disparities among the works is almost impossible. One can easily feel defeated by the sheer plenitude of variegated phenomena. But the response to that disconcertment should not be to blunt distinctions and impose order on the whole but to look at the more orderly parts of that whole and see what we can learn from them.

II. Remapping English Satire, 1658–1770

The material covered in this book is easier to understand if we take it in subperiods. In the beginnings and endings of the five survey chapters, I attempt to clarify and characterize the subperiods represented by those chapters and to distinguish them from the others. I will not repeat those discussions at length here, but let me offer a very brief (and necessarily somewhat crude) précis. The Carolean satire covered in chapter 3 is remarkable in its intensity, its energy, its particularity. Dominant in the reign of Charles II are personal lampoons, high-heat political invectives, and serious commentaries on increasingly dire sociopolitical circumstances; never again are those types so conspicuous, and never again do we find so few examples of abstract moral preachment or generalized denunciation of man. Satire at the end of the seventeenth century (chapter 4) is tamer and blander, at least in verse; the most forceful satires are those written for the stage, many critiquing very real social problems.

In the first quarter of the eighteenth century (chapter 5), "satire" comprises an astounding variety of distinct kinds, especially during the reign of Anne. In those years and only those years does monitory satire flourish. Here and only here do we find a concentration of difficult, sober, argumentative satires. Works like Defoe's *Jure Divino* and Arbuthnot's *Art of Political Lying* demand a lot of the reader; they are densely polemical in ways far removed from invective and lampoonery. In the period 1726–1745 (chapter 6), satire moves in two drastically different directions. Most of the works are either negatively judgmental (whether playfully undermining, sharply attacking, or somberly denouncing the target) or positive and sympathetic, educative rather than punitive. Straightforward cultural-cum-political critique looms large, much larger than at any other point in the long eighteenth century. Satire does not die in the twenty years or so after the deaths of Pope and Swift (chapter 7), but it does fragment. Satire in the 1750s and 1760s is on the whole much harder to characterize than in the previous subperiods. Nonpoliticized verse satire is more poetic than practically purposive; politicized verse satire is propagandistic and has some affinities with what we find in earlier chapters, but it is also a rarity. Dramatic satire can include gushy sentimentalism that mildly rebukes essentially likable people, as well as playful mockery, trenchant sociopolitical critique, and a variety of things in between. Satire in fiction is mostly diluted by plot and characters, but Smollett's morally outraged cynicism is not Lennox's substantive social commentary—and where does *Tristram Shandy* fit? This is not "chaos": it is multidirectionality, resulting from both literary and extraliterary changes, and it is unique to this subperiod. Practice at any given time is far from uniform, but if we take the material subperiod by subperiod, we find that patterns and clusters emerge that do make a good deal of sense.

What does recognizing the heterogeneity of the whole and the importance of subperiods tell us? The broadest conclusion is simply that, with all due respect to the enormous virtues of my predecessors, the explicit and implicit history found in past accounts is often quite misleading. Earlier scholars did not have the ready access to printed primary materials that we now enjoy, and using the new evidence leads us to some startling conclusions. I have been making a set of negative arguments throughout this book:

(1) We cannot use our favorite authors to characterize eighteenth-century satire. For literary scholars of the long eighteenth century, "satire" mostly means Dryden, Swift, and Pope, and other satirists get measured by the distance by which they failed to write *Gulliver's Travels* or *An Epistle to Arbuthnot*. Appreciating great works is good, but constructing a history that erases the contexts of these works is not. Without denying the possibilities of influence—whether in terms of emulation of or reaction against a predecessor—the fact remains that each of the major writers inhabits a particular satiric milieu. Some of these authors seem oddly disconnected from or irrelevant to that milieu (Pope in the first quarter of the eighteenth century is the best example), and some of them clearly belong to it and reflect its trends. Swift's early eighteenth-century satire shows tremendous range; he operates in different modes, many of which we find variously replicated among his contemporaries. Even when the writers "fit" their moments, we should not suppose that they typify the practice of the time: the full spread of what goes on in any given year or decade is not going to be demonstrated in the output of *any* single satirist.

(2) To assume some kind of organic development from Dryden to Swift to Pope to Fielding (and so on) and try to explain them in relation to one another is an essentially delusory enterprise. One can see where the impression of connectivity comes from: if one plucks out major canonical works and lays them side by side in glorious isolation, one tends to focus on their commonalities and to emphasize the correspondences among them. But how much does *Absalom and Achitophel* actually have to do with *A Tale of a Tub* or *Gulliver's Travels*, let alone Pope's Horatian imitations or *The Beggar's Opera*? Are these works really part of the same venture? Only very broadly and loosely, if that. What I have been arguing for is in part the restoration of writers to their (narrowly defined) "moments." Take characterizations of Dryden. In satire studies he is almost universally dealt with on the basis of two poems, which do not typify his output as a satirist and do not have much in common with each other. Trying to connect these works with any later canonical writer, if we wish to get beyond generalizations about the mock heroic, is hard going. We need to remember that the author of *Mac Flecknoe* is not producing the first installment of Augustan satire but is operating in the milieu of Carolean satire. From any account of satire yet written, one would get only a limited view of Dryden. He has been thoroughly sanitized, and he often comes across as dry, dull, and impersonal. But *Mac Flecknoe* is a dirty smear, and Dryden is having fun writing it. He can be bawdy, mean, and passionate, and he

has astonishing range. His practice of satire also changes beyond recognition in the 1690s. Carolean Dryden is aggressive, self-assured, and judgmental; under William he becomes indirect, subversive, and conscious of his own satiric impotence.

(3) Though we find thematic or typological clusters from subperiod to subperiod, we cannot really even speak of a "Carolean mode," much less a "Restoration mode," or of an early eighteenth-century mode. Within some of the chapters here—especially 3 and 5—we find significant changes. The complaints of the 1660s are not the sour criticisms of the early 1670s or the heated, terrified protests of 1678–1681. For a Cavalier to grumble about not being properly rewarded for his loyalty is one thing; for Dryden and other Tories to express dire concern with the fate of the country is something else again. The experimentation with irony and the difficult satires of Anne's reign would not have been written in 1700 or in 1720—they are a relatively short-lived phenomenon.

(4) There is no such thing as "eighteenth-century English satire," at least not as a unitary concept. Taken as a whole, this material is messy, confused, and discontinuous. It comprises a vast amount of material that appears in a variety of genres and subgenres; it comes in all sizes and shapes. Readers and viewers surely had preferences, but "satire" must have had a wide array of connotations for them. Satirists conceived of satire in very different ways, carrying out their enterprises for any number of reasons and for very different audiences.

These conclusions are pointing toward limitations and problems rather than toward positive insights, but they are not unproductive. We need to understand what a literary history cannot do—and why—before we can understand what it *can* do or should best try to do. David Perkins has argued that anyone operating in this realm faces a peculiar dilemma: "We must perceive a past age as relatively unified if we are to write literary history," but "we must perceive it as highly diverse if what we write is to represent it plausibly."[7] I have been arguing that in fact unity—especially implausible unity—is neither desirable nor helpful in a literary history of eighteenth-century English satire. What does a new and more plausible literary history, one based on diversity, look like?

One of the most positive conclusions of this study has huge implications for the nature of the kind of history we can write. That conclusion is simply this: *the dominant kinds of satire practiced at any point in the 1658–1770 period change—and often they do so rapidly and radically.* Carolean manuscript lampoons spring from a different world than the printed satires of the 1690s. The reign of Anne is not the reign of George I, let alone that of George II. To pick a work from the early 1680s, another from the early 1700s, and third from the late 1720s and lump them under a single heading is bad historical practice. Their sociopolitical worlds are just not the same. A certain amount of generalized social satire can be found throughout this period, but for a huge number of works, famous ones included, circumstances are the driving force. Reading and analyzing a lot of satires—and attending to the particular contexts whence they come—makes clear that there was no such thing as a dominant "Augustan mode."[8]

We need to remember what we are writing a history *of*. The preceding survey provides a history of *practice*, not a history of a single object or genre. "Satire" is not a coherent subject out of which a narrative can be made. That what one finds in this realm are wildly varied exemplars should be obvious from the survey chapters. Equally clear is the fact that significant connectives from work to work across the totality of the period at issue are not to be found. We cannot use the concept of a unified "mode" to organize our history. What I have been arguing is that we need to try to understand what generates the particular exempla that form the eighteenth-century satiric corpus. Individual works mostly do not—or not only—originate in a desire to take part in a grand tradition but are part of a reaction to immediate circumstances. Classical imitators like Pope and Johnson are operating in a recognizable tradition, but Pope's Horatian imitations are very much a product of the 1730s. Appealing to the classical tradition enriches interpretation in a variety of ways, but the *point* of the satire has largely to do with Pope's response to the events and frustrations of his own day. Most satire is circumstantial, written by and for people in the here and now.

Explication of almost all of the pieces covered in this survey—including the headliners—tends to be more effective if the explicator appeals to immediate contexts rather than to the masterpieces that form the rest of the eighteenth-century canon. *Absalom and Achitophel* is best understood as an Exclusion Crisis satire; *The Dunciad* is a product of the reign of Walpole; *The Rosciad* means more, in satiric terms, if one is thinking of the 1760s than if one is thinking of Churchill's inheritance from Pope. I see no particular reason that a piece written in, say, 1710 should have any formal relationship to one composed a generation later. If a satire belongs to a reasonably clear-cut genre, one can in some cases hypothesize (or even prove) the influence of earlier works upon later. If one is talking about 1690s social comedy, one can say that Congreve was Southerne's protégé and that Vanbrugh was familiar with the plays of both of them; they do not control what he does, though we can identify some evidence of impact. But where we have works in different genres, with how much certainty can we demonstrate influence? Can we say for sure what Fielding learned from Pope and Swift? Only if we rely on generalizations that may or may not be true and are certainly not provable. To claim that each of them mocked "low" cultural forms is fair enough—but that is not a feature of Popean satire as much as a vogue in the late 1720s and 1730s. Possibly Pope and Swift initiated the fad, but probably they did not. Writing satire does not always represent a literary activity carried out by people conscious of working in and adapting a tradition.

We need to appreciate two cruxes: (1) the material whose history I have been try-ing to write is astonishingly varied, and (2) immediate circumstances are vital to our understanding of individual pieces. The result is that a biological or evolutionary nar-rative will not work. My history is descriptive and analytic, an attempt to show what is there and to demonstrate when (and insofar as possible to explain why) satiric practice changed. "Satire" is a hydra-headed phenomenon, not a single definable entity in the process of readily traceable change; it is not legitimately treatable in its own terms, in isolation from its contexts. That satire is both a heterogeneous and a circumstantial mode makes for much complexity and even confusion—though we should remember that they are also part of the reason the great age of satire is so remarkable and so rich, so eminently worth our attention.

What I have been telling is not a "story" marked by development and sequential association. Sorting this material into a single narrative is not really possible, but this does not mean that we are simply left with disorder and incoherence, that lacking cohesion and connectivity we can offer nothing. "History-writing is not story-telling but problem solving," says David Hackett Fischer. "Sometimes the solution takes the form of a story. But often . . . a different kind of explanation-strategy is adopted" (xii). What I am offering is an "explanation-strategy" not cast in the form of a grand narrative.

The principal job of literary history is to represent what has come before. Someone wishing to provide a cohesive, developmental narrative can do so, but only by drop-ping much of the evidence out of sight and imagining or manufacturing connections, many of which are probably nonexistent or at least not provable. The story of "Augus-tan satire" from Dryden to Sterne has been told often enough, and the contention of this book is that there is no such story to tell. This does not mean we cannot represent eighteenth-century English satire. The true history of satire in its great age is not a history—it is a series of discontinuous little histories. These little histories (each what Lyotard calls a "*petit récit*") are complex but coherent, and though they are quite dif-ferent from each other, they can be read alongside one another in highly productive ways.[9] From them the bigger picture of eighteenth-century satiric practice emerges. If we want a history of that practice that is both comprehensible and plausible, then we must take it bit by bit.

The two broadest truths about eighteenth-century satiric practice are that it is highly diverse at all times and that it changes with bewildering speed from decade to decade. Both of them stem from the fact that satire is largely generated in response to its immediate circumstances. Eighteenth-century satire is not a matter of a dozen masterpieces that together exemplify a single mode; it is not a distinct literary form that develops apart from the world in which it was produced. Cherry-picking sources, treating them in generic and circumstantial isolation, and discovering tidy connectives between them is never wise, but in satire its results are particularly misleading. Literary critics are fond of asserting that the best satire transcends its moment, but satire is by and large a topical form, and the "moment" profoundly influences what satirists produce and why they produce it. Far more than the study of comedy, tragedy, lyric poetry, or fiction, the study of satire, especially satire in its greatest age, demands that we situate ourselves in the historical and generic contexts from which satires spring.

Standard Price Categories and Sample Titles

Where the price given comes from *The Luttrell File*—reflecting what Luttrell paid but not necessarily list price—I have marked the entry with an asterisk (*). Where the price comes from an advertisement, I have used a dagger (†), and where it comes from *The Term Catalogues*, I use a double dagger (‡). Otherwise, the price is given internally (usually on the work's title page, though sometimes listed on the half title or last page). For each category, I give the range of approximate value in present-day terms, using Hume's multipliers (two hundred to three hundred times the original price). Figures greater than about £10 are rounded to the nearest pound. Some titles are abbreviated here but are given in full in the bibliography.

1*d* [80 pence–£1.20]

An Excellent New Ballad between Tom the Tory, and Toney the Whigg (1678); 1/2°; 1 p.*
A Dialogue between Duke Lauderdale and the Lord Danby (1679/80); 1/2°; 2 pp.*
The Deliquium (1680?); 1/2°; 2 pp.*
The Devil Pursued: or, the Right Saddle Laid upon the Right Mare (1680); 1°; broadside.*
The Essex Ballad (1680); 1°; broadside.*
A Loyal Satyr against Whiggism (1682); 2°; 4 pp.*
[Arthur Maynwaring], *The King of Hearts* (1690); 2°; 5 pp.*
[Tom Brown], *A Satyr upon the French King* (1697); 1/2°; broadside.*
[Maynwaring?], *An Address to Our Sovereign Lady* (1704); 1/2°; broadside.*
The Dog in the Wheel (1705); 4°; 16 pp.*
The Long Vacation (1708); 8°; 16 pp.
[Joseph Browne], *The Circus: Or, British Olympicks* (1709); 8°; 16 pp.
[Defoe?], *A Letter to Mr. Bisset* (1709); 8°; 16 pp.
O Tempora! or a Satyr on the Times (1710?); 8°; 8 pp.
The Save-Alls (1710); 1/2°; 2 pp.*
[Swift], *The Fable of Midas* (1711); 1/2°; 2 pp.†
[Swift], *T[o]l[a]nd's Invitation to Dismal, to Dine with the Calves-Head Club* (1712); 1/2°; broadside.*

2*d* [£1.60–£2.40]

[Dryden], *Mac Flecknoe* (pub. 1682); 4°; 16 pp.*
[John Tutchin], *The Tribe of Levi* (1691); 8°; 16 pp.*

[Ned Ward], *A Walk to Islington* (1699); 8°; 16 pp.

Korath: or the Danger of Schism (1705); 4°; 8 pp.

The Republican Bullies Or, a sham Battel between two of a side (1705); 4°; 8 pp.

Bess o' Bedlam's Love to her Brother Tom (1709); 8°; 24 pp. (2nd ed. gives price)

[Swift], *A Meditation upon a Broom-stick* (1710); 8°; 16 pp.

[John Arbuthnot], *John Bull In His Senses* (part two of "John Bull"; 1712); 8°; 16 pp.

3d [£2.40–£3.60]

[Thomas Shadwell], *The Tory-Poets* (1682); 4°; 20 pp.*

[Richard Ames], *The Female Fire-Ships* (1691); 4°; 24 pp.*

A Search after Wit (1691); 4°; 24 pp.*

[Ward], *The Quack-Vintners* (1711); 8°; 24 pp.*

[Arbuthnot], *The Art of Political Lying* (1712); 8°; 24 pp.†

[Arbuthnot], *Law is a Bottomless-Pit* (part 1 of "John Bull"; 1712); 8°; 24 pp.

Brooke and Hellier (1712); 8°; 32 pp.† (Luttrell: *4d*)

[Thomas Brereton], *Charnock's Remains: Or, S[acheverel] his Coronation* (1713); 8°; 24 pp.

A Satyr upon Old Maids (1713); 4°; 12 pp.*

[Swift], *The First Ode of the Second Book of Horace Paraphras'd* (1713); 4°; 12 pp.

[Pope], *A Full . . . Account of a Horrid . . . Revenge by Poison, On the Body of Mr. Edmund Curll* (1716); 2°; 6 pp.

The Hell-Fire-Club (1721); 8°; 24 pp.

Belsize-House (1722); 8°; 32 pp.

British Worthies: or, Characters of the Age (1758); 8°; 15 pp.

4d [£3.20–£4.80]

R.D., *A Satyr against Satyrs: or, St. Peter's Vision Transubstantiated* (1680); 4°; 34 pp.*

Mercurius Menippeus . . . or, Hudibras in Prose (1682); 4°; 26 pp.*

[Ames], *Sylvia's Revenge* (1688); 4°; 32 pp.*

[Ames], *The Folly of Love* (1691); 4°; 32 pp.*

A Satyr against Painting (1697); 2°; 12 pp.*

[John Dennis?], *The Reverse: Or, The Tables Turn'd* (1700); 2°; 12 pp.*

A Satyr against Dancing (1702); 2°; 12 pp.*

[Defoe], *A Hymn to the Pillory* (1703); 8°; 16 pp.*

A Hymn to Money (1704); 8°; 28 pp.*

The Swan Tripe-Club in Dublin (1706); 4°; 20 pp.

[Arbuthnot], *John Bull Still In His Senses* (part three of "John Bull"; 1712); 8°; 32 pp.

[Swift], *Mr. C[olli]ns's Discourse of Free-Thinking, Put into plain English* (1713); 8°; 32 pp.

[Thomas Tickell], *An Imitation of the Prophecy of Nereus* (1715); 2°; 8 pp.†

A Satyr upon the Present Times (1717); 8°; 20 pp.

The Dancing-Master (1722); 8°; 20 pp.

The Citizen's Procession, or, the Smugler's Success and the Patriots Disappointment (1733); 2°; 8 pp.

6d [£4.80–£7.20]

[Dryden], *The Medall* (1682); 4°; 32 pp.*

[Ames], *The Search after Claret* (1691); 4°; 24 pp.*

Dryden, *Eleonora* (1692); 4°; 32 pp.*

[Ames], *Fatal Friendship; or, the Drunkards Misery* (1693); 4°; 32 pp.*

Tutchin, *A Pindarick Ode, in the Praise of Folly and Knavery* (1696); 4°; 22 pp.

[Ward], *A Trip to Jamaica* (1698); 2°; 16 pp. [advertised in other Ward works].

[Defoe], *The Pacificator* (1700); 2°; 16 pp.*

The Shoe-Maker Beyond his Last (1700); 2°; 16 pp.†

[Ward], *Labour in Vain, or, What Signifies Little or Nothing* (1700); 4°; 32 pp.†

[Ward], *The Rambling Rakes; or, London Libertines* (1700); 2°; 16 pp. [advertised in other Ward works].

Hob turn'd Courtier (1703); 2°; 16 pp. [advertised in other Ward works].

The Monster: Or, The World turn'd Topsy Turvy (1705); 4°; 24 pp.

Mirth in Ridicule: or, a Satyr against Immoderate Laughing (1708); 4°; 24 pp.

Deal in an Uproar (1713); 2°; 12 pp.

[Defoe], *Reasons against the Succession of the House of Hanover* (1713); 8°; 48 pp.

John Dunton, *King-Abigail: or, The Secret Reign of the She-Favourite* (1715); 8°; 32 pp.

Richard Savage, *The Convocation: or, a Battle of Pamphlets* (1717); 8°; 36 pp.

Human Passions . . . To which is added, An Ode to Impudence (1726); 2°; 12 pp.

[Fielding], *The Masquerade* (1728); 4°; 20 pp.

[Savage], *An Author to be Lett* (1729); 4°; 20 pp.†

Claudian's Rufinus: or, the Court-Favourite's Overthrow (1730); 8°; 32 pp.

[Fielding], *Tom Thumb* (1730); 8°; 24 pp.

[Swift], *A Libel on D[r] D[elany], and a Certain Great Lord* (1730); 8°; 32 pp.

[Arbuthnot], *A Brief Account of Mr. John Ginglicutt's Treatise Concerning the . . . Scolding of the Ancients* (1731); 8°; 30 pp.†

The City Triumphant: or, the Burning of the Excise-Monster (1733); 2°; 8 pp.

The Counterpart to the State-Dunces (1733); 2°; 10 pp.

The Neuter: or, a Modest Satire on the Poets of the Age (1733); 2°; 8 pp.

The Wooden Age (1733); 2°; 10 pp.

[Henry Carey], *The Tragedy of Chrononhotonthologos* (1734); 8°; 32 pp.

The Fair Thinker, or Reason Asserted: in a Dissection of Bigottry and Devotion (1740); 8°; 36 pp.

A Satirical Epistle to Mr. Pope (1740); 2°; 8 pp.

Fontenoy, A New Satiric Ballad (1745); 2°; 8 pp.

Ranelagh House (1747); 8°; 32 pp.

The Monosyllable If! (1748); 2°; 10 pp.†

John Taperell, *Swearing* (1751); 8°; 24 pp.

[John Hill], *The Smartiad* (1753); 2°; 8 pp. [advertised in *The London Magazine*; ECCO].

Patriotism! A Farce. As is acted by his Majesty's Servants (1763); 8°; 41 pp.

The Court and City Medley; or, Political Shaver (1764); 4°; 34 pp.† [advertised as "price only 6*d*"]

10*d* [£8–£12]

Behn, *The Widdow Ranter* (1690); 4°; 64 pp.*

Congreve, *The Old Batchelour* (1693); 4°; 68 pp.*

1*s* [£10–£15]

Shadwell, *The Sullen Lovers* (1668); 4°; 112 pp.‡

[Buckingham], *The Rehearsal* (1672); 4°; 60 pp.‡

Wycherley, *The Country-Wife* (1675); 4°; 108 pp.‡

Etherege, *The Man of Mode* (1676); 4°; 104 pp.‡

[Dryden], *Absalom and Achitophel* (1681); 2°; 38 pp.*

Dryden, *The Spanish Fryar* (1681); 4°; 94 pp.‡

[Dryden and Nahum Tate], *The Second Part of Absalom and Achitophel* (1682); 2°; 36 pp.*

[Multiple authors], *Commendatory Verses, on the Author of . . . the Satyr against Wit* (1700); 2°; 32 pp.*

[Defoe], *More Reformation* (1703); 4°; 60 pp.†

[Ward], *In Imitation of Hudibras. The Dissenting Hypocrite, or Occasional Conformist* (1704); 8°; 96 pp.

[Dunton], *The Pulpit-Fool* (1707); 4°; 72 pp.†

[Ward], *The Wooden World Dissected* (1707); 12°; 120 pp.†

[Luke Milbourne], *The Moderate Cabal* (1710); 8°; 64 pp.

Pope, *An Essay on Criticism* (1711); 4°; 48 pp.†

[Swift], *The Conduct of the Allies* (3rd ed.; 1711); 8°; 96 pp.†

Pope, *The Rape of the Lock* (1714 version); 8°; 56 pp.†

[Swift], *The Publick Spirit of the Whigs* (2nd ed.; 1714); 4°; 46 pp.

[Dunton?], *Mordecai's Memorial: or, There's Nothing done for him* (1716); 8°; 64 pp.

The Way of the Town: or, the Sham-Heiress (1717); 8°; 40 pp.

[Defoe?], *The Anatomy of Exchange-Alley* (1719); 8°; 66 pp.

[William Chetwood], *The Stock-Jobbers or, the Humours of Exchange-Alley* (1720); 8°; 48 pp.†

[Hugh] Chamberlen, *News from Hell: or, A Match for the Directors* (1721); 2°; 16 pp.

[Edward Young], *The Universal Passion. Satire II* (1725); 2°; 20 pp.†

Robin's Pathetick Tale (1727); 2°; 12 pp.

The Signal: or, a Satyr against Modesty (1727); 2°; 16 pp.

[Pope], *The Dunciad* (1728); 8°; 62 pp.†

Charles Forman, *Protesilaus: or, the Character of an Evil Minister* (1730); 8°; 62 pp.

[Fielding], *The Tragedy of Tragedies* (1731); 8°; 66 pp.

Verres and his Scribblers (1732); 8°; 80 pp.

[James Bramston], *The Man of Taste* (1733); 2°; 16 pp.

Pope, *The First Satire of the Second Book of Horace Imitated* (1733); 2°; 38 pp.†

[Swift], *On Poetry: A Rapsody* (1733); 2°; 28 pp.

[Paul Whitehead], *The State Dunces. Inscribed to Mr. Pope* (1733); 2°; 21 pp.

Pope, *An Epistle from Mr. Pope, to Dr. Arbuthnot* (1735); 2°; 24 pp.†

Discontent; or, an Essay on Faction (1736); 2°; 16 pp.

The Satirists: A Satire (1739?); 2°; 16 pp.

The State of Rome, under Nero and Domitian (1739); 2°; 18 pp.

Swift, *Verses on the Death of Dr. S[wift], D. S. P. D.* (1739); 2°; 20 pp.†

Laugh upon Laugh, or Laughter Ridicul'd (1740); 8°; 60 pp.

[McNamara Morgan], *The Causidicade* (1743); 4°; 32 pp.

William Whitehead, *An Essay on Ridicule* (1743); 2°; 20 pp.†

[John Brown], *An Essay on Satire: Occasion'd by the Death of Mr. Pope* (1745); 4°; 32 pp.

[Smollett], *Advice* (1746); 2°; 16 pp.

[Smollett], *Reproof* (1747); 2°; 14 pp.

Hogarth, *Beer Street* (1751) [some advertised for 1s 6d].†

Hogarth, *Gin Lane* (1751) [some advertised for 1s 6d].†

Richard Owen Cambridge, *A Dialogue between a Member of Parliament and His Servant* (1752); 4°; 28 pp.†

The Age of Dullness (1757); 4°; 27 pp.†

[Smollett], *The Reprisal: or, the Tars of Old England* (1757); 8°; 52 pp.

[David Garrick], *The Fribbleriad* (1761); 4°; 28 pp.

John Robinson, *Preferment* (1765); 4°; 22 pp.

Thomas Nevile, *The Fourteenth Satire of Juvenal Imitated* (1769); 4°; 18 pp.†

1s 6d [£15–£22]

[Brown?], *The Stage-Beaux toss'd in a Blanket* (1704); 4°; 76 pp.

[Susanna Centlivre], *The Basset-Table* (1705); 4°; 76 pp.

The General Cashier'd (1712); 4°; 72 pp.

The Comical Pilgrim; or, Travels of a Cynick Philosopher (1722); 8°; 112 pp.

[Defoe?], *Mere Nature Delineated* (1726); 8°; 128 pp.†

John Gay, *The Beggar's Opera* (1728); 8°; 64 pp.

[George Duckett], *Pope Alexander's Supremacy and Infallibility examin'd* (1729); 4°; 40 pp.

James Ralph, *The Fashionable Lady* (1730); 8°; 104 pp.

The Fall of Mortimer (1731); 8°; 68 pp.

Fielding, *The Modern Husband* (1732); 8°; 96 pp.

The Footman: An Opera (1732); 8°; 84 pp.

Fielding, *Pasquin* (1736); 8°; 72 pp.

[Fielding], *The Vernoniad* (1741); 4°; 40 pp.

Swift, *Directions to Servants* (1745); 8°; 96 pp.

George Alexander Stevens, *Distress upon Distress: or, Tragedy in True Taste* (1752); 8°; 100 pp.

[Allan Ramsay], *An Essay on Ridicule* (1753); 8°; 88 pp.†

The Devil upon Crutches in England, or Night Scenes in London (1755); 8°; 78 pp.†

A Satirical Review of the Manifold Falshoods . . . Hitherto publish'd concerning the Earthquake (1756); 8°; 96 pp.

Churchill, *The Rosciad* (2nd ed.; 1761); 8°; 23 pp.† [1st ed. printed in Dublin for 3*d*].

The Scrubs of Parnassus: or, All in the Wrong (1761); 4°; 37 pp.†

The Minister of State (1762); 4°; 38 pp.†

[Edward Burnaby Greene], *Friendship: A Satire* (1763); 4°; 32 pp.

The Triumph of Brutes, A Satire on this Caledonian Age (1763); 4°; 27 pp.

Liberty in the Suds; or, Modern Characters (1764); 4°; 24 pp.†

[Garrick], *The Sick Monkey* (1765); 4°; 28 pp.†

The Scourge (1765); 4°; 22 pp.†

George Caswall, *The Trifler* (1767); 4°; 28 pp.†

Liberty Deposed, or the Western Election (1768?); 8°; 58 pp.

Goldsmith, *Retaliation* (1774); 4°; 20 pp.†

2s [£20–£30]

Memoirs of the Court of Lilliput (1727); 8°; 168 pp.†

[Eliza Haywood], *The Adventures of Eovaai* (1736); 12°; 240 pp. [bound; 2*s* 6*d* bound in calf].†

[Corbyn Morris], *An Essay Towards Fixing the True Standards of Wit, Humour, Raillery, Satire, and Ridicule* (1744); 8°; 98 pp.†

[Thomas Warton], *New-Market* (1751); 2°; 18 pp.†

Christopher Smart, *The Hilliad* (1753); 4°; 49 pp.†

The Robin-Hood Society (1756); 8°; 112 pp.

[Edward Thompson], *The Meretriciad* (1761); 4°; 44 pp.

Folly, A Satire on the Times (1763?); 4°; 29 pp.

The Patriot Poet, A Satire (1764); 4°; 32 pp.†

[Evan Lloyd], *The Powers of the Pen* (1766); 4°; 45 pp.

2s 6d [£25–£37]

Whig and Tory: or Wit on both Sides (1712); 8°; 160 pp.† [bound; originally sold in 4
   separate pamphlets, 1710–11].

[Mary Davys], *The Accomplish'd Rake: or, Modern Fine Gentleman* (1727); 12°; 204 pp.
   [advertised in *The Monthly Catalogue*].

*Ranger's Progress: Consisting of a Variety of Poetical Essays, Moral, Serious, Comic, and
   Satyrical* (1760); 8°; 129 pp. [bound].†

Churchill, *The Prophecy of Famine* (1763); 4°; 32 pp.†

Churchill, *The Duellist* (1764); 4°; 50 pp.†

[Evan Lloyd], *The Methodist* (1766); 4°; 55 pp.†

[John Hall-Stevenson], *Makarony Fables; with the New Fables of the Bees* (1768); 4°; 58 pp.

3s [£30–£45]

[Delarivier Manley], *Secret Memoirs . . . Of several Persons of Quality . . . From the New
   Atalantis* (1709); 8°; 254 pp. [bound]†

Hogarth, *The Enraged Musician* (1741)†

[François Génard], *The School of Man . . . To which is prefixed, A Key to the Satyrical
   Characters Interspersed in this Work* (1753); 12°; 328 pp. [bound; sewed, 2s 6d].†

[John Slade], *The Transmigrating Soul; or, an Epitome of Human Nature* (1760); 12°; 257
   pp.†

3s 6d [£35–£52]

[Defoe?], *The Great Law of Subordination consider'd* (1724); 8°; 304 pp.

Young, *Love of Fame, The Universal Passion. In Seven Characteristical Satires* (1728); 8°; 188
   pp. [English ed.; advertised in *The Monthly Catalogue*].

4s [£40–£60]

[Swift], *A Tale of a Tub* (1704); 8°; 334 pp.‡

[Haywood], *Memoirs of a Certain Island Adjacent to the Kingdom of Utopia* (1725; with
   key); 8°; 298 pp.†

5s [£50–£75]

[Defoe?], *The Political History of the Devil* (1726); 8°; 316 pp.†

John Brown, *Essays on the Characteristics* (1751); 8°; 418 pp.†

[Christopher Anstey], *The New Bath Guide* (1766); 4°; 132 pp.†

[Sterne], *A Sentimental Journey through France and Italy* (1768); 8°; 2 vols. (242 pp. + 218
   pp.) [sewed].†

[Smollett], *Adventures of an Atom* (1769); 12°; 2 vols. (232 pp. + 191 pp.) [sewed].†

6s [£60–£90]

[Giles Jacob], *The Poetical Register: Or, the Lives . . . of the English Dramatick Poets* (1719–1720); 8°; 2 vols. (381 pp. + 376 pp.).†

[Fielding], *Joseph Andrews* (1742); 12°; 2 vols. (335 pp. + 310 pp.).†

[Smollett], *Roderick Random* (1748); 12°; 2 vols. (346 pp. + 380 pp.).†

[Charlotte Lennox], *The Female Quixote* (2nd ed.; 1752); 12°; 2 vols. (284 pp. + 319 pp.) [bound; sewed, 5s].†

[Smollett], *Ferdinand Count Fathom* (1753); 12°; 2 vols. (276 pp. + 325 pp.) [bound].†

[Goldsmith], *The Citizen of the World* (1762); 12°; 2 vols. (293 pp. + 257 pp.) [bound].†

[Goldsmith], *The Vicar of Wakefield* (1766); 12°; 2 vols. (210 pp. + 215 pp.) [bound; sewed, 5s].†

8s [£80–£120]

[John Shebbeare], *Letters on the English Nation* (1755); 8°; 2 vols. (295 pp. + 311 pp.) [bound; sewed, 7s].†

10s [£100–£150]

Smollett, *Travels through France and Italy* (1766); 8°; 2 vols. (376 pp. + 297 pp.) [bound].†

12s [£120–£180]

Hogarth, *Industry and Idleness* (1747).†

Fielding, *Tom Jones* (1749); 12°; 4 vols. (325 pp. + 342 pp. + 297 pp. + 359 pp.) [another edition advertised for 18s].†

[Smollett], *Peregrine Pickle* (1751); 12°; 4 vols. (296 pp. + 331 pp. + 308 pp. + 321 pp.) [bound; 10s 6d in boards].†

Fielding, *Amelia* (1751); 12°; 4 vols. (296 pp. + 270 pp. + 331 pp. + 302 pp.) [bound; 10s 6d in boards]†

15s [£150–£225]

[Defoe], *Jure Divino: A Satyr* (1706); 2°; 374 pp. in 12 parts [by subscription; pirated version, 5s].†

Hogarth, *Hudibras* illustrations (1726).†

Chapter 1 · Canonical and Noncanonical Satire, 1658–1770

1. Gill, *Cutting Edges*, ix.

2. Frye, *Anatomy of Criticism*, 224. Wendell V. Harris likewise concludes that "the essential ingredients of satire are humor, a target against which the humor is directed, and . . . an at least implicit ideal against which the target of the satire may be compared." *Dictionary of Concepts*, 358–359. See also Myers and Wukasch, *Dictionary of Poetic Terms*, 322–323; and Preminger and Brogan, *New Princeton Encyclopedia*, 1114–1117.

3. Morris, "American Satire," 377.

4. Connery and Combe, *Theorizing Satire*, 1; Test, *Satire*, 15.

5. Rosenheim, *Swift and the Satirist's Art*, 31.

6. Feinberg, *Introduction to Satire*, 258.

7. Griffin, *Satire*, 71.

8. Quintero, introduction to *Companion to Satire*, 1.

9. Olson, *Theory of Comedy*, 88–89.

10. Weinbrot, *Menippean Satire Reconsidered*, 2.

11. Fowler, *Kinds of Literature*, 110.

12. Dryden, *Discourse*, 4:41; *Kind Keeper*, 14:5; "The Authors Apology for Heroique Poetry," 12:89.

13. Kinservik, *Disciplining Satire*, 12.

14. The title page of this volume is dated 1693, but it actually appeared in October 1692.

15. *Poems on Affairs of State*, Yale edition, 5:xxvii. Hereafter *POAS-Y*.

16. Worcester, *Art of Satire*, 15.

17. Jack, *Augustan Satire*, x.

18. Bogel, *The Difference Satire Makes*, viii.

19. Seidel, "Satire, Lampoon, Libel, Slander," 33–57.

20. Hunter, "Political, Satirical, Didactic and Lyric Poetry," 204.

21. See Lord, *POAS-Y*, 1:xxvi.

22. I have not, for example, extended my research into the realms of woodcuts and almanacs, though there is certainly much satire to be found there.

23. Hume, "Economics of Culture." See pp. 490–492 for the difficulties of determining purchasing power of money.

24. Ibid., 492.

25. King, "Natural and Political Observations." Other major sources for such information are Vanderlint, *Money answers all Things* (1734) and Massie, *Calculations of the Present Taxes* (1761).

26. See especially Lindert and Williamson, "Revising England's Social Tables"; and Lindert and Williamson, "Reinterpreting Britain's Social Tables."

27. Hume, "Economics of Culture," 497.

28. St Clair, *The Reading Nation*, 42.

29. Love discusses the economics of manuscript production and circulation in *Scribal Publication*, 126–134.

30. St Clair, *The Reading Nation*, 26.

31. *The Third Volume of the Monthly Catalogue: being A General Register of Books . . . Printed and Published . . . in the Years 1727, and 1728* (1729). The advertisements for the *Miscellanies* are in no. 54 (March 1728, p. 26) and no. 50 (June 1727, p. 63).

32. Ward's individual pieces were almost all fairly cheap when sold singly (6*d* on average, or 1*s* for longer satires), but collections of his work were quite expensive. The complete *London Spy* is listed at 5*s* in 1703 (a second edition is advertised for the same price in 1704, and a fourth in 1711). The "second volume" of his works is (in 1704) also priced at 5*s*; the "fourth volume" is advertised for 6*s* in 1708. In 1713 *Nuptial Dialogues* (in 2 vols.; originally printed in 1710) goes for 10*s*.

33. *The Grub-street Journal*, no. 278 (24 April 1735).

34. McLaverty, *Pope, Print and Meaning*, 215.

35. Ibid., 216, 227. On Pope's subsequent octavos, see 231–241. *The General Evening Post* for 31 May 1743 (no. 1513) advertises several volumes of Pope's works at "underwritten Prices." The second volume of poetry is listed at 7*s* 6*d* in quarto and in a smaller format at 5*s*—previously priced, we are told, at £1 1*s* and 12*s*, respectively. Pope's *Iliad* (complete in six volumes), "formerly sold for 1*l*. 1*s*. per Vol. or 6*l*. 6*s*. the Whole," is now a sixth that price at £1 1*s*.

36. Richetti, *Life of Daniel Defoe*, 70, 61.

37. Furbank and Owens have provided the fullest account of the publishing history of Defoe's collected works in *Critical Bibliography*, 3–6.

38. The subscription price, as Furbank and Owens point out, was initially 10*s* (advertised in 1704); publication was delayed (for which Defoe was apologizing in the *Review* by January 1705), and when *Jure Divino* finally appeared, the price had risen to 15*s*. *Critical Bibliography*, 75–76.

39. *A Review of the State of the English Nation*, no. 87 (20 July 1706).

40. *The Satires of Decimus Junius Juvenalis* first appeared in October 1692. The ESTC reports a second edition in 1697, a fifth edition in 1726, and a sixth edition in 1735. The volume is published again in 1754.

41. Fludernik, review of *Satire, History, Novel*, 256.

42. Griffin, *Satire*, 190.

43. Eleven female satirists are cited in this book. Eight of them are included on the basis of fictional or dramatic works (Mrs. Aubert, Behn, Centlivre, Davys, Sarah Fielding, Haywood, Lennox, and Manley) and three because of verse (Egerton, Leapor, and Montagu). They are not all apolitical or nonaggressive—see Behn, Haywood, and Manley—but on the whole, sociomoral commentary and personal sparring are more prominent than political polemic.

44. Kupersmith, *Roman Satirists*, and Kupersmith, *English Versions of Roman Satire*.

45. See Haugen, "Imagined Universities"; and Money, *The English Horace*. Henderson, "Erudite Satire," is a thorough, careful investigation of satire by members of the universities or the Inns of Court and other learned writers.

46. See Orr, "Christopher Smart."

47. Fowler, *Kinds of Literature*, 38.

48. The dangers of broad overview are illustrated in Eric Rothstein's otherwise learned and judicious volume in *The Routledge History of English Poetry*. Rothstein divides a 120-year span in half, treating 1720 as an arbitrary break point. Within each sixty-year period works from different decades are promiscuously intermixed, obliterating subperiods and any sense of chronological change. See Rothstein, *Restoration and Eighteenth-Century Poetry*, chaps. 1 and 4.

49. For a discussion of this point, see Hume, "Construction and Legitimation," especially 648–649.

50. Crane, *Idea of the Humanities*, especially "Criticism as Inquiry" and "On Hypotheses in Historical Criticism" in vol. 2; Hume, *Reconstructing Contexts*; Hume, "Aims and Limits"; Hume, "Construction and Legitimation"; Hume, "Aims and Pitfalls."

51. Examples include Fischer, *Historians' Fallacies*; Levin, *New Readings vs. Old Plays*; Wellek, "Fall of Literary History"; Perkins, *Is Literary History Possible?*; and Skinner, *Visions of Politics*.

52. Latour, *Reassembling the Social*, 5.

53. Geertz, "Thick Description."

Chapter 2 · Contemporary Views on Satire, 1658–1770

1. Pope, *Epilogue to the Satires* (1738), dialogue II, l. 213.

2. See Griffin, *Satire*, 25.

3. A good discussion of the etymology of "satire" is Knoche, "Origin and Name of the *Satura*," in *Roman Satire*, 7–16.

4. See Dryden, *Discourse*, especially 4:28–29.

5. Griffin, "Dryden and Restoration Satire," 178. I agree with Griffin in finding the critical attempt "to apply [the *Discourse*] retrospectively . . . to the satires that Dryden himself and his contemporaries wrote" mostly unsuccessful.

6. Flecknoe, *Enigmaticall Characters*.

7. Morris, *Essay Towards Fixing the True Standards of Wit* (1744; 2s†), 50.

8. The author of *Biographia Classica* (1740) distinguishes between old and new satire (Horace and Juvenal) and suggests the limits of Horatian satire: "Horace was a slight superficial Satirist, who only laugh'd from the Teeth outward, whereas Juvenal bit to the very Bone, and did not often suffer his Prey to escape strangling and being put to death" (1:301).

9. *The Tatler*, 2:74 (10 November 1709).

10. *Ars Punica. Pars Altera* (1721), 7.

11. Dennis, *Critical Works*, 2:201.

12. Or, as Ned Ward says in *Durgen* (1729), "Pers'nal Reflections, Men of Art must own,/Cease to be Satyr, and become Lampoon" (12).

13. Bogel, *The Difference Satire Makes*, 258.

14. Poole, *The English Parnassus* (1657), 176.

15. See, for example, the anonymous *Raillerie a la mode Consider'd* (1673) and Richard Allestree's *The Government of the Tongue* (1667).

16. The quotations come from "The Publisher to the Reader" in Barrow's *Sermons*. In 1694, Daniel Burgess also publishes a sermon on *Foolish Talking and Jesting*, and five years later John Sergeant—like Glanvill and Barrow—connects railing with skepticism and atheism. See *Raillery Defeated by Calm Reason* (1699).

17. Grove, *Mirth's Madness*, 2, "Epistle Dedicatory" (unpaginated), 8.

18. *The Spectator*, 2:467 (15 December 1711). Addison's Sir Roger de Coverley, Paulson observes, is a "modern Quixote," whose creator "redefined satire to correspond to this flawed but lovable character, a figure who elicits sympathetic laughter instead of ridicule—laughter *with* instead of laughter *at* an object." *Don Quixote in England*, 23.

19. See also *The Scholar's Manual* (1733) and *Candour: Or, An Occasional Essay on the Abuse of Wit and Eloquence* (1739), the latter complaining that the satirist neither "spares the Altar, nor reveres the Throne" (3).

20. Elkin, *Augustan Defence of Satire*, 71, 72.

21. Other examples of a similar position include *Meditations of the Mirth of a Christian Life* (Oxford, 1653); *The Rule of Rejoycing* (1671); and *Wit and Mirth, an Antidote against Melancholy* (1682).

22. In a response to Shaftesbury, John Brown takes a similar position, refusing to condemn either jollity or sobriety wholesale. He maintains that "Mirth and Gravity are both harmless Things, provided they be properly applied: And we have seen that it is the Province of Reason alone, to determine when they are so." See "Essay on Ridicule considered as a Test of Truth," in his *Essays on the Characteristics* (1751; 5†), 69.

23. Oldham makes a similar point in the prologue to his *Satyrs upon the Jesuits* (1679–1681). He suggests that "mild fruitless methods" should be abandoned, because only "pointed Satyr" can do any good in attacks on Jesuits of hardened consciences (ll. 25, 26). In the "Advertisement" to the *Satyrs*, Oldham warns his readers that he will not offer the customary "Discourse of the Original, Progress, and Rules of *Satyr*," and neither will he demonstrate "that he has lately Read *Casaubon*." *Poems*, 3.

24. An excellent discussion of Shaftesbury and the debates about ridicule and religion is in Hudson, *Samuel Johnson and Eighteenth-Century Thought*, 28–37.

25. Sutherland, *English Satire*, 154.

26. Tottie, *Ridicule Consider'd and Censur'd*, 4, 6. Whitehead takes a similar position, voicing his concern—if less gravely than Tottie—that ridicule works against religious belief and truth: "Each laughing murders what he holds most dear." *Essay on Ridicule*, 6.

27. Brown, "Essay on Ridicule," in *Essays on the Characteristics*, 41, 47.

28. Asplin, *Alkibla* (1731), xi.

29. Sheffield and Dryden, *Essay upon Satire* (wr. 1679), ll. 12–13; Pope, *Epilogue to the Satires* (1738), dialogue II, l. 212.

30. Morris, *Essay Towards Fixing the True Standards of Wit*, 37.

31. Congreve, *Amendments* (1698), 8.

32. Fielding, *Contributions to "The Champion,"* 365–366, 367.

33. Both of these poems are printed in Defoe, *Satire, Fantasy and Writings on the Supernatural*, vol. 1, quotations at 37, 83.

34. Elkin, *Augustan Defence of Satire*, 1.

35. Marshall, "Daniel Defoe as Satirist."

36. *Some Critical and Politick Remarks*, 7.

37. Dennis, *A True Character of Mr. Pope* (1716), in *Critical Works*, 2:105.

38. Dennis, *An Essay upon Publick Spirit* (1711), 27.

39. Rapin's preference for Horace over Juvenal reflects the broader seventeenth-century French attitude toward satire. As Weinbrot has demonstrated, Casaubon, Dacier, and other French writers insisted upon satire's Roman origins and sought to elevate Horace's status as a satirist. In England, the "association with France, and especially with Dacier, clearly boosted Horace's already growing reputation." *Alexander Pope*, 12–19, quotation at 18. In *The Touch-Stone* (1728), James Ralph insists, contra Rapin and Blount, that "an open, sincere Countenance" is necessary to tell the "Truths of bold *Satire*" (106).

40. See also "Satire," in *Moral and Critical Reflections on Several Subjects* (1758): "The Satirist who really intends to benefit Mankind by making them ashamed of their Vices and their Follies, should mingle Honey with his Gall. He may attack the *Disease* with the Strength of a Lion, but he should treat the *Patient* with the Tenderness of a Lamb" (205).

41. Satirists do not always practice what they preach. The anonymous author of *The Satirists: A Satire* (1739?) suggests that abusive satire cannot do any good: "How base the Means! how impotent the End! / How vain th' Attempt to hope a moral Use, / And gain one Proselyte, by gross abuse" (4). The poet's own satire, however, is decidedly abusive; authors are alluded to by thinly disguised versions of their names (e.g., "P--e" for Pope).

42. Steele issues similar counsel in *The Spectator* (4 July 1712), suggesting that the best writer of raillery practices the "Art of keeping the Person he rallies in Countenance, by insinuating that he himself is guilty of the same Imperfection" (3:585).

43. See also *Hibernicus's Letters*, 1:105.

44. Another example is *The Satirist: A Poem* (1771), whose author contends that only "Satire's wrath" can "reclaim a harden'd race" (26).

45. Greene, *The Satires of Juvenal Paraphrastically Imitated* (1763), v, vi.

46. Or, in Aaron Hill's pithy decree, "WHEN FOLLIES ARE BECOME TOO GREAT FOR LAUGHTER, THEY ARE NO LONGER TO BE LAUGH'D AT." See *The Prompter*, no. 127 (27 January 1736).

47. "Letter to Euphronius," 159. The letter is attributed by the compiler to Thomas Fitzosborne and is part of a section headed "The publick advantage of well directed Satyr. The moral qualifications requisite to a Satyrist."

48. *The Toast* (1736), xxxix.

49. *Codrus: or, the Dunciad Dissected* (1728), 7–8.

50. *The Spectator*, 2:321 (30 October 1711).

51. How, *A Sermon Preach'd at Exon* (Exon, 1718), 29.

52. Addison, *Maxims* (1719), 74–75.

53. Ward, *Durgen*, 9. Especially in the mid-eighteenth century, several commentators insist, says William Webster, that satire "be pointed at the *Vice* more than at the *Man*." *Tracts Consisting of Sermons, Discourses, and Letters* (1745), 299.

54. Swift, preface to *The Battle of the Books*, 142.

55. *The Censor* (1717), 2:58–59.

56. Sir John Fielding, *The Universal Mentor* (1763), 234.

57. Scroope, *In defence of Satire*, ll. 80–81.

58. Beattie, *Dissertations Moral and Critical* (1783), 515–516. In her *Verses Address'd to the*

Imitator of the First Satire of the Second Book of Horace (1733), Lady Mary Wortley Montagu also opposes general satire, though for much different reasons: "*Satire* shou'd, like a polish'd Razor keen,/Wound with a Touch, that's scarcely felt or seen," but Pope's "is an Oyster-Knife, that hacks and hews;/The Rage, but not the Talent of Abuse" (4).

59. Brown, "Essay on Ridicule," in *Essays on the Characteristics*, 53. Brown's amplification is worth attention: "What is high Humour at *Wapping*, is rejected as nauseous in the *City*: What is delicate Raillery in *the City*, grows *coarse* and *intolerable* as you approach *St. James's*: And as many a well meant Joke, that passes unheeded in all these various Districts, would set an innocent Country Village in an Uproar of Laughter. THIS Subject might be much enlarged on: For the Modes and Objects of Ridicule are as indefinite as the imagined Combinations of Things" (54).

60. Gilbert, *Satire on All Parties* (1749), iv.

61. *The Repository, or General Review* (1756), 128.

62. *The Independent Whig* (1721), 304. See also *The Satirist: In Imitation of the Fourth Satire of the First Book of Horace* (1733): "Satire, to these, is monstrously ill-bred,/They wisely damn the Poet that they dread" (9).

63. Jacob, *The Poetical Register* (1719–1720; 6s†), 2:xxiii.

64. Charleton, *A Brief Discourse* (1669), 119.

65. Blount, *De Re Poetica*, 45; *Miscellanies By Normanby* (1702), 32.

66. In *Tears of the Muses* (1737), Aaron Hill implies that the satirist—because human—is guilty of the faults he censures: "Who is there, to say Truth, so unguilty of the Follies of Life, that he dares, in his own proper Person, stand out and justify the Right he assumes, of reproaching the Conduct of Others?" (viii).

67. Charleton, *A Brief Discourse*, 31.

68. Highet, *Anatomy of Satire*, 235.

69. Feinberg, *The Satirist*, 41, 335, 102.

70. Knight, *Literature of Satire*, 1, 3.

71. Griffin, *Satire*, 30.

72. Dickie, *Cruelty and Laughter*, 17, 3–4.

Chapter 3 · Satire in the Carolean Period

1. As Zimbardo suggests, "Whether positively, as the soil from which the eighteenth-century masterworks in time sprouted, or negatively, as the purgatory through which English culture passed to emerge as pure Augustan gold, we have understood the period only in relation to, and continuous with, the eighteenth century." *At Zero Point*, 1.

2. Rawson, *Satire and Sentiment*, 14.

3. Webster, "The 'Lustful Buggering Jew,'" 111.

4. Hume, "'Satire' in the Reign of Charles II," 348.

5. See Love, *Scribal Publication*. Some twenty-five hundred "state poems" survive only in manuscript form (Lord, *POAS-Y*, 1:xxvi).

6. On 4 March 1699, Dryden reported that the playbill for Congreve's *Double-Dealer* "was printed,—Written by Mr Congreve," remarking that "the printing an Authors name, in a Play bill, is a new manner of proceeding, at least in England." *Letters*, 113.

7. Hume, "'Satire' in the Reign of Charles II," 370.

8. Lord, *POAS-Y*, 1:li. Griffin discusses this issue usefully in *Satire*, chap. 5.

9. See Love, *English Clandestine Satire*, chap. 5. Love traces patterns of circulation and attribution, pointing out that "the bulk of the widely circulated lampoons were the work of a somewhat fractious and politically divided coterie of poets who nevertheless were in close enough touch with each other to be able to report with some authority in secondary lampoons on the authorship and circumstances of production of predecessor pieces." He also observes that "composition was as likely to be collaborative as solitary" (176).

10. Hume, "'Satire' in the Reign of Charles II," 338–343.

11. McKeon, "What Were Poems on Affairs of State?," 364–366; Hume, "'Satire' in the Reign of Charles II," 343–344.

12. Griffin makes this point effectively in "Dryden and Restoration Satire," 178.

13. Recent examples include Ogden, "Dryden's Satirical Tendency"; and Paulson, "Dryden and the Energies of Satire."

14. Hunter, "Political, Satirical, Didactic and Lyric Poetry," 189.

15. Winn, *Dryden and His World*, 292.

16. Dryden would say in the *Discourse* that lampoonery is "for the most part Unlawful," solemnly concluding that, "We have no Moral right on the Reputation of other Men" (4:59). The author of *Mac Flecknoe*, however, clearly had a great deal of fun besmirching his target—and he does not appear to have been fussed about his "Moral right" to do so.

17. *The Luttrell File*, 48.

18. Hume, "'Satire' in the Reign of Charles II," 345.

19. Zwicker, "Dryden and the Poetic Career," 141.

20. Harth, *Pen for a Party*, 169.

21. I agree with Wilding: "Dryden's political satires were political instruments. Whatever literary qualities we may admire in them, we need to remember their manipulative, political intent, their McCarthyite smearing." "Dryden and Satire," 210.

22. For this reading, see Milhous and Hume, *Producible Interpretation*, 143–149, quotation at 146.

23. Harth, *Pen for a Party*, 54–55.

24. Winn, *Dryden and His World*, 381; Dryden, *The Vindication* (1683; *Works*, vol. 14).

25. Hume, *The Rakish Stage*, 209.

26. Dennis, *Critical Works*, 2:201.

27. In ca. July 1677, Dryden described *The Kind Keeper* as "almost such another piece of businesse as the fond Husband, for such the King will have it, who is parcell poet with me in the plot." *Letters*, 11–12.

28. Griffin, *Satires against Man*, 285.

29. Griffin challenges what he suggests is too simplistic a reading of these satires, arguing that their playfulness should not be disregarded. *Satire*, 92–93.

30. Scroope took offense: to *On The Suppos'd Author*, he replied with *Answer By way of Epigram*, encouraging the "feeble scribler" to "Sitt swelling in thy hole like a vex'd Toad, / And full of pox, and Mallice, spitt abroad" (ll. 1, 3–4).

31. Many Carolean literary satires name names. Some focus exclusively on a single writer, as in a trio of satires on Edward Howard—Sackville's *To Mr. Edward Howard upon his "The British Princes"* (wr. 1669), Ashton's *On the Same Author upon His "British Princes"* (wr. 1669), and the anonymous *On the Same Author upon his "New Utopia"* (wr. 1671); Buckingham also

satirized *The Brittish Princes* in a short poem called *on these 2 V. of Mr Howards.* Also common are shotgun attacks on multiple authors, such as *Advice to Apollo* (wr. 1677) and *The Session of the Poets* (dated 1668 by Lord in *POAS-Y* but probably wr. 1664).

32. Thormählen, *Rochester*, 349.

33. Love collects the "impromptus" (*Works*, 289–301), including ten versions of the lines on Charles II; I quote the third version (292).

34. See, for example, Thormählen, *Rochester*, 298, and Webster, "Rochester's Easy King," 1–19.

35. Love includes several versions of the "scepter" lampoon (*In the Isle of Brittain*); my quotations come from his "Group-A text," ll. A22, A4, A31–33 (*Works*, 85–86).

36. Thormählen, *Rochester*, 14.

37. Vieth explains this poem as an example to Rochester's adversaries of how he could be vilified. See *Attribution in Restoration Poetry*, 202–203. Love calls the satire a "morbid piece of self-parody." *English Clandestine Satire*, 59.

38. Weinbrot emphasizes the devastating sadness of the *Letter from Artemiza*, maintaining that Rochester's satire is gloomier than either Swift's *Tale* or even the final *Dunciad*. See "The Swelling Volume," 21.

39. Thormählen, *Rochester*, 148.

40. Farley-Hills, *Rochester: The Critical Heritage*, 209, 240, 246.

41. Cousins, "Context, Design, and Argument," 433.

42. Griffin's emphasis on satire as inquiry or provocation is especially useful for Rochester: "Satire is often an 'open' rather than a 'closed' form . . . concerned rather to inquire, explore, or unsettle than to declare, sum up, or conclude." *Satire*, 95.

43. Rochester's readership extended beyond his coterie, as Love explains: "Poems written to wound enemies or to further his position at court would have failed in their aim if they had never spread beyond his own intimates." Love also demonstrates that the Earl meant his lampoons "not merely to amuse his friends but to mortify his victims, something which could only happen if they were made generally available at Whitehall." *Scribal Publication*, 247. Sitter argues that Rochester tries "to resist solidarity with the reader" of his satires, constantly subverting readers' ability to make sense of the works. "Rochester's Reader," 287.

44. See Eco, *The Role of the Reader*, chap. 1.

45. Hume and Love, *Plays, Poems, and Miscellaneous Writings Associated with Buckingham*, 1:341.

46. Ibid., 1:347.

47. On Duffett, see DiLorenzo's introduction to *Three Burlesque Plays of Thomas Duffett*; and West, "Dryden's *Mac Flecknoe*."

48. On the politics of the play, see McFadden, "Political Satire in *The Rehearsal*"; Stocker, "Political Allusion in *The Rehearsal*"; Hume and Love, *Plays, Poems, and Miscellaneous Writings Associated with Buckingham*, 1:349–355.

49. Buckingham, *Upon the Installment*, ll. 70–71. See Hume and Love's notes on the Danby poems (*Plays, Poems, and Miscellaneous Writings Associated with Buckingham*, 2:424–427). Hume and Love also print *A Supplement to the Chequer-Inne*, a short coda to another anti-Danby satire, *The Chequer Inn*. The attribution of the *Supplement* to Buckingham is not definite but not improbable (2:424); the text is at 2:17–18.

50. Wilson, *Court Satires*, 68.

51. For a full account of the suppression of the play and Coventry's disgrace, see Hume and Love, *Plays, Poems, and Miscellaneous Writings Associated with Buckingham*, 1:231–238.

52. Patterson has analyzed the ideological argument of *The Country Gentleman* convincingly and at length in "*The Country Gentleman*: Howard, Marvell, and Dryden."

53. What role Buckingham actually had in the composition of these works is impossible to determine. The standard edition includes those texts known to be "by" or partially by Buckingham but also works "associated with" him. Where authorship is completely uncertain, I use quotation marks ("Buckingham").

54. I quote from H. Gaston Hall's English translation of the play, printed as appendix V (at 2:341) of *Plays, Poems, and Miscellaneous Writings Associated with Buckingham*. The quotation is at 380.

55. Hume and Love, *Plays, Poems, and Miscellaneous Writings Associated with Buckingham*, 1:133–144.

56. Griffin, *Satire*, 150. More recently, Griffin has followed other critics in underscoring the political implications of some of Rochester's satires ("Dryden and Restoration Satire," 187–189).

57. Griffin, *Satires against Man*, 303.

58. On Marvell, see von Maltzahn, "Marvell's Ghost": "Marvell's small reputation as a poet can be contrasted with that of Rochester. . . . Marvell had nothing like such popularity, and nothing like such an identity as a poet or a protagonist in his poetry" (56).

59. Love, *English Clandestine Satire*, 105.

60. Ibid., 104; Love is quoting Keeble, "I Would Not Tell You," 129.

61. Patterson is mildly defensive about the neglect of Marvell's satires, complaining that even the best of these works have "damaged" his "reputation for delicacy of mind and sureness of touch." See *Marvell*, 72.

62. Smith, *Poems of Andrew Marvell*, 166.

63. Norbrook, *Writing the English Republic*, 168.

64. Patterson, *Marvell*, 73–74. Parts of *The Character of Holland* were published during the Second and Third Dutch Wars as anti-Dutch propaganda (though not by Marvell, who had a much more favorable attitude toward the Dutch at that time).

65. The poet of *The Downfall of the Chancellor* (wr. 1667) also attacks Clarendon, but he is not making an argument as much as he is voicing contempt after Hyde's fall: "This shrub of gentry," the satirist records with spiteful glee, "is tumbl'd down" (ll. 5–6).

66. Patterson, *Marvell*, 98.

67. See, for example, Chibnall, "Something to the Purpose"; Parkin, "Liberty Transpros'd"; and Hirst, "Parker, Marvell, and Political Culture."

68. Lord, "Satire and Sedition."

69. Ibid., 271. The attribution of this poem to Ayloffe is less definite than that of *Britannia and Raleigh*, though Ayloffe is the most plausible candidate, given the argument and tone of this poem (see also Mengel, *POAS-Y*, 2:393).

70. Others include *The Dream of the Cabal* (1672), *Advice to a Painter to Draw the Duke by* (wr. 1673), *Hodge* (wr. 1679), and *The Waking Vision* (1681).

71. The anonymous author of *The Waking Vision* warns Charles against both the "Roman gnat and the Dissenting moth" (l. 125). A non-Catholic Tory, the writer no doubt is genuinely

resistant to popery and anxious about Whig agitation, but the images of the "gnat" and the "moth" suggest nuisance rather than peril. This "vision" poem is tonally remote from *An Historical Poem* and in another universe altogether from Ayloffe's satire.

72. Lord, "Satire and Sedition," 268, 273.

73. Hammond, *John Oldham*, 1.

74. In *The Poems of John Oldham*, Brooks provides a detailed account of the publication history of these satires, which first appeared separately in pirated editions. He also points out that the original versions of these satires were more explicitly political (anti-York) than they were in the first authorized edition (1681). See especially xxx–xxxiv.

75. Brooks, *Poems of John Oldham*, xxix; Love, *English Clandestine Satire*, 126. Love is dealing in particular with the satires directed at the lord chief justice, Sir William Scroggs, though he also refers to Oldham's dramatic attack on the Jesuits.

76. Selden, "Oldham, Pope, and Restoration Satire," 114, 113.

77. Brooks, *Poems of John Oldham*, xxxii.

78. Ibid., xxix. *Sardanapalus* and *A Dithyrambique* were apparently written for Rochester and his circle, who had expressed appreciation of the *Satyr Against Vertue*.

79. Griffin, "Dryden and Restoration Satire," 189. Hammond had argued that "Oldham may have been attempting to emulate Rochester's 'sceptre' lampoon." *John Oldham*, 33.

80. Brooks is right to insist that "no poem of Oldham's is like a poem of Rochester's." *Poems of John Oldham*, xlv.

81. Selden suggests that "Oldham's indignation is often playful: he wears his pen like a sword and runs through 'each affronting Sot.'" "Oldham, Pope, and Restoration Satire," 125.

82. Griffin, "Dryden and Restoration Satire," 191. Selden argues for Rochester's influence on Oldham in "Rochester and Oldham." He grants that "Rochester's 'all-teaching tongue' cannot be given all the credit for Oldham's stylistic exuberance," and that "Oldham's own brand of heroic satire is not Rochester's" (102–103), but his emphasis on their similarities is nonetheless misleading.

83. Part I of *Hudibras* was available by the end of 1662 (Pepys bought a copy on 26 December); part II was available in late 1663 (Pepys borrowed a copy on 28 November). As Wilders points out in his introduction to *Hudibras*, the third part's title page lists 1678, but the first edition was available in print by 6 November 1677 (lvi). The *Term Catalogues* give a 1674 price (for parts I and II) of 3s 6d bound; four years later, parts I and II are listed at 4s. *Hudibras* is advertised throughout the eighteenth century in various formats and at various prices: in 1709 (3s in 1 vol. or 4s in 3 vols.), in 1710 (3s 6d), in 1714 (6s), in 1729 (by subscription for the dumbfounding sum of a guinea), in 1744 (12s unbound), in 1750 (2s 6d), in 1762 (3s 6d), in 1764 (12s), and in 1772 (3s 6d). Hogarth's *Hudibras* engravings sold by themselves for 15s in 1726.

84. Turner, "From Revolution to Restoration," 804.

85. Griffin, *Satire*, 150.

86. Marshall, "The Aims of Butler's Satire." The following discussion summarizes conclusions drawn in that article.

87. Lee, *The Cabal*, 243.

88. Durfey's *Butler's Ghost: or, Hudibras. The Fourth Part* (1682) is a slashing denunciation of the Whigs in general and of Shaftesbury in particular. This satire, like *Hudibras*, is written with at least an implicit positive agenda.

89. The satire in *The Geneva Ballad* (1674), sometimes attributed to Butler, functions simi-

larly. Its author scorches the nonconformists, but he also recalls the regicide and, like Butler, warns that all should not be forgiven and forgotten (ll. 22–23).

90. Selden, *English Verse Satire*, 89–100; Farley-Hills, *The Benevolence of Laughter*, 189.

91. Love, *English Clandestine Satire*, 19.

92. Hughes, *English Drama*, 56.

93. Ibid., 56–57.

94. Hirst, "Parker, Marvell, and Political Culture," 159. On Marvell's use of Buckingham's play, see Keeble, "Why Transpose *The Rehearsal?*"

95. Love recounts several instances of retaliation directed at authors of lampoons (*English Clandestine Satire*, 151–154). In Hume's discussion of John Crowne's *City Politiques*, he points out that the play was "unquestionably designed to mock Whig aims and politics in 1681–82. But to what degree its characters are intended to be identified as particular individuals is not so clear. In his pious and probably disingenuous note 'To the Reader' in the 1683 quarto, Crowne admits satirizing Titus Oates as Doctor Sanchy but protests innocence beyond that." Crowne's play, however, "invites applications, and right or wrong, they could produce reprisals." Crowne was beaten, probably by friends of the late Rochester, and lamented in the introductory note to *City Politiques*, that "Libels may prove costly things." See " 'Satire' in the Reign of Charles II," 357–358.

96. The anonymous *Satire* (1680)—an imitation of Juvenal's first satire—is a brief but sweeping list of offending individuals and types, and here as in *Utile Dulce* (1681), no single target seems especially significant. Both poets are complaining for the sake of complaining.

97. Summers, introduction to *Complete Works of Thomas Shadwell*, 1:xli.

98. Hume, " 'Satire' in the Reign of Charles II," 353. Pepys hated *The Sullen Lovers* upon his first two viewings (see 2 and 4 May 1668), but after being informed that "By Sir Positive At-all . . . is meant Sir Rob. Howard" (5 May), he changed his tune, enjoying the abuse of Howard and observing that Shadwell's representation "is most exactly true" (8 May). See *The Diary of Samuel Pepys*, 9:186, 191.

99. Love, "Charles, Viscount Mordaunt," 351.

100. Wilson, *Court Satires*, 47.

101. Love, *English Clandestine Satire*, 58.

102. Similar satires include *The Queen's Ball* (wr. 1670), attacking Queen Catherine, and Dorset's *Colin* (wr. 1679; also called *Colon*), a politicized invective directed at the Duchess of Portsmouth.

103. The author of *Acrostick* encourages the king to "Suffer not these base mercenary Whores / To rob thy kingdom & to drain thy Stores." British Library Add. MS 34,362, fol. 47r. The collection is dated 1679–1681, which seems plausible, and also includes *The Dissolution 1679* (fols. 48–49), whose author issues a similar warning. A king who "draws his Reasons from his breeches" endangers the country and himself: "Beware unthinking Charles beware / Consider & begin to feare." The satirist's distress is clear.

104. Other instances of this sort of purposive detraction include *A Dialogue between Duke Lauderdale and the Lord Danby* (1679); Shadwell's *The Medal of John Bayes* (1682); Settle's *Absalom Senior* (1682); and Shadwell's *The Tory-Poets: A Satyr* (1682; 3d*), a brutally clear attack on the Tories in general and on Dryden in particular.

105. I cite the version in *Plays, Poems, and Miscellaneous Writings Associated with Buckingham*, vol. 2, appendix II (quotation at 311). Hume and Love also print *A New Ballad to an*

Old Tune Call'd Sage Leafe (wr. 1673?), another smear job written against Buckingham with evident political purpose (see 2:498, 500). Among the most incisive satires on Buckingham is the character sketch penned by Butler, his sometime secretary. No man is a hero to his clerk, and "A Duke of Bucks" is a lacerating account of the shortcomings of "one that has studied the whole Body of Vice." Butler's other character sketches are all on types ("A Politician," "An Undeserving Favourite," "The Affected or Formal"); his treatment of the highly individual "Duke of Bucks" as a recognizable breed makes the satire even more stinging. Daves collects all 285 of Butler's known sketches in his edition of *Characters*. "A Duke of Bucks" is at 66–67, quotation at 66.

106. Satires on Monmouth are myriad, including *A Dialogue between Nathan and Absalom* (wr. 1680) and *The Great Despair of the London Whigs* (wr. 1683; pub. 1685). Shaftesbury is also much satirized, as in Nevil Payne's *The Siege of Constantinople* (perf. 1674; pub. 1675), John Caryll's *The Hypocrite* (1678), Behn's *The City-Heiress* (1682), and *The Last Will and Testament of Anthony King of Poland* (1682).

107. See Hume, *Development of English Drama*, 355.

108. *The Country-Wife* and *The Man of Mode* undoubtedly contain satiric elements—the question of whether they are "satires" has been much debated, probably insolubly so—but if either of them communicates a coherent satiric message, then that meaning has eluded scholars.

109. Canfield takes this play very seriously as a commentary on class warfare. See *Tricksters & Estates*, 87–88. Dawson has recently—and I think rightly—challenged Canfield's interpretation of city cuckolding comedy as oversimplified and badly misleading. See *Gentility and the Comic Theatre*, 42.

110. Hume, "Otway and the Comic Muse," 96. See also Hume, "Unconventional Tragedies of Thomas Otway," 74.

111. Hughes, *English Drama*, 230.

112. Hume, "The Satiric Design of *The Princess of Cleve*," 138.

113. Brooks, "English Verse Satire"; Doody, *The Daring Muse*, 30–56; Smith, *Literature and Revolution*, 295–319. Knoppers usefully crosses the false break point of 1660 in her study of satires on Cromwell, "Sing old Noll the Brewer."

114. *J. Cleaveland Revived: Poems, Orations, Epistles* (1659, 1660, 1662, 1668); *Poems by John Cleavland* (1661, 1662, 1665, 1669); *Clievlandi Vindiciae: or, Clieveland's Genuine Poems* (1677). Some of Cleveland's individual works reappear under slightly different titles in the Carolean period: his *The Hue and Cry after Sir John Presbyter* (a 1649 broadside) was reprinted as *The Loyal Livery-Mens Hue and Cry after Sir John Presbyter* (acquired by Luttrell in 1683). John Phillips's *A Satyr Against Hypocrites* (1655) is also reprinted several times in the Carolean period (1661, 1671, 1674, 1677, and 1680); Cowley's *Puritan and the Papist* is dated 1681/82.

115. Brooks, "English Verse Satire," 33, 36–37.

116. See Brome, *Poems*, 1:24. Brome's first satire was composed in 1643 and his last in 1661.

117. See, for example, Brome's *The Cavalier*, a short verse complaint penned by a disappointed loyalist soon after Charles's return. The rebels, the poet laments, "creep into profit and power," and the king's men "are low" (ll. 27). Brome still holds out hope, however, concluding with a tentative suggestion that the balance of power might eventually shift in favor of the royalists.

118. Lord, *POAS-Y*, 1:20.

119. See also *The Dream of the Cabal*, the context of which includes Charles's prorogation

of Parliament in 1671 and the negotiations occurring between England and France during that prorogation. At the end of the conference, six of the seven ministers have urged Charles to ally England with France—a course of action of which the satirist is clearly afraid. The poet awakens in the final lines, but far from dismissing the meeting as unreal, he foretells ominously, "'Tis ten to one but I shall dream again" (l. 384).

120. In "Satire and Sedition," Lord tentatively ascribes this poem to Ayloffe, largely because of the intensity of its bitterness ("the gods have repented the King's Restoration" [l. 162]) and its republican undertones.

121. For the text of and commentary on *A Raree Show*, see Schless, *POAS-Y*, 3:425–431.For a lengthy analysis of College's trial, see Weber, *Paper Bullets*, chap. 5.

122. The only serious analysis of this poem is Suarez, "A Crisis in English Public Life," a sensitive and judicious attempt to place it in its theological, political, and legal contexts.

123. Schless, *POAS-Y*, 3:345.

124. Harth's *Pen for a Party* is a good illustration of the utility of chronological precision. As Harth rightly argues, "the Tory propaganda" of late Carolean England "is by no means a single entity" (x). Attending to its three component "campaigns," as Harth's study demonstrates, allows us to understand Dryden's contributions as propagandist much more fully and accurately.

125. Selden, "Oldham, Pope, and Restoration Satire," 110.

126. Of the former, Love suggests that hearing it sung to its original tune ("Peggy's gone over sea with the soldier") "locates it socially as an improvisatorial drinking song in a way that gives point to what on the page is a rather tedious repetition of a rudimentary joke." *Scribal Publication*, 234.

127. See, for instance, *A Satire in Answer to a Friend* (wr. 1682?), whose author "shows his ultimate despair by rejecting the corrupt age in which he lives" (Schless, *POAS-Y*, 3:28). An earlier example is Brome's *The Satyr of Money* (wr. 1653?; pub. 1661), written during the Cromwellian regime, which reflects its author's bleak perception of moral and political topsy-turvydom.

128. Lord, *POAS-Y*, 1:168.

129. This event was connected to the assault on Coventry, as Lord explains: "Unchastened by the outraged public reaction to the attack on Sir John Coventry in December, Monmouth took part in a brawl inside a brothel . . . a few weeks later in which a beadle named Peter Vernell was murdered, 'praying for his life upon his knees'" (*POAS-Y*, 1:172). Lord is quoting a letter from Marvell to Mayor Ackham, 28 February 1671.

130. Nevo, *The Dial of Virtue*, 6. More recently, Hunter has argued that for these writers, "the inevitable other side of panegyric was satire: opposition, attack, derogation, lampoon, undermining—persuasion *against*, which was simply the opposite of celebration or argument in favour." "Political, Satirical, Didactic and Lyric Poetry," 184.

131. Griffin, *Satire*, 150–151. Griffin is challenging the notion that political satire is always "written from a clearly defined political position." He argues that "we should suspect that what looks like principle is often a blend of literary and political opportunity, personal circumstance, and an attempt to discredit a particular person or party or to advance a literary career" (150). I entirely agree with that warning, but replacing one generalization with another is problematic.

132. Lord, *POAS-Y*, 1:221.

133. Stranahan, "Bunyan's Satire and Its Biblical Sources," 60.

134. Forrest and Sharrock, *The Life and Death of Mr. Badman*, xxvi, xxviii.

135. Fielding, *The Champion*, 10 June 1740, in *Contributions to "The Champion,"* 365.

136. Brean Hammond has analyzed Bunyan's satire in *The Pilgrim's Progress*, explicating topical swipes in that text and describing the "castigatory spirit of the social critic." See "*The Pilgrim's Progress*: Satire and Social Comment," 131.

137. Wallace has argued persuasively that many seventeenth-century readers assumed the need to apply texts to contemporary circumstances, whatever the author's intention—that is, they read in a world in which history *applied*. See Wallace, "Dryden and History"; and Wallace, "Examples Are Best Precepts."

138. *Diary of Samuel Pepys*, 9:81 (20 February 1668).

139. Hughes, *English Drama*, 44–45.

140. *Diary of Samuel Pepys*, 8:167–168 (15 April 1667).

141. Pepys tells of Lacy's arrest: the actor "cursed" Howard ("it was the fault of his non-sensical play that was the cause of his ill usage") and told the playwright "that he was more a fool then a poet; on which Howard did give him a blow on the face with his glove; on which Lacy, having a cane in his hand, did give him a blow over the pate. Here, Rolt and others that discoursed of it in the pit this afternoon did wonder that Howard did not run him through, he being too mean a fellow to fight with—but Howard did not do anything but complain to the King of it; so the whole House is silenced." *Diary of Samuel Pepys*, 8:172–173 (20 April 1667).

142. For a useful discussion of the censorship of *Richard the Second* and other Exclusion Crisis plays, see Clare, "All Run Now into Politicks."

143. Griffin, "Dryden and Restoration Satire," 178, 179.

144. Selden, *English Verse Satire*, 73.

145. The phrase is from Miner, *Restoration Mode from Milton to Dryden*.

Chapter 4 · Beyond Carolean

1. Defoe's poetry has only recently started to receive serious critical attention. The first book-length study of the subject is Mueller, *A Critical Study of Daniel Defoe's Verse* (2010). Mueller mounts a strong case for engaging more seriously with Defoe's poetic output and for not measuring his verse according to the standards set by Pope.

2. Kishlansky, *A Monarchy Transformed*, 266.

3. Love provides a useful discussion of satires on William (and Mary) in *English Clandestine Satire*, 142–144. Paul Hammond deals helpfully with satires targeting William's homosexuality in *Figuring Sex*, especially 172–185.

4. Hume, "'Satire' in the Reign of Charles II," 341.

5. McKeon, "What Were Poems on Affairs of State?," 364–366; Hume, "'Satire' in the Reign of Charles II," 343–344.

6. Wilson, *Court Satires*, 159.

7. Love, *English Clandestine Satire*, 141.

8. Studies of early print media and of coffeehouse culture are numerous, and I need not rehearse their arguments here. On early newsbooks and newspapers, see Frank, *Beginnings of the English Newspaper*; Sutherland, *Restoration Newspaper and Its Development*; Cust, "News and Politics"; and Raymond, *Invention of the Newspaper*. On the role of coffeehouses in the transmission of news, see Pincus, "Coffee Politicians Does Create."

9. *A True Relation Of the several Facts . . . on Queen Elizabeth's Birth-day* (1711) on Wharton: "This Person, who has so often boasted himself . . . for making a certain Lilli bullero Song, with which, if you will believe himself, he sung a deluded Prince out of Three Kingdoms" (5).

10. *Bishop Burnet's History of His Own Time*, vol. 1 (1724), 792.

11. See Crump, *POAS-Y*, 4:310.

12. Ibid., 4:190.

13. Sackville, *Poems*, 138, ll. 38–39.

14. Brooks's *Dryden the Satirist* includes a chapter titled "The Satirist before the Satires," one titled "The Satirist after the Satires," and one on *The Hind and the Panther*, but he devotes most of his substantive analysis to *Mac Flecknoe, Absalom and Achitophel*, and *The Medall*. Brooks has little to say about any of Dryden's satires after *Absalom and Achitophel*, concluding (accurately) that in the late-life satires "we find him in topics and techniques little different from the satirist before the satires" (179). Ogden in "Dryden's Satirical Tendency" focuses exclusively on *Mac Flecknoe* and *Absalom and Achitophel*. Yu's coverage of Dryden's satire includes those two poems and *The Medall*. See *Nothing to Admire*, chap. 1. The same three poems figure in Griffin's "Dryden and Restoration Satire" and in Paulson's "Dryden and the Energies of Satire." Useful though these studies are, they are far from comprehensive. By my count, a full treatment of Dryden's satiric output would involve coverage of some twenty titles (including works for which he is solely responsible and those he coauthored).

15. Dryden's conversion attracted a good deal of mostly negative attention. The author of *To Mr. Dryden, Upon his Declaring himself a Roman Catholic* (wr. 1686) calls the poet a "Jack of all faiths" (l. 79), and in *The Town Life* (wr. 1686) Dryden is excoriated as a pen for hire: "Praise Cromwell, damn him, write the *Spanish Friar*—/ A Papist now, if next the Turk should reign,/ Then piously transverse the Alcoran" (ll. 20–23). The best-known satire on Dryden from this period is Prior and Montagu's *The Hind and the Panther Transvers'd*, a wickedly funny burlesque.

16. In the *Discourse* Dryden emphasizes as essential to satire a "principal Instructive Point" (4:80). He observes approvingly that "amongst the *Romans*," satire "was not only us'd for those Discourses which decry'd Vice, or expos'd Folly; but for others also, where Virtue was recommended" (48).

17. *Albion and Albanius* was written in 1684 for Charles II but not performed until June 1685, after his death.

18. For Dryden's quotation, see *The Hind and the Panther*, 3:119. Martin Clifford describes the author of *The Hind and the Panther* as a "*Satyrist*" and complains about "the *most noxious pieces* of his Satyr" in *Notes upon Mr. Dryden's Poems in Four Letters* (1687), 29, 34. In *The Hind and the Panther Transvers'd* (1687), Prior and Montagu also highlight the satiric nature of the poem (both in the preface and again at p. 14).

19. Winn, *Dryden and His World*, 423.

20. Bywaters, *Dryden in Revolutionary England*, 20–21.

21. The government had little tolerance for anti-Williamite satire. Brown and Tutchin were both arrested for their verses (Brown's *Satyr upon the French King* and Tutchin's *The Foreigners*, both discussed below). Ralph Gray was placed in the pillory for *The Coronation Ballad* (1689), which encourages the rabble to "make room for the clown," assails William's sexuality, and—most problematically—foretells his downfall: "Descended he is from an Orange tree,/ But if I can read his destiny,/ He'll once more descend from another tree" (ll. 75, 5–7).

22. Combe, "Clandestine Protest," 49.

23. Winn, *Dryden and His World*, 456.

24. Dryden, *Cleomenes*, 16:79.

25. Combe, "Clandestine Protest," 36.

26. The standard political reading of *Alexander's Feast* is Proffitt, "Political Satire in Dryden's *Alexander's Feast.*" Erskine-Hill maintains that "Alexander, not a portrait of William, was meant to remind of him." See *Poetry of Opposition and Revolution*, 44–46. On the anti-Williamite implications of Dryden's *Virgil*, see Zwicker, *Politics and Language*; and Winn, *Dryden and His World*, 487–489. The best recent account of the *Fables* is Gelineau, "Adorn'd with Labour'd Art."

27. *Amphitryon*, 15:233, I.i.78–79.

28. Winn, *Dryden and His World*, 446.

29. Milhous and Hume, *Producible Interpretation*, 226.

30. The play's political message has been much discussed. See Bywaters, *Dryden in Revolutionary England*, chap. 2; Schille, "Self-Assessment in Dryden's *Amphitryon*"; and Gelineau, "Identity in Dryden's *Amphitryon*." Hughes finds in the play broad applicability to historical circumstances: "Unsurprisingly, Dryden did not join Shadwell and Durfey in portraying the Revolution as a re-establishment of law. Law does not restrain power: it serves it." *English Drama*, 342.

31. For this reading, see Price, *Henry Purcell*, especially 290–295.

32. Hume, "Politics of Opera," 41.

33. Griffin, *Satire*, 21.

34. Winn, *Dryden and His World*, 444.

35. Dryden could almost certainly count on readers so inclined to make the application he invites. See Wallace, "Dryden and History"; and Wallace, "Examples Are Best Precepts."

36. Peterson explains the circumstances of Tutchin's dismissal from his post in the Victualling Office in his introduction to Tutchin's *Selected Poems*, vi. In *The Mouse Grown a Rat* (1702), Tutchin—a participant in Monmouth's rebellion, a champion of the Revolution, and a fierce opponent of Jacobitism—lamented that he had been "ruined for his country in James' reign, starved for his country in William's reign, and was liable to be hanged for his country in the next reign." Ellis, *POAS-Y*, 6:225. Peterson likens Tutchin to Oldham (introduction to Tutchin, *Selected Poems*, iii), but Tutchin resembles more closely Oldham's less well-known contemporary the vituperative anti-Stuart, anti-Catholic, republican Ayloffe.

37. Cameron, *POAS-Y*, 5:138.

38. An equally venomous (and equally resigned) anti-William poem is *Anno 1696*, a diatribe on William, under whose "tyranny" England has suffered "a lasting war," and who "never yet didst one kind thing" for his people. British Library Stowe 305, fols. 213v–214r.

39. See Cameron, *POAS-Y*, 5:309–310.

40. *The Luttrell File*, 145. *The Tribe of Levi* Luttrell explains as "A bitter poem on ye Clergy & Churchmen, expecially ye Bishops" (186).

41. See Bevil Higgons (?), *The Mourners*, and the anonymous *Upon Sorrel* (both 1702), both of which celebrate William's death and the horse that brought it about. Mandeville responds to William's opponents—somewhat after the fashion of Defoe—in *The Pamphleteers: A Satyr* (1703), another instance of strongly positive satire, defending the memory of the late king against his detractors.

42. *The Luttrell File*, 42.

43. Dennis (?) also responded harshly to Tutchin; his *The Reverse: Or, The Tables Turn'd* (1700; *4d**) is a point-by-point counterattack, as is the anonymous *The Natives: An Answer to The Foreigners* (1700).

44. Ellis, *POAS-Y*, 6:225.

45. Martin, "Gould's Attacks on the London Stage," 59. For a general account of Gould's life and writings, see Sloane, *Robert Gould*.

46. Martin, "Gould's Attacks on the London Stage," 60.

47. Much of Gould's work is of this kind. *A Satyr upon Man* (included in his *Poems*), a sort of sequel to *Love given o're*, excoriates men rather than women and concludes that mankind is uniformly despicable. See also *Jack Pavy, Alias Jack Adams* (in the 1689 *Poems*) and *The Corruption of the Times by Money* (1693); the former suggests that the more humans know the more they suffer, and in the latter, Gould complains bitterly about universal greed.

48. Nussbaum, *The Brink of All We Hate*, 31.

49. See also *The Lost Maiden-head* (1691), *The Restor'd Maiden-head* (1691), Ames's *The Female Fire-Ships* (1691; 3*d**), Gould's *A Satyr against Wooing* (1698), and the anonymous *Corinna; or, Humane Frailty* (1699; 4*d**).

50. Alan Marshall, *The Age of Faction*, 77, 78, 81.

51. Cook, *Sir Samuel Garth*, 15. *The Dispensary* was extremely popular: it went through three editions within five weeks, new editions appeared throughout the eighteenth century, and by 1768 it was in its eleventh London edition.

52. Terry, *Mock-Heroic from Butler to Cowper*, 59.

53. Quoted in Rosenberg, "London Dispensary," 48. Rosenberg cites the Royal College of Physicians *Minute Book*.

54. Bradham's facsimile edition is taken from the ninth edition (printed in Dublin in 1725), "selected because of the fullness of the *Compleat Key to the Dispensary* and because the *Key* in that edition was printed with the poem, not separately." The poem itself is substantively identical to the seventh London edition (1714), the last to appear in Garth's lifetime (9). The most substantial change the original version of *The Dispensary* underwent was in the second edition (also 1699), "a much expanded version of the first" (6).

55. Bradham, introduction to *The Dispensary*, 9. Such has been Garth's place in literary history: in 1974, in one of the few scholarly pieces to be devoted solely to Garth, Sena argued, "Like Dryden and Pope, Garth adopted the mock-heroic form as an effective means of defining the values of his world." "Samuel Garth's *The Dispensary*," 642.

56. Colomb, *Designs on Truth*, 98; Parker, "Modes of Mockery," 503. Parker explains Garth's poem as valuable primarily for its contribution to Pope's poetic education (500) and concludes that "Garth showed the way to illuminate through irony quotidian and contemporary objects by placing them in the scene—the imaginative field—of the heroic" (503).

57. Cook, *Sir Samuel Garth*, 58.

58. Johnson, *Lives*, 3:76.

59. Boys gives a full account of Blackmore's battle with the wits in *Sir Richard Blackmore and the Wits*, chap. 1.

60. Most of Ward's individual pieces went for 6*d*, though some longer works were 1*s*, as was his ninety-four-page *Dissenting Hypocrite* of 1704. Many of his publications include advertisements for his other works. The practice is by no means unique to him or to other commercial satirists, but it does make plain the desire to sell his product.

61. Brown, *To Sir R[ichard] B[lackmore], upon his unhappy Talent of Praising and Railing*, in *Works*, 1:11. The same volume includes several epigrams on Blackmore, including *On Job newly Travestied by Sir R[ichard] Bl[ackmore]*, *On Sir R[ichard] Bl[ackmore]'s Project to erect a Bank of Wit*, and *To Sir R[ichard] Bl[ackmore], on the two Wooden Horses before Sadlers-hall*.

62. Brown's personal attacks are often politically motivated, as in his blistering satires against Defoe. *Upon the Anonymous Author of, Legion's Humble Address to the Lords* and *To that Most Senseless Scondrel, the Author of Legion's Humble Address to the Lords* are vicious personal-cum-political derogations.

63. Ellis, *POAS-Y*, 6:3.

64. Boyce, *Tom Brown of Facetious Memory*, 60–63.

65. As Boyce explains, Brown's most memorable works "are of the seasonable variety—the scornful, stabbing lines on D'Urfey, the dramatic presentation of the dilemma of the Jacobites in 1697, an elegy on the death of Millington the auctioneer, and his best drinking songs." Ibid., 65–66. He "was busy digesting and presenting not immortal truth and beauty but rather the political and ecclesiastical developments of the moment" (68).

66. *The Devil's Journey to London* counters Ward from an apothecary's point of view, and *The Shoe-Maker Beyond his Last* was apparently written by a churchman.

67. Troyer, *Ned Ward of Grubstreet*, 15. The ESTC reports three editions of *A Trip to Jamaica* in 1698; it was in its seventh by 1700.

68. Other examples of Ward's journalistic/narrative satire include *A Trip to New-England* (1699), *A Frolick to Horn-Fair* (1700), *A Step to Stir-Bitch-Fair* (1700), *A Step to the Bath* (1700), *The Revels of the Gods* (1701), *The Rambling Fuddle-Caps* (1706), and—much later—*The Merry Travellers* (1721–1722).

69. Troyer, *Ned Ward of Grubstreet*, 61.

70. Boyce's description of Ward is apt: he "suffered, for reasons not wholly economic, from a *furor scribendi*, and since satire was then the thing, his flow of words often took that form. But his nature, being expansive and benevolent, was more suitable to the tavern-keeper than the satirist." *Tom Brown of Facetious Memory*, 128.

71. Hunter, "Political, Satirical, Didactic and Lyric Poetry," 193.

72. See, for instance, Ames's *The Search after Claret* (1691; 6d*), *Fatal Friendship; or, the Drunkards Misery* (1693; 6d*), *The Bacchanalian Sessions* (1693), and—a bit later—*A Satyr Against Wine* (1705).

73. Marsden, "Dramatic Satire."

74. Scouten, "Notes toward a History of Restoration Comedy"; Hume, *Development of English Drama*, introduction and chap. 9; Hughes, *English Drama*, especially chaps. 9 and 10.

75. Higden's quotation comes from the preface to his *The Wary Widdow: or, Sir Noisy Parrat* (1693).

76. An example of experimentation is Elkanah Settle's *New Athenian Comedy* (1693), a literary satire on John Dunton and the *Athenian Mercury* (1691–1696), which was never staged. See Cannan, *Emergence of Dramatic Criticism in England*, especially 148–149.

77. *The Humorists* (1670) similarly portrays a wide range of fools and fops, but the particularized personation so central to *The Sullen Lovers* is absent. In the preface, however, Shadwell complains that opposition to his satire had compelled substantial revisions: "I was forced, after I had finish'd it, to blot out the main design of it; finding, that, contrary to my intention, it had given offence" (1:183). He claims that he had not gone after individuals, but, as Hume says, the prefatory comments suggest "that Shadwell failed to get away with it a second time." *Development of English Drama*, 262. The original MS is extant; it has been printed by Richard Perkin (Dublin: Laurel House Press, 1975) but unfortunately without annotation of Shadwell's topical references.

78. See Borgman, *Thomas Shadwell*; Lloyd, "Shadwell and the Virtuosi"; and Gilde, "Shadwell and the Royal Society."

79. Hughes, *English Drama*, 160.

80. Bevis, *English Drama*, 92.

81. Hume, "The Change in Comedy," 116.

82. In the epilogue to *Love for Money*, the foregoing play is said to contain "Satyr"; in the preface to *The Campaigners*, Durfey writes of himself as a satirist and has much to say about satire (see especially 2–3) and particular satires.

83. McVeagh, *Thomas Durfey*, 113.

84. For a long time critics insisted that *The Relapse* represents a stinging rebuke of Cibber and the ethos of *Love's Last Shift*, though Cibber's enthusiastic participation as Lord Foppington suggests that this is not the way *he* perceived it. Vanbrugh might well be satirizing dramatic conventions that offer false solutions to insoluble problems, but he could just as likely be needling Cibber playfully rather than critically.

85. Milhous and Hume, *Producible Interpretation*, 298–299.

86. The most extensive treatment of marriage and law in plays from 1660–1714 is Alleman's *Matrimonial Law and the Materials of Restoration Comedy* . See also three books by Lawrence Stone: *The Family, Sex and Marriage in England*; *Road to Divorce*; and *Uncertain Unions and Broken Lives*.

87. Farquhar had clearly thought seriously about divorce. His debts to Milton's divorce tracts were pointed out by Larson in "The Influence of Milton's Divorce Tracts." See also Rothstein, *George Farquhar*, 147–149.

88. All references to *The Way of the World* are to *The Complete Plays of William Congreve*, ed. Davis (1967) . I cite this edition rather than *The Works of William Congreve*, ed. McKenzie (2011), because Davis based his text on the 1690s quartos, which bring us as close as we can get to what was performed in the theater. McKenzie's copy-text is the 1710 collected *Works*, in which the plays were revised and bowdlerized by Congreve when he created a literary monument for himself.

89. Bevis, *English Drama*, 153–154.

90. Love, *Congreve*, 88.

91. Southerne's *The Maid's Last Prayer* (1693) is an equally rigorous satire on high society that did not at all appeal to its audience. In *The Wives' Excuse*, Southerne presented predatory males taking advantage of women; *The Maid's Last Prayer*, as Jordan and Love point out, "counterbalances this by offering a picture of the ways in which women can manipulate their society, and trade upon the feelings of men." *The Works of Thomas Southerne*, 1:364.

92. Smith, *The Gay Couple*, 144.

93. Milhous and Hume, *Producible Interpretation*, 251.

94. As Kaufman concludes, "Southerne portrays . . . the wife's dilemma without recourse to the conventional conclusion which would satisfy the audience." "This Hard Condition of a Woman's Fate," 47.

Chapter 5 · Defoe, Swift, and New Varieties of Satire, 1700–1725

1. The distinctiveness of satire, particularly political satire, in the reign of Anne might reflect a trend Plumb called attention to almost half a century ago: "More general elections,

and more contests at these elections, took place between 1689 and 1715 than for the rest of the eighteenth century. Indeed, more general elections took place between 1688 and 1714 than at any other comparable period in the history of Parliament, excluding medieval times." *The Growth of Political Stability*, 10–11.

2. In the revised list of attributions accepted by Furbank and Owens in their *Critical Bibliography of Daniel Defoe*, satire occupies a surprisingly prominent place, but whether one accepts their drastically reduced canon (as I do) or rejects it, the fact remains that Defoe's corpus includes a substantial number of satires.

3. Marshall, "Daniel Defoe as Satirist."

4. Furbank and Owens, *Critical Bibliography*, 51. As a result of this satire and *Legion's Humble Address to the Lords* (also 1704), the authorities attempted to capture Defoe, but he managed to avoid arrest. Furbank and Owens, *Political Biography*, 40.

5. Two other examples are *An Account of the Great and Generous Actions of James Butler* (1715) and *The Danger of Court Differences* (1717), but those are only probable attributions.

6. DeLuna, "Yale's Poetasting Defoe," 352.

7. In *Defoe and the Idea of Fiction*, Sill discusses at length the antagonism between Defoe and Toland (130–136). See also Novak, "Defoe, the Occult, and the Deist Offensive."

8. In their *Critical Biography* Furbank and Owens include *The Political History of the Devil* as a "certain" attribution on the basis of a 1753 attribution to Defoe and the presence of several of Defoe's favorite allusions. I regard it as merely probable, though highly plausible.

9. In *A Sharp Rebuke From one of the People called Quakers to Henry Sacheverell* (1715), Defoe's Quaker accuses Sacheverell of being too fluent in "Subtilty and Equivocation" (8). Subtlety is also linked with diabolical cunning in *Memoirs of Count Tariff* (1713), *The Quarrel of the School-Boys at Athens* (1717), and *The Political History of the Devil* (1726), all merely probable attributions.

10. *Letter to Mr. Bisset* (1709), 10. This pamphlet is a probable rather than a certain attribution, though it is highly plausible.

11. Richetti, *Life of Daniel Defoe*, 21.

12. Novak, *Daniel Defoe: Master of Fictions*, 178–181.

13. I have made this argument at length in "The Generic Context of Defoe's *The Shortest-Way*."

14. See Downie, "Defoe's *Shortest Way*," 129.

15. Defoe, "A Brief Explanation of A late Pamphlet," 437.

16. A similar kind of satire is found in Prior's (?) *Dr. Sacheverell and Benjamin Hoadly* (wr. 1709) and Shippen's (?) *The Character of a Certain Whigg* (1712). *The Secret History of Queen Zarah and the Zarazians* (1705), sometimes attributed to Manley, includes politically motivated personal attack directed at the Churchills, Godolphin, Wharton, and others. See Downie, "Delarivier Manley."

17. Most exemplars of satiric grumbling occur in the first decade of the century. A rare later instance is the anonymous *Pasquin to the Queen's Statue at St. Paul's, during the Procession* (1715), a Jacobite poem expressing violent hostility to the new regime.

18. Also less common in this period than in late seventeenth-century satire is mere triumphalism, though a few exemplars exist, such as William Walsh's *Abigail's Lamentation for the Loss of Mr. Harley* (1708), *On My Lord Godolphin* (wr. 1710), and *Upon the Burning of Dr. Burgess's Pulpit* (wr. 1710).

19. Troyer, *Ned Ward of Grubstreet*, 90. Ward also thrashes the Whigs and the dissenters in *Hudibras Redivivus* (launched in 1705; all twenty-four parts were collected in the 1708 second edition).

20. *The Luttrell File*, 153.

21. Weinbrot, "Root Out This Cursed Race," 7. As Weinbrot also points out, the High Church "was equally frightened by the whiggish Dissenters' presumably genocidal urges against their true holy reformed religion" (8).

22. Ellis, *POAS-Y*, 7:43, 70.

23. Defoe's complaints about and attacks on the deception of his enemies recur throughout his career, but see, for example, *A New Discovery of an Old Intreague* (1691), *Reformation of Manners* (1702), *More Reformation* (1703), and *A Sharp Rebuke From one of the Quakers to Sacheverell* (1715).

24. Several satires at least ostensibly claim to be warning the queen against one group or another; see *On the New Promotion* (1705), *Fair Warning* (1710), and *Found on the Queen's Toilet* (1710).

25. Quoted by Ellis in *POAS-Y*, 7:388. Another overtly monitory piece is (Maynwaring's?) *An Excellent New Historical Ballad, To be sung at all the Elections in Britain* (1708?). The ballad—a warning that the Tories want to bring back the Pretender—was meant as election propaganda, urging support for "honest Whigs," who are most certainly not "Friends of old Louis." The manuscript (British Library Add. MS 61,462, fols. 17–18) is attributed to Maynwaring in an unidentified hand.

26. Ellis, *POAS-Y*, 7:160.

27. See Furbank and Owens, *Critical Bibliography*, 92–93.

28. Defoe uses the word "Subtilty" to describe Sacheverell in *A Sharp Rebuke From one of the Quakers to Sacheverell*: the divine speaks "Sentences of doubtful Interpretation, that so thou may'st reserve the Meaning thereof, as might best serve thy wicked Purposes" (8). In *The Pulpit-Fool* (1707; 1s†), Dunton denounces several particular clergymen as traitors, and his satire serves as a warning for credulous churchgoers: the pulpit-fool is "a Wolf in Sheeps Cloathing," hiding "*under Canonical Vestments*, that with more ease, and less Suspicion, he might seduce her Majesties Subjects from their Duty and Obedience" (preface).

29. Ellis, *POAS-Y*, 7:411.

30. Carolean exemplars are few; I would include *The King's Vows* (wr. 1670), *A Dialogue between Duke Lauderdale and the Lord Danby* (1679), and *On Plotters* (wr. 1680). Post-Carolean instances are more numerous, including *The Vindication* (wr. 1688), *The Female Casuist* (1690), *A Trimmer's Confession of Faith* (1694), and *St. Ignatius's Ghost* (1700).

31. Most of the monitory satires involving conformity/toleration issues are written by dissenters or their sympathizers against the High Church. An exception is the pro-Sacheverell *O Tempora! or a Satyr on the Times* (1710; 1d).

32. Ellis, *POAS-Y*, 7:55.

33. The irony of *A Great Noise About Nothing* is hard to interpret with confidence. Whether the satirist is voicing High Church anxieties or mocking them is not at all clear until the end, where the satirist defines the "Church" as "Persecution" (3). The implication is that what the High Churchmen are worried about is not the safety of their institution but the preservation of their prerogative for persecution. An angry High Churchman responded with *An Answer to the Great Noise about Nothing: or, a Noise about something* (1705).

34. Ellis, *POAS-Y*, 7:70.

35. See also Maynwaring's (?) *The History and Fall of the Conformity Bill* (1704), interpretation of which depends entirely on how we read its irony. The same could be said of Dunton's *A Cat may look on a Queen: or, a Satyr on her Present Majesty* (1705) and *The Manifesto of K. John the Second* (1715?).

36. Ellis, *POAS-Y*, 7:493.

37. Furbank and Owens, *Defoe De-Attributions*, 23 (entry no. 108).

38. Griffin, *Satire*, 39, 52.

39. Ellis, *POAS-Y*, 7:350.

40. This is exactly what the author of *The Devil Turn'd Limner* (1704) is worried about. He anxiously grumbles that Tutchin ("the Observator") and other journalists teach the people that they can make and unmake kings: "*Princes* to *Thrones* it is their Right to bring; / Thus all *Prerogative* is only lent, / Whilst they are pleased with their Government" (16).

41. See also *High-Church Miracles, or, Modern Inconsistencies* (wr. 1710), a bouncy poem whose author is clearly concerned with the implications of passive obedience and a divine right theory of kingship.

42. Defoe attempts to prevent an antigovernment reading of this satire, insisting in the preface, "If any are so weak as to suppose this is a *Satyr* against Kingly Government . . . I think I should sufficiently answer so foolish a Piece of Raillery, by saying only, *they are mistaken*" (38).

43. A similar example is *A New Ballad to ye Tune of ye Black Smith* (wr. 1710?), written upon Sacheverell's impeachment. Ballad form notwithstanding, this is textually dense, as for example:

> Says ye Rights of Church & this Teacher Mankind
> Are to God & their King by Contract confin'd
> Which if it be not Mutuall never can bind
> Which no Body dares deny.

British Library Add. MS 74,211. The satirist is arguing about divine right and objecting to the clergyman's interference in political debate.

44. The play was revised and performed under the title *Hampstead Heath*. Hume, *Development of English Drama*, 463.

45. Other satires on "types" include the toothless *A True Caracter of the Bread-street Tatlers* (1707) and the nastier *A Satyr upon Old Maids* (1713).

46. A similar satire is Ward's *The Modern World Disrob'd* (1708), which ridicules women (part I) and men (part II). A more concentrated character sketch is his earlier *The Rise and Fall of Madam Coming-Sir* (1703), a comical depiction of a barmaid.

47. See also *Parliament of Criticks, The Menippæan Satyr of Justus Lipsius in a Dream* (1702), Joseph Browne's *Liberty and Property* (1705), and *Belsize-House* (1722; 3*d*).

48. See Kinservik, *Disciplining Satire*, 12, and his "Censorship and Generic Change," 276.

49. Addison and Steele are in fact not identical satirists. In *The Spectator*, Bond explains, "Steele's point of view is generally more serious and straightforward, Addison's marked by greater variety and a spirit of comedy." For example, "the high ethical purpose of Steele's four critical papers on the drama . . . may be contrasted with Addison's high-spirited series on the absurdities of Italian opera." *The Spectator*, 1:lx. For a particularly good discussion of Addison's theory of satire, see Paulson, *Don Quixote in England*, 20–31.

50. Kinservik's discussion of Steele and Addison's program for satire is among the best; his emphasis is obviously on the ways in which this new notion of satire appears in drama. See "Censorship and Generic Change," especially 273–278.

51. *The Spectator*, 1:97 (27 March 1711); *The Tatler*, 3:241 (26 October 1710).

52. On Johnson as satiric playwright, see Kinservik, *Disciplining Satire*, 46. In *The Basset-Table*, Lord Worthy tries to reform Lady Reveller, a gambler and a coquette; the prim Lady Lucy seeks to reclaim the rowdy Sir James Courtly; a shopkeeper's wife, Mrs. Sago, is sharply satirized for living beyond her means. The three reformations are nicely moral, though *The Basset-Table* is more a comedy of manners than a piece of stodgy didacticism.

53. Victor, *An Epistle to Sir Richard Steele* (1722), 11.

54. Kenny, *Plays of Richard Steele*, 277.

55. Loftis, *Comedy and Society*, 83–86. As Hume points out, however, *The Squire of Alsatia* is "a stronger argument for Whig ideology than *The Conscious Lovers* (however defective we may think Shadwell's morality)." "Socio-Politics of London Comedy," 212.

56. Dawson, *Gentility and the Comic Theatre*, 27–28.

57. Dennis denigrates foreign influences on English culture in *An Essay on the Opera's after the Italian Manner* (1706) and in *An Essay upon Publick Spirit* (1711; 6d†), arguing in the latter for "the immediate Suppression [via taxation] of bare-fac'd Luxury, the spreading Contagion of which is . . . the greatest Extinguisher of *Publick Spirit*" (v–vi).

58. The South Sea Company (and all it stands for) is also targeted in a pair of satiric skits by Chetwood, *The Stock-Jobbers* (1720) and *South-Sea; or, the Biters Bit* (1720). The author of *Three Satires . . . to that Little Gentleman, of Great Vanity* (1719) also combines pointed attack (directed at Pope) with more general complaint (about widespread cultural collapse).

59. A less well-known example is *The Stage-Beaux toss'd in a Blanket* (1704; 1s 6d), a quasi-dramatic piece whose author (Thomas Brown?) ridicules Jeremy Collier and his followers. The characters rehearse at length arguments for and against the stage, and—despite the incisive caricatures and mocking tone—the satire reads more like a point-by-point animadversion than a lampoon.

60. Cook, *Bernard Mandeville*, 127.

61. Harth, "The Satiric Purpose of *The Fable of the Bees*," 333. Harth's study remains much the best account of Mandeville's satire, and I am indebted here to his discussion.

62. Harth, introduction to *The Fable of the Bees*, 23.

63. Spears, "The Meaning of Matthew Prior's *Alma*," 271, 290.

64. Rippy, *Matthew Prior*, 91.

65. I have discussed the "Scriblerus Club" and its influence at length in "The Myth of Scriblerus." The correspondence of Pope, Swift, Gay, Arbuthnot, and Parnell gives us very little grounds for assuming that the club's aims figured centrally in their lives. If any of our "Scriblerians" understood the meetings of 1714 as life changing or as the inspiration for later successes, we have no evidence of those sentiments. And, while some of their contemporaries certainly recognized the group members as personal friends and political allies, we have nothing to suggest that the men were seen as a "Scriblerian" cohort at any time during the century. (What spotty accounts we have of the "Club" meetings also suggest the possibility that Addison and Congreve were among the participants—two figures whom literary critics are none too eager to include among the "Scriblerian" ranks.) Satires signed by "Scriblerus" in the eighteenth century differ radically from one another: some attack pedantry, some attack Pope, and some

attack harsh satires on bad writers; some are gloomy and pessimistic, some are playful, and some are somewhere in between. Some writers connected Scriblerus to Pope and company, but that association was by no means invariable. The name "Scriblerus" clearly had some appeal (hence Fielding's adoption of "H. Scriblerus Secundus" in 1730–1731), but "Scriblerian" satire would not have meant to contemporaries what it means to us. Equally important is the fact that, however much help they gave each other, our "Scriblerians" produce very different kinds of work.

66. Damrosch, *Imaginative World of Pope*, 105.

67. Griffin, *Satire*, 40; Weinbrot, *Menippean Satire Reconsidered*, 213–230.

68. Sherburn, *Early Career*, 305.

69. Jack, *Augustan Satire*, 93.

70. Damrosch, *Imaginative World of Pope*, 111.

71. Mack, *Alexander Pope*, 296, 297. The full title of the poem is *To Mr. John Moore, Author of the Celebrated Worm-Powder*.

72. Mack, *Alexander Pope*, 298. The full title is *A Roman Catholick Version of the First Psalm*.

73. Sherburn, *Early Career*, 305.

74. Nokes, *John Gay*, 60.

75. Ibid., 58; Downie, "Gay's Politics," 47; Pellicer, "John Gay, *Wine* (1708) and the Whigs," 249. For more on the political import of *Cyder*, see Pellicer, "Harleian Georgic."

76. Lewis, "An Irregular Dog," 235.

77. *The Fan* "traces the social and verbal chiasmus between one person's toy and another's toil; between a fine lady's fashionable toilette and the toilsome labors of her servants. The grotto of Venus . . . is presented as a proletarian underworld of ceaseless toil." Nokes, *John Gay*, 132.

78. Armens describes the piece as "a pleasant poem of observation." *John Gay: Social Critic*, 73. McWhir admits the lightheartedness of much of the work but calls attention to its "moments of moral seriousness." "The Wolf in the Fold," 423. For a range of different interpretations, see Brant and Whyman, *Walking the Streets of Eighteenth-Century London*.

79. Copley and Haywood, "Luxury, Refuse and Poetry," 73.

80. The parts are *Law is a Bottomless-Pit* (pub. 6 March 1712; 3*d*), *John Bull In His Senses* (18 March; 2*d*), *John Bull Still In His Senses* (17 April; 4*d*), and *Lewis Baboon Turned Honest and John Bull Politician* (31 July; 6*d*).

81. Steensma, *Dr. John Arbuthnot*, 54.

82. The full title of the piece is *Proposals For Printing A very Curious Discourse, in Two Volumes in Quarto, Intitled, Pseudologia politice; or, a Treatise of the Art of Political Lying, with An Abstract of the First Volume of the said Treatise*.

83. Condren, *Satire, Lies and Politics*, 8–9.

84. Ibid., 36.

85. Carpenter has argued persuasively for the influence of late seventeenth-century Dublin paper wars on Swift's concept of satire. These performances, he says, were often parodic, as well as "brash, vulgar, confident, energetic, topsy-turvy, recognizing no bounds." "A School for a Satirist," 169. From my point of view, Carpenter's demonstration serves as a salutary reminder of Swift's seventeenth-century contexts, as well as another reason not simply to pigeonhole him as a "Scriblerian" writer.

86. Rawson, *Order from Confusion Sprung*, 158.

87. See, for example, the birthday poems to Stella, *To Stella, Who Collected and Transcribed*

his Poems (wr. 1720; pub. 1727); *Stella's Distress on the 3d fatal day of Octobʳ* (wr. 1723; pub. 1735); *A New-Year's-Gift for BEC* (wr. 1723; pub. 1765); and *Dingley, and Brent* (wr. 1724; pub. 1765).

88. The companion piece to this poem is *A Description of the Morning* (1709), a quietly humorous mock description that exposes, argues Downie, "the full range of discrepancies between actual and ideal." *Jonathan Swift, Political Writer*, 126.

89. Fabricant, *Swift's Landscape*, 85. What we are meant to see in *Description of a Salamander*, Fisher contends, "is a typical process which Cutts represents—the way in which it always happens, during wars, that 'reptiles' become the leaders of men." "Swift's Verse Portraits," 345.

90. Because this poem was not ascribed to Swift until it was first published in *The Gentleman's Magazine* of May 1764, the attribution has to be considered somewhat dubious. Why the poem was believed to be Swift's, *The Gentleman's Magazine* does not say.

91. Swift, *Journal to Stella*, 1:37.

92. See also Swift's *Verses on the upright Judge, who condemned the Drapier's Printer* (wr. 1724) and his attacks on Wood: *Wood, an Insect*; *On Wood the Iron-monger*; and *A Simile, on Our Want of Silver, and the only Way to remedy it* (all written in 1725).

93. Davis, "Poetry of Jonathan Swift," 108.

94. Ellis, *POAS-Y*, 7:524; Swift, *Journal to Stella*, 2:430.

95. Swift takes another shot at Nottingham ("double-Dismal") in *Peace and Dunkirk* (a 1712 broadside), which also mocks the fallen Godolphin ("Old *Godol[phi]n* full of Spleen, / Made *false Moves*, and lost his Queen") and other prominent Whigs (ll. 12, 15–16).

96. See Ellis, *POAS-Y*, 7:560.

97. See Gregg, *Queen Anne*, 344–346.

98. Ellis, *POAS-Y*, 7:553.

99. Real, "The Most Fateful Piece Swift Ever Wrote," 83.

100. Sales of this piece were evidently tremendous, despite the fact that the pamphlet cost a shilling (roughly £10–£15 in present-day terms). The first edition of a thousand copies sold out within two days, and the printer rushed a second edition into print. See the "Textual Account" of this work in Goldgar and Gadd, *English Political Writings, 1711–1714*, especially 341–342.

101. See Ehrenpreis, *Swift*, 2:491.

102. Winton, *Captain Steele*, 195, 198.

103. See Winton for a discussion what happened between the conception of *The Crisis* and its eventual publication, including the zealous promotion just before its appearance. *Captain Steele*, 185–196.

104. Ehrenpreis, *Swift*, 2:705–706.

105. Swift caused trouble for himself in this piece when he denounced the Scottish nobility, mocking the whole race, and grumbling about the Union. See the "Textual Account" in *English Political Writings, 1711–1714*, especially 449–454. The Scottish peers clamored for the prosecution of the author, and the Whigs were glad to press the issue. The government put a bounty on his head (£300, a huge amount of money), but no one squealed, and Swift managed to escape prosecution with Oxford's help. See Quinlan, "The Prosecution of Swift's *Public Spirit of the Whigs*."

106. Griffin, *Satire*, 151.

107. The most recent scholar to take up the subject is Hugh Ormsby-Lennon, whose *Hey Presto!* seeks to "resurrect the . . . verdict that *A Tale of a Tub* 'shews at bottom [the author's] contemptible Opinion of every Thing which is called Christianity,' a verdict passed by William

Wotton and the more conventionally pious among Swift's fellow-divines" (17). Ronald Paulson has convincingly argued that Swift is in *A Tale* undercutting some forms of Christianity. See *Sin and Evil*, 53–57.

108. Rosenheim, *Swift and the Satirist's Art*, 66–67.

109. Downie emphasizes the fact that Swift's satire "forces readers to think," compelling a more rigorously critical way of reading. *Jonathan Swift, Political Writer*, 96. Mueller argues similarly that Swift "feared the subversive effect of bad books on undiscerning readers. *A Tale of a Tub* . . . seeks to awaken its readers' discernment." "*A Tale of a Tub* and Early Prose," 208.

110. For an illuminating recent discussion of the politics and polemical strategies of the Bickerstaff pamphlets, see Rumbold, "Burying the Fanatic Partridge."

111. Mueller, "*A Tale of a Tub* and Early Prose," 214.

112. Paulson, *The Fictions of Satire*, 159.

113. Phiddian, "A Name to Conjure With," 141.

114. Weinbrot, *Menippean Satire Reconsidered*, 146.

115. In his life of Swift, Johnson observes that *A Tale* "is of a mode so distinct and peculiar, that it must be considered by itself; what is true of that, is not true of any thing else which he has written." *Lives*, 3:208.

116. Downie, *Jonathan Swift, Political Writer*, 92.

117. Weinbrot calls attention to the troubling effect of this satire and to Swift's "delicate balance between amusing and frightening his reader." *A Tale's* penultimate section is unsettling, ending "with the Church of England on the run, Dissent in authority over much of the nation, and the Modern narrator in authority over his imprisoned reader." *Menippean Satire Reconsidered*, 127, 159.

118. Phiddian, *Swift's Parody*, 68, 74.

119. Ellis, "*An Argument against Abolishing Christianity*," 135.

120. Bloom and Bloom, *Satire's Persuasive Voice*, 97.

121. Nokes, *Jonathan Swift*, 101.

122. Higgins, "*An Argument against Abolishing Christianity*." Higgins's excellent essay demonstrates that the *Argument* "is a brilliant appropriation of the . . . language and emphases of the Socinians," who accepted "the Church's anachronistic Trinitarian language precisely because the signification was verbal only" (215, 210). The *Argument*, Higgins rightly observes, includes a combination of "comic *élan*" and "real alarm," the latter resulting from the fact that, "as far as High Churchmen were concerned, the abolishing of Christianity *was* being proposed in print" (203, 207).

123. Suarez, "Swift's Satire and Parody," 112–113.

124. See Ehrenpreis, *Swift*, 2:284–285. This theme has been discussed at length by Steele in *Jonathan Swift: Preacher and Jester*.

125. Quintero, "Pope and Augustan Verse Satire," 215.

Chapter 6 · Harsh and Sympathetic Satire, 1726–1745

1. Hunter, *Occasional Form*, 9.

2. Examples are many, but see *The Oak, and the Dunghill* (1728), *The Levy-Haunter* (1729), and *The Citizen's Procession* (1733; 4*d*).

3. On the political satires of the major writers, see Goldgar, *Walpole and the Wits*; Gerrard,

Patriot Opposition to Walpole; and Pettit, *Illusory Consensus*. On the pro-ministerial writers, see Urstad, *Sir Robert Walpole's Poets*.

4. The most famous exemplar of this tendency is Baker, "Political Allusion." Goldgar rejected Baker's reading (of *The Author's Farce* in particular) in *Walpole and the Wits*, at 102–104, as did Cleary in *Henry Fielding, Political Writer* 28–32.

5. Few political satires are as good humored as Fielding's play. The author (Henry Carey?) of *A Learned Dissertation on Dumpling* (1726) indirectly but transparently satirizes ministerial corruption, attacking both parties as crooked and self-interested. But, however serious the satire's implications, the allegorical gimmick—"dumpling" represents aggregate political vice, and the targets are those ravenous for dumpling—is cheerfully silly.

6. *The Craftsman* was launched by Bolingbroke and Pulteney on 5 December 1726 and edited by Nicholas Amhurst; it ran until October 1752 (for a while under the title *The Country Journal, or, The Craftsman*). On visual satire against Walpole, see Carretta, *The Snarling Muse*, especially chap. 2. Beasley treats various examples of antiministerial prose satire in "Portraits of a Monster."

7. Earlier examples include Thomas Odell's *The Patron: or, the Statesman's Opera* (1729) and Pope's *The Impertinent, or a Visit to the Court* (pub. anonymously in 1733; printed in Pope's 1735 *Works* as *The Fourth Satire of Dr. John Donne*).

8. Much of the visual satire against Walpole is pretty standard fare, but one of the best-known pieces is particularly striking. *Idol-Worship; or, The Way to Preferment* (1740) depicts the colossal figure of Walpole astride the gate of St. James Palace with his breeches down and his rump uncovered. A toadying place-seeker, having mounted a pillar, is eye level with and preparing to kiss the ministerial backside.

9. William Havard's *King Charles the First* (1737), another dramatic satire against Walpole, suggests that corrupt ministers can bring about the downfall of kings. The published version of the piece "is at least as subversive as *The Fall of Mortimer*," but in performance, "a good deal of detail reinforcing the parallels to George II and Walpole was cut." Hume, *Henry Fielding*, 239.

10. Gay thought the scandal surrounding *Polly* would increase the play's marketability: the subscription price was a guinea, and the play with music was offered to other buyers for 6s. Gay was outraged when (within a week of its initial publication) pirates made it available for as little as 1s. He took legal action against this unauthorized competition but was forced to drop the quarto price to 2s 6d. See Sutherland, "'Polly' among the Pirates"; and Winton, *John Gay and the London Theatre*, especially 133–135.

11. The "majesty misled" theme also appears in Charles Forman's *Protesilaus: or, the Character of an Evil Minister* (1730; 1s), where the Great Man is defamed not at all subtly; Forman insinuates that the minister is guilty of treason and that George II would do well to realize the danger of letting him carry on unchecked.

12. Rawson reports that Walpole was sufficiently angered by *On Poetry: A Rapsody* and *An Epistle to a Lady* (both 1733) to consider ordering Swift's arrest. *Order from Confusion Sprung*, 175–176. The printers and publishers of these two satires were taken into custody; see Williams, *Poems of Jonathan Swift*, 2:629, 640.

13. In the *ODNB* entry on Whitehead, James Sambrook explains, "The House of Lords . . . ordered the author and publisher (Robert Dodsley) into custody. Whitehead decamped and Dodsley was not further prosecuted." Johnson suggested that "the whole process was probably intended rather to intimidate Pope than to punish Whitehead." *Lives*, 4:47.

14. A few satirists in this period object to the government's censorship of the stage or mock the paranoia that brings about such measures. In *A Compleat Vindication of the Licensers of the Stage* (pub. anonymously in 1739; 1s†), Samuel Johnson has his speaker argue ironically that, in Venturo's phrasing, "only suppression of the freedom of the press can bring 'peace' to Britain in these tempestuous times." *Johnson the Poet*, 65.

15. Weinbrot, *Alexander Pope*, 238.

16. *Epilogue to the Satires* actually comprises two "dialogues," printed separately in 1738 and then revised and published together under the title *Epilogue to the Satires* in 1740.

17. Johnson, *Lives*, 4:59.

18. Fabricant makes this point effectively in "Pope's Moral, Political, and Cultural Combat."

19. In this context, "low culture" refers to what someone like Pope despises and feels threatened by—the world of Manley, Haywood, Gildon, and Cibber, prolific scribblers and producers of "popular" entertainments. The milieu is richly described by Rogers in *Grub Street*.

20. See Lockwood, *Plays*, 1:364.

21. In Laetitia Pilkington's *Memoirs*, Swift is reported to have laughed only twice in his life, "once at some Trick a Mountebank's Merry-Andrew play'd; and the other time was at the Circumstance of *Tom Thumb*'s killing the Ghost" (1:312).

22. Fielding had also satirized popular entertainments and the beau monde in his poem *The Masquerade* (1728), delivering his critique with great bounce and energy.

23. Italian opera and its singers had many detractors in the second quarter of the eighteenth century, who felt that the "luxurious, irrational, effeminate import" had "insidious effects on British moral fibre, national identity, and the survival of native British drama." McGeary, "Verse Epistles," 29. McGeary provides a meaty discussion of the antecedents, characteristics, and varieties of anti-castrati satire, printing ten examples with annotations.

24. See also *The Opera of Operas; or, Tom Thumb the Great* (probably written by William Hatchett, perhaps in collaboration with others; 1733); Carey's *Margery; or, a Worse Plague than the Dragon* (1738), the sequel to *The Dragon of Wantley*; and *The Pigeon-Pye, or . . . Proper Materials For forming an Oratorio, Opera, or Play, According to the Modern Taste* (1738; 1s).

25. I note in passing that, while satire on pedantry is usually taken as a prominent enterprise in this period, in fact only a small percentage of satires have that as their target. Obviously *Peri Bathous* and *The Memoirs of Martinus Scriblerus* include satire of this sort, as does the 1729 *Dunciad*. Arbuthnot's very minor *A Brief Account of Mr. John Ginglicutt's Treatise* (1731) and *Virgilius Restauratus* (pub. 1732) are scrappy satires on learning, the first lightweight and amused, the other unfocused and less interesting. See also David Mallet's *Of Verbal Criticism: An Epistle to Mr. Pope* (1733), which defends Pope and criticizes Bentley, Theobald, and other so-called pedants. *A Tale of a Tub* is usually seen as an earlier exemplar of this sort of satire and *Tristram Shandy* as a later one, but satire on pedantry is surprisingly inconspicuous in this period.

26. Damrosch, *Imaginative World of Pope*, 120.

27. Says Mack, a touch too generously: "Whatever else the poem might be, it was a determined effort to settle scores with a mob of scribblers . . . who had made bold to sneer at him in print for nearly twenty years." *Alexander Pope*, 475. Weinbrot admits that Pope is after a fashion settling scores but also argues that his "personal motive is subsumed within the larger motive of public service—those proud of their vice should be exposed." *Menippean Satire Reconsidered*, 243.

28. Censorious responses to Pope, and to *The Dunciad* in particular, are legion. J. V. Gueri-not includes some 160 items in his *Pamphlet Attacks on Alexander Pope*. Some examples include James Ralph's *Sawney. An Heroic Poem Occasion'd by the Dunciad* (1728); the anonymous *The Female Dunciad* (1728); Ward's *Apollo's Maggot in his Cups* (1729; 1s); and Leonard Welsted's *One Epistle to Mr. A. Pope* (1730).

29. In *The Tears of the Muses* (1737), Aaron Hill laments the government's failure to provide patronage for high art. See also *Verres and his Scribblers* (1732) and Thomas Gilbert's *A Panegyric on a Court* (1739).

30. Brean Hammond, *Professional Imaginative Writing*, 242.

31. Pro-ministerial authors sometimes reversed the allegation, arguing that the opposition writers are untalented rabble-rousers pleased to rehearse popular charges. See for example *Discontent; or an Essay on Faction* (1736; 1s).

32. Swift has contempt aplenty for writers motivated by political ambition and those rewarded for loyalty rather than merit. He mocks Edward Young—whose *Love of Fame* satires had contained grand blandishment of Walpole—in *On Reading Dr. Young's Satires, called the Universal Passion* (wr. 1726), for instance, and he lampoons the Thresher poet (whom both he and Pope regarded as a bungling incompetent) in *On Stephen Duck, the Thresher and favourite Poet, a Quibbling Epigram* (wr. 1730). His most celebrated satire connecting bad literature and bad politics is *On Poetry: A Rapsody* (1733), a sour and wonderfully nasty piece of politicized lampoonery written against Dennis, Cibber, Fielding, and others, as well as party pens more generally.

33. Weinbrot, *Menippean Satire Reconsidered*, 253, 248.

34. Weinbrot, "Fielding's *Tragedy of Tragedies*," 20, 21.

35. Examples of lightweight social satire are *Vivitur Ingenio* (1726), full of satirical/comical maxims; Thomas Uvedale's *A Cure for Love* (2nd ed., 1732; 1s), a bouncy, nonbitter satire on women; and *A Trip Through the Town* (1735; 1s), a Ward-like piece of amused description. Dramatic examples include Dodsley's *Sir John Cockle at Court* (1738) and the anonymous *Bickerstaff's Unburied Dead* (1743); in both, "a wise man stands judge over a series of generalized London fools." Kinservik, *Disciplining Satire*, 130.

36. Montagu, *Complete Letters*, 2:93.

37. One of Fielding's satiric targets, as Hume points out, is the "crim. con." law: because wives were the property of husbands, they could not "consent" to extramarital sex; according to this law, therefore, a husband could collect damages for his wife's adultery from her sexual partner. *Henry Fielding*, 121–122.

38. Hunter, *Occasional Form*, 56.

39. Hogarth's *A Harlot's Progress* (1732) and *A Rake's Progress* (1735) both include pointed indictments of society and its inhabitants. Hogarth is objecting to a state of affairs he finds deplorable: the Harlot and the Rake, though not innocent, are also symptoms and victims of a dissipated society.

40. Other examples of harsh sociomoral satire are *Hell upon Earth: or the Town in an Uproar* (1729; 1s) and *Seasonable Admonitions* (1740; 1s).

41. Weinbrot, *The Formal Strain*, 138–139; the quotation from Pope is at l. 72.

42. Hume, *Rakish Stage*, 252. The quotation ("the World is all alike") is Macheath's conclusion in III.xiv (2:62).

43. Brecht's version (*Dreigroschenoper*) presumes outrage—he clearly wants his audience to

reject the grim message and to agitate for change. Gay, however, was not Brecht, and the satiric intent of *Dreigroschenoper* is not that of *The Beggar's Opera*.

44. Downie, *Jonathan Swift, Political Writer*, 216.

45. Rawson, *Order from Confusion Sprung*, 162.

46. Rosenheim, *Swift and the Satirist's Art*, 230.

47. Hammond is an exception: "contemporaries did not always regard Swift and Pope as entirely inseparable Siamese twins—the Castor and Pollux of Tory satire—as has been a prominent tendency amongst more recent readers." *Professional Imaginative Writing*, 238–239.

48. Paulson, *Hogarth's Harlot*, 68.

49. Weinbrot, *The Formal Strain*, 146, 148–149, 148.

50. This is Pope's phrasing in a 28 November 1729 letter to Swift. Pope, *Correspondence*, 3:81. Much the best discussion of Pope's use of Horatian satiric conventions in *Epistles to Several Persons* is Weinbrot's in *Alexander Pope*, chap. 6.

51. Weinbrot, *Alexander Pope*, 190.

52. On the "sermonic" nature of this poem, see Mack, *Alexander Pope*, 513.

53. Leranbaum, *Pope's "Opus Magnum,"* 102.

54. Weinbrot, *Alexander Pope*, 185.

55. Ibid., 331.

56. Ibid., 281.

57. Fabricant, *Swift's Landscape*, 85.

58. Downie, *Jonathan Swift, Political Writer*, 314. The *Libel* almost got Swift into trouble: the Irish parliament seriously considered prosecuting the printer and the author, though nothing came of it.

59. *Poems*, 3:824. Other examples include attacks on Richard Tighe (a member of the Irish Parliament) in *Mad Mullinix and Timothy* and *Tim and the Fables* (both 1728) and on Richard Bettesworth (another Irish MP and sergeant-at-law) in *On the Words—Brother Protestants, and Fellow Christians* (1733) and in *The Yahoo's Overthrow* (wr. 1734; pub. 1765).

60. As Rogers has recently demonstrated, however, Swift's most important poems in the late 1720s and 1730s tend either to concern England directly or at least to carry "English freight." "Swift and the Poetry of Exile," 128.

61. The best discussion of Swift's relationship to and attitude toward Walpole is the historian Paul Langford's "Swift and Walpole."

62. Rawson, *Order from Confusion Sprung*, 164.

63. See Swift's letter to Pope of 12 June 1732. *Correspondence*, 3:490.

64. *Directions to Servants* was published after Swift's death and two wildly variant manuscripts exist. On the fearful mess associated with this text, see Gaskell, *From Writer to Reader*, 80–100.

65. On the "checkered textual history" of the *Verses*, see Scouten and Hume, "Pope and Swift."

66. Karian has argued convincingly that "Swift intended his text to appear with gaps and blanks," thereby allowing different readers to fill in allusions in different ways. Parts of *Verses*, Karian concludes, might have "existed in either no authoritative form or in multiple authoritative forms." *Jonathan Swift in Print and Manuscript*, 196.

67. As Scouten and Hume observe, "The poem has been damned for exaggerated self-praise, defended for the 'ironic intention' of that praise, taken as a serious *apologia pro vita sua*,

and read as a seventeenth-century style religious meditation on death. No agreement at all has been reached about the basic nature of the poem." "Pope and Swift," 205.

68. Ibid., 231.

69. Swift disingenuously denied authorship of *Life*. On 1 May 1733, Swift insists to Pope that "in this Spurious piece, there is not a single line, or bit of a line, or thought, any way resembling the genuin Copy," a claim he repeats to Oxford on 31 May. *Correspondence*, 3:636, 651.

70. See Karian, *Jonathan Swift in Print and Manuscript*, 176, 180; Griffin, *Swift and Pope*, 172–175.

71. I have made this argument at length in "Swift on 'Swift.'"

72. Ehrenpreis *Swift*, 3:708.

73. Bevis, *English Drama*, 169.

74. The oddity in Gay's late-life career is *Achilles* (pub. posthumously in 1733), a ribald, farcical satire on sexual identity (the Homeric hero spends the play garbed in female attire), fashionable attitudes toward sex, and the ways of women. The piece includes political hits en passant, but the whole affair is pretty lightweight.

75. See Spacks, "John Gay," 164; and Nokes, *John Gay*, 385.

76. Gay, *Letters*, 122 (16 May 1732).

77. Nokes, *John Gay*, 505.

78. Ibid., 496.

79. Says Seidel in 2005 of the Scriblerians: "Theirs was a joint-venture company of abusive parody directed at popular public culture, government spoils and the expanded world of hack writers and periodical publishing." "Systems Satire: Swift.com," 250.

80. Kerby-Miller, introduction to *Memoirs of Scriblerus*, 50. An example of the speculation I am describing is at 315: "Though Swift never publicly said so," he asserts, "*it seems likely* that he actually began writing the travels as a direct contribution to the club scheme" (emphasis added). He offers no evidence to support this claim.

81. Pope, *Correspondence*, 2:426 (17 February 1727).

82. McLaverty, "The Failure of the Swift-Pope *Miscellanies*," 138–139. McLaverty's essay traces Swift's increasing resentment for Pope's editing of the 1727–1732 *Miscellanies*, convincingly suggesting that this experience led not only to Swift's assent to the Faulkner *Works* but also to the production of *The Life and Genuine Character of Dr. Swift* (pub. 1733). McLaverty also points out that the closeness between Pope and Swift that the *Miscellanies* were to reflect was a work of "myth-making" (132).

83. Harth, "Friendship and Politics." Griffin's *Swift and Pope*, published after I had completed my study, significantly extends and further documents the position sketched by Harth—a position with which I strongly concur.

84. *Memoirs of Scriblerus* was first published in Dublin; it was printed in London later the same year in the second volume of Pope's *Works*. That volume was wildly expensive, priced at £1 1s or, if one opted for the "cheaper" folio, a mere 10s 6d (somewhere between £100 and £150 in modern terms at the lower price). The ESTC does not report a separate London edition of this work.

85. Sherburn, *Early Career*, 305.

86. Harth, "Friendship and Politics," 240.

87. Swift's letter is at *Correspondence*, 3:245 (11 August 1729); the response is at 3:272 (28 November 1729).

344 Notes to Pages 218–223

88. Harth, "Friendship and Politics," 241.

89. Ibid., 247.

90. Johnson, *Lives*, 4:60.

91. Fabricant, *Swift's Landscape*, 197, 198.

92. Pope, *Correspondence*, 4:448 (24 March 1742/3).

93. Johnson, *Lives*, 4:47.

94. Harth, "Politics and Friendship," 247. Harth explains that Pope excluded Swift's *Libel on D[r] D[elany]* from their 1732 *Miscellanies* as part of an effort "to dissociate himself from the attitudes expressed in Swift's poem" (243). Pope lacked Swift's political temerity and was much more conservative in his political beliefs: "From such a perspective, how could he be expected to react with anything but surprise and puzzlement at such alarming political sentiments—not just their intemperate language—as he found expressed with increasing frequency in Swift's later political poems" (247).

95. Ehrenpreis, *Swift*, 3:556; Lund, "The Eel of Science," 20.

96. Weinbrot's recent study restores utility to the concept of Menippean satire, but the term has generally been applied so broadly as to become meaningless. Bakhtin and Frye defined Menippean satire so loosely that it became, in Weinbrot's phrasing, a voluminous "genre into which almost any work can be made to fit." *Menippean Satire Reconsidered*, 15.

97. Firth, "Political Significance"; Case, *Four Essays*; Harth, "Problem of Political Allegory"; Lock, *Politics of "Gulliver's Travels"*; Ehrenpreis, "Allegory of *Gulliver's Travels*."

98. Lock, *Politics of "Gulliver's Travels*," 2.

99. Varey, "Exemplary History," 41–42; Downie, "Political Significance of *Gulliver's Travels*," 14.

100. Knight, *Literature of Satire*, 68.

101. Hawes, "Three Times Round the Globe," 189.

102. Donoghue, *The Practice of Reading*, 182.

103. Fabricant, *Swift's Landscape*, 46.

104. Boyle, *Swift as Nemesis*, 38.

105. Reilly, *Jonathan Swift*; Chalmers, *Jonathan Swift and the Burden of the Future*.

106. Eddy, *"Gulliver's Travels": A Critical Study*, 189.

107. Wedel, "Philosophical Background"; Quintana, *Mind and Art*, 298.

108. Soft arguments include Ross, "Final Comedy"; Case, *Four Essays*, especially 117–126; Williams, "Voyage to the Houyhnhnms"; Tuveson, "The Dean as Satirist"; and Monk, "Pride of Lemuel Gulliver." For the hard-line approach, see Sherburn, "Errors Concerning the Houyhnhnms"; Crane, "The Houyhnhnms, the Yahoos, and the History of Ideas"; and Rosenheim, *Swift and the Satirist's Art*, especially 209–222. For a helpful overview of this debate, see Clifford, "Gulliver's Fourth Voyage."

109. Crane, "The Houyhnhnms, the Yahoos, and the History of Ideas," 263.

110. Rosenheim, *Swift and the Satirist's Art*, 219; Ehrenpreis, "Swiftian Dilemmas," 218.

111. Rawson, introduction to *English Satire*, vii.

112. Rawson, "Savage Indignation Revisited," 196.

113. Soft-school critics asked much the same questions in the mid-twentieth century, treating Don Pedro as a paragon of virtue whose humanity represents a happy alternative to Gulliver's misanthropy. Some satire theorists were then insisting that the genre must include an actual or implied *vir bonus*, which is far from universally true in this period. Be that as it may, Don

Pedro does come across as a good and decent man, and he strikes an odd note if the reader is meant to draw drastically misanthropic conclusions.

114. Rawson, *Gulliver and the Gentle Reader*, 28.

115. Ibid., 27, 28.

116. Rawson, *Order from Confusion Sprung*, 195.

117. Swift, *Correspondence*, 3:44 (3 November 1726); Ehrenpreis, "Show and Tell," 25.

118. Rawson, introduction to his and Higgins's *Gulliver's Travels*, xlii.

119. In "Swift's Satire," Elliott entertains a related possibility for a particular scene in part III when "Gulliver expresses contempt for the Laputans, then immediately praises them warmly, we are confused, and not in an artistic way: I would say Swift here has momentarily lost his footing" (415).

120. Swift, *Correspondence*, 2:352 (November/December 1720).

121. Ehrenpreis calls attention to an important difference between the *Travels* and Swift's other satires. By "connecting his attacks with their objects in the life of his time, we often infer the doctrines he is advocating; and he normally encourages us to proceed along such tracks." The *Travels*, Ehrenpreis concludes, "is less simple." *Swift*, 3:453.

122. Hunter, *Occasional Form*, 12.

123. Paulson, *Life of Henry Fielding*, 25.

124. What follows is a précis of my argument in "Henry Fielding and the 'Scriblerians.'"

125. Lockwood provides a detailed discussion of Fielding's allusions in *The Tragedy of Tragedies*. *Plays*, 1:500–504.

126. Hume, *Henry Fielding*, 89.

127. Critics have usually identified Ambrose Philips's *The Distrest Mother* (1712) as Fielding's primary target, but few audience members are likely to have made that connection. See Lewis, "Fielding's *The Covent-Garden Tragedy*."

128. Rivero, *Plays of Henry Fielding*, 138.

129. Cross, *History of Henry Fielding*, 1:172.

130. Bartolomeo, "Restoration and Eighteenth-Century Satiric Fiction."

131. Paulson, *Satire and the Novel*, 3, 5, 52. The point about Fielding's transition from satire to the novel is made at 99.

132. Paulson, *Sin and Evil*, 125.

133. Among the best studies of Fielding's attitude toward Parson Adams is Dickie's "*Joseph Andrews* and the Great Laughter Debate," chap. 4 of his *Cruelty and Laughter*. Dickie places Fielding's presentation of Adams in the context of eighteenth-century debates about "the ethics of laughter" (156).

134. Fielding, *Amelia* (1751), 2:24. I quote the original edition rather than that published by Battestin in 1983 because the Wesleyan standard edition is based—unfortunately—on the 1762 edition of *Amelia* (rather than the 1751 version). The alterations in the 1762 edition were, as Amory has demonstrated, almost certainly the work of Arthur Murphy rather than Fielding. See "What Murphy Knew."

135. McCrea, *Henry Fielding*, 168.

136. Hunter, *Occasional Form*, 3.

137. Rawson, *Gulliver and the Gentle Reader*, 93, 99.

138. Montagu, *Complete Letters*, 3:87 (22 September 1755).

139. Richetti, *English Novel in History*, 124.

140. Fielding's reader, as Reilly observes, must not "be simply well-meaning," but also "judicious, able to emancipate the inner truth from the surface appearance"; the reader must recognize that man "may be far better than his actual deeds." "Fielding's Magisterial Art," 77.

141. Fielding, "Cantos," in Grundy, "New Verse by Henry Fielding," 234 (canto 2, ll. 190, 238) and 236 (canto 3, l. 49).

142. The bleakness of *Amelia* has been much commented on, as have the disparities between it and Fielding's earlier novels. In *Amelia*, says Rawson, Fielding communicates "a sense that cruelties of circumstance, the general indecorum of things, is of an order of painfulness quite different from that normally exhibited in Fielding's work." "Fielding's Style," 172. For a full-dress study of Fielding's entire late career—placing *Amelia* and other late writings in the context of his service as a magistrate—see Bertelsen, *Henry Fielding at Work*.

143. Kinservik, *Disciplining Satire*, 13.

144. Hume, *Rakish Stage*, 201.

145. Nicoll, *History of English Drama*, 2:144.

146. Uglow, *Hogarth*, 244.

147. Paulson, *Popular and Polite Art*, 119.

148. Ogée has recently offered a reconsideration of "the nature of the similarities and differences" between Hogarth's and Fielding's "ways of seeing, or forms of looking." Granting correspondences among their works, he denies the utility of stressing a connection between Hogarth and Fielding: "a comparative survey . . . reveals that, while Hogarth was indeed addressing the disturbing issues at stake in the representation of the 'modern moral subject,' Fielding was . . . trying to breathe new life into the 'ancient moral subject.'" "O, Hogarth, Had I Thy Pencil," 201, 227.

149. Paulson, *Hogarth: His Life, Art, and Times*, 2:196, 197. As Paulson notes elsewhere, "Against Fielding's Christian solutions to the Problem of Evil, Hogarth posits the death and dissection of his evildoer here and now. . . . There is no reference in Hogarth's works to rewards (or punishments) in an afterlife; they simply do not appear, and the image of God is ordinarily elided." *Sin and Evil*, 135–136.

150. Bredvold, "Gloom of the Tory Satirists," 10.

Chapter 7 · Churchill, Foote, Macklin, Garrick, Smollett, Sterne, and Others, 1745–1770

1. Lockwood, *Post-Augustan Satire*, 3.

2. Ibid.; Bertelsen, *The Nonsense Club*.

3. Fisher, "Swift's Verse Portraits," 352.

4. The fullest account of this act is Liesenfeld, *The Licensing Act of 1737*.

5. Weinbrot, "Pope, His Successors, and the Dissociation of Satiric Sensibility," 196.

6. Elkin, *Augustan Defence of Satire*, especially 71–89.

7. Lockwood, *Post-Augustan Satire*, 21.

8. Other moralistic "satires on man" include George Canning's *Horace's First Satire Modernized* (1762; 1s); Bennet Allen's "To Mankind" (in his 1764 *Satirical Trifles*; 1s); and John Potter's sometimes venomous *The Hobby-Horse* (1766; 1s).

9. See Beatty, "Battle of the Players and Poets"; and Beatty, "Churchill's Influence." Bertelsen's discussion of the reaction to *The Rosciad* is excellent. *The Nonsense Club*, 78–90.

10. On Churchill's revisions of *The Rosciad*, see Smith, *Charles Churchill*, 28–30. Murphy was also satirized by the author of *The Murphiad* (1761).

11. Other disapproving responses to *The Rosciad* include *The Churchiliad* (a 1761 prose satire; 1s 6d) and *An Epistle to the Author of the Rosciad and the Apology* (also 1761). In the same year, Robert Lloyd defended Churchill in *An Epistle to C. Churchill*.

12. See especially chaps. 2 and 3 of Bertelsen, *The Nonsense Club*, for the literary/theatrical/journalistic satire.

13. Ibid., 21. On *The Drury-Lane Journal*, including a discussion of Thornton's fun spoof of *Amelia*, see 18–31.

14. Bertelsen, *Henry Fielding at Work*, 100. On this paper war, see also Goldgar, introduction to *"Covent-Garden Journal,"* xxxvi–xxxix.

15. See also Hugh Kelly's *Thespis* (1766) and the anonymous *Anti-Thespis* and *The Kellyad* (both 1767).

16. See Paul Baines's entry on Lauder in the *ODNB*.

17. Lockwood, *Post-Augustan Satire*, 79–80.

18. Similar examples are the anonymous *Progress of Lying* (1762; 1s), *The Quack Doctors* (1762), *A Poem on Satire* (1764), *The Demagogue* (1766), and *Liberty Deposed, or the Western Election* (1768; 1s 6d).

19. Lockwood, *Post-Augustan Satire*, 109.

20. Ibid., 22.

21. Ibid., 47.

22. I quote in passing an observation made by Smith in his discussion of *Night*: "A wide gap exists between Churchill and men like Dryden, Swift, and Pope with their faith in normalcy and their intolerance of aberration." *Charles Churchill*, 41. Dryden, Swift, and Pope are far from uniform in their worldviews, but distinguishing Churchill from his major satiric predecessors makes very good sense.

23. Sainsbury, *John Wilkes*, 97.

24. See Lockwood, *Post-Augustan Satire*, 26.

25. Ibid., 85. While the mockery in *The Ghost* is relatively light, some of its topical references are stingingly satiric, as in his portrayal of Samuel Johnson as "Pomposo." He depicts Pomposo as a powerful conversationalist and a genuinely erudite man (so far so good), but he also says that Pomposo "damns all Learning but his own" and describes him as having "Features so horrid, were it light, / Would put the Devil himself to flight" (II.666, 687–688).

26. Bertelsen, *The Nonsense Club*, 108–109.

27. Lockwood, *Post-Augustan Satire*, 8.

28. Most scholars assume that the relationship began in 1761–1762 (see Bertelsen, *The Nonsense Club*, 167), which seems likely. Nobbe suggests that the two men could have had occasion to meet in 1759. *"The North Briton": A Study*, 13–14.

29. *The North Briton* has been much studied. See Nobbe, *"The North Briton": A Study*; Thomas, *John Wilkes*, chaps. 2 and 3; and Cash, *John Wilkes*, chaps. 4 and 5.

30. Bertelsen, *The Nonsense Club*, 173. The appeal for a free press came in the opening line of *The North Briton*'s inaugural issue: "The *liberty of the press* is the birth-right of a BRITON, and is justly esteemed the firmest bulwark of the liberties of this country. It has been the terror of all bad ministers" (1:1).

31. Smith, *Charles Churchill*, 53; Nobbe, *"The North Briton": A Study*, 266. Nobbe lists

Churchill's contributions as nos. 7, 8, 10, 27, and 42; Smith attributes to Churchill nos. 8, 10, 18, 27, and 42.

32. Like the *North Briton* essays, the "Junius" letters (published in the *Public Advertiser* from 21 January 1769 to 21 January 1772) include derisive attack but were not necessarily conceived as satire. They represent political propaganda of a sort that is closely connected to the issues with which Wilkes and Churchill are so concerned and a stark contrast to the flabby literary satire covered in section I of this chapter.

33. See Thomas, *John Wilkes*, 28.

34. On Wilkes's pursuit of legal redress and the popular support of his actions, see ibid., 32–36.

35. Smith, *Charles Churchill*, 21.

36. "Patriotism" is obviously a vexed term and concept. See Griffin, *Patriotism and Poetry*, especially chap. 1. Churchill's admirers praise him as a patriot-poet; his detractors charge him and Wilkes with false patriotism. Examples of the latter are many, but see *The Conciliad: or the Triumph of Patriotism* (1761); *Patriotism! A Farce* (1763); Richard Bentley's *Patriotism, A Mock-Heroic* (1763); and *Churchill Dissected* (1764). These attacks tend to be fairly predictable, and often more personal than political.

37. Garrick, *Letters*, 1:378 (10 July 1763). Garrick added, "I am very desirous to know the opinion of the People, for I am really much, very much hurt at it—his description of his Age & infirmities is surely too shocking & barbarous—is Hogarth really ill, or does he meditate revenge?"

38. Paulson, *Art of Riot*, 33–34.

39. *Correspondence of Wilkes and Churchill*, 15.

40. In no. 17, Wilkes expresses regret at Hogarth's decision to join the controversy: "I am grieved to see the genius of *Hogarth* . . . sunk to a level with the miserable tribe of party etchers, and now, in his rapid decline, entering into the poor politics of the faction of the day, and descending to low personal abuse, instead of instructing the world, as he could once, by manly moral satire" (1:157).

41. See Carretta, *The Snarling Muse*; Carretta, *George III and the Satirists*; Donald, *Age of Caricature*; and Hunt, *Defining John Bull*. The Chadwyck-Healey series The English Satirical Print, 1600–1832, comprises thematic studies of visual satire, including Duffy's *The Englishman and the Foreigner* and Miller's *Religion in the Popular Prints, 1600–1832*. See also McCreery, *The Satirical Gaze*.

42. See Hunt, *Defining John Bull*, 12.

43. Carretta, *George III and the Satirists*, 53.

44. Both satires are from 1762; Carretta prints these (and a number of other examples) in *George III and the Satirists* (55 and 69 respectively) and discusses them at 54 and 68.

45. On *Scotch Paradice*, see Carretta, *George III and the Satirists*, 59, 63–64; he prints *John Bull's House sett in Flames* on 58, and the quotation comes from 57; on Hogarth's *The Times*, see 56–57.

46. See ibid., especially chaps. 2 and 3; and Carretta, *The Snarling Muse*, chap. 8 and epilogue.

47. Donald stresses the fact that visual satirists could use "emblematic shorthand" to avoid prosecution for libel (*Age of Caricature*, 54), a point Paulson makes with regard to Hogarth, who "demonstrates . . . that images are more indeterminate than words—they invite multiple

readings, a fact that he exploits outrageously and successfully. . . . Where the possibilities for meaning are many, a forbidden one can easily be hidden and overlooked." *Hogarth's Harlot*, 51.

48. See Thomas, *John Wilkes*, 38–56; Cash, introduction to *An Essay on Woman*, 55–68; and Cash, *John Wilkes*, 130–137, 144.

49. Cash, introduction to *An Essay on Woman*, 19.

50. Hume, *Henry Fielding*, 249.

51. Kinservik has made this argument in *Disciplining Satire*, effectively demonstrating the inapplicability of "the pejorative definition" of satire for many eighteenth-century playwrights and theatergoers (20).

52. *The Gentleman's Magazine* 17 (March 1747), 140. On the contemporary response, see Kinservik, *Disciplining Satire*, 120–128. Kinservik points out that *The Suspicious Husband* was the first successful satiric comedy following the passage of the Licensing Act, arguing that the censorship of the stage compelled playwrights to produce sympathetic and morally instructive rather than punitive satire.

53. Foote, *The Roman and English Comedy Consider'd and Compar'd* (1747), 27.

54. Hume, *Rakish Stage*, 349.

55. See Bevis, *The Laughing Tradition*, 203.

56. *What we must All come to* was immediately damned. See Dunbar, *Dramatic Career of Arthur Murphy*, 164–172. The play was revived (with moderate success) as *Marriage a-la-Mode* (1767) and as *Three Weeks After Marriage* (1776).

57. Boswell quotes Johnson as saying, in 1775, "I am told Foote means to *take me off*, as he calls it, and I am determined the fellow shall not do it with impunity." *Life of Johnson*, 2:299. On the sodomy trial, see Kinservik, "Satire, Censorship, and Sodomy."

58. Kinservik, *Disciplining Satire*, 150.

59. Conolly, *Censorship of English Drama*, 118, 121. On the controversy surrounding *The Minor* and Foote's revisions, see 117–122. For a list of some twenty topical and controversial contributions to the debate about *The Minor*, see Arnott and Robinson, *English Theatrical Literature*, nos. 2776–2796. On responses to Foote's play, see also Belden, *Dramatic Work of Samuel Foote*, 85–106.

60. As Kinservik concludes, "For most theatregoers, *The Minor* was another of Foote's plays that had a reputation for Aristophanic exposure of real people, but that had very little in the way of dragging actual miscreants before an audience for judgment." *Disciplining Satire*, 151.

61. *Piety in Pattens* is extant as Larpent MS no. 346 and Folger MS D.a.48. It was printed by Bogorad and Noyes in *Samuel Foote's "Primitive Puppet-Shew" Featuring "Piety in Pattens": A Critical Edition*, published as a special issue of *Theatre Survey* 14 (1973), no. 1a.

62. Bogorad and Noyes, *Foote's "Primitive Puppet-Shew,"* 15.

63. Conolly, *Censorship of English Drama*, 115. On the suppression of the play, see 114–117.

64. See Kinservik, *Disciplining Satire*, 152–155.

65. Bevis, *The Laughing Tradition*, 166.

66. Chatten, *Samuel Foote*, 109.

67. Both *A Will and No Will* and *The New Play Criticiz'd, or The Plague of Envy* (1747) were first published in the Augustan Reprint series, with an introduction by Kern.

68. No Larpent MS of this play exists, but there are two largely identical pirated printings of 1750. See Findlay, "Comic Plays of Charles Macklin," 401–402.

69. That the Irish Callaghan is the hero of the play is no surprise. Macklin's most famous

celebration of the Irish spirit is *The True-Born Irishman* (perf. 1762; pub. 1783), in which he savagely mocks the Anglophilia of Mrs. O'Dogherty, who changes her name to "Diggerty."

70. Two of Macklin's midcentury afterpieces are more particularized. *The New Play Criticiz'd, or The Plague of Envy* (perf. 1747; not pub. until the twentieth century) is a critical response to Hoadly's *The Suspicious Husband*. *Covent Garden Theatre, or Pasquin Turn'd Drawn-cansir* (perf. 1752; not pub. until the twentieth century) is a scattershot attack on a number of playwrights and on a host of other social follies. Its topicality was objected to by the censor. Conolly, *Censorship of English Drama*, 7.

71. Kinservik, *Disciplining Satire*, 183.

72. Findlay, "Comic Plays of Charles Macklin," 405.

73. Appleton, *Charles Macklin*, 212. On Macklin's revisions, see ibid., 211–213; and Kinservik, *Disciplining Satire*, 189–195. Five editions of *The Man of the World* were published in Dublin between 1785 and 1791, but the play was sufficiently toxic that it did not get printed in London until 1793.

74. One of the excised passages (which Bartley includes in brackets) is Sir Pertinax's call for Scottish solidarity: "Sir, Scotchmen—Scotchmen, sir—wherever they meet throughoot the globe—should unite and stick together, as it were in a poleetecal phalanx. Sir, the whole world hates us, and therefore we should loove yean anaither" (219).

75. Kinservik, *Disciplining Satire*, appendix. The manuscript is at the Pennsylvania State University, shelfmark PS-V-MS-61. My discussion of this satire is indebted to Kinservik; when I quote from this manuscript, I give the page number from his transcription.

76. Bevis, *The Laughing Tradition*, 146.

77. Garrick, "Part of a Prologue to *Harlequin's Invasion*," in *Poetical Works*, 1:158. For discussion of Garrick's speaking Harlequin, see Pedicord and Bergman, *The Plays of David Garrick*, 1:405. On Garrick's desire to compete with Rich, and on the effectiveness of the latter as a performer of mime, see Hume, "John Rich as Manager and Entrepreneur."

78. On the nationalism of *Harlequin's Invasion*, see O'Brien, *Harlequin Britain*, 135, 225–231.

79. Hume, *Rakish Stage*, 353.

80. John Lee had done much the same thing to Wycherley in his sanitized *The Country Wife* (1765; also staged at Drury Lane), though his play is a two-act farce rather than a full-length social comedy.

81. Wycherley, *Plays*, 480.

82. Pedicord, "*Ragandjaw*." The MS is Norfolk Record Office WKC 7/48, 404 x 2 (Ketton-Cremer).

83. Garrick, *Poetical Works*, 1:82.

84. *Theophilus Cibber, to David Garrick, Esq* (1759), 44–45.

85. Kinservik, *Disciplining Satire*, 138–139.

86. Stone and Kahrl, *David Garrick*, 478.

87. Kenrick, *A Letter to David Garrick* (1772), 7.

88. Davies, *Memoirs*, 2:276.

89. Garrick's best-known personal satire is *The Fribbleriad* (1761; 1s), part of an ongoing feud with the Irish critic Thaddeus Fitzpatrick, whom he mocks here as unlearned and effeminate. *The Fribbleriad*, though not an exercise in unprovoked meanness, is an energetic and cutting put-down of a personal and professional enemy.

90. Paulson, *Satire and the Novel*, 8, 9, prefatory note, 306, 309.

91. Palmeri, *Satire, History, Novel*, 273.

92. Palmeri, *Satire in Narrative*, 6. Palmeri attempts to revise Bakhtin's notion of parody, which simply "dislodges officialdom by means of carnival, its inverting opposite." Palmeri's theory of satiric narrative is that it parodies *both* the official world and its opposite: "Narrative satire presents a parodic antithesis to orthodoxy and then the negative of that antithesis; it describes a dialectic without a synthesis" (2, 3).

93. Smollett is probably also the author of a prose piece called *A Faithful Narrative of the Base and inhuman Arts That were lately practic'd upon the Brain of Habbukkuk Hilding* (1752; 6*d*), a savage attack on Fielding and Lyttelton. For attribution to Smollett, see Brack, "Tobias Smollett's Authorship of *Habbukkuk Hilding*." Chilton has recently offered a useful discussion of two other minor satires by Smollett, *Thomsonus Redivivus* (1746) and *Don Ricardo Honeywater Vindicated* (1748), both of which date from Smollett's early medical career. See "Smollett, the Picaresque, and Two Medical Satires."

94. Beasley, *Tobias Smollett*, 69.

95. Ibid., 223.

96. Many eighteenth-century printings of the *Atom* contained explanatory keys. Day, *Atom*, 249.

97. Ibid., lxi. On the publication and reception of the *Atom*, see lvii–lxii.

98. Hunter, *Occasional Form*, 209.

99. Goldgar, introduction to *"Covent-Garden Journal,"* xxxiv.

100. Battestin and Battestin, *Henry Fielding*, 545.

101. Goldgar, introduction to *"Covent-Garden Journal,"* xxvii; see also Battestin and Battestin, *Henry Fielding*, 542.

102. Bertelsen, *Fielding at Work*, 27, 4.

103. Another oddity is the nonfictional *The Journal of a Voyage to Lisbon* (pub. posthumously in 1755; 3*s*†), which combines social commentary and world-weariness with literary game playing, but that Fielding imagined this as satire I am inclined to doubt.

104. Keymer, introduction to *Laurence Sterne's "Tristram Shandy,"* 7. The standard study of *Tristram Shandy*'s reception is Howes, *Yorick and the Critics*. See also de Voogd and Neubauer, *Reception of Laurence Sterne*; and Bosch, *Labyrinth of Digressions*.

105. In Howes, *Sterne: The Critical Heritage*, 52. Subsequent citations will be given in the text, abbreviated *CH* with page number.

106. *London Chronicle*, 16–18 April 1765, 373.

107. Howes observes that eighteenth-century reviewers made no "extended mention of Locke," lamenting that "probably most readers did not understand this part of the plan of *Tristram Shandy*." *Yorick and the Critics*, 36.

108. Stedmond, "Satire and *Tristram Shandy*," 62.

109. New, *Laurence Sterne as Satirist*, 1–2, 2–3.

110. Parnell, "Swift, Sterne, and the Skeptical Tradition," 226–227.

111. Keymer, *Sterne, the Moderns, and the Novel*, 7, 16. Another recent attempt to "locate *Tristram Shandy* in relation to Scriblerian satire" is Regan, "Novelizing Scriblerus." Regan looks not only at affinities between "Scriblerian" satire and *Tristram Shandy* but at important differences as well. He concludes that placing Sterne in a tradition of learned wit is problematic

because "'Learned wit' . . . is not a unitary category" and that neither "is *Tristram Shandy* the kind of unitary *text* to which a single label . . . might be applied" (27). This seems sensible, though what we gain by calling *Tristram Shandy* "post-Scriblerian" is not clear to me.

112. Sterne, *Letters*, 116, 80 (30 January 1760; 23 May 1759).

113. Novak describes *Tristram Shandy* as a book in which "comedy is wrested from a view of life that is essentially sad," though he concludes that "Sterne's most powerful effects are achieved by the assumption that the feelings of the narrator and the characters are part of a real world that is best approached through comedy and laughter." "Satirical Form and Realistic Fiction," 137, 145.

114. Briggs, "Locke's *Essay* and the Tentativeness of *Tristram Shandy*," 495.

115. The most systematic study of Sterne's "skepticism" is Parker, *Scepticism and Literature*, chap. 5.

116. Weinbrot, *Menippean Satire Reconsidered*, 11.

117. Briggs, "Locke's *Essay* and the Tentativeness of *Tristram Shandy* ," 517–518.

118. Sterne, *Tristram Shandy*, 1:76.

119. Keymer, "*A Sentimental Journey* and the Failure of Feeling," 80.

120. Lamb, "Sterne and Irregular Oratory," 154. I confess to finding Lamb's argument ponderous, though some of the insights are sharp and provocative, as for example: "in *Tristram Shandy* Tristram defends the unimpeachable singularity of his characters against readers who might like to judge them according to an objective criterion" (157).

121. New, *"Tristram Shandy": A Book for Free Spirits*, 39.

122. Ibid., 32.

123. Keymer's *Sterne, the Moderns, and the Novel* offers the best discussion of just how much *Tristram Shandy* belongs to its moment.

124. Ross, *Laurence Sterne*, 4.

125. "Lennox's radical departure," Paulson argues, "is to have Dulcinea change places with Quixote and become the protagonist. . . . Arabella is both Quixote and Dulcinea—the roles being not exchanged but combined; and for this reason she worships herself." *Don Quixote in England*, 171.

126. Todd, *Sign of Angellica*, 159–160.

127. See Ross, "Mirror, Mirror"; and Rothstein, "Woman, Women, and *The Female Quixote*."

128. Hopkins, *True Genius of Goldsmith*, 27.

129. For some contextual background that helps explain Goldsmith's view of Dr. Primrose's moral responsibility, see Rothstein and Weinbrot, "The Vicar of Wakefield."

130. Quintana, *Oliver Goldsmith*, 108.

131. Gadeken, "Sarah Fielding," 552, 543–544.

132. Frye, "Towards Defining an Age of Sensibility," 144.

133. For Weinbrot's demolition of Frye's arguments, see "Northrop Frye and the Literature of Process Reconsidered."

134. For an excellent discussion of the "unsentimental" attitudes toward laughter in the mid- and later eighteenth century, see Dickie, *Cruelty and Laughter*. Dickie demonstrates that midcentury senses of humor are remarkably cruel and that "Eighteenth-century Britons—or a high proportion of them—openly delighted in the miseries of others" (1).

135. Black, introduction to *British Politics and Society*, 23.

Epilogue

1. Dennis, *Critical Works*, 2:201.

2. Said, "Swift's Tory Anarchy," 56.

3. See Hume, *Reconstructing Contexts*, 38–41.

4. Bredvold, "Gloom of the Tory Satirists," 3, 7.

5. See Williams, *Poetry and the Creation of a Whig Literary Culture*; and Womersley, "Cultures of Whiggism."

6. Hudson, review of Williams, *Poetry and the Creation of a Whig Literary Culture*, 456.

7. Perkins, *Is Literary History Possible?*, 27.

8. Throughout this study I have regularly rediscovered the truth of Levin's "two tentative principles" concerning the application of "literary historical contexts." The first is that "it would seem better to use a more proximate or specific genre (or subgenre) than a more general one within the same period—to use Elizabethan revenge tragedy, that is, rather than Elizabethan tragedy." And second, "it would seem better to determine the contemporary conception of that genre from the actual practice of the time, as seen in the works written within the genre, rather than from the theory promulgated in treatises on the subject." "The Problem of 'Context' in Interpretation," 93–94.

9. Lyotard, *The Postmodern Condition*, 60.

The bibliography is divided into two parts: Primary Sources from the Seventeenth and Eighteenth Centuries (both anonymous and attributed) and Criticism and Scholarship. Dates are of publication unless otherwise stated. Occasional broadsides and squibs were often published without date, and many of the hundreds of poems published in the original *Poems on Affairs of State* collections between 1689 and 1716 are from years or decades earlier and undatable except by deduction from content. As with play performance and publication, where there is a gap between a determinable date of composition and a known date of separate publication, I so indicate following the title of the work, but in many cases indeterminate dates make this impossible. I list first publication date where it differs from known composition date *only* when the work appeared separately—not when a work was first published in *State Poems* or other collections.

Poems reprinted with editorial apparatus in the seven-volume Yale *Poems on Affairs of State* (1963–1975) are usually cited from that source (*POAS-Y*) if printed from manuscript or broadside sources I have been unable to obtain through EEBO or ECCO. John Harold Wilson's *Court Satires of the Restoration* is abbreviated *CSR*. The Wing number is given for items separately published prior to 1701. Anonymously published or scribally circulated items are listed alphabetically by title in the "Anonymous" section, but where attributions have been offered, they are reported in brackets at the end of the entry. Such attributions are from *POAS-Y* if the work is cited from that source; otherwise the source is the English Short Title Catalogue. When there is widespread critical consensus on the authorship of anonymous works, those works are listed under the presumed author's name; otherwise they are listed in the "Anonymous" section, though sometimes with tentative attributions in brackets. Where good modern editions exist (e.g., the Oxford *Buckingham* and *Rochester*) items are cited from that source. A great many of the poems survive in manuscript, sometimes in a bewildering number of variant forms. I have usually cited printed versions when they exist on the theory that print usually involved wider dissemination. Insofar as possible, I have tried to cite the earliest separate published version rather than a text to be found in one or more of the original *Poems on Affairs of State* collections.

Primary Sources from the Seventeenth and Eighteenth Centuries

Anonymous

An Account of a Conference between His Grace George, late Duke of Buckingham, and Father Fitzgerald an Irish Priest (pub. 1705 in Buckingham's *Second Volume of Miscellaneous Works*).

Printed with apparatus in *Plays, Poems, and Miscellaneous Writings Associated with Buckingham.*

Acrostick (wr. ca. 1679–1681?). British Library Add. MS 34,362, fol. 47r.

An Address to Our Sovereign Lady. [London], 1704 [by Arthur Maynwaring?].

Advice to a Painter (wr. 1697). In *POAS-Y*, vol. 6.

Advice to a Painter to Draw the Duke by (wr. 1673). In *POAS-Y*, vol. 1.

Advice to Apollo (wr. 1677). In *POAS-Y*, vol. 1.

Advice to the Ladies. A Satyr. [London?], 1754.

Advice to the Painter, From a Satyrical Night-Muse, for Limning to the Life the Witnesses Against the Right Honourable, Anthony, Earl of Shaftesbury. London, 1681 [Wing A661].

The Age of Dullness. A Satire. By a Natural Son of the late Mr. Pope. London, 1757.

The Age of Wonders: To the Tune of Chivy Chase. [London], 1710.

Anno 1696 (wr. 1696). British Library Stowe 305, fols. 213v–214r.

An Answer to the Great Noise about Nothing: or, a Noise about something. [London], 1705.

Anti-Thespis: or, a Vindication of the Principal Performers at Drury-Lane Theatre from the False Criticisms . . . of a Poem lately published. . . . London, 1767.

Ars Punica. Pars Altera. or, Truth Vindicated from the Misrepresentations of the Dean of Worcester. Being a Faithful Collection of Ecclesiastical Puns, Quibbles, Græcisms, and Conundrums. . . . London, 1721.

The Bacchanalian Sessions; or the Contention of Liquors: with A Farewel to Wine. London, 1693 [Wing A2975] [by Richard Ames?].

A Ballad (wr. 1667). In *CSR*.

A Ballad Called Perkin's Figary, or, A ballad new which doth most plainly show How Seventy-Nine would fain be Forty-Two (wr. 1679). In *POAS-Y*, vol. 2.

A Ballad called the Haymarket Hectors (wr. 1671). In *POAS-Y*, vol. 1.

Ballad on Betty Felton (wr. 1680). In *CSR*.

The Banished Priests' Farewell to the House of Commons (wr. 1673). In *POAS-Y*, vol. 1.

Belsize-House. A Satyr . . . with the Rake's Song on the Falshood of Woman: The Libertine's Song: Another by a Rejected Virgin: And the Belsize Ballad. London, 1722.

Bess o' Bedlam's Love to her Brother Tom: With a Word in behalf of Poor Brother Ben Hoadly. London, 1709.

Bickerstaff's Unburied Dead. A Moral Drama. London, 1743.

Biographia Classica: The Lives and Characters of all the Classic Authors . . . With An Historical and Critical Account of Them and their Writings, 2 vols. London, 1740.

Bribery A Satire. London, 1750 [by César de Missy?].

The British Worthies: or, Characters of the Age. A Panegyrico-Satirical Poem. London, 1758.

Brooke and Hellier. A Satyr. London, 1712.

The Cabal. London, 1680 [Wing C179].

Candour: Or, An Occasional Essay on the Abuse of Wit and Eloquence. London, 1739.

A Canto on the New Miracle Wrought by the Duke of Monmouth (wr. 1681). In *POAS-Y*, vol. 2.

The Censor. 3 vols. 2nd ed. London, 1717.

Cethegus' Apology for Non-Appearance upon his Conjurer's Summons. London, 1682 [Wing C1784].

The Character (wr. 1679). In *POAS-Y*, vol. 2.

The Character of a Certain Whigg. [London], 1712.

A Character of the Church of Chichester (wr. 1673). In *POAS-Y*, vol. 1.

A Charge to the Grand Inquest of England (wr. 1674). In *POAS-Y*, vol. 1.

The Chequer Inn (wr. 1675). In *POAS-Y*, vol. 1.

The Church of England's Glory: or, the Vindication of Episcopacy. London, 1688 [Wing C4194].

The Churchiliad: or, a few Modest Questions proposed to the Reverend Author of the Rosciad. [London], 1761.

Churchill Dissected. London, 1764.

The Citizen's Procession, or, the Smugler's Success and the Patriots Disappointment. Being An excellent New Ballad on the Excise-Bill. London, 1733.

The City Triumphant: or, the Burning of the Excise-Monster. A New Ballad. London, 1733.

Claudian's Rufinus: or, the Court-Favourite's Overthrow. London, 1730.

The Clerical Cabal (wr. 1688). In *POAS-Y*, vol. 4.

The Club of Royalists (wr. 1681). In *POAS-Y*, vol. 2.

Codrus: or, the Dunciad Dissected. Bring the Finishing-Stoke. London, 1728 [by Edmund Curll and Elizabeth Thomas?].

The Comical Pilgrim; or, Travels of a Cynick Philosopher, Thro' the most Wicked Parts of the World . . . being A General Satyr on the Vices and Follies of the Age. London, 1722.

The Compleat Fop (wr. 1685). Folger MS M b 12, fols. 133v–134r.

The Conciliad: or the Triumph of Patriotism. London, 1761.

The Connoisseur. A Satire On the modern Men of Taste. London, 1735.

Corinna; or, Humane Frailty. A Poem. With an Answer to the E. of R[ochester]'s Satyr against Man. London, 1699 [Wing C6297].

The Counterpart to the State-Dunces. London, 1733.

The Country Parson's Advice to Those Little Scriblers Who Pretend to Write Better Sense Than Great Secretaries: Or, Mr. Stephens's Triumph over the Pillory. London, 1706.

The Court and City Medley; or, Political Shaver; Being a curious Collection of Satirical Originals, in Prose and Verse; adapted to the Present Times. London, 1764.

Crack upon Crack: or Crack-Fart Whipt with his own Rod. [London], 1680 [Wing C6738C].

The D: of B: Letany. Pub. 1679 as *The Litany of the D. of B.* In *Plays, Poems, and Miscellaneous Writings Associated with Buckingham*, appendix II.

The D[utch] Deputies. A Satyr. London, 1705.

The Dancing-Master. A Satyr. London, 1722.

Deal in an Uproar. A Satyr. London, 1713.

Declaration without Doors. [London, 1705].

The Deliquium: or, The Grievances of the Nation discovered in a dream. [London, 1680?] [Wing D908].

The Demagogue. London, 1766 [by William Falconer?].

The Devil Pursued: or, the Right Saddle Laid upon the Right Mare. A Satyr upon Madam Celliers. London, 1680 [Wing D1220].

The Devil Turn'd Limner: Or A Celebrated Villain drawn to the Life. With A Satyr against Loyalty, Suppos'd to be spoken By Bradshaw's Ghost to the Observator and Legion. London, 1704.

The Devil upon Crutches in England, or Night Scenes in London. A Satirical Work. London, 1755.

The Devil's Journey to London, or, The Visit Repaid Ned W[ar]d. Being a Satyr sent to Physicians College in Warwick-Lane. London, 1700 [Wing D1227A].

A Dialogue between Duke Lauderdale and the Lord Danby. [London], 1679 [Wing D309].

A Dialogue between Nathan and Absalom (wr. 1680). In *POAS-Y*, vol. 2.

A Dialogue between the Two Horses (wr. 1676). In *POAS-Y*, vol. 1.

Discontent; or an Essay on Faction: a Satire. Address'd to the Writers of the Craftsman, and other Party Papers. London, [1736].

A Discourse on Ridicule. London, 1716.

The Dissenters' Thanksgiving for the Late Declaration (wr. 1688). Pub. in collections in 1689. In *POAS-Y*, vol. 4.

The Dissolution 1679 (wr. 1679). British Library Add. MS 34,362, fols. 48–49.

The Divorce (wr. 1692). In *POAS-Y*, vol. 5.

The Dog in the Wheel. A Satyr. London, 1705.

The Downfall of the Chancellor (wr. 1667). In *POAS-Y*, vol. 1.

Dr. Sacheverell and Benjamin Hoadly (wr. 1709). In *POAS-Y*, vol. 7 [by Matthew Prior?].

The Dream of the Cabal: A Prophetical Satire Anno 1672 (wr. 1672). In *POAS-Y*, vol. 1.

An Epistle to the Author of the Rosciad and the Apology. London, 1761.

An Essay of Scandal (wr. 1681). In *CSR*.

The Essex Ballad to an old tune new reviv'd. London, 1680 [Wing E3341].

An Excellent New Ballad between Tom the Tory, and Toney the Whigg. London, 1678 [Wing E3803].

An Excursory View of the Present State of Men and Things. A Satire. In a Dialogue between the Author and his Friend. London, 1739.

The Fair Thinker, or Reason Asserted: in a Dissection of Bigottry and Devotion. A Satire. London, 1740.

Fair Warning. In *The Observator*, no. 24 (5 April 1710).

A Faithful Narrative of the Base and inhuman Arts That were lately practic'd upon the Brain of Habbukkuk Hilding, Justice, Dealer, and Chapman. London, 1752 [by Tobias Smollett?].

The Fall of Mortimer. An Historical Play. London, 1731.

The Fatal Union of France and Spain. A Satyr. London, 1701 [title page attribution to H. J. Esq.].

The Female Casuist, or Sherlock's Conversion (wr. 1690). In *POAS-Y*, vol. 5.

The Female Dunciad. London, 1728.

The Female Nine (wr. 1690). In *POAS-Y*, vol. 5 [by Charles Mordaunt, Earl of Monmouth?].

The Female Wits: or, the Triumvirate of Poets At Rehearsal (wr. 1696). London, 1704 [title page attribution to Mr. W. M.].

The Folly of Industry: or, the Busy Man Expos'd. A Satyr, Address'd to a Friend. London, 1704 [by William Wycherley?].

Folly, A Satire on the Times. Written by a Fool, and younger Brother to Tristram Shandy. London, [1763?].

Fontenoy, A New Satiric Ballad. London, [1745].

The Footman: An Opera. London, 1732.

Found on the Queen's Toilet (wr. 1710). In *POAS-Y*, vol. 7.

Fourth Advice to a Painter (1667). In *Directions to a Painter*, a small collection printed under Sir John Denham's name; the text of this poem is printed without a title at 16–18 and is run together with the text of the *Fifth Advice to a Painter* [Wing D998].

Garrick's Vagary: or, England Run Mad. London, 1769.

The General Cashier'd: A Play, As Design'd for the Stage. London, 1712.

The Geneva Ballad. To the Tune of 48. London, 1674 [Wing G516].

A Grammar of the English Tongue, With Notes, Giving the Grounds and Reason of Grammar in General. 2nd ed. London, 1712.

The Great Despair of the London Whigs (wr. 1683). Printed 1685 in *A Collection of 86 Loyal Poems . . . Collected by N. T.* [Wing T1005].

A Great Noise About Nothing: Or The Church's Danger. A Satyr. [London?], 1705.

Grimalkin, or, the Rebel Cat: A Novel. London, 1681 [Wing G2026].

A Health to the Tackers, or the Coventry Ballad. In *The Diverting Post*, no. 24 (31 March 1705). Reprinted in *POAS-Y*, vol. 7.

Hell upon Earth: or the Town in an Uproar. London, 1729.

The Hell-Fire-Club: Kept by a Society of Blasphemers. A Satyr. London, 1721.

An Heroic Poem 1681 (wr. 1681). In *POAS-Y*, vol. 2.

[Multiple authors]. *Hibernicus's Letters: or, a Philosophical Miscellany. Containing (among many others) Essays on the following useful and entertaining Subjects . . . Interspersed with several Original Poems and Translations*. 2nd ed. 2 vols. London, 1734.

High-Church Miracles, or, Modern Inconsistencies (wr. 1710). In *POAS-Y*, vol. 7.

The Highland Seer, or The Political Vision (1762). In Carretta, *George III and the Satirists*, 69.

An Historical Poem (wr. 1680). In *POAS-Y*, vol. 2.

The History of Insipids (wr. 1674). In *POAS-Y*, vol. 1.

The History of Seven (wr. 1710). In *POAS-Y*, vol. 7.

Hob turn'd Courtier. A Satyr. London, 1703 [by Edward Ward?].

The Hobby-Horse: A Characteristical Satire on The Times. London, 1766 [by John Potter?].

Hodge (wr. 1679). In *POAS-Y*, vol. 2.

The Honest Electors; or, the Courtiers sent back with their Bribes, A New Ballad Opera (not performed). London, 1733.

A Hue and Cry (wr. 1688). In *POAS-Y*, vol. 5.

Human Passions: A Satyr. London, 1726.

The Humble Address (wr. 1685). In *POAS-Y*, vol. 4.

The Humble Address of the Clergy of London and Westminster, Paraphras'd (1710). In *POAS-Y*, vol. 7 [by Arthur Maynwaring?].

The Humours of the Court: or, Modern Gallantry. London, 1732.

The Hungry Mob of Scriblers and Etchers (1762). In Carretta, *George III and the Satirists*, 55.

Idol-Worship; or, The Way to Preferment (1740). In Carretta, *The Snarling Muse*, 47.

The Important Triflers. A Satire: set forth In a Journal of Pastime A-la-mode, among Young-People of Fashion, in the Spring Season of the Year. London, 1748.

The Independent Whig. London, 1721.

John Bull's House sett in Flames (1762). In Carretta, *George III and the Satirists*, 58.

Julian's Farewell to the Coquets (wr. 1687). In *CSR*.

The Junto. [London, 1710] [by William Shippen?].

The Kellyad: or a Critical Examination into the Merits of Thespis. London, 1767.

The King's Farewell to Danby with His Speedy Recantation, and the Author's Paraphrase Thereupon (wr. 1679). In *POAS-Y*, vol. 2.

The King's Vows (wr. 1670). In *POAS-Y*, vol. 1.

Kitty's Stream: or, the Noblemen turned Fisher-Men. A Comic Satire. Addressed to The Gentleman in the Interest of the Celebrated Miss K[itt]y F[ishe]r. London, 1759.

Korath: or the Danger of Schism. A Satyr. [London], 1705.

Lampoon (wr. 1676). In *CSR*.

The Last Will and Testament of Anthony King of Poland. [London], 1682 [Wing L514aA].

Laugh upon Laugh, or Laughter Ridicul'd. A Poem, Ethi-Comico-Satyrical. Treating of the several Kinds or Degrees of Laughter. London, 1740.

The Law Corrupted; a Satire. London, 1706.

The Lawyers Answer to the Country Parson's good Advice to My Lord Keeper. London, 1706.

A Learned Dissertation on Dumpling; Its Dignity, Antiquity, and Excellence. With a Word upon Pudding. And Many other Useful Discoveries, of great Benefit to the Publick. London, 1726 [by Henry Carey?].

A Letter from a Gentleman in London, to his Friend in Pensylvania; with a Satire; containing Some Characteristical Strokes upon the Manners and Principles of the Quakers. London, 1756 [by William Smith?].

"Letter to Euphronius." In *English Originals in Prose and Verse Collected by I. L. Schulze, A.M.* 2nd ed. Hall [*sic*], 1766 [by Thomas Fitzosborne?].

Leviathan, or, a Hymn to Poor Brother Ben. London, 1710.

The Levy-Haunter, A Satire. London, 1729.

Liberty Deposed, or the Western Election. A Satirical Poem. London, [1768?].

Liberty in the Suds; or, Modern Characters. In a Letter to a Friend. London, 1764.

The Lion and Fox, or, the Matchievelian; A Satire. London, 1735.

A Litany (wr. 1672). In *POAS-Y*, vol. 1.

A Litany for the Monthly Fast (wr. 1692). In *POAS-Y*, vol. 6.

The Long Vacation. A Satyr. London, 1708.

Lord Blunder's Confession; or, Guilt makes a Coward. A New Ballad-Opera (not performed). London, 1733.

The Lost Maiden-head: or, Sylvia's Farewell to Love. A New Satyr against Man. London, 1691 [Wing L308].

A Loyal Satyr against Whiggism. London, 1682 [Wing L3365].

The Lunatick. A Comedy. Dedicated to the Three Ruling B——s at the New-House in Lincolns-Inn-Fields. London, 1705 [by William Taverner?].

Madam Le Croix (wr. 1686). In *CSR*.

The Man of Honour, Occasion'd by the Postscripts of Pen's Letter (wr. 1687) [by Charles Montagu?]. Published in collections in 1689. In *POAS-Y*, vol. 4.

Marvell's Ghost (wr. 1678). In *POAS-Y*, vol. 1. [by John Ayloffe?].

Marvell's Ghost (wr. 1691). In *POAS-Y*, vol. 5.

Meditations of the Mirth of a Christian Life. And the Vaine Mirth of a Wicked Life, with the Sorrowes of it. Oxford, 1653 [Wing B3441].

Memoirs of the Court of Lilliput . . . Containing an Account of the Intrigues, and some other particular Transactions of that Nation, omitted in the two Volumes of his Travels. London, 1727.

The Merchants Advocate, A Poem, In an Imitation of Juvenals XIII. Satyr. London, [1708].

Mercurius Menippeus. The Loyal Satyrist, or, Hudibras in Prose. London, 1682 [Wing B6325].

A Merry New Ballad: In Answer to Old Rowley the King (wr. 1683). In *POAS-Y*, vol. 3.

The Minister of State, A Satire. London, 1762.

Mirth in Abundance. Set forth and made manifest in many Jests, upon severall occasions, full of Wit and Truth . . . All of them New and Noble, free from Rayling, Baudery, Blasphemy, and Incivility. London, 1659 [Wing M2227].

Mirth in Ridicule: or, a Satyr against Immoderate Laughing. London, 1708.

Miscellanies in Prose & Verse, By the most honorable Marquis of Normanby . . . with Satyrs, Fables & Translations. London, 1702.

The Modern Englishman. A Satire. London, 1738.

Modern Virtue: A Satire. London, 1746.

Monmouth Degraded Or James Scot, the little King in Lyme. London, 1685 [Wing M2431].

The Monosyllable If! A Satire. London, 1748.

The Monster: Or, The World turn'd Topsy Turvy. A Satyr. London, 1705.

Moral and Critical Reflections on Several Subjects. Among which (by way of Illustration) various Characters Are occasionally interspersed. London, 1758.

Mordecai's Memorial: or, There's Nothing done for him. Being A Satyr upon Some-body, but I name No-body. London, 1716 [by John Dunton?].

The Mourners. Published in *The Observator*, no. 18 (20 June 1702). In *POAS-Y*, vol. 6 [by Bevil Higgons?].

The Murphiad. A Mock Heroic Poem. London, 1761.

The Natives: An Answer to The Foreigners. London, 1700 [Wing N238].

A Net for the D[evi]l: or, the Town Display'd. A Satyr. London, 1705.

The Neuter: or, a Modest Satire on the Poets of the Age. London, 1733.

A New Ballad, to an Old Tune, Call'd, I Am the Duke of Norfolk, etc. (wr. 1679). In *POAS-Y*, vol. 2.

A New Ballad of London's Loyalty To a Pleasant New Tune Called Burton Hall. London, 1681 [Wing N566].

A New Ballad to an Old Tune Call'd Sage Leafe (wr. 1673?). In *Plays, Poems, and Miscellaneous Writings Associated with Buckingham*, appendix II.

A New Ballad To the tune of The Irish Jig (wr. 1684). In *POAS-Y*, vol. 3.

A New Ballad to ye Tune of ye Black Smith (wr. 1710?). British Library Add. MS 74,211.

A New Ballad Writ by Jacob Tonson and Sung at the Kit Kat Clubb on the 8th of March 1705 (wr. 1705). In *POAS-Y*, vol. 7.

A New Catch in Praise of the Reverend Bishops (wr. 1688). Published in collections in 1689. In *POAS-Y*, vol. 4.

News from Hell: or, A Match for the Directors; A Satire. London, 1721 [title page attribution to Mr. Chamberlen].

The Nine (wr. 1690). In *POAS-Y*, vol. 5 [by John Sheffield, third Earl of Mulgrave?].

Nostradamus' Prophecy (wr. 1672). In *POAS-Y*, vol. 1 [by John Ayloffe?].

O Tempora! or a Satyr on the Times. [London, 1710?].

The Oak, and the Dunghill. London, 1728 [by William Broome?].

The Old Pack. [London], 1710. In *POAS-Y*, vol. 7, under the title *The Old Pack Newly Reviv'd.*

On My Lord Godolphin (wr. 1710). In *POAS-Y*, vol. 7.

On Plotters (wr. 1680). In *POAS-Y*, vol. 2.

On Several Women about Town (wr. 1680). In *CSR.*

On the Ladies of the Court (wr. c. 1663). In *CSR.*

On the Murder of Sir Edmund Berry Godfrey (wr. 1678). In *POAS-Y*, vol. 2.

On the New Promotion (wr. 1705). In *POAS-Y*, vol. 7.

On the Promoted Bishops (wr. 1691). In *POAS-Y*, vol. 5.

On the Queen's Speech (wr. 1710). In *POAS-Y*, vol. 7.

On the Same Author upon his "New Utopia" (wr. 1671). In *POAS-Y*, vol. 1.

On the Three Dukes Killing the Beadle on Sunday Morning, Feb. the 26th, 1671 (wr. 1671). In *POAS-Y*, vol. 1.

The Oxford Vision. April 1681 (wr. 1681). In *POAS-Y*, vol. 2.

The Oxfordshire Nine (1705). Printed from an undated broadside in *POAS-Y*, vol. 7 [by Charles Darby?].

A Panegyric (wr. 1681). In *POAS-Y*, vol. 2.

A Panegyrick On the Author of Absolom and Achitophel, occasioned by his former writing of an Elegy in praise of Oliver Cromwel. London, 1681 [Wing P260].

The Parliament Dissolved at Oxford (wr. 1681). In *POAS-Y*, vol. 2.

Parliament of Criticks, The Menippæan Satyr of Justus Lipsius in a Dream; Paraphras'd: in a Banter Upon the Criticks of the Age. London, 1702.

Pasquin to the Queen's Statue at St. Paul's, during the Procession, Jan. 20, 1715. [London, 1715].

The Patriot Poet, A Satire. Inscribed to the Reverend Mr. Ch[urchi]ll. London, 1764.

Patriotism! A Farce. As is acted by his Majesty's Servants. [London?], 1763.

The Pigeon-Pye, or, a King's Coronation, Proper Materials For forming an Oratorio, Opera, or Play, According to the Modern Taste: to Be Represented in Opposition to the Dragon of Wantley. London, 1738.

Plain Truth: A Satire. London, 1747.

The Plowman (wr. 1688). In *POAS-Y*, vol. 4.

A Poem on Satire. [London], 1764.

Poor Robins Dream, or the Visions of Hell: with a Dialogue Between the Two Ghosts of Dr. T. and Capt. B. London, 1681 [Wing P2884].

Popish Politics Unmasked (wr. 1680). In *POAS-Y*, vol. 2.

The Presbyterian Lash. or, Noctroff's Maid Whipt. London, 1661 [Wing K636] [by Francis Kirkman?].

The Progress (wr. 1688). In *POAS-Y*, vol. 4 [by Henry Mildmay?].

Progress of Lying. A Satire. London, 1762.

The Protestant Satire or Some Reason, Not all Rhyme In return to several late Popish libels Written in the year 1684 (wr. 1684). In *POAS-Y*, vol. 3 [by Thomas Shadwell?].

A Pulpit to be Let. London, 1665 [Wing P4204].

The Quack Doctors. A Satire. London, 1762.

The Quarrel between Frank and Nan (wr. 1681). In *POAS-Y*, vol. 2.

The Queen's Ball (wr. 1670). In *POAS-Y*, vol. 1.

Rabshakeh Vapulans: or, an Answer to the Tribe of Levi; in Vindication of the Clergy. London, 1691 [Wing R117].

Raillerie a la mode Consider'd: or the Supercilious Detractor. London, 1673 [Wing R139].

Ranelagh House: A Satire in Prose. London, 1747 [by Joseph Warton?].

Ranger's Progress: Consisting of a Variety of Poetical Essays, Moral, Serious, Comic, and Satyrical. London, 1760.

The Reflection (wr. 1689). In *POAS-Y*, vol. 5.

Reflections on the Council of Nine (wr. 1690). In *POAS-Y*, vol. 5.

The Repository, or General Review: consisting chiefly of a Select Collection of Literary Compositions. London, 1756.

The Republican Bullies Or, a sham Battel between two of a side, in a Dialogue between Mr. Review and the Observator. London, 1705.

The Restor'd Maiden-head. A New Satyr against Woman. London, 1691 [Wing R1177].

The Reverse: Or, The Tables Turn'd. A Poem Written in Answer . . . to a Late Scurrilous and Malicious Medly of Rhimes Called the Foreigners. London, 1700 [Wing D1041] [by John Dennis?].

Rightful Monarchy: or, Revolution Tyranny, A Satyr: being a Dialogue between High-Dutch Illustrious, and Low-Dutch Glorious. [London?], 1722.

The Robin-Hood Society: A Satire. With Notes Variorum. London, 1756.

Robin's Pathetick Tale, An Heroic Poem. London, 1727.

Rome, or Geneva: or, the True Church of England Without Either. London, 1717.

The Royal Buss (wr. 1675). In *POAS-Y*, vol. 1.

The Rule of Rejoycing; or, a Direction for Mirth, in a Sermon Preached upon Trinity-Sunday. London, 1671 [Wing S5806].

[Multiple authors]. *Rump: An Exact Collection of the Choycest Poems & Songs Relating to the Late Times.* 2 vols. London, 1662 [Wing B4851].

The Salamanca Doctor's Farewel: or, Titus's Exaltation to the Pillory, upon his Conviction of Perjury. [London], 1685 [Wing S368].

Satire, or Song (wr. 1682). In *POAS-Y*, vol. 3.

A Satire in Answer to a Friend (wr. 1682?). In *POAS-Y*, vol. 3.

A Satirical Epistle to Mr. Pope. London, 1740.

A Satirical Review of the Manifold Falshoods and Absurdities Hitherto publish'd concerning the Earthquake. London, 1756.

The Satirist: A Poem. London, 1771.

The Satirist: In Imitation of the Fourth Satire of the First Book of Horace. London, 1733.

The Satirists: A Satire. London, [1739?].

A Satyr against Brandy. London, 1683 [Wing H197] [by Joseph Hains?].

A Satyr against Coffee. [London], 1674 [Wing S709].

A Satyr against Confinement. London, 1702 [by Charles Hopkins?].

A Satyr against Dancing. London, 1702.

A Satyr against Ingratitude, With Some Reflections on the Wits of the Age. London, 1699 [Wing S709A].

A Satyr against Painting; In Burlesque Verse. London, 1697 [Wing S711].

A Satyr against Satyrs: or, St. Peter's Vision Transubstantiated. London, 1680 [Wing D83] [title page attribution to R.D.].

A Satyr Against Wine. With a Poem In Praise of Small Beer. London, 1705 [by Edward Ward?].

A Satyr on Lincolnshire; In a Letter from a Gentleman in Lincoln[shire] to his Friend in Wolverhampton, Staffordshire. 2nd ed. London, 1736.

A Satyr upon Old Maids. London, 1713.

A Satyr upon the Present Times. London, 1717.

A Satyrical Poem: or, the Beggar's-Opera Dissected. London, [1729].

The Save-Alls. Or, The Bishops Who Voted for Dr. Sacheverell. Pub. as *The Six Save-Alls.* [London, 1710]. In *POAS-Y*, vol. 7. The version printed in Edinburgh in 1710 (available on ECCO under the same title as the *POAS-Y* version) is quite different.

The Scamperers (wr. 1688). Printed in collections in 1689. In *POAS-Y*, vol. 4.

The Scholar's Manual. Being A Collection of Meditations, Reflections, and Reasonings, Design'd for Establishing and Promoting Christian Principles and Practice in Irreligious and Sceptical Times. London, 1733.

Scotch Paradice a View of the Bute[eye]full Garden of Edenborough (1763). In Carretta, *George III and the Satirists*, 63.

The Scourge, A Satire. Part I. London, 1765.

The Scrubs of Parnassus: or, All in the Wrong. A comi-tragical heroic Poem, in Hudibrastic Verse, addressed To the Authors of the Rosciad, the Fribbleriad, the Churchiliad, the Naiads of Fleet-Ditch, and the Gentlemen of both Theatres. London, 1761.

A Search after Wit; or, a Visitation of the Authors: in Answer to The late Search after Claret. London, 1691 [Wing A2991].

Seasonable Admonitions. A Satire. London, 1740.

The Secret History of Queen Zarah and the Zarazians; being a Looking-glass for —— —— In the Kingdom of Albigion. Albigion [London], 1705 [possibly by Delarivier Manley?].

Seigneur Dildoe (wr. 1673). Printed in Rochester's *Works*, "Disputed Works."

The Sentiments. To the Bishops (wr. 1688). In *POAS-Y*, vol. 4.

The Session of Ladies (wr. 1688). In *CSR*.

The Session of the Poets (dated 1668 by Lord in *POAS-Y* but probably wr. 1664). In *POAS-Y*, vol. 1.

The Seven Wise Men. London, 1704.

The Shoe-Maker Beyond his Last: or a satyr upon Scurrilous Poets, especially Ned W[ar]d. London, 1700 [Wing B5978].

Sic Transit Gloria Mundi (1762). In Carretta, *George III and the Satirists*, 62.

The Signal: or, a Satyr against Modesty. London, 1727 [by Francis Hawling?].

Sir Edmund Berry Godfrey's Ghost (wr. 1679). In *POAS-Y*, vol. 2.

Sir John Berkenhead Reviv'd, or a Satyr Against the late Rebellion. London, 1681 [Wing S3881].

Some Critical and Politick Remarks On a Late Virulent Lampoon, Call'd Faction Display'd. London, 1704.

St. Ignatius's Ghost, Appearing to the Jesuits; Upon the King's Signing the Act Against the Growth of Popery. A Satyr. London, 1700 [Wing S320].

The Stage-Beaux toss'd in a Blanket: or, Hypocrisie Alamode; Expos'd in a True Picture of Jerry C[ollier] a Pretending Scourge to the English Stage. London, 1704 [by Thomas Brown?].

The State of Rome, under Nero and Domitian: A Satire. London, 1739.

Strange's Case, Strangly Altered. [London], 1680 [Wing S5924].

A Summons from a True Protestant Conjurer to Cethegus' Ghost, to Appear September 19, 1682. London, 1682 [Wing S6176] [by Caleb Calle?].

Suum Cuique (wr. 1689). In *POAS-Y*, vol. 5 [by Arthur Maynwaring?].

The Swan Tripe-Club in Dublin. A Satyr. Dublin, 1706.

The Tack (wr. 1705). In *POAS-Y*, vol. 7.

The Tacking-Club: or, a Satyr on Doctor S[achevere]ll, and his Bulleys. [London?], 1710.

The Tale of a Nettle. Cambridge, 1710.

A Tale of the Tubs, or Rome's Masterpiece Defeated (wr. 1679). In *POAS-Y*, vol. 2 (dated 1680).

[Multiple authors]. *The Theatre of Wit, or a Banquet of the Muses*. London, 1746.

The Third Volume of the Monthly Catalogue: being A General Register of Books . . . Printed and Published . . . in the Years 1727, and 1728. London, 1729.

Three Satires. Most Humbly Inscribed and Recommended to that Little Gentleman, of Great Vanity, who has just published, A Fourth Volume of Homer. To which is added, A Character of the Nuns. A Satire. London, 1719.

To Mr. Dryden, Upon his Declaring himself a Roman Catholic (wr. 1686). In *POAS-Y*, vol. 4.

To the Loyal Londoners (wr. 1682). In *POAS-Y*, vol. 3.

The Toast. An Heroick Poem in four Books In four Books, Written originally in Latin, by Frederick Scheffer. Dublin and London, 1736.

The Town Life (wr. 1686). In *POAS-Y*, vol. 4.

The Tragick-Comedy of Titus Oates, Who sometime went under the Notion of The Salamanca Doctor. London, 1685 [Wing T2014].

A Treatise on Virtue and Happiness. 2nd ed. London, 1736 [by Thomas Nettleton?].

A Trimmer's Confession of Faith: Or, The True Principles of A Jack of Both-Sides. London, 1694 [Wing T2278].

A Trip Through the Town. Containing Observations on the Customs and Manners of the Age . . . Together with sundry other Curious and Diverting Particulars. London, [1735].

The Triumph of Brutes, A Satire on this Caledonian Age. London, 1763.

A True Caracter of the Bread-street Tatlers; Or, a Satyr against Impudence. London, 1707.

A True Relation Of the several Facts and Circumstances Of the Intended Riot and Tumult on Queen Elizabeth's Birth-day. [London], 1711.

The Tryal of Skill: or, A New Session of the Poets. Calculated for the Meridian of Parnassus (wr. 1704). In *POAS-Y*, vol. 6.

The Tune to the Devonshire Cant: Or, an Answer to the Parliament Dissolved at Oxford. London, 1681 [Wing T3251].

The Two Tom Lucys (wr. 1686). In *CSR*.

Upon his Majesty's being made Free of the City (wr. 1674). In *POAS-Y*, vol. 1.

Upon Sorrel. Printed without a title in *The Observator*, no. 4 (22 April 1702) . In *POAS-Y*, vol. 6 [by Thomas Smith?].

Upon the Beadle (wr. 1671). In *POAS-Y*, vol. 1.

Upon the Burning of Dr. Burgess's Pulpit (wr. 1710). In *POAS-Y*, vol. 7.

Utile Dulce (wr. 1681). In *CSR*.

Vanelia: or, the Amours of the Great. London, 1732.

Verres and his Scribblers; A Satire in Three Cantos. To which is added an Examen of the Piece, and a Key to the Characters and obscure Passages. London, 1732.

The Vindication (wr. 1688). In *POAS-Y*, vol. 5.

A Vision in the Tower to the Lord H[owar]d in His Contemplation. London, 1681 [Wing V658].

Vivitur Ingenio: being a Collection Of Elegant, Moral, Satirical, and Comical Thoughts, on Various Subjects. London, 1726.

Vox Clero, Lilli burlero, or, The Second Part of a Merry New Ballad (wr. 1689). In *POAS-Y*, vol. 5.

The Waking Vision; or, Reality in a Fancy. London, 1681 [Wing W282].

The Way of the Town: or, the Sham-Heiress. A Burlesque Poem. Being a Satyr on the Ladies of Pleasure and the Beaux's of the Town. London, 1717.

A Welcome to the Medal; or an Excellent New Song; Call'd The Constitution Restor'd, in 1711. Oxford [London?], 1711.

The Western Rebel; or, the True Protestant Standard set up. London, 1685 [Wing W1413].

The Westminster Combat. [London, 1710].

[Multiple authors]. *Whig and Tory: or Wit on both Sides.* London, 1712 [bound; originally sold in 4 separate pamphlets, 1710–1711].

The Whiggs Lamentation For the Death of their Dear Brother Colledge, The Protestant Joyner. London, 1681 [Wing W1660].

The Wiltshire Ballad. London, 1680 [Wing W2958].

Wit and Mirth, an Antidote against Melancholy. Compounded of Ingenious and witty Ballads, Songs, and Catches, and other Pleasant and Merry Poems. 3rd ed. London, 1682 [Wing P40].

The Wooden Age. A Satyrical Poem. London, 1733.

Attributed

Addison, Joseph. *Maxims, Observations, and Reflections, Divine, Moral, and Political*. London, 1719.

Allen, Bennet. "To Mankind." In his *Satirical Trifles: consisting of An Ode, written on the first Attack of the Gout. To Mankind, an Ode. The Farewell, written at Woodcote, near Epsom. Epigrams*. London, 1764.

Allestree, Richard. *The Government of the Tongue*. Oxford, 1667 [Wing A1138].

Ames, Richard. *Fatal Friendship; or, the Drunkards Misery: Being a Satyr against Hard Drinking*. London, 1693 [Wing A2978].

———. *The Female Fire-Ships. A Satyr against Whoring*. London, 1691 [Wing A2979].

———. *The Folly of Love, or, An Essay upon Satyr against Woman*. London, 1691 [Wing A2980].

———. *The Search after Claret; or, a Visitation of the Vintners*. London, 1691 [Wing A2989].

———. *Sylvia's Revenge, or, a Satyr against Man; in Answer to the Satyr against Woman*. London, 1688 [Wing A2992D].

Anstey, Christopher. *The New Bath Guide: or, Memoirs of the B[lunde]r[hea]d Family*. [London], 1766.

Arbuthnot, John. *A Brief Account of Mr. John Ginglicutt's Treatise Concerning the Altercation or Scolding of the Ancients*. London, 1731.

———. *John Bull In His Senses: being the Second Part of Law is a Bottomless-Pit*. London, 1712 [the second part of "John Bull"].

———. *John Bull Still In His Senses: being the Third Part of Law is a Bottomless-Pit*. London, 1712 [the third part of "John Bull"].

———. *Law is a Bottomless-Pit. Exemplify'd in the Case of The Lord Strutt, John Bull, Nicholas Frog, and Lewis Baboon*. London, 1712 [the first part of "John Bull"].

———. *Lewis Baboon Turned Honest and John Bull Politician. Being The Fourth Part of Law is a Bottomless-Pit*. London, 1712 [the fourth part of "John Bull"].

———. *Proposals For Printing A very Curious Discourse, in Two Volumes in Quarto, Intitled, Pseudologia politice; or, a Treatise of the Art of Political Lying, with An Abstract of the First Volume of the said Treatise [The Art of Political Lying]*. London, 1712.

———. *Virgilius Restauratus*. In Swift and Pope, *Miscellanies. The Third Volume* (1732).

Ashton, Edmund. *On the Same Author upon His "British Princes"* (wr. 1669). In *POAS-Y*, vol. 1.

Asplin, William. *Alkibla. Part II*. London, [1731].

Aubert, Mrs. *Harlequin-Hydaspes: or, The Greshamite. A Mock-Opera*. London, 1719.

Ayloffe, John. *Britannia and Raleigh* (wr. 1674–1675). In *POAS-Y*, vol. 1.

———. *Oceana and Britannia* (wr. 1681). In *POAS-Y*, vol. 2.

Baker, Thomas. *An Act at Oxford. A Comedy*. London, 1704.

Barrow, Isaac. *Several Sermons against Evil-Speaking*. London, 1678 [Wing B959].

Beattie, James. *Dissertations Moral and Critical. On Memory and Imagination. On Dreaming.*

The Theory of Language. On Fable and Romance. On the Attachments of Kindred. Illustrations of Sublimity. London, 1783.

Behn, Aphra. *The City-Heiress: or, Sir Timothy Treat-all.* London, 1682. In *Works*, vol. 7.

———. *The Luckey Chance, or an Alderman's Bargain* (perf. 1686). London, 1687. In *Works*, vol. 7.

———. *The Roundheads or, The Good Old Cause* (perf. 1681). London, 1682. In *Works*, vol. 6.

———. *The Widdow Ranter or, The History of Bacon in Virginia.* London, 1690. In *Works*, vol. 7.

———. *The Works of Aphra Behn.* Edited by Janet Todd. 7 vols. London: Pickering and Chatto; Columbus: Ohio State University Press, 1992–1996.

Bentley, Richard. *Patriotism, A Mock-Heroic. In Five Cantos.* London, 1763.

Bickerstaff, Isaac. *The Plain Dealer. A Comedy* (perf. 1765). London, 1766.

Bickham, George. *The Three False Brethren.* London, 1711. In *POAS-Y*, vol. 7.

Blackmore, Sir Richard. *A Satyr against Wit.* London, 1700 [Wing B3084].

———. "Upon Wit." In his *Essays upon Several Subjects. In Five Parts.* 2nd ed. London, 1716. Reprint, Dublin, 1716.

Blount, Sir Thomas Pope. *De Re Poetica: or, Remarks upon Poetry with Characters and Censures of the most considerable poets, whether ancient or modern.* London, 1694 [Wing B3347].

Boswell, James. *Boswell's Life of Johnson: Together with Boswell's Journal of a Tour to the Hebrides and Johnson's Diary of a Journey into North Wales.* Edited by George Birkbeck Hill, revised and enlarged by L. F. Powell. 6 vols. Oxford: Oxford University Press, 1934–1964.

Braithwaite, Richard. *The Chimneys Scuffle.* London, 1662 [Wing B4259].

Bramston, James. *The Man of Taste. Occasion'd by an Epistle Of Mr. Pope's On that Subject.* London, 1733.

Brereton, Thomas. *Charnock's Remains: Or, S[acheverell] his Coronation. A Satyr: Being a Parody upon Dryden's Mac-Fleckno.* London, 1713.

Brome, Alexander. *The Cavalier* (wr. 1660?). Published 1664 in his *Songs And other Poems*, 2nd ed. In *Poems*, vol. 1.

———. *Poems.* Edited by Roman R. Dubinski. 2 vols. Toronto: University of Toronto Press, 1982.

———. *The Satyr of Money* (wr. 1653?). Published 1661 in his *Songs and Other Poems.* In *Poems*, vol. 1.

Brown, John. *An Essay on Satire: Occasion'd by the Death of Mr. Pope.* London, 1745.

———*Essays on the Characteristics.* London, 1751.

Brown, Thomas. *Advice To the Kentish Long-Tails, By the Wise-Men of Gotham.* [London, 1701].

———. *Amusements Serious and Comical, Calculated for the Meridian of London.* London, 1700 [Wing B5051].

——— [et al.]. *Commendatory Verses, on the Author of the Two Arthurs, and the Satyr against Wit.* London, 1700 [Wing C5547].

———. *On Job newly Travestied by Sir R[ichard] Bl[ackmore]* (1707). In *Works In Prose and Verse*, vol. 1.

———. *On Sir R[ichard] Bl[ackmore]'s Project to erect a Bank of Wit* (1707). In *Works In Prose and Verse*, vol. 1.

———. *The Reasons of Mr. Bays Changing his Religion. Considered in a Dialogue between Crites, Eugenius, and Mr. Bays.* London, 1688 [Wing B5069].

———. *A Satyr upon the French King, Written by a Non-Swearing Parson, and drop'd out of his Pocket at Samm's Coffee-House.* London, 1697 [Wing S720].

———. *To Mr. Dryden, on his Conversion.* London, 1707. In *Works In Prose and Verse*, vol. 1.

———. *To Sir R[ichard] Bl[ackmore], on the two Wooden Horses before Sadlers-hall.* London, 1707. In *Works In Prose and Verse*, vol. 1.

———. *To Sir R[ichard] B[lackmore], upon his unhappy Talent of Praising and Railing.* London, 1707. In *Works In Prose and Verse*, vol. 1.

———. *To that Most Senseless Scondrel, the Author of Legion's Humble Address to the Lords.* London, 1707. In *Works In Prose and Verse*, vol. 1.

———. *To the Author of Gloriana. A Comical Pindaric Elegy* (wr. 1695). In *POAS-Y*, vol. 5.

———. *Upon the Anonymous Author of, Legion's Humble Address to the Lords.* London, 1707. In *Works In Prose and Verse*, vol. 1.

———. *The Works of Mr. Thomas Brown, In Prose and Verse . . . To which is prefix'd, A Character of Mr. Tho. Brown and his Writings, by James Drake.* 2 vols. London, 1707.

———. *The Works of Mr. Thomas Brown, Serious and Comical.* 4 vols. London, 1715.

Browne, Joseph. *The Circus: or, British Olympicks, A Satyr on the Ring in Hide-Park.* London, 1709.

———. *Liberty and Property. A Satyr.* London, 1705.

Buckingham, second Duke of. See Villiers, George, second Duke of Buckingham.

Bunyan, John. *The Life and Death of Mr. Badman* (1680). Edited by James F. Forrest and Roger Sharrock. Oxford: Clarendon, 1988.

———. *The Pilgrim's Progress from This World to That which is to come* (1678). Edited by James Blanton Wharey. Rev. ed. edited by Roger Sharrock. Oxford: Clarendon, 1960.

Burgess, Daniel. *Foolish Talking and Jesting Described and Condemned.* London, 1694 [Wing B5706].

Burnet, Gilbert. *Bishop Burnet's History of His Own Time.* Vol. 1. London, 1724.

Butler, Samuel. *Characters* (1759). Edited by Charles W. Daves. Cleveland: Press of Case Western Reserve University, 1970.

———. *Hudibras.* 3 parts (1662, 1663, 1677). Edited by John Wilders. Oxford: Oxford University Press, 1967.

Bysshe, Edward. *The Art of English Poetry: Containing, I. Rules for making Verses. II. A Dictionary of Rhymes. III. A Collection of the most Natural, Agreeable, and Noble Thoughts . . . that are to be found in the best English Poets.* London, 1702.

Cambridge, Richard Owen. *A Dialogue between a Member of Parliament and His Servant. In Imitation of the Seventh Satire of the Second Book of Horace.* London, 1752.

Canning, George. *Horace's First Satire Modernized, And Addressed to Jacob Henriques.* London, 1762.

Care, Henry. *Towser the Second a Bull-Dog. Or a short reply to Absalon and Achitophel.* London, 1681 [Wing C532].

Carey, Henry. *The Dragon of Wantley. A Burlesque Opera.* London, [1737].

———. *Margery; or, a Worse Plague than the Dragon: A Burlesque Opera.* London, 1738.

———. *The Tragedy of Chrononhotonthologos: being The most Tragical Tragedy, that ever was Tragediz'd by any Company of Tragedians.* London, 1734.

Caryll, John. *The Hypocrite: Written upon the Lord Shaftesbury in the Year 1678* (wr. 1678). In *POAS-Y*, vol. 1.

———. *Naboth's Vineyard: or, the Innocent Traytor.* London, 1679 [Wing C745A].

Caswall, George. *The Trifler. A Satire.* London, 1767.

Centlivre, Susanna. *The Basset-Table* (perf. 1705). London, 1706.

Charleton, Walter. *A Brief Discourse Concerning the Different Wits of Men.* London, 1669 [Wing C3663].

Chetwood, William. *South-Sea; or, the Biters Bit. A Tragi-comi-pastoral farce.* London, 1720.

———. *The Stock-Jobbers or, the Humours of Exchange-Alley.* London, 1720.

Churchill, Charles. *The Apology.* London, 1761.

———. *The Author.* London, 1763.

———. *The Candidate.* London, 1764.

———. *The Duellist.* London, 1764.

———. *An Epistle to William Hogarth.* London, 1763.

———. *The Ghost.* London, 1762–63.

———. *Night. An Epistle to Robert Lloyd.* London, 1761.

———. *The Poetical Works of Charles Churchill.* Edited by Douglas Grant. Oxford: Clarendon, 1956. All works by Churchill are cited from this edition.

———. *The Prophecy of Famine. A Scots Pastoral.* London, 1763.

———. *The Rosciad.* London, 1761.

———. *The Times.* London, 1764.

Cibber, Colley. *The Careless Husband* (perf. 1704). London, 1705.

———. *Love's Last Shift.* London, 1696. In *The Plays of Colley Cibber*, vol. 1. Edited by Timothy J. Viator and William J. Burling. Madison, NJ: Fairleigh Dickinson University Press, 2001.

Cibber, Colley, and Sir John Vanbrugh. *The Provok'd Husband; or, A Journey to London.* London, 1728. In Vanbrugh, *Complete Works*, vol. 3.

Cibber, Theophilus. *Theophilus Cibber, to David Garrick, Esq; with Dissertations on Theatrical Subjects.* London, 1759.

Cleveland, John. *Clievelandi Vindiciae: or, Clieveland's Genuine Poems, Orations, Epistles, &c. purged from The many False and Spurious Ones which had usurped his Name, And from innumerable Errours and Corruptions in the True Copies.* London, 1677 [Wing C4669].

———. *J. Cleaveland Revived: Poems, Orations, Epistles.* London, 1659 [Wing C4674].

———. *The Loyal Livery-Mens Hue and Cry after Sir John Presbyter.* London, 1683 (rpt. of *The Hue and Cry after Sir John Presbyter* [1649]) [Wing L3349].

———. *Poems by John Cleavland.* London, 1661 [Wing C4695].

———. *The Rebell Scot.* Published in *The Character of a London-Diurnall, with severall select Poems by the same Author.* London, 1647 [Wing C4663A].

———. *The Scots Apostacy.* London, 1647 [Wing C4699A].

Clifford, Martin. *Notes upon Mr. Dryden's Poems in Four Letters. By M. Clifford . . . To which are annexed some Reflections upon the Hind and Panther.* London, 1687 [Wing C4706].

College, Stephen. *Justice in Masquerade* (wr. 1679). London, 1680 [Wing J1248].

———. *Raree Show Or the true Protestant Procession.* [London], 1681 [Wing R2808].

———. *A Satyr against Injustice, or, Sc[rog]gs upon Sc[rog]gs.* [London], 1681 [Wing C5227].

———. *Truth Brought to Light Or Murder Will Out* (wr. 1679). In *POAS-Y*, vol. 2.

Colman, George. *The Deuce is in Him.* London, 1763.

———. *Polly Honeycombe, A Dramatick Novel of one act* (perf. 1760). London, 1761.

Congreve, William. *Amendments of Mr. Collier's False and Imperfect Citations, &c. From the "Old Batchelour," "Double Dealer," "Love for Love," "Mourning Bride."* London, 1698 [Wing C5844].

———. *The Complete Plays of William Congreve*. Edited by Herbert Davis. Chicago: University of Chicago Press, 1967. All plays by Congreve are cited from this edition.

———. *The Double-Dealer* (perf. 1693). London, 1694.

———. *Love for Love*. London, 1695.

———. *The Old Batchelour*. London, 1693.

———. *The Way of the World*. London, 1700.

———. *The Works of William Congreve*. Edited by D. F. McKenzie. 3 vols. Oxford: Oxford University Press, 2011.

Cooper, Anthony Ashley, third Earl of Shaftesbury. *A Letter Concerning Enthusiasm, to My Lord ******. London, 1708.

———. *Sensus Communis: An Essay on the Freedom of Wit and Humour*. London, 1709.

Cowley, Abraham. *Cutter of Coleman-Street* (perf. 1661). London, 1663 [Wing C6669].

———. *Puritan and the Papist. A Satyr*. London, 1681/2 [Wing C6685]. Reprint of the 1643 edition.

Crowne, John. *City Politiques*. London, 1683 [Wing C7378].

———. *The English Frier: or, the Town Sparks*. London, 1690 [Wing C7387].

Cumberland, Richard. *The West Indian*. London, 1771.

Davies, Thomas. *Memoirs of the Life of David Garrick, Esq. Interspersed With Characters and Anecdotes of His Theatrical Contemporaries*. 2 vols. London, 1780.

Davys, Mary. *The Accomplish'd Rake: or, Modern Fine Gentleman. Being An Exact Description of the Conduct and Behaviour of A Person of Distinction*. [London, 1727].

Dean, John. *Iter Boreale, or, Tyburn in Mourning For the Loss of a Saint*. London, 1682 [Wing D493].

Defoe, Daniel. *An Account of the Great and Generous Actions of James Butler*. London, 1715.

———. *The Address*. London, 1704. In *Political and Economic Writings*, vol. 2.

———. *The Anatomy of Exchange-Alley: or, A System of Stock-Jobbing*. London, 1719. In *Political and Economic Writings*, vol. 6.

———. *And What if the Pretender should come?* London, 1713. In *Political and Economic Writings*, vol. 1.

———. "A Brief Explanation of A late Pamphlet, Entituled, The Shortest Way with the Dissenters." In *A True Collection of the Writings of the Author of The True-Born English-man*. London, 1703.

———. *The Conduct of Christians made the Sport of Infidels*. London, 1717. In *Satire, Fantasy and Writings on the Supernatural*, vol. 5.

———. *The Consolidator: or, Memoirs of Sundry Transactions from the World in the Moon*. London, 1705. In *Satire, Fantasy and Writings on the Supernatural*, vol. 3.

———. *The Danger of Court Differences: or, the Unhappy Effects of a Motley Ministry: Occasion'd by the Report of Changes at Court*. London, 1717.

———. *The Dissenter Misrepresented and Represented* (wr. 1704). Published in *A Second Volume of the Writings of the Author of the True-Born Englishman*, 1705.

———. *An Elegy on the Author of the True-Born-English-Man. With An Essay On the late Storm*. London, 1704. In *Satire, Fantasy and Writings on the Supernatural*, vol. 1.

———. *An Encomium upon a Parliament* (wr. 1699). Published in *A True Collection of the Writings Of the Author of the True-Born English-man*, 1703. In *Satire, Fantasy and Writings on the Supernatural*, vol. 1.

———. *The Genuine Works of Mr. Daniel D'Foe, Author of the True-born English-Man.* 2 vols. London, 1721.

———. *The Great Law of Subordination consider'd.* London, 1724.

———. *A Hymn to the Pillory.* London, 1703. In *Satire, Fantasy and Writings on the Supernatural*, vol. 1.

———. *Jure Divino: A Satyr. In Twelve Books.* London, 1706. In *Satire, Fantasy and Writings on the Supernatural*, vol. 2.

———. *A Letter to Mr. Bisset.* London, 1709.

———. *Memoirs of Count Tariff, &c.* London, 1713. In *Satire, Fantasy and Writings on the Supernatural*, vol. 3.

———. *Mere Nature Delineated: or, a Body without a Soul.* London, 1726.

———. *The Mock Mourners. A Satyr, by Way of Elegy on King William.* London, 1702. In *Satire, Fantasy and Writings on the Supernatural*, vol. 1.

———. *More Reformation. A Satyr upon Himself.* London, 1703. In *Satire, Fantasy and Writings on the Supernatural*, vol. 1.

———. *A New Discovery of an Old Intreague: A Satyr.* London, 1691. In *Satire, Fantasy and Writings on the Supernatural*, vol. 1.

———. *The Pacificator.* London, 1700. In *Satire, Fantasy and Writings on the Supernatural*, vol. 1.

———. *The Political and Economic Writings of Daniel Defoe.* General editors W. R. Owens and P. N. Furbank. 8 vols. London: Pickering and Chatto, 2000.

———. *The Political History of the Devil, as well Ancient as Modern.* London, 1726.

———. *The Quarrel of the School-Boys at Athens, As lately Acted at a School near Westminster.* London, 1717. In *Satire, Fantasy and Writings on the Supernatural*, vol. 3.

———. *Reasons against the Succession of the House of Hanover.* London, 1713. In *Political and Economic Writings*, vol. 1.

———. *Reformation of Manners, a Satyr.* London, 1702. In *Satire, Fantasy and Writings on the Supernatural*, vol. 1.

———. *Satire, Fantasy and Writings on the Supernatural by Daniel Defoe.* General editors W. R. Owens and P. N. Furbank. 8 vols. London: Pickering and Chatto, 2003–2004.

———. *A Second Volume of the Writings of the Author of the True-Born Englishman.* London, 1705.

———. *A Sharp Rebuke From one of the People called Quakers to Henry Sacheverell, The High Priest of Andrew's Holbourn.* London, 1715.

———. *The Shortest-Way with the Dissenters: or Proposals for the Establishment of the Church.* London, 1702. In *Political and Economic Writings*, vol. 3.

———. *The Spanish Descent.* London, 1702. In *Satire, Fantasy and Writings on the Supernatural*, vol. 1.

———. *A True Collection of the Writings of the Author of the True Born English-man.* London, 1703.

———. *The True-Born Englishman.* London, 1701. In *Satire, Fantasy and Writings on the Supernatural*, vol. 1.

———. *Ye True-Born Englishmen Proceed* [sometimes called "A New Satyr on the Parliament"]. London, 1701. In *Satire, Fantasy and Writings on the Supernatural*, vol. 1.

Dennis, John. *The Characters and Conduct of Sir John Edgar.* London, 1720. In *Critical Works*, vol. 2.

———. *The Critical Works of John Dennis*. Edited by Edward Niles Hooker. 2 vols. Baltimore: Johns Hopkins Press, 1939–1943.

———. *An Essay on the Opera's after the Italian Manner, Which are about to be Establish'd on the English Stage*. London, 1706.

———. *An Essay upon Publick Spirit; being A Satyr in Prose Upon the Manners and Luxury of the Times, The Chief Sources of our present Parties and Diversions*. London, 1711.

———. *Remarks on Mr Pope's Rape of the Lock*. London, 1728. In *Critical Works*, vol. 2.

———. *A True Character of Mr. Pope, and his Writings*. London, 1716. In *Critical Works*, vol. 2.

Dillon, Wentworth, fourth Earl of Roscommon. *The Ghost of the Old House of Commons to the New One Appointed to Meet at Oxford*. London, 1681. In *POAS-Y*, vol. 2.

Dodsley, Robert. *The King and the Miller of Mansfield*. London, 1737.

———. *Sir John Cockle at Court. Being the Sequel of the King and the Miller of Mansfield*. London, 1738.

———. *The Toy-Shop. A Dramatick Satire*. London, 1735.

Dorset, sixth Earl of. See Sackville, Charles, sixth Earl of Dorset.

Dryden, John. *Absalom and Achitophel. A Poem*. London, 1681. In *Works*, vol. 2.

———, trans. *Aeneid*. London, 1697. In *Works*, vols. 5 and 6.

———. *Albion and Albanius: An Opera*. London, 1685. In *Works*, vol. 15.

———. *Alexander's Feast; or the Power of Musique. An Ode, In Honour of St. Cecilia's Day*. London, 1697. In *Works*, vol. 7.

———. *Amphitryon; or, The Two Socia's*. London, 1690. In *Works*, vol. 15.

———. "The Authors Apology for Heroique Poetry; and Poetique Licence." Prefixed to *The State of Innocence*. London, 1677. In *Works*, vol. 12.

———. *Cleomenes, the Spartan Heroe*. London, 1692. In *Works*, vol. 16.

———. *Discourse concerning the Original and Progress of Satire*. Prefixed to *The Satires of Decimus Junius Juvenalis*. London, 1693. In *Works*, vol. 4.

———. *Eleonora: A Panegyrical Poem: Dedicated to the Memory Of the Late Countess of Abingdon*. London, 1692. In *Works*, vol. 3.

———. *Fables Ancient and Modern*. London, 1700. In *Works*, vol. 7.

———. *The Hind and the Panther*. London, 1687. In *Works*, vol. 3.

———. *The Kind Keeper; or, Mr. Limberham* (perf. 1678). London, 1680. In *Works*, vol. 14.

———. *The Letters of John Dryden*. Edited by Charles E. Ward. 1942. Reprint, New York: AMS, 1965.

———. *Mac Flecknoe, or a Satyr upon the True-Blew-Protestant Poet, T. S.* London, 1682. In *Works*, vol. 2.

———. *Marriage A-la-Mode* (perf. 1671). London, 1673. In *Works*, vol. 11.

———. *The Medall. A Satyre against Sedition*. London, 1682. In *Works*, vol. 2.

———, trans. *The Satires of Decimus Junius Juvenalis. Translated into English Verse. By Mr. Dryden, and Several other Eminent Hands. Together with the Satires of Aulus Persius Flaccus*. London, 1693. In *Works*, vol. 4.

———. *The Spanish Fryar or, The Double Discovery*. London, 1681. In *Works*, vol. 14.

———. *The Vindication: or the Parallel of the French Holy-League and the English League and Covenant, Turn'd into a Seditious Libell against the King and his Royal Highness*. London, 1683. In *Works*, vol. 14.

———. *The Works of John Dryden*. Edited by H. T. Swedenberg Jr. et al. 20 vols. Berkeley: University of California Press, 1956–2000.

Dryden, John, and Nathaniel Lee. *The Duke of Guise. A Tragedy* (perf. 1682). London, 1683. In Dryden, *Works*, vol. 14.

Dryden, John, and Henry Purcell. *King Arthur: or, The British Worthy*. London, 1691. In Dryden, *Works*, vol. 16.

Dryden, John, and Nahum Tate. *The Second Part of Absalom and Achitophel*. London, 1682. In Dryden, *Works*, vol. 2.

Duckett, George. *Pope Alexander's Supremacy and Infallibility examin'd; And the Errors of Scriblerus and his Man William Detected*. London, 1729.

Duffett, Thomas. *The Mock-Tempest, or the Enchanted Castle* (perf. 1674). London, 1675. In *Three Burlesque Plays*.

——. *Psyche Debauch'd, A Comedy* (perf. 1675). London, 1678. In *Three Burlesque Plays*.

——. *Three Burlesque Plays of Thomas Duffett*. Edited by Ronald Eugene DiLorenzo. Iowa City: University of Iowa Press, 1972.

Dunton, John. *A Cat may look on a Queen: or, a Satyr on her Present Majesty*. London, 1705.

——. *Dunton's Whipping-Post: or, a Satyr upon Every Body*. Vol. 1. London, 1706.

——. *King-Abigail: or, The Secret Reign of the She-Favourite, Detected and Applied*. London, 1715.

——. *The Manifesto of K. John the Second . . . with A Satyr upon Royalty*. [London, 1715?].

——. *The Pulpit-Fool. A Satyr*. London, 1707.

Durfey, Thomas. *Butler's Ghost: or, Hudibras. The Fourth Part. With Reflections upon these Times*. London, 1682 [Wing D2703].

——. *The Campaigners: or, the Pleasant Adventures at Brussels. . . . With a Familiar Preface upon A Late Reformer of the Stage*. London, 1698 [Wing D2705].

——. *A Fond Husband: or, The Plotting Sisters*. London, 1677 [Wing D2724].

——. *Love for Money: or, the Boarding School*. London, 1691 [Wing D2740].

——. *The Progress of Honesty: Or, a View of a Court and City*. London, 1681 [Wing D2764].

——. *The Richmond Heiress: or, a Woman Once in the Right*. London, 1693 [Wing D2769].

——. *Sir Barnaby Whigg, or, No Wit like a Womans*. London, 1681 [Wing D2778].

Egerton, Sara Fyge. *The Female Advocate: or, an Answer to a Late Satyr against The Pride, Lust and Inconstancy, &c. of Woman*. London, 1686 [Wing F56].

Ellis, Clement. *The Vanity of Scoffing: or a Letter to a Witty Gentleman . . . Together with The Madness of the Scoffer's unchristian Choice*. London, 1674 [Wing E575].

Estcourt, Richard. *Prunella: An Interlude Perform'd in the Rehearsal, at the Theatre-Royal in Drury-Lane*. London, [1708].

Etherege, George. *The Man of Mode, or Sir Fopling Flutter*. London, 1676 [Wing E3374].

Farquhar, George. *The Beaux Stratagem*. London, 1707. In *The Works of George Farquhar*, edited by Shirley Strum Kenny. 2 vols. Oxford: Clarendon, 1988.

Fielding, Henry. *The Adventures of Joseph Andrews*. London, 1742. Edited by Martin C. Battestin. Oxford: Clarendon, 1967.

——. *Amelia*. 4 vols. London, 1752 [1751].

——. *An Apology for the Life of Mrs. Shamela Andrews*. London, 1741. In *Occasional Writings*.

——. *The Author's Farce*. London, 1730. In *Plays*, vol. 1.

——. "Cantos" on Pope's *Dunciad* (wr. 1729). Not published until the twentieth century. Cited from Grundy, "New Verse by Henry Fielding." Also in *Occasional Writings*.

——. *Contributions to "The Champion" and Related Writings*. Edited by W. B. Coley. Oxford: Clarendon, 2003.

———. *The Covent-Garden Journal.* London, 1752. In *"The Covent-Garden Journal" and "A Plan of the Universal Register-Office."* Edited by Bertrand A. Goldgar. Oxford: Clarendon, 1988.

———. *The Covent-Garden Tragedy.* London, 1732. In *Plays*, vol. 2.

———. *Don Quixote in England* (wr. 1729; perf. 1734). London, 1734. In *Plays*, vol. 3.

———. "An Epistle to Mr Lyttelton occasioned by two Lines in Mr Pope's Paraphrase on the first Satire of the 2d Book of Horace" (wr. 1733). Not published until the twentieth century. Cited from Grundy, "New Verse by Henry Fielding." Also in *Occasional Writings.*

———. *An Essay on Conversation.* London, 1743. In *Miscellanies*, vol. 1.

———. *An Essay on the Knowledge of the Characters of Men.* London, 1743. In *Miscellanies*, vol. 1.

———. *Eurydice, A Farce* (perf. 1737). London, 1743. In *Miscellanies*, vol. 2.

———. *Eurydice Hiss'd.* Published with *The Historical Register*, 1737. In *Plays*, vol. 3.

———. *The Historical Register, For the Year 1736.* London, 1737. In *Plays*, vol. 3.

———. *The History of Tom Jones: A Foundling.* London, 1749. Edited by Fredson Bowers, with an introduction and commentary by Martin C. Battestin. 2 vols. Oxford: Clarendon, 1975.

———. *The Journal of a Voyage to Lisbon* (pub. posthumously). London, 1755. In *Occasional Writings.*

———. *"The Journal of a Voyage to Lisbon," "Shamela," and Occasional Writings* [*Occasional Writings*]. Edited by Martin C. Battestin with Sheridan W. Baker Jr. and Hugh Amory. Oxford: Clarendon, 2008.

———. *A Journey from This World to the Next.* London, 1743. In *Miscellanies*, vol. 2.

———. *The Letter-Writers: Or, a New Way to Keep a Wife at Home. A Farce.* London, 1731. In *Plays*, vol. 1.

———. *The Life of Mr. Jonathan Wild the Great.* London, 1743. In *Miscellanies by Henry Fielding, Esq;*, vol. 3, edited by Hugh Amory, with notes and introduction by Bertrand A. Goldgar. Oxford: Clarendon, 1997.

———. *The Lottery.* London, 1732. In *Plays*, vol. 2.

———. *The Masquerade. A Poem. Inscrib'd to C[oun]t H[ei]d[eg]g[e]r.* London, 1728. In *Occasional Writings.*

———. *Miscellanies by Henry Fielding, Esq.* Vol. 1. Edited by Henry Knight Miller. Oxford: Clarendon, 1972.

———. *Miscellanies by Henry Fielding, Esq.* Vol. 2. Edited by Hugh Amory, with an introduction and commentary by Bertrand A. Goldgar. Oxford: Clarendon, 1993.

———. *The Modern Husband.* London, 1732. In *Plays*, vol. 2.

———. *The Old Debauchees.* London, 1732. In *Plays*, vol. 2.

———. *An Old Man taught Wisdom; or, the Virgin Unmask'd.* London, 1735. In *Plays*, vol. 3.

———. *Pasquin. A Dramatick Satire on the Times.* London, 1736. In *Plays*, vol. 3.

———. *Plays.* 3 vols. Edited by Thomas Lockwood. Oxford: Clarendon, 2004–2011.

———. *Rape upon Rape; or, the Justice Caught in his own Trap.* London, 1730. In *Plays*, vol. 1.

———. *"To John Hayes*, Esq;." London, 1743. In *Miscellanies*, vol. 1.

———. *Tom Thumb.* London, 1730. In *Plays*, vol. 1.

———. *The Tragedy of Tragedies, or the Life and Death of Tom Thumb the Great.* London, 1731. In *Plays*, vol. 1.

———. *Tumble-Down Dick: or, Phaeton in the Suds.* London, 1736. In *Plays*, vol. 3.

———. *The Universal Gallant: or, the Different Husbands*. London, 1735. In *Plays*, vol. 3.

———. *The Vernoniad*. London, 1741. In *Contributions to "The Champion" and Related Writings*.

———. *The Welsh Opera*. London, 1731.

———. *The Wesleyan Edition of the Works of Henry Fielding*. Executive editor W. B. Coley. Oxford: Clarendon, 1967–2011. Almost all references to works by Fielding are to this edition. *Amelia* is an exception because the Wesleyan edition uses the posthumous 1762 edition by Arthur Murphy rather than the 1751 original as copy text.

Fielding, Sir John. *The Universal Mentor; containing, Essays on the Most important Subjects in Life*. London, 1763.

Fielding, Sarah. *The Adventures of David Simple*. London, 1744. Edited by Malcolm Kelsall. London: Oxford University Press, 1969 (part 1 only).

———. *The Adventures of David Simple, Volume the Last*. London, 1753. Both parts are published in a two-volume edition in which the original text is reconstructed. Edited by Peter Sabor. Lexington: University Press of Kentucky, 1998.

Flecknoe, Richard. *Enigmaticall Characters, All Taken to the Life, from severall Persons, Humours, & Dispositions*. [London], 1658 [Wing F1213].

Foote, Samuel. *The Author*. London, 1757.

———. *The Bankrupt*. London, 1776.

———. *The Devil Upon Two Sticks*. London, 1778.

———. *The Englishman in Paris*. London, 1753.

———. *The Englishman return'd from Paris*. London, 1756.

———. *The Handsome Housemaid, or, Piety in Pattens* (perf. 1773). Published in Samuel N. Bogorad and Robert Gale Noyes, eds., *Samuel Foote's "Primitive Puppet-Shew" Featuring "Piety in Pattens": A Critical Edition*, special issue of *Theatre Survey* 14.1 (1973).

———. *The Knights*. London, 1754.

———. *The Lyar*. London, 1764.

———. *The Maid of Bath*. London, [1775?].

———. *The Mayor of Garratt*. London, 1764.

———. *The Minor*. London, 1760.

———. *The Nabob* (perf. 1772). London, 1778.

———. *The Patron*. London, 1764.

———. *The Roman and English Comedy Consider'd and Compar'd. With Remarks on the Suspicious Husband. And an Examen into the Merit of the present Comic Actors*. London, 1747.

———. *Taste*. London, 1752.

Forman, Charles. *Protesilaus: or, the Character of an Evil Minister*. London, 1730.

Garrick, David. "Address to the Town." London, 1763. In *Poetical Works*, vol. 1.

———. *The Country Girl*. London, 1766. In *Plays*, vol. 7.

———. "*Epigram*, written soon after *Dr. Hill's* Farce, called *The Rout*, was acted." In *Poetical Works*, vol. 1.

———. *The Fribbleriad*. London, 1761.

———. *The Guardian*. London, 1759. In *Plays*, vol. 1.

———. *Harlequin's Invasion* (perf. 1759). Not published until the twentieth century. In *Plays*, vol. 1.

———. *Lethe; or, Esop in the Shades* (perf. 1740). London, 1745. In *Plays*, vol. 1.

———. *The Letters of David Garrick*. Edited by David M. Little and George M. Kahrl. 3 vols. Cambridge, MA: Harvard University Press, 1963.

———. *Lilliput. A Dramatic Entertainment* (perf. 1756). London, 1757. In *Plays*, vol. 1.

———. *The Lying Valet*. London, 1741. In *Plays*, vol. 1.

———. *Miss in Her Teens; or, The Medley of Lovers*. London, 1747. In *Plays*, vol. 1.

———. "Part of a Prologue to *Harlequin's Invasion*." In *Poetical Works*, vol. 1.

———. *A Peep Behind the Curtain; or, The New Rehearsal*. London, 1767. In *Plays*, vol. 2.

———. *The Plays of David Garrick*. Edited by Harry William Pedicord and Fredrick Louis Bergmann. 7 vols. Carbondale: Southern Illinois University Press, 1980–1982.

———. *The Poetical Works of David Garrick, Esq; . . . with Explanatory Notes*. 2 vols. London, 1785.

———. *Ragandjaw* (private perf. 1746). First printed in Harry William Pedicord, "*Ragandjaw:* Garrick's Shakespearean Parody for a Private Theatre." *Philological Quarterly* 60 (1981): 197–204.

———. "A *Recipe* for a *Modern Critic*." In *Poetical Works*, vol. 1.

———. *The Sick Monkey, A Fable*. London, 1765.

Garrick, David, and George Colman. *The Clandestine Marriage, A Comedy*. London, 1766. In Garrick, *Plays*, vol. 1.

Garth, Sir Samuel. *The Dispensary*. London, 1699. Reprinted with an introduction by Jo Allen Bradham. Delmar, NY: Scholars' Facsimiles and Reprints, 1975.

Gay, John. *Achilles. An Opera*. London, 1733 (pub. posthumously). In *Dramatic Works*, vol. 2.

———. *The Beggar's Opera*. London, 1728. In *Dramatic Works*, vol. 2.

———. *The Distress'd Wife* (perf. 1734). London, 1743. In *Dramatic Works*, vol. 2.

———. *Fables*. London, 1727. In *Poetry and Prose*, vol. 2.

———. *Fables. By the late Mr. Gay. Volume the Second*. London, 1738. In *Poetry and Prose*, vol. 2.

———. *The Fan. A Poem. In Three Books*. London, 1713. In *Poetry and Prose*, vol. 1.

———. *John Gay, Dramatic Works*. Edited by John Fuller. 2 vols. Oxford: Clarendon, 1983.

———. *John Gay, Poetry and Prose*. Edited by Vinton A. Dearing with the assistance of Charles E. Beckwith. 2 vols. Oxford: Clarendon, 1974.

———. *The Letters of John Gay*. Edited by C. F. Burgess. Oxford: Clarendon, 1966.

———. *The Mohocks. A Tragi-Comical Farce*. London, 1712. In *Dramatic Works*, vol. 1.

———. *Polly: An Opera. Being the Second Part of the Beggar's Opera* (not perf. until 1777). London, 1729. In *Dramatic Works*, vol. 2.

———. *The Rehearsal at Goatham* (wr. ca. 1730; not perf.). London, 1754. In *Dramatic Works*, vol. 2.

———. *The Shepherd's Week. In Six Pastorals*. London, 1714. In *Poetry and Prose*, vol. 1.

———. *Three Hours after Marriage. A Comedy*. London, 1717. [With Pope and Arbuthnot?] In *Dramatic Works*, vol. 1.

———. *Trivia: Or, The Art of Walking the Streets of London*. London, 1716. In *Poetry and Prose*, vol. 1.

———. *The What d'ye Call It: A Tragi-Comi-Pastoral Farce*. London, 1715. In *Dramatic Works*, vol. 1.

———. *Wine a Poem*. London, 1708. In *Poetry and Prose*, vol. 1.

Génard, François. *The School of Man. Translated from the French*. London, 1753.

Gilbert, Thomas. *A Panegyric on a Court*. London, 1739.

———. *A Satire on All Parties: A Poem*. London, 1749.

Glanvill, Joseph. *A Blow at Modern Sadducism In some Philosophical Considerations about Witch-craft . . . With some Reflections on Drollery, and Atheisme*. London, 1668 [Wing G799].

Goldsmith, Oliver. *The Citizen of the World*. London, 1762. In *Collected Works*, vol. 2.

———. *Collected Works of Oliver Goldsmith*. Edited by Arthur Friedman. 5 vols. Oxford: Clarendon, 1966.

———. *The Good-Natur'd Man: A Comedy*. London, 1768. In *Collected Works*, vol. 5.

———. *Retaliation: A Poem*. London, 1774. In *Collected Works*, vol. 4.

———. *She Stoops to Conquer: or, The Mistakes of a Night*. London, 1773. In *Collected Works*, vol. 5.

———. *The Vicar of Wakefield*. London, 1766. In *Collected Works*, vol. 4.

Gould, Robert. *The Corruption of the Times by Money, a Satyr*. London, 1693 [Wing G1417].

———. *Jack Pavy, Alias Jack Adams*. In *Poems*.

———. *The Laureat*. [London], 1687 [Wing G1420].

———. *Love given o're: or, a Satyr against the Pride, Lust, Inconstancy, &c. of Woman*. London, 1682 [Wing G1422].

———. *Poems Chiefly consisting of Satyrs and Satyrical Epistles*. London, 1689 [Wing G1431].

———. *A Satyr against the Playhouse*. In *Poems*.

———. *A Satyr against Wooing: With a View of the Ill Consequences that attend it*. London, 1698 [Wing G1435].

———. *A Satyr upon Man*. In *Poems*.

Gray, Ralph. *The Coronation Ballad, 11th April 1689* (wr. 1689). In *POAS-Y*, vol. 5.

Greene, Edward Burnaby. *Friendship: A Satire*. London, 1763.

———. *The Satires of Juvenal Paraphrastically Imitated, And adapted to the Times*. London, 1763.

Grove, Edward. *Mirth's Madness, or, the Vanity of Mens Laughter, and of Their Merry Amusements in their Idle Hours. Consider'd in a Sermon Upon Ecclesiastes II. 1, 2*. London, 1702.

Hall-Stevenson, John. *Makarony Fables; with the New Fables of the Bees, in two cantos*. London, 1768.

Hatchett, Thomas [et al.?]. *The Opera of Operas; or, Tom Thumb the Great. Alter'd From the Life and Death of Tom Thumb the Great. And Set to Musick after the Italian Manner*. London, 1733.

Havard, William. *King Charles the First: An Historical Tragedy written in Imitation of Shakespear*. London, 1737.

Haywood, Eliza. *The Adventures of Eovaai, Princess of Ijaveo*. London, 1736.

———. *Memoirs of a Certain Island Adjacent to the Kingdom of Utopia*. London, 1725.

Hervey, John. *A Satyr. In the Manner of Persius. In A Dialogue between the Poet and his Friend*. London, 1730.

Higden, Henry. *The Wary Widdow: or, Sir Noisy Parrat*. London, 1693 [Wing H1945].

Hill, Aaron. *The Smartiad, a Satire. Occasioned by an Epic Poem, intitled The Hilliad*. London, 1753.

———. *The Tears of the Muses; in a Conference, between Prince Germanicus, and a Male-content Party*. London, 1737.

Hoadly, Benjamin. *The Suspicious Husband. A Comedy*. London, 1747.

Hogarth, William. *Beer Street* (1751). In Paulson, *Hogarth*, vol. 3.

————. *Gin Lane* (1751). In Paulson, *Hogarth*, vol. 3.

————. *A Harlot's Progress* (1732). In Paulson, *Hogarth*, vol. 1.

————. *Hudibras* (1725). In Paulson, *Hogarth*, vol. 1.

————. *Industry and Idleness* (1747). In Paulson, *Hogarth*, vol. 2.

————. *A Rake's Progress* (1735). In Paulson, *Hogarth*, vol. 2.

————. *The South Sea Scheme* (1721). In Paulson, *Hogarth*, vol. 1.

————. *Strolling Actresses in a Barn* (1738). In Paulson, *Hogarth*, vol. 2.

————. *The Times* (1762). In Paulson, *Hogarth*, vol. 3.

How, Jasper. *A Sermon Preach'd at Exon, May 7. 1718. Before an Assembly of the United Ministers of Devon and Cornwall.* Exon, 1718.

Howard, Edward. *The Change of Crownes* (perf. 1667). Not published until the twentieth century. Edited by Frederick S. Boas. London: Oxford University Press, 1949.

Howard, Sir Robert. *The Committee* (perf. 1662). Published in his *Four New Plays.* London, 1665 [Wing H2995].

————. *The Great Favourite, or the Duke of Lerma.* London, 1668 [Wing H2996].

Howard, Sir Robert, and George Villiers, second Duke of Buckingham. *The Country Gentleman* (scheduled for production in 1669 but banned and not published until 1976). In *Plays, Poems, and Miscellaneous Writings Associated with Buckingham,* vol. 1.

Jacob, Giles. *The Poetical Register: Or, the Lives and Characters of the English Dramatick Poets. With an Account of their Writings.* London, 1719–1720.

Johnson, Charles. *The Wife's Relief: or, The Husband's Cure. A Comedy.* London, 1711.

Johnson, Samuel. *A Compleat Vindication of the Licensers of the Stage.* London, 1739.

————. *The False Alarm.* 2nd ed. London, 1770.

————. *The Lives of the Most Eminent English Poets; With Critical Observations On Their Works.* Edited by Roger Lonsdale. 4 vols. Oxford: Clarendon, 2006.

————. *London, A Poem, In Imitation of the Third Satire of Juvenal.* London, 1738.

————. *The Vanity of Human Wishes. The Tenth Satire of Juvenal, Imitated.* London, 1749.

Johnson, Samuel (of Cheshire). *Hurlothrumbo: or, the Super-Natural.* London, 1729.

"Junius" [pseud.]. *The Letters of Junius* (pub. serially, 1769–1772). Edited by John Cannon. Oxford: Clarendon, 1978.

Kelly, Hugh. *False Delicacy: A Comedy.* London, 1768.

————. *Thespis: or A Critical Examination into the Merits of the Principal Performers belonging to Drury-Lane Theatre.* London, 1766.

Kenrick, William. *A Letter to David Garrick, Esq. occasioned by his having moved the Court of King's Bench against the publisher of Love in the suds.* London, 1772.

————. *Love in the Suds; A Town Eclogue being the Lamentation of Roscius for the Loss of his Nyky.* London, 1772.

————. *The Town. A Satire.* London, 1748.

Lacy, John. *The Old Troop: or Monsieur Raggou* (perf. 1664). London, 1672 [Wing L144].

Leapor, Mary. *The Works of Mary Leapor.* Edited by Richard Greene and Ann Messenger. Oxford: Oxford University Press, 2003.

Lee, John. *The Country Wife, A Comedy in Two Acts . . . Altered from Wycherley.* London, 1765.

Lee, Nathaniel. *The Princess of Cleve* (perf. 1682?). London, 1689. In *The Works of Nathaniel Lee,* edited by Thomas B. Stroup and Arthur L. Cooke, vol. 2 (1955). Reprint, Metuchen, NJ: Scarecrow Reprint, 1968.

Lennox, Charlotte. *The Female Quixote: or The Adventures of Arabella*. London, 1752. Edited by Margaret Dalziel. London: Oxford University Press, 1970.

———. *Poems on Several Occasions*. London, 1747.

Lloyd, Evan. *The Methodist*. London, 1766.

———. *The Powers of the Pen*. London, 1766.

Lloyd, Robert. *The Actor. A Poetical Epistle to Bonnell Thornton, Esq*. London, 1760.

———. *An Epistle to C. Churchill, Author of the Rosciad*. London, 1761.

———. *Poems. By Robert Lloyd, A. M*. London, 1762.

———. *The Progress of Envy a Poem, in Imitation of Spenser. Occasioned by Lauder's Attack on the Character of Milton*. London, 1751.

Loyd [*sic*], John. *A Satyr on the Times: And some of the Modern Plays*. [Dublin], 1730.

Macklin, Charles. *Covent Garden Theatre, or Pasquin Turn'd Drawncansir* (perf. 1752). Not published until the twentieth century. Printed (as transcribed from the Larpent manuscript in the Huntington Library) with an introduction by Jean B. Kern. Los Angeles: William Andrews Clark Memorial Library, University of California, 1965.

———. *The Fortune Hunters* (perf. 1748). There are two largely identical pirated printings, London, 1750.

———. *Four Comedies by Charles Macklin*. Edited by J. O. Bartley. London: Sidgwick and Jackson, 1968.

———. *Love à la Mode* (perf. 1759). London, 1779. In *Four Comedies*.

———. *The Man of the World* (perf. 1781). London, 1785. In *Four Comedies*.

———. *The New Play Criticiz'd, or The Plague of Envy* (perf. 1747). Not published until the twentieth century. Printed (as transcribed from the Larpent manuscript in the Huntington Library) with an introduction by Jean B. Kern. Los Angeles: William Andrews Clark Memorial Library, University of California, 1967.

———. *The School for Husbands, or the Married Libertine* (perf. 1761). Not published in the eighteenth century. In *Four Comedies*.

———. *The Spoild Child* (wr. late 1770s–early 1780s; incomplete MS). In Kinservik, *Disciplining Satire*, appendix.

———. *The True-Born Irishman* (perf. 1762). Dublin, 1783; London, 1784. In *Four Comedies*.

———. *A Will and No Will: or, A Bone for the Lawyers* (perf. 1746). Not published until the twentieth century. Printed with *The New Play Criticiz'd*.

Mallet, David. *Of Verbal Criticism: An Epistle to Mr. Pope. Occasioned by Theobald's Shakespear and Bentley's Milton*. London, 1733.

Mandeville, Bernard. *The Fable of the Bees: or, Private Vices Publick Benefits*. London, 1714.

———. *The Grumbling Hive: or, Knaves Turn'd Honest*. London, 1705.

———. *The Pamphleteers: A Satyr*. London, 1703.

Manley, Delarivier. *Secret Memoirs and Manners Of several Persons of Quality, of Both Sexes. From the New Atalantis*. London, 1709.

Marvell, Andrew. *The Character of Holland* (wr. 1653). London, 1681.

———. *Clarendon's Housewarming*. London, 1667.

———. *Flecknoe, an English Priest at Rome* (wr. 1646?). London, 1681.

———. *The Last Instructions to a Painter* (wr. 1667). Published in *The Third Part of the Collection of Poems on Affairs of State*. London, 1689.

———. *The Loyal Scot* (wr. 1667–1673). London, 1694.

————. *The Poems of Andrew Marvell.* Edited by Nigel Smith. 2003. Rev. ed., Harlow: Pearson Longman, 2007. All poems by Marvell are cited from this edition.

————. *The Rehearsal Transpros'd: Or, Animadversions upon a Late Book, Intituled, A Preface shewing What Grounds there are of Fears and Jealousies of Popery.* London, 1672. In *The Prose Works of Andrew Marvell,* vol. 1, edited by Martin Dzelzainis and Annabel Patterson. New Haven, CT: Yale University Press, 2003.

————. *The Second Advice to a Painter* (wr. 1666). London, 1667.

————. *The Statue in Stocks-Market* (wr. 1672–1674). London, 1689.

Massie, Joseph. *Calculations of the Present Taxes Yearly Paid by a Family of Each Rank, Degree, or Class.* 2nd ed. London, 1761.

Maynwaring, Arthur. *An Excellent New Historical Ballad, To be sung at all the Elections in Britain* (wr. 1708?). British Library Add. MS 61,462, fols. 17–18.

————. *The History and Fall of the Conformity Bill. Being an Excellent New Song To the Tune of the Ladies Fall.* [London, 1704].

————. *The King of Hearts.* London, 1690 [Wing M295A].

————. *The Life and Posthumous Works of Arthur Maynwaring, Esq; Containing Several Original Pieces and Translations, in Prose and Verse, never before Printed.* London, 1715 [compiled by John Oldmixon?].

————. *Tarquin and Tullia* (wr. 1689). In *POAS-Y,* vol. 5.

Milbourne, Luke. *The Moderate Cabal. A Satyr.* London, 1710.

Miller, James. *The Man of Taste. A Comedy.* London, 1735.

————. *Seasonable Reproof, A Satire, In the Manner of Horace.* London, 1735.

Montagu, Lady Mary Wortley. *The Complete Letters of Lady Mary Wortley Montagu.* Edited by Robert Halsband. 3 vols. Oxford: Clarendon, 1965–1967.

————. *Verses Address'd to the Imitator of the First Satire of the Second Book of Horace.* London, [1733].

Mordaunt, Charles, Earl of Monmouth. *The Ladies' March* (wr. 1681). In *CSR.*

Morgan, McNamara. *The Causidicade. A Panegyri-Satiri-Serio-Comic-Dramatical Poem.* London, 1743.

Morris, Corbyn. *An Essay Towards Fixing the True Standards of Wit, Humour, Raillery, Satire, and Ridicule.* London, 1744.

Murphy, Arthur. *The Citizen. A Farce.* London, 1761.

————. *Ode to the Naiads of Fleet-Ditch.* London, 1761.

————. *The Old Maid.* London, 1761.

————. *The Spouter: or, the Triple Revenge* (not performed). London, 1756.

————. *The Upholsterer, or, What News?* London, 1758.

————. *What we must All come to.* London, 1764.

Mulgrave, third Earl of. See Sheffield, John, third Earl of Mulgrave, and John Dryden.

Nevile, Thomas. *The Fourteenth Satire of Juvenal Imitated.* London, 1769.

Newcomb, Thomas. *Blasphemy As Old as the Creation: or, The Newgate Divine. A Satyr.* London, 1730.

————. *The Manners of the Age: In Thirteen Moral Satirs.* London, 1733.

O'Brien, Charles. *A Dialogue between the Poet and his Friend. A Satire.* London, 1755.

Odingsells, Gabriel. *Bays's Opera.* London, 1730.

Oldham, John. *The Careless Good Fellow.* London, 1680. Pub. as a broadside entitled *The Claret Drinker's Song.*

———. *A Dithyrambique on Drinking: Suppos'd to be spoken by Rochester at the Guinny-Club.* London, 1677.

———. *The Poems of John Oldham.* Edited by Harold F. Brooks. Oxford: Clarendon, 1987. All poems by Oldham are cited from this edition.

———. *Sardanapalus: An Ode* (probably wr. before spring 1679).

———. *A Satyr Against Vertue* [sometimes called *Aude aliquid. Ode*] (wr. 1676?). London, 1679.

———. *Satyrs upon the Jesuits.* London, 1679–1681.

———. *Upon a Bookseller, that expos'd him by Printing a Piece of his grosly mangled, and faulty* (wr. 1680). Pub. in *Satyrs upon the Jesuits . . . And some other Pieces By the same Hand*, 2nd ed., 1682, under the title "Upon a Printer."

———. *Upon a Woman who by her Falshood and Scorn was the Death of his Friend* (wr. 1678). Pub. in *Satyrs upon the Jesuits . . . And some other Pieces By the same Hand*, 2nd ed., 1682.

———. *Upon the Author of the Play call'd Sodom* (wr. 1678).

Otway, Thomas. *Friendship in Fashion.* London, 1678. In *Works*, vol. 1.

———. *The Souldiers Fortune.* London, 1681. In *Works*, vol. 2.

———. *Venice Preserv'd, or, A Plot Discovered.* London, 1682. In *Works*, vol. 2.

———. *The Works of Thomas Otway: Plays, Poems, and Love-Letters.* Edited by J. C. Ghosh. 2 vols. 1932. Reprint, Oxford: Clarendon Press, 1968.

Payne, Nevil. *The Siege of Constantinople* (perf. 1674). London, 1675 [Wing P893].

Pepys, Samuel. *The Diary of Samuel Pepys.* Edited by William Matthews and Robert Latham. 11 vols. London: G. Bell and Sons, 1970–1983.

Phillips, John. *A Satyr Against Hypocrites.* London, 1655 [Wing P2101].

Pilkington, Laetitia. *Memoirs of Laetitia Pilkington.* Edited by A. C. Elias Jr. 2 vols. Athens: University of Georgia Press, 1997.

Poole, Josua. *The English Parnassus: or, A Helpe to English Poesie.* London, 1657 [Wing P2814].

Pope, Alexander. *The Correspondence of Alexander Pope.* Edited by George Sherburn. 5 vols. Oxford: Clarendon, 1956.

———. *The Dunciad.* London, 1728. In *Pope's "Dunciad" of 1728: A History and Facsimile*, edited by David L. Vander Meulen. Charlottesville: University Press of Virginia, 1991.

———. *The Dunciad, in Four Books.* London, 1743. In *Twickenham Edition*, vol. 5.

———. *The Dunciad Variorum, with the Prolegomena of Scriblerus.* London, 1729. In *Twickenham Edition*, vol. 5.

———. *Epilogue to the Satires.* London, 1738. In *Twickenham Edition*, vol. 4.

———. *An Epistle from Mr. Pope, to Dr. Arbuthnot.* London, 1735. In *Twickenham Edition*, vol. 4.

———. *Epistle I (To Cobham) Of the Knowledge and Characters of Men.* London, 1734. In *Twickenham Edition*, vol. 3.2.

———. *Epistle II (To a Lady) Of the Characters of Women.* London, 1735. In *Twickenham Edition*, vol. 3.2.

———. *Epistle III (To Bathurst) Of the Use of Riches.* London, 1733. In *Twickenham Edition*, vol. 3.2.

———. *Epistle IV (To Burlington) Of the Use of Riches.* London, 1731. In *Twickenham Edition*, vol. 3.2.

———. *An Essay on Criticism.* London, 1711. In *Twickenham Edition*, vol. 1.

———. *An Essay on Man.* London, 1733–1734. In *Twickenham Edition*, vol. 3.1.

———. *The First Satire of the Second Book of Horace Imitated* (*Fortescue*). London, 1733. In *Twickenham Edition*, vol. 4.

———. *Fragment of a Satire*. Published in Swift and Pope, *Miscellanies, The Last Volume* 1727. In *Twickenham Edition*, vol. 6.

———. *A Full and True Account of a Horrid and Barbarous Revenge by Poison, On the Body of Mr. Edmund Curll, Bookseller*. London, 1716. In *Twickenham Edition*, vol. 5.

———. *The Impertinent, or a Visit to the Court. A Satyr*. London, 1733 (pub. anonymously). In *Twickenham Edition*, vol. 4, as *The Fourth Satire of Dr. John Donne*.

———. *The Memoirs Of the Extraordinary Life, Works, and Discoveries of Martinus Scriblerus*. London, 1741. Edited by Charles Kerby-Miller. New Haven, CT: Yale University Press, 1950.

———. *One Thousand Seven Hundred and Forty* (wr. 1740). London, 1797. In *Twickenham Edition*, vol. 4.

———. *Peri Bathous*. Published in Swift and Pope, *Miscellanies. The Last Volume*, 1727.

———. *The Rape of the Lock*. London, 1714 [early version]. In *Twickenham Edition*, vol. 2.

———. *A Roman Catholick Version of the First Psalm*. London, 1716. In *Twickenham Edition*, vol. 6.

———. *The Second Satire of the Second Book of Horace Paraphrased* (*Bethel*). London, 1734. In *Twickenham Edition*, vol. 4.

———. *Sober Advice from Horace*. London, 1734. In *Twickenham Edition*, vol. 4.

———. *To Mr. John Moore, Author of the Celebrated Worm-Powder* ["Worms"]. London, 1716. In *Twickenham Edition*, vol. 6.

———. *The Twickenham Edition of the Poems of Alexander Pope*. 11 vols. [in 12]. London: Methuen; New Haven, CT: Yale University Press, 1939–1969.

———. *The Works of Alexander Pope*. London, 1717.

———. *The Works of Alexander Pope, Esq; Vol. II. Containing his Epistles and Satires*. London, 1735.

Prior, Matthew. *Advice to the Painter. On the happy defeat of the Rebels in the West, and the Execution of the late Duke of Monmouth* (wr. 1685). In *Literary Works*, vol. 1.

———. *Alma: or, The Progress of the Mind. In Three Cantos*. London, 1718. In *Literary Works*, vol. 1.

———. *The Literary Works of Matthew Prior*. Edited by H. Bunker Wright and Monroe K. Spears. 2 vols. 1959. 2nd ed., Oxford: Oxford University Press, 1971.

———. *The Orange* (wr. 1688; pub. in several collections in 1689). In *Literary Works*, vol. 1.

Prior, Matthew, and Charles Montagu. *The Hind and the Panther Transvers'd to the Story of The Country-Mouse and the City-Mouse*. London, 1687. In Prior, *Literary Works*, vol. 1.

Ralph, James. *The Astrologer*. London, 1744.

———. *The Fashionable Lady; or Harlequin's Opera. In the Manner of a Rehearsal*. London, 1730.

———. *Sawney. An Heroic Poem Occasion'd by the Dunciad*. London, 1728.

———. *The Touch-Stone: or, Historical, Critical, Political, and Theological Essays on the Reigning Diversions of the Town*. London, 1728.

Ramsay, Allan. *An Essay on Ridicule*. London, 1753.

Randolph, Thomas. *The Muses Looking-Glass; (or, The Stage Re-View'd.) A Comedy*. London, 1706.

Ravenscroft, Edward. *The London Cuckolds* (perf. 1681). London, 1683 [Wing R333].

Robinson, John. *Preferment: A Satire*. London, 1765.

Rochester, second Earl of. See Wilmot, John, second Earl of Rochester.

Roscommon, fourth Earl of. See Dillon, Wentworth, fourth Earl of Roscommon.

Rowe, Nicholas. *The Biter. A Comedy* (perf. 1704). London, 1705.

Sackville, Charles, sixth Earl of Dorset. *Colon [Colin]* (wr. 1679). In *Poems*.

———. *A Faithful Catalogue of our Most Eminent Ninnies* (wr. 1688). In *Poems*.

———. *My Opinion* (wr. 1681). In *Poems*.

———. *On the Young Statesmen* (wr. 1680). In *Poems*.

———. *The Poems of Charles Sackville, Sixth Earl of Dorset*. Edited by Brice Harris. New York: Garland, 1979.

———. *To Mr. Edward Howard, on his Incomparable, Incomprehensible Poem Called "The British Princes"* (wr. 1669). Published 1680 in the *Poems* of "Rochester." In *Poems*.

Savage, Richard. *An Author to be Lett. Being A Proposal humbly address'd to the Consideration of the Knights, Esquires, Gentlemen, and other worshipful and weighty Members of the Solid and Ancient Society of the Bathos*. London, 1729.

———. *The Convocation: or, a Battle of Pamphlets*. London, 1717.

Scroope, Sir Carr. *Answer By way of Epigram* (wr. 1676?). In Rochester's *Works*.

———. *In defence of Satire* (wr. 1676?). In Rochester's *Works*.

Sergeant, John. *Raillery Defeated by Calm Reason: or, the New Cartesian Method of Arguing and Answering Expos'd*. London, 1699 [Wing S2586].

Settle, Elkanah. *Absalom Senior: or, Achitophel Transpros'd*. London, 1682 [Wing S2652].

———. *New Athenian Comedy, Containing The Politicks, Œconomicks, Tacticks . . . &c. Of that most Learned Society*. London, 1693 [Wing S2701].

Shadwell, Thomas. *Bury-Fair*. London, 1689. In *Complete Works*, vol. 4.

———. *The Complete Works of Thomas Shadwell*. Edited by Montague Summers. 5 vols. London: Fortune, 1927.

———. *Epsom-Wells* (perf. 1672). London, 1673. In *Complete Works*, vol. 2.

———. *The History of Timon of Athens, the Man-Hater*. London, 1678. In *Complete Works*, vol. 3.

———. *The Humorists*. London, 1671 (emasculated version as performed). In *Complete Works*, vol. 1. Also edited by Richard Perkin, transcribed from the original unpublished and unperformed MS version but printed without explanatory apparatus. Dublin: Laurel House, 1975.

———. *The Libertine* (perf. 1675). London, 1676. In *Complete Works*, vol. 3.

———. *The Medal of John Bayes: A Satyr against Folly and Knavery*. London, 1682 [Wing S2860].

———. *The Scowrers* (perf. 1690). London, 1691. In *Complete Works*, vol. 5.

———. *The Squire of Alsatia*. London, 1688. In *Complete Works*, vol. 4.

———. *The Sullen Lovers: or, the Impertinents*. London, 1668. In *Complete Works*, vol. 1.

———. *The Tory-Poets: A Satyr*. London, 1682 [Wing T1948].

———. *A True Widow* (perf. 1678). London, 1679. In *Complete Works*, vol. 3.

———. *The Virtuoso*. London, 1676. In *Complete Works*, vol. 3.

———. *The Volunteers, or the Stock-Jobbers* (perf. 1692). London, 1693. In *Complete Works*, vol. 5.

———. *The Woman-Captain* (perf. 1679). London, 1680. In *Complete Works*, vol. 4.

Shaftesbury, third Earl of. See Cooper, Anthony Ashley, third Earl of Shaftesbury.

Shebbeare, John. *History of the Excellence and Decline of the Constitution, Religion, Laws, Manners and Genius of the Sumatrans.* 2 vols. London, [1760?].

———. *Letters on the English Nation: by Batista Angeloni, A Jesuit.* 2 vols. London, 1755.

Sheffield, John, third Earl of Mulgrave, and John Dryden. *An Essay upon Satire* (wr. 1679). In *POAS-Y*, vol. 1.

Sheridan, Richard Brinsley. *The School for Scandal* (perf. 1777). Dublin, 1780; London, 1781 (no authorized text published in Sheridan's lifetime). In *The Dramatic Works of Richard Brinsley Sheridan*, vol. 1, edited by Cecil Price. Oxford: Oxford University Press, 1973.

Shippen, William. *Faction Display'd.* London, 1704.

Slade, John. *The Transmigrating Soul; or, an Epitome of Human Nature. A Moral Satire.* London, 1760.

Smart, Christopher. *The Hilliad: An Epic Poem.* London, 1753.

Smollett, Tobias. *The Adventures of Ferdinand Count Fathom.* London, 1753. Edited by O M Brack Jr. with introduction and notes by Jerry C. Beasley. Athens: University of Georgia Press, 1988.

———. *The Adventures of Peregrine Pickle.* London, 1751. Edited by James L. Clifford. London: Oxford University Press, 1964.

———. *The Adventures of Roderick Random.* London, 1748. Edited by O M Brack Jr. with an introduction and notes by James G. Basker, Paul-Gabriel Boucé, and Nicole A. Seary. Athens: University of Georgia Press, 2012.

———. *Advice: A Satire.* London, 1746.

———. *Don Ricardo Honeywater Vindicated.* London, 1748.

———. *The Expedition of Humphry Clinker.* London, 1771. Edited by Thomas R. Preston. Athens: University of Georgia Press, 1990.

———. *The History and Adventures of an Atom.* London, 1769. Edited by Robert Adams Day. Athens: University of Georgia Press, 1989.

———. *The Reprisal: or, the Tars of Old England.* London, 1757.

———. *Reproof: A Satire. The Sequel to Advice.* London, 1747.

———. *Sir Launcelot Greaves.* Pub. serially, 1760–1761. Edited by Barbara Laning Fitzpatrick, with an introduction and notes by Robert Folkenflik. Athens: University of Georgia Press, 2002.

———. *Thomsonus Redivivus: or, a Reply to W----m D--g--s, M.D.* London, 1746.

———. *Travels through France and Italy.* London, 1766. Edited by Frank Felsenstein. Oxford: Oxford University Press, 1979.

Southerne, Thomas. *The Maid's Last Prayer; or, Any Rather than Fail.* London, 1693. In *Works*, vol. 1.

———. *Sir Anthony Love: or, The Rambling Lady. A Comedy* (perf. 1690). London, 1691. In *Works*, vol. 1.

———. *The Wives' Excuse; or, Cuckolds make Themselves* (perf. 1691). London, 1692. In *Works*, vol. 1.

———. *The Works of Thomas Southerne.* Edited by Robert Jordan and Harold Love. 2 vols. Oxford: Clarendon, 1988.

The Spectator. Edited by Donald F. Bond. 5 vols. Oxford: Clarendon, 1965.

Steele, Sir Richard. *The Conscious Lovers* (perf. 1722). London, 1723 [1722]. In *The Plays of Richard Steele*, edited by Shirley Strum Kenny. Oxford: Clarendon, 1971.

Sterne, Laurence. *The Florida Edition of the Works of Laurence Sterne.* 8 vols. Edited by Melvyn New and Peter de Voogd. Gainesville: University Press of Florida, 1978–2009.

———. *The Letters*, part 1, *1739–1764. Florida Edition*, vol. 7.

———. *The Life and Opinions of Tristram Shandy, Gentleman* (pub. serially, 1759–1767). *Florida Edition*, vols. 1–3.

———. *A Political Romance, Addressed to* ——, *Esq; of York. To which is subjoined a Key.* York, 1759.

———. *A Sentimental Journey through France and Italy.* London, 1768. *Florida Edition*, vol. 6.

Stevens, George Alexander. *Distress upon Distress: or, Tragedy in True Taste. A Heroi-Comi-Parodi-Tragedi-Farcical Burlesque.* Dublin and London, 1752.

Swift, Jonathan. *Apollo Outwitted* (wr. 1709). Published in his *Miscellanies*, 1711. In *Poems*, vol. 1.

———. *An Argument against Abolishing Christianity* (wr. 1708). Published in his *Miscellanies*, 1711. In *Prose Works*, vol. 2.

———. *A Ballad on the Game of Traffick* (wr. 1702). Published in the Faulkner *Works*, vol. 8 (1746). In *Poems*, vol. 1.

———. *The Battle of the Books.* Published with *A Tale of a Tub*, 1704. In *A Tale of a Tub and Other Works.*

———. *Baucis and Philemon.* London, 1709. In *Poems*, vol. 1.

———. *A Beautiful Young Nymph Going to Bed* (wr. 1731). [London], 1734. In *Poems*, vol. 2.

———. Bickerstaff pamphlets. London, 1708–1709 (comprising *Predictions for the Year 1708, The Accomplishment of the First of Mr Bickerstaff's Predictions,* and *A Vindication of Isaac Bickerstaff Esq;*). In *Prose, Works*, vol. 2.

———. *Cassinus and Peter* (wr. 1731). Published with *A Beautiful Young Nymph*, 1734. In *Poems*, vol. 2.

———. *A Character, Panegyric, and Description of the Legion Club* [*The Legion Club*]. Published in *S[wif]t contra omnes. An Irish Miscellany*, Dublin, 1736. In *Poems*, vol. 3.

———. *The Character of Sir Robert Walpole* (wr. 1731). Not published in Swift's lifetime. In *Poems*, vol. 2.

———. *The Conduct of the Allies.* London, 1711. In *English Political Writings, 1711–1714.*

———. *The Correspondence of Jonathan Swift, D.D.* Edited by David Woolley. 4 vols. Frankfurt: Peter Lang, 1999–2007.

———. *A Description of a City Shower.* Published in *The Tatler*, no. 238 (17 October 1710). In *Poems*, vol. 1.

———. *The Description of a Salamander* (wr. 1705). Published in his *Miscellanies*, 1711. In *Poems*, vol. 1.

———. *A Description of the Morning.* Published in *The Tatler*, no. 9 (28–30 April 1709). In *Poems*, vol. 1.

———. *A Dialogue upon Dunkirk: Between a Whig and a Tory.* London, 1712. In *English Political Writings, 1711–1714.*

———. *Dingley, and Brent* (wr. 1724). Published in Deane Swift's edition of the *Works*, vol. 8 (1765). In *Poems*, vol. 2.

———. *Directions for a Birth-day Song* (wr. 1729). Published in Deane Swift's edition of the *Works*, vol. 8 (1765). In *Poems*, vol. 2.

———. *Directions to Servants.* Dublin and London, 1745. In *Prose Works*, vol. 13.

———. The Drapier's Letters (comprising *A Letter to the Shop-Keepers &c*; *A Letter to Mr Harding, Some Observations Upon a Paper, Call'd, The Report . . . Relating to Wood's Half-*

pence; *A Letter to the Whole People of Ireland*; *Seasonable Advice to the Grand-Jury*; and *A Letter To the right Honourable the Lord Viscount Molesworth*). Dublin, 1724–1725. In *Prose Works*, vol. 10.

———. *Epigram* ["As Thomas was cudgelld one day by his Wife"] (wr. 1723?). Published in Swift and Pope, *Miscellanies. The Last Volume*, 1727 . In *Poems*, vol. 1.

———. *An Epistle to a Lady*. Dublin and London, 1734 [for 1733]. In *Poems*, vol. 2.

———. *English Political Writings, 1711–1714: "The Conduct of the Allies" and Other Works*. Edited by Bertrand A. Goldgar and Ian Gadd. The Cambridge Edition of the Works of Jonathan Swift, vol. 8. Cambridge: Cambridge University Press, 2008.

———. *An Excellent New Ballad: or, The true En[gli]sh D[ea]n to be hang'd for a R[a]pe*. Dublin, 1730. In *Poems*, vol. 2.

———. *An Excellent New Song, being the Intended Speech of a famous Orator against Peace*. London, 1711. In *Poems*, vol. 1.

———. *An Excellent new Song on a seditious Pamphlet* (wr. 1720). Published in the Faulkner *Works*, vol. 2 (1735). In *Poems*, vol. 1.

———. *The Fable of Midas*. London, 1711. In *Poems*, vol. 1.

———. *The First Ode of the Second Book of Horace Paraphras'd: And Address'd to Richard St[ee]le, Esq;*. London, 1713. In *Poems*, vol. 1.

———. *A Hue and cry after Dismal*. London, 1712. In *English Political Writings, 1711–1714*.

———. *It's Out at Last*. London, 1712. In *English Political Writings, 1711–1714*.

———. *Journal to Stella*. Edited by Harold Williams. 2 vols. 1948. Reprint, Oxford: Clarendon, 1963.

———. *Judas* (wr. 1731/2). Published in the Faulkner *Works*, vol. 2 (1735). In *Poems*, vol. 3.

———. *The Lady's Dressing Room* (wr. 1730). London, 1732. In *Poems*, vol. 2.

———. *A Libel on D[r] D[elany], and a Certain Great Lord*. London and Dublin, 1730. In *Poems*, vol. 2.

———. *The Life and Genuine Character of Doctor Swift*. London, 1733. In *Poems*, vol. 2.

———. *Mad Mullinix and Timothy*. Published in *The Intelligencer*, no. 8 (29 June–2 July 1728). In *Poems*, vol. 3.

———. *Mary the Cook-Maid's Letter to Dr. Sheridan* (wr. 1718). Published in Swift and Pope, *Miscellanies. The Third Volume*, 1732. In *Poems*, vol. 3.

———. *The Mechanical Operation of the Spirit*. Published with *A Tale of a Tub*, 1704. In *A Tale of a Tub and Other Works*.

———. *A Meditation upon a Broom-stick* (wr. 1703). London, 1710. In *Prose Works*, vol. 1.

———. *Miscellanies in Prose and Verse*. London, 1711.

———. *A Modest Proposal For preventing the Children of Poor People From being a Burthen to Their Parents or Country, and for making them Beneficial to the Publick*. Dublin and London, 1729. In *Prose Works*, vol. 12.

———. *Mr. C[olli]ns's Discourse of Free-Thinking, Put into plain English*. London, 1713. In *Prose Works*, vol. 4.

———. *A New-Year's-Gift for BEC* (wr. 1723). Published in Deane Swift's edition of the *Works*, vol. 8 (1765). In *Poems*, vol. 2.

———. *On Mr. P[ultene]y being put out of the Council* (wr. 1731). Published in the Faulkner *Works*, vol. 2 (1735). In *Poems*, vol. 2.

———. *On Noisy Tom* (wr. 1736). Published in the Faulkner *Works*, vol. 10 (1762). In *Poems*, vol. 3.

————. *On Poetry: A Rapsody*. Dublin and London, 1733. In *Poems*, vol. 2.

————. *On Reading Dr. Young's Satires, called the Universal Passion* (wr. 1726). Published with *An Epistle to a Lady*, 1734. In *Poems*, vol. 2.

————. *On Stephen Duck, the Thresher and favourite Poet, a Quibbling Epigram* (wr. 1730). Published in the Faulkner *Works*, vol. 2 (1735). In *Poems*, vol. 2.

————. *On the Irish Bishops*. Published in *The Gentleman's Magazine*, June 1732. In *Poems*, vol. 3.

————. *On the Little House by the Church Yard of Castleknock* (wr. 1710). Published in the Faulkner *Works*, vol. 8 (1746). In *Poems*, vol. 1.

————. *On the Words—Brother Protestants, and Fellow Christians, so familiarly used by the Advocates for the Repeal of the Test Act in Ireland, 1733*. Published in *The Gentleman's Magazine*, supplement, 1733. In *Poems*, vol. 3.

————. *On Wood the Iron-monger* (wr. 1725). Published in the Faulkner *Works*, vol. 2 (1735). In *Poems*, vol. 1.

————. *Peace and Dunkirk; being an Excellent New Song upon the Surrender of Dunkirk to General Hill*. London, 1712. In *Poems*, vol. 1.

————. *Phillis, Or, the Progress of Love* (wr. 1719). Published in Swift and Pope, *Miscellanies. The Last Volume*, 1727. In *Poems*, vol. 1.

————. *The Poems of Jonathan Swift*. Edited by Harold Williams. 3 vols. 1937. 2nd ed., Oxford: Clarendon, 1958.

————. *Polite Conversation*. Dublin and London, 1738. In *Prose Works*, vol. 4.

————. *The Progress of Beauty* (wr. 1719). Published in Swift and Pope, *Miscellanies. The Last Volume*, 1727. In *Poems*, vol. 1.

————. *A Project for the Advancement of Religion, and the Reformation of Manners*. London, 1709. In *Prose Works*, vol. 2.

————. *A Proposal for the Universal Use of Irish Manufacture*. Dublin, 1720. In *Prose Works*, vol. 9.

————. *The Prose Works of Jonathan Swift*. Edited by Herbert Davis et al. 14 vols. Oxford: Basil Blackwell, 1939–1968; various reimpressions, sometimes corrected.

————. *The Publick Spirit of the Whigs: Set forth in their Generous Encouragement of the Author of the Crisis*. London, 1714. In *English Political Writings, 1711–1714*.

————. *A Satirical Elegy On the Death of a late Famous General* (wr. 1722). Published in *The Gentleman's Magazine* 34 (May 1764). In *Poems*, vol. 1.

————. *A Simile, on Our Want of Silver, and the only Way to remedy it* (wr. 1725). Published in the Faulkner *Works*, vol. 2 (1735). In *Poems*, vol. 1.

————. *Stella's Distress on the 3d fatal day of Octob'* (wr. 1723). Published in the Faulkner *Works*, vol. 2 (1735). In *Poems*, vol. 2.

————. *Strephon and Chloe* (wr. 1731). Published with *A Beautiful Young Nymph*, 1734. In *Poems*, vol. 2.

————. *A Tale of a Tub*. London, 1704. In *A Tale of a Tub and Other Works*.

————. *A Tale of a Tub and Other Works*. Edited by Marcus Walsh. Cambridge: Cambridge University Press, 2010.

————. *Tim and the Fables*. Published in *The Intelligencer*, no. 10 (13–16 July 1728?). In *Poems*, vol. 3.

————. *To Mr. Gay on his being Steward to the Duke of Queensberry* (wr. 1731). Published in the Faulkner *Works*, vol. 2 (1735). In *Poems*, vol. 2.

———. *To Stella, Who Collected and Transcribed his Poems* (wr. 1720). Published in Swift and Pope, *Miscellanies. The Last Volume*, 1727. In *Poems*, vol. 2.

———. *To Their Excellencies the Lord Justices of Ireland. The Humble Petition of Frances Harris, Who must Starve, and Die a Maid if it miscarries* [*Mrs. Harris's Petition*] (wr. 1701). Published with *Baucis and Philemon*, 1709. In *Poems*, vol. 1.

———. *T[o]l[a]nd's Invitation to Dismal, to Dine with the Calves-Head Club*. [London], 1712. In *Poems*, vol. 1.

———. *Traulus: The first Part*. [Dublin], 1730. In *Poems*, vol. 3.

———. *Traulus: The second Part*. [Dublin], 1730. In *Poems*, vol. 3.

———. *Travels into Several Remote Nations of the World. In Four Parts* [*Gulliver's Travels*]. London, 1726. In *Prose Works*, vol. 11.

———. *Verses on the Death of Dr. S[wift], D. S. P. D.* (wr. 1731). Dublin, 1739. In *Poems*, vol. 2.

———. *Verses on the upright Judge, who condemned the Drapier's Printer* (wr. 1724). In the Faulkner *Works*, vol. 2 (1735). In *Poems*, vol. 1.

———. *The Virtues of Sid Hamet the Magician's Rod*. London, 1710. In *Poems*, vol. 1.

———. *Whitshed's Motto On His Coach* (wr. 1724). Published in the Faulkner *Works*, vol. 2 (1735). In *Poems*, vol. 1.

———. *The W[in]ds[o]r Prophecy*. [London], 1711. In *Poems*, vol. 1.

———. *Wood, an Insect* (wr. 1725). Published in the Faulkner *Works*, vol. 2 (1735). In *Poems*, vol. 1.

———. *The Yahoo's Overthrow; or, The Kevan Bayl's New Ballad, upon Serjeant Kite's insulting the Dean* (wr. 1734). Published in Deane Swift's edition of the *Works*, vol. 8 (1765). In *Poems*, vol. 3.

Swift, Jonathan, and Alexander Pope. *Miscellanies in Prose and Verse. The First Volume*. London, 1727.

———. *Miscellanies. The Last Volume*. London, 1727.

———. *Miscellanies. The Second Volume*. London, 1727.

———. *Miscellanies. The Third Volume*. London, 1732.

Taperell, John. *Swearing, A Satire. With a Preface to the Swearer*. London, 1751.

Tate, Nahum. *The History of King Richard the Second* (banned December 1680; perf. January 1681 under the title *The Sicilian Usurper*). London, 1681 [Wing S2921].

Tatham, John. *The Rump: or The Mirrour of The late Times. A New Comedy*. London, 1660 [Wing T233].

The Tatler. Edited by Donald F. Bond. 3 vols. Oxford: Clarendon, 1987.

Taubman, Matthew. *Philander* (wr. 1680). In *POAS-Y*, vol. 2.

Thompson, Edward. *The Meretriciad*. London, 1761.

Thompson, Thomas. *Midsummer Moon: or, The Livery-Man's Complaint*. London, 1682 [Wing T1011].

Thornton, Bonnell. *Have At You All: or, The Drury-Lane Journal*. 16 January–9 April 1752.

Tickell, Thomas. *An Imitation of the Prophecy of Nereus. From Horace Book I. Ode XV*. London, 1715.

Tottie, John. *Ridicule, so far as it Affects Religion, Consider'd and Censur'd. A Sermon Preached before the University of Oxford, at St. Mary's, On Sunday, Dec. 8. 1734*. Oxford, 1734.

Tutchin, John. *The British Muse: or Tyranny Expos'd. A Satyr*. London, 1702.

———. *The Foreigners*. London, 1700 [Wing T3375].

———. *The Mouse Grown a Rat: or the Story of the City and Country Mouse Newly Transpos'd: in a Discourse betwixt Bays, Johnson, and Smith.* London, 1702.

———. *A Pindarick Ode, in the Praise of Folly and Knavery.* London, 1696 [Wing T3381].

———. *Selected Poems (1685–1700).* Introduction by Spiro Peterson. Los Angeles: William Andrews Clark Memorial Library, 1964.

———. *The Tribe of Levi.* London, 1691 [Wing T3384].

Uvedale, Thomas. *A Cure for Love: A Satyr in Imitation of Ovid.* 2nd ed. London, 1732.

Vanbrugh, John. *The Complete Works of Sir John Vanbrugh.* Edited by Bonamy Dobrée and Geoffrey Webb. 4 vols. 1927–1928. Reprint, New York: AMS, 1967.

———. *The Provok'd Wife.* London, 1697. In *Complete Works*, vol. 1.

———. *The Relapse; or, Virtue in Danger: Being the Sequel of The Fool in Fashion* (perf. 1696). London, 1697. In *Complete Works*, vol. 1.

Vanderlint, Jacob. *Money answers all Things.* London, 1734.

Victor, Benjamin. *An Epistle to Sir Richard Steele, On his Play, call'd, The Conscious Lovers.* London, 1722.

Villiers, George, second Duke of Buckingham. *Aduice to a Paynter, to draw the Delineaments of a Statesman, and his Vnderlings* (wr. ca. 1675?). In *Plays, Poems, and Miscellaneous Writings*, vol. 2.

———. *The Cabbin-Boy* (undatable). In *Plays, Poems, and Miscellaneous Writings*, vol. 2.

———. *The Ducks* (undatable). In *Plays, Poems, and Miscellaneous Writings*, vol. 2.

———. *The French Generall* (wr. 1685). In *Plays, Poems, and Miscellaneous Writings*, vol. 2.

———. *The Militant Couple* (pub. 1704 in *Miscellaneous Works*). In *Plays, Poems, and Miscellaneous Writings*, vol. 2.

———. *Miscellaneous Works, Written by His Grace, George, Late Duke of Buckingham.* London, 1704.

———. *On these 2 V. of Mr Howards* (wr. 1669?). In *Plays, Poems, and Miscellaneous Writings*, vol. 2.

———. *Plays, Poems, and Miscellaneous Writings Associated with George Villiers, Second Duke of Buckingham.* Edited by Robert D. Hume and Harold Love. 2 vols. Oxford: Oxford University Press, 2007.

———. *The Rehearsal* (perf. 1671). London, 1672. In *Plays, Poems, and Miscellaneous Writings*, vol. 1.

———. *The Second Volume of Miscellaneous Works, Written by His Grace, George, Late Duke of Buckingham.* London, 1705.

———. *Sir Politick Would-be* (wr. in French ca. 1662–1665). By Charles de Saint-Denis, Sieur de Saint-Évremond; Ludovic Stuart, Seigneur d'Aubigny; and Buckingham. Published in French in Saint-Évremond's *Œuvres meslées* (London, 1705). In *Plays, Poems, and Miscellaneous Writings*, vol. 1 (in French; English translation by H. Gaston Hall in vol. 2).

———. *A Song on Thomas Earl of Danby.* Scribally circulated, 1679. In *Plays, Poems, and Miscellaneous Writings*, vol. 2.

———. *A Supplement to the Chequer-Inne.* Scribally circulated, 1679. In *Plays, Poems, and Miscellaneous Writings*, vol. 2.

———. *Upon the Installment, of Sir [Thomas] Os[bor]n, and the Late Duke of New-castle* (wr. 1677). In *Plays, Poems, and Miscellaneous Writings*, vol. 2.

Walsh, William. *Abigail's Lamentation for the Loss of Mr. Harley.* London, 1708 (in *Poetical Reflexions . . . Part the Eleventh*). In *POAS-Y*, vol. 7.

Ward, Edward. *All Men Mad: or, England a Great Bedlam.* London, 1704.

————. *Apollo's Maggot in his Cups: or, the Whimsical Creation of a Little Satyrical Poet.* London, 1729.

————. *Bribery and Simony; or, a Satyr Against the Corrupt Use of Money.* London, 1703.

————. *Durgen. Or, a Plain Satyr upon a Pompous Satyrist.* London, 1729.

————. *Female Policy Detected. Or, The Arts of a Designing Woman Laid Open.* London, 1695 [Wing W734].

————. *A Frolick to Horn-Fair, With a Walk from Cuckold's-Point through Deptford and Greenwich.* London, 1700 [Wing W735].

————. *Hudibras Redivivus: or, a Burlesque Poem on the Times.* 24 parts. London, 1705–1707.

————. *In Imitation of Hudibras. The Dissenting Hypocrite, or Occasional Conformist; with Reflections On Two of the Ring-Leaders, &c.* London, 1704.

————. *A Journey to Hell: or, a Visit paid to the Devil.* 3 parts. London, 1700–1705.

————. *Labour in Vain, or, What Signifies Little or Nothing.* London, 1700 [Wing W744].

————. *The London Spy.* 18 parts. London, 1698–1703.

————. *The London Terrae-filius: or the Satyrical Reformer.* London, 1707–1708.

————. *Mars Stript of his Armour: Or, the Army Display'd in all its true Colours.* [London, 1708].

————. *The Merry Travellers: or, A Trip upon Ten-Toes, from Moorfields to Bromley.* Part I. London, 1721.

————. *The Modern World Disrob'd: or, Both Sexes Stript of their Pretended Vertue.* 2 parts. London, 1708.

————. *Nuptial Dialogues and Debates: or, an Useful Prospect of the Felicities and Discomforts of a Marry'd Life.* 2 vols. London, 1710.

————. *The Poet's Ramble after Riches, or, a Nights Transactions Upon the Road Burlesqu'd.* London, 1691 [Wing W748].

————. *The Quack-Vintners: or, a Satyr against Bad Wine. With Directions where to have Good.* [London], 1712.

————. *The Rambling Fuddle-Caps: or, A Tavern Struggle for a Kiss.* London, 1706.

————. *The Rambling Rakes; or, London Libertines.* London, 1700 [Wing W751].

————. *The Revels of the Gods: or, a Ramble thro' the Heavens.* London, 1701.

————. *The Rise and Fall of Madam Coming-Sir.* London, 1703.

————. *The Secret History of the Calves-Head Clubb, or, the Republican Unmasqu'd.* London, 1703.

————. *Sot's Paradise: or, The Humours of a Derby-Ale-House: with A Satyr upon the Ale.* London, 1698 [Wing W754].

————. *A Step to Stir-Bitch-Fair, with Remarks upon the University of Cambridge.* London, 1700 [Wing W757].

————. *A Step to the Bath: with A Character Of The Place.* London, 1700 [Wing W758].

————. *Three Nights Adventures: Or, Accidental Intrigues.* London, 1701.

————. *A Trip to Jamaica: With a True Character of the People and Island.* London, 1698 [Wing W761].

————. *A Trip to New-England. With a Character of the Country and People, both English and Indians.* London, 1699 [Wing W764].

————. *A Walk to Islington: with a Description of New Tunbridge-Wells, and Sadler's Musick-House.* London, 1699 [Wing W765].

———. *The Wooden World Dissected, in the Characters of 1. A Ship of War. 2. A Sea-Captain . . . &c.* London, 1707.

———. *Writings* [variously titled]. 4 vols. London, 1706–1709.

Warton, Thomas. *New-Market, A Satire.* London, 1751.

Wase, Christopher. *Divination* (wr. 1666). In *POAS-Y*, vol. 1.

Webster, William. *Tracts Consisting of Sermons, Discourses, and Letters.* London, 1745.

Welsted, Leonard. *One Epistle to Mr. A. Pope, Occasion'd By Two Epistles Lately Published.* London, [1730].

Wharton, Thomas. *Lilli burlero.* London, 1688. In *POAS-Y*, vol. 4, as *A New Song.*

Whitehead, Paul. *Manners: A Satire.* London, 1739.

———. *The State Dunces. Inscribed to Mr. Pope.* London, 1733.

Whitehead, William. *An Essay on Ridicule.* London, 1743.

———. *A Trip to Scotland* (perf. 1770). London, 1770.

Wild, Robert. *Iter Boreale.* London, 1660 [Wing W2132].

———. *The Loyal Nonconformist; or, An Account what he dare swear, and what not.* London, 1666 [Wing W2141].

Wilkes, John, and Charles Churchill. *The Correspondence of John Wilkes and Charles Churchill.* Edited by Edward H. Weatherly. New York: Columbia University Press, 1954.

———. *The North Briton.* 2nd ed. 3 vols. Printed by Wilkes on his private press and published in Dublin in 1763.

Wilkes, John, and Thomas Potter. *An Essay on Woman.* MS. Printed in *An Essay on Woman by John Wilkes and Thomas Potter: A Reconstruction of a Lost Book With a Historical Essay on the Writing, Printing, and Suppressing of this "Blasphemous and Obscene" Work.* Edited by Arthur H. Cash. New York: AMS, 2000.

Williams, David. *A Letter to David Garrick, Esq. On His Conduct as Principal Manager and Actor at Drury-Lane.* London, 1772.

Wilmot, John, second Earl of Rochester. *Allusion to Horace 10 Sat: 1st Book* (wr. 1675–1676?). In *Works*, 71–74.

———. *The Disabled Debauchee.* In *Works*, 44–45.

———. *An Epistolary Essay, from M.G. to O.B. upon their mutuall Poems.* In *Works*, 98–101.

———. *The Imperfect Enjoyment.* In *Works*, 13–15.

———. "Impromptus." In *Works*, 289–301.

———. *In the Isle of Brittain; in Works* [the "sceptre lampoon"]. Five versions printed in *Works*, 85–90. I cite "Group-A text."

———. *Letter from Artemiza in the Towne to Chloe in the Countrey.* In *Works*, 63–70.

———. *My Lord All-pride.* In *Works*, 93–94.

———. *On Poet Ninny.* In *Works*, 107–108.

———. *On The Suppos'd Author of A late Poem in Defence of Satyr.* In *Works*, 106–107.

———. *A Ramble in St. James's Park.* In *Works*, 76–80.

———. *Satyre against Reason and Mankind.* In *Works*, 57–63.

———. *To the Post Boy.* In *Works*, 42–43.

———. *Tunbridge Wells.* In *Works*, 49–54.

———. *Upon Nothinge.* In *Works*, 46–48.

———. *A very heroical epistle in answer to Ephelia* (wr. 1676?). In *Works*, 95–97.

———. *The Works of John Wilmot, Earl of Rochester.* Edited by Harold Love. Oxford: Oxford University Press, 1999. All poems by Rochester are cited from this edition.

Wilson, John. *The Cheats* (perf. 1663). London, 1664. Edited by Milton C. Nahm. Oxford: Basil Blackwell, 1935.

Wycherley, William. *The Country-Wife*. London, 1675. In *Plays*.

———. *The Plain-Dealer* (perf. 1676). London, 1677. In *Plays*.

———. *The Plays of William Wycherley*. Edited by Arthur Friedman. Oxford: Clarendon, 1979.

Yalden, Thomas. *Æsop at Court. Or, State Fables*. Vol. 1. London, 1702.

Young, Edward. *Love of Fame, The Universal Passion. In Seven Characteristical Satires*. 2nd ed. London, 1728.

———. *The Universal Passion. Satire I*. London, 1725.

———. *The Universal Passion. Satire II*. London, 1725.

Criticism and Scholarship

Abrams, M. H., with contributions by Geoffrey Galt Harpham. *A Glossary of Literary Terms*. 8th ed. Boston: Thomson Wadsworth, 2005.

Alleman, Gellert Spencer. *Matrimonial Law and the Materials of Restoration Comedy*. Wallingford, PA: privately printed, 1942.

Amory, Hugh. "What Murphy Knew: His Interpolations in Fielding's *Works* (1762), and Fielding's Revision of *Amelia*." *Papers of the Bibliographical Society of America* 77 (1983): 133–166.

Appleton, William W. *Charles Macklin: An Actor's Life*. Cambridge, MA: Harvard University Press, 1960.

Armens, Sven M. *John Gay: Social Critic*. New York: King's Crown, 1954.

Arnott, James Fullarton, and John William Robinson. *English Theatrical Literature, 1559–1900: A Bibliography*. London: Society for Theatre Research, 1970.

Baker, Sheridan. "Political Allusion in Fielding's *Author's Farce, Mock Doctor*, and *Tumble-Down Dick*." *PMLA* 77 (1962): 221–231.

Bartolomeo, Joseph F. "Restoration and Eighteenth-Century Satiric Fiction." In Quintero, *Companion to Satire*, 257–275.

Battestin, Martin C., and Ruthe R. Battestin. *Henry Fielding: A Life*. London: Routledge, 1989.

Beasley, Jerry C. "Portraits of a Monster: Robert Walpole and Early English Prose Fiction." *Eighteenth-Century Studies* 14 (1981): 406–431.

———. *Tobias Smollett, Novelist*. Athens: University of Georgia Press, 1998.

Beatty, Joseph M., Jr. "The Battle of the Players and Poets, 1761–1766." *Modern Language Notes* 34 (1919): 449–462.

———. "Churchill's Influence on Minor Eighteenth-Century Satirists." *PMLA* 42 (1927): 162–176.

Belden, Mary Megie. *The Dramatic Work of Samuel Foote*. 1929. Reprint, New York: Archon, 1969.

Bertelsen, Lance. *Henry Fielding at Work: Magistrate, Businessman, Writer*. New York: Palgrave, 2000.

———. *The Nonsense Club: Literature and Popular Culture, 1749–1764*. Oxford: Clarendon, 1986.

Bevis, Richard W. *English Drama: Restoration and Eighteenth Century, 1660–1789*. London: Longman, 1988.

———. *The Laughing Tradition: Stage Comedy in Garrick's Day*. Athens: University of Georgia Press, 1980.

Black, Jeremy, ed. *British Politics and Society from Walpole to Pitt, 1742–1789*. London: Macmillan, 1990.

Bloom, Edward A., and Lillian D. Bloom. *Satire's Persuasive Voice*. Ithaca, NY: Cornell University Press, 1979.

Bogel, Fredric V. *The Difference Satire Makes: Rhetoric and Reading from Jonson to Byron*. Ithaca, NY: Cornell University Press, 2001.

Bogorad, Samuel N., and Robert Gale Noyes, eds. *Samuel Foote's "Primitive Puppet-Shew" Featuring "Piety in Pattens": A Critical Edition*. Published as a special issue of *Theatre Survey* 14, no. 1a (1973).

Bond, Donald F., ed. *The Spectator*. 5 vols. Oxford: Clarendon, 1965.

———, ed. *The Tatler*. 3 vols. Oxford: Clarendon, 1987.

Borgman, Albert S. *Thomas Shadwell: His Life and Comedies*. New York: New York University Press, 1928.

Bosch, René. *Labyrinth of Digressions: "Tristram Shandy" as Perceived and Influenced by Sterne's Early Imitators*. Amsterdam: Rodopi, 2007.

Boyce, Benjamin. *Tom Brown of Facetious Memory: Grub Street in the Age of Dryden*. Cambridge, MA: Harvard University Press, 1939.

Boyle, Frank. *Swift as Nemesis: Modernity and Its Satirist*. Stanford, CA: Stanford University Press, 2000.

Boys, Richard C. *Sir Richard Blackmore and the Wits: A Study of "Commendatory Verses on the Author of the Two Arthurs and the Satyr against Wit" (1700)*. Ann Arbor: University of Michigan Press, 1949.

Brack, O M, Jr. "Tobias Smollett's Authorship of *Habbukkuk Hilding* (1752)." *Eighteenth-Century Intelligencer*, n.s., 20.3 (Sept. 2006): 5–17.

Bradham, Jo Allen. Introduction to *The Dispensary*, by Sir Samuel Garth. Delmar, NY: Scholars' Facsimiles and Reprints, 1975.

Brant, Clare, and Susan E. Whyman, eds. *Walking the Streets of Eighteenth-Century London: John Gay's "Trivia" (1716)*. Oxford: Oxford University Press, 2007.

Bredvold, Louis I. "The Gloom of the Tory Satirists." In *Pope and His Contemporaries: Essays presented to George Sherburn*, edited by James L. Clifford and Louis A. Landa, 1–19. Oxford: Clarendon, 1949.

Briggs, Peter M. "Locke's *Essay* and the Tentativeness of *Tristram Shandy*." *Studies in Philology* 82 (1985): 493–520.

Brooks, Harold F. *Dryden the Satirist*. Durham, UK: New Century, 1989.

———. "English Verse Satire, 1640–1660: Prolegomena." *Seventeenth Century* 3 (1988): 17–46.

———, ed. *The Poems of John Oldham*. Oxford: Clarendon, 1987.

Bywaters, David. *Dryden in Revolutionary England*. Berkeley: University of California Press, 1991.

Canfield, J. Douglas. *Tricksters & Estates: On the Ideology of Restoration Comedy*. Lexington: University Press of Kentucky, 1997.

Cannan, Paul D. *The Emergence of Dramatic Criticism in England: From Jonson to Pope*. New York: Palgrave, 2006.

Carpenter, Andrew. "A School for a Satirist: Swift's Exposure to the Wars of Words in Dublin in the 1680s." In *Reading Swift: Papers from The Fourth Münster Symposium on Jonathan Swift*, edited by Hermann J. Real and Helgard Stöver-Leidig, 161–175. Munich: Wilhelm Fink Verlag, 2003.

Carretta, Vincent. *George III and the Satirists from Hogarth to Byron.* Athens: University of Georgia Press, 1990.

———. *The Snarling Muse: Verbal and Visual Satire from Pope to Churchill.* Philadelphia: University of Pennsylvania Press, 1983.

Case, Arthur E. *Four Essays on "Gulliver's Travels."* Princeton, NJ: Princeton University Press, 1945.

Cash, Arthur H., ed. *An Essay on Woman by John Wilkes and Thomas Potter: A Reconstruction of a Lost Book With a Historical Essay on the Writing, Printing, and Suppressing of this 'Blasphemous and Obscene' Work.* New York: AMS, 2000.

———. *John Wilkes: The Scandalous Father of Civil Liberty.* New Haven, CT: Yale University Press, 2006.

Chalmers, Alan D. *Jonathan Swift and the Burden of the Future.* Newark: University of Delaware Press, 1995.

Chatten, Elizabeth N. *Samuel Foote.* Boston: Twayne, 1980.

Chernaik, Warren, and Martin Dzelzainis, eds. *Marvell and Liberty.* London: Macmillan, 1999.

Chibnall, Jennifer. "Something to the Purpose: Marvell's Rhetorical Strategy in *The Rehearsal Transpros'd.*" *Prose Studies* 9 (1986): 80–104.

Chilton, Leslie A. "Smollett, the Picaresque, and Two Medical Satires." In *New Contexts for Eighteenth-Century British Fiction: "Hearts Resolved and Hands Prepared": Essays in Honor of Jerry C. Beasley,* edited by Christopher D. Johnson, 219–230. Newark: University of Delaware Press, 2011.

Clare, Janet. "'All Run Now into Politicks': Theatre Censorship during the Exclusion Crisis, 1679–81." In *Writing and Censorship in Britain,* edited by Paul Hylands and Neil Sammells, 46–56. London: Routledge, 1992.

Cleary, Thomas R. *Henry Fielding: Political Writer.* Waterloo, ON: Wilfrid Laurier University Press, 1984.

Clifford, James L. "Gulliver's Fourth Voyage: 'Hard' and 'Soft' Schools of Interpretation." In *Quick Springs of Sense: Studies in the Eighteenth Century,* edited by Larry S. Champion, 33–49. Athens: University of Georgia Press, 1974.

Colomb, Gregory G. *Designs on Truth: The Poetics of the Augustan Mock-Epic.* University Park: Pennsylvania State University Press, 1992.

Combe, Kirk. "Clandestine Protest against William III in Dryden's Translations of Juvenal and Persius." *Modern Philology* 87 (1989): 36–50.

Condren, Conal. *Satire, Lies and Politics: The Case of Dr Arbuthnot.* London: Macmillan, 1997.

Connery, Brian A., and Kirk Combe, eds. *Theorizing Satire: Essays in Literary Criticism.* New York: Macmillan, 1995.

Conolly, L. W. *The Censorship of English Drama, 1737–1824.* San Marino, CA: Henry E. Huntington Library, 1976.

Cook, Richard I. *Bernard Mandeville.* New York: Twayne, 1974.

———. *Sir Samuel Garth.* Boston: Twayne, 1980.

Copley, Stephen, and Ian Haywood. "Luxury, Refuse and Poetry: John Gay's *Trivia.*" In *John Gay and the Scriblerians,* edited by Peter Lewis and Nigel Wood, 62–82. London: Vision, 1988.

Cousins, A. D. "The Context, Design, and Argument of Rochester's *A Satyr against Reason and Mankind.*" *Studies in English Literature* 24 (1984): 429–439.

Crane, R. S. "Criticism as Inquiry; or, The Perils of the 'High Priori Road.'" In Crane, *The Idea of the Humanities*, 2:25–44.

———. "The Houyhnhnms, the Yahoos, and the History of Ideas." 1962; Reprint in Crane, *The Idea of the Humanities*, 2:261–282.

———. *The Idea of the Humanities and Other Essays Critical and Historical.* 2 vols. Chicago: University of Chicago Press, 1967.

———. "On Hypotheses in 'Historical Criticism': Apropos of Certain Contemporary Medievalists." In Crane, *The Idea of the Humanities*, 2:236–260.

Cross, Wilbur. *The History of Henry Fielding.* 3 vols. 1918. Reprint, New York: Russell and Russell, 1963.

Cust, Richard. "News and Politics in Early Seventeenth-Century England." *Past and Present* 112 (1986): 60–90.

Damrosch, Leopold, Jr. *The Imaginative World of Alexander Pope.* Berkeley: University of California Press, 1987.

Davis, Herbert. "The Poetry of Jonathan Swift." *College English* 2 (1940): 102–115.

Dawson, Mark S. *Gentility and the Comic Theatre of Late Stuart London.* Cambridge: Cambridge University Press, 2005.

Day, Robert Adams, ed. *The History and Adventures of an Atom.* By Tobias Smollett. Athens: University of Georgia Press, 1989.

De Voogd, Peter, and John Neubauer, eds. *The Reception of Laurence Sterne in Europe.* London: Thoemmes Continuum, 2004.

DeLuna, D. N. "Yale's Poetasting Defoe." *1650–1850* 4 (1998): 345–362.

Dickie, Simon. *Cruelty and Laughter: Forgotten Comic Literature and the Unsentimental Eighteenth Century.* Chicago: University of Chicago Press, 2011.

DiLorenzo, Ronald Eugene, ed. *Three Burlesque Plays of Thomas Duffett.* Iowa City: University of Iowa Press, 1972.

Donald, Diana. *The Age of Caricature: Satirical Prints in the Reign of George III.* New Haven, CT: Yale University Press, 1996.

Donoghue, Denis. *The Practice of Reading.* New Haven, CT: Yale University Press, 1998.

Doody, Margaret Anne. *The Daring Muse: Augustan Poetry Reconsidered.* Cambridge: Cambridge University Press, 1985.

Downie, J. A. "Defoe's *Shortest Way with the Dissenters*: Irony, Intention and Reader-Response." *Prose Studies* 9 (1986): 120–139.

———. "Gay's Politics." In *John Gay and the Scriblerians*, edited by Peter Lewis and Nigel Wood, 44–61. London: Vision, 1988.

———. *Jonathan Swift, Political Writer.* London: Routledge and Kegan Paul, 1984.

———. "The Political Significance of *Gulliver's Travels*." In *Swift and His Contexts*, edited by John Irwin Fischer, Hermann J. Real, and James Woolley, 1–19. New York: AMS, 1989.

———. "What If Delarivier Manley Did *Not* Write *The Secret History of Queen Zarah*?" *Library* 5 (2004): 247–264.

Duffy, Michael. *The Englishman and the Foreigner.* Cambridge: Chadwyck-Healey, 1986.

Dunbar, Howard Hunter. *The Dramatic Career of Arthur Murphy.* New York: Modern Language Association, 1946.

Eco, Umberto. *The Role of the Reader: Explorations in the Semiotics of Texts.* Bloomington: Indiana University Press, 1979.

Eddy, William A. *"Gulliver's Travels": A Critical Study*. 1923. Reprint, New York: Russell and Russell, 1963.

Ehrenpreis, Irvin. "The Allegory of *Gulliver's Travels*." *Swift Studies* 4 (1989): 13–28.

———. "Show and Tell in *Gulliver's Travels*." *Swift Studies* 8 (1993): 18–33.

———. *Swift: The Man, His Works, and the Age*. 3 vols. Cambridge, MA: Harvard University Press, 1962–1983.

———. "Swiftian Dilemmas." In *Satire in the 18th Century*, edited by J. D. Browning, 214–231. New York: Garland, 1983.

Elkin, P. K. *The Augustan Defence of Satire*. Oxford: Clarendon, 1973.

Elliott, Robert C. "Swift's Satire: Rules of the Game." *ELH* 41 (1974): 413–428.

Ellis, Frank H. "*An Argument against Abolishing Christianity* as an Argument against Abolishing the Test Act." In *Reading Swift: Papers from The Second Münster Symposium on Jonathan Swift*, edited by Richard H. Rodino and Hermann J. Real, 127–139. Munich: Wilhelm Fink Verlag, 1993.

Erskine-Hill, Howard. *Poetry of Opposition and Revolution: Dryden to Wordsworth*. Oxford: Clarendon, 1996.

Fabricant, Carole. "Pope's Moral, Political, and Cultural Combat." *The Eighteenth Century: Theory and Interpretation* 29 (1988): 165–187.

———. *Swift's Landscape*. 1982. Reprint, South Bend, IN: University of Notre Dame Press, 1995.

Farley-Hills, David. *The Benevolence of Laughter: Comic Poetry of the Commonwealth and Restoration*. London: Macmillan, 1974.

———, ed. *Rochester: The Critical Heritage*. New York: Barnes and Noble, 1972.

Feinberg, Leonard. *Introduction to Satire*. Ames: Iowa State University Press, 1967.

———. *The Satirist: His Temperament, Motivation, and Influence*. Ames: Iowa State University Press, 1964.

Findlay, Robert R. "The Comic Plays of Charles Macklin: Dark Satire at Mid-Eighteenth Century." *Educational Theatre Journal* 20 (1968): 398–407.

Firth, Charles. "The Political Significance of *Gulliver's Travels*." In *Essays Historical & Literary*, 210–241. Oxford: Clarendon, 1938.

Fischer, David Hackett. *Historians' Fallacies: Toward a Logic of Historical Thought*. New York: Harper and Row, 1970.

Fisher, Alan S. "Swift's Verse Portraits: A Study of His Originality as an Augustan Satirist." *Studies in English Literature* 14 (1974): 343–356.

Fludernik, Monika. Review of *Satire, History, Novel*, by Frank Palmeri. *Eighteenth Century Fiction* 18 (2005): 255–257.

Forrest, James F., and Roger Sharrock, eds. *The Life and Death of Mr. Badman*. By John Bunyan. Oxford: Clarendon, 1988.

Fowler, Alastair. *Kinds of Literature: An Introduction to the Theory of Genres and Modes*. Cambridge, MA: Harvard University Press, 1982.

Fox, Christopher, ed. *The Cambridge Companion to Jonathan Swift*. Cambridge: Cambridge University Press, 2003.

Frank, Joseph. *The Beginnings of the English Newspaper, 1620–1660*. Cambridge, MA: Harvard University Press, 1961.

Frye, Northrop. *Anatomy of Criticism: Four Essays*. Princeton, NJ: Princeton University Press, 1957.

———. "Towards Defining an Age of Sensibility." *ELH* 23 (1956): 144–152.

Furbank, P. N., and W. R. Owens. *A Critical Bibliography of Daniel Defoe*. London: Pickering and Chatto, 1998.

———. *Defoe De-Attributions: A Critique of J. R. Moore's "Checklist."* London: Hambledon, 1994.

———. *A Political Biography of Daniel Defoe*. London: Pickering and Chatto, 2006.

Gadeken, Sara. "Sarah Fielding and the Salic Law of Wit." *Studies in English Literature* 42 (2002): 541–557.

Gaskell, Philip. *From Writer to Reader: Studies in Editorial Method*. Oxford: Clarendon, 1978.

Geertz, Clifford. "Thick Description: Toward an Interpretive Theory of Culture." In *The Interpretation of Cultures: Selected Essays*, 3–30. New York: Basic Books, 1973.

Gelineau, David. "'Adorn'd with Labour'd Art': The Intricate Unity of Dryden's Fables." *Modern Philology* 106 (2008): 25–59.

———. "Identity in Dryden's *Amphitryon*: Cuckolds of Order." *Studies in English Literature* 38 (1998): 427–445.

Gerrard, Christine. *The Patriot Opposition to Walpole: Politics, Poetry, and National Myth, 1725–1742*. Oxford: Clarendon, 1994.

Gilde, Joseph M. "Shadwell and the Royal Society: Satire in *The Virtuoso*." *Studies in English Literature* 10 (1970): 469–490.

Gill, James E., ed. *Cutting Edges: Postmodern Critical Essays on Eighteenth-Century Satire*. Knoxville: University of Tennessee Press, 1995.

Goldgar, Bertrand A., ed. *"The Covent-Garden Journal" and "A Plan of the Universal Register-Office."* By Henry Fielding. Oxford: Clarendon, 1988.

———. *Walpole and the Wits: The Relation of Politics to Literature, 1722–1742*. Lincoln: University of Nebraska Press, 1976.

Goldgar, Bertrand A., and Ian Gadd, eds. *English Political Writings, 1711–1714: "The Conduct of the Allies" and Other Works*. By Jonathan Swift. Cambridge: Cambridge University Press, 2008.

Gregg, Edward. *Queen Anne*. 1980. 2nd ed., New Haven, CT: Yale University Press, 2001.

Griffin, Dustin. "Dryden and Restoration Satire." In Quintero, *Companion to Satire*, 176–195.

———. *Patriotism and Poetry in Eighteenth-Century Britain*. Cambridge: Cambridge University Press, 2002.

———. *Satire: A Critical Reintroduction*. Lexington: University Press of Kentucky, 1994.

———. *Satires against Man: The Poems of Rochester*. Berkeley: University of California Press, 1973.

———. *Swift and Pope: Satirists in Dialogue*. Cambridge: Cambridge University Press, 2010.

Grundy, Isobel M. "New Verse by Henry Fielding." *PMLA* 87 (1972): 213–245.

Guerinot, J. V. *Pamphlet Attacks on Alexander Pope, 1711–1744: A Descriptive Bibliography*. New York: New York University Press, 1969.

Hammond, Brean S. "*The Pilgrim's Progress*: Satire and Social Comment." In *The Pilgrim's Progress: Critical and Historical Views*, edited by Vincent Newey, 118–131. Liverpool: Liverpool University Press, 1980.

———. *Professional Imaginative Writing in England, 1670–1740: "Hackney for Bread."* Oxford: Clarendon, 1997.

Hammond, Paul. *Figuring Sex between Men from Shakespeare to Rochester*. Oxford: Clarendon, 2002.

———. *John Oldham and the Renewal of Classical Culture*. Cambridge: Cambridge University Press, 1983.

Harris, Wendell V. *Dictionary of Concepts in Literary Criticism*. Westport, CT: Greenwood, 1992.

Harth, Phillip. "Friendship and Politics: Swift's Relations with Pope in the Early 1730s." In *Reading Swift: Papers from The Third Münster Symposium on Jonathan Swift*, edited by Hermann J. Real and Helgard Stöver-Leidig, 239–248. Munich: Wilhelm Fink Verlag, 1998.

———, ed. *The Fable of the Bees*. By Bernard Mandeville. 1970. Reprint, New York: Penguin, 1989.

———. *Pen for a Party: Dryden's Tory Propaganda in Its Contexts*. Princeton, NJ: Princeton University Press, 1993.

———. "The Problem of Political Allegory in *Gulliver's Travels*." *Modern Philology* 73 (1976): S40–S47 (supplement festschrift issue).

———. "The Satiric Purpose of *The Fable of the Bees*." *Eighteenth-Century Studies* 2 (1969): 321–340.

Haugen, Kristine. "Imagined Universities: Public Insult and the *Terrae Filius* in Early Modern Oxford." *History of Universities* 16.2 (2000): 1–31.

Hawes, Clement. "Three Times Round the Globe: Gulliver and Colonial Discourse." *Cultural Critique* 18 (1991): 187–214.

Henderson, Felicity. "Erudite Satire in Seventeenth-Century England." PhD diss., Monash University, 2002.

Higgins, Ian. "*An Argument against Abolishing Christianity* and Its Contexts." In *Reading Swift: Papers from The Fifth Münster Symposium on Jonathan Swift*, edited by Hermann J. Real, 203–223. Munich: Wilhelm Fink Verlag, 2008.

Highet, Gilbert. *The Anatomy of Satire*. Princeton, NJ: Princeton University Press, 1962.

Hirst, Derek. "Samuel Parker, Andrew Marvell, and Political Culture, 1667–73." In *Writing and Political Engagement in Seventeenth-Century England*, edited by Hirst and Richard Strier, 145–164. Cambridge: Cambridge University Press, 1999.

Hopkins, Robert H. *The True Genius of Oliver Goldsmith*. Baltimore: Johns Hopkins Press, 1969.

Howes, Alan B., ed. *Sterne: The Critical Heritage*. London: Routledge and Kegan Paul, 1974.

———. *Yorick and the Critics: Sterne's Reputation in England, 1760–1868*. New Haven, CT: Yale University Press, 1958.

Hudson, Nicholas. Review of *Poetry and the Creation of a Whig Literary Culture 1681–1714*, by Abigail Williams. *Age of Johnson* 18 (2007): 453–457.

———. *Samuel Johnson and Eighteenth-Century Thought*. Oxford: Oxford University Press, 1988.

Hughes, Derek. *English Drama, 1660–1700*. Oxford: Clarendon, 1996.

Hume, Robert D. "The Aims and Limits of Historical Scholarship." *Review of English Studies*, n.s., 53 (2002): 399–422.

———. "The Aims and Pitfalls of 'Historical Interpretation.'" *Philological Quarterly* 89 (2010): 353–382.

———. "'The Change in Comedy': Cynical versus Exemplary Comedy on the London Stage, 1678–1693." *Essays in Theatre* 1 (1983): 101–118.

———. "Construction and Legitimation in Literary History." *Review of English Studies*, n.s., 56 (2005): 632–661.

————. *The Development of English Drama in the Late Seventeenth Century.* Oxford: Clarendon, 1976.

————. "The Economics of Culture in London, 1660–1740." *Huntington Library Quarterly* 69 (2006): 487–533.

————. *Henry Fielding and the London Theatre, 1728–1737.* Oxford: Clarendon, 1988.

————. "John Rich as Manager and Entrepreneur." In *The Stage's Glory: John Rich (1692–1761)*, edited by Jeremy Barlow and Berta Joncus, 29–60. Newark: University of Delaware Press, 2011.

————. "Otway and the Comic Muse." *Studies in Philology* 73 (1976): 87–116.

————. "The Politics of Opera in Late Seventeenth-Century London." *Cambridge Opera Journal* 10 (1998): 15–43.

————. *The Rakish Stage: Studies in English Drama, 1660–1800.* Carbondale: Southern Illinois University Press, 1983.

————. *Reconstructing Contexts: The Aims and Principles of Archaeo-Historicism.* Oxford: Oxford University Press, 1999.

————. " 'Satire' in the Reign of Charles II." *Modern Philology* 102 (2005): 332–371.

————. "The Satiric Design of Nat. Lee's *The Princess of Cleve.*" *Journal of English and Germanic Philology* 75 (1976): 117–138.

————. "The Socio-Politics of London Comedy from Jonson to Steele." *Huntington Library Quarterly* 74 (2011): 187–217.

————. "The Unconventional Tragedies of Thomas Otway." In *Du verbe au geste: Mélanges en l'honneur de Pierre Danchin*, 67–78. Nancy, France: Presses Universitaires de Nancy, 1986.

Hume, Robert D., and Harold Love, eds. *Plays, Poems, and Miscellaneous Writings Associated with George Villiers, Second Duke of Buckingham.* 2 vols. Oxford: Oxford University Press, 2007.

Hunt, Tamara L. *Defining John Bull: Political Caricature and National Identity in Late Georgian England.* Aldershot, UK: Ashgate, 2003.

Hunter, J. Paul. *Occasional Form: Henry Fielding and the Chains of Circumstance.* Baltimore: Johns Hopkins University Press, 1975.

————. "Political, Satirical, Didactic and Lyric Poetry (I): From the Restoration to the Death of Pope." In Richetti, *Cambridge History of English Literature*, 160–208.

Jack, Ian. *Augustan Satire: Intention and Idiom in English Poetry, 1660–1750.* Oxford: Clarendon, 1952.

Jordan, Robert, and Harold Love, eds. *The Works of Thomas Southerne.* 2 vols. Oxford: Clarendon, 1988.

Karian, Stephen. *Jonathan Swift in Print and Manuscript.* Cambridge: Cambridge University Press, 2010.

Kaufman, Anthony. " 'This Hard Condition of a Woman's Fate': Southerne's *The Wives' Excuse.*" *Modern Language Quarterly* 34 (1973): 36–47.

Keeble, N. H. " 'I Would Not Tell You Any Tales': Marvell's Constituency Letters." In *The Political Identity of Andrew Marvell*, edited by Conal Condren and A. D. Cousins, 111–134. Aldershot, UK: Scolar, 1990.

————. "Why Transpose *The Rehearsal*?" In Chernaik and Dzelzainis, *Marvell and Liberty*, 249–268.

Kenny, Shirley Strum, ed. *The Plays of Richard Steele.* Oxford: Clarendon, 1971.

Kerby-Miller, Charles, ed. *The Memoirs Of the Extraordinary Life, Works, and Discoveries of Martinus Scriblerus*. New Haven, CT: Yale University Press, 1950.

Kernan, Alvin B. *The Plot of Satire*. New Haven, CT: Yale University Press, 1965.

Keymer, Thomas, ed. *Laurence Sterne's "Tristram Shandy": A Casebook*. Oxford: Oxford University Press, 2006.

———. "*A Sentimental Journey* and the Failure of Feeling." In *The Cambridge Companion to Laurence Sterne*, edited by Thomas Keymer, 79–94. Cambridge: Cambridge University Press, 2009.

———. *Sterne, the Moderns, and the Novel*. Oxford: Oxford University Press, 2002.

King, Gregory. "Natural and Political Observations and Conclusions upon the State and Condition of England." In *Two Tracts by Gregory King*, edited by George E. Barnett, 16–56. Baltimore: Johns Hopkins Press, 1936.

Kinservik, Matthew J. "Censorship and Generic Change: The Case of Satire on the Early Eighteenth-Century London Stage." *Philological Quarterly* 78 (1999): 259–282.

———. *Disciplining Satire: The Censorship of Satiric Comedy on the Eighteenth-Century London Stage*. Lewisburg, PA: Bucknell University Press, 2002.

———. "Satire, Censorship, and Sodomy in Samuel Foote's *The Capuchin* (1776)." *Review of English Studies*, n.s., 54 (2003): 639–660.

Kishlansky, Mark. *A Monarchy Transformed: Britain, 1603–1714*. New York: Penguin, 1996.

Knight, Charles. *The Literature of Satire*. Cambridge: Cambridge University Press, 2004.

Knoche, Ulrich. *Roman Satire*. Translated by Edwin S. Ramage. Bloomington: Indiana University Press, 1975.

Knoppers, Laura Lunger. " 'Sing Old Noll the Brewer': Royalist Satire and Social Inversion, 1648–64." *Seventeenth Century* 15 (2000): 32–52.

Kupersmith, William. *English Versions of Roman Satire in the Earlier Eighteenth Century*. Newark: University of Delaware Press, 2007.

———. *Roman Satirists in Seventeenth-Century England*. Lincoln: University of Nebraska Press, 1985.

Lamb, Jonathan. "Sterne and Irregular Oratory." In *The Cambridge Companion to the Eighteenth-Century Novel*, edited by John Richetti, 153–174. Cambridge: Cambridge University Press, 1996.

Langford, Paul. "Swift and Walpole." In *Politics and Literature in the Age of Swift: English and Irish Perspectives*, edited by Claude Rawson, 52–78. Cambridge: Cambridge University Press, 2010.

Larson, Martin A. "The Influence of Milton's Divorce Tracts on Farquhar's *Beaux' Stratagem*." *PMLA* 39 (1924): 174–178.

Latour, Bruno. *Reassembling the Social: An Introduction to Actor-Network-Theory*. Oxford: Oxford University Press, 2005.

Lee, Maurice, Jr. *The Cabal*. Urbana: University of Illinois Press, 1965.

Leranbaum, Miriam. *Alexander Pope's "Opus Magnum," 1729–1744*. Oxford: Clarendon, 1977.

Levin, Richard. *New Readings vs. Old Plays: Recent Trends in the Reinterpretation of English Renaissance Drama*. Chicago: University of Chicago Press, 1979.

———. "The Problem of 'Context' in Interpretation." In *Shakespeare and Dramatic Tradition: Essays in Honor of S. F. Johnson*, edited by W. R. Elton and William B. Long, 88–106. Newark: University of Delaware Press, 1989.

Lewis, Peter. "Fielding's *The Covent-Garden Tragedy* and Philips's *The Distrest Mother*." *Durham University Journal*, n.s., 37 (1975): 33–46.

———. " 'An Irregular Dog': Gay's Alternative Theater." *Yearbook of English Studies* 18 (1988): 231–246.

Liesenfeld, Vincent J. *The Licensing Act of 1737*. Madison: University of Wisconsin Press, 1984.

Lindert, Peter H., and Jeffrey G. Williamson. "Reinterpreting Britain's Social Tables, 1688–1913." *Explorations in Economic History* 20 (1983): 94–109.

———. "Revising England's Social Tables, 1688–1812." *Explorations in Economic History* 19 (1982): 385–408.

Lloyd, Claude. "Shadwell and the Virtuosi." *PMLA* 44 (1929): 472–494.

Lock, F. P. *The Politics of "Gulliver's Travels."* Oxford: Clarendon, 1980.

Lockwood, Thomas, ed. *Plays*. By Henry Fielding. 3 vols. Oxford: Clarendon, 2004–2011.

———. *Post-Augustan Satire: Charles Churchill and Satirical Poetry, 1750–1800*. Seattle: University of Washington Press, 1979.

Loftis, John. *Comedy and Society from Congreve to Fielding*. Stanford, CA: Stanford University Press, 1959.

Lord, George de Forest. "Satire and Sedition: The Life and Work of John Ayloffe." *Huntington Library Quarterly* 29 (1966): 255–273.

Love, Harold. "Charles, Viscount Mordaunt and 'The Ladies' March.'" *Review of English Studies*, n.s., 55 (2004): 346–354.

———. *Congreve*. Oxford: Basil Blackwell, 1974.

———. *English Clandestine Satire, 1660–1702*. Oxford: Clarendon, 2004.

———. *Scribal Publication in Seventeenth-Century England*. Oxford: Clarendon, 1993.

Lund, Roger D. "The Eel of Science: Index Learning, Scriblerian Satire, and the Rise of Information Culture." *Eighteenth-Century Life* 22 (1998): 18–42.

The Luttrell File: Narcissus Luttrell's Dates on Contemporary Pamphlets, 1678–1730. Edited by Stephen Parks, assisted by Earle Havens. New Haven, CT: Beinecke Rare Book and Manuscript Library, 1999.

Lyotard, Jean-François. *The Postmodern Condition: A Report on Knowledge*. 1979. Translated by Geoff Bennington and Brian Massum. Minneapolis: University of Minnesota Press, 1984.

Mack, Maynard. *Alexander Pope: A Life*. New Haven, CT: Yale University Press, 1985.

Marsden, Jean I. "Dramatic Satire in the Restoration and Eighteenth Century." In Quintero, *Companion to Satire*, 161–175.

Marshall, Alan. *The Age of Faction: Court Politics, 1660–1702*. Manchester: Manchester University Press, 1999.

Marshall, Ashley. "The Aims of Butler's Satire in *Hudibras*." *Modern Philology* 105 (2008): 637–665.

———. "Daniel Defoe as Satirist." *Huntington Library Quarterly* 70 (2007): 553–576.

———. "The Generic Context of Defoe's *The Shortest-Way with the Dissenters* and the Problem of Irony." *Review of English Studies*, n.s., 61 (2010): 234–258.

———. "Henry Fielding and the 'Scriblerians.'" *Modern Language Quarterly* 72 (2011): 19–48.

———. "The Myth of Scriblerus." *Journal for Eighteenth-Century Studies* 31 (2008): 77–99.

———. "Swift on 'Swift': From *The Author upon Himself* to *The Life and Genuine Character*." *Huntington Library Quarterly* 75 (2012): 327–364.

Martin, Susan M. "Robert Gould's Attacks on the London Stage, 1689 and 1709: The Two Versions of 'The Playhouse: A Satyr.'" *Philological Quarterly* 82 (2003): 59–86.

McCrea, Brian. *Henry Fielding and the Politics of Mid-Eighteenth-Century England.* Athens: University of Georgia Press, 1981.

McCreery, Cindy. *The Satirical Gaze: Prints of Women in Late Eighteenth-Century England.* Oxford: Clarendon, 2004.

McFadden, George. "Political Satire in *The Rehearsal.*" *Yearbook of English Studies* 4 (1974): 120–128.

McGeary, Thomas. "Verse Epistles on Italian Opera Singers, 1724–1736." *RMA Research Chronicle* 33 (2000): 29–88.

McKeon, Michael. "What Were Poems on Affairs of State?" *1650–1850* 4 (1998): 363–382.

McLaverty, James. "The Failure of the Swift-Pope *Miscellanies* (1727–32) and *The Life and Genuine Character of Doctor Swift* (1733)." In *Reading Swift: Papers from The Fifth Münster Symposium on Jonathan Swift*, edited by Hermann J. Real, 131–148. Munich: Wilhelm Fink Verlag, 2008.

———. *Pope, Print and Meaning.* Oxford: Oxford University Press, 2001.

McVeagh, John M. *Thomas Durfey and Restoration Drama: The Work of a Forgotten Writer.* Aldershot, UK: Ashgate, 2000.

McWhir, Anne. "The Wolf in the Fold: John Gay in *The Shepherd's Week* and *Trivia.*" *Studies in English Literature* 23 (1983): 413–423.

Milhous, Judith, and Robert D. Hume. *Producible Interpretation: Eight English Plays, 1675–1707.* Carbondale: Southern Illinois University Press, 1985.

Miller, John. *Religion in the Popular Prints, 1600–1832.* Cambridge: Chadwyck-Healey, 1986.

Miner, Earl. *The Restoration Mode from Milton to Dryden.* Princeton, NJ: Princeton University Press, 1974.

Money, D. K. *The English Horace: Anthony Alsop and the Tradition of British Latin Verse.* Oxford: Oxford University Press for the British Academy, 1998.

Monk, Samuel. "The Pride of Lemuel Gulliver." *Sewanee Review* 63 (1955): 48–71.

Morris, Linda A. "American Satire: Beginnings through Mark Twain." In Quintero, *Companion to Satire*, 377–399.

Mueller, Andreas K. E. *A Critical Study of Daniel Defoe's Verse: Recovering the Neglected Corpus of His Poetic Work.* Lampeter: Edwin Mellen, 2010.

Mueller, Judith C. "*A Tale of a Tub* and Early Prose." In Fox, *Cambridge Companion to Jonathan Swift*, 202–215.

Myers, Jack, and Don Charles Wukasch. *Dictionary of Poetic Terms.* 1985. Reprint, Denton: University of North Texas Press, 2003.

Nevo, Ruth. *The Dial of Virtue: A Study of Poems on Affairs of State in the Seventeenth Century.* Princeton, NJ: Princeton University Press, 1963.

New, Melvyn. *Laurence Sterne as Satirist: A Reading of "Tristram Shandy."* Gainesville: University of Florida Press, 1969.

———. *"Tristram Shandy": A Book for Free Spirits.* New York: Twayne, 1994.

Nicoll, Allardyce. *A History of English Drama, 1660–1900.* Rev. ed. 6 vols. Cambridge: Cambridge University Press, 1952–1959.

Nobbe, George. *"The North Briton": A Study in Political Propaganda.* 1939. Reprint, New York: AMS, 1966.

Nokes, David. *John Gay: A Profession of Friendship.* Oxford: Oxford University Press, 1995.

———. *Jonathan Swift, a Hypocrite Reversed: A Critical Biography.* Oxford: Oxford University Press, 1985.

Norbrook, David. *Writing the English Republic: Poetry, Rhetoric and Politics, 1627–1660*. Cambridge: Cambridge University Press, 1999.

Novak, Maximillian E. *Daniel Defoe: Master of Fictions*. Oxford: Oxford University Press, 2001.

———. "Defoe, the Occult, and the Deist Offensive during the Reign of Queen Anne." In *Deism, Masonry, and the Enlightenment: Essays Honoring Alfred Owen Aldridge*, edited by J. A. Leo Lemay, 93–108. Newark: University of Delaware Press, 1987.

———. "Satirical Form and Realistic Fiction in *Tristram Shandy*." In *Approaches to Teaching Sterne's "Tristram Shandy,"* edited by Melvyn New, 137–145. New York: Modern Language Association, 1989.

Nussbaum, Felicity. *The Brink of All We Hate: English Satires on Women, 1660–1750*. Lexington: University Press of Kentucky, 1984.

O'Brien, John. *Harlequin Britain: Pantomime and Entertainment, 1690–1760*. Baltimore: Johns Hopkins University Press, 2004.

Ogden, James. "Dryden's Satirical Tendency." *Forum for Modern Language Studies* 31 (1995): 215–222.

Ogée, Frédéric. "'O, Hogarth, Had I Thy Pencil': Delineations of an Alleged Friendship." In *Henry Fielding (1707–1754): Novelist, Playwright, Journalist, Magistrate*, edited by Claude Rawson, 201–229. Newark: University of Delaware Press, 2008.

Olson, Elder. *The Theory of Comedy*. Bloomington: Indiana University Press, 1968.

Ormsby-Lennon, Hugh. *Hey Presto! Swift and the Quacks*. Newark: University of Delaware Press, 2011.

Orr, Leah. "Christopher Smart as a Christian Translator: The Verse *Horace* of 1767." *Studies in Philology* 108 (2011): 439–467.

Palmeri, Frank. *Satire, History, Novel: Narrative Forms, 1665–1815*. Newark: University of Delaware Press, 2003.

———. *Satire in Narrative: Petronius, Swift, Gibbon, Melville, and Pynchon*. Austin: University of Texas Press, 1990.

Parker, Blanford. "Modes of Mockery: The Significance of Mock-Poetic Forms in the Enlightenment." In Quintero, *Companion to Satire*, 495–509.

Parker, Fred. *Scepticism and Literature: An Essay on Pope, Hume, Sterne, and Johnson*. Oxford: Oxford University Press, 2003.

Parkin, Jon. "Liberty Transpros'd: Andrew Marvell and Samuel Parker." In Chernaik and Dzelzainis, *Marvell and Liberty*, 269–289.

Parnell, J. T. "Swift, Sterne, and the Skeptical Tradition." *Studies in Eighteenth-Century Culture* 23 (1994): 221–242.

Patterson, Annabel. "*The Country Gentleman*: Howard, Marvell, and Dryden in the Theater of Politics." *Studies in English Literature* 25 (1985): 491–509.

———. *Marvell: The Writer in Public Life*. London: Longman, 2000.

Paulson, Ronald. *The Art of Riot in England and America*. Baltimore: Owlworks, 2010.

———. *Don Quixote in England: The Aesthetics of Laughter*. Baltimore: Johns Hopkins University Press, 1998.

———. "Dryden and the Energies of Satire." In *The Cambridge Companion to John Dryden*, edited by Steven N. Zwicker, 37–58. Cambridge: Cambridge University Press, 2004.

———. *The Fictions of Satire*. Baltimore: Johns Hopkins Press, 1967.

———. *Hogarth: His Life, Art, and Times*. 3 vols. New Brunswick, NJ: Rutgers University Press, 1991.

———. *Hogarth's Harlot: Sacred Parody in Enlightenment England*. Baltimore: Johns Hopkins University Press, 2003.

———. *The Life of Henry Fielding: A Critical Biography*. Oxford: Blackwell, 2000.

———. *Popular and Polite Art in the Age of Hogarth and Fielding*. Notre Dame, IN: University of Notre Dame Press, 1979.

———. *Satire and the Novel in Eighteenth-Century England*. New Haven, CT: Yale University Press, 1967.

———. *Sin and Evil: Moral Values in Literature*. New Haven, CT: Yale University Press, 2007.

Pedicord, Harry William. "*Ragandjaw*: Garrick's Shakespearean Parody for a Private Theatre." *Philological Quarterly* 60 (1981): 197–204.

Pedicord, Harry William, and Fredrick Louis Bergmann, eds. *The Plays of David Garrick*. 7 vols. Carbondale: Southern Illinois University Press, 1980–1982.

Pellicer, Juan Christian. "Harleian Georgic from Tonson's Press: The Publication of John Philips's *Cyder*, 29 January 1708." *Library* 7 (2006): 185–198.

———. "John Gay, *Wine* (1708) and the Whigs." *British Journal for Eighteenth-Century Studies* 27 (2004): 245–255.

Perkins, David. *Is Literary History Possible?* Baltimore: Johns Hopkins University Press, 1992.

Peterson, Spiro. Introduction to *Selected Poems (1685–1700)*, by John Tutchin. Los Angeles: William Andrews Clark Memorial Library, 1964.

Pettit, Alexander. *Illusory Consensus: Bolingbroke and the Polemical Response to Walpole, 1730–1737*. Newark: University of Delaware Press, 1997.

Phiddian, Robert. "A Name to Conjure With: Games of Verification and Identity in the Bickerstaff Controversy." In *Reading Swift: Papers from The Second Münster Symposium on Jonathan Swift*, edited by Richard H. Rodino and Hermann J. Real, 141–150. Munich: Wilhelm Fink Verlag, 1993.

———. *Swift's Parody*. Cambridge: Cambridge University Press, 1995.

Pincus, Steve. "'Coffee Politicians Does Create': Coffeehouses and Restoration Political Culture." *Journal of Modern History* 67 (1995): 807–834.

Plumb, J. H. *The Growth of Political Stability in England 1675–1725*. London: Macmillan, 1967.

Poems on Affairs of State: Augustan Satirical Verse, 1660–1714 [*POAS-Y*]. General editor George deF. Lord. 7 vols. Vol. 1 edited by Lord. Vol. 2 edited by Elias F. Mengel Jr. Vol. 3 edited by Howard H. Schless. Vol. 4 edited by Galbraith M. Crump. Vol. 5 edited by William J. Cameron. Vols. 6–7 edited by Frank H. Ellis. New Haven, CT: Yale University Press, 1963–1975.

Preminger, Alex, and T. V. F. Brogan, eds. *The New Princeton Encyclopedia of Poetry and Poetics*. Princeton, NJ: Princeton University Press, 1993.

Price, Curtis Alexander. *Henry Purcell and the London Stage*. Cambridge: Cambridge University Press, 1984.

Proffitt, Bessie. "Political Satire in Dryden's *Alexander's Feast*." *Texas Studies in Literature and Language* 11 (1969–1970): 1307–1316.

Quinlan, Maurice J. "The Prosecution of Swift's *Public Spirit of the Whigs*." *Texas Studies in Literature and Language* 9 (1967): 167–184.

Quintana, Ricardo. *The Mind and Art of Jonathan Swift*. Oxford: Oxford University Press, 1936.

———. *Oliver Goldsmith: A Georgian Study*. New York: Macmillan, 1967.

Quintero, Ruben, ed. *A Companion to Satire*. Malden, MA: Blackwell, 2007.

———. "Pope and Augustan Verse Satire." In Quintero, *Companion to Satire*, 212–232.

Rawson, Claude, ed. *English Satire and the Satiric Tradition*. Oxford: Basil Blackwell, 1984.

———. "Fielding's Style." In *The Cambridge Companion to Henry Fielding*, ed. Rawson, 153–174. Cambridge: Cambridge University Press, 2007.

———. *Gulliver and the Gentle Reader: Studies in Swift and our Time*. London: Routledge and Kegan Paul, 1973.

———. Introduction to *Gulliver's Travels*, by Jonathan Swift. Edited by Claude Rawson and Ian Higgins. Oxford: Oxford University Press, 2005.

———. *Order from Confusion Sprung: Studies in Eighteenth-Century Literature from Swift to Cowper*. London: Allen and Unwin, 1985.

———, ed. *Politics and Literature in the Age of Swift: English and Irish Perspectives*. Cambridge: Cambridge University Press, 2010.

———. *Satire and Sentiment 1660–1830: Stress Points in the English Augustan Tradition*. 1994. Rev. ed., New Haven, CT: Yale University Press, 2000.

———. "Savage Indignation Revisited: Swift, Yeats, and the 'Cry' of Liberty." In Rawson, *Politics and Literature in the Age of Swift*, 185–217.

Raymond, Joad. *The Invention of the Newspaper: English Newsbooks, 1641–1649*. Oxford: Clarendon, 1996.

Real, Hermann J. " 'The Most Fateful Piece Swift ever Wrote': *The Windsor Prophecy*." *Swift Studies* 9 (1994): 76–99.

Regan, Shaun. "Novelizing Scriblerus: *Tristram Shandy* and (Post-) Scriblerian Satire." *Shandean* 17 (2006): 9–33.

Reilly, Patrick. "Fielding's Magisterial Art." In *Henry Fielding: Justice Observed*, edited by K. G. Simpson, 75–100. London: Vision, 1985.

———. *Jonathan Swift: The Brave Desponder*. Manchester: Manchester University Press, 1982.

Richetti, John, ed. *The Cambridge History of English Literature, 1660–1780*. Cambridge: Cambridge University Press, 2005.

———. *The English Novel in History, 1700–1780*. London: Routledge, 1999.

———. *The Life of Daniel Defoe*. Oxford: Blackwell, 2005.

Rippy, Frances Mayhew. *Matthew Prior*. Boston: Twayne, 1986.

Rivero, Albert J. *The Plays of Henry Fielding: A Critical Study of His Dramatic Career*. Charlottesville: University Press of Virginia, 1989.

Rogers, Pat. *Grub Street: Studies in a Subculture*. London: Methuen, 1972.

———. "Swift and the Poetry of Exile." In *Swift's Travels: Eighteenth-Century British Satire and Its Legacy*, edited by Nicholas Hudson and Aaron Santesso, 124–142. Cambridge: Cambridge University Press, 2008.

Rosenberg, Albert. "The London Dispensary for the Sick-Poor." *Journal of the History of Medicine and Allied Science* 14 (1959): 41–56.

Rosenheim, Edward W., Jr. *Swift and the Satirist's Art*. Chicago: University of Chicago Press, 1963.

Ross, Deborah. "Mirror, Mirror: The Didactic Dilemma of *The Female Quixote*." *Studies in English Literature* 27 (1987): 455–473.

Ross, Ian Campbell. *Laurence Sterne: A Life*. Oxford: Oxford University Press, 2001.

Ross, John F. "The Final Comedy of Lemuel Gulliver." In *Studies in the Comic*, by Bertrand H. Bronson et al., 175–196. Berkeley: University of California Press, 1941.

Rothstein, Eric. *George Farquhar*. New York: Twayne, 1967.

———. *Restoration and Eighteenth-Century Poetry, 1660–1780*. London: Routledge and Kegan Paul, 1981.

———. "Woman, Women, and *The Female Quixote*." In *Augustan Subjects: Essays in Honor of*

Martin C. Battestin, edited by Albert J. Rivero, 249–275. Newark: University of Delaware Press, 1997.

Rothstein, Eric, and Howard D. Weinbrot. "The Vicar of Wakefield, Mr. Wilmot, and the 'Whistonean Controversy.'" *Philological Quarterly* 55 (1976): 225–240.

Rumbold, Valerie. "Burying the Fanatic Partridge: Swift's Holy Week Hoax." In Rawson, *Politics and Literature in the Age of Swift*, 81–115.

Said, Edward W. *The World, the Text, and the Critic.* Cambridge, MA: Harvard University Press, 1983.

Sainsbury, John. *John Wilkes: The Lives of a Libertine.* Aldershot, UK: Ashgate, 2006.

Schille, Candy B. K. "Self-Assessment in Dryden's *Amphitryon*." *Studies in English Literature* 36 (1996): 545–560.

Scouten, A. H. "Notes toward a History of Restoration Comedy." *Philological Quarterly* 45 (1966): 62–70.

Scouten, A. H., and Robert D. Hume. "Pope and Swift: Text and Interpretation of Swift's Verses on His Death." *Philological Quarterly* 52 (1973): 205–231.

Seidel, Michael. "Satire, Lampoon, Libel, Slander." In *The Cambridge Companion to English Literature 1650–1740*, edited by Steven N. Zwicker, 33–57. Cambridge: Cambridge University Press, 1998.

———. *The Satiric Inheritance: Rabelais to Sterne.* Princeton, NJ: Princeton University Press, 1979.

———. "Systems Satire: Swift.com." In Richetti, *Cambridge History of English Literature*, 235–258.

Selden, Raman. *English Verse Satire, 1590–1765.* London: Allen and Unwin, 1978.

———. "Oldham, Pope, and Restoration Satire." *Yearbook of English Studies* 14 (1984): 109–126.

———. "Rochester and Oldham: 'High Rants in Profaness.'" *Seventeenth Century* 6 (1991): 89–103.

Sena, John F. "Samuel Garth's *The Dispensary*." *Texas Studies in Literature and Language* 15 (1974): 639–648.

Sherburn, George. *The Early Career of Alexander Pope.* Oxford: Clarendon, 1934.

———. "Errors Concerning the Houyhnhnms." *Modern Philology* 56 (1958): 92–97.

Sill, Geoffrey M. *Defoe and the Idea of Fiction, 1713–1719.* Newark: University of Delaware Press, 1983.

Sitter, John. "Political, Satirical, Didactic and Lyric Poetry (II): After Pope." In Richetti, *Cambridge History of English Literature*, 287–315.

———. "Rochester's Reader and the Problem of Satiric Audience." *Papers on Language & Literature* 12 (1976): 285–98.

Skinner, Quentin. *Visions of Politics.* Vol. 1, *Regarding Method.* Cambridge: Cambridge University Press, 2002.

Sloane, Eugene Hulse. *Robert Gould, Seventeenth Century Satirist.* Philadelphia: privately printed, 1940.

Smith, John Harrington. *The Gay Couple in Restoration Comedy.* 1948. Reprint, New York: Octagon Books, 1971.

Smith, Nigel. *Literature and Revolution in England, 1640–1660.* New Haven, CT: Yale University Press, 1994.

———, ed. *The Poems of Andrew Marvell.* Rev. ed. Harlow: Pearson Longman, 2007.

Smith, Raymond J. *Charles Churchill*. Boston: Twayne, 1977.

Spacks, Patricia M. "John Gay: A Satirist's Progress." *Essays in Criticism* 14 (1964): 156–170.

Spears, Monroe K. "The Meaning of Matthew Prior's *Alma*." *ELH* 13 (1946): 266–290.

St Clair, William. *The Reading Nation in the Romantic Period*. Cambridge: Cambridge University Press, 2004.

Stedmond, J. M. "Satire and *Tristram Shandy*." *Studies in English Literature* 1 (1961): 53–63.

Steele, Peter. *Jonathan Swift: Preacher and Jester*. Oxford: Clarendon, 1978.

Steensma, Robert C. *Dr. John Arbuthnot*. Boston: Twayne, 1979.

Stocker, Margarita. "Political Allusion in *The Rehearsal*." *Philological Quarterly* 67 (1988): 11–35.

Stone, George Winchester, Jr., and George M. Kahrl. *David Garrick: A Critical Biography*. Carbondale: Southern Illinois University Press, 1979.

Stone, Lawrence. *The Family, Sex and Marriage in England, 1500–1800*. New York: Harper and Row, 1977.

———. *Road to Divorce: England 1530–1987*. Oxford: Oxford University Press, 1990.

———. *Uncertain Unions and Broken Lives: Intimate and Revealing Accounts of Marriage and Divorce in England, 1660–1857*. Oxford: Oxford University Press, 1995.

Stranahan, Brainerd P. "Bunyan's Satire and Its Biblical Sources." In *Bunyan in Our Time*, edited by Robert G. Collmer, 35–60. Kent, OH: Kent State University Press, 1989.

Suarez, Michael F., S.J. "A Crisis in English Public Life: The Popish Plot, *Naboth's Vineyard* (1679), and Mock-Biblical Satire's Exemplary Redress." *Huntington Library Quarterly* 67 (2005): 529–552.

———. "Swift's Satire and Parody." In Fox, *Cambridge Companion to Jonathan Swift*, 112–127.

Summers, Montague, ed. *The Complete Works of Thomas Shadwell*. 5 vols. London: Fortune, 1927.

Sutherland, James. *English Satire*. Cambridge: Cambridge University Press, 1958.

———. " 'Polly' among the Pirates." *Modern Language Review* 37 (1942): 291–303.

———. *The Restoration Newspaper and Its Development*. Cambridge: Cambridge University Press, 1986.

Tave, Stuart M. *The Amiable Humorist: A Study in the Comic Theory and Criticism of the Eighteenth and Early Nineteenth Centuries*. Chicago: University of Chicago Press, 1960.

The Term Catalogues, 1668–1709. Edited by Edward Arber. 3 vols. London: privately printed, 1903–1906.

Terry, Richard. *Mock-Heroic from Butler to Cowper: An English Genre and Discourse*. Aldershot, UK: Ashgate, 2005.

Test, George A. *Satire: Spirit and Art*. Tampa: University of South Florida Press, 1991.

Thomas, Peter D. G. *John Wilkes: A Friend to Liberty*. Oxford: Clarendon, 1996.

Thormählen, Marianne. *Rochester: The Poems in Context*. Cambridge: Cambridge University Press, 1993.

Todd, Janet. *The Sign of Angellica: Women, Writing, and Fiction, 1660–1800*. London: Virago, 1989.

Troyer, Howard William. *Ned Ward of Grubstreet: A Study of Sub-Literary London in the Eighteenth Century*. Cambridge, MA: Harvard University Press, 1946.

Turner, James Grantham. "From Revolution to Restoration in English Literary Culture." In *The Cambridge History of Early Modern English Literature*, edited by David Loewenstein and Janel Mueller, 790–833. Cambridge: Cambridge University Press, 2002.

Tuveson, Ernest. "Swift: The Dean as Satirist." *University of Toronto Quarterly* 22 (1953): 368–375.

Uglow, Jenny. *Hogarth: A Life and A World.* New York: Farrar, Straus, and Giroux, 1997.

Urstad, Tone Sundt. *Sir Robert Walpole's Poets: The Use of Literature as Pro-Government Propaganda, 1721–1742.* Newark: University of Delaware Press, 1999.

Varey, Simon. "Exemplary History and the Political Satire of *Gulliver's Travels.*" In *The Genres of "Gulliver's Travels,"* edited by Frederik N. Smith, 39–55. Newark: University of Delaware Press, 1990.

Venturo, David F. *Johnson the Poet: The Poetic Career of Samuel Johnson.* Newark: University of Delaware Press, 1999.

Vieth, David M. *Attribution in Restoration Poetry: A Study of Rochester's "Poems" of 1680.* New Haven, CT: Yale University Press, 1963.

Von Maltzahn, Nicholas. "Marvell's Ghost." In Chernaik and Dzelzainis, *Marvell and Liberty,* 50–74.

Wallace, John M. "Dryden and History: A Problem in Allegorical Reading." *ELH* 36 (1969): 265–290.

———. "'Examples Are Best Precepts': Readers and Meanings in Seventeenth-Century Poetry." *Critical Inquiry* 1 (1974): 273–290.

Weber, Harold M. *Paper Bullets: Print and Kingship under Charles II.* Lexington: University Press of Kentucky, 1996.

Webster, Jeremy W. "The 'Lustful Buggering Jew': Anti-Semitism, Gender, and Sodomy in Restoration Political Satire." *Journal for Early Modern Cultural Studies* 6 (2006): 106–124.

———. "Rochester's Easy King: Rereading the (Sexual) Politics of the Scepter Lampoon." *English Language Notes* 42 (2005): 1–19.

Wedel, T. O. "On the Philosophical Background of *Gulliver's Travels.*" *Studies in Philology* 23 (1926): 434–450.

Weinbrot, Howard D. *Alexander Pope and the Traditions of Formal Verse Satire.* Princeton, NJ: Princeton University Press, 1982.

———. "Fielding's *Tragedy of Tragedies*: Papal Fallibility and Scriblerian Satire." *Harvard Library Bulletin,* n.s., 7 (1996): 20–39.

———. *The Formal Strain: Studies in Augustan Imitation and Satire.* Chicago: University of Chicago Press, 1969.

———. *Menippean Satire Reconsidered: From Antiquity to the Eighteenth Century.* Baltimore: Johns Hopkins University Press, 2005.

———. "Northrop Frye and the Literature of Process Reconsidered." *Eighteenth-Century Studies* 24 (1990–1991): 173–195.

———. "Pope, His Successors, and the Dissociation of Satiric Sensibility: A Hypothesis." In *Eighteenth-Century Satire: Essays on Text and Context from Dryden to Peter Pindar,* 186–203. Cambridge: Cambridge University Press, 1988.

———. "'Root Out This Cursed Race': Defoe's *Shortest Way with the Dissenters* and his Longer Way with Himself." In *Anglistentag 2006 Halle: Proceedings,* edited by Sabine Volk-Birke and Julia Lippert, 7–23. Trier: Wissenschaftlicher Verlag, 2006.

———. "The Swelling Volume: The Apocalyptic Satire of Rochester's *Letter from Artemisia In The Town to Chloe In The Country.*" *Studies in the Literary Imagination* 5 (1972): 19–37.

Wellek, René. "The Fall of Literary History." In *The Attack on Literature and Other Essays,* 64–77. Chapel Hill: University of North Carolina Press, 1982.

West, Michael. "Dryden's *Mac Flecknoe* and the Example of Duffett's Burlesque Dramas." *Studies in English Literature* 18 (1978): 457–464.

Wilders, John, ed. *Hudibras*. By Samuel Butler. Oxford: Oxford University Press, 1967.

Wilding, Michael. "Dryden and Satire: 'Mac Flecknoe, Absalom and Achitophel, the Medall,' and Juvenal." In *John Dryden*, edited by Earl Miner, 191–233. Athens: Ohio University Press, 1972.

Williams, Abigail. *Poetry and the Creation of a Whig Literary Culture, 1681–1714*. Oxford: Oxford University Press, 2005.

Williams, Harold, ed. *The Poems of Jonathan Swift*. 3 vols. 1937. 2nd ed., Oxford: Clarendon, 1958.

Williams, Kathleen M. "Gulliver's Voyage to the Houyhnhnms." *ELH* 18 (1951): 275–286.

Wilson, John Harold. *Court Satires of the Restoration*. Columbus: Ohio State University Press, 1976.

Winn, James Anderson. *John Dryden and His World*. New Haven, CT: Yale University Press, 1987.

Winton, Calhoun. *Captain Steele: The Early Career of Richard Steele*. Baltimore: Johns Hopkins Press, 1964.

———. *John Gay and the London Theatre*. Lexington: University Press of Kentucky, 1993.

Womersley, David, ed. *"Cultures of Whiggism": New Essays on English Literature and Culture in the Long Eighteenth Century*. Newark: University of Delaware Press, 2005.

Worcester, David. *The Art of Satire*. 1940. Reprint, New York: Russell and Russell, 1960.

Yu, Christopher. *Nothing to Admire: The Politics of Poetic Satire from Dryden to Merrill*. New York: Oxford University Press, 2003.

Zimbardo, Rose A. *At Zero Point: Discourse, Culture, and Satire in Restoration England*. Lexington: University Press of Kentucky, 1998.

Zwicker, Steven N. "Dryden and the Poetic Career." In Richetti, *Cambridge History of English Literature*, 132–159.

———. *Politics and Language in Dryden's Poetry: The Arts of Disguise*. Princeton, NJ: Princeton University Press, 1984.

A question mark following an author's name signals a tentative attribution. The letter P following a title in the "Defoe" section indicates works whose attribution is considered merely "probable" (as established by Furbank and Owens, *Critical Bibliography of Daniel Defoe*).